María de Zayas
Tells Baroque Tales of Love
and the
Cruelty of Men

PENN STATE STUDIES
in ROMANCE LITERATURES

Editors

Frederick A. de Armas   *Alan E. Knight*

María de Zayas
Tells Baroque Tales of Love
and the
Cruelty of Men

Margaret Rich Greer

The Pennsylvania State University Press
University Park, Pennsylvania

Publication of this book has been aided
by a grant from the Program for Cultural
Cooperation between Spain's Ministry of
Culture and United States Universities.

Library of Congress Cataloging-in-Publication Data

Greer, Margaret Rich.
    Desiring readers : Maria de Zayas tells baroque tales of love and the cruelty
of men / by Margaret Rich Greer.
          p.   cm. — (Penn State studies in Romance literatures)
    Includes bibliographical references (p.   –   ) and index.
    ISBN 0-271-01987-5 (cloth : alk. paper)
    1. Zayas y Sotomayor, María de, 1590–1650—Criticism and interpretation.
I. Title.   II. Title: Maria de Zayas tells baroque tales of love and the cruelty of
men.   III. Series.
PQ6498.Z5G74   2000
    863'.3—dc21   99-29789
                                                                    CIP

It is the policy of The Pennsylvania State University Press to use acid-free paper for
the first printing of all clothbound books. Publications on uncoated stock satisfy
the minimum requirements of American National Standard for Information
Sciences—Permanence of Paper for Printed Library Materials, ANSI Z39.48–1992.

Contents

APPENDIXES

2   Plot Summaries   361
3   Charts of Stories   381

    Notes   397
    Works Cited   449
    Index   463

List of Illustrations

In loving memory of

Dorothy Rose Rich
and
J. Arthur Rich
and
Margaret Helen Rose

Acknowledgments

It is with pleasure that I acknowledge my debt to family, friends, students, and colleagues who have contributed to this project in a variety of ways. My thanks go first to Judith Whitenack and Amy Williamsen for organizing a panel dedicated to Zayas at the Kentucky Romance Languages Conference in April 1989, and for inviting me to participate. It was a wonderful session and the excitement it generated encouraged me to take on a lengthy study of her work.

I owe a great deal to students in classes at Princeton and New York University for their enthusiastic attention to Zayas's work and their insightful readings. My debt to them, particularly to Belén Atienza, Laura Bass, María Caba-Rios, José Antonio Rodríguez-Garrido, and Molly Pelz, goes far beyond the specific acknowledgments in some notes,

Elisa Rhodes provided many useful leads to sources on early Spanish women's lives and spirituality. Guiomar Hautcoeur generously shared with me part of her dissertation project on the influence of the Spanish novella in France. Bruce Wardropper contributed leads on questions of Golden Age poetry and kindly gave me a copy of Amezúa's edition of the *Novelas amorosas,* long out of print. Mercedes Dexeus and Jaime Moll provided invaluable bibliographic assistance and personal support in Spain. Matt Stroud pushed me to a better comprehension of Lacan with tough questions in Kentucky in 1989 and the example of his own Lacanian studies of Golden Age drama. Henry Sullivan not only provided a model and guide with his work on Lacan, but also kindly read portions of this manuscript and made a number of valuable corrections and suggestions. Laura Bass read the entire manuscript carefully and her good eye and intelligent questions have strengthened it greatly. Bob Blue's thorough reading and good suggestions also improved the manuscript, and I thank both Fred de Armas and Bob for their support in bringing it to press and Shannon Pennefeather and Romaine Perin for guiding it well through the publishing process. Stephanie Sieburth also read part of the manuscript and, along with Hortensia Calvo, Helen Solterer and Leslie Damasceno, provided both intellectual and personal support at critical junctures. Gonzalo Pontón also provided an important correction to Chapter 6. I thank all the members of the North Carolina Research Group on Medieval and Early Modern Women for welcoming me into an intellectual and personal community that I treasure, for the wit, the wisdom—and the good food. More specifically, their readings, critique, and suggestions were invaluable in revising Chapter 3. Particular thanks to Liz Clark and Irene Silverblatt for generosity with their time and advice, and to Monica Green for connecting me with Montserrat Cabré, whose input has also much strengthened Chapter 3.

Sections of Chapters 4 and 5 have been published in *María de Zayas: Dynamics of Discourse,* edited by Judith Whitenack and Amy Williamsen (London, University Presses of America, 1995). A portion of Chapter 10 has appeared in *Echoes and Inscriptions: Comparative Approaches to Early Modern Hispanic Literature,* edited by Barbara Simerka and Christopher B. Weimer (Lewisburg: Bucknell University Press, 2000) and also in the first issue of *Laberinto,* an on-line journal (http://www.utsa.edu/academics/cofah/laberinto) launched by Simerka and Weimer. My thanks to those editors for permission to reprint the sections in their present form.

I am grateful to Princeton University for the sabbatical leave during which much of this book was written, and to Duke University for an initial semester free of teaching obligations that enabled me to finish the manuscript while we were relocating to North Carolina.

Finally, I thank my husband, Bob, and our son and daughter, Jim and Emily, who as intelligent listeners, questioners, and readers helped me shaped my ideas into coherent form. The whole family thanks our friends in Tarcento and Mels—especially Ida—who nourish our spirits and our bodies. And a particular thanks to Bob for providing the retreat where I wrote the first sentence of this book while watching the sparrows peck away the golden persimmons outside my window in January 1995 and the last as the blackbirds gorged themselves on elderberries in August 1998.

Titles of Zayas and Cervantes Novellas in English Translation

María de Zayas y Sotomayor

When my translaton differs from that of H. Patsy Boyer, mine is given in parentheses and hers is included in brackets.

Novelas amorosas y examplares (Amorous and Exemplary Novels) [The Enchantments of Love. Amorous and Exemplary Novels]

1. *Aventurarse perdiendo* (Venturing and Losing) [Everything Ventured]
2. *La burlada Aminta y venganza del honor* (Aminta Deceived and Honor's Revenge)
3. *El castigo de la miseria* (The Miser's Reward)
4. *El prevenido engañado* (Forewarned but Not Forearmed)
5. *La fuerza del amor* (The Power of Love)
6. *El desengaño andando y premio de la virtud* (The Road to Disillusionment and the Prize for Virtue) [Disillusionment in Love and Virtue Rewarded]
7. *Al fin se paga todo* (Just Desserts)
8. *El imposible vencido* (Triumph over the Impossible)
9. *El juez de su causa* (The Judge in Her Own Case) [Judge Thyself]
10. *El jardín engañoso* (The Garden of Deceit) [The Magic Garden]

Parte segunda del Sarao y entretenimiento honesto (Desengaños amorosos) (The Disenchantments of Love)

Desengaño 1 (*La esclava de su amante*) (Slave to Her Own Lover)
Desengaño 2 (*La más infame venganza*) (Most Infamous Revenge)
Desengaño 3 (*El verdugo de su esposa*) (His Wife's Executioner)
Desengaño 4 (*Tarde llega el desengaño*) (Too Late Undeceived)

Desengaño 5 (*La inocencia castigada*) (Innocence Punished)
Desengaño 6 (*Amar sólo por vencer*) (Love for the Sake of Conquest)
Desengaño 7 (*Mal presagio casar lejos*) (Marrying Afar: Portent of Doom)
[Marrying Abroad: Portent of Doom]
Desengaño 8 (*El traidor contra su sangre*) (Traitor to His Blood)
Desengaño 9 (*La perseguida triunfante*) (Triumph over Persecution)
Desengaño 10 (*Estragos que causa el vicio*) (The Ravages of Vice)

Miguel de Cervantes Saavedra

Novelas ejemplares (Exemplary Novels) Editor B. W. Ife

1. *La gitanilla* (The Little Gypsy Girl)
2. *El amante liberal* (The Generous Lover)
3. *Rinconete y Cortadillo* (Rinconete and Cortadillo)
4. *La española inglesa* (The English Spanish Girl)
5. *El licenciado Vidriera* (The Glass Graduate)
6. *La fuerza de la sangre* (The Power of Blood)
7. *El celoso extremeño* (The Jealous Old Man from Extremadura)
8. *La ilustre fregona* (The Illustrious Kitchen Maid)
9. *Las dos doncellas* (The Two Damsels)
10. *La señora Cornelia* (Lady Cornelia)
11. *El casamiento engañoso* (The Deceitful Marriage)
12. *Novela y coloquio que pasó entre Cipión y Berganza* (The Dialogue of the Dogs)

PART I

The Subject in Question

Introduction: Desiring Readers

> Yo adoro lo que no veo
> y no veo lo que adoro,
> de mi amor la causa ignoro
> y hallar la causa deseo.
> Mi confuso devaneo
> ¿quién le acertará a entender?,
> pues sin ver, vengo a querer
> por sola imaginación,
> inclinando mi afición
> a un ser que no tiene ser.
>
> (I adore what I cannot see,
> I cannot see what I adore,
> my love's cause I do not know,
> and to find that cause I long.
> My confused delirium—
> who might comprehend it?
> without seeing, I have come to love
> by imagination alone,
> turning my affection
> to a being who has no being.)
> —Jacinta, in María de Zayas y
> Sotomayor, *Novelas amorosas y
> ejemplares*

A Book About María de Zayas?

"You're writing a book about María de Zayas? *Everybody's* working on María de Zayas!"[1]

During the past few years, reference to my current project has frequently elicited some variety of that response. Sometimes it is delivered with names of specific individuals, or the observation that scads of graduate students are writing their dissertations on Zayas, but often it is a bare generalization pronounced with overtones of astonishment, amusement, or cautionary skepticism. The spoken or unspoken subtexts that I hear in this reaction are bemusement that a little-known seventeenth-century woman writer of novellas could suddenly attract so much interest, and a tactful warning that we may be overdoing it. Can such a peripheral writer of prose from Spain's Golden Age, the era of Cervantes, Calderón, Lope, Quevedo, Góngora, Gracián, and so on, really merit not just one book, but many?

The Attraction of Zayas

How to explain this upsurge of interest in the prose fiction of María de Zayas y Sotomayor? I think three principal factors contribute to her rediscovery by late twentieth-century readers and the fascination she arouses in her renewed public. The first is undoubtedly the emergence of feminism. Two decades ago most canonical reading lists, such as those given to graduate students at American universities, included in the portion dedicated to the Hispanic Golden Age at best two women writers, both nuns: Saint Theresa of Avila and Sor Juana Inés de la Cruz.[2] Readers seeking to recover feminine voices from the past find in Zayas an important addition, a secular writer who was a significant contributor to the novella tradition shaped by Boccaccio, Bandello, Cinzio, and Cervantes. Furthermore, her works are relatively accessible, as her two-volume novella collection, the *Novelas amorosas y ejemplares* (Amorous and Exemplary Novels) (1637) and the *Desengaños amorosos* (Disenchantments of Love) (1647) has seen numerous editions and translations over the intervening centuries, and has recently been published in modern translations in English and Italian by Patsy Boyer and Sonia Piloto di Castro, respectively. Her play *La traición en la amistad* (Friendship Betrayed), first published by Serrano y Sanz in his 1903 collection of Spanish women writers and reissued in 1975, now also appears in two new anthologies of plays by Golden Age women dramatists, one published in Spain by Felicidad González Santamera and Fernando Doménech (1994), and another in the United States by Theresa Soufas (1996b). A company that had begun to record books on tape was advertising at the 1994 Feria del Libro in Madrid that the next author to be so published, after Cervantes and García Lorca, would be María de Zayas; and a Fundación Cultural María de Zayas, established in the Salamanca district of Madrid, supports a Web site (www.zayas.net) as well as a library and a series of cultural activities. Despite the importance of feminism in leading a new public to Zayas and despite her ardent defense of women's rights, however, she does not fit neatly into twentieth-century feminist molds, as we will see in following chapters. Nevertheless, the current debate over whether she should be considered a feminist writer augments rather than diminishes her interest for present-day readers.

Second, the rediscovery of Zayas and many lesser-known women writers of her era both contributes to and benefits from a more generalized broadening of traditional literary canons and a rethinking of our understanding of the texture of life and of the alleged ideological uniformity of earlier periods, in Spain as in other national traditions. Literary critics, historians, and sociologists are calling attention to a variety of voices marginal to the dominant discourse, in terms of gender, sexual orientation, or religious or political philosophy. On rereading canonical authors, we are also seeing evidence of contradiction or dissension even in the works of authors conceived to be as conservative and as supportive of absolutism and Counterreformation philosophy as Quevedo or Calderón.[3] María de Zayas, combining as she does a radical overt defense of women's rights with an otherwise conservative ideological posture, adds a new perspective to our awareness of the complexities of subject positioning in Baroque Spain.

The third factor in the renewed appreciation of the writings of Zayas is our changing concept of the nature of subjectivity. The long-prevailing idea of an essential, autonomous, thinking self in the Cartesian tradition has largely given way to a postmodern concept of an inherently problematic, divided subjectivity. We understand human beings to be "sub-ject" to systems resistant to rational control: more thought than freely, "objectively" thinking out their own place in the world, more determined by language and by the Symbolic order in a larger sense than in command of it, whether in the structures of the unconscious or of national, transnational, and global socioeconomic and political systems. This postmodern sense of the human subject, curiously, makes possible a renewed comprehension, visceral as well as logical, of wo/man's sense of place in early modern Spain.[4] When don Quixote, or don Gutierre and doña Mencía of Calderón's drama *El médico de su honra* (The Surgeon of His Honor) pronounce "Soy quien soy" (I am who I am), they voice a self-concept determined by intersections of gender, class, family name, political obligation, and related categories that determine, however conflictively, the role that the subject can and must play in society.[5] I recently saw a striking echo of this self-definition in Tony Kushner's epic drama *Angels in America,* a smash hit in London and on Broadway. In the play, when Roy Cohn, the Washington lawyer who gained enormous influence in the McCarthy era, is diagnosed as having AIDS, he roars his rejection, saying that only homosexuals get AIDS, and although he does sleep with men, "homosexuals are men who know nobody and who nobody knows. Who have zero clout. Does this sound like me?" That apparently bizarre self-definition was front-page news for the *New York Times* Theater section (16 May 1993), but it sounds hauntingly familiar to any devotee of Golden Age literature. Cohn opposes a system that classifies individuals on the basis of sex and sexual preference with another system based on position in the sociopolitical hierarchy. In neither configuration does a concept of an interiorized moral or rational "selfhood" play a determining role.

As any current moviegoer knows, the refocusing of the subject, the recognition of the blurred boundaries between self and other, has been accompanied by a fascination with the erotic, with the supernatural, and with violence. All three have to do with the irrational nature of human relationships, and all three are present in abundance in the stories of María de Zayas. Centuries before viewers flocked to such films as *Blue Velvet, The Crying Game,* or *The Silence of the Lambs,* Zayas was exploring the irrational origins of sexual desire, the social construction of gender roles, the multiple varieties of sexual obsession, and the violence it provokes. Those drawn to the blending of supernatural forces and passion in novels or films such as *The Witches of Eastwick, Dracula,* or *The Night of the Living Dead* can find in Zayas's work tales of lovers controlled by black magic or saved by miraculous divine intervention, and uncanny stories of the power of the "not-quite-dead" over the living. It is, in fact, precisely these elements that provoked her erasure from the national literary canon formulated in nineteenth-century Spain and that now lure a late twentieth-century reading public.

"Desiring Readers"

Zayas—like virtually all writers—designed her tales to do just that, to lure readers. However, as a woman writing in an overwhelmingly masculine literary tradition, in an era in which literate males outnumbered reading women by at least five to one and in a largely misogynist, patriarchal culture that enjoined women to silence, her first words in her prologue address the daring of her endeavor.[6] Employing the subjunctive mode, she gives it the heading "Al que leyere"—"To the reader," or, more literally, "To him who may read":

> Quién duda, lector mío, que te causará admiración que una mujer tenga despejo, no sólo para escribir un libro, sino para darle a estampa. . . . Quién duda, digo otra vez, que habrá muchos que

atribuyan a locura esta virtuosa osadía de sacar a luz mis borrones, siendo mujer, que, en opinión de algunos necios, es lo mismo que una cosa incapaz. (*Novelas,* 21)

(No doubt, dear reader, it will amaze you that a woman should have the nerve, not just to write a book but actually to have it printed. . . . No doubt, I repeat, there will be many who will attribute to madness my righteous audacity in bringing my scribbles to light, being a woman, which in the opinion of some fools, is the same as being incompetent.)

In this preface and in the frame narrative that surrounds the collection and links the stories, Zayas repeatedly demonstrates her concern for establishing and maintaining contact with a "listening" or reading public, male as well as female. Although her stated objective is to address *women,* to warn them of the dangers of sexual desire, her implied addressee is as often, if not more frequently, male, as in the following closing lines of her preface:

Con mujeres no hay competencias. . . . Y así, pues, no has de querer ser descortés, necio, villano, ni desagradecido. Te ofrezco este libro muy segura de tu bizarría, y en confianza de que si te desagradare, podías disculparme con que nací mujer, no con obligaciones de hacer buenas novelas, sino con muchos deseos de acertar a servirte. Vale. (*Novelas,* 23)

(With women, there is no competition. . . . And therefore, in consequence, you will not want to be discourteous, foolish, common, nor ungrateful. I offer you this book with the assurance of your gallantry and with the confidence that if it should displease you, you can excuse me on the grounds that I was born a woman, not with the obligation of making good novels but with great desire to succeed in serving you.)

Her male-directed forms of address range from aggressive, or at least hostile, admonitions to subtly seductive forms of flattery.[7]

Zayas's concern for entertaining her readers is also demonstrated by her awareness of "what sells." In her preface, she justifies her choice to serve her readers an "insubstantial" but "appetizing" plate in the form of novels, because a book without erudition can be good if the topic is right, while "otros llenos de sutilezas se venden, pero no se compran, porque la materia no es importante o es desabrida" (other books full of subtleties are put on sale but never bought because the subject is unimportant or disagreeable) (*Novelas*, 23).[8] The first purport of the title of my Introduction, "Desiring Readers," therefore, refers to Zayas's desire for readers.

At the same time, I choose that title to invoke the role of desire in narration, in reading, and in interpretation. Desire and narrativity are intimately linked, as Peter Brooks and a number of other critics point out.[9] For Brooks, desire is the motor, the driving force of narrative. "Narratives both tell of desire—typically present some story of desire—and arouse and make use of desire as dynamic of signification. Desire is in this view like Freud's notion of Eros, a force including sexual desire but larger and more polymorphous" (Brooks 1985). Within the plot, it is the desire for an object; driving the plot, both for teller and hearer/reader, it is the desire for meaning, the ordering force that narrative provides for temporal existence.

Zayas offers her readers twenty stories of sexual desire, while reiterating from beginning to end that the purpose of her narration is to warn them against the power and danger of that desire. Through the device of the male and female characters in the overarching narrative frame who narrate, listen to, and criticize those stories, Zayas demonstrates how gender and one's position within and toward the circuit of desire condition the construction of meaning, by both the narrators and the interpreters of their tales. We may believe ourselves to speak and read with conscious processes, but as Zayas shows, the energy and much of the shape and direction of that speaking and telling emerge from the place of the unconscious. The first episode in Zayas's first story is an exploration of the mysterious origins of sexual desire, as a lonely young woman brings her lover to life and then to death in two violent dreams, and sings the song whose opening lines serve as the epigraph to this Introduction. It was my own first experience of reading this story with students, and our attempts to "acertar a entender" (manage to understand) the knowledge, conscious and unconscious, with which Zayas animates her fictions, that launched me on an investigation of that other avenue of exploration of desire, psychoanalytic theory. This course led me from Freud's explanation of the unconscious and its symbolic expression in dreams and creative daydreams; to Lacanian theory of the crucial role of language in the formation of gendered, desiring subjects; and thence to feminist critiques of Freudian and Lacanian theory, on the one hand, and on the other, back to Zayas's day and to the philosophical/theological and medical explanations of the psyche that were available to her and to her readers.

I opt to read Zayas's stories from the perspective of Lacanian psychoanalytic theory, bringing that theory into dialogue with rereadings of Freud and Lacan by Kristeva and other women who have made significant contributions to psychoanalytic discourse, as well as with theories of the psyche and of sexual difference current in Golden Age Spain. In doing so, I am consciously duplicating the conflictive position from which Zayas wrote in the seventeenth century. She sought to express herself and to communicate with readers both from within and against an overwhelmingly masculine philosophical and literary tradition. The importance and persuasive power of that tradition was undeniable for women of literary inclinations, and although Zayas argued that women were misunderstood and misrepresented within it, she had no other source from which to draw the concepts, literary motifs, and rhetorical tools that she redeployed in her attempt to give voice to an alternative feminine perspective. Similarly, psychoanalytic theory as developed by Freud and Lacan may be at one and the same time a twentieth-century patriarchal discourse, permeated by phallocentrism, *and* a fascinating, philosophically powerful tool of crucial importance for women who seek to comprehend and convey their own sense of being.[10] From Melanie Klein to Julia Kristeva, women who feel that psychoanalytic discourse imperfectly or unjustly represents women's subjectivity have contributed important corrections and alternative theories, but they necessarily depart from and dialogue with the fundamental discoveries of Freud and Lacan. Therefore, just as Zayas drew on and reworked well-known motifs from a masculine literary tradition, and staged a dialogue between male and female narrators, so will I begin with Freud and Lacan and bring into dialogue with them concepts drawn from Kristeva and other women, as each proves useful to illuminating the fictions of María de Zayas.

Opting for such eclecticism does not eliminate the obligation to acknowledge the conflicting claims of different theories. As is often noted, the unconscious is not directly observable, nor its earliest stages of structuration in infancy recuperable; these can only be construed or reconstructed on the basis of observation and interpretation of its effects in later life. The perspectivism implicit in gender position inevitably biases the observer's understanding, as Freud himself acknowledged in admitting that female sexuality remained for him a dark continent that would have to be explored by female analysts.[11]

Lacanian theory does not simplify the problem of perspectivism, but it does address its importance. In "The Agency of the Letter in the Unconscious," Lacan tells the story of a young boy and girl, brother and sister, seated opposite each other in a train car looking out the window as the train pulls into the station. "'Look,' says the brother, 'we're at Ladies!';

'Idiot!' replies his sister, 'Can't you see we're at Gentlemen.' " Lacan continues: "For these children, Ladies and Gentlemen will be henceforth two countries towards which each of their souls will strive on divergent wings, and between which a truce will be the more impossible since they are actually the same country and neither can compromise on its own superiority without detracting from the glory of the other" (Lacan 1977, 152). Ragland-Sullivan (1991, 50–51) cautions that the positioning of these children should not be reduced to a binary opposition based on anatomical difference, for either can line up on one side or the other of the phallic signifier of difference.[12] The children could, as it were, change seats so that each would see the other sign; what they cannot do is *not* take a seat, not assume a gendered and hence partial—in both senses of the word—perspective.

Recognition of the structuring of the unconscious around the problem of sexual difference is, I believe, precisely what makes psychoanalytic theory a fruitful avenue of approach to a greater appreciation of Zayas's tales of the perils of sexual desire. Knowing that it is an avenue that some critics resist taking, however, I offer the following story to skeptics of both genders. Let us begin by imagining that Zayas's frame heroine Lisis is bringing her rival, Lisarda, up-to-date on modern psychiatric terminology. Lisis asks Lisarda: "Do you know the definition of a neurotic?' Lisarda: "No." Lisis: "That's someone who builds castles in the air. Then do you know how to recognize a psychotic?' Lisarda: "No." Lisis: "That's someone who *lives* in those castles. And you don't know what a psychiatrist is either?" "No." Lisis: "That's the person who collects the rent."[13]

That story is offered as an acknowledgment of the liabilities of what Françoise Meltzer has called the "totalizing teleology of psychoanalysis" (1987, 217). When psychoanalytic theories are brought to bear on literary works, they often arrive to "collect the rent," to constitute themselves as the owners of meaning, the master plot—usually Oedipal—that rents out small pieces to literary artists.[14] The rich ambiguities of the literary creation can be lost in the process, for as Peter Brooks points out, the traditional psychoanalytic approach often "displaces the object of analysis from the text to some person, some other psychodynamic structures," making of its object of analysis either "the author, the reader, or the fictive person of the text" (Brooks 1987, 334–35). Paul Julian Smith similarly criticizes "would-be psychoanalytic critics . . . [who] seek to dissect the author or character, as if the first were immediately accessible and the second endowed with autonomous existence" (Smith 1989, 69).

Author, character, or reader analysis may, in fact, be inevitable in psychoanalytic criticism of narrative, and in any other critical school that focuses at least in part on the constitution of the human subject in literature rather than restricting its gaze solely to formal structures. Subjectivity is constructed, in lived experience as in fictional narratives and in their interpretation, within what Lacan calls the Borromean knot of the Symbolic, Imaginary, and Real orders. In explaining the interrelationship of the Imaginary and Symbolic, I find useful an anecdote from my own son's childhood. As infants enter the mirror stage, becoming aware of their separateness from the (m)Other, the primary nurturer, they "put on," rather like a suit of borrowed clothes, a bodily image that will henceforth form the core of identity. This is an alienated image, formed not as a direct reflection of intimate experience of the bodily organism, but by analogy with the child's perception of other human bodies, and by recognition of his or her own external, mirror image. This "image-suit," cut to the measure of the incorporated images of others, is at the same time a mis-recognition and a fantasy, an anticipatory formulation of the ego ideal that the child strives to establish or live up to. The leitmotiv repeated incessantly by my son at about eighteen months was "Me do it BIG self." To an external observer, this small, roly-poly toddler was neither big nor self-sufficient. But because he was by this stage able to use Symbolic-order language to project, to translate to us that Imaginary identity, we were able to interpret it as an assertion of autonomy important to the achievement of a concept (however illusory) of self-mastery. Writing and reading fictions involves a similar process of the projection and reception in the Symbolic-order text of identities shaped and understood in the Imaginary order.[15]

The relational and identificatory function of the Imaginary order that grounds unconscious *moi* fictions also underpins the writing and reading of narrative fictions and is inseparable from the explanatory, interpretative logic of the Symbolic text. The reception of narrative involves the same interweaving of the Imaginary and Symbolic orders that Ragland-Sullivan summarizes in relation to the "self": "Without the imaginary there would be no sense of identity, no basis for Desire, no representational reference point for reality perception, no mechanism by which to anchor language to any coherent sense of being a 'self.' But without the Symbolic to stabilize, give form to, and 'translate' the Imaginary, man would remain at the same perceptual level as common animals that lack speech. The Imaginary must be sought, then, not just as a separate category, but at the join between Real events and Symbolic naming" (1986). Smith (1989, 102), in fact, observes that our sense of the "realism" of an accomplished author such as Galdós derives from his skillful suture of the Imaginary and Symbolic, of the play of identification and alienation inherent in their functioning.[16]

The Imaginary lure of author/character analysis might be seen, then, not as a "trap," unless the critic stays to "live in that castle," but an appropriate way station in the elucidation of the literary structure in question.

Both Brooks and Smith maintain the validity of psychoanalytic perspectives in literary study on the grounds that they are useful in understanding literary as well as psychic structures. In Brooks's opinion, "the materials on which psychoanalysts and literary critics exercise their powers of analysis are in some basic sense the same: that the structure of literature is in some sense the structure of mind—'the mental apparatus,' . . . the dynamic organization of the psyche, a process of structuration."[17] The structural similarity on which he focuses is that between the transactions of writing and reading and the transference that occurs between analysand and analyst.[18] For Smith, "The object of study will become not the author or character but the structure of the text itself; and the quest for stable or original meaning abandoned for the movement of desire in language" (Smith 1989, 69–70).

Kristeva empties out the identificatory lure of a personalized focus of transference between reader and author or character in her discussion of the signifying practice of texts.[19] In this practice as in the analytic situation, says Kristeva, the subject is realized within language, as the analysand assumes the power of discourse initially attributed only to the analyst; but in the text,

> the absence of a *represented* focal point of transference prevents this process from becoming locked into an identification that can do no more than adapt the subject to social and family structures. To hamper transference, the text's analysis must produce the certainty that the analyst's place is empty, that "he" is dead, and that rejection can only attack signifying structures. . . .
>
> The text . . . comes to be the empty site of a process in which its readers become involved. The text turns out to be the analyst and every reader the analysand. But since the *structure and function of language take the place of the focus of transference* in the text, this opens the way for all linguistic, symbolic, and social structures to be put in process/on trial. (Kristeva 1984, 209–10; emphasis in the original)

Zayas's novellas are much more conventional, at least superficially, than the sort of avant-garde writing Kristeva had foremost in her mind in drawing this analogy, but as I will argue in subsequent chapters, they too require an active participation of the reader in the signifying process.

The structure of María de Zayas's stories presents the critic with two problems: first, the loose, episodic nature of a number of her stories;[20] and second, the apparent discrepancy between the quite ardent feminism expressed in the prologue "Al que leyere" and some sections of the frame narrative and the relative conservatism of the plotting of male-female relations in the enclosed tales. While these characteristics could be explained simply as defects in Zayas's narrative talents, such a dismissal seems less than satisfactory given the success of her stories in her own era and their ability to recapture a modern audience, after a two-century banishment from the literary canon. Were they—and are we—only undemanding or forgiving readers, who like her tales despite these "flaws"? Or are her collections constructed on another logic than that of the dominant narrative tradition, a difference that enhances rather than diminishes their narrative lure? In the chapters that follow I seek to demonstrate that psychoanalytic criticism can help us find meaning in Zayas's supposed flaws and can help us understand the unconscious logic of her simultaneous divergence from the dominant narrative tradition and adherence to conservative values.

Since my object of study is Zayas's fiction, not psychoanalytic theory in itself, I will cite different theorists—primarily Freud, Lacan, and Kristeva—somewhat eclectically, as they seem most helpful in elucidating the structures in question, but I will acknowledge relevant divergent or conflicting explanations in the Notes. I do not presume to address myself to experts in psychoanalytic theory nor pretend to offer a full presentation of any school. Rather, imagining a reader primarily interested in Zayas, I aim at an intelligible presentation of those concepts useful to fuller understanding of Zayas's narrative strategies and I confine the most basic theoretical explanations to the Notes so that they will be available for those whose familiarity with psychoanalysis is limited, yet not distracting to readers more conversant with—or resistant to—psychoanalytic theory.[21] The Notes and Works Cited should serve to lead those interested in fuller explanations to the sources that I have found most useful in explicating the theorists utilized in this study.

In the remainder of Part I, which I have titled "The Subject in Question," I present Zayas from several angles. I survey her biography, documented and speculative, in Chapter 1, and in Chapter 2, the publication history of her *Novelas amorosas* (1637) and *Desengaños amorosos* (1647), as well as the history of her reception. In Chapter 3, I offer an extended analysis of the content and logic of the feminist apology in her prologue.

In Part II, "The Mother Plot," I describe the overall pattern of maternal absence and presence in her stories in relation to her insight into the unconscious roots of sexual desire, her attempts to refigure narratives of desire from a feminine perspective, and the literary and social pressures that limited her capacity to do so. In Chapter 4, I analyze the first story, *Aventurarse perdiendo* (Venturing and Losing) at length, exploring the working-through of desire as Jacinta brings love to life and puts it to death in melodramatic dreams, finds and loses another love, and finally retires to a convent as a lay resident. The significance of maternal presence and maternal voice in other stories is treated in Chapter 5.

In Chapter 6, "Phallic Woman; or, The Laugh of the Medusa," of Part III, "Border Crossings," I examine Zayas's occasional reversal of masculine dominance in stories told by male narrators that, in alternation with female-narrated stories of male abuse of women, set up a fictionalized dialogue between masculine and feminine fantasies of the danger posed by the opposite sex. In Chapter 7, "The Sexual Masquerade: Cross-Dressing and Gender Definition," I study how Zayas uses cross-dressing—primarily female to male in the *Novelas,* and male to female in the *Desengaños*—to challenge the stability of gender definition, the "naturalness" of the social roles assigned to each sex, and the relationship of attire and identity. In Chapter 8, "The Undead and the Supernatural," I consider her violation of other frontiers, those that separate natural and supernatural causality and the divide between life and death. In Chapter 9, "Familiar Enemies," I study Zayas's presentation of sexual violence against women in relation to sociopolitical structures and historical events of her day, her fictional answer to the question of whether that violence comes from "without" or "within."

Finally, in Chapter 10, "Framing the Tale," I analyze Zayas's use of the frame-tale format, her relationship to the tradition of exemplary literature, and her construction and confusion of narrative levels. I suggest that she employs the frame narrative as a polemical strategy in an effort to enhance the power of narrative to transcend the limits of fiction and reorganize her readers' modes of thought.

In an attempt to limit repetition and confusion while discussing twenty multiepisode stories, I have included as appendixes both narrative plot summaries and charts of characters, familial relationships, historical settings, and other elements germane to my analysis.

Quotations from Zayas's novellas are given both in Spanish and English. The translations are my own. They are in some cases more literally than artistically rendered, to give English-speaking readers an equivalent of the exact wording on which my interpretations are based, and a feeling for her flowing yet convoluted style. However, I gratefully acknowledge my debt to H. Patsy Boyer's translation, which I have frequently consulted. With the recent publication of these very readable translations (published under the titles *The Enchantments of Love* and *The Disenchantments of Love*), it is hoped that Zayas will join the too limited number of Spanish writers who have "crossed the Pyrenees," still apparently a formidable cultural or linguistic barrier for readers who persist in viewing the literary tradition of Renaissance and early modern Europe almost exclusively in terms of the literatures of Italy, France, and England.

As her frame heroine Lisis withdraws to the security of a convent at the end of the collection, Zayas adds a final paragraph signed with her own name in which she invites a mysterious "Fabio" to come visit her in that "free" female haven. She invites a continuation of the discussion of whether, given the difficulties of sexual relationships between men and women, that withdrawal is a tragic or happy solution. Many aspects of those relationships have changed in the intervening centuries, but as late twentieth-century readers rediscover the fascination of her stories of love and hate, of courtly rhetoric and graphic violence against women, the front-page stories of our newspapers demonstrate the continuing relevance of that discussion.

1

The Biographical Puzzle

Just who was this woman, María de Zayas y Sotomayor? The scraps of information we have are far too few for us to piece together a coherent picture of her life. We know with absolute certainty little more than that she lived in the first half of the seventeenth century and in Madrid. We do not even know whether these tales of passion were penned by a single or married woman. Now if we were able to accept the name María de Zayas, simply as a marker of an "author function" as described by Foucault (1984), as an organizing principle of a certain body of literary discourse, this should not influence our encounter with her fictions. Yet readers shaped by our cultural tradition insistently attempt to explain their own understanding of fictional discourse by reference to an author as historical subject, somehow known or reconstructed, whose unique situation is then read back into the text as the reader attempts to comprehend or contain its puzzling and contradictory aspects. Amezúa concludes his introduction to her *Novelas* with the statement

> Y es lástima, a la verdad, que sepamos tan poco de su carrera humana, cuyo conocimiento tanto nos hubiera ayudado a juzgar su obra literaria; porque si el novelista fabrica sus libros pidiendo a la realidad sus materiales, para trabarlos y revestirlos, ha de valerse de la argamasa de su sangre, de sus ideas y sentimientos, a fin de que, acendrándolos después en el crisol del Arte, logren así su gloriosa perennidad. (*Novelas,* xlv)

> (And it is a pity, in fact, that we know so little of her human existence, knowledge of which would have helped us so much to judge her literary work; because if the novelist fabricates her books drawing from reality the materials to join and clothe them, she has to take advantage of the mortar of her blood, her ideas and feelings, so that, refined later in the crucible of Art, they may thus achieve their glorious perpetuity.)

Given the scarcity of documentary sources on María de Zayas, many readers have turned to circumstantial and textual evidence to fill in the gaps in their constructions of this enigmatic figure. "Carentes asimismo de otras noticias ajenas coetáneas" (Lacking other contemporary information as well), says Amezúa, "no nos queda más recurso que el de acudir a sus propias obras, para rastrear en ellas las pasajeras y superficiales referencias que de sí misma hizo" (we have no other recourse than to turn to her own works, in order to comb them for fleeting and superficial references that she made to herself) (*Novelas,* ix). Susan Griswold (1980), however, offers a healthy corrective to readings that uncritically construct this loop between fictive texts and an Imaginary biography. Analyzing the multiple levels of authorial discourse in Zayas's fiction, Griswold points out how Zayas distances herself from her fictions through several layers of narrators and Griswold objects to the tendency to read the ideas or lives of Zayas's heroines as direct reflections of those of the author herself. This is a valid and important objection; yet as we will see in the final chapter of this study, Zayas also breaks that distancing repeatedly and invites a conflation of those several narrative levels in an allusive but enigmatic final paragraph signed with her own name. Furthermore, as we will see below, the most recently discovered testimony of her life tempts us again to see autobiographical elements in her second volume of stories.

According to a baptismal certificate published by Manuel Serrano y Sanz, Zayas seems almost certainly to have been born in 1590, the daughter of Fernando de Zayas y Sotomayor and María de Barasa.[1] Fernando de Zayas was an infantry captain who served as administrator for the seventh count of Lemos, Pedro Fernández de Castro, and was awarded the habit of the elite military-religious Order of Santiago in 1628 (Barbeito Carneiro 1992, 166–67). Ten years later, he was named corregidor of the *encomienda* (estate) of Jeréz de los Caballeros of that order, but apparently enjoyed that post briefly, as another man was named to it in 1642 (Yllera 1983, 16). Textual evidence supports this documentary testimony of her probable membership in the aristocracy of Madrid; her narrators repeatedly voice invectives against servants and hostility toward those who illegitimately assume the use of *don* to indicate nobility.

Zayas set her stories in cities across the breadth of the Spanish Habsburg empire in Europe, from Flanders to Naples and Sicily, as well as in all the major cities of the peninsula. Combining her textual rendering of those cities with circumstantial evidence, literary historians have speculated that Zayas may have lived for periods of her life outside Madrid, in Valladolid, Zaragoza, Naples, and Barcelona.[2] She sets one novella, *Al fin se paga todo* (Just Desserts), in Valladolid during the period from 1601 to 1606 when Philip III moved his court to that city from Madrid, and it has been postulated that Fernando de Zayas might have taken his family there during those years. However, her descriptions of Valladolid, and of Zaragoza as well, seem too formulaic to offer convincing proof of personal acquaintance with those cities.

While both volumes of her stories were first published in Zaragoza rather than in Madrid, factors in the history of publication rather than residence may have determined this choice, at least in the case of the first volume. As part of the reform campaign instituted by the duke of Olivares in the early years of the reign of Philip IV, publication of collected volumes of *comedias* and of most novels was banned in the realm of Castile from 1625 to 1634, when Zayas was preparing her first volume for publication (Yllera 1983, 16). Furthermore, as Sylvania (1922) and Yllera (1983, 18) point out, it may have been easier to find a publisher in Zaragoza than in the court at Madrid, where both literary and official publications filled the presses to capacity.

Arguments for her residence in Naples are based on her father's service as administrator to Pedro Fernández de Castro, the seventh count of Lemos, who was viceroy in Naples from 1610 to 1616, and might have been accompanied to that post by Fernando de Zayas and his family. Zayas situates part or all of three stories in Naples during the viceroyalty of the seventh count of Lemos,[3] and details of the description of a chapel in the story *La fuerza del amor* (The Power of Love) do convey a greater sense of personal familiarity with particular geographic details. Montesa Peydro (1981, 23) suggests that her description of the participation of marriageable women in courtly festivities in Naples may reflect her personal experience, as may the narrator of the ninth *desengaño,* who says that she saw the manuscript of the life of the saintly queen Beatriz when she was in Italy with her parents. Yllera (1983, 17), however, finds the description of Naples as conventional as that of other cities in which she sets her novels, and points out that the description of the chapel may have been drawn from a secondary source.

Whether or not Zayas ever lived outside Madrid, that court city was the center of her literary life in her formative years as a writer. She was certainly resident there in 1617, when her signature appears along with that of other associates—secular and religious, male and female—of the Brotherhood of the Defenders of the Immaculate Conception (Barbeito Carneiro 1992, 166–67). Between 1621 and 1632, she wrote laudatory poems included in the preliminaries of books by several authors,[4] a custom that many repaid in preliminary verses for her *Novelas amorosas.* She also wrote a play—perhaps *Traición en la amistad* (Friendship Betrayed), which survived in manuscript and was published at the beginning of this century by Serrano y Sanz.

Zayas is said to have participated in one or more of the literary academies that flourished in Madrid in these decades, although the precise nature of her participation is uncertain. The "Prólogo de un desapasionado lector" (Prologue by a Dispassionate Reader) to her *Novelas amorosas* says that Zayas has been "much applauded and celebrated by the learned Academies of Madrid" (*Novelas,* 25), and Willard King (1963, 59 n. 81) states that she was permitted to participate in the activities of the Madrid academy sponsored by Francisco de Mendoza and perhaps that of Sebastián Francisco de Medrano as well. The Medrano group met between about 1617 and 1622 and was followed in 1623 by the Mendoza Academy, which lasted until at least 1637 (King 1963, 49–62).

When the vogue of literary academies spread from Italy to Spain and France in the sixteenth century, women did not acquire in Spanish academies the importance they enjoyed in their Italian and French counterparts, and the studies of Willard King and José Sánchez list virtually no women as regular members. Her relationship to them may not have extended beyond participation in the poetic competitions they sponsored, in which visitors, including women, were invited to participate (King 1963, 54). Pérez de Montalbán, who placed considerable value on membership in academies (King 1963, 96–97), praises Zayas's participation in poetic competitions but does not attribute academy membership to her. On the other hand, in *El diablo cojuelo* (The Crippled Devil), Luis Vélez de Guevara does make the woman dramatist and poet from Seville Ana Caro de Mallén an active participant in his fictional academy, which may have been based on a group extant in Seville.[5] Other women present there sit veiled and silent on the floor, except for singing the ballad finale of the meeting (Vélez de Guevara 1984, 157–60). Another fictional doña Ana, described as "sola, rica, y discreta, / su honestidad conocida, / y el empleo de su vida / le da al estudio" "single, rich and prudent, known for her decorum, who devotes her life to study" (Moreto y Cabaña 1828, 5) hosts an academy in her own home in Moreto's *comedia, No puede ser* (It Cannot Be).[6] The *gracioso* (comic character) Tarugo makes an extended joke of the impossibility of combining poetic talent and wealth, but no one in the play questions the combination of poetic gifts, femininity, and full participation in such a gathering. Moreto's doña Ana launches the action with a poetic enigma of her own composition that compares a woman in love to smoke that can only be contained by her own concern for her honor, not by sentinels imposed by tyrannical males, and refuses to marry her fiancé until he has learned that lesson. Judging by the evidence of Zayas's participation in a poetic competition sponsored by the Academy of Saint Thomas Aquinas in Barcelona in 1643, to be discussed at greater length below, she, like those Anas, participated fully at least in the competition, although she took no prizes either for her looks or her poetry; in contrast, other women's poetic gifts are praised but they are assigned a more marginal as well as more decorative role in the events, like the ballad singers in *El diablo cojuelo*.

During the decades of the 1620s and 1630s, Zayas garnered the praise of a number of the well-known writers of her day, including Lope de Vega, Castillo Solórzano, and Pérez de Montalbán. Lope, in his *Laurel de Apolo* (1630), carried his display of classical erudition to such lengths in praise of Zayas that one suspects an ironic intent:

> ¡Oh dulces Hipocrenides hermosas!
> los espinos Pangeos
> aprisa desnudad, y de las rosas
> tejed ricas guirnaldas y trofeos

> a la inmortal doña María de Zayas,
> que sin passar a Lesbos, ni a las playas
> del vasto mar Egeo,
> que hoy llora el negro velo de Theseo,
> a Sapho gozará Mytilenea,
> quien ver milagros de mujer desea;
> porque su ingenio vivamente claro
> es tan único y raro, que ella sola pudiera,
> no solo pretender la verde rama,
> pero sola ser sol de tu ribera,
> y tú por ella conseguir más fama,
> que Napoles por Claudia, por Carnelia
> la sacra Roma, y Thebas por Targelia"
> (165)

(Oh, beautiful, sweet Muses of Hippocrene, strip thorny Pangaion Oros [the mountain in Greece whose peak was the home of the cult of Dionysius] and from its roses weave garlands and trophies for the immortal doña María de Zayas, for whoever wishes to see womanly wonders, without traveling to Lesbos nor the beaches of the vast Aegean Sea that today weep Theseus's black sail, will enjoy a Mytilenean Sappho, because her lively clear talent is so unique and rare that she alone could aspire to the green bough, she alone could be the sun to your shores, and you through her secure more fame than Naples for Claudia, holy Rome for Cornelia and Thebes for Targelia.)[7]

She also enjoyed the admiration and friendship of Ana Caro de Mallen, who had achieved some recognition in literary circles and had been invited to Madrid to chronicle festivities in the Buen Retiro in 1637 (Caro 1993, 19–13). Caro de Mallen wrote a laudatory preliminary poem for Zayas's *Novelas amorosas,* and Zayas returned her compliments through the voice of the narrator of her fourth *desengaño,* who included Caro de Mallen in her list of illustrious women, describing her thus:

> La señora doña Ana Caro, natural de Sevilla: ya Madrid ha visto y hecho experiencia de su entendimiento y excelentísimos versos, pues los teatros la han hecho estimada y los grandes entendimientos le han dado laureles y vitores, rotulando su nombre por las calles." (*Desengaños,* 230)

(Doña Ana Caro, native of Seville. Madrid has already seen and experienced her learning and her superb poetry; her works have been celebrated in the theaters and great minds have lauded and cheered her, sounding her name through the city streets.)

Castillo Solórzano combines another fictional testimony to their friendship with praise for both women writers in *La Garduña de Sevilla,* His character Monsalve prefaces the reading of his own novella by saying:

> Es atrevimiento grande escribir en estos tiempos, cuando veo que tan lúcidos ingenios sacan a luz partos tan admirables cuanto ingeniosos, y no sólo hombres que profesan saber y humanidad, sino también damas ilustres, pues en estos tiempos luce y campea con felices aplausos el ingenio de doña María de Zayas y Sotomayor, que con justo título ha merecido el nombre de Sibila de Madrid, adquirido por sus admirables versos, por su felice ingenio y gran prudencia; habiendo sacado de la estampa un libro de diez novelas, que son diez asombros para los que escriben este género; pues la meditada prosa, el artificio de ellas y los versos que interpola es todo tan admirable, que acobarda las más valientes plumas de nuestra España. Acompáñala en Madrid doña Ana Caro de Mallen, dama de nuestra Sevilla, a quien se deben no menores alabanzas, pues con sus dulces y bien pensado versos suspende y deleita a quien los oye y lee. (Moreto y Cabaña 1828, 5)

> (It is very daring to write in these times, when I see such lucid talents give birth to creatures as admirable as they are witty, and not just men who profess knowledge and learning, but also illustrious ladies, since in these days doña Maria de Zayas y Sotomayor's talent shines out, having brought from the presses a book of ten novellas that are ten wonders for those who cultivate this genre; for the meditated prose, their craft, and the verses she intersperses in them are all so admirable that they intimidate our Spain's most courageous pens. Accompanying her in Madrid is doña Ana Caro de Mallen, a lady of our Seville to whom no lesser plaudits are due, for with her sweet and well-considered verses she astounds and delights all those who hear and read them.)

And during that same period, as Pérez de Montalbán testifies in *Para todos* (For Everyone) (1632), Zayas was composing her first novellas:

> Doña María de Zayas, dézima Musa de nuestro siglo, ha escrito a los
> certámenes con grande acierto, tiene acabada una comedia de ex-
> celentes coplas y un libro para dar a la estampa en prosa y verso de
> ocho Novelas exemplares. (Cited in Moll 1982, 178)

> (Doña María de Zayas, tenth muse of our century, has entered po-
> etic competitions with great success, has completed a *comedia* in ex-
> cellent verse, and has ready for publication a book of eight novellas
> in prose and verse.)

As Jaime Moll reconstructs events, Zayas apparently had a volume of eight
stories ready for publication in 1626 and had secured the necessary license
and approval, only to find her way blocked by the ban on publication in
Castile of works of entertainment. The Aragonese publisher Pedro de Esquer, postulates Moll, then took the manuscript to Zaragoza and secured
the necessary licenses for publication of the stories in Aragonese territory.

Zayas's first volume of novellas, the *Novelas amorosas y exemplares,* as it appeared in Zaragoza in 1637, contained ten stories, as did her second, published ten years later in that same city with the title *Parte segunda del Sarao, y
entretenimiento honesto,* and generally known as the *Desengaños amorosos.*[8] In
fact, the two tomes constitute a single collection, for the framing narrative
begun in the first part is only concluded at the end of the second volume.
Zayas's tone changed in the intervening decade; the invective against male
abuse of women is much more bitter and male violence against women
reaches almost grotesque levels in the *Desengaños.* Whether Zayas had
planned this progression from the outset, or whether personal experiences
may have contributed to the darkness of her second volume we do not
know; the intervening decade was, however, one in which the pessimistic
mood and sense of national decline characteristic of seventeenth-century
Spain increased markedly with a string of serious defeats in the monarchy's
several overseas campaigns, with economic and political turbulence at
home, and with the revolt of Cataluña and Portugal in the crisis year of
1640, which brought war within the boundaries of the peninsula (Elliott
1990, 341–49).

If Zayas published any more preliminary poems for other authors after
the publication of her first volume of stories in 1637, they have not survived. She did participate in volumes of homage to Lope de Vega and Montalbán after their deaths, in 1636 and 1639, respectively.[9] Zayas's invisibility
thereafter and the somber vision of her second volume of stories have

given rise to highly speculative biographical inventions, often involving reading the fate of selected Zayas protagonists as that of the author herself. Amezúa (1948, xvi) and Martínez del Portal (Zayas y Sotomayor 1973, 29), among others, have suggested that Zayas was reflecting a disappointment in love. However, Yllera (1983, 19) and Montesa (1981, 27) point out sensibly that this seems an improbable explanation for a woman approaching or past fifty years of age. More commonly, readers have concluded that Zayas followed the path she marked out for several of her heroines, including Lisis, the heroine of the overarching frame narrative, who retreat from marriage and choose to live as nuns or secular residents of a convent. Barbeito Carneiro (1992, 180–81) goes so far as to suggest that three Zayas heroines may reflect three phases of the life of their author: Lisis, whose retreat to secular life in the convent would explain Zayas's silence between 1639 and 1646; Isabel, the heroine of the first *desengaño;* who took the habit after telling her story of enslavement to love and whose story supposedly justifies Zayas's cautionary literary farewell; and Estefanía, the persecuted queen who also retreated to the convent and took the habit after the death of her husband. Not surprisingly, Barbeito Carneiro does not link with Zayas the heroine of the last story, who also becomes a nun, but only after seducing her brother-in-law and causing the deaths of a whole household. Montesa (1981, 31) and Barbeito Carneiro further suggest that Zayas may have elected to live in a Concepcionista convent. Barbeito Carneiro (1992, 181) suggests in particular the convent of the Concepción Jerónima, but says that she has been unable to locate documentation to prove this hypothesis. Amezúa (1950, xxii) carries speculation to an extreme. To the hypothesis that she might have withdrawn to a convent, he adds (1) that she may well have been ugly, since the authors who praised her never mentioned beauty, in an era when that was customary; and (2) that the inability to find a husband may have joined her deep religious faith in her choice of that retreat (*Desengaños,* xxii).

Some of these speculations can now be definitively laid to rest, but others promise to take on new life following Kenneth Brown's 1987 publication of Francesc Fontanella's manuscript *Vejamen* (Vexation), a poetic "roast" of Zayas and other poets that was written and read at the conclusion of a poetic competition celebrated by the Academy of Saint Thomas Aquinas in Barcelona in 1643. That academy, founded in 1538 at the instigation of Saint Francis of Borja with the obligation of organizing festivities to honor Saint Thomas (Brown 1987, 180–81), was made up of monks of the Dominican convent of Santa Caterina (or Santa Catalina) in which it had its seat, together with university professors and students. The 1643 festivities, which took place while French and Spanish troops fought outside Barcelona for control of Cataluña, were organized to celebrate the donation of a relic of the saint by the convent of Saint Thomas of Tolosa. After sermons, masses, processions, and fireworks, a poetic competition was held in the first two days of the event. Along with Zayas, participants in the competition included an architect, a historian, a goodly number of authors of ecclesiastic works, university students and aspiring poets (Brown 1987, 182). The festivities concluded on the eighth and last day with the reading of a *vejamen* composed by the young secretary of the academy, Francesc Fontanella, who had received his degree in civil and canon law the year before (Brown 1987, 174, 176).

Like the *vejámenes* that concluded poetic competitions in many other literary academies of the era, that of Fontanella parades before its author in an allegorical dream the participants in the competition—plus a few poets apparently invented for the sake of wordplay on their names—painting a satirical portrait of the poetic failings of each, and in the case of Zayas, of her physical characteristics as well.[10] The *Vejamen* opens with a "Sentencia," or pronouncement directed to his audience, the poets of Barcelona, soon to be satirically portrayed.[11] The opening pronouncement, which is not ironic, lavishes grandiloquent praise on that city as a majestic center of urbanity, civility, and beauty (Brown 1987, vv. 36, 38) despite the "external hostilities" waged on it by "barbaric arrogance" (vv. 71, 79). The city enjoys the protection of two stars: the scientific Mercury, Saint Thomas, who defends the citizens of Barcelona against the "barbaric fury of servile ignorance" (vv. 145–46) and Mars—armed with the fleur-de-lis of the French kings (vv. 122–24). The poetic competition is thus presented as a literary extension of the War of Secession, fought against the forces of Castile. After Latin verses by the poets of the academy (not included in the text), the satiric "vexation" itself begins, as the author falls asleep thinking of the competition.

In Fontanella's "dream," Apollo appears, fully armed and furious because Barcelona has scorned its poets, his followers, enclosing them in a hospital for the insane (Brown 1987, 231–90). Apollo urges the author to visit them but he resists, protesting that the hospital is populated by "semmaneras," women whose sole objective is to "deflower" the virginal closure of the purses of impoverished poets (304–14). The *semmaneras* will reappear at the end of the satire as the women invited to be marginal, decorative participants in the competition. Their burlesque introduction, an inversion of the poetic conventions of courtly love traditional in Catalonian poetry, initiates a misogynist strain that permeates the satire as a whole and anticipates the treatment that Zayas will be accorded.[12] Apollo reassures him that a poet can compensate the *semmaneras* with the rich gifts of his flattering language: "agués semmaneras / un poeta pot donar / en lo riquíssim discurs / de dos cobles de romans, / o los rubins de un Abril, / o de una font [lo] cristall, / o las perlas de la aurora, / o los celestes diamants" (a poet, in his very rich discourse, with two couplets in romance can give these "women-of-the-week" either the jewels of an April or the crystal of a spring or the pearls of dawn, or celestial diamonds). The dreamer then finds himself before the portals of the hospital and is easily admitted, despite its Latin inscription warning that none who are not poets and hence insane will be admitted.

The hospital that he tours is divided into three major wards, according to the language in which the poets write: Latin, Catalán, or Castilian, each overseen by the greatest poet in that tongue: Virgil, Ausiàs March, and Garcilaso, respectively. There is also a fourth room of Catalan ballad writers presided over by one "Pastor" (shepherd) Garceni, the bucolic pseudonym of the Rector of Vallfogona, Vicente Garcia (Brown 1987, 193–94 and vv. 841–51). Among the "turba llatinant" (Latinizing throng) (494) of poets who write in Latin, mostly university professors and students, one is charged with being more a grammarian than a poet (vv. 403–6), another with following an outmoded, "rancid" muse (vv. 411–12), others for substituting a Greek for a Latin *y* to make an anagram work, for writing from a dictionary, or for misuse of Latin words and abuse of classical mythology. Fontanella also pokes fun at the misuse of that ancient tongue by punctuating the *Vejamen* with passages of macaronic Latin.

The most illustrious poets are to be found in the next and most architecturally elegant ward, that of the Catalans, and the new classical model that Fontanella proposes is Ausiàs March, sincerely lauded as "poeta cast y eloqüent, / com a Phènix dels antichs, / com a Pare dels moderns" (pure and eloquent poet, [appearing] as a Phoenix [arising] from the ancients, a Father of modern poets) (vv. 537–40). According to Fontanella, the poets of Barcelona should take as inspiration only the models of their own land, but this is unfortunately not the case. As Brown notes (1987, 225 n. 36), Catalonian poets of the sixteenth and seventeenth centuries were given to imitation of Castilian models and gongorine elaboration. Fontanella criticizes them for filling their verses with words borrowed from Castilian and for metric deficiencies and false rhymes due to their inadequate knowledge of Catalan.

The poets in the Castilian ward in which Zayas is an inmate draw

Fontanella's satire first for being "castellans fingits" (sham Castilians), that is, for writing in Castilian although they are Catalan by birth. They are enclosed behind "un portal rumbant / hont lo artífice subtil / a las difunctas estàtuas / volgué donar esperit" (an ostentatious portal whose subtle artifice tried to give life to defunct statues). In other words, the insanity of Catalan poets who write in Castilian is that they seek admiration by cultivating artifices in an attempt to give a semblance of life to an alien, dead tradition. Their poems are called glosses, not original creations but only reworkings or copies of that old school. These characters include a Montañes anchorite preoccupied with penning verses with a pedantic and outmoded calligraphy (vv. 693–708); a poet who strays from the tradition of Garcilaso to copy Góngora and makes obscure, twisted glosses; others who limp blindly (on deficient poetic "feet"); another who steals the fruits of "la Vega" (Lope de Vega) (vv. 761–64), an "alchemist" poet who tries to give his simplistic verse refinement by passing it through a colorist alembic; and finally, a "don Diego de Noche," who came from Vich to learn to gloss but only dares appear at night because he is ashamed of his ill-polished verse. As Brown points out (1987, 233 n. 50), this fictitious poet is a figure of those who falsely attached the title "don" to their names. Hence, all the poets in the Castilian ward are falsifiers, usurpers in some fashion of a discourse that is not their own. Zayas is a usurper of another kind, as we will see when we set her portrait in the context of the *Vejamen* as a whole.

From the Castilian ward, Fontanella goes on to another room of "cathalans romansistas" (Catalan ballad writers), whom he satirizes for their pompous style (v. 862), for using Castilian words and images, for gongorism (vv. 879–80), for lame meters, and for indecorous comparisons (v. 895). In this section he also paints a satirical self-portrait, calling himself a shepherd, Pastor Fontano, who writes in a macaronic language and will have no hope of advancement, since his satire is sure to provoke the enmity of the judges as well as of the other poets he caricatures (vv. 917–24).

Leaving the last ward, Fontanella finds the patio or garden of the hospital filled with many *semmaneras*, women who are not regular members of the academy but are invited to participate at some level in the week's activities. If in Fontanella's burlesque opening of the dream they appear as greedy courtesans who deflower poor poets, here he heeds Apollo's advice to pay them gallant poetic praise. They are called "sovereign flowers" in a blessed spring garden (vv. 942–44), an army of suns gathered by the God of Love (vv. 945–48). He lists some eight women, with brief and stereotypical praise of their beauty and discretion. They are in the hospital to beg charity for the poets, but also bring him their own verses, demanding that he give them the best prizes (vv. 985–93). He defers to the judges, saying that if he were a judge, he would, like Phebo, rain crowns on them—perhaps returning thereby to a sexual innuendo in the form of an allusion to the golden rain of Jupiter that impregnated Danae. The women grow angry, and he awakens from this section of his dream, having escaped from a feminine menace similar to that which inaugurated his oneiric excursion.

Concluding the *Vejamen*, Fontanella begs forgiveness for his satire and describes Apollo's triumph, in which he frees the poetic inmates of the hospital. As secretary of the Academy, Fontanella distributes the prizes, three in each of four categories, including one to Sor Theodora Molera, one of the *semmaneras* who wins the last prize in the category of the Catalan ballad writers, and whom he lauds as "gloriosament singular / en ingeni y en bellesa" (gloriously unique in wit and beauty). In closing, he encourages the Catalan poets to continue writing, lauds his "ever-victorious Barcelona" and Saint Thomas, and again asks pardon for his "musa ronca," his hoarse, satirical muse.

This, then, is the context in which Fontanella's burlesque portrait of María de Zayas appears: (1) a roast in verse of all the participants in an academic "joust," in a tradition of satirical conclusions of literary competitions that is at least as old as the satyr plays that ended Greek theatrical festivals; (2) written by a nationalistic Catalan during the War of Secession; (3) in which the worst sins are that of aping languages and poetic traditions— Latin and Castilian—he paints as defunct or alien or both; and (4) and in which women appear as sexual and economic predators or as marginal, decorative beings to be "bought off" with trite flattery. Although burlesque caricatures of physical characteristics were standard in other *vejámenes*, perhaps even more common than satire of poetic peccadilloes or other distinguishing characteristics, according to Carrasco Urgoiti (1965, 107), only Zayas merits such treatment in Fontanella's dream. Her usurpation is yet more fundamental than that of Catalans whose verse makes them "sham Castilians"; he paints her as a bewhiskered woman who tries to usurps masculine discourse for which she does not have the "physical equipment," that is, a "sword" under her "sayas" or skirts:

> Doña María de Sayas
> viu ab cara varonil,
> que a bé que "sayas" tenia,
> bigotes filava altius.

> Semblava a algun cavaller,
> mes jas' vindrà a descubrir
> que una espasa mal se amaga
> baix las "sayas" femenils.
> En la dècima tercera
> fou glosadora infeliz,
> que mala tercera té
> quant lo pris vol adquirir.
> O! Senyora Doña Saÿa [*sic*],
> per premiar sos bons desitgs
> del sèrcol de un guardainfant
> tindrà corona gentil!
>
> (vv. 725–40)

(I saw Doña Mary of the Skirts with a manly face, who although she has "skirts," twirls a haughty mustache. She looked like a gentleman, but it will be discovered that a sword can hardly be hidden under feminine skirts. In the third décima, she was unfortunate at glossing and she has a poor procuress if she wants to win a prize. Oh, Lady Dame Skirt, to reward your good desires, you will have a charming crown [made of] the hoop of your farthingale.)

Along with the obvious play with Zayas/sayas/skirts that he repeats twice, Fontanella builds a sexual wordplay on the meanings of "third" as both ordinal number and "third" in the sense of go-between or procuress. Her third *décima* (a poetic form consisting of ten-line strophes) will be a poor procuress in securing the satisfaction of her desires, whether the prize she seeks be a literary award or erotic satisfaction. The only reward she will win is a crown made from the frame of the hoop of her own skirts. Brown (1987, 231 n. 47) suggests that Fontanella must have known Zayas quite well, because otherwise his jokes on her would be in bad taste. While the logic of that deduction is questionable, he does demonstrate the probability of a personal connection by pointing out that a second edition of her *Desengaños,* published in Barcelona by Sebastian de Cormellas in 1649, was approved for publication in 1648 by one Maestro Fray Pío Vives, prior of the convent of Santa Catalina Mártir of Barcelona, the convent in which the academy met, and by Fontanella's older brother, who signed as "Fontanella Regens. 23 septemb. 1648."

This burlesque portrait is both a treasure and a puzzle that raises more

questions than it settles. We can be more sure than before that Zayas did
not, or at least had not yet, joined a convent, since Fontanella twice addresses one of the *semmaneras,* the only woman to receive a prize, as "sor
Theodora Molera" (965, 1145), whereas he calls Zayas "doña María" or
"Senyora Doña Saya" (725, 735). This does not, however, eliminate the possibility that she was living as a secular resident of a convent. We can be absolutely sure that she did reside outside Madrid at least in this period, if
not before. But *why* was she, a true rather than a sham Castilian, in
Barcelona during the war? The lure of reading her novellas autobiographi-
cally raises its head again, from a new corner. The heroine of her first *desengaño* moves to Zaragoza because her father has been appointed a com-
mander of the forces sent to put down the rebellion, and she and her
mother accompany him as far as Zaragoza. Could this have any sort of autobiographical inspiration? Zayas's father, who was born in 1566, was
named administrator of an estate of the Order of Santiago in 1638 but another man replaced him in that post in 1642. Is it possible that a man of
seventy-six did occupy some military or administrative post at the front,
and that Zayas as an unmarried daughter of fifty-two accompanied him? Or
that she traveled to Aragon in the company of a husband, brother, or some
other relative so occupied? Or had she been resident there before the war?
Did she indeed publish the first two or three editions of both volumes in
Zaragoza and Barcelona because of that residence? The poems she contributed to the volumes in honor of Lope and Pérez de Montalbán published in Madrid in 1636 and 1639 could have been solicited from her in
absence from the court city. If she was resident in Zaragoza, however, she
seems not to have been active in literary circles in that city, because she did
not participate in the two poetic competitions published there in 1644 and
1646, although both included a number of women poets.[13] Although her
first novella opens in Montserrat, none of her fictional narrators identify
with the cause of Catalan nationalism; rather, the voice of Lisis in the concluding frame section speaks from the perspective of Castilian loyalties as
she rails against effeminate gentlemen who will not abandon the pleasures
of court even to accompany their king in defense of their women threatened by the advance of the (French) enemy (see Chapter 10 below).

More intriguing yet is the question of how much truth and what significance we should read in Fontanella's portrayal of her as a bewhiskered
woman of manly face and deportment. He is certainly presenting her as a
sexually ambiguous creature, in an age that exhibited women with beards
and mustaches as freaks of nature. Of the several portraits made of

bearded women, the most famous is José Ribera's 1631 painting of Magdalena Ventura, now in the Lerma-Medinaceli Collection in Toledo, Spain, showing her with a long beard and nursing a baby, with her bemused-looking husband standing behind her (see Fig. 7 below). There were also bearded women saints such as Saint Paula of Avila, called "Santa Barbacia," who had asked to be thus deformed in order to be freed of the love of men (Brown 1987, 180–81). That much maligned figure the *dueña* (duenna) is often portrayed in Golden Age literature as whiskered because of her age, which makes it impossible for her to satisfy her sexual desires except by serving as a go-between for young women in her charge.[14] Fontanella's joke about Zayas needing a better "tercera" than her poetry to win the prize she desires implies frustrated sexual as well as literary ambitions on her part. Celestina is also portrayed by Rojas as repulsive and sexually ambiguous, still sexually desirous and finding pleasure in touching young women. But they are not at the same time portrayed as masculine in all aspects but dress and phallus, as Fontanella figures Zayas.

The passage that Fontanella places immediately after that of Zayas also plays with ambiguities of gender and of order. He says that Melànio's poetry begins with two pretty *quintillas* (five-line strophes) but ends poorly, that it is like the statue of Nabucco, with a head of gold and feet of clay, or "com la engañosa sirena / entre lo espumat zafir / ques' en los principis ninfa / y en los fins mònstruo marí" (like the deceitful siren in the sapphire foam, who is a nymph above and a sea monster below) (vv. 745–49). Fontanella attaches that monstrosity only to Melànio's *poetry,* however, whereas in Zayas's case, he affixes it to her flesh.

Should we read this portrait as a reliable indication that Zayas was "butch" in appearance and perhaps in sexual orientation? Lope de Vega compared her talents to those of Sappho (see page 22 above), a fairly common standard of reference for women poets in her day, but Zayas omitted Sappho from the list of "foremothers" she included in her preface "Al que leyere" (see Chapter 3 below). In *Desengaño 6, Amar sólo para vencer* (Love for the Sake of Conquest), she raises and then rejects the possibility of sexual love between women, but includes an episode of male homosexuality in the following story (see Chapter 7 below). Reading these clues together with the portrait, we might conclude that Zayas was carefully avoiding the admission of lesbian attraction. In an era in which homosexuality was severely punished in Spain, by burning recognized homosexuals, by putting them on public exhibition in processions—or by committing them to mental institutions[15]—Fontanella's portrait may be seen as an insinuation that Zayas is in the hospital for sexual deviance as well as for poetic madness.

On the other hand, we can also read the portrait as a backhanded compliment, a masculinization of Zayas in the flesh that is a grotesque admission of her effective intrusion in the realm of literary discourse generally considered a masculine preserve. Zayas is the only woman who is an inmate with the male poets in the hospital wards and is included in the *Vejamen* as a full-fledged participant in the poetic competition. Although one *semmanera*, Sor Theodora Molera, does take last prize in the ballad contest, as a group they are marginalized—admitted only to the garden of the hospital—and either categorized as predators or dismissed with stereotypical flattery. Fontanella directs his satire of the male poets only at their poetic defects, not at their persons. He says that she was a "glosadora infeliz" (unhappy or unfortunate in glossing) in her third *décima*, but he does not specify defects of meter, of rhyme, or of indecorous images, as he does in the case of male poets. Rather, with his play on "third," he turns his critique of her poetry into an insinuation of sexual and literary frustration. Her verse may well have been less than inspired; she is certainly a better storyteller than poet. Or it may have been a poor procurer of favors for her because it challenged the male participants in its content or form. Fontanella may be satirizing Zayas for not having a sword hidden under her skirts precisely because she does wield visibly and with formidable effect the pen she has in hand.

Just when did Zayas take that pen in hand to write the second part of her *Sarao?* Yllera (1983, 17 n. 32) reads the declaration by Lisis in the closing frame of the *Desengaños* that the *sarao* began on Carnival Tuesday, 1646, as marking the beginning of Zayas's composition of the volume. This may be a questionable elision of authorial voices, but it is one that Zayas's own practice often encourages. It would mean that, after a decade-long silence, Zayas composed her entire second volume in the space of six or seven months, as the approval of the censors are dated 28 October and 11 November 1646. If she was indeed resident in Barcelona or elsewhere in Aragon during this period, her removal from the literary circles of Madrid would explain the absence of the conventional laudatory verses of fellow authors in the preliminaries of her *Desengaños*. That volume is prefaced only by a letter from one Inés de Casamayor to the duke of Hijar. The letter recommends its publication and seeks the duke's protection against envious, misogynistic detractors:

> para asegurarle de las sombras de envidiosos maldicientes que, a fuer de fantasmas nocturnas, hacen espantos de que nuestro sexo haya merecido tan generales aplausos, ceñídole tan debidos laure-

les y eternizándose con tan subido punto de honores de tan lucido e inmortal ingenio. Como si estuvieran vinculados a solos varones sus ventajosos lucimientos y se opusiera algún estoque de fuego que le impidiera o imposibilitara al discurso femenino la entrada del paraíso de las letras, o algún dragón sólo para los hombres reservara la fruta de oro de las Ciencias. (Cited in Barbeito Carneiro 1992, 174–75)

(in order to protect it from the threat of envious backbiters who, in the manner of nocturnal shadows, are horrified that our sex should have merited such generalized applause, been decked with such well-earned laurels, and earned itself lasting fame with honors so high in such a shining, immortal talent. As if these profitable distinctions were linked only to males and some fiery sword blocked or forbade entrance to the paradise of letters to feminine discourse, or some dragon reserved the golden fruit of Learning for men only.)

Investigators have not been able to identify an Inés de Casayamor, but Barbeito Carneiro suggests as a "remote possibility" that the name might be an anagram of Inés de Çayas y Sotomayor (1986, 835). In the light of Fontanella's satire, this possibility seems less remote. The letter could well be a rejoinder by Zayas herself or some friend or relative to the *Vejamen*, recasting the allegorical dreamer Fontanella as a misogynistic nocturnal phantom.[16] While the reference to being "crowned with well-earned laurels" may be conventional, it could also be a response to his jibe that her only prize would be the crown of her farthingale.

We have as yet no further trace of Zayas thereafter, nor any definitive documentation of the place or date of her death, although Barbeito Carneiro (1986, 175–76) concludes from the phrasing of the recommendation for the 1659 publication of a combined volume of her works that she was still alive at that date. Serrano y Sanz (1975, 2:583–87) published two death certificates issued in Madrid for women named María de Zayas, dated 1661 and 1669. The first is for a María de Zayas, widow of Juan Valdés, who died in the parish of San Sebastián on 11 January 1661. She leaves all her possessions to one Bartolomé de Çaragoça and his wife, Laura Grasa. These include the right to collect from the heirs of "Magdalena of Ulloa, Marquise of Malagón, my lady," who is also referred to as "Countess," the daily one and a half *reales* she had specified should be paid to this María de Zayas for the remainder of her life, but which had not been paid for the past five years. She concludes both her will and *poder,* or proxy, by saying that although she knows how to read, because of her grave illness and vision loss, she has had a witness sign the documents. The other María de Zayas was the wife of Pedro Balcazar y Alarcón, leaving as heir don Alonso Martínez, of the Capilla Real, in whose house on the "calle del Relox" (Street of the Clock) she died on 26 September 1669. She was buried in San Martín. Barbeito Carneiro is incorrect in saying that Serrano y Sanz concludes that neither death certificate is that of the author; he publishes them without evaluating commentary other than observing the difficulty that the name María de Zayas was common in seventeenth-century Madrid.

Given the evidence of the *Vejamen,* the search for further documentation of her last years and her death should probably be extended to Barcelona and Zaragoza. We can hope that a combination of luck and diligence may produce new testimonies as interesting as that satirical portrait. Meanwhile and in the final analysis, our most valuable witness to the importance of Zayas is the fascinating compound voice that addresses us in the two volumes of her stories.

2

The Writer and Her Reception

Zayas in the Novella Tradition

Zayas's collection of tales is at the same time unique *and* highly conventional, both in its overall structure and in narrative content. She draws on a tradition of familiar tales and narrative motifs, recombining, reworking, and augmenting them with stories partly or wholly of her own invention. Elements of her stories can be traced at least as far back as *Kalilah et Dimnah* and the *Disciplina clericalis* of Petrus Alfonsi (see Chapter 10 below). But the fundamental model for the frame-tale tradition to which Zayas's fictions belong was, of course, that established by Boccaccio's *Decameron* (1353), in which seven young women and three men withdraw from plague-wracked Florence to the countryside and entertain themselves by telling stories, ten each day for ten days.

Although the narrative frame within which Zayas encloses her novellas is a literary descendant of that of Boccaccio, she alters the model by adding to the frame a plot that is important to the didactic or polemical purpose of her collection. Four beautiful young noblewomen and five gallant noblemen gather to celebrate the Christmas season and to entertain their friend Lisis, who is recovering from an illness, by telling two stories a night over five nights. The cause of Lisis's illness is unrequited love for don Juan, one of the noble guests, who prefers her cousin Lisarda. In the first volume, the "maravillas" (marvels), as the stories are termed,[1] are narrated on the first and third nights by women, on the second and fourth by men, and the fifth by don Juan and Lisis's mother, doña Laura. As don Juan continues to prefer Lisarda, Lisis accepts the attentions of don Diego and the first collection ends with the promise of their betrothal on New Year's Day and a second round of storytelling to conclude with Lisis's wedding.

In that second round of storytelling, the second volume of her collection, the opening frame section sets a marked change of tone and time. The storytelling has been postponed for more than a year because of a recurrence of Lisis's illness. When she recovers and the *sarao* (soirée) is resumed during the carnival season (*carnestolendas*), the tales are no longer called *maravillas;* Lisis specifies instead the narration of "desengaños," stories dedicated to "disenchanting," or "disillusioning"—to opening the eyes of all to the dangerous illusions of love and the faithlessness and cruelty of men. This time, Lisis dictates that only women will narrate the disenchantments, to defend the reputation of women, so maligned that virtually no one speaks well of them. The narrators added for this purpose include, among others, a beautiful Moorish "slave" whose own story is the first disenchantment; a nun who tells the ninth tale; and Lisis, who narrates last and, profiting from that story and all the preceding examples, chooses at the end not to marry don Diego but to withdraw from the world of men to secular life in a convent. Zayas thus took Boccaccio's frame as model but reshaped both its content and its ultimate signifying function.[2]

She also drew from Boccaccio and other authors in the Italian novella tradition many of the narrative building blocks with which she constructed the tales related within that frame. Parts of a number of her stories can be traced to Boccaccio's *Decameron,* to the *Novelle* of Matteo Bandello that were such a rich source of plots for Spanish dramatists,[3] to Masuccio's *Novellino,* and possibly to works of other Italian *novellieri* as well.[4]

The vogue of the novella arrived rather belatedly in Spain, vis-à-vis its development in Italy and France. With scattered exceptions, such as the *El pa-*

trañuelo (Tall Tales) (1567) of Joan Timoneda and the *Noches de invierno* (Winter Nights) (1609) of Antonio de Eslava, the novella form only gained popularity with Spanish writers and readers after Cervantes provided a new model in his *Novelas ejemplares* (Exemplary Novels) (1613). In the following decades, particularly in the 1620s and 1630s and in spite of the ban restricting their publication in Castille, the short story rivaled the *comedia* (play) in popular favor. Zayas, too, apparently began writing her novellas in the 1620s, in the shadow of Cervantes' success, and the third story in each of her two volumes is a reworked Cervantine tale. Her debt to Lope de Vega's ironic contribution to the short-story genre, the *Novelas a Marcia Leonarda* (Stories for Marcia Leonarda) (1621/1624) is equally clear; Lope is the only living author other than Ana Caro singled out by name for praise by a Zayas narrator, and she rewrites his story *Las fortunas de Diana* (The Fortunes of Diana) as her ninth novella, *El juez de su causa* (The Judge in Her Own Case) taking her title too from an early Lope play.[5] Less obvious, but not necessarily less significant, is the intertextuality between Zayas's fictions and the stories of Castillo Solórzano, the most prolific author of story collections, and of Pérez de Montalbán, whose two collections were the most popular in Spain if one can judge by the frequency of their republication. As well as similarities in the overall structure of their "novelas cortesanas" (courtly tales), there are resemblances of plots or subplots between these three and other Spanish *noveleros* of the era. Tracing lines of transmission for narrative motifs is a difficult if not futile undertaking, however, for the stories circulated widely both in the written and oral tradition. Nevertheless, as I will show in subsequent chapters, studying Zayas's handling of traditional tales in relation to her male counterparts illuminates the particularities of her vision and presentation.

Reception of Zayas

Sales and Censors

Zayas's novellas were extremely popular in her day; she herself reports in the *Desengaños* on the enthusiastic reception of her first volume: "Si unos le desestimaron, ciento le aplaudieron, y todos le buscaron y le buscan, y ha gozado de tres impresiones, dos naturales y una hurtada" (If a few thought little of it, a hundred applauded it, and all sought it out and continue to seek it, and it has enjoyed three printings, two legitimate editions and one pirated) (Zayas y Sotomayor 1983, 258). More than twenty editions of one or both parts were printed between 1637 and 1814.[6] A number of her novellas circulated in French, German, English, and Dutch, either in direct translations or, more frequently, through French adaptations by Paul Scarron and others, in which Zayas's authorship was not generally acknowledged. Through this route, her stories also found their way into comic plots on the French stage.[7] According to J. A. van Praag, after the *Novelas ejemplares* (Exemplary Novels) of Cervantes, those of Zayas were the best known in western Europe in her day.[8] Judging by the number of editions alone, Zayas's novellas reached a height of popularity with readers in the eighteenth century (Yllera 1983, 64, 76). The steady republication of her complete works ended early in the nineteenth century, as sociopolitical changes impacted the formulation of national literary canons, and complete editions did not reappear until the mid-twentieth century. Nevertheless, her tales' enduring popularity with segments of the reading public was evident in the continuing publication of certain stories in collected volumes.

Trying to understand how Zayas's work has been read over the three and a half centuries since their publication requires some inventive sleuthing, for until recent decades, her tales have occasionally been condemned, and more largely ignored, by critics. Piecing together evidence from scattered remarks or significant silences tells as much about the tastes of the age and its receptivity or hostility to women writers in general as it does about readings of Zayas in particular. Commentary on her novellas has generally centered on three areas, in varying combinations over the years: (1) the moral or didactic worth of her stories; (2) their nature and value as literary works; and (3) whether they qualify as "feminist" or protofeminist texts.

In Zayas's own era, precise critical commentary on contemporary authors was rare, outside of polemical literary debates such as that over *culteranismo*.[9] The praise Zayas earned from fellow authors speaks unspecifically of her "ingenio vivamente claro" (lively clear wit) (Vega Carpio 1776, 165), her "admirables versos, . . . felice ingenio y gran prudencia" (admirable verses . . . felicitous wit and great prudence), her "diez novelas, que son diez asombros" (ten novellas, which are ten wonders), their "artificio" (artifice) and "meditada prosa" (meditated prose) (Castillo Solórzano 1854, 184). Such praise was, however, always coupled with reference to her gender, a fact that reveals how deeply rooted was the belief that women's creative capacities were inherently inferior and Zayas was therefore exceptional as a *woman* writer.

While most censorial approvals are equally general and conventional, some censors did use this platform for more specific observations on the nature of the text and their reasons for granting it license for publication. The censors for the first editions of Zayas's works added brief but significant judgments. Approving the license for the first edition of the *Novelas*, Juan Domingo Briz appended to the standard declaration that the work contained nothing against the Catholic faith and good customs the affirmation "antes gustosa inuentiua y apacible agudeza, digna del ingenio de tal Dama" (rather delightful inventiveness and gentle wit, worthy of the talent of such a Lady) (Zayas y Sotomayor 1637b, fol. q3r). Joseph de Valdivielso, perhaps responding to the demands Zayas advanced in her "Al que leyere" preface terms his approval a necessary courtesy to a woman writer: "Y quando a su Autora, por ilustre emulación de las Corinnas, Saphos, y Aspasias, no se le deviera la licencia que pide, por Dama, y hija de Madrid, me parece que no se le puede negar" (And even if a license were not due to the Authoress as an illustrious emulator of Corinas, Sapphos, and Aspasias, then as a Lady and daughter of Madrid, it seems to me that it cannot be denied to her) (Zayas y Sotomayor 1637b, fol. q2r). Domingo Briz, approving a 1646 Barcelona edition of the *Novelas;* Juan Francisco Ginovés, who approved the *Desengaños* in 1646; and Pío Vives, authorizing a second edition in Barcelona in 1649, all praise the didactic value of her fictions, and the latter two see them as providing gender-specific moral correction. To the standard approvals, Briz adds: "majormente llegintse ab animo candido, desirjant lograr lo rato de la lectura pues a vista de tants desenganys, será la ganancia segura" (particularly as they reach a candid spirit, desiring to take advantage of the time for reading, since the gain is assured in view of so many disenchantments) (1646, fol. A2v). Ginovés continues with the comment that

> le veo lleno de exemplos, para reformar costumbres, y digno de que se dé á la Estampa, que en él (ya que el ocio de las mugeres ha crecido el número á los libros inútiles) la que se ocupare en leerle tendrá exemplos con que huir los riesgos, á que algunas desatentas se precipitan. Assi lo siento.[10]

> (I see it full of examples to reform customs and worthy of being printed, since with it—now that women's idleness has increased the

number of useless books—she who occupies herself in reading it will have examples with which to flee the dangers into which some unheeding women rush headlong. This is my view.)

Whereas Ginovés only expresses concern for reforming idle and heedless women given to reading "useless books," Vives thinks Zayas's have utility for both sexes:

> En él veo un asilo donde puede acogerse la femenil flaqueza más acosada de importunidades lisonjeras, y un espejo de lo que más necesita el hombre para la buena dirección de sus acciones. Y así, le juzgo muy provechoso y digno de comunicarse al mundo por la estampa. (1649, fol. A2r)

> (I see in it a sanctuary in which the womanish weakness most besieged by flattering importunities can find refuge, and a mirror of that which man most needs for the right ordering of his actions. Therefore, I judge it most beneficial and worthy to be transmitted to the world in print.)

Since later editions either repeated early licenses and censorial approvals or omitted such preliminaries, they do little to illuminate the continuing history of Zayas's reception—with one delightful exception. In approving a one-volume 1712 edition of both parts in Valencia, Fray Vicente Bellmont added to the earlier censorial approvals his own savored appreciation of her stories.[11] Seeing verisimilitude in these apparently fabulous tales, he embroiders on the Horatian dictum of sweet utility in literature, comparing Zayas to an ingenious bee in her sweetness and her sting:

> He leído lo que este Libro contiene, y en su Sarao divertido, y provechoso, que mezcla lo vtil con lo dulze, en los desengaños que trae, y novelas que refiere (que aunque parecen fabulosos sucessos, muestran mucho de veridicos;) y aviendolo mirado bien, no hallo cosa, que à la Fè Catolica, buenas costumbres, y Regalias de su Mag. se oponga; y assi puede darse la licencia de reimprimirse; conformandome con las Aprobaciones que ya muy de antes contiene; y aplaudiendo à la Authora [sic] Doña Maria, de argumentosa Aveja, que en lo picante, dulze, y provechoso, si no la aventaja, la emula.

> (I have read what this book contains, and in its entertaining and beneficial *Sarao* that combines the useful with the sweet, in the dis-

enchantments it presents and the novels it recounts—which, although they appear to be fictional stories, reveal much about true events—and having examined it well, I find nothing opposed to the Catholic faith, good customs, and privileges of his Majesty; and thus I authorize its license for reprinting; agreeing with the approvals that it has long contained, and applauding the Authoress doña María, who emulates if not surpasses the busy, ingenious Bee in her sting, sweetness, and worth.)[12]

Zayas's narrative gifts also earned her two citations by Nicholas Antonio, the originator of Spanish literary historiography, in his 1694 volume *Bibliotheca Hispana nova, sive Hispanorum scriptorum qui ab anno MD ad MDCLXXXIV floruere notitia*. He includes her in his alphabetical (by first name), listing of both male and female authors: "D. Maria de Zayas et Sotomayor, Matritensis, amoeni ingenii femina, scripsit: *Novelas amorosas y exemplares*, Tum alibi, tum Caesaraugustae 1638, in 8o; *Novelas y Saraos, Segunda arte*. Caesaraugustae 1647" (D. María de Zayas y Sotomayor, of Madrid, a woman of delightful wit, wrote, *Amorous and Exemplary Novellas*, first elsewhere [*sic*], then in Zaragoza in 1638, in 8o; *Novellas and Soirées, Part Two*, Zaragoza, 1649 [*sic*]) (Antonio 1783–88, 88). The addition of the phrase "amoeni ingenii femina" is at least a small indication of respect for her talents; Mariana de Carvajal merits no such crumb of praise added to his citation of her *Navidades de Madrid* (Christmas in Madrid), but the compliment pales in comparison to his more extended praise of women who write hagiographic works and to the three full pages he devotes to Saint Teresa's life and works. Antonio also adds to this volume an appendix in which he lists some 50 literary women (not necessarily writers).[13] Repeating his citation of Zayas therein, he adds to it that she has earned the praise of her contemporaries, and quotes Lope verses about her in his *Laurel de Apolo* (see Chapter 1, pages 21–22 above) (Antonio 1783–88, 352).

Continued editions of her complete novellas throughout the eighteenth century are the best testimony we have to her popularity with readers.[14] As essayists such as Manuel Benito Fiel de Aguilar and Xavier Lampillas began to build the idea of a national literary canon toward the end of the century (Baker 1990, 16), however, Zayas found a mixed reception. Fiel de Aguilar's *La literatura española demostrada por el erudito don Nicolas Antonio*, a free rendition of the Latin biobibliography, eliminated women writers from the main body of the work and excised Zayas from the appendix of "sabias" (learned women) listed by categories: theology, philosophy, mystic theology, jurisprudence, mathematics, science, and *bellas letras* (which include epistolary correspondence, rhetoric and "other arts") (1787, 99–105). Lampillas, in contrast, accords her high praise in his *Ensayo histórico-apologético de la literatura española contra las opiniones preocupadas de algunos escritores modernos italianos*. Criticizing Bandello for taking only filth and ugliness from Boccaccio and praising a sixteenth-century Spanish translation for cleaning them up, he lauds the stylistic and moral superiority of sixteenth- and early seventeenth-century Spanish novellas:

> La fama que grangearon nuestros noveladores entre los italianos y franceses no la debieron a la licencia contra la honestidad de costumbres, sino a la delicadeza de sus moderados afectos, a la fecundidad de invenciones bien ordenadas, y a la elegancia del estilo. Se haría interminable este párrafo, si diese razón del crecido número de Novelas Españolas que salieron de aquellos tiempos, y fueron traducidas a los idiomas más cultos de Europa. El que deseare hacer el paralelo con los inumerables cuentecillos entretenidos que se publican cada día, hallará que apenas hay invención, desenlace, acontecimiento, ni desenredo de sucesos que no esté en las antiguas Novelas Españolas. En ellas se hicieron famosos Lope de Vega, Juan Pérez de Montalván, Alonso Castillo Solórzano, y la erudita Doña María de Zayas, cuyas Novelas están escritas con tanta gracia, que en el curso de pocos años se hicieron siete reimpresiones, y traducidas en Francés se publicaron en París en dos tomos en los años 1656, 1680 y 1711. (Lampillas 1789, 5:185–86)[15]

> (The fame that our novella-writers earned among the Italians and the French they owed not to offenses against honest customs but to the delicacy of their moderate affections, to the fertility of their well-made plots, and to their stylistic elegance. This paragraph would become endless if I recounted the large number of Spanish Novellas that appeared in those times and that were translated to the most cultured languages of Europe. He who would compare them to the innumerable little entertaining stories that are published every day would scarcely find any invention, denouement, event, or plot development that is not in the old Spanish Novellas. Lope de Vega, Juan Pérez de Montalbán, [and] Alonso Castillo Solórzano became famous for them, and the erudite Doña María de Zayas, whose Novellas are written so gracefully that seven reprints were made of them within the space of a few years and translated

into French, they were published in Paris in two volumes in 1656, 1680, and 1711.)

Could Zayas Have Written *Gil Blas*?

The nineteenth century, however, brought two apparently contradictory changes with regard to Zayas's work: the steady editorial pattern came to a halt in 1814, just as the first critical debate over her literary talents was born. When we examine the underlying causes, however, it is clear that they are not in fact contradictory, nor is it a mere chronological coincidence that republication of her complete works ended just two years after the Constitution of Cadiz in 1812 set out (at least as a project) the construction of a constitutional monarchy in an effort to bring liberal democracy to Spain. The struggle to replace absolutism with a liberal regime was protracted, and replacement of the traditional oligarchic social structure by a bourgeois society took place slowly. But some of the cultural changes that elsewhere accompanied those processes anticipated their consolidation in Spain. One such change was the institution of "literature" being formulated as an aesthetic category distinct from other discourses within the larger, traditional category of arts and letters and a concurrent erasure of women writers as significant contributors to that institution (see Baker 1990 and Jagoe 1993). The institution of literature—mostly fiction—was one of the cultural tools with which an ascendant bourgeoisie defined its superiority against, on the one hand, an aristocracy it viewed as corrupt and artistically uncouth, and on the other, an illiterate and immoral lower class. Baker takes the view that "el surgimiento de un mercado literario y cultural crea el espacio social . . . donde el nuevo hombre de letras puede existir y, con el tiempo, ejercer una especie de soberanía entre intelectual y política en el terreno de una incipiente y también precaria opinión pública (the rise of a literary and cultural market creates the social space . . . in which the new man of letters can exist and, in time, exercise a kind of sovereignty at once intellectual and political in the field of an incipient and also precaria public opinion) (1990, 15). The periodical press, which experienced a meteoric rise in the 1840s, served as a preferred medium in which these new illustrated critics defined the national canon and set its aesthetic criteria, partitioning off "high" literary art from worthless if not corrupting works of pure entertainment, literature for popular consumption (Baker 1990, 15; Jagoe 1993, 226).

As industrial capitalism gained a foothold in Spain and the reading public grew, the novel achieved a preeminent position in the publishing industry and, in the second half of the century, a new critical importance. Whereas in 1822 the periodical *La Censura* stated that "la novela es un género poco importante en literatura" (the novel is a genre of little importance in literature), in 1860 the duke of Rivas termed it the most important literary form (Jagoe 1993, 226). In the same year that *La Censura* voiced its low opinion of the novel, J. A. Llorente planted the seed for the implication of Zayas in a critical debate associated with the rise of the novel and the establishment of a national literary canon. Llorente included Zayas in a list of thirty-seven Spanish authors who he thought might possibly have written the original Spanish version of the *Bachilier de Salamanque* that he considered the model for Alain René Lesage's picaresque vision of French society, *Gil Blas de Santillane*. He saw in her two volumes of novellas "assez de talent pour composer le *Bachiler* et *Gil Blas,* si elle se fût adonnée à des histoires fabuleuses plus longues et plus liées qu'une nouvelle isolée" (enough talent to compose the *Bachelor* and *Gil Blas,* if she had dedicated herself to writing longer fictions, more connected than an isolated novella) (1822, 196). Llorente's judgment furnished a topic for critical debate about Zayas that lasted into the twentieth century.

We can see these processes at work and observe their effect on the evaluation of Zayas in two brief citations by Alberto Lista and Antonio Gil y Zárate. Although in his critical essays Lista paid considerably more heed to poetry and drama than to the novel, he did write a series of four essays on the novel in response to an 1840 discussion of the parallels between novels of chivalry and the historical novel. Tracing the history of the novel from its infancy in the novels of chivalry, he says that after Cervantes buried the "monstrous" novels of chivalry with his pen, "los escritores de novelas se dedicaron al género moral o satírico. . . . Aparecieron entonces las *novelas* de Doña María de Zayas, el *escudero Marcos de Obregón, el Diablo Cojuelo, la pícara Justina, Guzmán de Alfarache,* y otras muchas" (novel writers dedicated themselves to moral or satirical forms. . . . There then appeared the novellas of Doña María de Zayas, the *Squire Marcos de Obregón, The Rogue Justina, Guzmán de Alfarache,* and many others) (Lista y Aragón 1844, 157). Lista does not discriminate between novellas and novels, and adds no weighted qualifying adjectives to separate "high" from "low" forms.

Gil y Zárate, however, in his 1844 manual of literature (repeatedly republished throughout the nineteenth century) reflects the novel's gain in stature. He lauds the picaresque novel and the works of Cervantes as the two pillars on which Spanish pride in the genre could rest. Prior to Cervantes, the Spanish novel followed one of two routes, says Gil y Zárate: in pastoral and chivalric novels, "se había engolfado en un mundo ideal donde nada se presentaba de cuanto existe en la naturaleza" (it had embarked in an ideal world where nothing that exists in the world of nature was present), whereas in picaresque novels, "se arrastraba en lodazales inmundos, pintando los seres más abyectos de las sociedad" (it dragged itself through filthy quagmires, describing the most abject beings in society). Gil y Zárate much prefers the picaresque novels, of which he says, "España tuvo . . . la gloria de ser la creadora de este género de novelas; y si no es enteramente suya la mejor que se conoce [*Gil Blas*], suministró al menos sus materiales" (Spain had . . . the glory of being the creator of this genre of novels; and if the best of them known [*Gil Blas*] is not entirely hers, she at least furnished its materials) (Gil y Zárate 1844, 244). His favorites were *El diablo cojuelo* and *El escudero Marcos de Obregón,* which he thinks the most likely sources for Lesage's *Gil Blas* and deserving of as much appreciation as the French work then so popular in Spain. To his list of picaresque novels Gil y Zárate adds a brief mention of the

> novelas cortas . . . en cuyo género, introducido por Cervantes, se ejercitaron también Lope de Vega, Montalván, Alonso del Castillo Solórzano, Tirso de Molina, no faltando algunas mujeres, como doña María de Zayas y doña Mariana Carvajal y Saavedra. Muchas de estas novelas, como las de Montalván, están mezcladas de versos; pero aunque sus autores dan prueba de ingenio, y se pueden sacar de ellas buenos trozos de prosa, deben considerarse en lo general como obras de entretenimiento más bien que literarias. (Gil y Zárate 1844, 243)

> (novellas . . . a genre, introduced by Cervantes, also practiced by Lope de Vega, Montalbán, Alonso de Castillo Solórzano, Tirso de Molina, including some women, like doña María de Zayas and doña Mariana Carvajal y Saavedra. Many of these novellas, such as those of Montalbán, have verse interspersed in them, but although their authors show evidence of inventiveness and one can find good prose passages in them, they should in general be considered as entertaining rather than literary works.)

Thus, while Gil y Zárate did not specifically reject the possibility that Zayas might have furnished the materials for *Gil Blas,* he demoted the whole

novella genre in which she wrote to the subliterary classification of entertaining works.

Eustaquio de Fernández de Navarrete did, however, specifically refute
Llorente's assertion in 1854. In his one-hundred-page historical survey of
the Spanish novel that prefaced Rosell y López's *Novelistas posterios a Cervantes,* Fernández de Navarrete dedicated two concluding pages to women
writers, centering on Zayas. He considered her a "fácil poetisa, con instruc-
ción no vulgar en las letras humanas" (a facile poetess, with an uncommon
education in human letters) (1854, xcvii). With a chivalrously ironic distaste for learned women, he calls her a "rare anomaly" in a land in which

> no parece sino que rechazan nuestras costumbres que las que nos
> roban los corazones con sus encantos aspiren también con su saber
> a cautivar nuestro entendimiento. Una literata ofrece en general a
> los ojos del vulgo cierto no sé qué de hombruno, que le quita parte
> de los hechizos de su sexo. (xcvi)

> (it seems that our customs deny that the women who steal our
> hearts with their charms should also aspire to capture our under-
> standing with their learning. A literary women generally appears in
> the eyes of the masses to have some sort of mannishness that takes
> away part of the charms of their sex.)

Fernández de Navarrete concedes that talent has no gender and that many
women possess a great degree of talent, particularly for the "imaginative
arts," and therefore, "no hay justicia para que neguemos a la mitad del
género humano espaciarse por los amenos campos de la poesía y de la novela, ni para que nos privemos por una necia altivez del placer que po-
dríamos encontrar en sus delicados escritos" (it would be unjust for us not
to allow half of the human race to expatiate in the pleasant fields of poetry
and the novel, and to deprive ourselves through a foolish arrogance of the
pleasure that we could find in their delicate writings) (xcvi) One wonders
how he defined "delicate writings" in light of the following four Zayas novels: *El castigo de la miseria* (The Miser's Punishment) and *Tarde llega el desengaño* (Too Late Undeceived), along with *La fuerza del amor* (The Power of
Love) and *El juez de su causa* (The Judge in Her Own Case).

With the typical attitude of nineteenth-century adherents to concepts of
the possible and proper spheres for feminine creative activity,[16] Fernández
de Navarrete discounts the idea that Zayas—or any other woman—could
have written *Gil Blas:*

Carecía de la observación y de aquel íntimo conocimiento de las escenas del mundo que sólo puede adquirir un hombre, y de que está
privada una señora por el retiro y circunspección en que la obliga a
vivir el decoro de su sexo. A éste no le es permitido penetrar en los
palacios de los príncipes sino en días de teatral ceremonia; nunca
en el sucio asilo del vagabundo y pordiosero, en el garito de los
tahures, ni en el burdel de la cortesana corrompida. No ve el
mundo cual es, sino tal cual en el trato superficial y poco franco se
le ofrece a sus ojos; los hombres, por el respeto que se merece, se
presentan siempre ante una mujer con hipócrita compostura; y así,
antes puede adivinarlos que conocerlos. Malas circunstancias son
las que refiero para escribir novelas, cuyo principal mérito consiste
en el profundo conocimiento de las costumbres de las distintas
clases de la sociedad; conocimiento que se adquiere, más que en la
meditación del gabinete, siendo actor o espectador a lo menos de
los lances que se describen o de otros idénticos. (xcvii-xcviii)

(She lacked observation and that intimate knowledge of scenes of
the world that only a man can acquire, and of which a lady is de-
prived by the retirement and circumspection in which the decorum
of her sex requires her to live. That sex is not permitted to penetrate the palaces of princes except in days of theatrical ceremony;
never in the dirty refuge of the vagabond and beggar, in the gambling den, nor in the brothel of the corrupt courtesan. She does not
see the world as it is but as it is offered to her eyes in superficial,
controlled acquaintance; men, out of the respect that they deserve,
always present themselves before women in a hypocritical pose;
thus, she can at best guess about rather than know them. The circumstances I relate are bad for writing novels, whose principal
merit consists of profound knowledge of the customs of the different clases of society; a knowledge that is acquired less in meditation
in the study than in being an actor or at least a spectator of the inci-
dents that are described, or of other identical ones.)

He credits her instead with a flowing, elegant, and interesting narrative
style, as well as with clarity of expression, the last of which many later critics
and translators would dispute. He chides her, however, for sometimes pro-
moting "vulgar concerns" such as the prodigious effects of magic in *La inocencia castigada* but concedes that this philosophical defect does not detract from the pleasure her works provide.

Fernández de Navarrete's patronizing and partial (in two senses) judgment reflects not only bourgeois ideology regarding the nature and proper role of women, but also the complex history of women's role in the rise of the novel.[17] Jagoe (1993, 226) points out that the novel was one of the first cultural forms to achieve mass production and distribution, through delivery to subscribers' homes by installment and through serialization in periodicals. At midcentury it was still considered by many Spanish commentators not only a frivolous genre but also one dangerous to morals, particularly among women, the young, and the lower classes (Jagoe 1993, 227). Its readership did include an increasing number of women, and beginning in 1841, a significant number of women also wrote and published novels. In Jagoe's words,

> These female authors played a significant role in ridding the novel of the stigma of immorality. Their insecurity about wielding the figuratively phallic pen rather than the prescribed feminine needle caused them to downplay the novel's history of political subversiveness and licentiousness, and to advertise instead its potential for spreading rather than subverting conventional middle-class values. Far more constricted than their male counterparts in educational and commercial opportunities as well as permissible vocabulary and subject matter, they set out to identify themselves as the blameless apologists of respectability, writing apolitical, "educational" novels that catered to an apparently innocuous readership of young ladies and respectably married women. (229)

As a number of popular male novelists also addressed themselves to a presumably feminine audience, whether or not women truly constituted the novel's primary readers, the genre came to be viewed as feminine.

As the novel acquired increasing dominance in the literary market, some middle-class liberals began to defend serial novels, seeing in their broad popularity a social and politically useful medium for propagating nationalism and moral values in all classes. Desire on the part of a male intellectual elite to exert control over novel reading and writing resulted on the one hand in the "wholesale censorship" of novels in the 1850s and a ban on women's publishing without their husbands' consent, and on the other, in a call for an aesthetic reform that would masculinize the novel form (Jagoe 1993, 229). That reform, as theorized and practiced by Galdós and other male novelists, called for the replacement of idealism, the mode previously considered more noble and worthy, with a realism that presumably only male writers could produce. Thus novels were divided into two classes: low, idealist, and feminocentric works of entertainment devoured by uncritical readers, and high literary art, realist novels for educated, serious readers seeking edification rather than diversion (234–40).[18]

In sum we can say that the emergence of a substantial number of women novelists in the nineteenth-century literary market may be part of the reason for the lengthy interruption in publication of Zayas's novellas; the availability of new works by women writers would logically decrease the demand for new editions of a long-familiar writer. At the same time, a new critical establishment interested in a masculinization of the novelistic discourse was unlikely to view her works impartially, nor to accept Llorente's suggestion that Zayas as a woman writer might possibly have contributed to the creation of that pillar of the national canon, the picaresque novel.

Pardo Bazán: An Aristocratic Picaresque

Not surprisingly, it was Pardo Bazán, who, near the turn of the century, countered both the editorial and critical trends in Zayas's reception. She published eight Zayas tales in the third volume of the Biblioteca de la Mujer series that she directed, with a preface in which she took issue with Fernández de Navarrete's evaluation of Zayas and with the selection of novellas published in *Novelistas posteriores a Cervantes*.[19] She quotes his discussion of Zayas in full, and then challenges his idea that women cannot observe the "real" world, which she links with the prejudices of "contemporary pseudorealists" who think that "only scenes from the gambling den, the brothel, or the hospital are realism" (c. 1892, 12). Zayas was neither a poor observer nor timorous in her expression; rather "that frank, dry, rather cynical note" that characterized picaresque narratives "sounds out more clearly in the writings of *Lisis* than in any of her contemporaries" (13). She gives us, says Pardo Bazán, a picaresque literature of the aristocracy:

> Lo que distingue las *Novelas* de doña María de Zayas entre las de los demás autores picarescos también clásicos y venerados por su donaire y sanidad de lengua, es que la ilustre dama pinta las costumbres de una esfera social que podemos llamar aristocrática. . . . Doña María no pinta el pueblo, y por lo mismo sus obras son un documento precioso, pues demuestran a todo el que se tome la molestia

de cotejarlas con las populares de entonces, que el espíritu pi-
caresco y de bellaquería no era fenómeno peculiar de las clases in-
feriores, sino que se encontraba difuso en todas las esferas sociales.
(13–14)

(What distinguishes the *Novelas* of doña María de Zayas from those
of the other classic picaresque authors, also venerated for the grace
and soundness of their language, is that the illustrious lady paints
the customs of a social sphere we can call aristocratic. . . . Doña
María does not paint common people, and for that in itself her
works are a precious document, as they demonstrate to anyone who
will take the trouble to compare them with then-popular works that
the roguish picaresque spirit was not a phenomenon unique to the
lower classes, but diffused among all social spheres.)

Pardo Bazan ranks Zayas's best stories with those of Cervantes and argues
that for the author of *El castigo de miseria* (The Miser's Reward), writing *El
Bachiller de Salamanca* (The Salamanca Graduate) or *La pícara Justina* (The
Rogue Justina) would not have been an arduous enterprise. She defends
Zayas's use of magic and the marvelous, saying that the trick the wise "Lisis"
[*sic*] uses on the miser of *El castigo* is no more reprehensible than Cervantes' use of magic in the *Coloquio de los perros* (The Colloquoy of the
Dogs). Nor was she "más supersticiosa de lo que somos las que hoy
seguimos y respetamos las huellas de su pie de Musa" (more superstitious
than those of us who today follow in her footprints and respect her as our
Muse) (13). Citing use of the marvelous by contemporary writers such as
Teófilo Gautier, Próspero Merimée, and Ivan Turgenev, Pardo Bazán con-
tends that it was a response to the taste of the public of their day, and
moreover, to "las perennes exigencias de la imaginación de los lectores en
todo tiempo" (the perennial demands of the imagination of readers of all
times) (13).

In line with this judgment, Pardo Bazán includes *La inocencia castigada*
(Innocence Punished) and another Zayas tale involving magic, *El desengaño
amando y premio de la virtud* (The Road to Disillusionment and the Prize for
Virtue), in her selection.[20] Despite having linked Zayas with the picaresque,
citing the "tyranny of custom," she regretfully omitted two of her tales that
most clearly resemble that mode, *El prevenido engañado* (Forewarned but
Not Forearmed) and *Al fin se paga todo* (Just Desserts) and another "pretty"
novella "because of their crudeness." Given the increase in "external mod-

esty" since Zayas's day, says Pardo Bazán, "me temo . . . que se la juzgue mal por culpa de algunas frases vivas y algunas escenas poco veladas (aunque nunca relamente licenciosas), que pueden encontrarse en sus escritos" (I fear . . . that she be judged ill on account of some lively phrases and imprudent—although never really licentious—scenes that can be found in her writings) (15).

Applauding her vigorous advocacy of women's rights, Pardo Bazán summarizes the pleasure she finds in her work:

De mí sé decir que doña María me deja en el paladar el gratísimo sabor del Jerez oro, aromático y neto. Su ingenuidad templada por la discreción; su agudeza y vivacidad propiamente femeniles; su aplomo y señorío de distinguida dama y su completa ausencia de sentimentalismo y gazmoñería, me cautivan y enamoran. (16)

(As for me, I can say that doña María leaves on my palate the welcome flavor of Sherry, golden, aromatic, and genuine. I am captivated and enamored by her candor tempered with discretion, her truly feminine wit and vivacity, her poise and dignity as a distinguished lady, and her complete lack of sentimentality and priggishness.)

The Victorian View: An Indecent Zayas

If a reader such as Pío Vivas in Zayas's day saw her tales as a salutary sanctuary for women, a corrective mirror, readers schooled in restrictive Victorian standards of decency saw them very differently indeed, as even Pardo Bazán indicated in her selection. George Ticknor, while acknowledging Zayas as a "sturdy defender of women's rights," thinks *El prevenido engañado,* although written by " 'a lady of the court,' . . . one of the most gross I remember to have read," and he criticizes Scarron for not mitigating "its shameless indecency" in his version of the story (1866, 3:143).

Ludwig Pfandl is in 1933 yet more extreme in his condemnation of Zayas's art on both moral and literary grounds. While admitting that these "libertine histories" are "entertaining and almost always interesting" (369), he criticizes them for lack of unity, for excessive, sadistic realism, for obscenity, and for repetition of well-known motifs, and he compares her work to "un edificio gótico estropeado por arquitectos renacentistas y barrocos" (a Gothic edifice ruined by Renaissance and Baroque architects) (Pfandl 1933, 36). He takes issue with an unnamed "modern American writer" who describes doña María as the first Spanish feminist, and says that Zayas is at best an inconsistent feminist if one takes into account some of the figures with which she populates her stories. Finally, he concludes: "¿Se puede dar algo más ordinario y grosero, más inestético y repulsivo que una mujer que cuenta historias lascivas, sucias, de inspiración sádica y moralmente corrompidas?" (Can there be anything more common and gross, more unaesthetic and repulsive, than a woman who writes lascivious, dirty, sadistic, and morally corrupt stories?) (370).[21]

Lena E. V. Sylvania, the critic whom Pfandl disdained to name, raised the issue of feminism in the first monograph dedicated to Zayas, published in 1922, just after women in the United States secured the right to vote. She asserts that Zayas "can well be classed with those who first braved public opinion to assert and maintain, by force of argument, that women have certain rights and that, as human beings, they are not inferior to men" (13:197). Sylvania does admit that Zayas's "sprightly" novellas are "sometimes a little crude, but scarcely objectionable enough to be termed licentious" (Sylvania 1922, 14:206). Reading the novellas as portraits of the society, manners, and moral standards of the age,[22] she sees Zayas as an "ardent Christian" and a didactic writer whose occasional crudeness is "justified by the loftiness of her underlying purpose, namely, the enlightenment of her sex, and by her effective protest against the tyranny of man and the warning note she sounds to women to beware of the snares and temptations of the world" (14:206). Sylvania also studies possible Italian and Spanish sources for several Zayas stories, and their subsequent reworking by other authors, an effort greatly extended by Edwin Place. He seconds Sylvania's evaluation of the intent of Zayas's novellas, which, taken as a whole, "constitute a strong argument against the current opinion of that age that women were designing, weakminded creatures of very unstable morals" (Place 1923, 8). Some of her stories were too strong for his stomach, however. Of *Mal presagio casar lejos* (Marrying Afar: Portrait of Doom), a *desengaño* that involves multiple murders and a homosexual scene, he says: "For this revolting story of cruelty I have no source to offer. It may have been a tale invented by the Spanish to justify the cruelty of the Duke of Alba, if we are to regard Zayas' explanation, given at the end of the story, as having any significance. At any rate, the story may be classed as more feministic propaganda, and is moreover, the most blood-curdling of the whole collection" (47).

Literary Psychology

Angel Valbuena Prat, writing with his usual critical acumen in his *Historia de la literatura española,* published in Republican Barcelona in 1937, shifted the terms for judging Zayas's tales away from moralistic criteria to an appreciation of her tales for their literary merit, psychological insight, and "fine sensuality." He describes Zayas as

> un temperamente finamente sensual; y a los motivos amorosos, en los que por un lado no temía lo escabroso, y de otro penetraba en exquisitas idealizaciones, debe sus éxitos más vivos. Algunos procedimientos, literariamente bellos, interesan además, por ser anticipaciones del mundo del subconsciente, hoy puesto en primer plano en la escuela de Freud. (1937, 105) ˈ

> (a finely sensual temperament; she owes her liveliest successes to amorous themes, in which, on the one hand, she was not afraid of scabrous things, and on the other, filled them with exquisite idealizations. Some elements of her stories, beautiful in literary terms, are also interesting as anticipations of the world of the subconscious, today advanced by the Freudian school.)

In that vein, he describes at length the dreams of Jacinta in Zayas's first story (see Chapter 4 below), and delights in the satirical and psychological force of *El castigo de la miseria,* whose Cervantine inspiration he recognizes. Valbuena agrees with Sylvania that Zayas is interesting as a "true and enthusiastic feminist" who preached a concept of women that was freer and more modern than that of her times, and he characterizes as "pre-Romantic" her outpourings of violence, tears, and sexual daring.

> Distinguida, fina de alma, y exquisitamente erótica, supo dar una vida a los cuadros realistas y a las desmelenadas aventuras trágicas, que la convierten, para mi gusto, en la mejor derivación del Cervantes de las «Ejemplares» cuyos límites amplía en la dirección que pudiéramos llamar prerromántica. (106)

> (Distinguished, a refined spirit, and exquisitely erotic, she knew how to give life to realistic scenes and untrammeled tragic adventures that, in my opinion, make her the best successor to the Cer-

vantes of the "Exemplary Novels," whose limits she expanded in a
direction that we might call pre-Romantic.)

Zayas as Realist

At midcentury Agustín de Amezúa gave readers the first complete modern
editions of the *Novelas amorosas* (1948) and the *Desengaños amorosos* (1950),
with an extensive introduction to the first volume.[23] Furthermore, he provided a new focus for the critical debate over her works with his insistent
characterization of Zayas as a "realistic" writer. Discounting source studies
such as that of Place and taking at face value the declarations of Zayas's
narrators that they are recounting true stories, Amezúa considered her stories a faithful reflection of the tumultuous reality of Golden Age Spain.[24] At
the same time, he saw her characters as a mimetic representation of her
own feminine temperament, or vice versa.[25] He followed some ideas suggested earlier by Valbuena Prat, calling her pre-Romantic in her use of
magic and mystery, and citing her psychological insight. The latter is for
Amezúa, however, not an anticipation of Freud's investigation of the unconscious, but a subset of his own theory of narrative realism and innate
feminine insight, which makes women both more sensitive and more credulous than men.[26] Amezúa calls Zayas an "intransigent feminist" (1948,
xxi), and describes as surprising her defense of women's equality on the
basis of material and spiritual identity with men (1948, xxv). In his introduction to the *Desengaños* (1950, xxi), he cites Marivaux's "curious theory"
that literary styles have "their own sex"; if so, he says, that of Zayas is "fran-
camente femenino, por su ligereza, nerviosidad e impresionismo, trasunto
del alma de una mujer" (frankly feminine, for its lightness, nervous flexibility, and impressionism, a likeness of a woman's soul.) Accepting as fact
her authorial declaration that she writes in a natural style, he praises her
avoidance of *culteranismo*. At the same time, however, he finds that style imperfect:

> Páginas escritas al correr de la pluma, en las que la fuerza y calor del
> relato vencen a la preocupación estilística. . . . De ahí nacen, en
> consecuencia, sus defectos también; las oraciones largas, demasiado
> largas, con períodos intercalados en el principal, que a veces hacen
> oscuro el sentido y dificultan no poco la buena puntuación; ciertas
> incorrecciones y descuidos gramaticales, repeticiones innecesarias;
> *ques* expletivos, y tal cual solecismo, por fin, lunarcillos y tachas de

su estilo, que peca acaso de demasiado familiar, pero, por eso
mismo, más valioso también para la historia del lenguaje. (1950,
xxi)

(Pages written as fast as the pen can move, in which the vigor and
warmth of the narrative prevail over stylistic concerns . . . As a result, from this too spring her defects; long sentences, too long, with
clauses inserted in the main sentence that sometimes obscure its
meaning and pose no small difficulty for good punctuation; exclam-
atory "whiches" and an occasional solecism, in all, small blemishes
and flaws in her style, which perhaps sins in overfamiliarity, but is
for that in itself more valuable for the history of the language.)

Although Amezúa makes Zayas a full participant in the "great age of
faith," when saving one's soul was the primary goal, and a didactic, moralizing writer, he cannot shake a discomfort with some of her fictions, which
he says should not be put in the hands of all readers (xxxiv).[27] "Pecan
muchas veces de escabrosos y lúbricos, y . . . más de una de sus novelas no
se cohonestan, por su atrevimiento, con el calificativo de *ejemplares* y *honestas* con que ella las rotuló" (They are often very scabrous and lubricious
and . . . more than one of her novellas in their daring do not jibe with the
qualifiers *exemplary* and *honest* with which she labeled them) (1948, xxxi).
Yet he maintains that Pfandl went too far in his condemnation and failed
to understand that the "realism" of Zayas "no era exagerado, sino verdadero; que la sociedad española del siglo XVII presentaba aquellos mismos acres contrastes . . . entre religiosidad y lujuria, lujo y miseria, devoción y galanteria" (was not exaggerated but truthful; that Spanish society of
the seventeenth century presented those same sharp contrasts . . . between
religiosity and lust, luxury and misery, devotion and galantry) (1948,
xxxiv).

Structuralism: Conventional Crucigrams

Amezúa's insistence on Zayas's "realism" stimulated a flurry of opposing
evaluations by readers of the 1970s, which were guided by formalist and
structuralist theories of literature. Juan Goytisolo lead the way with a
provocative essay in which he portrays Amezúa's reading as symptomatic of
a retrograde, "decimonónico" (nineteenth-century) tradition of Spanish
literary criticism that ignores the fact that literary works engage more with
literary traditions than with any reflection of "reality." Mocking Amezúa for

taking on faith Zayas's declaration that the stories are true, he compares her plots to the "argumentos crucigramas" (crossword-puzzle plots) of detective novels and Westerns in which novelty resides in the disposition of well-known elements, the small variations introduced and the particular solution arranged (1977, 65–73). Zayas employed without irony or major alteration the available elements in the literary arsenal of her day and populated her stories with two-dimensional characters, functional pieces in an "ars combinatoria" of didactic design, says Goytisolo. Her fictions, he finds, are polar opposites of the realism Amezúa exalted.

Alessandra Melloni (1976), in studying Zayas's narrative technique from the perspective of the narratological and semiotic theories of Genette and Eco, is even more insistent than Goytisolo on the conventionality of Zayas's fictions.[28] Sandra Foa (1979), on the other hand, accepts the idea of Zayas's "realism," but does point out that the desire to convince readers of the truth of her stories is part of her didactic purpose. Foa also describes Zayas's use of rhetorical devices, the subordination of character to idea, and her debt to previous writers from Boccaccio to Lope de Vega. Marcia Welles proposes that Zayas's *novelas cortesanas* should be evaluated according to the genre to which they rightly belong, that of the idealized conventions of the romance as defined by Northrup Frye. For Welles, the tales lack any form of external realism, but "they nevertheless reveal an internal realism corresponding to the mythic level of universal truth" (Welles 1978, 307).

Hans Felten (1978), in a rather forced association of Zayas's fictions with "moralistic" literature from Machiavelli to Gracián, suggests that the very use of the word "exemplary" in her title is conventional. He thinks she is less interested in supplying ethically exemplary tales, or even in a thoroughgoing "suffragette" defense of women, than she is in presenting a morally-neutral description of human customs, a study of appearance and discretion, of deceit and its unmasking and the cleverness required to prevail in amorous relationships in a world ruled by deception.

By far the most complete study of Zayas from the structuralist era is that of Montesa Peydro (1981), which he calls rightly calls a multiperspectivist approach, availing itself of sociology and semiology as well as structuralism. Not a book that can be succinctly summarized, it will continue for some time to be a significant contribution to Zayas studies. While keeping in view the importance of convention in her stories, he sets them in the context of the social realities of her day and believes that she reflects the state of mind of the most penetrating Spaniards of her century in the pessimism of her works, in which the omnipresence of war and the consciousness of national decline are so evident. Particularly valuable is his concluding analysis of narrative voices and levels, as well as his survey of extant editions, complete and partial, of her works.

Poststructuralism: Desire and the Patriarchy

Goytisolo also led the way in another reevaluation of Zayas's fiction, that of the eroticism criticized by readers from Ticknor to Amezúa.[29] Despite her "feminist crusade," he says, Zayas created female characters who operate as actively desiring subjects as well as objects of desire, and whose sexuality sometimes makes passive objects of males, thus blurring the difference between genders (1977, 97–103). The repressive social norms of her century prevented the expression of eroticism possible in *La Celestina* (Celestina) or *La lozana andaluza* (Portrait of Lozana, the Lusty Andalusian Woman); nevertheless, says Goytisolo, in Zayas's tales, "la procesión iba por dentro y el fuego que corroe a los personajes femeninos se trasluce en visiones, pesadillas y sueños que parecen directamente extraídos del consultorio siquiátrico de algún estudioso de Freud" (the procession went on within and the fire that gnaws at feminine characters is translated in visions, nightmares and dreams that seem to be drawn straight from the psychiatric clinic of some student of Freud) (97). For Goytisolo, her combination of the erotic with burlesque touches, magic and violence is what makes her fictions live for readers today; he concludes: "En un país cuya literatura ha servido desde siglos de vehículo transmisor—a menudo admirable—a la institucionalización de sus complejos y frustraciones sexuales, las *novelas* de María de Zayas se destacan de modo señero y nos conmueven aún con la frescura de su insólito y audaz desafío" (In a country whose literature has for centuries served as a transmitter—often an admirable one—for the institutionalization of its sexual complexes and frustrations, the novels of María de Zayas alone stand out and still move us with the freshness of her singular and daring challenge) (109).

This "desafío"—the nature and limits of Zayas's challenge to patriarchal institutions—has been the focus of recent critics, who have brought a variety of poststructuralist theoretical perspectives to readings of her fictions. Rather than attempting to describe here the studies multiplying in articles, conference papers, and book projects, I leave reference to them for appropriate points in the chapters to follow.[30] A few suggestive studies deserve particular recognition, however. Paul Julian Smith (1989), studying "the enabling conditions for sexual difference itself" and the problem of female resistance, bodily and textual, to a male authority "always already in place," reads Zayas in the light of the theories of Julia Kristeva and Luce Irigaray and finds covert contradictions in her superficially conservative text that sometimes mimics, sometimes subverts the masculine tradition. Bruce Gartner (1989) couples René Girard's model of triangulated desire with a Derridean interest in textual inscriptions and economies of exchange and with feminist perspectives on the possibilities of an alternative feminine discourse in a dissertation one hopes will appear as a published monograph. Lou Charnon-Deutsch (1991), in a richly insightful article, demonstrates the ways in which Zayas subverts the gendered relationships of dominance and challenges a sexual economy based on the exchange of women, seen as passive, idealized objects. Focusing primarily on *La esclava de su amante* (Slave to Her Own Lover) and *El juez de su causa,* she shows how Zayas introduces subtle but significant alterations in traditional narrative patterns that allow feminine agency as women take in their own hands the redress of masculine abuse, failures of marriage contracts and the inconstancy of male desire.

My own reading of Zayas shares with theirs a combination of psychoanalytic and feminist perspectives on the logic, drive, and intent of Zayas's narratives, but I broaden that focus through a multivalent attention to historical context. I put twentieth-century psychoanalytic explanations in dialogue with explanations of the human psyche and of sexual difference current in Zayas's day, and I read her reworking of familiar narrative elements intertextually, against the novella tradition she inherited. I explore the play of historical events in her work, considering first how the multiple crises Spain faced in the 1640s may have impacted the darkened tone of her second volume. Second, I show how she reconfigured and redeployed the heroes, allies and enemies of the Spanish monarchy as she traced out a psychic map of the dilemma of women in the patriarchal family. Finally, I connect her narration of that dilemma to the fundamental ideological tension that pervades and animates her stories—the impasse between gender and class identity for this aristocratic, protofeminist writer.[31] While she painted in lurid colors the unjust treatment of women as a group, she defended with equal passion the superiority of her aristocratic class. With that defense, Zayas paradoxically accepted the legitimacy of the institutions that supported the aristocracy, the very institutions that also prescribed the repression of women whose injustice she protested.

3

The Prologue "Al que leyere" and the Question of Zayas's Feminism

¿Qué razón hay para que no tengamos promptitud para ~~los hombres~~ los libros?
(What reason is there that we women should not have readiness ~~for men~~ *for books?*)

Zayas a Feminist?

Concluding the previous chapter, I described Zayas as an aristocratic, protofeminist writer, torn between gender and class identity. Another tension too pervades and shapes her novellas: her sometimes complementary, sometimes conflicting, ambitions to secure greater respect for all women and, at the same time, recognition for her own merits as a writer, within a thoroughly masculine literary tradition. The phrase I quote as an epigraph for this chapter appears near the conclusion of the authorial preface to her first volume of stories; I foreground it here because I believe that the slip of the pen between "men" and "books" that she corrected between the first and second editions of 1637 reveals that tension at work, as I will explain at greater length below. While she speaks on behalf of women and often to them, the judge and jury whom she implicitly or explicitly seeks to persuade are masculine. Recognition of that tension in her writerly ambitions can help us understand both the underlying logic of her protofeminist arguments and the debate surrounding her classification as a feminist.

Numerous readers of Zayas, from Pío Vives through poststructuralists, have considered her a "feminist" writer, seeing her as a spokeswoman for women, a writer who addresses specifically feminine experience and whose objective is that of improving the lot of women. With the exception of Sylvania, however, many others have found her a flawed feminist. The first mark registered against her status as a feminist was the objection that she writes about "bad" women. Readers from Pfandl to Griswold have asked how Zayas can be considered a legitimate, effective, or sincere defender of women's rights when a number of her female characters are less than ideal models of moral conduct. Pfandl, for example, concedes that Sylvania's description of Zayas as a feminist is legitimate up to a point

> en cuanto la Zayas sabe encontrar no pocas frases bellas y acertadas contra los rígidos preceptos que regulaban las relaciones entre hombres y mujeres en la España de aquel tiempo. Pero no debe olvidarse, en el entusiasmo de una tesis preconcebida, que la misma Zayas, ya sea por descuido o con intención . . . introduce una serie de figuras que ponen muy en duda la formalidad de sus teorías. (1933, 370)

> (inasmuch as Zayas knows how to find not a few beautiful and accurate phrases against the rigid precepts that regulated relations between men and women in the Spain of her time. But it should not be forgotten, in enthusiasm for a preconceived thesis, that the same Zayas, whether carelessly or intentionally . . . introduces a series of figures that cast much doubt on the seriousness of her theories.)

The stories most often cited in this regard are the novelas *El prevenido, engañado* (Forewarned but not forearmed)and *Al fin se paga todo* (Just Desserts),[1] in which female protagonists actively pursue satisfaction of their desires, deceiving or making fools of a series of men in so doing. Amezúa defends these characters as a "realistic" reflection of women in Zayas's day, while Felten sees them as evidence of Zayas's nonjudgmental "moralistic" observation of female as well as male use of deceit in amorous relationships, which takes priority over her feminist objectives (1978, 124). What critics scandalized by these stories have not noticed is that Zayas tells them through male narrators, thus creating an ironically double-voiced perspective, the significance of which will be discussed in Chapter 6 of this study.

Griswold, reading with much more sensitivity to the literary structure of the *Sarao,* also questions the characterization of Zayas as a feminist writer. She suggests that Zayas's reputation as a feminist propagandist is in large part a result of a patronizing attitude toward women writers and of naive, intentionalistic readings that attribute all profeminist opinions in the *Sarao* to the author, overlooking the complex literary structure of the work and the ironic distances she opens up between the multiple layers of narrators and audiences within it (1980, 99–101). Even Lisis, despite her authorial function in the frame narrative, should not be presumed to be an alter ego for Zayas, says Griswold; the concluding *desengaño* that Lisis relates, *Estragos que causa el vicio,* centering as it does on a desiring woman who causes the death of a whole household, is "a dubious contribution" to the defense of women (109), one that contributes more to the antifeminist position that, in Griswold's view, is stated with equal vigor in the work.

As Foa, Melloni, and Griswold all point out, Zayas participated in a long-standing literary and philosophical debate concerning the nature and rights of women.[2] Situating Zayas as a feminist writer in relation to the *Querelle de femmes,* to the view of women in Neoplatonism and Christian humanism, and to Cervantes, Lope, and Quevedo, Foa finds Zayas's passionate, artistic treatment of the feminist theme original and virtually unique in an era characterized in Spain by pessimism, political decadence, and a recrudescence of misogyny. Melloni, on the other hand, feels that even in the debate about the nature and rights of women, Zayas did not alter either the literary or ideological canons of her era, except perhaps in the fervor with which she called women to arms against men (1976, 89–103). Griswold proposes that Zayas used the feminist-antifeminist debate, a long-standing literary topos, as a central *literary* structure with which to treat a "more fundamental opposition" (1980, 110), applicable to both sexes, that between will and reason, head and heart. In Griswold's opinion, "Zayas' personal feminism is a highly dubious matter, and one must reject the notion that feminism is the central impulse of her writing. Surely it is *not* an obsessive thesis for which the *novelas* provide pamphleteering support, nor can Zayas' work be said, by any stretch of the imagination, to be an intrepid defense of women's rights. At best, feminism and antifeminism are counter-themes which provide an important structuring element to the book and a concrete articulation of a more abstract theme" (113).

The Feminist Logic of "Al Que Leyere"

Any judgment of Zayas as a feminist necessarily begins with the theses she presents in the "Al que leyere" (To the reader) preface to the *Novelas*. Only in this preface and in a brief postscript signed in her own name at the end of the *Desengaños* does Zayas speak in her own voice.[3] The arguments that Zayas presents therein place her right in the center of a more recent debate of vital concern to feminism, that between the validity of "essentialist" and of "constructionist" definitions of women. For Diane Fuss, this debate reflects the "difficulty of theorizing the social in relation to the natural" (1989, 1).[4] Essentialists define women on the basis of a biological nature, finding the essence of the feminine in that which is presumed to be outside the social, untainted if perhaps repressed by patriarchal order. Luce Irigaray deploys an essentialist view of women in her lyrical evocation of "two lips that speak together," and similar assumptions generally underlie the idea of *écriture féminine*, of a particular kind of writing inherent to women.[5] For constructionists, on the other hand, definitions of a feminine essence are culturally and historically produced (Fuss 1989, 2). As Thomas Laqueur argues in his book *Making Sex*, definitions of the nature of the flesh and of sexual difference are always rendered within and in the service of a particular social order.[6] Yet Fuss finds that even in the most radically constructionist views of sexual difference, traces of essentialism linger.[7] Although Zayas grounds her defense of women primarily in constructionist assertions, more than a trace of essentialism surfaces in her argument.

"Al que leyere" is, in its rhetorical strategy, the linguistic equivalent of hurling a guantlet at one's opponent and then curtseying to him. (The implied reader to whom Zayas directs her preface is clearly masculine; hence my pronoun choice.) The force of her self-justification as a woman writer derives from her impassioned tone and mobile, cumulative style of argumentation rather than from philosophical consistency. Her opening address to the reader challenges the masculine injunction to feminine silence and the general presumption of women's (intellectual) incapacity, then shifts to a demand for the courtesy that all gentlemen owe to women.

> Quién duda, lector mío, que te causará admiración que una mujer tenga despejo, no sólo para escribir un libro, sino para darle a la estampa. . . . Quién duda, digo otra vez, que habrá muchos que atribuyan a locura esta virtuosa osadia de sacar a luz mis borrones,

siendo mujer, que, en opinión de algunos necios, es lo mismo que una cosa incapaz; pero cualquiera, como sea no más de buen cortesano, ni lo tendrá por novedad ni lo murmurará por desatino. (*Novelas,* 21)

(No doubt, my reader, you will be amazed that a woman should have the nerve, not only to write a book but to have it published. . . . No doubt, I repeat, many will attribute to madness this virtuous audacity of printing my scribbles, being a woman which, in the opinion of some idiots, is the same as being incompetent; but even if only as a good gentleman, no one will consider it a novelty nor whisper about it as a folly.)

As Zayas summons arguments against female inferiority to men, she first asserts their material and spiritual identity with men:

porque si esta materia de que nos componemos los hombres, y las mujeres, ya sea una trabazón de fuego, y barro, o ya una masa de espíritus, y terrones, no tiene más nobleza en ellos que en nosotras, si es una misma la sangre, los sentidos, las potencias y los órganos por donde se obran sus efetos, son unos mismos, la misma alma que ellos, porque las almas ni son hombres ni mujeres; ¿qué razón ay para que ellos sean sabios y presuman que nosotras no podemos serlo? (*Novelas,* 21)

(because if this matter of which we are made, men and women, whether it be a union of fire and clay or an amalgamation of spirits and clods of earth, has no more nobility in them than in us, if it is the same blood, the same senses, powers and organs through which they work their effects, because souls are neither male nor female; what reason is there that they should be wise and presume that we cannot be so?)

Next she adds to this a striking, pure constructionist argument that women's apparent deficiencies are due to inadequate education and social constraints, saying that

esto no tiene, a mi parecer, más respuesta, que su impiedad, o tiranía en encerrarnos, y no darnos maestros: y así la verdadera causa de no ser las mujeres doctas, no es defecto del caudal, sino falta de la aplicación, porque si en nuestra crianza, como nos ponen el cambray en las almohadillas, y los dibuxos en el bastidor, nos dieran libros, y preceptores, fuéramos tan aptas para los puestos, y para las Cátedras, como los hombres. (*Novelas,* 21–22)

(in my opinion, there is no other explanation for this than their cruelty or tyranny in enclosing us and in not giving us teachers; and thus the true reason why women are not learned is not a defect in their resources, but lack of application, because if in our upbringing they gave us books and preceptors as they supply us with chambray for sewing cushions and designs for embroidery frames, we would be as well suited for posts and professorships as men.)

At this crucial point, however, Zayas shifts to an apparently contradictory, essentialist definition of feminine superiority in terms of bodily humors, describing women as

quizá más agudas, por ser de natural más frio, por consistir en humedad el entendimiento, como se ve en las respuestas de repente, y en los engaños de pensado, que todo lo que se haze con maña, aunque no sea virtud, es ingenio. (*Novelas,* 22)

(perhaps sharper, being by nature of a colder temperament, since the intellect consists of dampness [humoral wetness], as can be seen in [our] quick replies and [our] intentional deceptions, for everything that is done skillfully, even if not virtuous, is wit.)[8]

Although this particular combination of arguments is unique to Zayas, only the last might qualify as her addition to the traditional debate over the nature of women; it is probably a response to the influential treatise of Huarte de San Juan, *Examen de ingenios para las ciencias* (1575).[9]

Zayas's assertion of the material and spiritual identity of men and women is an extension of the Christian doctrine of the fundamental equality of all human beings, created by God and in his image. Materially, said don Juan Manuel in his *Libro de los estados,* all men are equally composed of the four humors made of the four elements, and metaphysically, they are all so far removed from the power of God that one is no greater than the other (Vigil 1994, 5). Since this doctrine coexisted with a belief in a divinely ordered hierarchy in earthly existence, gender differentiation generally involved qualification of either material or spiritual elements that gave males superiority over females. Traditional arguments in defense of women often relied at least in part on variant interpretations of the prevailing story of the creation.[10] Zayas, instead, took on the "scientifically" misogynistic account of human nature of Huarte de San Juan, a widely read renewal and reformulation of the humoral theory of medicine that had prevailed in antiquity (Arquiola 1988, Soufas 1996a).

If we set Zayas's defense against Huarte's formidably argued depreciation of women's intellectual capacity, we can see the emotional logic of her apparently contradictory line or argumentation. Huarte was, in Daniel Heiple's words, "a convinced biological determinist" (Heiple 1991, 122) whose work constitutes "one of the most devastating attacks on women in Spanish Golden Age letters" (125–26). He used an apparently closely reasoned, scientific argument to demonstrate that an individual's mental capacities depend on the humoral composition of the body, the balance of heat and cold, dryness and wetness, a balance in which, as we will see, he finds women necessarily inferior.

Zayas begins on common ground with Huarte in her declaration that men and women possess the same blood, senses, faculties, and organs. In the alternate formulations for that material equality of the sexes that she offers—an amalgam either of "fuego y barro" (fire and clay) or "espíritus y terrones" (spirits and clods of earth), however, we can glimpse the diversity of discourses dealing with sexual difference that she, like Huarte, inherited, and whose discrepancies and inconsistencies she could exploit to reverse his arguments. "Barro" (clay) reflects the biblical tradition and "terrones" (earth) that of natural philosophy (Cadden 1993, 74–75). Explanations in medical treatises, works of natural philosophy, and biblical and theological formulations differed in purpose, form, and content, and "knowledge" accumulated, disappeared, was recovered and reformulated, crossing discourses as it did so, from the fifth-century B.C. Hippocratic corpus to Aristotle, Galen, and the church fathers forward to early modern Europe without ever achieving a coherent description of the nature and fundamental identity or polarity of the sexes (Cadden 1993). Fundamental differences included whether both men and women contributed "seed" for procreation (as suggested by Hippocratic writers), or only men; whether women were only passive participants, material supports, in that process, with men taking the active and formative role, as in Aristotle's hierarchical explanation, and the nature and relative valuation of their physical consistutions in the humoral theory of medicine systematized by Galen. Hence, writers on sexual difference could draw on various authorities who gave differing and sometimes internally contradictory accounts to support their own visions. Huarte was a formidable spokesman for what has been called the "one-sex" model of human sexuality, which saw women as imperfect males, possessing the same organs, but inside rather than outside the body, due to a lack of heat.[11] There was not a technical term for the vagina or ovaries until the eighteenth century; in Latin, Greek, and the modern European languages, the ovaries were called testicles,[12] and the vagina and uterus were represented in words and drawings as analogous to the penis. In Huarte's formulation,

> el hombre, aunque nos parece de la compostura que vemos, no difiere de la mujer, según dice Galeno, más que en tener los miembros genitales fuera del cuerpo. Porque, si hacemos anatomía de una doncella, hallaremos que tiene dentro de sí dos testículos, dos vasos seminarios, y el útero con la mesma compostura que el miembro viril sin faltarle ninguna deligneación.
>
> Y de tal manera es esto verdad, que si acabando Naturaleza de fabricar un hombre perfecto, le quisiese convertir en mujer, no tenía otro trabajo más que tornarle adentro los instrumentos de la generación; y si hecho mujer, quisiese volverla en varón, con arrojarle el útero y los testículos fuera, no había más que hacer. (1989, 608)

> (a man, although his composition seems to us to be what we see, is no different from a woman, according to Galen, except in having his genitals outside his body. Because if we dissect a maiden, we will find that she has within herself two testicles, two seminal vessels, and the uterus with the same composition as the virile member, not lacking a single delineation.
>
> And this is true in such a way that if Nature, having finished making a perfect man, should want to convert him into a woman, it would require no other work than turning the generative instruments within; and if having made a woman, should wish to change her into a man, after pushing outside the uterus and testicles, [Nature] would have nothing more to do.)

The determination of whether a creature is male or female depends on the quantity of heat it contains (and Huarte provides detailed instructions about whom to marry and how to undertake the procreative act in order to conceive male children):

Pues qué sea la razón y causa de engendrarse los miembros geni-
tales dentro o fuera, o salir hembra y no varón, es cosa muy clara sa-
biendo que el calor dilata y ensancha todas las cosas, y el frío las de-
tiene y encoge. Y así, es conclusión de todos los filósofos y médicos
que si la simiente es fría y húmida, que se hace hembra y no varón, y
siendo caliente y seca se engendrará varón y no hembra. De donde
se infiere claramente que no hay hombre que se pueda llamar frío
respecto de la mujer, ni mujer caliente respecto del hombre.
(609–10)

(Therefore the reason and cause why the genital organs are engendered within or without, or coming out a female and not a male is
very clear, knowing that heat dilates and enlarges everything and
cold stops and shrinks them. And thus, the conclusion of all
philosophers and doctors is that if the seed is cold and wet, it becomes a female and not a male, and in being hot and dry, it will en-
gender a male and not a female. From which can be clearly inferred
that there is no man who can be called cold in relation to woman,
nor woman hot in relation to man.)

This balance in woman is necessarily cooler, since she must be cold and wet
to be fertile, to possess the required quantity of "sangre flemática" "phleg-
matic blood" to have the menstrual blood to nourish the fetus, and milk
after its birth (610–14). But this coldness and wetness inhibits the development of intellectual faculties, said Huarte: "De cuatro calidades que hay
(calor, frialdad, humidad y sequedad) todos los médicos echan fuera la frialdad por inútil para todas las obras del ánima racional" (Of the four qualities that exist—heat, cold, wetness and dryness—all doctors discard coldness as useless for all works of the rational spirit) (327).[13] Not all women
are equally cold and damp, and it is possible for a woman who possesses
only the first degree of these qualities to have greater mental powers than
the most imperfect male, Huarte concedes, citing as examples Judith and
Deborah of Old Testament history. Nevertheless, "quedando la mujer en su
disposición natural, todo género de letras y sabiduría es repugnante a su
ingenio. Por donde la Iglesia católica con gran razón tienen prohibido que
ninguna mujer pueda predicar ni confesar ni enseñar; porque su sexo no
admite prudencia ni disciplina" ([for] the woman conserving her natural
disposition, all types of letters and wisdom are repugnant to her wit. For
which the Catholic church with good cause prohibits any woman preach-

ing or serving as confessor or teaching; because her sex does not permit prudence or discipline) (615).

Huarte, as a biological determinist, assured the king and other readers that education was wasted on those who lacked the proper (warm) humoral temperament to achieve distinction in the exercise of the faculties of the rational soul. Zayas's arguments constitute a double-barreled reversal of the good doctor's thesis on this account. She declares eloquently that if women were given books and tutors rather than embroidery hoops, they would prove themselves the intellectual equals or even the superiors of males. Furthermore, while she agrees with Huarte that women's humoral balance is colder than that of men, she assigns an opposite value to coldness and wetness, making them the condition for greater understanding that would give women an advantage over men in official and university posts if they were afforded a proper education.

On what grounds could Zayas perform this apparently arbitrary reversal? In the first place, she could point to inconsistencies in Huarte's own treatise, for at several points he links relative coldness with the highest mental faculty, *entendimiento* (understanding or judgment).[14] Inconsistencies abound in the definitions of the sexual composition of men and women, as we have seen. Although the majority of writers assigned a positively valued heat to men, others—including Hildegard of Bingen—attributed heat to women and relative cold to men (Cadden 1993, 17, 79). Isidore of Seville maintained three different propositions regarding procreative seed: (1) that only men have sperma—hence noblemen pass their blood to sons; (2) that only women have sperma—a sperma that contaminates an illegitimate child, or *spurius*—born to a noblewoman of an ignoble father; and (3) that both have sperma, a proposition that served to explain why a child is a boy or a girl, according to the relative potencies of male and female semen (Laqueur 1990, 55–56). In Laqueur's words, "These three distinct arguments about what we might take to be the same biological material are a dramatic illustration that much of the debate about the nature of the seed and of the bodies that produce it—about the boundaries of sex in the one-sex model—are in fact not about the bodies at all. They are about power, legitimacy, and fatherhood, in principle not resolvable by recourse to the senses" (57).

In effect, the standard procedure, in Huarte as in Zayas, in defenders of women as well as in antifeminist writers, was to proceed from hierarchically-valued gender assumptions to a definition of sexual anatomy, not the reverse. Juan de Espinosa, in his *Diálogo en laude de las mugeres* (Dialogue in

Praise of Women) (1580), had similarly reworked the valoration of another anatomical "fact"—that male children were generated in the right
testicle and carried in the right side of the uterus, and females in the left.
This was in accord with the standard symbolic assignation of space, in
which higher or right was superior to lower and left. Espinosa maintained
the left-right assignments but reversed their values, saying that the presence of the heart makes the left side more noble and the left-side position
therefore a mark of superiority (1990, 149). Zayas's seeming construction-
ist/essentialist shift—first attributing women's apparent intellectual inferiority to educational disadvantages, then claiming that women's coldness
and dampness make them potentially men's intellectual superiors—are
thus, in fact, two different attacks on constructed gender hierarchy, first as
it operated in social practice, and second, as inscribed in scientific or
philosophical discourse.

What sort of proofs were offered for the truth of this relation between
gender, physiological composition, and intellectual potential? Huarte did
not suggest that an individual's humoral balance could be quantitatively
measured; rather, it is inferred by "señales" (signs) visible in his behavior,
both intellectual and moral, and in his accomplishments. Zayas follows a
similar procedure, but again reorders Huarte's categories of humoral
cause and mental capacity. Having declared women's potential superiority
on the basis of associating their cold and humid temperament with *entendimiento* (understanding), she continues, claiming that this "se ve en las
respuestas de repente, y en los engaños de pensado, que todo lo que se
haze con maña, aunque no sea virtud, es ingenio" (can be seen in our
quick replies and in our intentional deceptions, for everything done with
artfulness, while it may not be virtuous, is a product of wit) (*Novelas*, 22).
This demonstration, which seems to wield a double-edged sword in the defense of women, is again a case of starting from grounds men would generally concede and then shifting the direction of the argument. As any devotee of the *comedia* knows, women were regularly depicted as possessing this
sort of verbal, strategic ingenuity. Huarte himself describes it, with a mixture of aversion and admiration. In his thesis, women who behave this way
possess the lowest degree of the requisite feminine coldness and humidity
and demonstate a "mala condición," the deviation of the *ingenio*, or imagination, toward duplicity, astuteness, caviling, and *maña*, or cunning (1989,
616). "Ninguna cosa pasa por alto la que tiene este punto de frialdad y humidad; todo lo nota y riñe, y así no se puede sufrir. Suelen ser las tales de
buena conversación, y no se espantan de ver hombres, ni tienen por mal

criado al que les dice un requiebro" (Nothing escapes the woman who possesses this grade of coldness and humidity; she observes and argues everything, and is thus insufferable. They are usually good at conversation, and aren't afraid of seeing men, nor consider themselves ill served by those who pay them a compliment) (1989, 616).[15] Zayas appropriates this commonplace, ambivalent conception of women's cleverness and uses it to argue that even in the absence of equal education, women regularly demonstrate with their quick-wittedness the compatibility of a cold, damp temperament and intellectual capacity.

Foremothers

With a concession that not everyone may consider this quick wit a credit to women, Zayas next turns to a time-honored tactic for establishing legitimacy of a given praxis, that of citing the authority of illustrious forefathers—or foremothers, as the case requires. Zayas, like many women writers before and after her, draws up a list of learned women whose recognized distinction serves "para exemplar de mis atrevimientos" (as a model for my daring).[16]

> Veremos lo que hicieron las que por algún accidente trataron de buenas letras, para que ya que no baste para disculpa de mi ignorancia, sirva para exemplar de mis atrevimientos. De Argentaria, esposa del poeta Lucano, refiere él mismo que le ayudó en la corrección de los tres libros de *La Farsalia,* y le hizo muchos versos que pasaron por suyos. Temistoclea, hermana de Pitágoras, escribió un libro doctísimo de varias sentencias. Diotima fué venerada de Sócrates por eminente. Aspano hizo muchas leciones de opinión en las academias. Eudoxa dexó escrito un libro de consejos políticos. Cenobia, un epítome de la *Historia Oriental.* Y Cornelia mujer de Africano, unas epístolas familiares, con suma elegancia. (*Novelas,* 22)

> (Let us see what was done by those who through some accident dealt with literature, so that while they may not be sufficient to excuse my ignorance, they may serve as a model for my daring. Of [Pola] Argentaria, wife of the poet Lucan, he himself relates that she helped him correct the three books of the *Pharsalia* and wrote many verses that were taken as his. Themistoclea, sister of Pythago-

ras, wrote a most learned book of maxims. Diotima was esteemed
for her eminence by Socrates. Aspano [Aspasia] gave many influential lessons in the academies. Eudocia left a book of political counsel. Cenobia, a compendium of the *Eastern History*. And Cornelia,
wife of Africano, [wrote] family letters of great elegance.)

Male counselors or champions of women had long compiled lists of illustrious women, mythical and historical, lists that center on feminine defense of virtue, fidelity, maternal devotion, and piety, and to a lesser extent,
on models of feminine courage and wisdom. When Alvaro de Luna, following the example of Boccaccio's *De claris mulieribus*, compiled his *Libro de las
virtuosas é claras mujeres* (1466), he organized it into three sections, beginning with Mary and ending with the mother of Saint John the Baptist:
women of the Bible, women of antiquity, and saints of the church. This is a
variant of the tradition in medieval texts of citing "Nine Heroes," three
each from the Old Testament, antiquity and the medieval era (Scott 1994,
207). Zayas does not follow this triparatite scheme in her prologue, in
which she only names women from classical Greece and Rome and the
early Christian era. In the opening of *Desengaño cuarto,* however, she adds a
number of distinguished women from her own age, ranging from the intellectually gifted and politically empowered sisters of Carlos V to learned
nuns—Eugenia de Contreras, of the convent of Sor Juana de la Cruz in
Salamanca, and María de Barahona, of the convent of the Concepción
Jerónima in Madrid—and women poets, including her friend from Seville,
Ana Caro Mallén de Soto.[17]

Zayas's brief list of foremothers is tellingly distinct from the masculine
model in selection, organization and objectives. First, and most important,
she is primarily and overtly concerned in this apologetic preface with
women as writers and as teachers of men. Second, she begins her two sub-
groups of writers with the woman closest to her either in space or time, and
then moves farther afield. Third, we can find the connective logic in the
progression of her list as much in what she leaves unsaid about the women,
probably presuming that her readers already know it, as in what she says.
That is, she begins with a woman whose gifts as a writer contributed to her
husband's fame, then lists three women known as teachers of great
philosophers. The last of these, Aspano, or Aspasia, was a woman of considerable political influence, as were all the women in her following sub-
group of early Christian women. Furthermore, her selection and tele-
graphic description of the women raise a number or intriguing questions

about just how much she did know about her models. Finally, although Zayas concludes her list with a woman writer famous as a mother, she passes over in silence the exemplary maternity for which she was primarily remembered.

Although the logical starting point for Zayas's list might seem to be Sappho, to whom Lope had compared Zayas in the accolade to her in his *Laurel de Apolo,* Zayas does not mention the Greek poet of Lesbos. In view of the sexual innuendos in Fontanella's poetic roast of her (see Chapter 1 above), and Zayas's declared rejection of the possibility of sexual attraction between women (see Chapter 7 below), her omission of Sappho invites speculation. Is this an innocent or a telling omission? And if the latter, does it too reflect a true rejection of lesbian love, or rather a careful omission of a sexual as well as artistic "foremother"? Other women writers did acknowledge her. When Christine de Pizan in *La cité des dames* (1405) asks her allegorical interlocutor if women have a "clever enough mind" for "high understanding and great learning," Lady Reason describes Sappho's accomplishments at length (1982, 63–68). The Peruvian woman poet who wrote in the early seventeenth century under the name Clarinda does mention Sappho, as well as Pola Argentaria (Sabat-Rivers 1987, 283). Sor Juana, on the other hand, like Zayas, omitted Sappho from her list, and Scott suggests that the omission was a strategic distancing, since a number of her love poems were addressed to women.

Skipping Sappho, Zayas begins close to home, with (Pola) Argentaria, wife of the Spanish-born poet Lucan. Lucan, born in Córdoba in A.D. 39, wrote the epic poem *Bellum civile,* more popularly known as the *Pharsalia,* an account of the war between Caesar and Pompey. The poem was left unfinished when Lucan was forced to commit suicide in A.D. 65 at the age of twenty-six, along with his uncle, Lucius Annaeus Seneca, and others, when his participation in a plot to assassinate Nero was discovered. With Virgil and Ovid, he was one of the authors most frequently studied in medieval halls of rhetoric, and long passages of the *Pharsalia* were incorporated into the *Primera crónica general* ordered compiled by Alfonso el Sabio (Lida de Malkiel 1975, 368). Even if Zayas did not read Latin, she could have read the poem in Juan de Jáuregui's 1614 translation (Lida de Malkiel 1975, 370; Lucan 1993, xvi n. 14). In Zayas's account, a share of the credit for his poetic accomplishments was due to his wife, Pola Argentaria.[18] While that alone would qualify her for Zayas's list, David Quint's work on Lucan's position in the epic tradition raises intriguing questions of just what else Zayas might have seen in the *Pharsalia.* For Quint, in *Epic and Empire,*

Lucan creates an anti-Virgilian "epic of losers," a genre that resists the linear narrative, the conservative teleology of Virgilian epic, and the triumphalist portrayal of the classic heroes of imperial domination. In its resistance to linearity, that anti-epic moves toward the wandering and digressive structure of romance, or toward the destruction of form itself, toward formlessness, suggests Quint. Yet as poetic spokesman of the aristocratic oligarchy of republican Rome, Lucan could not fully divorce himself from the imperialist venture any more than could Ercilla in the *Araucana* (Quint 1993, 1–40, 131–85). That sort of ideological division parallels similar tensions we can see at work both in Zayas's episodic narrative constructions and in their ideological underpinnings—in Zayas's case, the division between gender and class, and her resistance to but incomplete break from masculine narrative paradigms. And the puzzle of Zayas's presence in Barcelona in 1643 and possible ties through the duke of Hijar to groups opposing the Olivares regime in Madrid[19] suggests that Zayas might have felt a political kinship with the parodying of tyrannical rulers penned by Lucan—with the help of his wife.

From this "woman behind the poet" Zayas moves to "women behind philosophers," Themistoclea, Diotima, and Aspano, or Aspasia. Themistoclea (or Aristocleia) was a Delphic priestess said to have taught Pythagoras (c. 582–500 B.C.) much of his doctrine (Smith 1849, 1:302) (Diogenes Laertius 1931, bk. 8, chap. 1, para. 8, 21). Zayas describes her not as a Delphic priestess, but as a sister of Pythagoras and author herself of a collection of a philosophical miscellany.

Zayas's laconic reference to Diotima raises more intriguing questions. What did she know of this figure who was central to Plato's exposition in the *Symposium* of eros as an ascent from physical beauty to philosophical creativity and virtuous contemplation of Beauty as an ideal form? She clearly believed Diotima to have been a historical figure, rather than the fictional creation she is considered by most, if not all, modern commentators (Halperin 1990, 119–24; Plato 1989, 45). Castiglione, in the closing pages of *Il cortegiano*—a book that, in contrast to the *Symposium*, Zayas is likely to have read—also refers to Diotima as an actual person: "Socrates himself confessed that all the mysteries of love that he knew had been revealed to him by a woman, the famous Diotima" (Castiglione 1967, 344). Did she know that the "mysteries of love" expressed by Diotima/ Socrates/Plato were built on a model of homosexual love? Presumably not, since the Neoplatonic philosophy of love that was common currency among Renaissance poets had been reframed in heterosexual terms; but

Desengaño 6, in which Zayas makes most use of that philosophy of love, is a story in which a male, crossed-dressed as a female, argues for the possibility of an ideal love between women. The denouement of the tale, however, is an implicit rejection of the Neoplatonic philosophy of love as one among many amorous discourses men use to betray women, as we will see in Chapter 7. Intriguing as these questions may be in the light of contemporary feminist discussions of the role of Diotima in the founding moments of Western philosophy,[20] in all likelihood, Zayas saw in her no more than a woman known as the teacher of a preeminent male thinker.

Zayas's reference to "Aspano" poses a similar puzzle. She says, "Aspano hizo muchas lecciones de opinión en las academias" (Aspano gave many influential lessons in the academies) (*Novelas,* 22).[21] I have found no record of a learned "Aspano," but in citing her after Diotima, Zayas surely meant to indicate Aspasia, who was indeed an influential figure in Athenian political and intellectual life. Halperin, in fact, suggests that she may have been the model who inspired Plato's creation of Diotima.[22] She was a Milesian woman who came to live in Athens and became the mistress of Pericles, whose impassioned love she earned for her intellectual gifts as well as her beauty (Smith, 1849, 1:386). Socrates calls her his instructor in rhetoric in Plato's dialogue *Menexenus,* and says she has made many other men good orators; a lost Socratic dialogue by Aeschines titled *Aspasia* credits her with making a good orator and first man of Athens of an undistinguished dealer in cattle, Lysicles, with whom she lived briefly after the death of Pericles (Smith 1849, 1:386; Halperin 1990, 123). According to Smith, "The house of Aspasia was the great centre of the highest literary and philosophical society of Athens" (1:386) and she was considered to have exercised considerable political influence as well.

The final three learned foremothers that Zayas lists—Eudoxa, Cenobia and Cornelia—were also women of political influence, but from the early Christian era. As in the case of the first four women, Zayas begins with the most recent and moves backward in time. Eudoxa, or Eudocia, was the wife of the emperor Theodosius, in the fifth century A.D. She was born in Athens, the daughter of the sophist Leontius, and given the name Athenais. Versed in Greek and Latin literature, rhetoric, astronomy, and geometry, she was also a famous beauty. Her father therefore left all of his property to her two brothers at his death, saying that her good fortune and education would be a sufficient inheritance for her (Smith 1849, 2:78). She went to Constantinople to appeal against her brothers and there met Theodosius's sister Pulcheria, who was instrumental both in her marriage and her conversion to Christianity, whereupon Eudoxa took the name Eudocia. Historical chronicles say that she administered the affairs of Constantinople for seven years, and became a patron of Jerusalem, where she spent the end of her life. She was indeed an author, as Zayas says of her. She wrote four long works in heroic verse: *A Poem on the Victory Obtained by theTroops of Her Husband Theodosius over the Persians* (A.D. 421 or 422), *A Paraphrase of the Octateuch, A Paraphrase of the Prophecies of Daniel and Zechariah,* and *A Poem on the History and Martyrdom of Cyprian and Justina;* and in some editions of the *Homero-Centones,* a much published poem on the history of the fall of humankind and its redemption by Jesus Christ, made up of verses from Homer, she is also credited as its author (Smith 1849, 2:79).

The last two women Zayas cites were often included in lists of illustrious women, albeit with different emphasis that that given them by Zayas. Cenobia, or Zenobia, the third-century A.D. queen of Palmyra, who figures in all such lists, is presented first and foremost as a model of courage, strength, and chastity. From Boccaccio (1881, 2:343–52) forward, her biography begins with her youthful disdain for feminine pastimes, when she preferred to dedicate herself to hunting and to a Spartan outdoor life. As an adult, she served as a captain in the army of her husband, Odaenathus, her bravery helping him reconquer the eastern portion of the Roman empire. After his death, she proclaimed herself regent in the name of her young sons and extended her domains through Egypt and much of Asia Minor. She was eventually defeated by the Roman emperor Aurelian, captured while fleeing with her sons, and taken to Rome to grace his triumphal procession, wherein she appeared so richly attired that she figured more as victor herself than as vanquished, according to Boccaccio. Alvaro de Luna and Christine de Pizan omit this final episode from their accounts of her life.[23] They follow Boccaccio closely, however in prasing her chastity. Reluctant to marry, she purportedly would sleep with her husband only for the purpose of procreation. Luna abbreviates Boccaccio's description of her learning in Egyptian and Greek,[24] but this aspect of her character is the climax of Pizan's description of Zenobia's virtues. She notes "her profound learnedness in letters, both in those of the Egyptians and in those of her own language. When she rested, she diligently applied herself to study and wished to be instructed by Longinus the philosopher, who was her master and introduced her to philosophy. She knew Latin as well as Greek, through the aid of which she organized and arranged all historical works in concise and very careful form. Similarly, she desired that her children, whom she raised with strict discipline, be introduced to learning" (1982, 55). Zayas passes over all this in silence, saying succinctly that Zenobia wrote "a compendium of the *Eastern History*."[25]

When Cornelia (second century B.C.), Zayas's last foremother appears in lists of famous women, she earns her place precisely as a famous mother. She was the daughter of the general Scipio Africanus, and later the mother-in-law of Scipio Africanus the Younger, not "mujer de Africano" (wife of Africanus) (*Novelas*, 22), as Zayas calls her. Cornelia married Tiberius Sempronius Gracchus, whose death left her a widow with twelve children. She refused all offers to remarry—including one from Ptolemy—and devoted herself to her children. Her two sons, Tiberius and Caius, known as the Gracchi, became famous Roman statesmen and distinguished orators. A learned woman, well versed in both Greek and Roman literature, she was indeed known for the excellence of her letters, as Zayas says. According to Smith, "Her letters, which were still extant in the time of Cicero, were models of composition" (1849, 1:855). But it was as a mother that she was most remembered. Alvaro de Luna (1891, 171–72) includes her as an example of virtuous disdain for worldly riches, ignoring all aspects of her life other than a much told incident in which, when another woman displayed her wealth to Cornelia, she had her sons brought before her and told the other woman that they were her only jewels. She exercised considerable influence over her statesmen sons: "It was related by some writers that Tiberius Gracchus was urged on to propose his laws by the reproaches of his mother, who upbraided him with her being called the mother-in-law of Scipio and not the mother of the Gracchi" (Smith 1849, 1:855). After the death of her sons, she retired to Misenum for the remainder of her life—which in Smith's description bears interesting similarities to the retirement to secular life in a convent in which Zayas leaves several protagonists and which she praises in her authorial voice in the closing paragraph of her *Desengaños:* "Here she exercised unbounded hospitality; she was constantly surrounded by Greeks and men of letters; and the various kings in alliance with the Romans were accustomed to send her presents, and receive the like from her in return. Thus she reached a good old age, honoured and respected by all, and the Roman people erected a statue to her, with the inscription, CORNELIA, MOTHER OF THE GRACHI" (Smith 1849, 1:855).

Zayas concludes her list of foremothers with a rhetorical "etcetera" indicating that the list could be extended indefinitely: "Y otras infinitas de la antiguedad, y de nuestros tiempos, que paso en silencio por no alargarme, y

porque ya tendrás noticias de todo, aunque seas lego, y no hayas estudiado"
(and a infinite number of other women of antiquity and our own times
whom I pass over in silence in order not to be too lengthy, and because you
must already know all this, even if you are a layman and uneducated).[26]

Having concluded her list, Zayas adds two other justifications for
women's capacity to enter the literary world as autodidacts, even in a society that bars access to formal education for women.[27] "Y que después que
hay *Polianteas* en latín, y *Sumas morales* en Romance, los seglares, y las mujeres pueden ser letrados" (And now that there are *Polyantheas* in Latin and
Summae of Morals in the vernacular, laymen and women can be learned)
(*Novelas,* 22). Polyantheas were a kind of encyclopedic compendium of
knowledge, of the sort parodied by Cervantes in the "Prólogo" to *Don
Quixote.*[28] They existed in Spanish as well as in Latin, a good example being
the *Para todos* of Zayas's friend Pérez de Montalbán. The *Summas* in Spanish were comprehensive surveys of religious doctrine intended for laymen,
in contrast to *Summae* in Latin, written either for theologians or for the use
of secular clergy. Without the irony of a Cervantes or Lope, Zayas first sees
in these tools a medium in which women can find the learning to enter the
literary world. Second, she says that voracious reading habits such as her
own can teach women literary skills,

> si todas tienen mi inclinación, que en viendo cualquiera nuevo o
> antiguo, dexo la almohadilla y no sosiego hasta que le paso. Desta
> inclinación nació la noticia, de la noticia el buen gusto; y de todo
> hacer versos, hasta escribir estas novelas. (*Novelas,* 22)

> (if all women have my inclination, for seeing any new or old book, I
> leave my sewing cushion and don't rest until I have reviewed it. From
> this inclination came information, from information good taste, and
> from all that, writing verse and then writing these novellas.)

Between these two clauses, however, Zayas inserts a rhetorical question
regarding women's proficiency with . . . books? that contains the fascinating slip of the pen with which I opened this chapter. In the first edition of
1637, the phrase is as follows: "Pues si esto es verdad, ¿qué razón hay para
que no tengamos promptitud para *los hombres?* y más si todas tienen mi inclinación . . ." (Well if this is true, what reason is there that we should not
have readiness *for men,* especially if all women have my inclination . . .)
(Zayas y Sotomayor 1637b, fol. q7r; emphasis added). In the second edi-

tion of 1637, which states on the title pages that the novellas are "de nuevo corretas, y enmendadas por su misma Autora" (again corrected and emended by the author herself), Zayas changes the word "hombres" (men) to "libros" (books), which is the more logical continuation of the sentence. The error, however, is a classic Freudian slip that shows that a masculine judge and jury were ever present in her mind as controllers of access to the literary and intellectual elite she sought to enter.

Two other alterations made between the first and second editions of the work also merit attention. After defending her determination to write a novel as perhaps easier, perhaps more appealing, than other sorts of books full of subtleties that no one buys, she continues in the first edition:

> Esto es dezir, que el libro a que te combido, puede servir por fruta entre otros platos de mas sustancias, que está el gusto humano tan achacoso, y con tanto hastío de ver las cosas que pasan en el mundo, que ha menester valerse de saynetes para quitar los amargores, o para tragar los sobresaltos. (Zayas y Sotomayor 1637b, fol. q7r)

> (This is to say that the book that I offer you can serve as a fruit between other more substantial dishes, for human taste is so sickened and so revolted from seeing the things that happen in the world that it needs to avail itself of farces to relieve its bitterness and to digest its shock.)

Similar defenses of literature of entertainment are common among authors of novellas or *comedias*. Why she should include it in her first version and remove it shortly thereafter is hard to say. Perhaps after seeing the volume in print, she no longer felt the need to defend it with such a clichéd modesty about the nature of her offering. Or she may have removed it in connection with the second substantial excision.

That second emendation will take us back to the question of the value and legitimacy of essentialist definitions or strategies for women writers. Fuss, after concluding that in philosophical terms, neither radical essentialism nor radical constructionism are tenable, argues as does Gayatri Spivak that the *strategic* use of essentialism by subaltern groups is legitimate and may be an effective way of establishing a position from which a counterhegemonic discourse can be sustained. Women, blacks, Native Americans, or other marginalized groups may use an essentializing self-definition to define and defend their specificity over and against the dominant groups. In the words of Fuss: "In the hands of a hegemonic group, essentialism can be employed as a powerful tool of ideological domination; in the hands of the subaltern, the use of humanism to mime (in the Irigarian sense of to undo by overdoing) humanism can represent a powerful displacing repetition. The question of the permissibility, if you will, of engaging in essentialism is therefore framed and determined by the subject-position from which one speaks" (1989, 32).

As we have seen in considering Zayas's answer to Huarte de San Juan, she was willing to employ both constructionist and essentialist arguments—in their seventeenth-century equivalents of educational inequalities and biological determinism—in contesting women's inferior situation in the hierarchical "one-sex" model from which prevailing definitions of sexual difference derived. She shifts women up or down the hierarchical ladder of gender as she builds her case. I would argue that "hombres"/"libros" (men/books) slip of the pen marks the turning point in her rhetorical tactic, her shift from an aggressive assertion of feminine intellectual strength to an almost coquettish appeal for the courtesy all gentlemen owe to women, an appeal that implicitly invokes the concept of women as defenseless beings whom superior males must honor and protect. The slip in the first edition reveals that although she meant to talk about women's capacity to deal with books, she was thinking about dealing with men as she made this tactical shift.[29] In effecting this turn, Zayas moves first into a standard topos of authorial modesty, calling her book an insubstantial but comforting "dish," as we have seen. Next, she engages another prefatorial topos, that of the book that stands or falls on its own merit, but then shifts the focus of that apology from the independent quality of the book to an assertion of its right to a protected status as the product of a woman writer. From that stance, she continues with the two sentences, in italics below and omitted from the corrected edition, that reveal her conscious deployment of a subaltern strategy:

> No es menester prevenirte de la piedad que debes tener, porque si es bueno, no harás nada en alabarle, y si es malo, por la parte de la cortesía que se le debe a cualquiera muger, le tendrás respeto. *Las sátiras, y las furias no se hizieron para los rendidos, sino para los soberbios. Quien tiene honra, da lo que tiene, cada uno hace como quien es.* (1637b, fol. q7r-v)

> (It is unnecessary to warn you of the charity that you should have, because if it is good, you will have done nothing in praising it, and if it is bad, out of the courtesy owed to any woman, you will respect it.

Satires and rages weren't made for the humble but for the haughty. He who
has honor gives what he has, everyone acts according to who he is.)

In other words, satire and anger should not be directed against the weak
but against the strong and proud, and honorable gentlemen will extend
that honor to others and will treat subordinates with respect. These sentences have a double edge, a passive-aggressive quality, for the converse is
that any man (the implied reader of this preface clearly being masculine)
who does not treat a woman (writer) with respect demonstrates that he is
not honorable. It may well have been discomfort with this double edge, on
Zayas's part, or that of first readers, or both, that motivated the excision of
these two sentences from the corrected edition. And she might then have
removed the "insubstantial dish" topos to maintain a balance between ag-
gressivity and modesty.

Zayas's closing argument is that male obligation to respect women is not
only the chivalrous obligation to protect the weak, but also the practical
recognition of their need for women. In the final analysis, Zayas argues,
male respect for women is the debt they owe their mothers—an argument
whose significance I will explore in the following chapter.

> Con mujeres no hay competencias; quien no las estima, es necio,
> porque las ha menester: y quien las ultraja, ingrato, pues falta al re-
> conocimiento del hospedaje que le hicieron en la primer jornada.
> (Zayas y Sotomayor 1637b, fol. q7r-v)

> (With women there is no competition; he who does not esteem
> them is stupid, because he needs them: and whoever abuses them,
> an ingrate, for he fails to recognize the lodging that they gave him
> on his first day's journey.)

Then, in a "correlación cuatrimembre" (a four-part correlation) (Alonso
1976, 412) worthy of Calderón, she summarizes the positions gentle male
readers must avoid: "Y así, pues no has de querer ser descortés, necio, villano, ni desagradicido . . ." (Therefore, since you will not wish to be discourteous, lumpish [ignorant], vulgar, nor ungrateful . . .) (*Novelas*, 22).
The neatness of this correlation is effaced by the erasure of two sentences
in the corrected edition, but in the first version, it summarizes concisely
four arguments she had just made: (1) "la cortesia . . . a cualquiera mujer"
(gentlemen owe all women courtesy), therefore you will not wish to be "de-

scortés," (discourteous); (2) "las sátiras . . . no se hicieron para los rendidos" (satire should not be used against the humble [submissive]), therefore you will not wish to be "necio" (ignorant and imprudent, or lumpish); (3) "quien tiene honra, da lo que tiene, cada uno hace como quien es" (he who has honor, gives what he has, everyone acts according to who is), therefore you will not wish to be "villano" (ignoble or vulgar), lest you present yourself as a man who has no honor to give; and (4) all men need women, and are of women born, therefore you will not wish to be "desagradecido," or ungrateful.

Last, Zayas closes with a flattering rhetorical curtsey to her implied male reader, saying that "te ofrezco este libro, muy segura de tu bizarría, y en confiança, de que si te desagradare, podrás disculparme con que nací mujer, no con obligaciones de hazer buenas Nouelas, sino con muchos deseos de acertar a seruirte. Vale." (I offer you this book, sure of your gallantry and with confidence that if it should displease you, you will pardon me since I was born a woman, not with the obligation to create good Novelas, but with a great desire to serve you. Farewell) (Zayas y Sotomayor 1637b, 23).

In sum, I believe that an attentive reading of Zayas's "Al que leyere," carried out with one eye on the context in which she wrote and the other informed by modern insights into the historical construction of gender and subject positions, can reveal an unspoken logic in this preface that seems at first sight so contradictory. In an age in which in both religious and philosophical discourses feminine inferiority was grounded in a belief in divinely or naturally instilled essential differences, she opens her case by arguing essential identity, material and spiritual, and advances a constructionist argument to explain women's disadvantaged position. Taking up current scientific discourse, she then turns the determinist argument of humoral difference on its head, backing it up with a list of illustrious foremothers. Finally, Zayas makes a strategic concluding retreat to an implicitly essentialist posture as she appeals to the chivalrous respect men owe to women.

PART II

The Mother Plot

4

Aventurarse perdiendo

For I am the first and the last.
I am the honored one and the scorned one.
I am the whore and the holy one.
I am the wife and the virgin . . .
I am the barren one, and many are her sons . . .
I am the silence that is incomprehensible . . .
I am the utterance of my name.
                            —*Thunder: Perfect Mind*

Reading with Mother in Mind

According to Peter Brooks, "Most viable works of literature tell us something about how they are to be read, guide us toward the conditions of
their interpretation" (1985, xii). As we have seen, in the "Al que leyere"
preface to her *Novelas amorosas,* Zayas climaxes her appeal for a sympathetic reading with the argument that the reader owes a woman writer this
courtesy, in the last analysis, out of respect and gratitude to his mother.

> Con mujeres, no hay competencias; quien no las estima es necio,
> porque las ha menester; y quien las ultraja ingrato, *pues falta al re-
> conocimiento del hospedaje que le hicieron en la primera jornada.* Y así,

pues, no has de querer ser descortés, necio, villano, ni desagradecido . . . (Zayas y Sotomayor 1637b, fol. q7r–v; emphasis added)

(With women there is no competition; he who does not esteem
them is stupid, because he needs them: and whoever abuses them,
an ingrate, *for he fails to recognize the lodging that they gave him on his
first day's journey.* Therefore, since you will not wish to be discourteous, lumpish [ignorant], vulgar, nor ungrateful . . .)

Zayas thus tells her readers at the outset to remember their debt to their
mothers as they read.[1]

As a literary genre, the novella could be said to have assumed, in its
primera jornada (first act), an ironic stance toward mothers. In the first story
of the first day of the *Decameron,* Boccaccio's miscreant protagonist Ciappelletto secures acceptance as a saint by confessing a series of minor sins
for which he purportedly feels a hyperbolic sense of guilt. The climactic sin
in the litany he confesses, with long and loud weeping, is that of having
once as a boy cursed his mother.[2] His confessor assures him that in an age
when men curse God himself all day and are forgiven, his sin is inconse-
quential. Yet Ciappelletto wails on: "Alas, father! What are you saying? My
sweet mother, who carried me in her womb nine months, day and night,
and who took me in her arms more than a hundred times! Cursing her was
too evil, and the sin was too great; and if you do not pray to God on my behalf, He will not forgive me" (Boccaccio 1982, 29). Boccaccio scholars continue to debate long and loudly the meaning of this story.[3] But as the good
father absolved Ciappelletto of all guilt and spread the news of his holi-
ness, we can say that along with the delivery of a false saint through whom
God purportedly worked true miracles, a new narrative era was born in a
supremely ambiguous speech act directed against the mother.

If the *Decameron* constitutes the *primera jornada* of the novella, then for
our purposes, its *segunda jornada* opens in Spain with the 1613 publication
of Cervantes' *Novelas ejemplares.* In the complex novella that closes that collection, *El coloquio de los perros* (The Dialogue of the Dogs), cursing the
mother is portrayed as yet more fundamental to language, part and parcel
of inherited original sin, and concurrent with the debut of the individual
subject in speech. Berganza observes to Cipión that

el hacer y decir mal lo heredamos de nuestros primeros padres y lo
mamamos en la leche. Vése claro en que apenas ha sacado el niño

el brazo de las fajas cuando levanta la mano con muestras de querer vengarse de quien, a su parecer, le ofende; y casi la primera palabra articulada que habla es llamar puta a su ama o a su madre. (1990, 457)

(saying and doing wrong is something we inherit from our first parents and drink with our mother's milk. This can clearly be seen in the fact that the child no sooner takes its arm out of its blankets than it raises its hand as if to seek to exact vengeance on whoever he thinks has offended him; and almost the first word he says is to call his nurse or mother a whore.) (1992, 101)

In Berganza's words, then, cursing the mother is the original speech act.[4]

Cervantes' *Novelas* were an immediate success, and other authors quickly followed his lead between 1620 and midcentury.[5] In the height of its popularity in Spain, the novella thus shares the stage, so to speak, with that other much favored genre, the *comedia*. Lope, in his *Novelas a Marcia Leonarda,* suggests that the novella and the *comedia* are akin in their freedom from subjection to traditional precepts, and in their obligation to please their public.[6] With the partial exception of Cervantes' novellas, we find in novella collections significant correspondences to the *comedia* in characterization, theme, and structure.[7] Francisco de Lugo y Dávila's 1622 collection blended the two genres in its very title: *Teatro popular: Novelas morales,* and a number of Zayas novels have a roughly tripartite plot structure akin to the three-act *comedia*.[8] And it is a truism of *comedia* studies that, except for a few mythical goddesses and queens, mothers are conspicuous for their absence in Golden Age drama (Soufas 1997).[9]

This maternal absence is a feature the *comedia* shares with American popular films of the thirties and forties and with novels by nineteenth-century women writers. In the films, as Naomi Scheman (1988) has pointed out, the consummation of heterosexual love for daughters, or the remarriage of mothers, depends in a patriarchal society on the suppression of the powerful maternal bond. In the novels, according to Marianne Hirsch, the very existence of plot requires that suppression: "In order to write, nineteenth-century women writers reenact the breach that, in the terms of culture and of the novel, alone makes plot possible. To do so they must separate their heroines from the lives and the stories of their mothers. Plot itself demands maternal absence" (1989, 67). Recent fiction by women writers, particularly that of "hyphenated" women writers, those between two cultural traditions, however, demonstrates quite another relationship between mothers and narrativity. For writers such as Isabel Allende, Judith Cofer, Cristina Garcia, Toni Morison, or Amy Tang, for instance, the maternal tradition is more the source of storytelling than its obstacle.

Two major psychic and social structures are involved in these instances of maternal presence or absence: one concerns women as subjects or objects in the circuit of desire, and the other the performance of women as speaking, or better said, writing subjects. Since published and publicly performed Golden Age dramas were written almost exclusively by men, only the first structure is clearly germane to maternal absence in the *comedia*.[10] In past years, the few *comedia* critics who have commented on this lack have attributed it to various factors: the influence of the Italian novella and Italian theater companies in the formative years of Spanish popular theater, the practical effect of the structures of theatrical companies (McKendrick 1991, 75) or the powerlessness of women in the patriarchal society of Hapsburg Spain, which rendered the mother a superfluous presence in the dramatic economy. More recently, Emilie Bergmann (1991) has described the restricted if not negative role accorded mothers in sixteenth-century treatises on feminine comportment by Juan Luis Vives and Fray Luis de León, and Ruth Anthony [El Saffar] (1993) has cast maternal absence in the *comedia* as an erasure motivated by the psychic power of the maternal figure, repressed in a Counter-Reformation society that made her the symbol of the violence of sexual desire.

We might expect that maternal absence would be equally characteristic of the Spanish novella tradition, since the *comedia* and the novella were directed toward largely the same public, written within the same cultural context, and nourished by similar if not identical elements in the literary tradition. This does not, however, prove to be the case. Cervantes, for example, in *La Gitanilla* (The Little Gypsy Girl), the novella that opens his collection, has Preciosa sing poetic hymns to ideal mothers both holy and political, Santa Ana and Queen Margarita; and in his closing story, *El coloquio*, Berganza paints in grotesque detail their polar opposites, the witch-mothers Cañizares and la Montiela. Maurice Molho (1993), Andre Bush (1993), and María Antonia Garcés (1993) read those demonically threatening figures as indicative of a Cervantine unease with the maternal figure, psychically akin to that which Ruth Anthony [El Saffar] found in the maternal erasure in *La vida es sueño*. Between those saintly and demonic polarities, nevertheless, Cervantes includes a number of more human mothers,[11] from Preciosa's mother, who kicks off her *chapines* (high heels) in delight at finding her long-lost daughter, to Estefanía, Rodolfo's mother in *La fuerza de la sangre,* who stages a carefully crafted dramatic spectacle to bind her errant son to Leocadia.[12] Significantly, however, Estefanía, functions as mother of a son.[13] In Cervantes' tales, as in the films of the 1930s and 1940s, a fundamental pre-history to virtually every love story involves separation of the daughter from her mother, either by the kidnapping of the daughter[14] or the death of the mother.[15] The repetition of this pattern in these love stories should *not* be attributed, I would suggest, to the weight of the Italian novella nor to a flight from what Kristeva describes as the maternal abject, however accurate that may be as a reading of the grotesque portrayal of Cañizares.[16] Rather, I believe, it represents a case of Cervantes' perspicacity regarding the configuration of desire within the human condition. That insight will be elaborated with greater complexity from a feminine perspective by María de Zayas.

Mothers Present and Absent

In Zayas's collection of novellas, mothers are notable *both* for their presence and for their absence. Like Cervantes, Zayas makes the absence of the mother figure a precondition for the first heterosexual commitment by her first heroine, Jacinta, and by the great majority of her heroines.[17] Yet in the overarching frame narrative set up at the beginning of the *Novelas amorosas,* the *sarao* in the home of the frame heroine Lisis, just the opposite is the case.[18] In this courtly gathering, all five women narrators have mothers, and all five male narrators have fathers, death having claimed the opposite-sex parents in each group. As Zayas puts it, "convidaron a los padres de los caballeros y a las madres de las damas, por ser todas ellas sin padres y ellos sin madres, que la muerte no dexa a los mortales los gustos cumplidos" (they invited the gentlemen's fathers and the ladies' mothers, for all the ladies were without fathers and the gentlemen without mothers, since death does not allow full pleasure to mortals) (*Novelas,* 31).

Mothers, then, are strikingly present at the scene of narration, and significantly absent in the stories actually told, particularly in those told by female narrators. In examining this dichotomy, let us begin with presence, the replication of the female and male narrators by their same-sex parents. As a formal device, this makes the scene of narration a dramatic ceremonial pattern appropriate to the courtly *sarao* it claims to be, an entertainment whose restrained conventionality counterpoints and highlights the violent passions in the tales told therein. As the male and female narrators center their purported tales of love on a war between the sexes of escalating intensity, the reader comes to see the deployment of the male and female groups as strategic, a clear demarcation of two hostile camps.[19] Near the midpoint of the *Desengaños,* Zayas explicitly paints an atmosphere of antagonistic expectancy at the outset of the second night of storytelling. Word of the previous night's disenchantments having spread through the court, a larger public had gathered early, although, she says,

> no sé si muy gustosos, por estar prevenidos de que las desengañadoras, armadas de comparaciones y casos portentosos, tenían publicada la guerra contra los hombres. . . . ¿Quién ignora que habría esta noche algunos no muy bien intencionados? Y aun me parece que los oigo decir: ¿Quién las pone a estas mujeres en estos disparates? ¿Enmendar a los hombres? Lindo desacierto. Vamos ahora a estas bachillerías, que no faltará ocasión de venganza. Y como no era ésta fiesta en que se podía pagar un silbo a un mosquetero, dejarían en casa doblado el papel y cortadas las plumas, para vengarse. (*Desengaños,* 258)

> (I don't know if [they gathered] happily, having been warned that the [lady] disillusioners, armed with comparisons and portentous cases, had announced war against men. . . . Who doubts that there would have been some that night with not very good intentions? And I even seem to hear them say: Who stirs up these women in this tommyrot? Reform men? A pretty blunder. Let's have at this prattle, as we won't lack a chance for revenge. And since it wasn't an affair in which one could pay a groundling to whistle, they would have left the page marked and the pens trimmed at home to avenge themselves.)

The expectation that embattled male listeners will return home to work their revenge with pen and paper points beyond the tensions of social and courtship rituals to the deeper significance of this formal male-female division, the manner in which it is linked to language, and how it is perpetuated within that medium. The split between a mother-daughter contingent and a father-son contingent effectively represents the manner in which cultural constructs assign speaking positions to human subjects. Infants born into a world of preexisting language are immediately labeled as male or female according to the visible anatomy of the biological organism: "It's a girl," or, "It's a boy." As the Symbolic order intervenes to break the Imaginary (m)Other-child dyad, children acquire a self-concept structured by and in language—language of sexual difference—as they learn the grammatical paradigms I/you/he/she. "I'm a girl, you're a boy." Except in the most thoroughgoing cases of transexuality, speaking subjects retain the gender pronouns assigned to match their biological anatomy. Albeit with much more varying degrees of thoroughness and less universality, the majority of human subjects also form an Imaginary identification with the parental figure designated as the same gender, and absorb the cultural myths assigned to that position. "I'm a girl, I'll be the mommy; you're a boy, you be the daddy." Now, as we all know, *pace* Napoleon and Freud, biology is *not* destiny.[20] As Lacan demonstrates, any subject can take up a position on either side of the masculine-feminine gender divide, But since the language that shaped our self-concept obliges us to employ gender pronouns, as "he's" and "she's" in this world, we are effectively (if somewhat shakily) divided into two camps. Thus I read the social organization of Zayas's framing *sarao* as a recognition that as sub-jects of language, we speak in the shadow, if not the literal presence, of the language-anchored image of our same-sex parent.

But that is only the beginning of the narrative organization of experience. Although as narrators the women speak in the presence of their mothers, within the tales they tell most female characters function in the *absence* of their mothers, an absence that Zayas emphasizes just as I emphasize the word here. By my statistical analysis, of the forty-seven significant female agonists of these tales of love and death, only thirteen have living mothers (see charts in Appendix). As a first level of explanation, we can say that Zayas, like Cervantes, nineteenth-century women writers, and creators of 1930s films, saw it necessary to separate mother and daughter in order to initiate a history of desire. But there is more. Of those thirteen girls with living mothers, six are in four of the six tales narrated by men,[21] two are in a story told by a mother, one commits suicide, one is pushed into desire by rape, one is beheaded while nursing her child, one is seduced by a man posing as a woman, and the last is saved from blinding, rape, and death only by repeated interventions of the Virgin Mary—the Mother of God. By analyzing the overall pattern of maternal absence and the specific instances of maternal presence, we can discover Zayas's insight into the unconscious roots of sexual desire, comprehend her attempt to refigure narratives of desire from a feminine perspective, and appreciate the literary and social pressures that limited her capacity to do so.[22]

Aventurarse perdiendo

> . . . the poets among us can be
> "literalists of
> the imagination"—. . .
> . . . can present
>
> for inspection, imaginary gardens with real toads in them
> Marianne Moore, "Poetry"

Desire and Narrative

Zayas's first enclosed narrator declares her didactic purpose in the opening sentence of the first tale, *Aventurarse perdiendo* (Venturing and Losing). Her story, Lisarda tells us, is about desire, about the dangers that the unrestrained energy of [sexual] desire poses for both sexes.[23] While no example may be sufficient to save a star-cursed woman, her story should serve as a warning to other women, "de aviso para que no se arrojen al mar de sus desenfrenados deseos, fiadas en la barquilla de su flaqueza, temiendo que en él se aneguen, no sólo las flacas fuerzas de las mujeres, sino los claros y heroicos entendimientos de los hombres, cuyos engaños es razón que se teman" (*Novelas,* 37) (as a warning not to throw themselves into the sea of their unbridled desires, trusting in the fragile bark of their weakness, for fear that it should swamp not only women's frailty, but also the clear and heroic wisdom of men, whose deceptions are rightly to be feared).

Not only does Zayas, through her first narrator, foreground the role of desire in organizing the plot; she also makes explicit the desire for meaning as the motor of narration, through the voice of the first incorporated listener within that tale. Fabio, a handsome, virtuous, and wise young nobleman, on a pilgrimage to the sanctuary of Montserrat, discovers the beautiful Jacinta disguised as a boy,[24] and urges her to tell her tale:

> Me has puesto en tanto cuidado y deseo de saberla, que si me pensase quedar hecho salvaje a morar entre estas peñas, mientras estuvieres en ellas, no he de dejarte hasta que me la digas, y te saque, si

puedo, de esta vida, que sí podré, a lo que en ti miro, pues a quien tiene tanta discreción, no será dificultoso persuadirle que escoja más descansada y menos peligrosa vida, pues no la tienes segura, respecto de las fieras que por aquí se crían, y de los bandoleros que en esta montaña hay; que si acaso tienen de tu hermosura el conocimiento que yo, de creer es que no estimarán tu persona con el respeto que yo la estimo. No me dilates este bien, que yo aguardaré los años de Ulises para gozarle. (*Novelas,* 43)

(You have aroused in me so much concern and desire to hear your story, that even if I thought I'd turn into a savage to dwell among these peaks, as long as you are here, I shall not leave you until you tell it to me so that I can extricate you from this way of life if I can, [and] I will be able to, from what I see in you, for it won't be hard to persuade someone who possesses such discretion to choose a more pleasant and less dangerous life, for yours is not safe, considering the wild animals and the bandits who inhabit these wilds; if they discover your beauty, as I have, you can be sure they won't show the same respect for your person as I do. Please don't delay doing me this favor, as I will wait all Ulysses' years to enjoy it.)

Brooks, in his "transactional model" of reading that likens the processes of writing and reading to the transference that occurs between analysand and analyst, says that framed narratives—such as in Zayas's collection—or others that include a fictional listener like Fabio—foreground the fact that for all narrative, "shape and meaning are the product of the listening as of the telling" (1985, 236). A similarly ordered relationship between viewer, text, and social structures has been posited by Claire Johnston with regard to feminist film: "In order to counter our objectification in the cinema, our collective fantasies must be released: women's cinema must embody the working through of desire: such an objective demands the use of the entertainment film" (cited in de Lauretis 1984, 107). Johnston proposes an interactive signifying process, one in which the fantasies embodied in the text stimulate a working-through of desire by the viewer and a critical focus on the interaction of traditional social structures and narrative paradigms. In the pages that follow, I suggest that the structure of Zayas's first story and of the collection as a whole encourages a working-through of desire that takes us, through a series of erotic fantasies, back to "la que nos dio la primera jornada"—to the house of the mother. I will discuss this story at considerable length, because it sets the tone for the whole two-volume collection.

The journey through desire on which Zayas leads her readers is, in a sense, a circular voyage, one that begins as well as ends in the "house of the mother." Immediately after defining the didactic purpose of the story, that of warning against succumbing to "unbridled desire," Zayas situates it physically, in the "ásperas peñas de Montserrat" (craggy peaks of Montserrat), which she describes as "suma y grandeza del poder de Dios y milagrosa admiración de las excelencias de su divina Madre" (summit and greatness of the power of God and *wondrous miracle of the perfections of his divine Mother*) (*Novelas*, 37; emphasis added). Of all the marvels in the sacred temple, she continues, "el mayor de todos [es] aquel verdadero retrato de la Serenísima Reina de los Angeles y Señora nuestra" (the greatest of all is that true portrait of the Our Lady, the most Serene Queen of the Angels) (*Novelas*, 37–38), and Fabio begins his pilgrimage by worshiping her, offering her his soul and examining attentively the walls covered with shrouds and crutches and with "otras infinitas insignias de su poder" (an infinity of other insignia of her power) (*Novelas*, 38). Thus, Zayas has Fabio discover the jilted Jacinta not in the Sierra Morena that gave shelter to the embattled lovers don Quixote, Cardenio, and Dorotea,[25] but in Montserrat, amid the rugged peaks of Spain's most famous sanctuary to the "divine Mother."[26]

The value of this opening setting in Montserrat is, furthermore, twofold and paradoxical. As a religious retreat, it establishes a sacred affiliation with the maternal; but in its physical configuration, this strange mountain stands as a landscape of desire. As Foa observes, scenic description in Zayas is generally minimal and either utilitarian or formulaic; in the rare instances of extended scenic description, "it is clearly symbolic or atmospheric, and functional, in relation to the central action" (1979, 110). One of these instances, as Foa also points out, is the setting of Montserrat. Of all the mountainous regions of Spain that Zayas could have picked, this is the most suggestive in potential symbolism of unconscious desire. Montserrat is a location richly layered in meanings: first, as Zayas describes it, as a religious retreat dedicated to "the divine Mother," one that drew illustrious pilgrims from all over Europe in Zayas's day;[27] second, as the symbol of Catalan nationalist sentiments that it has become. But before the region came to embody either of those meanings, it contained a forest sacred to the rites of Venus. According to the *Enciclopedia universal ilustrada . . . Espasa-Calpe* (s.v. "Monserrat"):

Santa María of Montserrat, Cataluña, Spain. Engraving. Courtesy of the Monastery of Montserrat

The Virgin of Montserrat and pilgrims on the road to the monastery. Engraving.
Courtesy of the Monastery of Montserrat

No es . . . de maravillar que ya en las remotas épocas precristianas ejerciera esta montaña una sugestión atrayente sobre las almas de los supersticiosos paganos y que dado lo aficionados que eran éstos a dedicar los lucus o bosques sagrados a alguna divinidad, consagraran alguno de los bosquecillos que los hermosean, a la más risueña y poética de sus divinidades, a Venus, la diosa del amor y de las gracias que debía más tarde ser suplantada y sustituida por la graciosa María, divina Madre del Amor Hermoso, de toda gracia y bondad.

(It is . . . not surprising that already in remote pre-Christian eras this mountain should exert such an attractive suggestiveness over the souls of superstitious pagans and that, given their fondness in dedicating *luci* or sacred groves to some divinity, they should consecrate some one of the little woods that beautify it to the most smiling and poetic of divinities, Venus, the goddess of love and of grace, who would later be supplanted and replaced by the gracious Mary, divine Mother of Beautiful Love, all grace and goodness.)

The sixteenth- and seventeenth-century engravings in Figures 1–3 convey better than modern photos the effect of seeing from afar the fantastic formation of Montserrat, rising mysteriously tall, round, and alone from the surrounding landscape. Zayas calls attention to its solitary height, describing it as "un empinado monte a quien han desamparado los demás" (a towering mountain forsaken by all the rest) (*Novelas*, 37). Hicks describes it more scientifically: "Its rock formation rises upward to a maximum height of 1,224 meters above sea level at the crest of Saint Jerome. Its form is the result of the slow action of geological transformations in which the surrounding land settled leaving the mountain which had formed from molten stone. Its jagged outline is the work of eons of sun and rain, wind and ice" (Virués 1984, 21). The *Espasa-Calpe* article offers no explanation why Montserrat should have been sacred to the rites of Venus, but given the frequent appearance of phallic objects in the fertility rites of pagan religions, the physical contours of the mountain may well have encouraged this use.

The subsequent substitution of a shrine to the Virgin Mary for an erotic pagan cult—and the very language with which the *Enciclopedia Espasa-Calpe* reports it—accord with Kristeva's account of the psychological foundation of the cult of the Virgin. Says Kristeva: "The story of the virginal cult in

Montserrat at the end of the seventeenth century. Engraving from 1691. Courtesy of the Monastery of Montserrat

Christianity amounts in fact to the imposition of pagan-rooted beliefs in, and often against, dogmas of the official Church" (1987, 237) The father-centered law of monotheistic Judaism, in combating the surrounding cults of the mother-goddess, banished the "unclean" female from the sacred space of the temple; the cult of the Virgin, however, by cleansing the mother-figure of the contamination of flesh and death, made possible a symbolic recovery of the feminine as ideal mother-wife-daughter (1982, 113; 1987, 95–97, 234–63).

Superposition of the cult to the Virgin did not, however, abolish all association of Montserrat with subjection to Venus. The legendary origins of the monastery link the mountain retreat with sexual temptation as well as with purgation and healing. In *El Monserrate segundo* (1602), Cristobal de Virués's epic account of the monk Garin, the devil, offended by the asceticism of this hermit's life in a Montserrat cave, lures him into raping a beautiful young woman, then killing and burying her and leaving the mountain. The penance eventually imposed on him by the pope includes crawling from Rome back to Montserrat on all fours. When Garin reveals his crime to her father and leads him to disinter her, they find her miraculously resurrected with only a shining mark on her white neck as witness to her decapitation. She elects to stay in Montserrat, serving in the chapel dedicated to the recently discovered image of the Virgin, and Garin prophesies the future grandeur of the monastery her father founds there. The mountain continued to be known for the ascetic rigors—and demonic temptations—undergone by hermits who resided there.[28]

Zayas is not the only writer to select Montserrat as a retreat for frustrated lovers. Another famous pilgrim of love, that of Lope de Vega in *El peregrino en su patria,* also withdraws to this region in the second book, and interspersed between religious stories and acts of devotion, Lope recounts several tales of sexual sin and frustrated love, including a long and closely autobiographical story of his love of Elena Osorio (Vega Carpio 1971, 257–73). In Castillo Solórzano's *Lisardo enamorado,* virtually all the surviving lovers of the interlocking stories are reunited at the end on pilgrimages to Montserrat.[29] Nor is the association of Montserrat with desire confined to Spanish writers. In story 26 of Marguerite de Navarre's *Heptameron* the young protagonist d'Avannes, trying to devise a way to be alone with a flighty young married woman whom he desires, first thinks of a feigned pilgrimage to the monastery of Our Lady of Montserrat (Navarre 1984, 294).

The Birth of Desire: Jacinta's Dream

Within this symbolic physical landscape, Zayas narrates the birth of feminine desire in a first-person retrospective account by Jacinta that paints maternal absence as the emotional setting for the generation of desire. Jacinta, like most of Zayas's heroines in stories told by female narrators, is launched on the "sea of desire" after her mother's death. Her father, furthermore, is unconcerned with her well-being. Zayas makes it clear that the emotional vacuum is as important as the resulting lack of parental guidance and control, naming the loss of the mother's company before that of her guidance, and dwelling on Jacinta's resentment of her father's disinterest and preference for her brother:

> Faltó mi madre al mejor tiempo, que no fue pequeña falta, pues su compañía, gobierno y vigilancia fuera más importante a mi honestidad, que los descuidos de mi padre, que le tuvo en mirar por mí y darme estado (yerro notable de los que aguardan a que sus hijas le

tomen sin su gusto). Quería el mío a mi hermano tiernísimamente, y esto era sólo su desvelo, sin que se le diese yo en cosa ninguna, no sé qué era su pensamiento, pues había hacienda bastante para todo lo que deseara y quisiera emprender. (*Novelas,* 44)

(My mother died at the worst time, and it was no small loss because her company, guidance, and vigilance would have been more important for my purity than my father's neglect to look out for me and arrange my marriage—a notorious error on the part of those who wait for their daughters to do it without their approval. My father loved my brother tenderly—he was my father's one and only concern, without a thought for me, and I have no idea what his intentions were, since there was an estate sufficient to do anything he might have wanted or desired to undertake.)

In this emotional vacuum, Zayas animates desire in the form of a fantasy within a fantasy. The first episode that Jacinta tells to Fabio opens with her account of a dream in which she, Pygmalion-style, brings to life her first love object. As we will see, that object is always a fantasy—an image of the beloved that the subject holds rather than his/her substantial "reality." Hence we could also say that this fictional dream is a literalization of the psychic process that takes place in the first identification of an object of desire.

Diez y seis años tenía yo cuando una noche estando durmiendo, soñaba que iba por un bosque amenísimo, en cuya espesura hallé un hombre tan galán, que me pareció (¡ay de mí, y cómo hice despierta experiencia dello!) no haberle visto en mi vida tal. Traía cubierto el rostro con el cabo de un ferruelo leonado, con pasamanos y alamares de plata. Paréme a mirarle, agradada del talle y deseosa de ver si el rostro confirmaba con él; con un atrevimiento airoso, llegué a quitarle el rebozo, y apenas lo hice, cuando sacando una daga, me dió un golpe tan cruel por el corazón que me obligó el dolor a dar voces, a las cuales acudieron mis criadas, y despertándome del pesado sueño, me hallé sin la vista del que me hizo tal agravio, la más apasionada que puedas pensar, porque su retrato se quedó estampado en mi memoria, de suerte que en largos tiempos no se apartó ni se borró della. Deseaba yo, noble Fabio, hallar para dueño un hombre de su talle y gallardía, y traíame tan fuera de mí esta imaginación, que le pintaba en ella, y después razonaba con él, de suerte que a pocos lances me hallé enamorada sin saber de qué, porque me puedes creer que si fue Narciso moreno, Narciso era el que vi. (*Novelas*, 44–45)

(I was sixteen when, one night while I was sleeping, I dreamed I was going through a lovely forest, in whose depths I found a man so handsome, that it seemed to me (woe is me! and even when I was awake I relived that dream!) I had never seen his like in all my life. His face was covered by the edge of a tawny-colored cape with braided trim and catches of silver. I stopped to look at him, pleased by his build and wanting to see if his face matched it; with a graceful boldness I drew near to pull back his cloak, and no sooner had I done that than, drawing a dagger, he stabbed it so cruelly into my heart that the pain made me cry out and all my maids came running, and waking up from this dark dream, I found myself, without the sight of the one who had done me such an injury, the most impassioned woman you can imagine, because his image remained engraved on my memory so that it did not vanish or fade away for ever so long. I yearned, noble Fabio, to find a man with his striking appearance and physique to be my husband, and this fantasy had me so beside myself that I drew him in my imagination and then talked with him, so that in no time I was in love without knowing with whom, because if you can believe me that Narcissus was dark, then the man I saw was Narcissus.)

How, as twentieth-century readers of a seventeenth-century fiction, should we interpret this dream? Critics from Valbuena Prat and Goytisolo forward have found it a sign of Zayas's psychological insight, but does this do anachronistic violence to the understanding of dreams in her day? The dream is replete with symbolism whose sexual nature seems almost painfully obvious to a present-day reader, for whom, as Peter Gay says, "Freud is inescapable" (Freud 1989, xiii), albeit in trivialized form. In *The Interpretation of Dreams,* Freud recognized the dream as expressing a wish fulfillment, in disguised or undisguised form. Thoughts repressed into the unconscious emerge with the slackening of censoring psychic defense mechanisms in sleep. Their expression operates through the processes of condensation and displacement, so that several dream thoughts are condensed in one image or word, and the latent dream thought that carries the greatest psychic intensity may be displaced to an apparently subordinate element of the dream. The psychic censor is not inactive in a dreaming state, however, but operates in a variety of ways to distort disturbing latent dream content into more acceptable form. To take Jacinta's dream as an example, up-and-down inversions are a common form of distortion, serving here to veil the phallic symbolism of Jacinta's "bold" action in drawing back the stranger's cape to reveal his "face," thereby initiating his violent attack. The condensation of several dream thoughts in the mystery man's covered face will be discussed below.

Rather than trying to "escape" from Freud, escape from our own reading context, we should, I believe, put contemporary understandings of dream symbolism in dialogue with symbolic language and oneiric interpretations current in seventeenth-century Spain to illuminate regions of commonality and complementarity in their explanations of the dream, as well as areas of divergence.[30] For example, long before readers learned from Freud's *The Interpretation of Dreams* to see pointed objects as phallic symbols and wooded landscapes as the *crines pubis*,[31] the erotic nature of Jacinta's dream was clearly indicated by its setting in "un bosque amenísimo," a standard indication of the *locus amoenis* for Zayas's readers. That such fictional dreams often paralleled Freud's own explanation of the revelation of unconscious desires in dreams he attributed to poetic insight, which had intuited psychic operations that he slowly came to understand through case studies.[32]

There have been wide variations over the centuries in the understanding of the nature of dreams and the ways of interpreting them, of course. From ancient times to that of Zayas, some kinds of dreams were thought to be an imaginative, figural discourse through which divine knowledge could be imparted to the human soul while the body slept. Calderón dramatized the process in a marvelously staged scene in his mythological court play, *Las fortunas de Andrómeda y Perseo,* in which Perseus's half brother and sister Mercury and Pallas use a dream to inform him diplomatically of his divine origins. Mercury and Pallas appear on cloud *tramoyas* (stage machines) and sing their plan in recitative, the harmonious discourse of divinity, then have him lured into the grotto of Morpheus, where, with the help of a drop-in stage set, the audience sees the scene of Jupiter's seduction of Perseus's mother, Danae, as Perseus, asleep on the side of the stage, dreams it.[33] They choose that medium as the best way to explain to him why his proud heart rebels against his apparent peasant status, imparting to him the knowledge that Jupiter was his father so that he will feel empowered to undertake great actions, but with an ambiguity that they hope will deter him from incurring the wrath of the jealous Juno by openly revealing the secret of his parentage.

Calderón's dream scene accords with Freud's usage of dreams as a window into the psyche's past that will permit the dreamer to better govern his or her present and future conduct. More commonly, however, a division was made between "mundane" dreams that relate to the dreamer's past or present physical and emotional state, and divinely inspired dreams with a predictive value. Artemidorus, the second-century physician from Asia Minor whose *Oneirocritica* was the most popular guide to dream interpretation in sixteenth-century Europe (Kagan 1990, 36–37), drew such a distinction. Dreams that were the product of psychobiological processes he called *enhypnia.* They can be the product of the dreamer's body, registering in sleep, hunger, or thirst, or the effects of overeating, or the product of the mind, or of both body and mind, as "when a lover dreams that he is in the company of his beloved" (Artemidorus Daldianus 1975, 14). He continues, saying that "of those dream experiences which pertain to the mind, some are due to one's fears, while others are due to one's hopes" (14). If these "anxiety dreams and petitionary dreams" (20) related to the sleeper's present state end when he awakens, Artemidorus considers them unimportant. His interest centers on the predictive value of the *oneiros,* his second category, which "[calls] to the dreamer's attention a prediction of future events; . . . after sleep, it is the nature of the *oneiros* to awaken and excite the soul by inducing active undertakings" (14–15).

In contrast to Aristotle, who considered all dreams to be of psychobiological origin rather than godsent, and dream divination therefore a pseudoscience (Miller 1994, 44–46), Artemidorus says he is unconcerned with their origin: "I do not, like Aristotle, inquire as to whether the cause of our dreaming is outside of us and comes from the gods or whether it is motivated by something within, which disposes the soul in a certain way and causes a natural event to happen to it. Rather, I use the word in the same way that we customarily call all unforeseen things god-sent" (20–21).

In the Christian era, the question of the origin of dreams was again of crucial importance, however. Although some apologists such as Clement of Alexander linked dream divination with the foolishness of polytheism (Miller 1994, 64), respect for the possible divine inspiration of dreams continued, given the authority of such biblical dreamers as Joseph and Jacob, and of martyrs such as Saint Perpetua.[34] However, the possibility that dreams and visions were demonically inspired loomed large as well, particularly during the Counter-Reformation era in which Zayas lived, with its dedication to rooting out any spiritual heterodoxy and its rejection of pleasures of the flesh as temptations of the devil. In Zayas's times, dreams were considered matters of importance, finds Richard Kagan. Innumerable marketplace dream analysts or village wisewomen were available to interpret dreams and Catholic priests were instructed to inquire about parishioners' dreams in the confessional and guard against dreams of possible demonic inspiration (1990, 37). Zayas would probably have known of the case of Lucrecia de León, whose prophetic dreams critical of the policies of Philip II took her into the circles of power in Madrid before her arrest and trial by the Inquisition in 1590 (Kagan 1990).[35]

Artemidorus classified some *oneiros* as "theorematic," or directly predictive, as when a person at sea dreams of a shipwreck and the ship later sinks, while others are allegorical, in that they "signify one thing by means of another: . . . through them, the soul is conveying something obscurely by physical means" (1975, 15). He also points out that some dreams convey "many things through a few images" (19). Artemidorus traveled widely and compiled an encyclopedic collection of recurrent dream motifs and brief

José de Ribera, *The Dream of Jacob*. Oil on canvas. Museo del Prado, Madrid

"case histories," which he offers to assist other interpreters, yet he stresses that the interpreter of dreams must take into account the dreamer's social context and personal habits to read dreams rightly. Reading Artemidorus, then, we can see that the psychic mechanisms of dream imagery were recognized long before Freud labeled them as displacement and condensation; and that another master dream-reader, like Freud, was ambivalent about whether one could rely on a dictionary-like classification of dream symbolization, or whether dreams could only be understood individually, contextually, and interactively between dreamer and analyst.

On the other hand, we can appreciate two major divergences between the ancient dream book and Freud: first, the appreciation of dreams as prognostic rather than diagnostic tools, and second, the role played by sexual imagery. For Freud, as Wilson illustrates, an infinite diversity of images serve to represent sexual thoughts and wishes, whereas in Artemidorus, sexual activity is presented directly and pragmatically, but "one might say that there is no group of ideas that is incapable of representing *economic* facts and wishes" (Wilson 1993, 67); "sex for Artmeidorus' dreamers . . . was a screen, a predictable disguise, for the issues that *really* mattered" (69), and they were economic. Wilson finds that Cervantine dreamers stand at an intersection, looking both backward toward Artemidorus and forward toward Freud in terms of the relative weight of sexual and economic anxiety. She posits in the form of questions the suggestion that the condemnation of bodily pleasures, the doctrines of asceticism formulated in the fourth century by such church fathers as Saint Jerome and Saint Augustine, may have played a significant role in the alteration of subjectivity through a repression of carnality that made sexuality assume a more weighted and screened role by Spain's Golden Age (Wilson 1993, 69–70). In Jacinta's two dreams, the weight clearly falls on veiled erotic wishes, screened in part behind images of wealth.

Patricia Cox Miller, in her study of dreaming in late antiquity, concludes that despite significant differences in evaluations of dreams over the centuries in Graeco-Roman culture, "in situations of personal crisis—whether of conscience or erotic desire . . . dreaming provided an ideational ground for the negotiation and expression of emotion and idea" (1994, 65) and a medium that brought dreamers' submerged thoughts and fears to conscious awareness and provoked them to new forms of interaction with the world. She cites as one example the dreams Saint Jerome recorded in the late fourth century, in a letter to the virgin Eustocium about the difficulties of the ascetic life. He recounted that he had dreamed of dancing girls and

of being beaten by a judging Christ for continuing to read secular literature. The effects of this dream, like that of Zayas's Jacinta, lingered after
awakening: Saint Jerome reported awakening with his body black and blue
from the beating. Furthermore, he presents as a dream his vision of Eustocium in the king's bridal chamber, of the Song of Songs, in an erotic
oneiric scene that has much in common with that which Zayas creates for
Jacinta: "The secrets of your bedchamber always guard you; your bridegroom always sports with you on the inside. Do you pray?: you speak to the
bridegroom. Do you read?: he speaks to you. And, when sleep comes upon
you, he will come behind the wall and put his hand through the opening
and touch your inner body, and trembling you will rise up and say, 'I am
wounded by love' " (Jerome, *Epistula* 22.25.1 in *Corpus scriptorum ecclesiasti-
corum latinorum* 54.178–79, cited in Miller 1994, 231).

Saint Jerome's dream is part of the well-recognized phenomenon of the
mystical appropriation of the language of human love and eroticism as the
only medium in which to attempt to communicate the ineffable. But the
movement of imagery from the sphere of human to divine love need not
be seen as unidirectional. The wounding of love in the transverberation
scene in Saint Teresa's *Libro de su vida* (Book of Her Life) bears a significant resemblance to Jacinta's dream of being stabbed in the heart by a
handsome stranger, crying out with pain, and awakening totally enamored
of him:

> En esta visión quiso el Señor le viese [al ángel] ansí; no era grande
> sino pequeño, hermoso mucho, . . . Veíale en las manos un dardo
> de oro largo, y al fin del hierro me parecía tener un poco de fuego.
> Ese me parecía meter con el corazón algunas veces, y que me lle-
> gaba a las entrañas: al sacarle me parecía las llevaba consigo, y me
> dejaba toda abrasada en amor grande de Dios. Era tan grande el
> dolor, que me hacía dar aquellos quejidos, y tan excesiva la suavidad
> que me pone este grandísimo dolor, que no hay desear que se quite,
> ni se contenta el alma con menos que Dios. (Teresa de Jesús 1972,
> 238)[36]

> (In this vision the Lord wanted him [the angel] seen thus; he was
> not large but small, very beautiful, . . . I saw in his hands a long
> golden spear, and at the tip, it seemed to me to have a little fire. He
> seemed to put this into my heart several times, and it penetrated to
> my innards: when he took it out it seemed to take them with it, and

it left me completely afire with a great love of God. The pain was so great that it made me make those moans, and so extreme the gentleness that this very great pain created in me that there was no desiring it to be removed, nor could the soul be content with anything less than God.)

Saint Teresa's desire is for the death of the self in spiritual *jouissance* of God.[37] Zayas, in animating feminine desire for a very human male, used similar imagery to bring desire back to earth. Dream imagery is drawn from the culture of the dreamer, and the language in which it is reported bears the marks of the literature of its era, religious as well as secular.[38]

Given the above evidence of a centuries-old understanding of the link between dreams and psychic concerns, and the use of similar symbolic language in discourses of desire, both erotic and religious, we can assume that Zayas's seventeenth-century readers would likely have shared with us the understanding of Jacinta's dream as the expression of a submerged sexual wish. Her contemporaries would have differed from a post-Freudian audience, however, in reading that dream as predictive, as a supernatural "advance notice" of the advent of her lover.

Left in an emotional vacuum by the death of her mother and the disregard of her father, Jacinta dreams herself into love; her own interpretation of her dream expounds at length on the causative role played by her fantasy. Asking, "¿Quién vió, Fabio, amar una sombra . . . ?" (Who, Fabio, ever heard of anyone loving a mere shadow?), she compares herself to Pygmalion and other mythical lovers whose passion for impossible objects was less mad than her obsession with a mere fantasy. She recites for Fabio the poem that served as the epigraph to our Introduction, a poem she wrote to her "beloved ghost," analyzing the madness of loving a phantom traced by her own soul, and praying that heaven might fulfill her desire:

> Dame, cielo, si has criado
> aqueste ser que deseo,
> de mi voluntad empleo,
> y antes que nacido, amado;
> . . . .
> ¿a quién le sucedió,
> de amor milagro tan nuevo,

Gianlorenzo Bernini, *Ecstasy of Saint Teresa*, Santa Maria della Vittoria, Rome
(photo: Art Resource, New York)

que le ocupase el deseo
amante que en sueños vió?
(*Novelas,* 46–47)

(Grant me, heaven, if you have made him, this being I desire, object
of my will, though yet unborn, adored. . . . To whom has there be-
fallen a miracle of love so new, as to be possessed by desire for a
lover seen only in dreams?)

Jacinta's understanding listener Fabio provides no answer for her
rhetorical questions,[39] but Zayas's generation of desire in a fantasy anticipates Lacan's explanation of the figuration of the object of desire in the
Imaginary order. This figuration both precedes and exceeds any particular
object that a given subject may identify as embodying the (im)possible satisfaction of desire. It is grounded in the lack-in-being that Jacinta attributes
to the material death of her mother—the perceived loss caused by recognition of separation from the original object of desire, the first nurturer or
(m)Other, upon entry into the Symbolic order of language and sexual difference. As a stand-in for that lost object, the object of desire can never satisfy the desiring subject's demand for love; like Jacinta's first love object,
it is thus wrought in a compensatory fantasy and destined for eventual
shipwreck.

How, then, does Zayas configure this "object of will" in Jacinta's dream?
As noted, the dream begins in a classic *locus amoenus,* the thickness of a
beautiful forest. In this space, Jacinta dreams of seeing a figure more handsome and masculine than any she has ever seen, a man who hides his face
behind the corner of his cape.[40] The cape may protect his identity but the
description of it, in the coded language of dress so important in Zayas
(Kaminsky 1989), reveals the fact that he is well-to-do, a significant fact in
the attachment of the feminine subject to the Symbolic order that we will
later explore in the last section of this chapter. He wears "un ferruelo leonado, con pasamanos y alamares de plata" (a tawny-colored cape, with
braided trim and catches of silver) (*Novelas,* 45). If in analyzing the description of this dream cape we focus not on the overt imagistic content
but on the language in which it is described, we can see the cape itself as a
signifier of aggression and captivation. According to the *Diccionario de Autoridades,* "ferruelo" derives from the Latin word *ferrus,* iron, iron weapon,
or sword; "leonado" means the tawny gold of the lion, "animal ferocísimo,
y mui generoso y de noble condición" (a very ferocious animal, and very

generous and of a noble disposition); "alamares" may, according to Covarrubias, derive from the Latin *hamus,* meaning "hook"; "pasamanos"—literally "pass-hands"—requires no comment. Jacinta, pleased by his figure,
stops to gaze at him. Wanting to know if his face is as handsome as his
physique, she approaches him and pulls back the cape with, as she says,
"un atrevimiento airoso" (a graceful boldness) (*Novelas,* 45). In the instant
she exposes his face, he pulls out a dagger and stabs her a "cruel" blow to
the heart. The pain causes her to cry out and as her servants come to
awaken her from her "pesado sueño" (dark dream),[41] she finds herself
without the "sight" of her assailant, but impassioned by his image, engraved in her memory.

Aggression: Scopic and Physical

Two actions in this dream deserve careful attention, Jacinta's bold gaze and
the reactive blow it provokes. Eyes and the power of looking are a significant leitmotiv or symbolic code throughout Zayas's tales. In part, Zayas's
accentuation of eyes partakes of the conventional poetic topos of the eyes
as the portal of the soul, the pathway through which a lover's soul passes
into the possession of the beloved. But her unconventional emphasis on
the power of the gaze from the perspective of feminine desire in Jacinta's
dream alters the traditional gendered encoding of scopic activity. She depicts what Emilie Bergmann has called the "transgressive female gaze," an
act of looking in which the woman is the sexual aggressor rather than the
passive object, or the mock-passive lure, of the male gaze.[42]

Zayas's recoding is not a simple passive-active role reversal in which
women actively contemplate males as sexual objects; rather, she depicts
scopic activity as a bidirectional captivation, in which women look and are
caught by what they see.[43] Jacinta prefaces telling her life story to Fabio by
attributing women's frailty and vulnerability to their eyes in that "tenemos
ojos, que, a nacer ciegas, menos sucesos hubiera visto el mundo, que al fin
viviéramos seguras de engaños" (we have eyes, because, if we were born
blind, the world would have seen fewer [novel] events, for we at least
would live safe from deceptions) (*Novelas,* 44). Women have eyes with
which to see, and it is their looking that exposes them to deceits, deceits
that are, furthermore, *seen* by the world. Jacinta, in her dream, boldly approaches the handsome *galán* and pulls back his cape to see his face but is,
as a consequence, obsessed by the image she has revealed. She says she
awakens to find herself without "la vista del que me hizo tal agravio" (the

sight of the man who did me such injury) (*Novelas,* 45), at once suffering from the pain inflicted, from the lack of his "sight," and from its lingering imprint. The word for sight, in Spanish as in English, means both the act of seeing and the object of vision, and thus functions as an ambivalent expression of visual direction.

When the man of her dreams, don Félix, appears in the flesh in the street below her balcony, Jacinta repeats her dream-looking in a more socially approved fashion. She says that "pude . . . poner los ojos en las galas, criados y gentil presencia, y deteniéndome en ella más de lo justo, vi tal gallardía en él. . . . Vi en efecto el mismo dueño de mi sueño, y aun de mi alma" (I could . . . rest my eyes on his finery, his servants and his gallant bearing, and lingering on it longer than was fitting, I saw such a handsome figure in him. . . . I saw in effect, the very lord of my dreams, and of my soul as well) (*Novelas,* 48). As in her dream, she notes first the signs of his social status, his finery and the servants accompanying him,[44] then turns her eye on his handsome form, on which she confesses having dwelt at unseemly length. Drawn by her gaze, don Félix looks up at the balcony, and this time, the arrow of love strikes him: "Miró don Félix al balcón, viendo que sólo mis ojos hacían fiesta a su venida. Y hallando amor ocasión y tiempo, executó en él el golpe de su dorada saeta" (don Félix looked at the balcony, seeing that only my eyes danced at his arrival. And finding the moment and the opportunity, love struck him a blow with his golden arrow) (*Novelas,* 49). Throughout the remainder of the tale, eyes often stand in for the subjects themselves, sometimes speaking a more eloquent and captivating code than language itself. And when, at the end of the story, Jacinta despairs of securing reciprocation by her second love, Celio, and retires to live as a *seglar* (lay resident) in a convent where Fabio says Celio will visit her, Jacinta says: "Si tú haces que Celio me vea, con eso estoy contenta, porque como yo vea a Celio, eso me basta . . . por lo menos comerá el alma el gusto de su vista" (If you arrange for Celio to see me, I will be content with that, because as long as I see Celio, that will be enough for me . . . at least my soul will feed on the pleasure of his sight) (*Novelas,* 78).[45]

Looking, then, exposes both the subject and the object of the look to captivation by desire, and we can in this light understand the logic of the defensive/aggressive response that Zayas assigns to Jacinta's dream man. Even in fantasy, the birth of desire is a violent and painful affair from a feminine perspective.[46] Jacinta underlines this in the poem she writes to her fantasy lover: "¿Mas cómo puedo pedir / vida ni muerte a un sujeto, / que no tuvo de perfecto, / más ser que saber herir?" (But how can I ask for life or death from a being whose only perfection is knowing how to wound?) (*Novelas,* 47). The violence of this dreamed encounter raises from the outset the question of the relationship between the much noted level of violence against women in Zayas's novellas and the position of the feminine narrator and reader.

Both de Lauretis and Bersani find a close link between desire, sadistic violence, and narrativity. De Lauretis compares the standard definition of narrative with Laura Mulvey's description of sadism: "Sadism demands a story, depends on making something happen, forcing a change in another person, a battle of will and strength, victory/defeat, all occurring in a linear time with a beginning and an end" (de Lauretis 1984, 103). Bersani (1969) writes: "Literature . . . is not merely instructive *about* desire; in a sense, desire *is* a phenomenon of the literary imagination. Desire is an activity within a lack; it is an appetite stimulated by an absence. But it is never only a lack. Desire is a hallucinated satisfaction in the absence of the source of satisfaction. In other words, it is an appetite of the imagination. . . . In the same way that literary works are always critical revisions of other literary works, our desires reformulate both other desires and the pleasures which are at the source of all desire" (11). Because desire is inherently insatiable, it is also inherently violent, because it attempts to eliminate everything alien to it, and to take revenge on a resisting world (13). Reiterating the meaning-making value of myth, folktale, and all subsequent narrative, de Lauretis emphasizes that narrativity is embedded in social practice, and in turn contributes to the reinforcement of those practices. Jerome Bruner also posits, from the perspective of developmental psychology, the circularity between narrative and social reality. Bruner says that "there is compelling evidence to indicate that narrative comprehension is among the earliest powers of mind to appear in the young child and among the most widely used forms of organizing human experience" (1991, 9). Narrative is a fundamental tool in what Bruner calls the "cultural tool kit" with which we achieve a knowledge of social reality. We organize our lives by telling them as stories, to ourselves and to others.

The converse of this is that narrative paradigms have a powerful effect on social practice, particularly on the relationships between men and women. Bruner is not concerned with the gender coding of narrative, but for de Lauretis, its basic structure is a two-person drama that, "regardless of the gender of the text-image" (1984, 119) requires a male subject, an active, differentiating principle of culture, and a female object, "female-obstacle-boundary-space" (121) that he overcomes. In formulating this conceptualization, de Lauretis draws on the narrative typology of Jurij Lot-man, who reduces the conflict of narrative to two fundamental dramatis personae, hero and antagonist or obstacle, and to two repeatable functions: "entry into a closed space, and emergence from it. . . . Inasmuch as closed space can be interpreted as 'a cave,' 'the grave,' 'a house,' 'woman' (and, correspondingly, be allotted the features of darkness, warmth, dampness), entry into it is interpreted on various levels as 'death,' 'conception,' 'return home' and so on; moreover all these acts are thought of as mutually identical" (Lotman quoted in de Lauretis 1984, 118). What position does this structure leave for the female writer/teller and—since the production of meaning requires the active participation of the reader/hearer —the female reader?

Masochism and Narcissism

If the nature of the text-generating desire in the fundamental, masculine Oedipal plot can be described as sadistic, would its feminine version then be masochistic?[47] Freud, who maintained that there was only one kind of libido, that it is masculine, active, and aggressive, said: "The suppression of women's aggressiveness which is prescribed for them constitutionally and imposed on them socially favors the development of powerful masochistic impulses, which succeed . . . in binding erotically the destructive trends which have been diverted inwards. Thus masochism . . . is truly feminine" (1974, 22: 166).[48] The predominance of stories in Zayas's collection that recount male violence—either psychological or physical—against women might suggest that she conceives of female desire and its effects in fundamentally masochistic terms, and that she facilitates a masochistic identification with feminine suffering for her readers. In the second part of her collection, the *Desengaños amorosos,* the level of violence against women reaches the level of the grotesque. Even in the relatively nonviolent second episode of *Aventurarse perdiendo,* in which the desire is Jacinta's, the narrator describes love itself as a war waged by men against women, in which women are both objects to be defeated and spaces to be invaded:[49]

> ¡Ay de mí! que cuando considero las estratagemas con que los hombres rinden las mujeres, digo que todos son traidores, y el amor guerra y batalla campal, donde el amor combate a sangre y fuego al honor, alcaide de la fortaleza del alma. (*Novelas,* 71)

>(Woe is me! For when I think about the tricks and strategies men
use to conquer women, I say they are all traitors, and love is war and
a battlefield where love with blood and fire combats honor,
guardian of the fortress of the soul.)

Lacan, however, cautioned against assumptions of an essential link between masochism and passivity in women other than through fantasies related to the effect of the signifier in the unconscious and to the prejudice
of analysts similarly conditioned.[50] And recent film criticism has problema-
tized the simplicity of early feminist accounts of gendered authorial or
camera-eye positioning and of audience identification and response.[51]
Even in viewing or reading traditionally Oedipal narratives, audience
response is not a straightforward polarity between voyeuristic/mascu-
line/sadistic and objectified/feminine/masochistic positions. Both masculine and feminine subjects, as narrators and viewers or readers, can and
do identify across gender lines, and audience responses indicate that they
shift identificatory positioning as narratives proceed.[52]

Authorial and audience capacity for cross-gender identification seems
much greater than the gender flexibility of representational paradigms,
however, which persistently portray power and aggression as masculine and
fear, exploitation, and weakness as feminine. Speaking theoretically and
polemically in her preface, Zayas posits women's spiritual and material
equality with men as well as their capacity to take up arms and to replace
men in university posts, yet on moving into the storytelling mode, she has
her first enclosed narrator counterpose in the first sentence "las flacas
fuerzas de las mujeres" (women's slender forces) and the "claros y heroicos
entendimientos de los hombres" (men's clear and heroic understanding).
Within the plots of her tales, Zayas does sometimes reverse, at least temporarily, gender-coded action by allowing women to dress and act as males.
As Smith says, however, this occasional feminine adoption of the "law of
the dagger and the phallus" does not by itself modify gendered role paradigms (1989, 33).

Yet Jacinta's dream does indicate the operation of a more subtle psychic
stratagem for effecting cross-gender identification and undermining the
firm boundaries and polarities of gender paradigms. Jacinta describes the
man of her dreams as Narcissus and comments that "si fue Narciso
moreno, Narciso era el que vi" (if Narcissus was dark, then the man I saw
was Narcissus)" (*Novelas*, 45). Given the range of mythic figures of masculine beauty, Narcissus seems an unlikely choice. Male writers of Golden

Age Spain did sometimes use Narcissus similarly as a figure for masculine beauty.[53] But evocations of Narcissus in Zayas's era in Spain, as elsewhere, normally served to represent self-absorbed beauty, unresponsive to love. In the world of drama, for example, Narcissus might figure as the self-absorbed fop of Guillén de Castro's *El Narciso en su opiníon,* or the tragic character of Calderón's court drama *Eco y Narciso.* Zayas displays him in this stance too, in a poem in *El castigo de la miseria* (A Miser's Reward) constructed as a gloss on the refrain "Murmurad a Narciso/que no sabe amar" (Whisper to Narciso / who knows not how to love) (*Novelas,* 130–33). Yet Zayas also chooses Narcissus to designate an idealized male object of love, in gender-crossing songs of jealous lovers, as we will see. Half a century later, Sor Juana Inés de la Cruz would choose Narcissus to figure not an ideal human lover, but Christ himself, in the lovely *auto sacramental* titled *El divino Narciso.*

Why should Narcissus play such a significant and positive role in the literary imaginations of these two women writers? Ludwig Pfandl considered it symptomatic of a narcissistic neurosis in Sor Juana's case, reflective of a psychic division and strong masculine tendencies. While Octavio Paz (1988) criticizes the limitations of Pfandl's biographical and psychological reading of *El divino Narciso,* he reiterates the same theme of a "movement toward the masculine," and a "narcissistic" personality.[54] Pfandl and Paz are both reading Sor Juana's use of Narcissus through the lens of Freud's conception of narcissism as pathological and narcissistic desire to be loved as characteristic of a passive feminine position (Young-Bruehl 1990, 31).[55] For Lacan and Kristeva, however, narcissism plays a positive rather than a regressive or pathological role, and is not particular to the feminine subject. Rather, narcissistic identification is a feature in the formation of all human identity (Ragland-Sullivan 1986, 39–41, 270). Primary narcissism contributes to the creation of a child's corporeal image in the mirror stage; secondary narcissism "concerns the dialectic of love and aggression in all human relations" (Wright 1992, 272). Identification with others outside the self is crucial to the foundation of our sense of being (see Introduction, note 16 in the present volume), as well as the cause of sexual drive. Like Jacinta, ensnared by the figure in her dreams, it involves captivation by the other's image, or by one's own image as reflected in others (Wright 1992, 272–73). Furthermore, Kristeva considers narcissistic identification the psychic bond that underlies all love. "It is essential for the lover to maintain the existence of that ideal other [the paternal pole of primary identification], and to be able to imagine himself similar, merging with him, and even indistinguishable from him"; "the amatory experience rests on *narcissism* and its aura of emptiness [the sense of separation from the mother], seeming, and impossibility, which underlies an *idealization* equally and essentially inherent in love" (1987, 33, 267). Seeing the positive contribution of narcissistic identification helps us understand why Zayas selected Narcissus as a model for imagining her dream man, and why Sor Juana would use the same myth as an allegorical representation of the specular bonding of Christ and Human Nature.[56] I suggest that both women writers display in this choice not neurotic yearnings to transform themselves into masculine subjects, but rather a poetic intuition into the process of cross-gender identification that makes love possible, and that can therefore serve as a model for the transcendence of the greater divide between the human and the divine.

We can indeed see the designation of the ideal veiled lover in Jacinta's dream as Narcissus as being indicative of Zayas's poetic intuition into the positive role of narcissistic identification. Understanding that dreamers commonly represent themselves simultaneously in different guises in more than one character in their dreams, I suggest that the mysterious ideal object first appeared with a cape masking his face because he was in a sense the male Jacinta might wish to be, the male who would have earned her father's love, now totally dedicated to her brother. And it is revealing his nonidentity with her that provokes the painful wound. Given the condensation of dreamwork, this would not exclude the more obvious phallic desire symbolized by the wounding dagger, but would render her desire more complex. Hence we can read Jacinta as dreaming an Imaginary duplication of herself as both male and female, both subject and object of desire.

Zayas uses Narcissus to represent an ideally beautiful male lover who invites an even more radical transcendence of gender difference in a ballad in *El desengaño andando, y premio de la virtud*. This erotic ballad paints a pastoral scene of the reciprocal love of Anarda and "un gallardo pastorcillo, / que por ser Narciso en gala, / será su nombre Narciso" (A gallant little shepherd who, because he was like Narcissus in charm, will be named Narcissus) (*Novelas,* 280). The handsome shepherd is next likened to Adonis, and then, much more surprisingly, to Hermaphroditus, the son of Hermes and Aphrodite beloved by the water nymph Salmacis, who became joined with her in a single, bisexual person.[57]

> Y por quien Salmacis bella
> tomara por buen partido

en su amada compañia
ser eterno hermafrodito
(*Novelas,* 280)

(And for whom beautiful Salmacis will decide to become an eternal hermaphrodite in his beloved company).

The context in which this ballad is sung presents the reader with a positively dizzying crisscrossing of gender and perspective. In an episode told by a female narrator, doña Clara's husband has been lured away from her by another women who holds him with magic powers. Doña Clara traces them to another city and there finds her husband half naked in her rival's living room singing the foregoing ballad, in which Anarda steals away from her jealously watchful husband for a love tryst with this Narcissus/Adonis/Hermaphroditus who is evoked through the gaze of Venus and Salmacis. This Narcissus, however, does not drown in his own reflection, but sates his thirst with the nectar of coral lips. As if laughing at her own vertiginous play with gender, Zayas ends the poem on a comic note: "Al campo cerró las puertas / el rapaz, de Venus hijo, / que poner puertas al campo / sólo pudiera Cupido. / Lo demás que sucedió; vieron los altos alisos, / haciendo sus hojas ojos / y sus cogollos oídos" (The lad, son of Venus, closed the meadow gates; for only Cupid could put gates on a meadow. The tall birches saw the rest that followed, turning their leaves into eyes and their shoots into ears) (*Novelas,* 281).

Zayas repeats this dizzying blur of gender identification through Narcissus and Hermaphrodite in another poetic complaint by a jealous lover in *Desengaño 6* (*Amar sólo para vencer*) (Love for the Sake of Conquest). Significantly, that jealous lover is a male, cross-dressed as a maidservant, "Estefanía," to gain proximity and court Laurela. When Laurela returns from visiting the man her parents want her to marry, s/he sings a lengthy poetic complaint that concludes with a list of divine lovers made into models of their relationship. Heading that list is Narcissus as model for the rival, whom Estefanía hopes will turn as deaf an ear to Laurela's love as Narcissus did to Echo's. As the climactic image, the singer figures her/himself as Hermaphrodite, dismembered by the beloved's faithlessness, which s/he cannot avenge:

Desháganse los lazos
del leal y dichoso Hermafrodito,

pues en ajenos brazos
a mi hermoso desdén estar permito
(*Desengaños*, 316)

(Untie the bonds of loyal and blessed Hermaphroditus, since I
allow my lovely rejecter to be in another's arms)

This twice-repeated association of Narcissus and Hermphroditus confirms,
I believe, the element of androgyny and cross-gender identification underlying the depiction of Jacinta's dream man as Narcissus.

Yet despite the bisexual process of characterization, her dream fantasy
nevertheless retains a fundamentally masochistic shape when viewed from
the feminine position: as the principal, active, invading figure, she constitutes "herself" as male; figured as female, however, her desiring activity is
limited to drawing back what we might call the veil of modesty, which unleashes upon her a violent attack.

Thus, while we recognize that Zayas provides in Narcissus a figure of
cross-gender identification for Jacinta and places women in both subject
and object positions in relation to desire in plotting her stories; and while
we acknowledge that reader identification with the feminine or masculine
protagonists is not limited by sex or gender either, we cannot ignore the
fact that the great majority of her stories depict the heroine as the misused
object of male violence. Most also include an active, aggressively desiring
woman—usually in the stance of a shameless antagonist. In a few stories—
told by male narrators—in the first volume of the collection, she does paint
successfully desiring women in a more positive light, for reasons we will explore in subsequent chapters. When the heroine of a Zayas tale is the originator of the desiring action, however, she almost inevitably becomes its victim as well.[58] In the majority of her plots—most particularly those narrated
by women—active libido is presented as appropriate for the male, and not
for the female.

Within the confines of the sexual stereotypes of her day, Zayas provides
a "working-through of desire" as a twice-rendered fantasy in the dreams of
Jacinta. Jacinta brought desire to life in her first dream, as her dreamed
Narcissus literally took on flesh as don Félix, who upon first sight of her on
her balcony, says, "Tal joya será mía, o yo perderé la vida" (That jewel will
be mine, or I will perish) (*Novelas*, 49). The "jewel" is withheld but briefly,
for as she comments to Fabio, he offers exactly what she desires—"la
ocasión de casarse, y más del mismo que ama" (the chance to get married,

and moreover to the one she loves), the very bait that lures any woman to her downfall. (*Novelas*, 50–51). When a threat to that marriage prospect intervenes in the form of Adriana, a beautiful cousin of don Félix who falls in love with him, the jealous Jacinta, on a promise of marriage witnessed by a servant, gives herself to Félix, "body and soul": "Le di la posesión de mi alma y cuerpo, pareciéndome que así le tendría más seguro" (I gave him possession of my soul and my body, thinking that way I would be more sure of him) (*Novelas*, 53). The despairing cousin writes a note to Jacinta's father telling him to guard his house more carefully, because "había quien le quitaba el honor" (there was someone who was stealing his honor) (*Novelas*, 55) and then she commits suicide. Fleeing Jacinta's father's wrath, the lovers take refuge in the convent where two of Félix's aunts are nuns, and Félix, after killing her brother in self-defense, leaves the country. Thinking him dead, Jacinta becomes a nun, but when he reappears six years later, they resume their sexual union and she abandons the convent. They obtain a papal dispensation from her vows and blessing for their marriage, but are required not to cohabit for a year, and don Félix leaves Jacinta with relatives in Madrid while he goes to achieve honor serving in Mamora.

Eros and Thanatos

As Jacinta gave life to the object of her desire in a dream, so in parallel fashion, during his second enforced absence, she "annihilates" desire in her second melodramatic and prophetic dream: "(porque como la Fortuna me dio a don Félix en sueños, quiso quitármele de la misma suerte) soñaba que recibía una carta suya, y una caxa que a la cuenta parecía traer algunas joyas, y en yéndola a abrir, hallé dentro la cabeza de mi esposo" (because as Fortune had given me don Felix in a dream, she wanted to take him away from me the same way, I dreamt that I received a letter from don Felix and a box that looked as if it brought some jewels, and on opening it, I found within it my husband's head) (*Novelas*, 67). Dreaming of finding words of love accompanied by jewels, she finds death in the form of a severed head.

Why should the death of love, like its birth, be revealed in a dream? Because dreams—for their classical interpreters as for psychoanalysts—offer access to knowledge unreachable through rational discourse alone. Jacinta tells Fabio that she had been living with a foreboding of catastrophe even before the dream, because "no hay más ciertos astrólogos que los amantes" (there are no surer astrologers than lovers) (*Novelas*, 67). Lovers know irrationally, intuitively, the logic of the stars, the order of the universe, the *logos* that threatens their vision of happiness and fulfillment. But it is the divine/unconscious discourse of dreams that brings the letter of the truth of its fatal end,[59] the beheading of the dream man, the shipwreck that awaits those who "se arrojen al mar de sus desenfrenados deseos" (throw themselves into the sea of unrestrained desire), as Lisarda warned in her opening sentence.

In *Beyond the Pleasure Principle*, Freud (1974, 18:34–43) postulates as the two fundamental drives the death instinct and sexual desire, Thanatos and Eros, and in his interpretation of the three caskets in *The Merchant of Venice* (1974, 12:291–301) shows how they become intertwined in the human psyche, in various registers. What the ego fears most is annihilation or separation, which is also experienced as a kind of death.[60] In complex organisms, according to Freud, the death instinct strives to decompose the organism, to achieve a state of inorganic stability. Libido counters the destructive force in the unconscious by directing it outward, in the form of sadism, or inward in the form of masochism (1974, 18:36, 53–57). The relevance of that observation to the dagger blow of Jacinta's first dream needs no explanation.

The emotional context that Zayas creates for Jacinta's second dream is as telling as that she set for the first dream. Jacinta finds herself again in an emotional void. She lives, in a sense, the third repetition of the emotional trauma of separation. The first was the lost of the first love object, the mother, and frustration with the unresponsiveness of her father; from this sense of lack, desire was born in her first dream. The desire that animates such an Imaginary fantasy is always a vision of wholeness and security that will cover over the lack-in-being caused by the original loss.[61] But that fantasy has now been shattered twice: Félix left her with his aunts in a convent and disappeared for six years. There, as a nun, she reestablished a substitute feminine community, with the company of Félix's sister Isabel. Félix reappears and ruptures that tranquillity, then leaves her again with relatives while he goes to Mamora. She spends months waiting without a word from him, lamenting her sense of inconsolable emptiness (*Novelas*, 67).

The death drive also works through a subject's sense of guilt in relation to cultural norms and laws, a sense of guilt that Jacinta had expressed in various ways. When she first fled home, she expressed approval of her father for taking vengeance in his own hands, calling it an "acción noble" (a noble action) a "propósito honrado" (honorable aim) for the loss of "la mejor joya de su casa y la mejor prenda de su honra" (the best jewel of his house and the best security of his honor) (*Novelas*, 63). When Félix reappeared the first time, she procured a key to a door of the convent for her lover, and speaking retrospectively with Fabio, registers both their sexual pleasure and her sense of guilt. With that key, Félix found himself, she says,

> más glorioso que con un reino. ¡Oh caso atroz y riguroso! Pues todas o las más noches entraba a dormir conmigo. Esto era fácil, por haber una celda que yo había labrado de aquella parte. Cuando considero esto no me admiro, Fabio, de las desdichas que me siguen, y antes alabo y engradezco el amor y misericordia de Dios, en no enviar un rayo contra nosotros. (*Novelas,* 63)

> (more in glory than with a kingdom. Oh, what a harsh and awful affair! For every night or almost every night he came in to sleep with me. This was easy, because there was a cell that I had had built on that side. When I think about this I am not surprised, Fabio, about the misfortunes that follow me; rather I praise and exalt the love and mercy of God in not sending a bolt of lightning against us.)

Under the pressure of the death drive emanating from the pain of separation and the weight of guilt, Jacinta's dreamwork is an attempt to extinguish desire so she may return to an unfeeling stability. She had expressed just such a wish for emotional peace in regard to the false earlier news of his death, commenting that "en seis años no se acordó de España ni de la triste Jacinta que había dejado en ella: pluguiera a Dios se estuviera hasta hoy, y me hubiera dejado en mi quietud, sin haberme sujetado a tantas desdichas" (in six years he never remembered Spain or the sorrowful Jacinta he had left there. Would to God he had stayed there forever and left me to my peace and quiet without subjecting me to so many misfortunes!) (*Novelas,* 61).

The imagery of Jacinta's two dreams possesses interesting symmetries. In the first, she pulled back the cape to reveal his face, which initiated the wound of love. In the second, she opened the box and saw his severed head, and as the image of his face is engraved on her soul when she awakens from the first dream, so she repeatedly sees his severed head after waking from the second: "Pareciéndome que a todas partes que volvía la cabeza, vía la de don Félix" (Wherever I turned my head I seemed to see that of don Félix) (*Novelas,* 68). When she sees the box in her dreams, she thinks Félix is sending her jewels, just as she first noted the silver decora-

tions on his cape in the first dream, and the luxury of his attire when he appeared in the street. The interpenetration of symbols of riches and sex is
not surprising. As Diana de Armas Wilson has pointed out (1993, 70, 77)
there was widespread linguistic ambiguity between the sexual and the economic in Golden Age Spain, when, as Javier Herrero says, love and cash
were competing for attention.[62] A famous example is "Dulcinea's" demand
for six reales from don Quixote in the Cueva de Montesinos episode. For a
noblewoman, the choice of an appropriately well-to-do and noble partner
was obviously a consciously expressed interest. But it also has unconscious
roots in the nature of feminine desire, which we will explore below.

The Desire to Be Desired

As Jacinta found, desire is not easily annihilated. While Jacinta's experience with Félix might serve to work through desire perceived as biological
energy shaped by social structures, such as it was characterized by Freud (at
least in his later years), desire has other roots. Zayas demonstrates these
psychic roots of desire in the second episode of *Aventurarse perdiendo* in a
poetic intuition that anticipates yet more clearly Lacanian explanations of
the cause of desire.

Lacan reread Freud's idea of *Trieb* (Drive) as a complex of Need, Desire,
and Demand that seeks constantly and fruitlessly to fill the void left by consciousness of the separation from the (m)Other, to regain *jouissance,* the
ecstatic sense of fusion of the pre-mirror-stage infant.[63] Since the *moi,* the
specular unconscious subject, the locus of the primary identifications that
construct individuality, and of primary libido, is constituted by the reflected and internalized gaze of the Other (see Introduction, pages 10–11
above), this insatiable complex of Need, Desire and Demand operates primarily as the demand for recognition, the "Desire to be desired" as
Ragland-Sullivan puts it (1986, 73).[64] "In Lacan's dialectical context Desire
emanates first from the *moi*'s thrust toward recognition of/from/about/to
the Other(A): Who am I? What am I of you? The space between the *moi*
and the Other(A) is, therefore, Desire, a space that widens throughout life.
Human conflict and anxiety are bound, then, to arise both intrapsychically
and intersubjectively. An alien Desire resides at the center of one's being, a
Desire whose text is repressed" (Ragland-Sullivan 1986, 76–77). Jacinta's
initiation as a desiring dreamer, we recall, was set in the context of the
physical as well as psychic loss of her mother and paternal indifference to
her well-being.

The sense of separation, of division from the loved/loving other is felt as psychic death in the threatened disintegration of the *moi* (Ragland-Sullivan 1986, 72–73, 118). Although the expression is conventional, it is nevertheless significant that Zayas paints each separation of Jacinta from her lover in terms of death. When Félix flees to Flanders, Jacinta says that her tears and lamentations were such "que fué mucho no costarme la vida" (that it all but cost my life) (*Novelas*, 59). His second departure, for Mamora, causes her, again, three months of life-threatening illness (*Novelas*, 65). And just before the second dream, she says:

> En todo este tiempo no tuve cartas de don Félix, y aunque pudieran consolarme las de su padre y hermana, . . . no era posible que hinchiesen el vacío de mi cuidadosa voluntad, la cual me daba mil sospechas de mi desdicha, porque tengo para mí, que no hay más ciertos astrólogos que los amantes. (*Novelas*, 67)

> (In all this time, I received no letters from don Felix, and although those of his father and sister might have consoled me . . . it was impossible for them to fill the void of my anxious desire, which gave me a thousand suspicions of my misfortune, because as for me, I believe there are no better astrologers than lovers.)

She reiterates the significant reference to the need to "fill the void," recounting how she spent three years lamenting Félix's death, unable to find another love object that could, as she puts it, "satisfaciese mis ojos ni hinchiese el vacío de mi corazón" (satisfy my eyes or fill the emptiness of my heart) (*Novelas*, 69).

Significantly, Zayas depicts the origin of her second love in terms of a triangular inspiration, a displaced reenactment of the Oedipal mother-father-daughter triad,[65] in which awareness of another's unsatisfied desire awakens her own. She has felt no amorous inclination toward Celio until she hears him boasting of his coldness to another woman's love:

> Jamas miré a Celio para amarle [hasta] . . . un día, que nos contó como era querido de una dama, y que la aborrecía con las mismas veras que le amaba, gloriándose de las sinrazones con que pagaba sus ternezas. ¿Quién pensara, Fabio, que esto despertara mi cuidado, no para amarle, sino para mirarle con más atención que fuera justo? De mirar su gallardía renació en mí un poco de deseo, y

con desear se empezaron a enjugar mis ojos, y fui cobrando salud
(*Novelas*, 70).

(I never looked at Celio with love [until] . . . one day . . . he told us
how he was loved by a lady and how he despised her with the same
intensity as she loved him, boasting of the slights with which he repaid her endearments. Who would think, Fabio, that this would
awaken my interest, not to love him, but to look at him more attentively than was fitting? Regarding his fine figure, a bit of desire was
reborn in me, and with desire, my tears began to dry and I started
recovering my health.)

Not only does another's unsatisfied desire for Celio awaken that of Jacinta,
but Zayas has Jacinta disclose her love to him in the form of a poem supposedly about yet another woman, who falls in love when she is captivated
by her lover's gaze reflected in a mirror.

In the Jacinta-Celio episode, as in Lacanian theory of psychic development, the mirror serves as an important metaphor for the phenomenon of
the perception of identity in alienated form, in the space of the Other, and
as the captivating reflector of the desired/desiring gaze.[66] In simplified, ex-
periential terms, the mirror functions as a metaphor for the fact that a
baby, previously an undifferentiated site of sensations, learns its identity as
a physically integrated and separate being by seeing itself in a "mirror."
The physical presence of a true mirror is not necessary; s/he can acquire
the same sense of identity in alienation by analogy, from observing other
human beings over time, but we can more easily visualize how s/he learns
in front of a mirror. Imagine Jacinta's mother, holding her up to a mirror;
as the image of Jacinta and her mother catches the infant Jacinta's eye, the
mother says, "That's you," or more likely, "That's Jacinta." She first sees
herself from the perspective of another, from the space of the (m)Other,
who directs her gaze and attaches to the image she sees a name, a Symbolic-order designation, a signifier for the subject she is becoming.

Now let us imagine that Jacinta's mother is summoned by someone
else—perhaps Jacinta's father—and sets her by herself in front of the mirror. Although Jacinta may be content for a time, touching the mirror,
noticing how the "other" baby moves as she does, we can imagine that she
would soon lose interest, feel that something was missing. As a baby already
capable of sitting by herself, she will have learned over previous months to
associate satisfaction of her physical wants with the responsive gaze of the

mother or her substitutes. She will try to summon back that gaze by crying. We can then imagine the mother returning, picking her up and producing a happy smile when their gazes meet in the mirror, then playing a game of mirror peek-a-boo, appearing and disappearing from the mirror as the puzzled Jacinta gazes from the mother in the mirror to the mother in the flesh. She thus learns very effectively that she and the mother are separate beings, that there is a space between them, and that she cannot dominate that space, cannot assure that the mother's gaze will meet hers.

With that consciousness of separation, desire enters, the demand for recognition, the question "Who am I for you?" in Ellie Ragland-Sullivan's description. And Jacinta inevitably learns that the mother's desire is at least partly elsewhere, that she comes and goes, that she responds to another's call. Who or what is it that the mother wants? Classically, the father, or some other social form of the third term that breaks the infant-mother dyad. We can picture our infant Jacinta, playing mirror peek-a-boo with the mother, only to have the game interrupted by the father's entry into the room. Jacinta can no longer summon the mother's gaze, either to her or to the mirror, and follows that maternal gaze to see what it is the mother wants. The infant's desire is at this stage the mother's desire—in French, *désir de la mère*, playing on the ambiguity of the preposition to communicate the fact that it is at once the infant's desire *for* the mother and an identification with her desire, with the desire *of* the mother (Fink 1995, 57).

Why should another woman's desire awaken that of Jacinta? The reasons are incomprehensible to Jacinta as a conscious subject, buried in her "pre-history" as a speaking subject. In Kristeva's mother-centered psychoanalytic theory, feminine desire does not consist "simply" of the desire to be desired by the father figure; it results rather from identification with the desire of the mother, a primary identification of the *moi* destined for repetition in displaced form in adult life:

> Let me now point out that the most archaic unity that we thus retrieve—an identity so autonomous that it calls forth displacements—is that of the Phallus desired by the mother. It is unity of the imaginary father, a coagulation of the mother and her desire. The imaginary father would thus be the indication that the mother is not complete but that she wants . . . Who? What? The question has no answer other than the one that uncovers narcissistic emptiness; "At any rate, not I." Freud's famous "What does a woman want" is perhaps only the echo of the more fundamental "What does a

mother want?" It runs up against the same impossibility, bordered on one side by the imaginary father, on the other by a "not I." And it is out of this "not I" (see Beckett's play with that title) that an Ego painfully attempts to come into being. (Kristeva 1987, 41)

If we read in this light the structure of desire that Zayas has constructed between Jacinta and Celio, we can see that her desire for Celio emerges in this triangular situation through identification with the other woman's desire, as a repetition of the primary attempt to fill the *manque-à-être*. It emerges as "a recapitulation of her identification with the mother's *desire*" (Chase 1989, 80). She had learned to identify the father (and substitute masculine subjects) as object of desire by following the direction of her mother's gaze, and her interest in Celio is aroused by seeing him as the object of another woman's desire.

With a poetic intuition of this structure, Zayas shows Jacinta revealing her newly reawakened desire in a sonnet[67] on the dazzling power of a mirror-reflected gaze, a sonnet that ostensibly speaks of its effect on another woman.

[Celio me pidió] que hiciera un soneto a una dama, que mirándose a un espejo, dio en él el sol, y la deslumbró. Y yo aprovechándome de ella, hice este soneto:

> En el claro cristal del desengaño
> Se miraba Jacinta descuidada,
> Contenta de no amar sin ser amada,
> Viendo su bien en el ageno daño.
> Mira de los amantes el engaño,
> la voluntad, por firme, despreciada,
> y de haberla tenido escarmentada,
> huye de amor el proceder extraño.
> Celio, sol de esta edad, casi envidioso
> De ver la libertad con que vivía,
> Exenta de ofrecer a amor despojos,
> Galán, discreto, amante y dadivoso,
> Reflejos que animaron su osadía,
> Dio en el espejo, y deslumbró los ojos.
> Sintió dulces enojos,
> Y apartado el cristal, dijo piadosa:
> Por no haber visto a Celio fui animosa.

Y aunque llegué a abrasarme,
No pienso de sus rayos apartarme.
(*Novelas*, 70–71)

([Celio] asked me to compose a sonnet for a lady who, looking at herself in a mirror, was struck by a ray of sunlight which dazzled her. Taking advantage of her, I composed this sonnet:

In the clear looking glass of disenchantment, Jacinta regarded herself, unconcerned, happy neither to love nor be loved, seeing her good in others' suffering.

She observes the deception of lovers, a heart's desire, for its faithfulness, despised, and chastised for having felt it, she flees love's strange procedures.

Celio, the sun of this age, almost envious at seeing the freedom in which she lived, exempt from offering spoils to love,

Gallant, discreet, generous, loving, cast reflections that animated his [her?] daring in the mirror and dazzled her eyes.

She felt a sweet annoyance and, setting aside the glass, said devotedly:

Not having seen Celio, I was courageous, and although I came to be inflamed, I do not intend to retreat from his rays.)

The desire to be desired is not unique to feminine subjects of course, and Zayas shows Celio as much captured by that need as captor. The ambiguous reference of Spanish pronouns, frequently accentuated by Zayas, serves her well here, as "su" could indicate that his handsome reflection in the mirror encouraged either his own or her daring, thus condensing the intersubjective captivation of the reflexive gaze.

The entire episode with Celio rests on the desire to be desired. Jacinta says that the reason for Celio's pleasure at her sonnet was that "a nadie le pesa de ser querido" (no one is averse to being loved) (*Novelas*, 71), and when Fabio reveals to her that Celio is in any case inaccessible because he has already taken religious orders, he says that given his friend's nature, "sólo este estado le conviene, porque imagino que si tuviera mujer propia, a puros rigores y desdenes la matara, por no poder sufrir estar siempre en una misma parte, ni gozar una misma cosa" (this is the only status that suits him, because I imagine that if he had a wife, he would kill her through sheer harshness and contempt, since he can't stand to stay long in the same place nor always to enjoy the same thing) (*Novelas*, 76).

Whereas the "other woman" through whom Jacinta's desire is awakened is totally anonymous in the Celio episode, strategically placed "other women" for Zayas's heroines have a significant familial connection. In the frame tale, Lisis's competitor is her cousin Lisarda, and an enviously desiring sister unchains disaster in the last story in each volume (see the discussion of *El jardín engañoso* in Chapters 5 and 9 of this study). The very first "other woman" in this opening story is also a cousin, not of Jacinta but of don Félix. From Jacinta's perspective, Adriana possesses an "inside track" advantage in the presence and assistance of her mother, who is a sister of Félix's father. Maternal presence in this significant form in the first plotted episode represents, I believe, a complex displacement of mother-daughter identification and rivalry onto the place of the "other woman." Kristeva, in "Stabat Mater," links the difficulty in recognizing and addressing the "other woman" to the painful establishment of identity for feminine subjects in a problematic mother-daughter relationship of symbiosis, loss, and resentment.[68] Adriana is the unfair competitor who is trying to "have it both ways"—to retain her bond to her mother and have the desired man as well. Zayas has her commit suicide, after a tearful farewell to her mother, with a poison that not only kills her but also destroys her beauty, causing her body to swell and turn black.[69]

It is a straightforward circumstance of triangulated desire, however, that brings Jacinta to the nadir of exile by and from love in which Fabio discovered her. After Jacinta declares her love for Celio and her hope to become his wife, she basks briefly in his attentions, then suffers his neglect, and finally, hearing that he is courting another woman in Salamanca, sets out to pursue him in that city. Misled toward Barcelona, robbed of her money and jewelry and abandoned in the wilds by the "gentleman" chosen to accompany her on the journey, she cuts her hair, dresses as a boy, and takes refuge in Montserrat working as a shepherd for the monks. With the resolve never to return to be wounded by Celio's faithless gaze, she joins a long poetic tradition of the suffering exiles of love.

The working-through of desire is, nevertheless, left in abeyance at the end of this first story. When Fabio has, on the one hand, assuaged Jacinta's wounded ego by telling her that Celio holds her in high esteem and that his mistreatment of her was characteristic of his behavior toward all women and, on the other hand, disabused her of any hope of marriage with Celio, who has accepted holy orders, Jacinta gladly agrees to return to society. Fabio brings her back not to Baeza, but to the very center of society, to the court in Madrid, and to "un Monasterio principal" (one of the best convents) (*Novelas*, 77).[70] Calling herself a "Phoenix of love" who will always persist in her hopeless devotion to the disloyal Celio, she chooses to lead a secular life in the convent, rejecting the two alternatives proposed by Fabio, that she become a nun or marry someone else. With brotherly visits from Celio and the sisterly company of doña Guiomar, who joined her upon the death of her mother, she continues to live there, says the narrator, "tan contenta, que le parece que no tiene más bien que desear, ni más gusto que pedir" (so happy that it seems to her that there is nothing better to desire nor other pleasure to ask) (*Novelas,* 79).

An interesting structural device, however, ties Jacinta's fate and choice to the frame story, thus in effect keeping the working-through of desire an open question until Lisis's final choice at the end of the collection. At the end of the opening frame scene, Lisis, sad because don Juan only has eyes for Lisarda and has worn her colors, sings a lament about a fickle lover, *Celio,* which reminds don Juan of his ingratitude. Lisarda then tells the first story, and don Juan's extravagant praise of her narrative again wounds Lisis. She takes up a guitar and sings verses that as clearly apply to her situation as to that of Jacinta, a sonnet about constant women who love ungrateful men, and for whom the only reward is love itself. The text underlines the self-referentiality of Lisis's sonnet (a previous reader of my library copy of the *Novelas* had written "cf Jacinta" in the margin). She then appears to follow the opposite strategy from that of Jacinta, encouraging don Diego's attentions in order to arouse don Juan's jealousy, and the first volume closes with the promise of her proximate betrothal to don Diego; the second, however, concludes with her announcement that, profiting by the stories told, she has chosen to renounce the treachery of men and to take refuge in a convent where, like Jacinta, she will lead a secular life in the company of women.

Sexual Difference and Object Choice

What, then, is the logic in the sequence of episodes in this story? What sort of "working-through of desire" is Zayas offering us in the progression of Jacinta's experiences? I believe that its narrative sequence charts a progression of human bonding for the woman that proceeds not from mother through father to husband (as Freud and Oedipal fictional plots assume), nor from mother to God, as moralists and mystics proposed, but from mother through men back to women.[71]

Heroines in Zayas tales narrated by women, with only three exceptions, follow either this circular route, from mother to men and back to feminine

Men Women

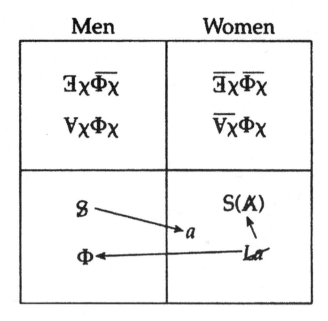

$$\exists x \overline{\Phi x} \qquad \overline{\exists x} \overline{\Phi x}$$

$$\forall x \Phi x \qquad \overline{\forall x} \Phi x$$

$$\$ \qquad S(\cancel{A})$$

$$\Phi \qquad \mathit{La}$$

community, or a tragic straight line from mother to husband or lover to violent death. Only in the stories Zayas tells through a masculine narrator can feminine desire begin in the presence of a living mother and end in successful, socially approved marriage. Her revision of the masculine-inscribed master plot demonstrates a poetic intuition into the nature of sexual difference and object choice.[72] We can find this illustrated visually by reference to the lower half of the diagram of the Lacanian schema of sexuation (see diagram above).[73]

For those subjects on the masculine side of the graph there is only one arrow, pointing toward an *objet a* of desire on the feminine side. A masculine subject, forced by the *Nom/Non du père* to identify with difference, away from the maternal, seeks to recoup that loss by pursuing a substitute object on the feminine side. When Zayas through her masculine narrators imaginarily assumes the perspective of a masculine subject, the presence of the mother of the woman who embodies his *objet a* does not, therefore, represent an obstacle, a competing locus of attachment. Rather, she serves as the model by which girls learn to be "just like their mothers," like the forbidden (m)Other whose lack he seeks to recoup.[74] (Zayas's double-voiced presentation of this masculine perspective will be the topic of Chapter 6.) On the feminine side of the graph, however, there are two arrows. One points toward the symbolic phallus on the masculine side—which in Lacanian theory is not an appendage, nor even the man associated with it, but something more like the attachment to the social, to the Symbolic order that that signifier represents. It is the signifier of desire itself.

As a dutiful daughter subject to Symbolic-order law in a patriarchal system, Jacinta expects her father to "mirar por mí y darme estado" (look after me and give me "status"), in other words, the status of marriage. The first scene of courtship, at a grilled window in her house, is an emblematic illustration of the operation of that arrow. Don Félix offers Jacinta "amor . . . y esta mano" (love and this hand), the hand constituting the promise of marriage. In describing her reactions, Jacinta names the desire for marriage itself before desire for this particular man, and calls that promise a *cebo* (bait) that leads to the perdition of a woman—a perdition, however, that she judges such a blessing that she attaches no conditions to her surrender to that loss. And so she extends her hand through the bars, symbolically joining herself to the phallus across the sexual divide:

> ¿Quién se viera rogado con lo mismo que desea, amigo Fabio, o qué mujer despreció jamás la ocasión de casarse, y más del mismo que ama, que no acepte luego cualquier partido? Pues no hay tal cebo para en que pique la perdición de una mujer que éste, y así no quise poner en condición mi dicha, que por tal la tuve, y tendré siempre que traiga a la memoria este día. Y sacando la mano por la rexa, tomé la que me ofrecía mi dueño. (*Novelas,* 50–51)

> (What woman, being entreated to do the very thing she desires, friend Fabio, ever disdained the chance to get married, and particularly to the one she loves, what woman doesn't accept any match right away? Because there is no better bait with which to lure a woman to her perdition than this one, and thus I did not want to put any conditions on my blessedness, for that is what I considered it, and always will whenever I recall that day. And extending my hand through the grate, I took that which my lord offered me.)

Furthermore, that arrow remains in place for Jacinta, even in her outcast state and masculine disguise; that fantasy of wholeness in the promise of marriage still seems to her a moment of blessedness. As Zayas constitutes her first heroine, desire is heterosexual, and sexual choice lies on the other side of the sexual graph even when the fantasy of enduring wholeness in such relationships has twice failed.

The other arrow stays on the feminine side. That arrow indicates a drive toward a fantasy of *jouissance* beyond the phallus, a recognition of the lack in the phallic signifier, the inadequacy of the *Nom/Non du père* that dictates separation from the primary matter, the (m)Other. It may be read as asexual, as aimed at religious ecstasy, or both, but however interpreted, it means that feminine subjects have a partner on both sides of the sexual graph (Fink 1991). To launch a girl in the circuit of desire from the imaginary perspective of a feminine narrator, then, the attachment on the feminine side must ordinarily be suppressed by the removal of the mother. And at the failure of a heterosexual relationship and the fantasy of wholeness achieved through attachment to the phallus, that other arrow exercises its pull toward the opposing magnetic pole of feminine *jouissance*.

Recognizing the two magnetic poles that attract/attach the feminine subject helps us understand why in Zayas's plot structures we find the alternation between attraction to men and retreat to a safe feminine haven that characterizes the movement of *Aventurarse perdiendo* (Venturing and Losing) and of other Zayas stories. The precondition she creates for the first heterosexual commitment by Jacinta and the great majority of her other heroines is the absence of the mother figure. Each subsequent crisis of love turns Jacinta back to female society, which she often describes in terms of a substitute mother-love. When she flees her house and don Félix has to leave Spain, Félix leaves her in the convent with his aunts, whom Jacinta says "me querían como hija" (loved me like a daughter) (*Novelas*, 58). Although the convent is technically a "house of God," Zayas does not underline religious devotion in the choice of convent life, except in *Desengaño 9*, which is told by a nun.[75] The retreat to a convent is depicted more as an emotional—or physical—safe haven in which a substitute female family is reconstituted.[76] When Jacinta first believes Félix dead, she elects to stay in his aunts' convent, saying that "tomé el hábito de religiosa, y conmigo para consolarme y acompañarme doña Isabel, que me quería tiernamente" (I took a nun's habit, and to console me and keep me company, doña Isabel, who loved me tenderly [took one] with me) (*Novelas*, 60). In registering her choice, she mentions not religious conviction but rather the loving companionship of Félix's sister. After his actual death, she chooses not to return to the convent, but to stay with his widowed relative and her daughter, "doña Guiomar, y su madre, que me tenían en lugar de hija" (doña Guiomar and her mother, who treated me as her daughter) (*Novelas*, 69).

5

Mothers Otherwise

The Mother's Story: *El jardín engañoso* (The Garden of Deceit)

To launch a girl in the circuit of desire from the imaginary perspective of a feminine narrator, who knows the strength of the attachment on the feminine side, its magnetic pull must ordinarily be suppressed by the removal of the mother. As Hirsch points out, however:

> For female writers, motherlessness means freedom not only from constraint but also from the power that a knowing connection to the past might offer, whether that past is powerful or powerless. . . . if daughters knew the mothers' stories, they might not repeat them. But for that suppressed mother-daughter connection to make its way into fiction, either the oedipal originals of plot would have to

be reimagined and transformed, or oedipal paradigms abandoned altogether. Narrative itself would have to be enabled, at least in part, by maternal presence rather than absence. (1989, 67)

We see such enablement occurring in some contemporary fiction by women writers, but Zayas anticipated this intuition centuries ago. The closing story of her first volume is a kind of miracle tale, the one story told by a woman that ends in successful, enduring, socially approved marriage for two sisters, with the classic happy ending "vivieron muchos años con hermosos hijos" (they lived many years and had beautiful children).[1] And it is told by a mother. Laura, the mother of the frame heroine Lisis, tells a story in which another mother, Fabia—a widow, like the narrator—plays a critical role in securing an ideal husband for Fabia's elder daughter.

In this tale, it is the heroine's father who dies early in the story. With the intercession of her mother, the heroine, Constanza, marries an ideal husband, don Carlos. When a passionate former suitor, don Jorge, then reappears and through a Faustian pact creates in January a beautiful Maytime garden that Constanza had laughingly set as the price of her admission of don Jorge's desires, the generosity of her husband Carlos is such that it shames both don Jorge and the devil himself into good actions. The devil relinquishes don Jorge from payment with his soul and he at last agrees to marry the younger sister, Teodosia, whose love he had previously spurned. Zayas inherited from Boccaccio the basic elements of this plot—the suitor, the generous husband, and the May-in-January garden created by a magician.[2] But with her additions, Zayas makes that story an implicit reversal of the biblical story of the fall of humanity into original sin and death.[3]

In her version, the "original sin," as it were, arises in fratricidal conflict over the object of desire, while the father still lives and his law prevails. In prefacing her story, Laura underlines the originary nature of fratricide and sisterly betrayal motivated by jealousy, love, and envy, saying that "desde el principio del mundo ha habido hermanos traidores y envidiosos, como nos dicen dos mil exemplos que hay escritos" (since the beginning of the world there have been treacherous and envious brothers, as two thousand written examples tell us) (Novelas, 400). As Charnon-Deutsch points out, Zayas's stories locate evil not outside but within the family unit, in the sexual difference that threatens women's well-being (1991, 24). That threat does not emerge exclusively from the masculine sex, however; in Zayas's plots, it resides as well in feminine rivalry and betrayal in the pursuit of sexual desire. In the story, Teodosia, although loved by don Jorge's younger brother Federico, is secretly and passionately in love with don Jorge, and suggests to him that Constanza's reserve in returning his demand for love is caused by a secret love for Federico. Don Jorge, whose rivalry with his brother predates this challenge, then kills his younger brother in a Cain-and-Abel-style fit of jealousy over, not the favor of God, but that of Constanza.[4]

Zayas also makes the magician the devil himself, and the price of the garden not just a great sum of money, but one's very soul. The garden thus becomes a false earthly paradise created by carnal desire, one made by the devil rather than by God, and its disappearance is not a punishment for sin but redemption from committing it. And in Zayas, it is a mother who tells the story and another mother who weds her daughter to the man whose generosity defeats the devil of illicit desire.

The price of sexual favors is underlined linguistically in this story, as Gartner observes: "*El jardín engañoso* meticulously describes the amorous maneuverings in the language and terms of trade and barter . . . in a constant traffic for the object of desire" (1989, 94). Reference to favors in terms of exchange value—"precio" (price), various forms of "pagar" (to pay), and "cambio" (exchange) is much more insistent in this story than in others. But an interesting change of linguistic register occurs in midstory. After don Jorge kills his brother and flees the city with his crime undetected, the father dies and Fabia is left in charge of the estate and of her daughters. Their relationship is described as follows:

> En este tiempo murió su padre, dexando a sus hermosas hijas con gran suma de riqueza, y a su madre por su amparo. La cual, ocupada en el gobierno de su hacienda, no trató de darlas estado en más de dos años, ni a ellas se les daba nada, ya por aguardar la venida de su amante, y parte por no perder *los regalos* que de su madre tenían. (*Novelas*, 407)[5]

> (Her father died in this time, leaving his handsome daughters with a great quantity of riches, and with their mother as their protector. She, occupied with managing the estate, did not try to arrange marriages for them in more than two years, nor did it matter to the ladies, whether because they were waiting the arrival of their lover, or in part in order not to lose the *comforts* their mother *gave* them.)

At this point in the story, don Carlos appears, takes up residence across the street from Fabia and her daughters, and the term *regalo* or *regalar* (gift or to give) replaces the use of *precio* and *pagar* (price and to pay) for a time.

Carlos, knowing that his prospects as a poor *hidalgo* (gentleman) are not promising, makes his approach through Fabia. He begins to "*regalarla* con algunas cosas que procuraba para este efecto, haciendo la noble señora en agradecimiento lo mismo" (give her things he secured for that end, the appreciative noble lady doing the same [for him]) (*Novelas*, 407). He also gives "un gran *regalo*" (a big gift) (*Novelas*, 408) to a doctor who agrees to treat him for a false illness.[6] Appearing to be at death's door, he begs Fabia to allow him to leave his entire estate to Constanza for her dowry. After his miraculous "recovery," Fabia marries Constanza and Carlos, and he earns Constanza's love "con tantos *regalos* y caricias" (with so many gifts and caresses) (*Novelas*, 410) that when he reveals to them his trick—that both the illness and his wealth were fictitious—both Constanza and Fabia accept the outcome as "la voluntad del cielo" (heaven's will) (*Novelas*, 410). *Regalar*, according to the *Diccionario de autoridades*, means "agasajar, o contribuir a otro con alguna cosa, voluntariamente o por obligación" (to regale with gifts, entertain splendidly, or contribute something to another, voluntarily or by obligation), or "halagar, acariciar, o hacer expresiones de afecto y benevolencia" (to flatter, treat tenderly, or express affection and goodwill).

Under the mother's tutelage, the linguistic register used to describe human relationships shifts to one of generosity and affection rather than of prices and payment.[7] It is what Cixous describes as an *économie féminine*, a feminine, or gift, economy (1988, 80–81, 86–88). When don Jorge reappears, the word *regalo* (gift) is used one more time, in the description of his intense courtship of Constanza. But when Teodosia falls ill of despair over his rejection of her love and Constanza tries to redirect his desire toward her sister, the vocabulary of exchange replaces it. Telling don Jorge that her honor prevents her from giving him the "reward" that his perseverance merits, she continues: "Me ha parecido *pagaros* con dar en mi lugar *otro yo*, que de mi parte *pague* lo que en mí es sin remedio. En concederme este *bien* me *ganáis*, no sólo por verdadera amiga, sino por perpetua *esclava*" (I had decided to *pay you* by giving you in my stead *another me*, who will *pay* on my behalf what for me is impossible. In granting me this *good* you *win* me, not only as a true friend but as your eternal *slave*) (*Novelas*, 413). This monetary register continues, centering particularly around the description of don Jorge's pact with the devil and Carlos's speech to Constanza about the *price* and *reward* of virtue and love, and coming to a close only when don Jorge and finally the devil address the *cost* of a soul, a *jewel* that cost the death of God on the cross.

The regime of generosity inaugurated by the mother is not a pure, uninterested generosity, however. Zayas's storytelling widow links it with the verb "granjear," (to earn, win, or capture [friendship or sympathy]) to describe Carlos's strategy: "granjeando este bien por medio de su engaño, y Constanza tan contenta, porque su esposo sabía granjear su voluntad con tantos regalos y caricias" (winning this good by means of a trick, and Constanza very happy, because her husband knew how to win her favor with so many presents and caresses) (*Novelas*, 410). Furthermore, she prefaces the account of Carlos's generosity in sparing Constanza's life at the cost of his honor or life with an analysis of the role of wealth and virtue in marital relationships:

> Viendo Carlos un caso tan extraño, considerando que por su esposa se veía en tanto aumento de riqueza, cosa que muchas veces sucede ser freno a las inclinaciones de los hombres la desigualdad, pues el que escoge mujer más rica que él ni compra mujer sino señora, de la misma suerte, como aconseja Aristóteles, no trayendo la mujer más hacienda que su virtud, procura con ella y su humildad granjear la voluntad de su dueño. (*Novelas*, 419)

> (Carlos, seeing such a strange event, [and] considering that thanks to his wife he saw himself so increased in wealth, inequality being something that often succeeds in restraining men's inclinations, since he who chooses a woman richer than he buys not a wife but a lady [owner], by the same token, as Aristotle advises, when the woman brings no other estate than her virtue, she attempts to earn with it and her humility the favor or her lord.)

Carlos's willingness to sacrifice his honor is grounded in a reversal of the usual power relationships between the sexes in marriage, a reversal that stems from his economic dependence on Constanza.[8]

There is no absolutely free gift, says Cixous, but there can be one that does not aim at a phallocentric *plus de jouir,* surplus value, a profitable supplementary return. "All the difference lies in the why and how of the gift, in the values that the gesture of giving affirms, causes to circulate; in the type of profit the giver draws from the gift and the use to which he or she puts it." The masculine economy is organized around gaining "more masculinity: plus-value of virility, authority, power, money, or pleasure. . . . A man . . . has to . . . show up the others. Masculine profit is almost always mixed up with a success that is socially defined." A woman too "gives *for.*

She too . . . gives herself—pleasure, happiness, increased value, enhanced self-image. But she doesn't try to 'recover her expenses.' She is able not to return to herself, never settling down, pouring out, going everywhere to the other" (Cixous and Clément 1988, 87). Zayas's tale, like Cixous's comments, suggests the possibility of another kind of commerce governed by women, with "a more supple relationship to (emotional and material) property that can stand separation and detachment, and can bear the freedom of the other" (Wright 1992, 91–92).

And what of the language of love in the presence of the mother? Another linguistic peculiarity of this ending novella is the absence of inserted songs and poetic formulations of amorous discourse. Gartner, who reads this story through a Girardean perspective focused on the triangulation of desire (1989, 76), sees their absence as indicative of don Jorge's inability to confront and express his desire. But relating this story to *Desengaño* 7 in which both the discourse of courtly love and the displays of patriarchal power are carried to extremes (see Chapters 7 and 9 below), we can read the relative merits of absent and present discourse of love quite differently. In fact, the narrator says that don Jorge regularly gives voice to his amorous intent, particularly after he returns, when his open courtship of Constanza causes murmurs through the city. But the narrating mother gives primacy of expression to Constanza's prudent regulation of his courtship, both initially, when both her parents were living and she awaits parental selection of a husband, and after his return, when she jokingly sets a supposedly impossible price on her favors. The despairing don Jorge accepts the devil's offer as a result of the *resistance* to seduction by the traditional masculine codes of courtship on the part of this daughter who lives her story in the presence rather than the absence of her mother. The exploding disappearance of the demonic garden of desire leaves behind a dense, stinking smoke and don Jorge on his knees in tears and thankful prayer to God, in which he is joined by all the assembled feminine company.

To provide, from the perspective of a feminine narrator, a "happy ending" for her first volume of love stories, Zayas doubles maternal presence in her fictional reversal of the expulsion from paradise. Yet at both the beginning and the end of this fantasy of the reordering of sexual relationships and of the language of love in a matriarchal regime, Zayas's narrating mother undercuts the authority of this mythical "(m)Other plot." Rather than opening her tale with the standard assertion of its veracity, Laura admits to her "discreto auditorio" (prudent listeners) that she is not "selling them as proven truth" all the events she will recount. She credits as verisimilar all the events except the possibility of the devil doing a good work, which she can only attribute to "otras secretas causas, que nosotros ignoramos" (other secret causes, of which we are ignorant) (*Novelas*, 400).[9] So saying, she leaves it to her audience to believe what they will of her story: "En esto no os obligo a creer más de lo que diere gusto; pues el decirla yo no es más de para dar exemplo y prevenir que se guarden de las ocasiones" (In this I do not oblige you to believe more than what you please, since telling it is only to provide an example and warn you to guard against dangers) (*Novelas*, 400). Deceits and lies prevail to the very end of the story, as neither don Jorge's killing of his brother nor Teodosia's original lie is revealed until after the death of each. And at the conclusion of the tale, as Zayas moves the reader back "out" through the various levels of narration, from Teodosia's account, through Laura's, to the frame-tale setting and to her own concluding authorial voice, all maternal authority for the "maravilla" (marvel) worked is effaced. As in Boccaccio's versions of the tale, Teodosia invites her readers, and Lisis invites her companions, to debate whether the greatest credit should go to Carlos, don Jorge, or the devil.

Why would Zayas thus subvert her own subversion of the patriarchal narrative?[10] Perhaps because of "desiring readers," her desire as author to please her readers, to provide an ending that would lure both male and female readers on to the second volume she promised in her concluding paragraph.[11] Perhaps her own implicit understanding of the nature of desire across the sexual divide—of feminine attraction to the phallus as signifier of authority, and masculine attraction to a feminine *objet a* of desire— made a fundamental reordering of authority between the two genders unimaginable for her within the confines of patriarchal society. Perhaps because her complicity in the ideological structure of that society made it possible for her to criticize its effects on women but not to re-imagine it beyond the realm of theory and fantasy.[12] Hirsch suggests that suppression of the mother-daughter connection condemns women to repeating the mother's (Oedipal) story. Perhaps Zayas knew that the converse is true as well; that a mother such as Laura, who wishes her daughter to marry, must tell her story as a half-truth, a story that acknowledges by indirection the lies and (self)delusions on which sexual relations are founded. The knowing mother mediates her daughter's accession to heterosexual marriage by herself accepting the false promise of patrimony and wedding her daughter to that false promise, then passing over her own role in silence as she teaches her daughters to entertain the fantasy of a happily-ever-after ending, but with an ironic caution toward the untruth at its core.

In the real world of Golden Age Spain, one mother was severely punished for opposing a father's authority, even after his death, to dispose of
his daughter in a marriage of his choosing. Mary Elizabeth Perry describes
a case in 1620 in which a widow helped her daughter, Catalina de Mesa,
marry a man of her own choosing rather than the man specified in her
father's will. The marriage was sustained, but the widow was sentenced to
life in prison by the Inquisition (Perry 1990, 67–68).

In Zayas's second volume, the *Desengaños amorosos,* the real world of the
disastrous decade of the 1640s in Spain is very much present in the settings
of her *Disenchantments.* And in the violent world of these stories, maternal
presence works no such "marvels" even as temporary fantasies. The heroine of the first story, Zelima/Isabel Fajardo, is separated from her mother
not by the natural cause of her mother's death, but by rape, by a doubled
rebellion within the house of patriarchy (see Chapter 9 below). Zayas in
this volume carries to such extremes her depiction of the violence of the
patriarchal order against women that it seems to threaten the very survival
of that order, if not of the human species itself.[13]

Readers of Zayas's stories often note the overall absence therein of any
significant representation of maternal nurturing. The primary importance
of mother-daughter relationships in her stories indeed centers on the presence or absence of mothers to daughters of marriageable age rather than
on the mother-child relationship. The majority of Zayas's heroines never
have children and only occasionally does the narrator comment on that absence as a perceived lack. Their lack is registered, however, at the end of
the second novella, *La burlada Aminta* (Aminta Deceived) where Zayas
writes that "sólo le falta a esta buena señora tener hijos, para ser del todo
dichosa" (this good lady only lacks having children to be completely
blessed) (*Novelas,* 119). Aminta has gone outside the law, cross-dressing
and giving up her claim to her paternal inheritance—both her family
name and the inherited wealth due her. Her childlessness is surely linked
to that voluntary exile from the patriarchal order whose continuation depended on obedient feminine reproduction.[14] The last five works in the
Novelas amorosas do end with the acknowledgment that the marriage produces children. All but one of the heroines who have children in these stories also have living mothers, and the exception, doña Clara, is partially
protected from her husband's neglect by surrogate mother figures—her
mother-in-law while she lives,[15] and later by doña Juana, a former lover of
her husband who has become a nun and who takes Clara's two daughters
as her own and gives Clara money to follow the husband who has aban-

doned her. The one story that depicts a young mother fully committed to nurturing her child is *Desengaño 8,* in which a nursing mother is decapitated, leaving her one-year-old son to awaken crying with hunger.[16] Significantly, the maternal grandmother is present to respond to the cries of that child—the only surviving direct descendant of any protagonist of the *Desengaños.* Hence we can conclude that Zayas in her plots recognizes that the continuation of the species depends on the maintenance of the connection with the maternal that is disparaged if not literally decapitated in the patriarchal order.

At the same time, however, Zayas seems to connect active mothering with a kind of servile degradation, not fully appropriate to the dignity of a noble lady.[17] The two heroines (doña Clara, and doña Ana of *Desengaño 8*) who have children early in their respective episodes are both then reduced to poverty, to doing their own housework, even to selling handwork. Doña Clara, the daughter of a merchant, was married to don Fernando on the promise of a rich dowry;[18] and doña Ana, who is noble but poor, is judged by her husband's father to be socially as well as economically unsuitable and he disinherits his son on learning of their marriage. We never see in Zayas's stories a grotesque mother such as Cañizares in Cervantes' *Coloquio de los perros* (Dialogue of the Dogs), but the distancing from material mothering in her stories may also have its roots in maternal abjection. Except in her prefatory reminder to male readers of their debt to their mothers, she rarely stresses the social importance of women's reproductive capacity. Yet in *Desengaño 8,* there is a fascinating, if unspoken, symbolic polarity between blood and milk, in which the first represents both death and a hyperbolic concern for the preservation of the paternal legacy, and the second the importance of the maternal nurture that patriarchy both requires and menaces, the feminine power that haunts the patriarchal Imaginary (see Chapters 8 and 9 below).

Saved by the Mother of God: *La perseguida triunfante*

The contrast between threatening masculine violence and comforting, protective mothers is raised to a cosmic level in the next-to-last story in the collection. *Desengaño 9, La perseguida triunfante* (Triumph over Persecution) tells the story of a beautiful queen, Beatriz, happily married to King Ladislao but pursued also by the latter's younger brother, Federico.[19] In the king's absence, the prince's amorous advances become so insistent that

Beatriz has him shut up in a golden cage. When the king returns, he believes Federico's accusations that it was Beatriz who tried to seduce him, and orders her blinded and abandoned to savage beasts and starvation in the wilds.[20] There follow a series of trials instigated by Federico with the assistance of a demonic doctor of magic. Beatriz is always miraculously rescued by a mysterious and beautiful lady who eventually reveals herself to be "la Madre de Dios" (the Mother of God). She then gives Beatriz, who has been living for eight years as a hermit, both masculine garb and the magic herb with which she will work her redemption.[21] The story is narrated by a nun, Estefanía, who says that she read the story in manuscript in Italy, where Beatriz is considered a saint.[22] In fact, *Desengaño 9* is a reworking of a popular story known as "The Chaste Wife Accused by Her Brother-in-Law" or the "Crescentia legend" that circulated widely throughout Europe from as early as the twelfth century. Zayas herself may well have read the story of Beatriz in Italy while there as a girl with her parents, as her narrator claims. She almost certainly knew it also from a variety of sources in Spain, including the *Cantigas de Santa María* of Alfonso el Sabio, the medieval romance "Fermoso cuento de una santa emperatrís que ovo en Roma & de su castidat" (Beautiful Story of a Holy Empress of Rome and of Her Chastity)[23] and "Patraña 21" of Timoneda's *El patrañuelo* (Tall Tales). The episodic structure of *Desengaño 9* clearly shows the influence of hagiographic literature as well, as Grieve (1991) points out.[24]

Zayas could draw from these sources the building blocks of her cosmic confrontation, but the skillful construction of the narrative toward its dramatic climax is her unique contribution. Early in its European circulation, the story of Beatriz became linked with the medieval tradition of narratives of miracles performed by the Virgin. The fifth *cantiga* of Alfonso el Sabio is titled "Esta é como Santa Maria ajudou a emperadriz de Roma a sofre-las grandes coitas per que passou" (This Is How Holy Mary Helped the Empress of Rome Suffer the Great Tribulations Through Which She Passed.) In the Alfonsine version, the empress is named Beatriz, and when the Virgin supplies her with the magic herb she will use to cure her brother-in-law both physically and spiritually, her benefactor is identified as "la Madre de Dios" (the Mother of God).[25] Although Timoneda's version (the penultimate story in his collection, as Zayas's is in hers) is the closest to Zayas in time and in the novella tradition, it includes no divine intervention and the tale is naturalized; Geroncia, as the queen is named, has been abandoned on a deserted island, where she sees a snake use the herb to cure its wounds. Beatriz has no name, being identified only by her position as

"saintly empress" in the medieval romance, a thoroughly misogynist narrative that stresses the uniqueness of her chastity in contrast to the sinful
practices of most women. That narrative foregrounds from the outset the
role of the devil, albeit not in personalized form but in his power over the
hearts and sexual natures of men and women.[26] Zayas, however, personifies
the devil in the form of the mysterious doctor. He appears to Federico in
the same place in which her beautiful benefactor first rescues Beatriz, but
in a contrasting guise: "[Federico] vio bajar por una senda . . . un hombre
vestido a modo de escolástico, de horrible rostro, y que parecía de hasta
cuarenta años. Traía un libro en la mano, dando con él muestra de que
profesaba ciencia" (Federico saw descending a path . . . a man dressed in
the style of a scholastic, with a horrible face, perhaps forty years of age. He
carried a book in his hand, demonstrating with it that he professed learning) (*Desengaños*, 437). As a "doctor" his malefic and imperfect knowledge
and medical powers are juxtaposed with the curative power the Mother of
God gives to Beatriz. At the same time, Zayas demonstrates her narrative
skill in delaying to the climactic confrontation the revelation of his identity, thus leaving her readers the pleasure of anticipating the identification
of both the demon-male and the divine mother.

Foa, Welles (1978, 306–7), Grieve, and other commentators on this
story usually refer to Beatriz's divine protector as the Virgin Mary, which,
while technically correct, overlooks the significance of Zayas's insistence
on calling her the Mother of God. Once she has revealed her identity to
Beatriz, the narrator refers to "la Madre de Dios" seven times within the
space of five paragraphs, varying this appellation only to call her once
"Reina de los Angeles" (Queen of the Angels), and once "Señora nuestra"
(our Lady) (*Desengaños*, 457–59); she interrupts her narration with a long,
direct address to her female readers about the dangers of the world of
men, in which even such a good queen can only be saved by the divine
mother:

> Pues mirad cómo esta reina que, pues merecía tener el favor de la
> Madre de Dios, buena era; pues si siendo buena tuvo necesidad de
> que la Madre de Dios la defendiese de un hombre, vosotras, en
> guerra de tantos y sin su favor, ¿cómo os pensáis defender? (*Desen-
> gaños*, 459)

> (For see how good this queen was, who merited the favor of the
> Mother of God; then if being so good she needed the Mother of

God to defend her against a man, you, at war with so many men and without Her favor, how do you expect to defend yourselves?)

The confrontation between the demonic in masculine garb and the divine maternal protector climaxes in a face-to-face victory of the latter before the assembled court:

> Viendo todos . . . cómo la Madre de Dios, Reina de los Angeles y Señora nuestra, tenía puesta su divina mano sobre el hombro dere-cho de la hermosa reina Beatriz, a cuya celestial y divina vista, el doctor que, sentado en una silla, estaba cerca de la cama de Fed-erico, dando un gran estallido, como si un tiro de artillería se dis-parara, daba grandes voces, diciendo:
> —¡Venciste, María, venciste! ¡Ya conozco la sombra que amparaba a Beatriz, que hasta ahora estuve ciego!
> Desapareció, dejando la silla llena de espeso humo, siendo la sala un asombro, un caos de confusión, porque a la parte que estaba Beatriz con su divina defensora era un resplandeciente paraíso, y a la que el falso doctor y verdadero demonio, una tiniebla y oscuridad. (*Desengaños*, 465)

> (Everyone seeing . . . how the Mother of God, Queen of the Angels and our Lady had placed her divine hand on the right shoulder of the lovely queen Beatriz, at which celestial and divine vision, the doctor who was seated in a chair, close to Federico's bed, giving out a great explosion as if a gunshot had been fired, shouted loudly, say-ing: "You won, María, you won! Now I recognize the shadow that sheltered Beatriz, if until now I was blind!"
> He disappeared, leaving the chair full of dense smoke, the hall having been a marvelous sight, a confused chaos, because on the side where Beaters was with her divine defender it was a resplendent paradise and on that of the false doctor and true devil, darkness and obscurity.)

In a resolution common in the lives of married saints, not only Beatriz but also her loving husband then renounce the world and the flesh and retire to monasteries. Beatriz does not go alone, however; the narrating nun doña Estefania tells us that she took with her "todas sus damas que quisieron ser sus compañeras" (all her ladies-in-waiting who wanted to be her companions) (*Desengaños*, 466), all of whom became nuns with her.[27]

A (m)Other Plot?

This pattern is repeated over and over in Zayas's stories; at the failure of a heterosexual relationship, the heroine retreats either temporarily or permanently to a convent, where she is often joined by female relatives or friends. It is on an amplified version of this withdrawal from male society that the entire collection closes, as the framing heroine Lisis chooses that haven over the love of don Diego:

> Lisis y doña Isabel, con doña Estefanía, se fueron a su convento con mucho gusto. Doña Isabel tomó el hábito, y Lisis se quedó seglar. Y en poniendo Laura la hacienda en orden, que les rentase lo que habían menester, se fue con ellas, por no apartarse de su amada Lisis, avisando a su madre de doña Isabel, que como supo dónde estaba su hija, se vino también con ella, tomando el hábito de religiosa. (*Desengaños*, 510)

> (Lisis and doña Isabel went with doña Estefanía to her convent with great pleasure. Doña Isabel took the habit and Lisis remained a laywoman. And Laura, having put her estate in order so that it might yield the income they needed, went with them, in order not to separate herself from her beloved Lisis, notifying doña Isabel's mother too, who as soon as she found out where her daughter was, also joined her, taking the nun's habit.)

The overall movement of Zayas collection, then, proceeds from the house of the father to the house of God, which, in terms of psychic attachment, is a conditional return to the house of the mother.[28]

The constitution of a (m)Other plot in Zayas collection is not a radical overturning of the Oedipal paradigm, either in this penultimate story or in the collection as a whole, but a working *through* it in two senses of the word. Given the mutually reinforcing effect of social practice and culturally embedded narrative structure, her own complicity with the ideology of Counter-Reformation Spain, and her implication in the signifying structures of desire, María de Zayas could not abolish the Oedipal model. Rather, she depicts the working-through of desire as a struggle that must be waged over and over, for every human subject, as the motor of every narrative. The majority of the plotted episodes follow that Oedipal paradigm, but their framing within individual stories and in the *Sarao* as a whole repeatedly challenges the validity of the "master plot," suggesting that it is only part of the story.

What part does this hagiographic novella play in that challenge? Foa attributes to Zayas the addition of a feminist message to the hagiographic model in the frequent interpolations of the narrator, Estefanía, denouncing the cruelty and injustice of men. Such a feminist message was, in fact, a standard element of female saints' lives; their biographies regularly focused on male abuses of women and the struggle for freedom from male authority figures (Heffernan 1988, 189, 266–69, 292–95).[29] Grieve goes much further than Foa, suggesting that Zayas availed herself of the hagiographic model not only in this but also in other tales; that by borrowing from hagiography stock motifs and the overt depiction of violence against the flesh and transferring them into the context of marriage in a series of texts centered on "martyrdom within marriage" (1991, 88), she created a "feminized novella," a new shape or new garment woven of "time-honored, Church-sanctioned cloth" (104). Grieve is certainly right in calling these revisionist texts, and in explaining the major role in their subversiveness played by the explicit and insistent display of violence against female flesh that is sublimated in Cervantine novellas and in Zurbarán's visual portrayals of female martyrs (103). (The psychical complexities of that display will be explored in Chapter 8.) But if desire is, as Brooks says, both the matter and the motor of narrative, to what extent could Zayas cut the matter differently? What, precisely, could that "new shape" be?

Zayas uses the motor of Oedipal desire to drive narrative, but extends its route beyond the traditional happy ending of a love story. In her collection the dream of love and the fulfillment of sexual satisfaction is a fantasy that must be lived through in some form, but marriage is more often a way station then a final destination in the narratives of women's lives. Love fades, or is serialized, or brings death in its wake. In the words of Charnon-Deutsch, "Men in general are a metaphor for the disillusionment adult women face after the age of puberty" (1991, 24) and the crux of the story is how—and whether—women survive it. We might relate her reshaping of the novella form to Susan Winnette's analysis of traditional narratology that builds the pleasure of the text on an Oedipal model of masculine sexual pleasure—one structured linearly from arousal and tumescence to orgasm, a linear structure of building from beginning, through a swelling middle to a climax that gives retrospective significance. Winnett argues that a woman's sexual pleasure is different; it invokes the tumescence and detumescence of breast-feeding and pregnancy as "radically *pro*spective, full of the incipience that the male model will see resolved in its images of detumescence and discharge. Their ends (in both senses of the word) are, quite literally, beginning itself" (Winnett 1990, 509). In Shelley's *Franken-stein,* for example, emphasis falls on what follows birth, when a male "mother" refuses responsibility for his creation. This, says Winnett "poses questions not accommodated in a *Master*plot and gestures toward an economy in which another consideration of the relations among beginnings, middles, and ends would yield radically different results" (510–11). Winnett concludes:

> The meanings generated through the dynamic relations of beginnings, middles, and ends in traditional narrative and traditional narratology never seems to accrue directly to the account of the woman. At best, they point toward a rereading that evaluates the ideology of narrative dynamics according to whose desires they serve, rendering us suspicious of our complicity in what has presented itself to us as the pleasure of the text. We have been taught to read in drag and must begin to question seriously the determinants that govern the mechanics of our narratives, the notion of history as a sense-making operation, and the enormous investment the patriarchy has in maintaining them. (516)

In my experience of reading Zayas with students, the response to her first novella, *Aventurarse perdiendo* (Venturing and Losing) is often discomfort at the serial nature of Jacinta's loves. Women readers have indeed been taught by the traditional narrative "to read in drag," and as Jacinta falls in love with Celio, they question the sincerity of her love for Félix. Male readers, from the Victorian era to the present day, can be equally discomfited by don Fadrique's fate at the hands of serial mistresses in *El prevenido engañado* (Forewarned but Not Forearmed) (see Chapters 1 and 3 above). But as students continue to read her tales, they cease to voice such unease. We might conclude, therefore, that Zayas succeeds in educating her readers toward another economy of beginnings, middles, and ends. But given the philosophy of *desengaño* to which she subscribed and the distance from material mothering we have noted, we cannot ascribe that reordering to the same relationship to the female flesh and feminine sexual pleasure that Winnett describes.

Cutting the matter of sexual desire differently involved, in various ways, cutting (back) through to the *mater.* Unquestionably, the cult of the Vir-

gin—the "Mother of God," the "Queen of Heaven," who defeated the devil
to save Beatriz—played a fundamental role in both the feminine and masculine imaginary in Zayas's era; her membership in a religious brotherhood dedicated to the defense of the doctrine of the Immaculate Conception is representative of the importance of Spanish devotion to that
concept. The growth of the cult of the Virgin from the twelfth century forward allowed the humanization of Christianity through the reintroduction
of the feminine excluded from the Holy Trinity and silenced in the early
centuries of the established church by a combination of political interests
and the asceticism of church fathers, particularly Saints Augustine and
Jerome (Pagels 1988; Sullivan 1989). This occurred through the reabsorption of the feminine in the maternal, but a virginal maternal cleansed of
the stain of sin and freed from death (Kristeva 1987, 238–40).[30] "Alone of
all her sex" she attracted women's identification, as Kristeva says,

> by suggesting the image of A Unique Woman: alone among women,
> alone among mothers, alone among humans since she is without
> sin. But the acknowledgement of a longing for uniqueness is imme-
> diately checked by the postulate according to which uniqueness is
> attained only through an exacerbated masochism: a concrete
> woman, worthy of the feminine ideal embodied by the Virgin as an
> inaccessible goal, could only be a nun, a martyr, or, if she is married,
> one who leads a life that would remove her from that "earthly" con-
> dition and dedicate her to the highest sublimation alien to her
> body. (258)

Acceptance of this model involves a symbolic elimination of the feminine
of the flesh, the material maternal, akin to the physical elimination of the
material mother Ana in *Desengaño 8*.

Beatriz, with the assistance of the Mother of God, symbolically leaves behind her fleshly feminine identity as she passes through the stages of her
martyrdom, changing names and clothing.[31] She begins as the beautiful
queen and beloved wife Beatriz, a name she shares with Dante's beloved
guide, from the Latin word *beatrix*, "blessed," or in the genitive, "one who
brings joy." Cast out from this happy condition, blinded, and abandoned to
the beasts of the forests, she has her sight restored by the Virgin and is
found by a Duke Octavio who takes her to live in his palace. She adopts the
name Rosismunda, which suggests "rose of this world," and sheds her
queenly attire: "quitándose los ricos vestidos que llevaba, los guardó, vis-
tiéndose de otros que le dio la duquesa, más honestos" (removing the rich

garments that she wore, she put them away, dressing herself with other, more modest clothes that the duchess gave her). (*Desengaños,* 434). When Federico and his "doctor" cause her to be accused of treachery to the duke and to be returned to the fountain where they found her, she finds the queenly attire she had left in the duke's palace magically restored to her, as it is at each stage of her martyrdom, signifying in Zayas's code of sartorial symbolism that with the divine protection of the Virgin Mother, she retains her queenly identity throughout her trials.

In the palace of the emperor and empress of Germany, where she becomes a surrogate mother to the prince, she takes the name Florinda. Broken down as "Flor" + "inda," its ending, like "linda," suggests again "lovely flower" but also links her to the Roman goddess Flora, goddess of flowers, and by extension, of all vegetation, and of fertility.[32] She is not a mother of the flesh, however, but of the spirit. At first sight of her, the prince threw his arms about her and refused to be separated from her, and she in turn "amaba al príncipe más que si fuera su hijo" (loved the prince more than if he had been her son) (*Desengaños,* 449). When Federico kills the prince and leaves the dagger in the hand of the sleeping "Florinda," the Mother of God restores the prince to life and rescues her from her executioners, taking her to live in a hermit's cave, where she changes her regal attire for a rough woolen habit and a headdress of coarse linen. After eight years, the Virgin appears again, identifying herself as the Mother of God, recalls Beatriz from the ecstasy her revelation produced, and instructs her to don the masculine attire she brings and return to Hungary with her salvific herbs. The "Most Holy Virgin" sets Beatriz on that path, telling her: "Anda, hija, con la bendición de Dios y mía, y sanarás a todos los que hicieron lo que te he dicho, en el nombre de Jesús, mi amado Hijo" (Go forth, daughter, with God's blessing and mine, and you will cure all those who do as I have told you, in the name of Jesus, my beloved Son)—a blessing that in implication incorporates the Mother of God in the place of the Holy Spirit in the Trinity.[33] Beatriz arrives at court, summoned for her fame as "el médico milagroso" (the miraculous doctor) having left behind her feminine identity and attire, exchanged for a divine power to give life or death, physical and spiritual.

In the medieval romance, the empress is not freed from her perilously luring feminine identity by cross-dressing but rather undergoes a literal transformation of the flesh:

> Tanto trabajó su cuerpo en velar & en orar & en ayunar & en orar, que la su faz clara & vermeja tornó negra & fea. Non quería loor nin

losenja de cosa que feziese; & asy fue demudada su faz & el fermoso
paresçer del su rostro que non semejava en cosa la enperatrís que
tanto solía ser fermosa, que de su beldat corría nonbrada por todo
el mundo. Mas la graçia del Santo Spíritu le escalentó asy la voluntad que non dava cosa por la beldat del cuerpo por su alma salvar.
Ningunt viçio non quería para su carne, ca bien sabía que quanto el
cuerpo más martiriase tanto esclareçería más la alma. (Benaim de
Lasry 1982, 179)

(She worked her body so hard in watching and praying and fasting
and praying, that her clear and ruddy face turned black and ugly.
She wanted neither praise nor compliments for anything she did
and thus her face was changed and the beautiful appearance of her
countenance so that it did not resemble in any way the empress who
used to be so handsome that her beauty was renowned throughout
the world. But the grace of the Holy Spirit so inflamed her will that
she cared nothing for the beauty of her body in order to save her
soul. She desired no vice of the flesh, for she knew well that
the more her body was martyred, the more her soul would be
enlightened.)

Although the emperor begs her to resume married life after she reveals
her identity, she refuses, even when the pope adds his plea to that of the
emperor. Not only does she retire to a convent, but she persists in the mortification of her flesh by cutting off her beautiful hair and choosing to live
as an "emparedada," walled up in a small space, the fate involuntarily inflicted on the heroine of *Desengaño 5,*

> ca bien sabía la santa dueña que quien bien quier pensar de su
> alma, que le conviene enmagreçer el cuerpo & afanar & trabajar, ca
> sienpre la carne es contra el alma. . . . Por ende non deve dar la
> dueña a su cuerpo ningunt buen comer, mas apretarlo assy por abs-
> tenançia que le non rodeen nin la tiente contra la alma nin cosa,
> nin lo enbolver en paños de seda, nin en cosa de que a la alma mal
> pueda venir. (Benaim de Lasry 1982, 225)

> (for the saintly lady knew well that for whoever wants to think well
> of her soul, it is best to thin down her flesh, because the flesh is al-
> ways against the soul. . . . Therefore, the lady should not give her
> body anything good to eat, but to discipline it severely though absti-

nence, so that nothing surrounds nor tempts the soul, and not wrap it in cloth of silk, nor in anything by which evil can come to the soul).

In contrast, Zayas's ending of this story in effect symbolically redeems Beatriz's feminine identity in the flesh. When the Mother of God appears to her in her cave, she tells Beatriz that her Son wants her to restore her honor in this world:

> Quiere mi Hijo que sus esposas tengan buena fama, y por eso muchas a quien el mundo se le ha quitado, aun después de la última jornada de él, permite que con averiguaciones bastantes, como las que se hacen en su canonización, se la vuelva el mismo que se la ha quitado. Mas de ti quiere que tú la restaures y quites a tu mismo enemigo el peligro que tiene de condenarse, y a tu esposo y padres, junto con los dos reinos de Inglaterra y Hungría, en la mala opinión que te tienen. (*Desengaños,* 460)

> (My son wants his brides to have good reputation and therefore for many from whom the world has taken it away, even after the last act of life, he allows that what has been taken from them be restored with sufficient proofs such as those that are carried out in canonization. But in your case he wants you to restore it and to remove from your own enemy the danger he faces of being condemned, and from your husband and parents, together with the two kingdoms of England and Hungary, the bad estimation they have of you.)

Other Zayas victim-heroines, "martyrs of marriage" (Grieve 1991), have their redemption written in their flesh after death (see Chapter 8 below), but in this penultimate tale, the Mother of God gives Beatriz the means to redeem herself in life—masculine garb and the magic herb. When Federico confesses and is cured and Beatriz reveals her identity, her vindication is instantly inscribed on her body:

> Apenas la reina dijo esto, cuando se vio, y la vieron todos, con los reales vestidos que sacó de palacio cuando la llevaron a sacar los ojos y se habían quedado en la cueva, sin faltar ni una joya de las que le quitaron los monteros; tan entera en su hermosura como

antes, sin que el sol, ni el aire, aunque estuvo ocho años en la cueva, la hubiese ajado un minuto de su belleza. (*Desengaños*, 465)

(No sooner had the queen said this than she saw herself, and everyone saw her, with her royal garments that she wore when they took her out of the palace to take out her eyes, and that she had left behind in the cave, not lacking even one of the jewels that the huntsmen had taken away from her; her beauty as complete as before, without either sun or air having withered her beauty one minute, despite her having been in the cave for eight years.)

The miraculous preservation of her purity and perfection is thus testified to in the beauty of her body, and the reappearance of the regal garments and jewelry marks her right to the rank of queen. Now the Mother of God appears for all to see, and places her hand on Beatriz's shoulder. Restored to full enjoyment of her social identity as a woman of the highest rank, Beatriz nevertheless chooses to remove herself from the circuit of earthly desire and, not wanting to spend even one night in the palace, she retires to a convent with her ladies-in-waiting.

And then what? Is there a story beyond desire? Opening the third night of the *Desengaños*, even the prospective nuns Lisis and Isabel present themselves as participants in the sexual masquerade, whose value is written in terms of their beauty and desirability, heightened rather than effaced by inaccessibility. Concluding a lengthy and detailed description of their gleaming, bejeweled white attire, Zayas writes that "en la belleza imitaban a Venus, y en lo blanco la castidad de Diana" (in their beauty they imitated Venus, and in their whiteness the chastity of Diana) (*Desengaños*, 405). The nun Estefanía describes how nuns reverse the terms between the sexes, occupying the role of *engañadores* (deceivers) of the men who court them:

La hacienda que primero aprendemos [es] el engañar, como se ve en tantos ignorantes, como asidos a las rejas de los conventos, sin poderse apartar de ellas, bebiendo, como Ulises, los engaños de Circe, viven y mueren en este encantamiento, sin considerar que los engañamos con las dulces palabras y que no han de llegar a conseguir las obras. (*Desengaños*, 408–9)

(The first occupation we learn is deceiving, as you see by all those ignorant men who, as if rooted at the grates of the convents unable to pull themselves away from them, drinking in Circe's tricks, like

Ulysses, live and die in this enchantment, without considering that
we deceive them with sweet words and that they will not get as far as
securing deeds.)

These women seek no sexual relation, yet Zayas shows their power enhanced by their knowing use of the sexual masquerade (see Chapter 7
below). Even in this hagiographic story, she leaves in place the structures
(narrative and sexual) of desire, and returns to them with a bang for her
final tale (see Chapter 9 below).

When Zayas heroines retreat behind convent walls, withdrawing to the
feminine side of the sexual divide, they are—almost—silenced.[34] In most
cases, their stories end with a one-sentence epilogue on their saintly life
and death. Inasmuch as we hear more of them, it is as they maintain some
limited contact across the sexual divide, either to converse with men, as in
the case of Jacinta, or to assist other victims of male abuse, as does Juana in
El desengaño andando (Disillusionment in Love) when she makes herself
surrogate mother to Clara's daughters while Clara pursues her errant
husband.

And what of mystic love, mystic desire for union with God? In "God and
the Jouissance of Woman" Lacan posits a specifically feminine *jouissance,
jouissance* of the body, beyond the phallus, that he connects with mystic
jouissance. It is a *jouissance* that a woman knows inasmuch as she ex-sists, not
all castrated within the phallic function, but that she cannot articulate, because it is outside the domain of phallic signification (1975, 68–71; 1982,
144–47). This is not *literally* true; Saint Teresa, Sor María de Agreda, and
other female (and male) mystics do articulate their experience, but they
appropriate metaphorically the language of human desire to do so.[35] Several of Zayas's nuns or prospective nuns speak of "el mejor esposo, Dios"
(the best husband, God) but she builds no story on such mystic *jouissance*
of God.

Zayas's narrating nun Estefanía does give us at least a glimpse of feminine rapture in the presence of the Mother of God. When Beatriz recognizes her in the full panoply of her attributes as the Virgin of the Immaculate Conception—"en el diáfano manto azul, en los coturnos de la plateada
luna, en la corona de estrellas, en el clarísimo resplandor de su divino y
sagrado rostro, en los angélicos espíritus que la cercaban" (in her di-
aphanous blue cloak, in the curve of the silver moon, in the crown of stars,
in the bright splendor of her divine and sacred face, in the angelic spirits
that surrounded her), she is transported by the vision. "Puestos los ojos en

ella, así como estaba de hinojos, se quedó inmóvil y elevada, gran rato absorta en tan gloriosa vista" (Her eyes fixed on her, on her knees as she was,
she remained motionless and elevated, long absorbed in that glorious vision.) The narrator, however, turns her gaze away from that experience:
"Goce Beatriz este favor tan deseado, mientras que yo pondero este misterioso suceso" (Let Beatriz enjoy this long-desired favor, while I ponder this
mysterious occurrence) (*Desengaños,* 458). Rather than "pondering" the
occurrence, she turns to a lengthy tirade on the helplessness of less-favored
women in the world of men, returning two pages later to say, "Ahora volvamos a Beatriz, que la dejamos elevada y absorta en aquella divina vista"
(Now let us return to Beatriz, whom we left elevated and absorbed in that
divine vision.) After another paragraph about the savage jungle of men's
hearts, she returns yet a third time to the scene of the enraptured Beatriz:

> Pues, como digo, estaba Beatriz arrodillada, y tan fuera de sí, mi-
> rando aquella Divina Señora, de quien tan regalada se hallaba, que
> se estuviera allí hasta el fin del mundo, si la Santísima Virgen no le
> dijera:
> —Vuelve en ti, amiga Beatriz. (*Desengaños,* 460)

> (Well, as I say, Beatriz was kneeling, and so beside herself seeing
> that Divine Lady, by whom she found herself so generously treated
> that she would have been there until the end of the world, if the
> Most Holy Virgin had not said to her: "Come out of your trance,
> friend Beatriz.")

The Virgin, leading her hand-in-hand, sets her on the path back to Hungary, gives her the blessing of the unorthodox familial "Trinity" (see page
151 above), and departs, leaving Beatriz much moved and paralyzed by her
departure:

> Y dejándola así, arrodillada, se desapareció, quedando la santa
> reina tan enternecida de que se hubiese partido de ella, que no ac-
> ertaba a levantarse, ni quitar la boca del lugar adonde había tenido
> sus gloriosos pies. Y así estuvo un buen espacio. (*Desengaños,* 461)

> (And leaving her thus, kneeling, she disappeared, the saintly
> queen remaining so much moved that she had departed from her
> that she could not stand up, nor take her mouth away from the spot
> where she had had her glorious feet. And she stayed in that state for
> a good time.)

Thus Zayas gives us at least a glimpse of a totally feminine *jouissance* in communion with the divine Mother. It is brief, external, and intermittent, as the narrator turns back and forth from describing the enraptured Beatriz to lecturing her worldly listeners and readers. That it is no more intimate nor extended should not surprise us. Such a feminine discourse, could it be located, would not fit easily within the frame of the novella tradition in which Zayas elected to write. Nor have succeeding generations of spokeswomen for the feminine experience found it easy to express. Kristeva, in the divided columns of her essay "Stabat Mater" reaches for a way in which to express a barred or inchoate feminine/maternal discourse. It is a moving essay, but it is also a divided discourse that communicates not in isolation but in dialogue with an appropriated masculine voice. We will examine Zayas's two-edged dialogue with that voice in the following chapter.

And so, as Zayas brings her heroines through Oedipal desire and back to silent enjoyment of the House of the Mother, I return to the lines of the mystic poet of *Thunder: Perfect Mind:*[36]

> For I am the first and the last.
> . . . .
> I am the silence that is incomprehensible . . .
> I am the utterance of my name.

PART III

Border Crossings

6

Phallic Woman; or, The Laugh of the Medusa

Narrating from the Masculine Perspective

Not all narrators are alike in Zayas's tales. While Zayas tells no stories from behind the convent walls and gives us no more than a visual hint of a purely feminine *jouissance* of union with the Mother of God, she does cross the sexual divide and situate her narrative voice imaginarily in the masculine position. She switches seats in the train car, as it were,[1] and the plots she creates from that seat arrive at quite different destinations from those told by feminine narrators.

Although the majority of Zayas's stories depict women as powerless victims of male abuse and thus demonstrate female fear and resentment of male dominance in the seventeenth century, her occasional reversal of that dominance offers us an interesting feminine construction of masculine anxiety fantasies, one written with a double-edged pen, one might say. In the first volume, several stories show aggressive, desiring and clever women who, for good or ill, control the males in their lives. All of these stories are narrated by men, roughly in alternation with female-narrated stories of male abuse of women. Although the narrators are not clearly individualized as are those of Marguerite de Navarre in the *Heptameron*,[2] the stories in themselves set up a kind of fictionalized dialogue between male and female fantasies of the danger posed by the opposite sex. The dialogue of perspectives she creates in so doing, however, has been largely ignored to date. Welles specifically denies any differentiation of narrative voice in the twenty tales, "each narrator being indistinguishable from the other and functioning as a 'second self' of María de Zayas" (Welles, 1978, 302). Griswold, Montesa, Williamsen, and others discuss the nature and function of the interplay of various levels of narration, but they do not comment on distinctions between the narrators other than to note the exclusion of male narrators in the *Desengaños* or consider the relationship between Lisis and Zayas's authorial voice.[3]

The first male-narrated story, *El castigo de la miseria* (A Miser's Reward), is a radical revision of Cervantes' paired stories *El casamiento engañoso* (The Deceitful Marriage) and *El coloquio de los perros* (The Dialogue of the Dogs), in which Cervantes' talking dogs are replaced by a tortured cat.[4] Although it ends with the male protagonist's death, this story as well as *El prevenido, engañado* (Forewarned but Not Forearmed), and *Al fin se paga todo* (Just Desserts) contains very humorous scenes as well, a relatively rare quality in Zayas's writing.[5] Hence the subtitle of the present chapter. Freud compared the horror of the sight of the severed head of Medusa with its writhing, snakelike hair to the sight of the female genitals for the young boy; seeing the absence of the penis, a "nothing to see" surrounded by hair, he is horrified by the possibility of his own castration (equivalent for him to decapitation) (see "Medusa's Head," Freud 1974, 18:273–74). Hélène Cixous, in the classic essay "The Laugh of the Medusa," flaunts the petrifying Medusa's head, turning parody and irony on the phallocentric castration anxiety in Freudian and Lacanian constructions of women. Cixous, urging women to write themselves, from a positive valuation and assertion of the woman's body, turns the Medusa's Head around: "Too bad for them if they fall apart upon discovering that women aren't men, or that the mother doesn't have one. But isn't this fear convenient for them? Wouldn't the worst be, isn't the worst, in truth, that women aren't castrated, that they have only to stop listening to the Sirens (for the Sirens were men) for history to change its meaning? You only have to look at the Medusa straight on to see her. And she's not deadly. She's beautiful and she's laughing" (Cixous 1980, 255). A feminine text, says Cixous, written without the masculine fear of castration, crumbles and holds up to ridicule the "bar of separation"; it is free "to smash everything, to shatter the framework of institutions, to blow up the law, to break up the 'truth' with laughter" (258). Although Zayas through male narrators presents the masculine perspective of woman as lure and threat, she, like Cixous, and Luce Irigaray and Jane Gallop as well,[6] turns the tables on that perspective with laughter in the first volume.

In the second volume, all the explicit narrators of all the tales are women, but inner male narrators relate the actions of the fourth, *Tarde llega el desengaño*. Humor virtually disappears from this much darker, violent collection of stories. The two episodes of *Tarde llega el desengaño* (Too Late Undeceived), through parallel situations of enclosure and life-threatening domination by the opposite sex, make clear the anxiety fantasy organizing the other male-narrated stories of feminine desire and feminine power.

Desire, in these male-narrated stories, departs from a different station in life from that in the female-told tales. The principal feminine protagonists of novellas told by men have living mothers as well as fathers, with the exception of *El castigo de la miseria,* in which the significant parentage is the characterization derived from a literary parent, Cervantes. As we have seen in the previous chapter, a masculine subject, forced by the *Nom/Non du père* to identify with difference, away from the maternal, seeks to recoup that loss by pursuing a substitute object on the feminine side. When Zayas through her narrator imaginarily assumes the perspective of a masculine subject, the presence of the mother of the woman who embodies his *objet a* does not, therefore, represent an obstacle, a competing locus of attachment, but rather the model by which girls learn to be "just like their mothers," like the forbidden (m)Other whose lack he seeks to recoup. This seems to me to explain why half of the Zayas heroines with living mothers who enter into a relationship of desire are found in the few stories told by male narrators. I should note, however, that in none of these stories does the mother play a significant role such as that of Cervantes' doña Estefanía in *La fuerza de la sangre* (The Power of Blood). Rather, on imaginarily crossing the bar and assuming the masculine perspective, Zayas can leave the mother in place because she transfers feminine power—both as lure and threat—to the daughter.

In describing Zayas's literary constructions of that lure and threat through the image of the "phallic woman," I do not mean to invoke the ambivalently androgynous female of the Covarrubias emblem or Ribera's Magdalena Ventura, nor do I refer to the Freudian notion of a stage in the

Sebastian de Covarrubias, Emblemas morales, Emblem 64, "Hic, & haec & hoc."
Engraving. Biblioteca Nacional de Madrid

José de Ribera, *Magdalena Ventura with Her Husband and Child*. Oil on canvas. Collection of the Duchess of Lerma, Toledo (photo: Fundación Casa Ducal de Medinaceli)

(male) child's development in which he assumes that women—including most particularly his mother—also possess a penis.[7] Rather, I employ the term *phallus* as it functions as signifier in the Symbolic order of Lacanian theory, in which it is not an appendage, nor even the man associated with it, but something more like the attachment to the social, to the Symbolic order that that signifier represents. As the privileged signifier, the marker of sexual difference, it marks the access of the child to subjectivity in and through lack, language, and desire. It is the signifier of desire itself. As Lacan says in *Encore*, women can also place themselves on the "having" side of the phallic function, on the left side of our chart: "On s'y range, en somme, par choix—libre aux femmes de s'y placer si ça leur fait plaisir. Chacun sait qu'il y a des femmes phalliques et que la fonction phallique n'empêche pas les hommes d'être homosexuels" (1975, 67); translated by Jacqueline Rose as "On the whole one takes up this side by choice—women being free to do so if they so choose. Everyone knows that there are phallic women and that the phallic function does not prevent men from being homosexual" (Lacan 1982, 143). In rough terms, this means that a woman can identify with the phallic position, which in patriarchal culture as we know it signifies possession of authority and knowledge, with the illusion (for either sex) of *having* the phallus—or she can figure the male fantasy that it is Woman as object of his desire who possesses this knowledge, this authority, who *is* the Phallus. "Because her very body serves as a lure to desire, Woman is essentialized by males as containing secret truths, the answers to enigmas, answers from, or to, the Otherness that the masculine denies and rejects and projects onto others. In this sense she is the phallus" (Ragland-Sullivan 1991, 60).

As Zayas's male-narrated stories illustrate, the imago of such a phallic woman in the imaginary realm of the male is for him both a lure and a threat that must be punished or contained.[8] She is so because of her relation to the unconscious and to the inevitable trauma that constitutes the self as an alienated being, the subject of an insatiable circuit of demand and desire, a subject for whom the maintainance of "normalcy" and stable gender identity demands repression of the *metaphorical* castration he/she has undergone. Ragland-Sullivan explains this in terms of what she calls a "double Castration":

> At the Real structural level of primary Castration, both males and females experience loss of the symbiotic attachment to the mother as a kind of Castration. At the secondary or substantive level, Imaginary representations and social meanings are attributed to the

mother and father in an effort to understand or explain the separation drama. Secondary Castration inheres in Imaginary and Symbolic efforts to explain a Real effect. The Other(A) is the place of
the unconscious and thus is either a dark-faced and absent part of
oneself which one must flee or a mysterious force which one renders divine and proceeds to worship. The primordial (m)Other at
the mirror-stage, structural base of the ego becomes confused with
woman; and women are consequently seen as secretly powerful. The
mother within both sexes therefore implies an unseen dominance.
This makes woman—as her displacement—someone to be feared,
denied, ignored, denigrated, fought, and conquered—or conversely worshipped and enshrined. But whether woman is generi-
cally feared or extolled, the individual's attitude toward women
implies a position toward their own unconscious. Either posture—
woman as insufficient and inferior or woman as mysterious and
superior—testifies to the division *(Ichspaltung)* in the subject that
reveals the unconscious as a sense of Otherness or absence.
(1986, 297)

Whereas the acceptance of phallic separation and differentiation is abstract and is operated on and through entry into the Symbolic order, the
experience of mirror stage identification with the (m)Other exists in the
Imaginary, and is corporeal, grounded in the nostalgia for the symbiotic
union with the maternal body. The lure and threat of the (m)Other is,
therefore, always there in the mirror that is the body. Kristeva, in her
mother-centered rewriting of Lacanian theory, has expounded at length
on the perceived menace of identity loss through absorption in the bound-
aryless maternal body in a series of works: *Pouvoirs de l'horreur, Histoires
d'amour, Soleil noir.*[9] K. Silverman, in *The Acoustic Mirror* (1988), develops an
account of the psychic factors underlying the enclosure—both physical
and diegetic—of the female in Hollywood film. But long before that male
camera eye was invented, María de Zayas had created a series of male narrators and protagonists who convey the same fantasies of luring yet threatening women and similar strategies for their containment.

El castigo de la miseria

Whereas the female narrator of *Aventurarse perdiendo* (Venturing and Losing) presented her story as a warning to women against giving in to de-

sire,[10] don Alvaro in narrating *El castigo de la miseria* (A Miser's Reward) introduces his story as a cautionary tale against the misplaced desire represented by miserliness. At the outset, then, sexual desire is presented as dangerous in women, while in men the danger is posed not by the presence of desire but by its misdirection. "Es la miseria la más perniciosa costumbre que se puede hallar en un hombre, pues en siendo miserable, luego es necio, enfadoso y cansado, y tan aborrecible a todos, sin que haya ninguno que no guste de atropellarle, y con razón" (Miserliness is the most pernicious habit that one can find in a man, for by being miserly, he is consequently foolish, annoying and tiresome, and abominable to all, and there is no one who doesn't enjoy knocking him down, and rightly so) (*Novelas*, 123). The protagonist, don Marcos, son of a poor *hidalgo*, has risen from the position of page to the rank of gentleman-in-waiting, and has amassed the small fortune of six thousand ducats by dint of a lifestyle of penury in the extreme.

The narrator calls his manhood into question on a variety of counts in addition to those raised in the introduction cited above. On his promotion to "gentilhombre" (gentleman-in-waiting), he adds that "haciendo en esto su amo en él lo que no hizo el cielo" (his master [is] doing for him what heaven had not done). Eating virtually only when he can do so at others' expense, don Marcos has descended the chain from *Homo sapiens* to vegetable, as "con la sutileza de la comida, se vino a transformar de hombre en espárrago" (with the slenderness of his diet, he came to transform himself from a man into an asparagus) (*Novelas*, 126).

More comically yet, and more significant, he is equally stingy with his "output" as he is with "input": "Llevaba un pícaro de cocina que lo hacía todo, y le vertiese una extraordinaria vasija en que hacía las inexcusables necesidades; era del modo de un arcaduz de noria, porque había sido en un tiempo jarro de miel, que hasta en verter sus excrementos guardó la regla de la observancia" (He employed a kitchen boy who did everything for him, and emptied out the unusual receptacle in which he made his unavoidable necessities; it was in the manner of a waterwheel bucket, having been at one time a honey pot, because even in dumping out his excrement, he maintained a rule of parsimony) (*Novelas*, 126–27). The recycled honey pot becomes an "arcaduz de noria," which the *Diccionario de autoridades* defines as "el que lleno viene vacio torna. Refrán que se puede apropriar a los que van a las Cortes a pleitos y pretensiones impertinentes, que gastan su hacienda, y vuelven vacios, sin haver conseguido cosa alguna" (that which comes full and returns empty. A proverb that can be applied to those who go to Court with suits and impertinent pretension, who spend their estate and return empty-handed, without having achieved a thing).

In his investigation of fantasies of the unconscious, Freud found a repeated link between money and feces, which seemed almost interchangeable in their link to sexual neuroses.[11] Excrement is also one of the *objects a,* or part objects, in Lacanian theory because toilet training marks the first instance in which a social demand is made of the infant by the (m)Other to yield an object (at approximately the end of the mirror stage and the beginning of its induction into the Symbolic order). The child satisfies this demand by producing feces and thus enters the desire/demand circuit and the reciprocity of exchange (see Lacan 1981, 180, 195–96, 100). Hoarding feces/money signifies the rejection of this demand for social and, ultimately, sexual interaction. Zayas intuits the same linkage between money, feces, social interaction, and sexual desire, and has her male narrator open this tale by saying that the worst thing a man can be is a miser, that it makes him abominable to all and the appropriate target of the worst punishment.

Don Marcos has evinced a similar resistance to sexual outlay, lest it cost him money. He has reached the age of thirty without ever being married or "amancebado" (living with a concubine), although numerous marriages had been proposed to him. He remained "el hombre más reglado de los que se conocían en el mundo; porque guardaba castidad, que decía él, que en costando dineros, no hay mujer hermosa, y en siendo de balde no la hay fea" (the most restrained man known in the world, because he maintained chastity, for he said that in costing money, there is no lovely woman, and being free, there is no ugly one) (*Novelas,* 128). But like Campuzano in Cervantes' *El casamiento engañoso* (The Deceitful Marriage), he is finally lured by marriage to Isidora, an unscrupulous older woman posing as a wealthy widow. Unlike Campuzano, don Marcos is not presented as a deceiver deceived; rather, he is something of a simpleton undone by his single-minded love of money. He is not attracted by the glimpse of a white hand, as was Cervantes' Ensign Campuzano, but by the promise of her fortune and the lavishness of her table. On marrying her, he is contemplating not sensual gratification but ways to save yet more money, and perhaps even spare himself the need for procreative outlay. Isidora lives with a handsome young "nephew," Agustín, and don Marcos comments that should God not grant them children, "pues doña Isidora tenía aquel sobrino, para él sería todo, si fuese tan obediente, que quisiese respetarle como a padre" (since doña Isidora had that nephew, for him he would be everything if he were obedient enough, for he wanted him to respect him like a father) (*Novelas,* 137).

Extended play on words indicates don Marcos's sexual disinterest or impotence, in contrast to the prowess of the "nephew" Agustinico. The Narcissus myth appears in its traditional form, here in a complaint against a self-absorbed lover that Isidora has her maid Marcela sing to entertain don Marcos; it is a *letra* (rondeau) glossing the refrain "Murmurad [fuentecillas] a Narciso / que no sabe amar" (Murmur, [fountains], to Narcissus, who does not know how to love) (*Novelas,* 130–32). When Isidora proposes a card game called "jugar al hombre" (to play the man) after the courting banquet she has offered him, don Marcos interprets "playing the man" solely as a threat to his money. and rejects the invitation saying that

> no tan solamente no sabía jugar al hombre, más que no conocía ni una carta, y que verdaderamente hallaba por su cuenta que valía el no saber jugar muchos ducados por año.
>
> —Pues el señor don Marcos—dixo doña Isidora—es tan virtuoso que no sabe jugar, que bien le digo yo a Agustinico que es lo que está mejor al alma y a la hacienda. (*Novelas,* 139)

> (not only did he not know how to play the man, but he didn't know a single card, and that he truly found on his account that not knowing how to play saved him many ducats a year.
>
> "Since don Marcos," said doña Isidora, "is so virtuous that he doesn't know how to play, although I keep telling Agustinico that it is what is best for one's soul and pocketbook.")

The joke on Don Marcos's innocence continues as he launches into a tirade proposing to keep Agustín from "playing," or going out at night, by nailing shut the house doors, which is of course locking in the threat to his manly honor, not out, since every reader/listener understands what sort of games transpire between Isidora and Agustín. But in any case, don Marcos is fixated not on sexual fidelity but on his money; as he says, "su honra era su dinero" (his honor was his money) (*Novelas,* 154).[12]

After his deceivers have fled with his fortune, leaving him penniless and hounded by bill collectors seeking payment for the borrowed accoutrements that Isidora has used to lure him, don Marcos finds her maid Marcela. Marcela poses as a fellow victim of her mistress and convinces him to pay for a magic seance, staged by her lover, in which a devil is to appear to tell don Marco where Isidora and her beau have gone with his money.[13]

The devil, whose appearance climaxes the séance, is in fact a cat, trained through torture, that bursts into the room with its fur aflame and exploding firecrackers tied to its tail and claws Marcos's face so severely before escaping through a window to expire in the street outside that don Marcos is left in a nearly fatal swoon. He recovers to receive a letter from "Doña Isidora de la Venganza" (Doña Isidora the Avenger) saying that she has only given just desserts to "don Marcos Miseria" (don Marcos Miser) and offering to repeat the lesson if he saves another six thousand ducats. Among his sins of miserliness toward himself and others, Isidora includes a repetition of the image of his excremental parsimony. The letter is as follows:

> A don Marcos Miseria, salud: Hombre que por ahorrar no come, hurtando a su cuerpo el sustento necesario, y por interés de dineros se casa, sin más información que si hay hacienda, bien merece el castigo que vuestra merced tiene, y el que se le espera andando el tiempo. Vuestra merced, señor, no comiendo sino como hasta aquí, ni tratando con más ventajas que siempre hizo a sus criados, y como ya sabe la media libra de vaca, un cuarto de pan, y otros dos de ración *al que sirve y limpia la estrecha vasija en que hace sus necesidades* vuelva a juntar otros seis mil ducados, y luego me avise, que yo vendré de mil amores a hacer con vuestra merced vida maridable, que bien lo merece marido tan aprovechado.—Doña Isidora de la Venganza. (*Novelas*, 163; emphasis added)

> (To don Marcos Miser, greetings: A man who, to save money, doesn't eat, robbing his body of its necessary sustenance, and who marries for money without knowing anything except that there is property, well deserves the punishment that your grace has had, and that which awaits you as time goes on. Your grace, sir, eating only as you have so far and not treating your servants more liberally than you always have—you know, the half pound of beef, a penny loaf of bread, and another pittance *to the boy who works for you and cleans the narrow vessel in which you do your necessities,*—get together another six thousand ducats and then let me know, and I will come with the greatest of pleasure to live a married life with your grace, for a man so thrifty well deserves it.—Doña Isidora the Avenger.)

With this shock, he sickens and dies—or in the first edition of 1637, he commits suicide with a rope furnished to him by the marriage broker who arranged the fatal match.

El castigo de la miseria bears an interesting relation to Cervantes' *El casamiento engañoso*. The Cervantine tale is linked, as a sort "marco," or "frame," to *El coloquio de los perros*. Zayas makes her protagonist a "Marco" antonomastically as don Marcos.[14] Whereas Cervantes' philosophizing dogs work a "talking cure" on Campuzano, Zayas makes a tortured cat an important agent in don Marcos's fatal disillusionment. In part, we might attribute this alteration to the increasingly pessimistic climate of seventeenth-century Spain,[15] as well as to Zayas's gender perspective. But why the change from dogs to a cat? The first answer might be that there is a cruelly comic logic to the use of a cat to chastise a simpleton who has so amply illustrated the dangers of buying "gato por liebre" (a cat for a hare). Furthermore, however, looking at the historic association between cats, magic, and women and, more specifically, female sexuality, discloses a more interesting explanation, one more revealing of Zayas's understanding of male attitudes toward women.[16]

As Robert Darnton has amply illustrated in *The Great Cat Massacre*, cats have fascinated men[17] over the centuries, from ancient Egypt to Baudelaire and Manet, and have had important ritual value in a variety of cultures (89). Darnton attributes this to their mysterious bearing, their apparently semihuman intelligence, and their ambiguous ontological status. Seymour Menton reached a similar conclusion in studying the importance of cats for writers in the mode labeled magic realism, in which he finds that cats have an emblematic status equal to that of the swan in Hispanic modernism. Their inscrutability makes them a fertile object for the exercise of the human imagination and invites the attribution of magic qualities to them, as Borges gave to the enormous cat who occupies a pivotal position in "El Sur." Like "una divinidad desdeñosa," the cat allows clients to stroke it, but Juan Dahlman finds it separated from his touch as if by a glass, "porque el hombre vive en el tiempo, en la sucesión, y el mágico animal, en la actualidad, en la eternidad del instante (Borges 1956, 180). The use of a cat in the magic seance staged for Don Marcos is predictable, for cats were regularly associated with witchcraft. In ancient Egypt, cats were worshipped and women in particular considered them their special special protectors; in contrast, by the tenth century, cats had become identified with witchcraft. Hundreds were burned as witches in disguise; the Inquisition prosecuted owners of cats in the fourteenth and fifteenth centuries, and by the end of the fifteenth, the devil was frequently painted as a cat (Menton 1998, 37). Darnton provides horrifying particulars of the process:

Witches transformed themselves into cats in order to cast spells on their victims. Sometimes, especially on Mardi Gras, they gathered for hideous sabbaths at night. They howled, fought, and copulated horribly under the direction of the devil himself in the form of a huge tomcat. To protect yourself from sorcery by cats there was one, classic remedy: maim it. Cut its tail, clip its ears, smash one of its legs, tear or burn its fur, and you would break its malevolent power. A maimed cat could not attend a sabbath or wander abroad to cast spells. (1984, 93–94)

The persisting association of the malevolence of the cat with women surfaces in an early magic realist painting, *Rheingasse* (1917) by the Swiss painter Niklaus Stöcklin: through a window above a laundry, a cat appears juxtaposed to an old woman with the features of a witch; the cat gazes menacingly at a bird at the outer edge of the painting. Menton lists multiple associations of cats and women that followed in paintings and fictions in this mode, including the works of Fernando Botero and, in Cortázar's *Rayuela*, repeated links between the protagonist's lover la Maga (literally, woman magician) and cats (Menton 1998, 38).[18]

Outside the context of witchcraft, cats have also been intimately associated with female sexuality. In French, *le chat*, *la chatte*, and *le minet* all have the double meaning of "pussy" in English. That particular polysemy does not appear to exist in Spanish, but the association of women and cats in sexual contexts certainly does. Lope, who said that a generic characteristic of women is having the soul of a cat, plays on the double meaning of the word "gato" as animal or "bolso o talego en que se guarda el dinero" (purse or poke in which money is kept) in *La Dorotea* in an interchange between Laurencio and Don Bela:

Lau. . . . de los gatos se saca el algalia.
Bel. Dorotea huele bien naturalmente.
Lau. Por lo que tiene de gato, y al fin lo vendrá a ser de tus doblones.
(Vega Carpio 1980, 275, 275 n. 139)

(*Lau.* . . . civet is extracted from cats.
Bel. Dorotea's scent is naturally sweet.
Lau. Say she's a cat in clawing at doubloons, not in giving off perfumes.)
(Vega Carpio 1985, 137)

In Lope's *El castigo sin venganza,* the gracioso Batín comments skeptically on the duke's supposed conversion from rogue to dutiful husband by telling the following story about the transformation of a feline into a woman:

> ¡Plega al cielo que no sea,
> después destas humildades,
> como aquel hombre de Atenas,
> que pidió a Venus le hiciese
> mujer, con ruegos y ofrendas,
> una gata dominica,
> quiero decir, blanca y negra!
> Estando en su estrado un día,
> con moño y naguas de tela,
> vio pasar un animal
> de aquestos, como poetas,
> que andan royendo papeles,
> y dando un salto ligera
> de la tarima al ratón,
> mostró que de naturaleza
> la que es gata será gata,
> la que es perra, será perra,
> in secula seculorum.
> (ll. 2374–91)

(May heaven grant, after these humilities, that he not be like that man from Athens who asked Venus, with pleas and offerings, to turn into a woman his Dominican—I mean white and black—pussycat! In her drawing room one day, with a topknot and cloth petticoats, she saw passing by one of those animals that, like poets, go around gnawing on paper, and giving a quick jump from the dais onto the rat, showed that by nature, she who is a cat will be a cat, she who is a bitch will be a bitch, *in secula seculorum.*)

In Burgundy, to mock a cuckold, young people would "faire la chat,"—pass a cat around, pulling its fur to make it howl. Germans called charivaris *Katzenmusik,* perhaps because they involved the literal torture of cats, or howling like cats under the windows of newly remarried widows or cuckolds. Celebrations of the summer solstice, so widely linked with lovers, involved in France a horrifying variety of tortures to cats, tying them in bags, suspending them from ropes, setting them on fire and chasing them through the streets, or driving them into the traditional bonfire with a ceremonious volley of rifle fire (Darnton 1984, 83–85).

The particular cat massacre that inspired Darnton's research took place in a print shop in Paris in the 1730s, and consisted of a large cat hunt and massacre by the print shop apprentices. It culminated in the mock trial and assassination of *la grise* (the gray), the favorite cat of the master's wife. By killing *la grise,* says Darnton, the workers in effect accused the mistress of being a witch and of sexual infidelity. Continues Darnton: "It was metonymic insult, the eighteenth-century equivalent of the modern schoolboy's taunt; 'Ah, your mother's girdle!' But it was stronger, and more obscene. By assaulting her pet, the workers ravished the mistress symbolically. At the same time, they delivered the supreme insult to their master. His wife was his most precious possession, just as her *chatte* was hers. In killing the cat, the men violated the most intimate treasure of the bourgeois household and escaped unharmed" (99).

I believe that Darnton's suggested metonymic reading is also valuable in understanding *El castigo de la miseria* and other Zayas stories. There is no overt link between don Marcos, doña Isidora, and the particular cat tormented in this story, as there was in the print-shop massacre between the master, his wife, and her cat. The only connection is don Marcos's fortuitous encounter with Marcela. This is characteristic of the loosely episodic structure of most Zayas stories, whose meaningful elements accumulate paratactically in a (dis)order similar to the rambling construction of her long, looping sentences. I suggest, however, that if we read Zayas stories metonymically, looking for the relation of contiguity between the more-or-less discontinuous elements, we find a meaning that is as much repressed as revealed by their articulation. Paul Julian Smith (1989, 38) has connected the disrupted syntax of both Saint Teresa and Zayas with a feminine language such as that described by Irigaray that makes its gender felt within the masculine mold of language through gaps and ruptures, negation and strategic silence. I believe that this disjunctive signifying process extends beyond the level of the sentence to the articulation of the narrative as a whole, and is what requires a metonymic reading; in other words, one that locates the central object not in a locus that is textually labeled as such, but rather represented by laterally related allusion.

Whereas Jakobson connects metonymy with the realistic novel,[19] it seems to me that its function therein is different from that which is operative in Zayas's work; that in the realistic novel, it is deliberately productive of meaning, encouraging the reader to complete imaginatively a "possible world" of the novel from the partial, or synecdochic descriptions actually present. The metonymical articulation of Zayas's stories would seem to function as much to repress as to produce meaning, to say without saying what cannot be directly confronted in the female psyche under patriarchy or contained in the rational mold of the master plot.

By such a metonymic reading, we can find in the articulation of this tale Zayas's intuition of the unconscious logic behind masculine anxiety fantasies regarding the opposite sex. The logic is that imputed to her male narrator, who would punish "pussy" to evoke and exorcize the devil from it that makes a fool of man, while punishing the man as well for being such a fool. Isidora, the particular "pussy" who was don Marcos's downfall, and who sealed his death warrant with the insulting letter she signed "Doña Isidora de la Venganza," does have the tables turned on her at the end. As Agustín, Isidora, and the maid Inés waited in Barcelona for a ship to Naples, Inés and Agustín stole off one night while doña Isidora was sleeping, taking with them don Marcos's six thousand ducats. Doña Isidora returned to Madrid, says the narrator, where she was reduced to begging for alms. In comparison with the violence done to women in subsequent Zayas novellas, this is a mild punishment. It is in keeping with the light tone of the story, in which the explicit target of criticism is misdirected male desire. The libidinally invested object for don Marcos was not the opposite sex, says Zayas, but money.

By introducing a male narrator for this third tale, Zayas creates a framework within which to represent masculine ambivalence toward feminine sexuality, a theme that will be repeated in the succeeding "phallic woman" tales. Male narrators both evoke female desire and attempt to contain or punish it.

Desengaño 4 (Tarde llega el desengaño)

The containment strategies are made most evident in *Tarde llega el desengaño* (Too Late Undeceived), in the linked episodes recounted through two inner male narrative voices, a shipwrecked traveler, don Martín, whose third-person account encloses the first-person narrative of don Jaime de Aragón. Contrary to Pfandl's opinion that the two adventures recounted by don Jaime "no tienen ninguna relación entre sí, y necesitan del apoyo de una breve narración que las encuadre" (are unrelated and need the support of a brief narrative that frames them) (1933, 369), I suggest that there is an intimate, if unstated, connection between the episodes and the prefatory frame.

That frame consists of a reiteration of Zayas's arguments in "Al que leyere" (To the Reader) for women's intellectual potentialities, updated and intensified in the voice of Filis, the explicit narrator of the tale. The rhetorical structure of this frame is akin to the advance/retreat strategy of "Al que leyere" in alternately courting and accusing male readers. Filis opens by suggesting that men are not so culpable for the prevailing deceitful relations between the sexes, that it is women who allow themselves to be deceived, or who deceive themselves. For example, she cites a "bachillera" (prattler) whose reaction to a story of one wife's misfortune with her husband was to say: " 'Bueno fuera que por una nave que se anega, no navegasen las demás' " (It would be a fine thing if because one ship sinks, the rest shouldn't sail) (*Desengaños*, 228). This image of a ship on a threatening sea both prefigures the shipwreck that will initiate the tale to come and recalls the opening warning of the first novella against embarking on the "sea of unbridled desires . . . in a fragile barque" (*Novelas*, 37). Recalling the murder of innocent wives in the two previous *desengaños*, she excuses/accuses the male sex by saying that despite the purported existence of free will, some women seem condemned by fatal stars, and their two husbands' cruel natures may well *not* be characteristic of all men. Next she invokes masculine superiority as natural, as their birthright: "Ellos nacieron con libertad de hombres, y ellas con recato de mujeres" (They [men] were born with men's freedom, and the women with women's reserve) and "los hombres, con el imperio que naturaleza les otorgó en serlo" (men, with the dominion that nature granted them in so being") (*Desengaños*, 228). But in the next breath she annuls that "natural" male superiority, as she continues in the same sentence to characterize male vituperation and restriction of women as a socially organized defense mechanism against the threat of feminine power, explaining that men are

> temerosos quizá de que las mujeres no se les quiten, pues no hay duda que si no se dieran tanto a la compostura, afeminándose más que naturaleza las afeminó, y como en lugar de aplicarse a jugar las armas y a estudiar las ciencias, estudian en criar el cabello y matizar el rostro, ya pudiera ser que pasaran en todo a los hombres. Luego

el culparlas de fáciles y de poco valor y menos provecho es porque
no se les alcen con la potestad. Y así, en empezando a tener discurso
las niñas, pónenlas a labrar y hacer vainillas, y si las enseñan a leer,
es por milagro, que hay padre que tiene por caso de menos valer
que sepan leer y escribir sus hijas, dando por causa que de saberlo
son malas, como si no hubiera muchas más que no lo saben y lo son,
y ésta es natural envidia y temor que tienen de que los han de pasar
en todo. Bueno fuera que si una mujer ciñera espada. sufriera que
la agraviara un hombre en ninguna ocasión; harta gracia fuera que
si una mujer profesara las letras, no se opusiera con los hombres
tanto a las dudas como a los puestos; según esto, temor es el abatir-
las y obligarlas a que ejerzan las cosas caseras. (*Desengaños,* 228–29)

(fearful perhaps that women might take it away from them, because
there is no doubt that if they didn't devote themselves so much to
appearance, effeminizing themselves more than nature effeminized
them, and if they set themselves to practicing with arms and studying sciences instead of studying how to take care of their hair and
paint their faces, it could well be that they would outstrip men in
everything. Therefore accusing them as facile, of little value and less
use, is so they won't make off with their authority. And thus, as soon
as girls begin to speak and reason, they set them at embroidering
and doing hemstitching, and if they teach them to read, it's a miracle, for there are fathers who think it's of little worth that their
daughters learn to read and write, giving the excuse that knowing it
makes them bad, as if there weren't many more women who don't
know how and are bad, and this is natural envy and fear they have
that they will outdo them in everything. It would be a fine thing for
a woman, if she wore a sword, to allow a man to injure her on any
occasion; it would be funny indeed, should a woman be lettered,
that she shouldn't compete with men over doubtful issues as well as
over offices; accordingly, it's out of fear that they beat them down
and oblige them to do household tasks.)

Offering proof of that feminine capacity, Filis then gives a list of outstanding women, this time drawn not from ancient or classical history, but from
a group of women who in Zayas's own era were living proof of the feminine
capacity to govern[20] and to achieve distinction in learned fields[21] and as
poets and dramatists.[22]

Filis caps the theme of male fear of women with a striking final comparison, in which she equates men's depriving women of books and arms with the literal castration of men: "De manera que no voy fuera de camino en que los hombres de temor y envidia las privan de las letras y las armas, como hacen los moros a los cristianos que han de servir donde hay mujeres que los hacen eunucos por estar seguros de ellos" (And so I am not off the track in saying that men deprive them of letters and arms out of fear and envy, as the Moors make eunuchs of the Christians who are to serve where there are women so they can be sure of them) (*Desengaños*, 231). The privileged object in the second half of her equation is access to women as sexual object; in the first half, it is access to Symbolic-order power. As the Moors castrate their Christian captives to protect their power over women as sexual object, so men, she says, protect their dominion by denying women access to words and swords, the signifiers of phallic power. This equation is, in my opinion, an uncanny anticipation of the operation of secondary castration, the acceptance of sexual difference on the basis of "having" versus "being" the phallus, and of its unequal effects in the hierarchization of gender roles in patriarchal culture.

Exhorting women to a Cixous-like smashing of the bar of gender separation, Zayas's narrator Filis tells them: "¡Ea, dejemos las galas, rosas y rizos, y volvamos por nosotras: unas, con el entendimiento, y otras, con las armas! Y será el mejor desengaño para las que hoy son y las que han de venir" (Come on, women, let's forget the finery, roses, and curls and stand up for ourselves: some with learning, others with arms! And it will be the best disenchantment for women of today and those to come) (*Desengaños*, 231). Her own contribution to this disenchantment, in accord with Lisis's commandment, will be directed against men, she says, and she concludes her preface, not with the rhetorical curtsy to a masculine audience that concluded the "Al que leyere," but with an aggressive apology rather in the style of an Amazon remembering that she may someday require male service: "Por si algún día los hubiere menester, les pido perdón y licencia" (In case someday I should have need of them, I ask their pardon and permission) (*Desengaños*, 231).

In the preface to this *desengaño*, then, the explicit feminine narrator Filis, using an alternately luring and threatening rhetorical strategy, openly addresses the fear of feminine power that underlies masculine containment strategies. To shift the reader smoothly into the diegetic episodes told from a masculine perspective, Zayas takes advantage of the ambiguous pronominal address of courtly love poetry. She accomplishes an expertly faded-in transition to the voice of the first masculine enclosed narrator, as Filis sings a song of longing for an absent love, addressed in the ninth and sixteenth line as "dueño mío." The perspective pivots on the second invocation of "my master/beloved," the first heptasyllabic line of the song, toward the cry to "señora mía" (my lady) in the penultimate couplet. As prose resumes and storytelling begins, the readers learns that that song was sung by "don Martín, caballero mozo, noble, galán y bien entendido," (don Martín, a young gentleman, noble, handsome, and intelligent) on shipboard, returning from military service in Flanders to Toledo, to marry his beloved cousin.

The opening setting of this story—like that of *Aventurarse perdiendo* one of relatively few instances of extended scenic description in Zayas—has clear symbolic value. Don Martín's ship is caught in a violent storm, driven for days by the furious power of wind and water and finally wrecked on a mountainous coastline, but with the help of a board and "Heaven's protection," don Martín and another man survive the waves—"furiosas y fuera de madre" (ferocious beyond the measure [literally, furious and "out of mother"]) and take shelter in a shoreline cave, not knowing whether they are on Christian or Moorish soil. As Foa points out, this opening displays for the reader a scene of human beings driven by violent forces beyond their control, in an atmosphere of fear, darkness, and mystery appropriate to the events to follow (1979, 159–60). Furthermore, don Martín's shipwreck dramatically illustrates the well-worn metaphor of the vulnerability of human life on a stormy sea, an image that Zayas's narrators repeatedly invoke to warn against the power of sexual desire. His shipwreck is physical and he survives; venturing inland he finds the castle of don Jaime de Aragón, in which he will witness the tragic tale of a figurative shipwreck of desire, of what don Jaime recalls as "los naufragios de su vida" (the shipwrecks of his life) (*Desengaños*, 250).

With the telling and playing out of don Jaime's story, the reader, through the gaze of the witness-participant don Martín, is drawn into a contracting vortex of passion and death in the two love stories of his life. First, the physical setting is compressed into ever smaller spaces: from the sea to the island Gran Canaria, into a castle whose drawbridge is then pulled closed defensively and into a dining hall therein; off this hall, a small door opens and from it emerges a beautiful but pale and emaciated woman dressed in sackcloth, who crawls under the dining table to be fed table scraps disdained by dogs. From another door, in melodramatic, chiaroscuro contrast, a jet black woman ceremoniously enters, her way lit by candelabras borne by two damsels. Don Martín and his friend are astounded by the contrast between her ugliness, described as bestial if not demonic, and her bejeweled, rich attire and the attention lavished on her by their host. After the meal, the black woman departs with equal ceremony and the white woman crawls out from under the table, is served water in a skull she carries, and is then locked into the tiny room from which she entered. The history of love and hate that don Jaime recounts for his guests as a means to explain this bizarre scene is a two-chapter story, containing two parallel situations of enclosure and life-threatening domination by the opposite sex that make clear the anxiety fantasy organizing both this and other male-narrated stories of female desire.

The first episode is a version of the Pysche-Cupid myth told by Apuleius in the *Golden Ass,* in the gender-reversed form that De Armas calls "The Invisible Mistress" story. As told by Apuleius, the Psyche and Cupid myth is a story of feminine sexual initiation and of love nearly destroyed by feminine curiosity and jealousy.[23] In the gender-reversed form in which it circulated beginning with the twelfth-century French romance *Partonopeus de Blois,* masculine and feminine roles were reversed; a handsome young man is drawn into the abode of an invisible mistress and his attempt to identify her threatens their love, and perhaps his life as well.[24]

The adventure that don Jaime recounts to don Martín began when, as a gallant twenty-four-year-old captain serving in Flanders, he received an intriguing invitation to a nighttime rendezvous. An elderly servant came to lead him blindfolded on a long and labyrinthine route to a house, up a staircase and down a corridor, where a woman dressed in rustling silks took his hand and lead him through three more rooms to her *estrado* (drawing room). If earlier he had thought he might be led to "infernales abismos" (infernal abysses), he now imagines that he is in the arms of a goddess because of "la gloria que siento en el alma" (the glory I feel in my soul), the scent and sweetness of the lodgings, and the "partes tan realzadas" (preeminent parts) he is invited to explore by touch in the darkness. She tells him that her love for him has driven her to bring him to her thus in secret, and that he must never attempt to see her, nor divulge their secret to anyone. When, after he enjoys her "regaladísimos favores" (most generous favors), she fills his pockets night after night with money and jewels, he concludes that she must be a "mujer poderosa" (powerful woman). His nightly rendezvous with his "dama encantada" (enchanted lady) continue for more than a month, until don Jaime reveals his secret to a friend to defend his reputation against charges that his new wealth comes from nightly robbery.

With the friend's help, he marks the door of his lady's house with a bloody sponge as he enters that night and discovers the next day that it is the residence of a powerful old prince who has only one daughter, a young widow. Pressed by don Jaime, she reluctantly allows him to see her beauty in the light the next night and tells him who she is: "Madama Lucrecia, . . . princesa de Erne. . . . Mi padre es muy viejo, no tiene otro heredero sino a mí, y aunque me salen muchos casamientos, ninguno acepto ni aceptaré hasta que el Cielo me dé lugar para hacerte mi esposo" (Madam Lucrecia, . . . princess of Erne . . . My father is very old, he has no other heir but me, and although many marriage offers come to me, I accept none nor will I accept any until Heaven permits me to make you my husband) (*Desengaños*, 244). Ignoring her injunction of secrecy, don Jaime begins to court her openly and she sends assassins to kill him. He survives the attack but his commanding general has been warned to send him home because the offended party, a woman, will continue to seek revenge against him as a madman and "mal celador de secretos" (bad keeper of secrets) (*Desengaños*, 246). He returns to his home in Gran Canaria to find that his mother has died; his father dies within a year, leaving him a wealthy man of thirty-three,[25] but unreceptive to the many advantageous marriages offered him because he remains obsessed with the memory of Lucrecia: "porque aún vivía en mi alma la imagen adorada de madama Lucrecia, perdida el mismo día que la vi; que aunque había sido causa de tanto mal como padecí, no la podía olvidar ni aborrecer" (because there still lived in my soul the adored image of Madam Lucrecia, lost the very day I saw her; for although she had been the cause of so much trouble that I suffered, I could not forget her or hate her) (*Desengaños*, 246–47).

Zayas's "Invisible Mistress" story is not, in itself, radically different from numerous other versions; its uniqueness derives rather from certain telling details, and from its linkage to the story of don Jaime's second love.[26] Together, they suggest that Zayas intuited what psychoanalytic theory has labeled the repetition compulsion, the endeavor to master the trauma of loss that is linked at one pole to the fiction of wholeness connected with the image of the phallic mother and, at the other, to the death drive. Elizabeth Bronfen provides a clear and concise summary of the central elements of this compulsion:

> The satisfaction that repetition, informed by the death drive, affords is that it serves as a fulfilment of two fundamental desires: for an absence of tension and for the re-finding of lost wholeness. If we

recall that the finding of a love-object is, in fact, a re-finding of the lost maternal body, another connection between the death drive and femininity emerges. The return to a prior state involves the maternal body in a threefold sense: as the real material body lost with birth, as the fiction of a whole body that the phallic mother represents during primary narcissism, and in the image of which surrogate love-objects are chosen, and as trope for the dust to which the human being is forced to return. (Wright 1992, 55)

Illustrating how Zayas's intuition of the repetition compulsion organizes *Desengaño 4* will require a certain patience in crisscrossing the two stories, as well as fictional and historical sources on which they draw, to gather the clues to the unconscious processes that lead to don Jaime's madness and his wife's death.

The most obvious clue is that phenomenon we have all witnessed in everyday experience, that of choosing a second love object solely on the basis of a physical resemblance to a lost love. At mass one Holy Week, don Jaime tells don Martín,

> vi un sol: poco digo, vi un ángel; vi, en fin, un retrato de Lucrecia, tan parecido a ella, que mil veces me quise persuadir a que, arrepentida de haberme puesto en la ocasión que he dicho, se había venido tras mí. Vi, en fin, a Elena, que éste es el nombre de aquella desventurada mujer que habéis visto comer los huesos y migajas de mi mesa. Y así que la vi, no la amé, porque ya la amaba: la adoré. (*Desengaños*, 247)

> (I saw a sun; I understate, I saw an angel; I saw, in sum, a portrait of Lucrecia, so like her that a thousand times I wanted to persuade myself that, sorry for having put me in the situation I've related, she had come after me. I saw, in sum, Elena, for this is the name of that unfortunate woman you have seen eating the bones and crumbs from my table. And as soon as I saw her, I didn't fall in love with her, because I already loved her: I adored her.)

Elena is a physical copy of Lucrecia but her opposite in other ways: she is a virgin whose only wealth is her beauty and her virtue; her father is dead and her mother is "una honrada y santa señora" (an honorable and saintly lady) (*Desengaños*, 247). After they have been happily wed for six years, her

mother dies and two years later a black woman servant accuses Elena of infidelity with a handsome young cousin who lives with them. He kills the
cousin and locks up his wife, sustaining her only with water served in the
skull of her dead cousin and scraps he serves to her under the table, as don
Martín saw, while the black servant occupies her place as lady of the house.
In the versions of this story told earlier by Bandello (1990, novella 12, part
2), and Marguerite de Navarre (1984, story 43), the wife was guilty of adultery but Elena was innocent, as the servant reveals in a deathbed confession the very night that don Jaime tells don Martín his story. When the
men rush to release Elena from her prison, they find her dead in a saintly
pose, and don Jaime goes mad.

Zayas offers us a second clue in the names she gives her characters:
Elena, Lucrecia, princess of Erne, and don Jaime de Aragón. Elena is also
the name that Boccaccio gives to the young widow who is at first sexual
tease and tormentor, and then victim, of a scholar, Ranieri, in the *Decameron*, day 8, story 7. Both in its bipartitite structure and in the erotically
charged, symbolic use of space, this story is akin to Zayas's tale. Whereas
various critics have read Boccaccio's tale as misogynistic, autobiographical,
or both, Almansi suggests that it should be seen as an illustration of his use
of the traditional Dantean literary model of *contrappasso*, "rapporto diretto
o inverso tra colpa e pena, per cui la pena è analoga o opposta, come
natura e qualità, alla colpa" (a direct or inverse relationship between guilt
and punishment, in which the punishment is analogous or opposite in nature and quality to the guilt) (*Vocabulario italiano* 1993, s.v. "contrapasso")
Boccaccio does indeed introduce the story as an example of "retaliation"
and of "just revenge dealt to a woman of our own town whose trick, when
turned around and used against her, almost caused her death" (1982, 504).
Boccaccio's Elena is a handsome young widow who has chosen not to remarry, but to enjoy herself with a young lover she has chosen, when Ranieri
falls in love with her. A vain and flirtatious woman, she encourages his attentions, to the extent of telling him to come into her courtyard the night
after Christmas. On that cold and snowy night, she keeps him locked up in
her snowy courtyard while she enjoys herself inside the house with her
lover, occasionally sending encouraging messages to the scholar that she
will come as soon as her "brother" leaves, while she and her lover laugh at
the scholar's dancing attempts to keep from freezing to death. Some time
later, Elena's lover leaves her, and her maidservant, who believes that the
scholar is versed in magic arts as well as philosophy, asks him to help her
draw that lover back to her. The scholar tricks Elena into spending a night

naked in a tree, then has her immerse herself in a stream, climb a tower, and repeat an incantation. Seeing her naked beauty from his hiding place, the scholar is "suddenly attacked by the desires of the flesh which caused a certain part of him which had been resting to stand up straight, [and] he was tempted to leave his hiding place, seize her, and fulfill his desires. . . . But when he recalled who he was, the injury that was done him, why he had received it, and from whom, his indignation was fired up again, both his compassion and his lust were driven away, and he remained firm in his resolution" (1982, 513). He chooses, rather than pleasure of sexual possession, the sadistic delight of revenge, torturing her flesh on the roof of a hot tower as she had tormented him in a frozen courtyard. He removes the ladder from the tower, leaving her to be seared by the sun at the top of it all the following July day. When Ranieri reveals himself, she begs him for mercy, but in prolonged harangues he reminds her how she had frozen him and his desire for her in her courtyard, curses women who choose younger men to "warm their wool," and suggests that she either pray to her lost lover for help or throw herself off the tower to break her neck where her soul will be welcomed in the devil's arms. He tells her that the sight of her death would be a pleasure for him, and that "when I consider in what peril you placed my life, it would not be enough for me to take your life by way of revenge, nor the lives of a hundred other women like you, for I would be killing only one vile, evil, and wicked woman" (1982, 516). All teasing, cold hussies are one and the same, as it were. Boccaccio's prolonged description of Elena's suffering and thirst as horseflies settle on her cracked flesh, her pleas, and his harsh sermons to her are the narrative equivalent of the lingering death that don Jaime inflicts on Elena in Zayas's story.

Finally Ranieri has Elena's clothes sent to the maidservant (the same one who helped keep him locked in the garden), who with a peasant's help, brings her down from the tower but breaks her own leg in the process, which completes Ranieri's pleasure. Boccaccio's tale concludes with a warning for other ladies against playing such tricks: "So, then, this is what became of the foolish young woman and her tricks when she thought she could play around with a scholar the way she might with any other man, for little did she know that scholars—not all of them, I say, but the majority—know only too well *where the Devil hides his tail*. And so, ladies, beware of playing such tricks, especially on scholars" (1982, 524; emphasis added).[27]

If the Boccaccio story is a symmetrical *contrappasso*, then we might say that Zayas structures her bipartite tale as a *trapasso*, in the sense of both transfer and death. Boccaccio's Elena tortured Ranieri by inviting him into her inner courtyard and freezing him there, whereupon he sent her up a tower to fry. In Zayas, however, the torture is not turned back on its originator, but rather transferred, as Elena pays for the nearly fatal wound inflicted by another woman, akin to her only in her physical similarity, but her opposite in innocence and powerlessness. And where Boccaccio inverts the sexually-charged spatial setting (courtyard to tower), Zayas repeats it. As don Jaime narrates his first entry into Lucrecia's house, he describes at length how he is drawn deep into the interior, as

> entrando en el zaguán . . . [el criado] me asió de la mano y me subió por unas escaleras. . . . Acabamos de subir, y en medio de un corredor, . . . con una llavé que traía abrió una puerta, y trasladando, al entrar por ella, mi mano, que en la suya llevaba otra, . . . sin hablar palabra, volvió a cerrar y se fue, dejándome más encantado que antes; porque la dama a quien me entregó, según juzgué por el crujir de la seda, fue conmigo caminando otrás tres salas, y en la última, llegando a un estrado, se sentó y me dijo que me sentara. (*Desengaños*, 240)

> (entering the doorway . . . [the servant] took hold of my hand and led me up some stairs. . . . We stopped climbing up, and in the middle of a corridor, . . . with a key he carried he opened a door, passing my hand as he went through it to another hand which his held, . . . without uttering a word, he closed the door again and went away, leaving me more enchanted than before; because the lady to whom he delivered me, as I judged from the crackle of silk, went walking with me through three other rooms and in the last one, arriving at a dais, seated herself and told me to sit down.)

When she tries to kill him for violating the secrecy of these nightly encounters, don Jaime remains possessed by her memory. She can only be dispossessed by a physical look-alike, a physically identical *objet a* who fills his lack—as long as no shadow casts a doubt over his total possession: "Elena era mi cielo, Elena era mi gloria, Elena era mi jardín, Elena mis holguras, Elena mi recreo" (Elena was my heaven, Elena was my glory, Elena was my garden, Elena my enjoyment, Elena my recreation) (*Desengaños*, 247). But when that shadow is cast, she receives, as a woman, the hatred never turned on Lucrecia: "Ya es Elena mi asombro, mi horror, mi aborrecimiento; fue mujer Elena, y como mujer ocasionó sus desdichas y las mías" (Now Elena is my fright, my horror, my hatred; Elena was a woman, and as a woman caused her misfortunes and mine) (*Desengaños,* 247). As in Ranieri's harangue in Boccaccio, the woman who destroys his illusion of having the phallus, who is no longer the *objet a* of desire that fills lack but instead the intolerable signifier of lack itself, becomes a condensation of all women and the threat they pose to the masculine fantasy of dominance.

Don Jaime's reactions to the reported offense spring straight from the unconscious. First, he is tempted to cut out the maidservant's tongue, as if he could thus erase the signified psychic wound that her words produced by excising the signifying instrument. Second, he thinks of killing every living thing in the household, as if that would excise the living place of the wound. Controlling this desire lest he "espantar la caza" (frighten the prey) (*Desengaño* 249), he chooses instead to transport the household to the country castle. This is not only to effect prudent distance from the city where he is free to exercise his revenge unquestioned; it also functions as an attempt to alleviate the intolerable "gaze of the other" that redoubles the visibility of his injured honor to his own sight.[28] The offending gaze is multiple for don Jaime. It emerges from his lost *objet a,* Elena, whose offense he cannot bear to see, "no teniendo paciencia para aguardar a ver mi agravio a vista de ojos" (not having the patience to wait to see my injury before my eyes) (*Desengaños,* 249).[29] It is lodged most offensively in the gaze of the black maidservant, who has become a kind of anamorphic object, functioning like the dark, elongated skull crossing the foreground in Holbein's painting the *Ambassadors*—a blot first meaningless in itself, but that once perceived from a certain viewing angle, transforms the meaning of the entire field of vision.[30] Her report, even untested and potentially meaningless in itself, changes his whole mode of being: "tuve cautela y disimulación, que ya para mí es [cierto], aunque pudiera ser que no fuera: que al honor de un marido sólo que él lo sospeche basta, cuanto y más habiendo *testigo de vista*" (I was cautious and dissimulating, now that it was certain for me although it could have been that it didn't exist: for a husband's honor, that he only suspects it is enough, much more so having *an eyewitness*) (*Desengaños,* 249; emphasis added). And the gaze (in don Jaime's Imaginary) resides finally in the big Other, the social order, from which he tries to hide "the prodigious history" in the castle, as he told don Martín at the beginning of his narrative:

> Sois los primeros a quien la he dicho y han visto lo que en este castillo pasa; porque desde que me retiré a él de la ciudad, no he

consentido que ninguno de mis deudos o amigos que me vienen a
ver pasen de la primera sala, ni mis criados se atreverán a contar a
nadie lo que aquí pasa, pena de que les costara la vida. (*Desengaños*,
238)

(You are the first to whom I have told it and who have seen what
goes on in this castle; because since I withdrew to it from the city, I
have not permitted any of my relatives or friends who come to see
me to pass beyond the first room, nor would my servants dare tell
anyone what occurs here, on pain of their lives.)

Closing the entire transported household off from the outside world in the
castle, he burns the suspected cousin alive, reserving his skull, makes Elena
witness the transfer of all her wifely privileges to her accuser, and then
locks Elena into the tiny room from which don Martín saw her emerge, to
have her degradation specularly and spectacularly renewed nightly.[31] Don
Jaime seeks to deflect toward Elena the wounding gaze of the Other that
haunts his Imaginary by making the cousin's skull the anamorphic object
for *her* rather than for him, the memento mori that will remind her constantly of her sin, and by subjecting her to the nightly sight of her ac-
cuser/supplantor, "viendo cada día la esclava que ella más aborrecía, ador-
nada de sus galas y en el lugar que ella perdió en mi mesa y a mi lado"
(seeing every day the slave she most abhorred adorned with her finery and
in the place that she lost at my table and by my side) (*Desengaños*, 249). In
don Jaime's words, he saved the skull "para que le sirva de vaso en que
beba los acíbares, como bebió en su boca las dulzuras" (so that it might
serve as the cup in which to drink bitterness as she drank sweetness from
his mouth) In her tiny cell, "su compañía es la calavera de su traidor y
amado primo" (her company is the skull of her betraying and beloved
cousin) (*Desengaños*, 249). In Bandello's tale, the sight and stench of the
rotting body of the wife's lover is to play this role; Zayas apparently drew
the use of the skull from Marguerite de Navarre's version of the story in the
Heptameron. François Rigolot (1994) links that skull with the iconography
of repentant sinners, particularly as formulated in the image of Mary Magdalene holding a skull, and perhaps also by the use of the skull as icon of
the redemption from sin through Christ's crucifixion.[32] The irony of its use
in Zayas is that the skull becomes a demonstration of the slippage between
signifier and signified. Only in don Jaime's fantasy can it represent both his
dishonor and Elena's penitence for sin; for don Martín and other view-

ers/readers, it signifies rather the sacrifice of Elena and her cousin to his irrational cruelty.

Elena's name thus furnishes a partial explanation for the relationship between the two episodes in *Desengaño 4*. In the first half of the Boccaccio tale, as in the "Invisible Mistress" story, a woman lures a man into a sexually charged inner space where he is in her power; its second half centers on a torturing confinement of a woman, also the nucleus of the Bandello story. Zayas's use of the name Elena suggests that it was her familiarity with Boccaccio's story that inspired her to link the Bandello tale with the "Invisible Mistress" story. In joining them, Zayas remodels Boccaccio's masculine *contrapasso* into a *trapasso* in which she shows how masculine anxiety that is provoked by the sexual lure and threat posed by one powerful woman is paid for by another woman, powerless and innocent.

The conjunction of two other names provides a clue to Zayas's intuition into the deeper roots of that masculine anxiety, an intuition that may have been unconscious rather than conscious, given the partial displacement of meaning in the *sens*, or signifying direction, of her use of the two names. The meaningful conjunction is that of the name of the protagonist, don Jaime de Aragón, with that of the woman in the first episode, "Madama Lucrecia, princesa de Erne." Obviously, this Lucrecia is no spiritual kin to the virtuous, self-sacrificing Lucrecia much loved as a model of feminine chastity, the Roman matron who committed suicide after being raped by Tarquin.[33] A more succinct writing of Zayas's version of the name Lucrecia, with its appended title, would be Lucrecia de Erne, but for two letters, homophonous with another famous Lucrecia, Lucrezia d'Este, better known as Lucrezia Borgia (1480–1519). That Lucrecia, born to the then-powerful Roman branch of the Aragonese Borja clan, was the daughter of Pope Alexander VI (Rodrigo Borgia) and his longtime mistress, Vannozza Cattanei; and sister to the equally famous and ambitious Cesar. She was legendary for her beauty, her elegance, her participation in the family's crimes and excesses, and the enduring rumors of her incestuous relationships with her brother and her father. They made and broke her several engagements and marriages in their pursuit of political power. She was successively betrothed to two Spanish nobles in 1491, but when Alexander became pope in 1492, fighting with the Sforza family in Milan against the Aragonese dynasty in Naples, she was wed to Giovanni Sforza, duke of Pesaro. Alexander then allied himself with Naples and Milan against the French, and Giovanni fled Rome in fear of his life. Their marriage was annulled in 1497, on the doubtful grounds of nonconsummation; Giovanni later charged the existence of incest between Lucrezia and Alexander. The latter, to strengthen his alliance with Naples, in 1498 married Lucrezia to the seventeen-year-old Alfonso de Aragón, duke of Bisceglie, the illegitimate son of Alfonso II of Naples. Her brother César sent four men to attack and kill Alfonso de Aragón on the steps of St. Peter's;[34] although Alfonso survived that attack, while he was recuperating, a servant of Cesar's killed him, suffocating him with a pillow. Lucrezia was subsequently seen with a mysterious child named Giovanni, whose father was first reputed to be César, later Alexander. The pope then married her to Alfonso d'Este, duke of Ferrara, on December 30, 1501. Alexander died in 1503; the new pope, Julius II, had Cesar arrested; and with his death, Lucrezia withdrew from political activity and dedicated herself to the cultivation of the arts and letters in the court of Ferrara.

In Zayas's "Invisible Mistress" story, we have Lucrecia d'Erne, a rich and powerful young woman living in the house of her aged father, "un príncipe y gran potentado de aquel reino" (a prince and great potentate of that kingdom), "viuda, mas muy moza, por haberla casado niña, de las más bellas damas de aquel país" (a widow, but a very young girl, having been married as a child, one of the most beautiful ladies of that country) (*Desengaños*, 244). Lucrezia Borgia was first engaged at eleven years of age, then wed to Giovanni Sforza at twelve. Zayas's Lucrecia promises don Jaime *de Aragón* that she will make him her husband when her father's death leaves her free to choose. When don Jaime risks courting her openly, six (rather than four) men attack him, and narrowly miss killing him. He is more fortunate than the historical Lucrezia's second husband, Alonso *de Aragón,* in that during don Jaime's recuperation, he is warned in time that he must flee the country to save his life. Zayas adds no open charge of incest in this episode—that accusation is displaced to the second episode, in which the maidservant accuses Elena of an affair with her cousin. In previous versions of this second episode in Bandello and Marguerite de Navarre, the young lover was, respectively, a vassal of the elderly husband and a young gentleman brought up in the husband's household. It is Zayas who makes him a "primo hermano," (first cousin), young, handsome, and "bien entendido" (learned), but poor, whom don Jaime has brought into his household and treated "en lugar de hijo," (as a son) (*Desengaños,* 4). She has thus displaced the idea of incest from the Lucrecia story to its sequel.[35] Although in various Zayas stories, brothers or sisters compete for the same love object, this is the only Zayas story in which the possibility of incestuous desire is raised, however indirectly.[36]

To explain the link between this hint of incestuous desire and Zayas's construction of the masculine anxiety that leads some men to circumscribe women's scope of action, whether it be by denying them access to books and arms, or by imprisoning and starving them within the household, as don Jaime does Elena, I would begin again with everyday experience. It is a common adage of popular psychology that men tend to marry women like their mothers—or polar opposites of them. Adult object choices, according to Freud, are bound to infantile sexual drives and to unresolved attachments to infantile object cathexes. Adult sexuality can never be fully satisfying, because of the irresolvable clash between the Oedipal injunction against incest and the pre-Oedipal object choice, the search for a substitute for the lost primary maternal love object (Grosz 1990, 115). In "The Theme of the Three Caskets" Freud suggests that the three caskets between which Bassanio chooses in *The Merchant of Venice* represent the choice between three forms of woman, or of the mother: "What is represented here are the three inevitable relations that a man has with a woman—the woman who bears him, the woman who is his mate and the woman who destroys him; . . . they are the three forms taken by the figure of the mother in the course of a man's life—the mother herself, the beloved one who is chosen after her pattern, and lastly the Mother Earth who receives him once more" (1974, 12:301). Adult sexual relations are fraught with unnamable "ghosts," the never-quite remembered attachments of the pre-Oedipal past (Grosz 1990, 133). In Zayas's story of successive failures of the sexual relation narrated from the male perspective, it is the not-quite-namable ghost of underlying maternal attachment that hovers on the thresholds of the two episodes of the plots, displaced and condensed as in dream imagery, but retrievable through analysis of the "dream thought," the "grammatical" connection between the elements of the dreamwork.

Lucrecia is related to the lost maternal object not only in the associations of incest attached to her name discussed above, but also in the mythic structure of the "Invisible Mistress" story itself.[37] A young man is mysteriously summoned into a house for a sexual encounter with a woman of great wealth and power whom he must neither see nor name as long as the father lives. As he is drawn deep into the interior of the house, he describes his fear, then the sensual pleasures he finds at its center. The fear as well as pleasure associated with this penetration, and the necessary invisibility of the love object, are both characteristic of the masculine compromise between pre-Oedipal attachment to the mother and the Oedipal injunction against incest. According to Freud, in physically possessing a woman, a man is confronted by the "lack" in her, which he temporarily fills, thus achieving sexual gratification and momentary reassurance of his possession of the phallus, but also receiving a reminder of the possibility of his own castration.[38]

The value of the mystery that draws don Jaime to his assignation, the masking or veiling the object of desire, is also linked to the masculine compound of desire for and fear of this encounter. "The woman can be his object of desire in so far as she 'veils' the 'mysteries' for which he searches, only, that is, in so far as her 'lack' is veiled or hidden. . . . The imaginary vacillation between a yearning for, and fear of, incorporation by the other provides the structural framework within which his fantasies and practices are developed" (Grosz 1990, 136).

The subject's fear of absorption is traced further back into the pre-Oedipal period by Kristeva, in her theory of abjection, the process by which the future subject first endeavors to separate itself from the all-enveloping maternal body, which becomes a sort of "pre-object" or "fallen object." Fear and dread of reabsorption within the unbounded "me"/"not me" space sets the precondition for subsequent castration anxiety and generates rituals of purification that in turn establish sexual difference and a hierarchical sexual order.[39] In Timoneda's *Patraña 16*, threatening/luring female sexuality is much more blatantly revealed—literally as well as figuratively. Threatened by a prediction that his daughter's child would displace him as king, Astiages marries his daughter to a low-ranking man in a faraway country, then orders a trusted servant, Harpago, to kill his newborn grandson. Harpago spares and eventually allies himself with the grandson, Ciro, to overthrow Astiages. In the decisive battle, Astiages

> juntó muy gran hueste y vino sobre Ciro y Harpago y llevándolos de vencida a los soldados que iban huyendo salían las madres y sus mujeres al encuentro, que volviesen a la batalla; y viendo que no querían, alzándose las madres sus haldas y mostrando su [*sic*] vergüenzas, a voces altas decían:
>
> —¿Qués esto? ¿Otra vez queréis entrar en los vientres de vuestras madres?
>
> "Los soldados de vergüenza desto, volvieron a la batalla con gran ánimo. (1986, 258–59)
>
> (assembled a very large force and came against Ciro and Harpago, and facing defeat, the mothers and wives of the soldiers who were

fleeing came out to meet them, [urging them] to return to the battle; and seeing that they didn't want to, their mothers, raising their skirts and showing their genitals [shameful parts], yelled at them: "What is this? Do you want to go back again into the bellies of your mothers?"

The soldiers from shame at this, returned to the battle with great spirit.)

María Antonia Garcés points up the phenomenon of abjection in Cervantes' grotesque scene of Berganza's repulsion at the vision of Cañizares, with her female sexuality "veiled" by the folds of her pendulous stomach, and his horror at enclosure in her tomblike room as she carries out her (Imaginary?) sexual congress with the devil. He drags her and himself out of that enclosure, exposing her diabolic sexuality.

In Zayas's story, the enveloping feminine figure Lucrecia is anything but grotesque; don Jaime describes her "soberanos favores" (unsurpassed—or sovereign—favors) and the "partes realzadas" (preeminent parts) by which he judges her to be "una deidad" (a goddess) and she sends him off with purses full of money and jewels every night. She is a repetition of the nurturing primary maternal figure whom he enjoys in darkness and secrecy, a repetition of the mythical *jouissance* prior to the intromission of the Third term, the paternal law that marks separation, the death of *jouissance* imposed by the *Nom/non du père,* and the emergence of the subject in the Symbolic order.[40] In a characteristically lyrical passage, Kristeva depicts the process of abjecting the maternal as a kind of saving death of the body (me/not me; mother/infant) that illustrates the nearly fatal effect of don Jaime's separation from Lucrecia once he turns toward paternal order law. "An Ego is a body to be put to death, or at least to be deferred, for the love of the Other and so that Myself can be. Love is a death sentence that causes me to be. When death, which is intrinsic to amorous passion, takes place in reality and carries away the body of one of the lovers, it is at its most unbearable; the surviving lover then realizes the abyss that separates the imaginary death that he experienced in his passion from the relentless reality from which love had forever set him apart: saved" (Kristeva 1987, 35–36). The speaking subject recognizes that this mythical *jouissance* is fleeting and ultimately illicit. Don Jaime concludes: "Mas como las venturas fundadas en vicios y deleites perecederos no pueden durar, cansóse la fortuna de mi dicha, y volvió su rueda contra mí" (But since happiness founded on perishable vices and pleasures cannot last, fortune tired of my blessing and turned her wheel against me) (*Desengaños,* 242).

Whereas in the original Psyche myth, the idyllic hidden relationship between Eros and Psyche was interrupted by the jealous "concern" of
Psyche's sisters, in Zayas's story the disruption emanates from envious male
friends. Observing his nightly absences and his newfound wealth, they
speculate that he spends his nights robbing and stealing (*Desengaños*, 243),
and his comrade Baltasar urges him to "volver por vuestra perdida
opinión" (defend your lost reputation)—in effect, to remember and to defend his name, his social position, to acknowledge his subjection to Symbolic-order law. In a comment that recalls Psyche's sisters, he suggests that
"para seguridad de vuestra vida" (for the safety of your life) they must identify the residence of his "amada prenda" (beloved jewel), situate her too
within the Symbolic order. And he offers a telling method of effecting this
identification; he supplies don Jaime with a blood-soaked sponge to mark
the doorway of her house as he enters or leaves. Blood, as we have seen
(see Chapter 5 above), serves as symbol both of violence and of inscription
under the paternal name, in the sacred order. Like the death by bleeding
of doña Mencía in *Desengaño 8,* this blood-marked doorway is powerfully
reminiscent of Calderón's *El médico de su honra* (The Surgeon of His
Honor). Here, I suggest, it functions polysemically, perhaps as another
anamorphic blot that colors the scene differently according to the desiring
perspective of the viewer. It marks an inscription in the patriarchal order
that either prevents or requires the slaughter of the innocent,[41] according
to whether the viewer/hearer/reader associates this stain with the ritual of
Passover or the honor code of *El médico* as dominant referent. Having thus
marked her door, don Jaime presses her to lift the "veil" of darkness and
mysterious anonymity, and the next day begins parading past her windows
in the street, in the company of his friend Baltasar, courting her from outside the house, according to the established codes of courtship, precipitat-
ing her attack against him as a bad keeper of secrets.

   The underlying conflation of mother, phallic mother, and the threat of
death is registered in don Jaime's description of his return to the Gran Canaria on learning that, in his words, "mi amada señora [fue] el juez que me
condenaba a tan precisa y cercana muerte" (my beloved lady [was] the
judge who was condemning me to such a sure and near death) (*Desengaños,* 245). Returning home he finds that "la airada parca había cortado el
hilo de la vida a mi madre" (angry Fate had cut the thread of my mother's
life) (*Desengaños,* 245). The close narrative proximity of these two events
suggests that the near deathblow dealt him by another angry goddess of his
fate, Lucrecia, kills, in a sense, not him but the mother within, to whom his

attachment was nearly fatally repeated in his affair with Lucrecia. His father's death follows within a year, leaving don Jaime rich, at the best of ages, and the object of many marriage proposals. He has survived the Oedipal crisis, but not the repetition compulsion, "porque aún vivía en mi alma la imagen adorada de madama Lucrecia" (because the adored image of Madam Lucrecia still lived in my soul) (*Desengaños*, 246).

As his attachment to Lucrecia was a reduplication of the primary maternal attachment, so Elena is a duplicate of Lucrecia, the beloved chosen in the pattern of the mother, rendered apparently nonthreatening by her powerlessness, her virginity, her poverty, and the living presence of her honorable and saintly mother. His happiness with Elena is undisturbed during the six years that her mother lives. When she dies, don Jaime reports, "sentílo yo más que ella" (I felt it more than she did); the saintly mother serves in his mind as model and insurance of the virtue of the daughter. But two years thereafter, when Elena is for the first time showing symptoms of possible pregnancy, the menace of incest raises its head again, this time as a presumed Oedipal rival in the love affair that the maidservant alleges Elena is carrying on with her first cousin. This raises the other threat posed by the interiority of women's sexuality—that it can harbor another man's child.[42] It is the threat "within the house," so to speak, just as Elena's cousin is a traitor within don Jaime's household, not an external rival. Don Jaime's irrational, instinctive reaction is to physically enclose the feminine sexuality he believes to have escaped his control, forcing her to drink water from the skull of her "lover" as he believes her to have drunk his kisses in life.

In choosing to believe the black servant's accusation rather than Elena's assertion of innocence and in putting her in Elena's place in the household, don Jaime is choosing the "third casket," the third form of woman, the woman who destroys him, woman as the death that inhabits every subject from the moment of birth. She was born in his very household, he says, "nació en mi casa de otra negra y un negro, que siendo los dos esclavos de mis padres los casaron" (born in my house of another black woman and a black man, both of them my parents' slaves, whom they married) (*Desengaños*, 248). As black as Elena is pure white, the servant is described in hyperbolic animalistic terms, giving a portrait of demonic, animalistic sexuality itself. Like the dying black man in the stable who has been the object of Beatriz's passion in *El prevenido engañado* (Forewarned but Not Forearmed), she represents the deathly enslavement to animalistic desire. She is a form of the "enemy within" whom we will encounter again in the final *desengaño* (see Chapter 9 below). But death is the final "feminine" form that don Jaime can neither evade nor confine. He stabs the black maidservant to death, with the wish that she had yet more lives he could take away; but then he finds Elena dead as well, in her cell, a perfect icon of saintly death, God having giving her the reward for the martyrdom to which he subjected her. All don Jaime can do is cry for an equal punishment and for death itself to join him to her again. This too is beyond his control, as don Martín has taken away his dagger and he is reduced to tearing out his beard and hair and ranting incomprehensibly as his reason snaps. The very fear of women that Filis named in the preface as the reason for men's "castration" of women, forbidding them arms and letters, has turned back on him, leaving don Jaime with neither weapons nor the power of rational speech.

Turning Other Tales

In other male-narrated stories, Zayas more subtly turns the tale back against the man who tells it, against the literary model from which it derives, or against both. Frequently, the subversive elements involve some combination of physical confinement of men and feminine laughter at their predicament. The "obscenity" that such readers as Ticknor and Pfandl attributed to the fourth and seventh novellas, *El prevenido engañado* (Forewarned but Not Forearmed) and *Al fin se paga todo* (Just Desserts), may well have been a response to this combination as much as to the sexual content of the stories.[43] If we read *El prevenido* as a picaresque tale, then it is a reworking of the model in which the protagonist is not a poor orphan who becomes a "mozo de muchos amos" (servant of many masters) like Lazarillo, but a young nobleman who is a "mozo de muchas amas" (young man with many mistresses). At the same time, one might follow Grieve's suggestion that Zayas's basic model is the hagiographic tale and see this story in a parodic relationship with saints' lives, particularly given the parade of women who educate/victimize don Fadrique beginning with *Serafina* and ending with her daughter *Gracia*. It shares the highly episodic nature of both genres. The name of his second ladylove is also ironic; this Beatriz does not lead him to a vision of heaven as does Dante's, but down into the back rooms of a stable where he sees her passion for a dying black servant. In the next-to-last episode, a duchess locks him in a cupboard while she makes fun of both don Fadrique and her husband. And the last episode ridicules through literalization the masculine preoccupation with women's obligation to guard men's honor, as don Fadrique sets Gracia to patrolling the bedroom in armor while he sleeps.

The humorous scenes of a man literally entrapped by desire for a woman most proliferate in *Al fin se paga todo*. Here don Gaspar is, in rapid narrative succession, caught in doña Hipólita's garden when her husband returns home unexpectedly; locked in her burning house from which he barely escapes; caught so tightly climbing in a window that he has to run away, frame and all, and get a carpenter to saw him out; and finally, locked in a trunk when her husband comes hurrying home "pidiendo a gran priesa en que hacer las necesidades ordinarias" (asking in a great hurry for something in which to do the ordinary necessities) (*Novelas,* 312). He nearly suffocates in the trunk and revives in the house of her brother-in-law, who threatens to kill him, a combination that finally causes him to renounce his pursuit of her. He makes off only with her "real" jewels (when she flees her house and seeks his protection), not the "jewel" of her honor.[44] That jewel is stolen by her brother-in-law, who sneaks through the attic and slips into her bed after letting the horses out of the stables to draw her husband away. When she realizes the bed-switch that has occurred, she follows the same attack route and kills him, then flees to don Gaspar for protection, only to be robbed, beaten, and thrown out in the street. Another man rescues her and eventually marries her when her husband dies and she inherits his wealth. As are characters in many other Zayas tales, doña Hipólita is involved in several amorous relationships. Charnon-Deutsch suggests that the serial relationships of Zayas's heroines constitute in themselves a subversion of masculine discourse and a potential challenge to patriarchal monogamy. They demonstrate that for both sexually passive and aggressive feminine protagonists, "their sexuality is unrelated to conventional exchange practices and female reproductive functions. Both learn first hand that marriage arrangements are transactions which are irrelevant to their own sexuality" (1991, 25).

In its plot structure, *Al fin se paga todo* would seem to constitute a subtle mockery of the male fantasy of rescuing a beautiful damsel in distress, and of earning the reward of sexual satisfaction, prosperity, and fame to boot.[45] Don Garcia, only "medianamente rico" (moderately wealthy), gets money as well as the lady. Her husband leaves her "heredera de toda su hacienda" (*Novelas,* 326); and she marries him, "haciéndole señor de su belleza y de su gruesa hacienda, que sólo ésta le faltaba para ser en todo perfecto, pues aunque tenía una moderada pasadía, no era bastante a suplir las faltas, que siendo tan noble era fuerza tuviese" (making him lord of her beauty and of her large estate, the only thing he lacked to be absolutely perfect, since although he had enough to get by fairly well, it wasn't enough to supply all the needs which, being so noble, he necessarily had) (327). Various critics have noted the discord between the didactic cliché of the title—reiterated in various ways in the text itself—and the negative exemplarity of the events narrated. Punishment and reward are continually displaced rather than returning to the originator of the censorious or meritorious act.

That masculine fantasy is also visible in the following novella, *El imposible vencido,* although the overall structure therein is not mocking, humorous, or ironic, but a kind of miracle tale of love overcoming death itself. Only one episode contains comic overtones, as the hero don Rodrigo unveils (or unsheets) an embodied "ghost" of desire, an adulterously desiring neighbor who haunts the widowed doña Blanca.[46] Nor is there any humor in the last male-narrated tale in the first volume, *El juez de su causa* (The Judge in Her Own Case). Many readers find the narrative deviation from the traditional Oedipal plot in that tale "sadistic" rather than comic, as the heroine-viceroy Estela prolongs her male disguise and her trial of her lover Carlos (see Chapter 7).

As Zayas articulates the masculine perspective on the relationship between the sexes, she both gives and takes away. She gives voice to masculine desires and fears, conscious and unconscious, following apparently traditional narrative motifs and structures. But in part or in whole, in a variety of ways, in one manner or another, every male-narrated story turns back on its narrator or narrative model to expose the psychic origins of male (mis)treatment—verbal and physical—of the women the men love and fear. The Medusa, cross-voiced, laughs. Yet dares not allow herself the last laugh.

7

The Sexual Masquerade

Cross-Dressing and Gender Definition

Classifying and Declassifying.

How do we grasp what constitutes the being we call "woman"? The first question typically asked about every newborn human being is one of categorization by sex: Is it a boy or a girl? Anxious parents may precede this question with a query about whether the child is healthy or normal. But this is the exception that provides the humor in an old joke about a certain powerful but homely politician. As the story goes, when he was born, his father asked the doctor, " '¿Es hombre o mujer?' El doctor quedó pensando unos momentos y luego contestó lentamente: 'Pues, si en dentro de 10 minutos, no ladra, entonces es hombre.' " ("Is it a boy or a girl?" The doctor stood thinking a few moments before answering slowly: "Well, if within ten minutes, it doesn't bark, then it's a boy.") We might say that the joke therein plays on the human need to categorize, or what Foucault identified as the grounding of culture in the "dividing practices" (1982, 208). The doctor turns the presumably ground-zero question about human nature, Is it a man or a woman? into the yet more basic question, Is it human or animal? The new father surely expected the doctor to base his answer on observation of external bodily characteristics—specifically, the genital formation of the newborn. But the doctor, finding visual clues too ambiguous, had recourse to another, less tangible signifying system—the nature of the creature's "speech," as it were.

The unexpected shift in categorizing and signifying systems that provides the humor in this joke raises a serious issue: the relationship of "nature" and "culture," or of the biological organism and the Symbolic order in the constitution of the human subject. The age-old question of what creates and what signifies the division between man and woman and the nature of gender definition has been variously focused and defined, but the opposing terms all revolve in some sense around delimiting the sphere of operation of the "natural" or morphological and the social—in facetious terms—whether we separate men from women by the nature of the body or how they've been taught to bark. As studies such as those of Fuss, Laqueur, Butler, and many others have shown, however, we can no longer set "nature" or a prediscursive, biologically given sex against a culturally assumed "gender," since the definitions of "nature" and of "sex" have a history that demonstrates their implication in any given socio-political order.[1] While such dissection of the terms of the debate may be new, the issue itself is not: Zayas addressed it both explicitly and implicitly in her preface "Al que leyere" (To the Reader), arguing from both essentialist and constructionist positions without reconciling their logical contradictions, as we have seen.

In several of her tales, Zayas uses cross-dressing to elaborate and personify the interrogation of binary and essentialist gender categories set out in "Al que leyere." The authors of ever increasing numbers of critical studies assert that, however parodically or playfully cross-dressing may be presented, it is at base a serious challenge to stable categorization of gender identity. Zayas also poses this implicit challenge in several of her novellas, demonstrating that it is the roles that are socially prescribed along with the dress assigned to men and women that restricts women's capacities to act, not some inherent intellectual or moral weakness.

Women Dressing Up: *El juez de su causa*

Three stories in the *Novelas amorosas* include cross-dressing episodes in which women dress as men. This female-to-male cross, common in Golden Age *comedias* where it afforded male viewers the pleasure of seeing female legs, was presumably an acceptable transformation for male readers and viewers (strict moralists excepted) because it could be easily explained instrumentally, not as an end or pleasure in itself, but as dressing "up" in the gender hierarchy (Garber 1992, 22, 41, 52–53), and thus a validation of the superiority of the masculine position. Furthermore, from a masculine perspective, it is a doubly validating move, because the young woman in question typically dons male dress in pursuit of a masculine love object. We can see Zayas's implicit recognition of the masculine pleasure in this validation of male superiority in the fact that the one story in which two women don masculine attire, *El juez de su causa* (The Judge in Her Own Case), is told by a male narrator. This is also the only Zayas story in which a woman—the antagonist Claudia rather than the heroine Estela—cross-dresses to pursue the man she loves.

The three Zayas heroines who adopt male dress differ from Claudia in that they do so not assertively but reactively, as a self-defense strategy after they have been made social outcasts by the effects of masculine desire, and by their admission of that desire. The first occurrence is the opening of the first story, *Aventurarse perdiendo* (Venturing and Losing), in which Fabio finds Jacinta dressed as a shepherd boy in Montserrat. Jacinta's male dress is an anomaly in the instances of transvestism in the collection as a whole, since Fabio penetrates her disguise, as do observant characters in Cervantes' tale *Las dos doncellas* (The Two Damsels). Following the sound of her song of lament over Celio's disdain, Fabio tells her that

> viendo en tu rostro y en tu presencia que tu ser no es lo que muestra tu traje, porque ni viene el rostro con el vestido, ni las palabras [de tu canción] con lo que procuras dar a entender, te he buscado, y hallo que tu rostro desmiente a todo, pues en la edad pasas de muchacho, y en las pocas señales de tu barba no muestras ser hombre. (*Novelas*, 42)

> (seeing in your face and in your bearing that your being is not what your attire exhibits—because neither your face matches your dress, not the words [of your song] what you are trying to give one to un-

derstand—I looked for you, and I find that your face gives the lie to everything, for your age is beyond that of a boy, and with little sign of a beard, you do not show yourself to be a man.)

Jacinta's male dress is also anomalous in that it is *purely* defensive, a protective cover for her vulnerability as a woman. Having been rejected by Celio and robbed when she tried to follow him to Salamanca, to buy male clothes she sells a ring the robbers overlooked, cuts her hair, and makes a pilgrimage to Montserrat where she prays to the "Holy Image" for three days and stays there when the friars from whom she begs food offer her the job of shepherd (*Novelas,* 75). Thus, she only hides behind male dress when she has given up active pursuit of satisfaction of her desire.

In the other two works in the *Novelas,* as in most uses of this device by other Golden Age authors of novellas and *comedias,* the heroine succeeds in passing as a male. Given the fact that the role assigned to women in Golden Age Spain dictated for them a social invisibility—silence and withdrawal, humility and modesty—the irony in this impenetrable masculine disguise is that it is on changing to male dress that the woman literally achieves invisibility, for no one sees through the clothes. As Eric Nicholson comments in his survey of early modern European theatre, "The joke is on the male characters, who cannot anticipate such a complete reversal of gender-determination, and hence rarely see through the 'masculine' exterior. At another level, the joke is on members of the audience who would similarly judge identity on the basis of gender roles, and gender on the basis of clothing" (1993, 303). Perhaps to counter the potential discomfort of that "joke" on the audience, female-to-male transvestism in *comedias* frequently includes scenes in which a woman becomes enamored of the cross-dressed *galán* (gallant), a device that situates the ridicule for not penetrating the disguise on women rather than men.[2] Zayas shuns the use of this device against women, but she does "cross-dress" it to ridicule men, as we will see.

In contrast to Jacinta, the heroines of *La burlada Aminta* (Aminta Deceived) and *El juez de su causa* who cross-dress as men take on masculine psychic attributes along with male attire, as well as the freedom of movement allowed only to men. Aminta, the seduced and abandoned heroine of *La burlada Aminta,* even takes on the very pseudonym used by her seducer, Jacinto, when she cross-dresses to pursue him and exact her revenge.[3] Refusing to allow her second admirer and eventual husband don Martín to avenge her, she insists on redressing the stain on her honor herself by stabbing him and his lover Flora to death. The narrator comments on Aminta/"Jacinto's" first encounter with "Jacinto"/Francisco: "Es de creer, que fue necesario el ánimo que el traje varonil le iba dando, para no mostrar su sobresalto y flaqueza" (We can believe she needed the courage the manly attire gave her not to show fear and weakness) (*Novelas*, 110). Paul Julian Smith, noting the superficial conservatism of Zayas's texts, says that an occasional female rebellion such as that of Aminta does not provide an alternative social model in her stories: "The woman displaces the man, but only by reproducing masculine actions and values. Zayas implies an acceptance of the patriarchal code of honor. . . . Women are thus permitted to adopt a travesty of man, but cannot transgress the law of the dagger and the phallus" (1989, 33). More accurate would be to say that, aside from the polemical attacks on that order in frame sections of the collection, Zayas gives us no diegetic vision of women definitively *overturning* that law. Her interrogation of its legitimacy appears, rather, in subtle modifications in traditional narrative paradigms, including her use of the motif of cross-dressing.

Zayas, as noted, restricts her use of the classic formula of a cross-dressed woman pursuing an elusive male lover to a feminine antagonist. Claudia, in *El juez de su causa*, dresses as a page boy to enter the service of don Carlos in hopes of turning his affections away from Estela, the heroine of the story. When this fails, she renounces the Christian faith in order to marry a Moor. She is eventually condemned by the good Moorish prince Xacimín to die on a stake. According to Zayas's stated code of sexual ethics, a woman who would take off her "traje y opinión por seguir [su] gusto" (dress and reputation to follow her pleasure) (*Novelas*, 378) and then renounce her faith to boot was dying the death appropriate to a renegade (*Novelas*, 388). She has renounced the feminine position of "being" the Phallus, the object of masculine desire, to pursue her desire actively, thus adopting the masculine position vis-à-vis desire as well as attire, and she dies impaled on Symbolic-order law.

Immediately after Claudia meets this death, Estela elects to dress as a man and go to serve the emperor Carlos V in Tunis rather than return directly to Spain with the escort that the Moorish prince had provided for her. Comparison of this story with Lope's version in *Las fortunas de Diana* is instructive.[4] Despite Lope's running play with literary models and satire of the conventions of the novella, he rationalizes and naturalizes the progression of Diana to the exalted post of viceroy. Her adoption of male dress is a logical step after she has given birth to Celio's child in the country and, to make her cross-dressing visually plausible for the reader, he says: "Era Diana bien hecha y de alto y proporcionado cuerpo, no tenía el rostro afeminado, conque pareció luego un hermoso mancebo" (Diana was well built, with a tall and well-shaped body, [and] she didn't have an effeminate face, and thereby she looked right away like a handsome youth) (1988, 74). With wit, artistic talent, and skill at arms, she wins the attention of ever higher nobles, and Lope even justifies her skill with arms by saying that she had in her home used the arms with which her brother practiced fencing. Much of this "realism" is tongue-in-cheek, of course, and Lope twice underlines the fictionality of its conclusion. Although Diana finds Celio in jail in Cartagena, she does not reveal her identity to him until they have returned to Seville and kissed the king's hand. Lope explains the delay in another *intercolunio* or metaliterary commentary:

> Pienso, y no debo de engañarme, que vuestra merced me tendrá por desalentado escritor de novelas, viendo que tanto tiempo he pintado a Diana sin descubrirse a Celio después de tantos trabajos y desdichas; pero suplico a vuestra merced me diga, si Diana se declarara y amor ciego se atreviera a los brazos, ¿cómo llegara este gobernador a Sevilla? (1988, 99)

> (I think, and I doubt I'm wrong, that your grace probably considers me a dispirited story writer, seeing that I have gone on so long painting Diana not revealing herself to Celio, after so many trials and misfortunes; but I beg your grace to tell me, if Diana declares who she is and blind love held out its arms, how would this governor reach Seville?)

And he ends the story by asking his beloved fictional reader to imagine the happiness of the lovers for herself while he leaves for Toledo to tell her mother and brother of the happy outcome. Lope thus plays with making the inconceivable aspect of such a gender cross almost verisimilar.

Zayas, in contrast, offers no motivation for Estela's decision to become a soldier nor any explanation of why her physical transformation is convincing. With equally unmotivated abruptness, when Estela as viceroy finally reveals her identity, pardons Carlos, and rejects the count to whom her parents had promised her in marriage, she says that:

> ella era mujer de Carlos, por quien quería cuanto poseía, y que le pesaba no ser señora del mundo para entregárselo todo; pues sus valerosos hechos nacían todos del valor que el ser suya le daba, suplicando, tras esto, a su padre lo tuviese por bien. (*Novelas*, 398)

(she was the wife of Carlos, for whom she desired everything she possessed, and was sorry she couldn't be mistress of the world to give it all to him; for her courageous acts were all born of the courage that belonging to him gave her, begging, thereafter, that her father should approve of it.)

Her post as viceroy of Valencia is then transferred to Carlos along with the habit of Santiago she had been awarded, while she is made princess of Buñol. The most striking aspect of this episode is the lengthy ordeal to which Estela subjects Carlos, delaying for months the revelation of her identity, raising his hopes of a pardon, and then keeping him on his knees before her in fear for his life during his trial while she as viceroy denounces him for doubting the loyalty of Estela. This episode is an ordeal for many readers as well. Pfandl called it a "sádica y espeluznante historia" (sadistic and horrifying story) (1933, 369) and Chevalier's judgment is similar: compared to Lope's *Las fortunas de Diana*, Zayas "acentúa el carácter artificial del episodio la delectación morosa de Estela—hablaría de sadismo si la palabra no estuviera ya desvirtuada por el uso y abuso que se hace de ella—, cuya justificación se le escapa al lector, dado que no se ve claramente en qué pecó Carlos contra las leyes del amor" (Estela's lingering enjoyment accentuates the artificial character of the episode—I would speak of sadism if the word had not already been made meaningless by the use and abuse made of it—whose justification escapes the reader, since he does not see clearly in what manner Charles sinned against the laws of love) (Chevalier 1982, 31). Pardo Bazán finds it perhaps the weakest of Zayas's stories: "Si *El castigo de la miseria* es una perla, *El juez de su causa* me parece muy endeble y asaz embrollada fábula; tal vez en ninguna de sus narraciones dormitó así doña María" (If *A Miser's Reward* is a pearl, *The Judge of Her Own Case* seems to me a very weak and entangled tale; perhaps in no other narrative is Zayas so caught napping) (c. 1892, 14–15).

Critics interested in feminine narrative strategies, however, are now showing us that such "defects" may be deliberate. Charnon-Deutsch makes a persuasive case for regarding Estela's delay in returning power to its "proper" male locale as a feminist subversion of traditional masculine (narrative) structures, however partial and limited by Zayas's inscription in a conservative, patriarchal ideology. Patricia Parker traces out a relationship over the centuries of verbal *copia*, or excess, ascribed to women with a similarly gendered strategy of *dilatio* and deferral,[5] of not proceeding quickly and economically to the (phallic) point either verbally or erotically, but rather entangling the thread of discourse and prolonging the consummation:[6] "The final context for 'dilation' is an erotic one within a specific masculinist tradition—the putting off of coitus or consummation which Andres Capellanus describes as a feminine strategy in the art of love, a purportedly female plot in which holding a suitor at a distance creates the tension of a space between as well as an intervening time" (Parker 1987, 16). Such "dilation" affords a certain power to the feminine position, a "Penelope's web" of prattle that holds off suitors, and can even constitute a kind of feminine rebellion, as in *A Midsummer Night's Dream*. This is so however provisionally and inevitably curtailed it may be, in a masculine tradition, by the reassertion of the telos of feminine submission to masculine dominance (Parker 1987, 18–20).

At the same time, if we remember that the story is narrated by don Juan, we can again see Zayas's understanding of unconscious male fears of powerful women operative in the extension of Estela's "sadistic" manipulation of the vulnerable Carlos. Using a male narrator is a psychologically inspired way of escaping from the impasse of imagining such feminine possession of power in the social structures that Zayas knew; inconceivable as a logical possibility from a conservative feminine position, such empowerment could be imagined through a male narrator, for whom it would exist in unconscious fantasies.

Comparative examination of pronoun usage and related grammatical markers of gender can also tell us something about Zayas's play with gender categories in these episodes. Marjorie Garber in her study of transvestism and transsexuality states that pronoun usage is as significant as surgical intervention in the transformation of sexual identity (1992, 100, 117). Describing Jacinta dressed as a shepherd boy in Montserrat in the first episode of *Adventurarse perdiendo* (Venturing and Losing), Zayas uses masculine nouns and pronouns, but only after Fabio has heard her gentle, delicate voice singing of Celio's fickle ingratitude. She plays off references to the "mozo" (youth) and "hermoso zagal" (handsome lad) against other classic markers of feminine beauty—her snow white hands and beautiful complexion untouched by the sun that clearly mark this as a traditional scene of a lovelorn lady, a narrative cousin of the cross-dressed Dorotea in *Don Quixote* whom Cardenio found bathing her snow white feet in the Sierra Morena (Cervantes Saavedra 1971, 176).

In narrating the story of *La burlada Aminta* (Aminta Deceived) crossdressed as Jacinto, Zayas regularly calls her Aminta and "ella," the procedure that Lope also consistently follows in *Las fortunas de Diana*. Saying that her masculine dress has given her boldness, Zayas invests with dramatic irony Aminta/Jacinto's meeting with her seducer Jacinto/don Francisco, as the latter says that s/he resembles a person whom he loved for twenty-four hours, and that "porque tú le pareces tanto, quiero que me sirvas, por verme servido de un retrato, de quien yo serví, que es gloria ver rendido a quien ha sido señor, aunque sea en figura" (because you look so much like her, I want you to serve me, to see myself served by a portrait of the one whom I served, because it's glorious to see someone humbled who has been one's master, even if it's only in a likeness) (*Novelas,* 111). To this, Aminta responds that "si por ser retrato de esa persona, me recibas en tu servicio, tengo que agradecer a naturaleza, que me ha hecho en su estampa, porque de mí te digo, que desde el punto que te vi, te quise bien" (if for being a portrait of that person, you receive me into your service, I must thank nature, which has made me in her likeness, because as for me, I say that from the moment I saw you, I loved you well) (*Novelas,* 111). His lover Flora, less deceived by her male disguise, strongly suspects that "Jacinto" really is Aminta, but fears to tell him that lest it remind him of his previous passion for Aminta.

In the Claudia/Claudio cross portion of *El juez de su causa,* the narrator employs "Claudio" and "él" only when s/he is clearly being viewed through the eyes of another character who sees her as male, and the same procedure applies to the cross-dressed Estela while she is don Fernando. When she is made viceroy, however, that procedure changes, and the transitional procedure is highly significant. The passage is as follows:

> Ve aquí a *nuestra Estela Virrey de Valencia,* y a don Carlos su Secretario y el más contento del mundo, pareciéndole que con el padre alcalde no tenía que temer a su enemigo, y así se lo dió a entender *su señor.*
>
> Satisfecho iba don Carlos de que *el Virrey* lo estaba de su inocencia en la causa de Estela, con lo cual ya se tenía por libre, seguro de sus promesas.
>
> Partieron, en fin, con mucho gusto, y con el mismo llegaron a Valencia, donde fué recibido *el Virrey* con muestras de grande alegría. (*Novelas,* 391–92; emphasis added)
>
> (Here you see *our Estela Viceroy of Valencia,* and don Carlos her/his[7] Secretary and the happiest man in the world, believing that with "his father as mayor" he did not have to fear his enemy, and he indicated this to *his lord.*

Don Carlos went along satisfied that *the Viceroy* was convinced of his innocence in Estela's case, with which he considered himself free, sure of his/her promises.

They departed, finally, with much pleasure, and with the same pleasure arrived in Valencia, where *the Viceroy* was received with shows of great happiness.)

The first reference directed to the reader is to the dual figure Estela/Virrey de Valencia; the next names only the viceroy, seen by Carlos as his lord. The third is to the viceroy seen in "his" popular welcome to Valencia. From this point forward, over and over, Zayas has her narrator refer to "el Virrey" and "él," only twice naming Estela from the narrator's point of view to call forth the woman within the official viceregal body. There are, of course, numerous references to "Estela" from the third-person perspective both by the viceroy and by Carlos, when they discuss the history of his case. But only when Estela finally reveals her identity to Carlos and the assembled audience at the end of the trial is a feminine pronoun again applied to her. In her final diatribe against Carlos for suggesting that Estela might have left with the page Claudio, "ella mujer y él hombre. Quizá . . ." (she a woman and he a man. Perhaps . . .) (*Novelas*, 397), Estela attacks his assumption that sexual difference determines conduct. She focuses on ethical and class qualities that prevail over sex or gender role played:

Ni Estela era mujer ni Claudio hombre; porque Estela es noble y virtuosa, y Claudio un hombre vil, criado tuyo y es heredero de tus falsedades. Estela te amaba y respetaba como a su esposo, y Claudio la aborrecía porque te amaba a ti. Y digo segunda vez que Estela no era mujer, porque la que es honesta, recatada y virtuosa, no es mujer, sino ángel. Ni Claudio hombre, sino mujer, que enamorada de ti, quiso privarte della, quitándola delante de tus ojos. Yo soy la misma Estela, que se ha visto en un millón de trabajos por tu causa, y tú me lo gratificas en tener de mí la falsa sospecha que tienes. (*Novelas*, 397)

(Neither was Estela a woman nor Claudio a man; because Estela is noble and virtuous, and Claudio a common man, your servant and inheritor of your falsehoods. Estela loved you and respected you as her husband and Claudio hated her because she loved you. And I say again that Estela wasn't a woman, because she who is honest, modest, and virtuous is not a woman but an angel. Nor was Claudio a man, but rather a woman who, in love with you, wanted to steal you from her, taking her away before your very eyes. I am that same Estela, who has seen a million trials for your sake, and you thank me for it with the false suspicions you hold.)

Blaise Pascal, in "Three Discourses on the Condition of the Greats," tells the story of a commoner shipwrecked on an island who was proclaimed king when the populace saw in him a duplicate of their lost king.[8] By a similar process, Estela becomes the (masculine) body of Symbolic power, of phallic authority, when she is so (mis)recognized by others. At least in this story, Zayas's pronoun usage shows gender identity and the different roles culturally attached to them as a fiction, as little motivated by any essential difference in the two sexes as her manner of plotting Estela's transformation. If Aminta, within masculine dress, drew courage from it to assume the phallic role culturally ascribed to the masculine position, Estela in masculine dress finds her authorization in the gaze of the Other.

Do Clothes Make the Woman? *Desengaño 5, La inocencia castigada*

Clothes sometimes do indeed make the man, Zayas would seem to indicate—but do they make the woman? In the *Desengaños amorosos,* the primary transvestite mode is reversed, since, in two stories, males cross-dress as females.[9] Such transformations were rare both on the Golden Age stage and in the novella tradition. Alan Paterson, studying androgynous characters in three dramas of Tirso, comments: "The contrast between the frequency of female transvestite roles and infrequency of the male equivalent is enough to suggest a censoring mechanism in the anthropology of that society; maleness implied an essential security (legal, civil, religious) which was not to be exposed to enquiry on the public forum of the stage" (Paterson 1993, 106). But two notable women writers did expose maleness to that sort of inquiry—Sor Juana, in *Los empeños de una casa,* and Zayas, in her *Desengaños.*[10]

The reversal begins with the second story, *Desengaño 2, La más infame venganza* (The Most Infamous Revenge), a story of vengeance carried out by means of cross-dressing that parallels in reverse gender Aminta's re-

venge in the second novella, *La burlada Aminta*. While Don Juan is out of
the country, his beautiful sister Octavia has been seduced on promise of
marriage by the son of a rich senator of Milan, Carlos. Under pressure
from his father, Carlos eventually sends her to a convent so that he may
marry a richer, though plain and innocent, young woman named Camila.
Summoned back to the country by Octavia when she learns of the marriage, Don Juan attempts to exact revenge not by killing Carlos but by
courting and seducing Camila. When she ignores his attentions, he dresses
in one of his sister's best dresses and, presenting himself as a noblewoman
who must keep her face and identity veiled by a cape, gains access to
Camila's chamber and rapes her at the point of a dagger. Then with the
cape thrown back, he stalks out of the house ordering all who heard him in
the house and through the city streets to tell Carlos that "ya yo me he ven-
gado quitándole el honor con su mujer, como él me le quitó a mí con mi
hermana; que yo soy don Juan hermano de Octavia" (I have now avenged
myself taking away his honor with his wife, as he took away mine with my
sister; that I am don Juan, brother of Octavia) (*Desengaños*, 193). Camila
takes refuge in a convent and when the senator convinces his son that he
should bring her back to live as his wife, he refuses to eat or sleep with her,
and eventually poisons her. Rather than her dying immediately, her whole
body swells monstrously, causing her six months of suffering before her
death. Both Carlos and don Juan disappear and the senator, having no
other sons, remarries to sire new male offspring.

The form in which Zayas narrates this episode illuminates from several
angles the paradox voiced by so many heroes of Golden Age dramas, who
ponder why a man's honor is lodged in such a "fragile vessel" as woman.
From a Lacanian perspective, the basic answer to that query is easier to see.
The masculine subject has undergone a double (symbolic) castration—
first, the loss of the mythical *jouissance* of infant union with the (m)Other
and his emergence as subject of language; and second, the relinquishing
of his incestuous desire for the maternal body in exchange for the identification with the Name-of-the-Father that undergirds his masculine gender
identity. Thereafter, having surrendered a pre-Oedipal and Oedipal *jouissance* of the phallic mother, his maintenance of the masculine illusion of
having the phallus is heavily invested in defending his right to the enjoyment of a restricted set of feminine substitutes and of prohibiting access to
them by any competitors. Since Carlos has violated don Juan's phallic authority by seducing his sister, he takes revenge not by killing him but by violating Camila. Zayas has Lisis recognize the nature of this investment in

her concluding frame-tale absolution of Camila (see below). Retaliatory enjoyment of another man's woman is neither new nor necessarily tragic in the novella tradition. Boccaccio's *Decameron,* day 8, story 8, is a comic version that ends in a happy decision to continue wife-sharing. What is interesting about the Zayas story is the way in which she dresses this offense in women's clothes, figuratively as well as literally. The story is narrated by Lisarda, Lisis's cousin and rival for the affections of another don Juan, who takes pains not to alienate him with her storytelling:

> Ocupó la hermosa Lisarda el asiento situado para las que habían de desengañar, temerosa de haber de mostrarse apasionada contra los hombres, estando su amado don Juan presente; mas, pidiéndole licencia con los hermosos ojos, como si dijera: "Más por cumplir con la obligación que por ofenderte hago esto," empezó así. (*Desengaños,* 171)

> (The lovely Lisarda occupied the seat put in place for the women who were to be disenchanters, fearful of having to display herself impassioned against men, in the presence of her beloved don Juan; but begging license with her lovely eyes, as if saying: "I do this more to fulfill my obligation than to offend you," she thus began).

Lisarda introduces her story with hyperbolic expressions of humility and an apology for speaking without personal experience, since she has neither been disillusioned nor misused by men. Throughout her narrative, she shifts a significant part of the blame for the victimization of innocent women such as Camila to other women, for allowing themselves to be deceived and for the way they do or do not seek revenge.[11] At the conclusion of her story, she repeats this tactic, saying:

> No tengo que decir a las damas otro desengaño mayor que haber oído el que he contado, mas de que ni las culpadas ni las sin culpa están seguras de la desdicha, que a todas se extiende su jurisdicción; y si esta desdicha la causan los engaños de los hombres o su flaqueza, ellas mismas lo podrán decir, que yo, como he dicho, si hasta ahora no conozco los engaños, mal podré avisar con los desengaños. (*Desengaños,* 196)

> (I don't have to tell ladies another and greater disillusionment than having heard the one I have told, except that neither guilty women

nor blameless ones are safe from misfortune, whose jurisdiction extends to all; and if that misfortune is caused by the deceits of men
or by their own weakness, they themselves can say, for I, as I have
said, not having known deceits thus far, can ill advise them with
disillusionments.)

With this disclaimer, she concludes, "congojada y sonrosada . . . por ir
huyendo de culpar de todo punto a los hombres en las desdichas que suce-
den a las mujeres, por no enojar a don Juan" (anxious and blushing . . . to
escape from blaming men on all counts for the misfortunes that happen to
women, in order not to anger don Juan) (*Desengaños,* 196). By having Lisarda narrate this "disillusionment" from such an ambivalent position,
Zayas demonstrates the complicity of desiring women—Lisarda as well as
Octavia—in the perpetuation of a system that makes women both victims
of male misuse and instruments of the victimization of other women.
Camila, however, rejects all don Juan's attentions, stepping out of this lop-
sided circuit of desire. Therefore, he must *literally* don women's clothes to
overcome her inaccessibility. Even so, numerous voices throughout the
city—including the frame character doña Isabel (erstwhile "slave" of her
lover and future nun)—attach some blame to her for not informing her
husband of don Juan's courtship, and even suggest that Carlos had the
right to kill her. Zayas gives Lisis the last word to refute this idea, however,
and to place blame on men, for their competitive investment in enjoyment
of women, and for the mobility of their desire:

> El celoso, no porque ama más guarda la dama, sino por temor de
> perderla, envidioso de que lo que es suyo ande en venta para ser de
> otro, y así, no mató a Camila eso, que siento que hizo como cuerda
> y honesta, pareciéndole, como lo hiciera si el falso don Juan no bus-
> cara aquella invención diabólica para su venganza, que su resisten-
> cia y recato la libraran del deshonesto amor de don Juan. No la
> mató, como digo, sino la crueldad de Carlos, que como se cansó de
> Octavia, siendo hermosa y no teniéndola por propia, hastío que em-
> palaga a muchos o a todos, también le cansaría Camila. (*Desengaños,*
> 196)

> (The jealous man doesn't guard his lady because he loves her more,
> but rather for fear of losing her, envious that what is his might be on
> the market to belong to another, and thus [not telling Carlos about

don Juan] didn't kill Camila, for I think that she acted wisely and honestly, in the opinion that—as would have been the case if the false don Juan had not employed that diabolic invention for his revenge—her resistance and modesty would free her from the dishonest love of don Juan. Nothing killed her, as I say, except Carlos's cruelty, for as he tired of Octavia, being lovely and not being his own wife, a surfeit that is cloying to many or all men, he probably tired of Camila as well.)

This cross-dressing episode in *Desengaño 2* is brief, and while its consequences temporarily disrupt orderly succession within the paternal order, it never threatens the stability of the binary system of gender categories. Such a destabilization does occur, however, in *Desengano 6, Amar sólo por vencer* (Love for the Sake of Conquest), which involves a lengthy and elaborate transvestite sequence. A young man, Esteban, disguises himself as Estefanía to be close to Laurela, the girl he desires and whom he successfully seduces and then abandons. In order to explain Zayas's allusive-elusive interrogation of gender identification and object choice in this tale, however, we must consider this story in sequence, in the light of the preceding and following novellas.

The preceding *Desengaño 5, La inocencia castigada* (Innocence Punished) also involves the symbolic, instrumental and imaginary value of a woman's clothes. A young gallant, don Diego, falls in love with doña Inés, a beautiful and virtuous young married woman. She pays no attention to his courtship, but a woman neighbor notices his campaign and arranges for don Diego to enjoy "the lady" several nights in a dark, remote trysting place. "The lady" is, in fact, not doña Inés, but "una mujer de oscura vida" (a woman of a low life) dressed in doña Inés's dress, which the neighbor has borrowed for two weeks. Learning eventually that he has had no more of doña Inés than her dress, don Diego renews his courtship of the lady herself, again in vain, despite her husband's absence from the city. Don Diego then has recourse to a Moorish magician who makes him a wax effigy of doña Inés, naked and with an arrowlike pin in her heart, which has the power to summon her to his bed whenever he lights a candle on top of it. She arises from her own bed in a trance, puts on no more than a petticoat and comes to do his bidding until he sends her home, where she awakens as if from a bad dream. Although don Diego finds these favors "muertos" (lifeless), because the lady never speaks, he summons her repeatedly over a month until one night her brother and the corregidor see her in the street in her nightgown. She is declared innocent of guilt for her actions while enchanted, but her brother, husband, and sister-in-law wall her up in a chimney where she can only stand or squat in the dark, losing her sight and the flesh of her legs, gradually consumed by her own excrement, as the sister-in-law keeps her alive on scraps of food and water to prolong her agony.[12] After six years, she is rescued when a widow given the room adjacent in the neighboring house hears her lamenting prayers through the wall and notifies the lady of the house, who summons the religious and legal authorities. After they nurse her back to health, her beauty returns but not her eyesight, and Inés goes to live in a convent, while her brother, husband, and sister-in-law are executed for their cruelty.

I read this story as a fascinating study of the futile attempt to grasp the "essence" of woman. Lacan argues that there is no signifier for *The* woman, that she is, within the phallic function *not all*—not all bounded by Symbolic order language and law:

> When any speaking being whatever lines up under the banner of women it is by being constituted as not all that they are placed within the phallic function. It is this that defines the . . . the what?— the woman precisely, except that *The* woman can only be written with *The* crossed through. There is no such thing as *The* woman, where the definite article stands for the universal. There is no such thing as *The* woman since of her essence—having already risked the term, why think twice about it?—of her essence, she is not all. (Lacan 1982, 144)

She is not less complete than man, nor lacking anything in the Real; rather, there is in the feminine position something more, the possibility of a *jouissance* beyond the phallus, beyond symbolization within the phallic function of language. For the masculine subject, who *is* wholly alienated within language, she represents the enigma of the lack-in-being (*manque-à-être*) that initiates desire and the site/sight on which he elaborates the fantasy of wholeness in a sexual relationship that would somehow "plug up" that gap in being. But the two sexes are not complementary, except in fantasy; each seeks in a sexual partner not the particularity of an individual being but an image of the Other sex that would fill his or her lack.

Laura, the narrator of this tale, recognizes that even harmonious relationships between the sexes rest on deception and pleasure-producing delusions. Lisis's widowed mother prefaces her tale with the statement that she cannot "disenchant" from personal experience because she lived "dulcemente engañada" (sweetly deceived) with her husband, whose loving nature gave her no cause to know and recount disenchantments. Furthermore, she says, both men and women deceive each other, and ignore contrary evidence to persist in that state of delusion:

> Y así, las mujeres se quejan de sus engaños, y los hombres de los suyos. Y esto es porque no quieren dejar de estarlo; porque paladea tanto el gusto esto de amar y ser amados que, aunque los desengaños se vean a los ojos, se dan por desentendidos y hacen que no los conocen. (*Desengaños*, 262)

> (And thus, women complain of their [men's] deceits, and men of those of women. And this is because they don't want to stop being deluded; because this loving and being loved is so savory to their taste that, although the disillusionments may be right before their eyes, they pretend not to understand and act as if they didn't recognize them.)

The phrase that Zayas employs in describing this willed delusion makes a striking connection between an infant being encouraged to nurse and a pleasurable, deceptive substitution. The *Diccionario de Autoridades* (1737) gives two meanings for the verb "paladear": (1) "poner al recien nacido miel u otra cosa suave en el paladar, para que con aquel dulce o sabor se aficione al pecho y mame sin repugnancia ni dificultad" (to put honey or some other sweet thing on a newborn's palate, so that with that sweet or flavor he develops a liking for the breast and nurses without repugnance or difficulty); and (2) "metafóricamente, vale aficionar a alguna cosa, o quietar el deseo de ella, por medio de otra, que dé gusto y entretenga" (metaphorically, it means to induce a liking for something or to calm the desire for it by means of something else that gives pleasure and entertains).

Don Diego, having fixed on Inés as the object of his desire, is delighted with his trysts with the woman masquerading as Inés in her dress and manner. Thus, Zayas demonstrates that it is not the particularity of a woman's being that the man seeks, but the form that fits his fantasy.[13] Like the *objet a* that is the cause of masculine desire, Inés's dress is an empty form filled out by his fantasy of the ideal woman, the cause of his desire. On the Lacanian diagram of the relationship of the drive around the goal of *jouissance* in its relationship to the three orders, Inés's dress would occupy the

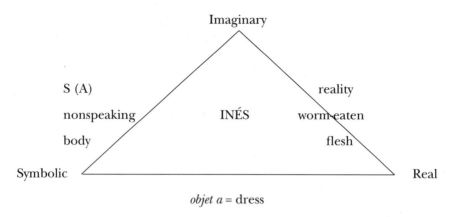

objet a = dress

position of the *objet a,* the masculine drive to reach the Real from the Symbolic order (see diagram).

With the help of the Moorish magician, don Diego next succeeds in the reverse: summoning Inés's body without the dress. Although he can "light her flame," draw her physical being to his bed at will, don Diego finds that it too is less than satisfying, since it/she will not speak. He can command her flesh with this "demonic enchantment" but not her reason, judgment, or will. When he asks her to confirm that having her in his arms and in his bed is not a dream,

> doña Inés no respondía palabra; que viendo esto el amante, algo pesaroso, por parecerle que doña Inés estaba fuera de su sentido con el maldito encanto, y que no tenía facultad para hablar, teniendo aquéllos, aunque favores, por muertos, conociendo claro que si la dama estuviera en su juicio, no se los hiciera. (*Desengaños,* 277–78)

> (doña Inés didn't utter a word; and seeing this the lover, somewhat sorrowful, for it seemed to him that doña Inés was out of her senses with the accursed spell, and she had no capacity to speak, [therefore] considered those actions lifeless, although they were favors, recognizing clearly that if the lady were in her right mind, she would not grant them.)

He comes little closer to possessing Inés in her flesh than he did when enjoying the prostitute in her dress. "She" is elsewhere. On our diagram, this nonspeaking body would fall on the slope between the Symbolic and the

Imaginary, in the position of the barred truth of the Other. When the patrolling officers and her brother see Inés, entranced and in her nightdress on her way to don Diego's house, her brother proclaims her innocent, and the legal system concurs. The Moorish magician having disappeared, only don Diego is condemned by the Inquisition.

But doña Inés has violated the paternal law, the *Nom-du-Père*, and her relatives, not content with the legal verdict, "grasp" her physically and wall her in, condemning her to a death-in-life, as the flesh that had escaped their control is consumed and the darkness blinds her to the world. Zayas describes in revolting detail her appearance when she is rescued from her stinking tomb in the wall: blind, her blond hair turned white and teeming with vermin, her deathly pallor and cadaverous emaciation, the furrows tears have made in her face, and worst of all, the worm-eaten wounds to the bone on her legs and thighs.

> En primer lugar, aunque tenía los ojos claros, estaba ciega, o de la oscuridad . . . u de llorar, . . . Sus hermosos cabellos, que cuando entró allí eran como hebras de oro, blancos como la misma nieve, enredados y llenos de animalejos, que de no peinarlos se crían en tanta cantidad, que por encima hervoreaban; el color, de la color de la muerte; tan flaca y consumida, que se le señalaban los huesos, como si el pellejo que estaba encima fuera un delgado cendal; desde los ojos hasta la barba, dos surcos cavados de las lágrimas, que se le escondía en ellos un bramante grueso; los vestidos hechos ceniza, que se le veían las más partes de su cuerpo; descalza de pie y pierna, que de los excrementos de su cuerpo, como no tenía donde echarlos, no sólo se habían consumido, mas la propia carne comida hasta los muslos de llagas y gusanos, de que estaba lleno el hediondo lugar. (*Desengaños,* 287)

(In the first place, although her eyes were clear, she was blind, either from the darkness . . . or from crying. . . . Her lovely tresses, which when she entered were strands of gold, white as the very snow, tangled and full of little animals that breed in such quantity when hair is not combed, that teemed on top of it; her color, the color of death, so thin and emaciated that her bones showed as if the skin on top of them were but a thin veil; from her eyes to her chin, two furrows dug by her tears, as if a thick cord lay hidden in them; her clothes turned to ashes so that most parts of her body were visible; her feet and legs bare, because the excrement from her body, since she had nowhere to dispose of it, had not only eaten into them, but her very flesh was eaten up to the thighs with wounds and worms, which filled the stinking place.)

She is made a vision of the horror of human death and decomposition, as her flesh nourishes the lowest form of animal life. On our graph, this vision of Inés resides on the slope between the Real and the Imaginary, the reality of the death that inhabits life and the life that inhabits death, closely associated in the unconscious and multiple cultural images with woman as *mater* and matter.

Some aspect of doña Inés as woman is contained in each of these images, as she is (mis)recognized by other subjects in the Imaginary and Symbolic orders, and each of these images is in part an effect of the Real as it is distorted in the phantasmatic, subjective perception of "reality." But no one image, nor the overlapping of the three, contains her totality. We can situate the hypothetical essence Inés in the center of the triangle, as the Being whose full enjoyment is the object around which the drives of others circulate but that they never attain. Her "essence" as Woman resists symbolization, it "ex-sists" in the Lacanian sense described by Zizek. The impossibility of fully grasping "Inés" in any of these images shows us "this exsistence of the real, of the Thing embodying impossible enjoyment, that is excluded by the very advent of the symbolic order. . . . it is precisely woman that 'exsists,' i.e., that persists as a leftover of enjoyment beyond meaning, resisting symbolization, which is why, as Lacan puts it, woman is 'the *sinthome* of man' "[14]

Yet doña Inés does survive to be rescued by another woman, a widow like the narrator, who from a physically and socially marginal position overhears her lament and prayers for release through the wall. Does Zayas mean us to read that there is some inner, essential bond between women, which can rescue womanhood if we can break through the isolating walls imposed by patriarchal order? This would be a satisfying reading for political feminism, and would seem to be supported by a number of explicit statements by Zayas's female narrators. Yet she undercuts it within the framework of this same story, identifying other women as her cruelest enemies—the neighbor who borrowed her dress for gain and the heartless sister-in-law, whose excuse is that she only did her husband's bidding, but was the first to suggest that Inés might have been enjoying herself under false cover of enchantment.[15] Furthermore, the moralizing commentary of the framing listeners speaks as much of bad women as of good, and Zayas implicitly contrasts the justice and charity of doña Inés's treatment by the higher religious and legal *institutions* of patriarchy with the cruelty and egotism of individuals linked to her by sexual desire and by family ties.

Significantly, although this story is told by Laura, Lisis's mother, her narrative shows us Inés primarily through masculine eyes and the collective eye of the patriarchal social order and its legal institutions.[16] First we see her through don Diego's eyes, then through those of the assemblage of men who see her wandering the streets in her chemise at night, and then through the eyes of her brother and husband, as well as the sister-in-law allied with their cruel punishment. When the narrator departs from this collectivized or individualized masculine point of view, she marks the new viewing perspective, but she never gives us a full "reverse" shot from the point of view of doña Inés herself. Her closest approach to such a viewpoint is the most artificially marked, in fact. After don Diego's first experiment with the statue/candle, to show us doña Inés's reaction, she underlines her narrative presence as guide and conduit of the reader's (external) line of sight: "Estése [don Diego] con ella [la vela-estatua] lo que le durare, y vamos a doña Inés, que como estuvo en su cama y la vela se apagó, le pareció, cobrando el perdido sentido, que despertaba de un profundo sueño" (Let [don Diego] be with it [the candle-statue] however long it lasts, as we go to doña Inés to whom, when she was in her bed and the candle went out, it seemed as she recovered her lost senses, that she was awakening from a deep sleep) (*Desengaños,* 278). At subsequent points, the narrator describes how the neighboring widow hears doña Inés through the wall, then calls for a generalized "piedad" (compassion) to witness her wasted body, and gives the concluding moralizing summary to the nun Estefanía, who compares the welcoming and forgiving arms of her divine Husband with the cruelty of human consorts and the injustice toward women of human tongues. Even so, don Juan has the final word, and he likens the habit of speaking ill of women to the popular and "civilized" vice of using tobacco. I take this marking of any deviation from the standard masculine presentation of women as a problematic departure from the ingrained tradition of Symbolic-order language, which always views women as the enigmatic sexual Other who can only be symbolized in alienated form, can never be captured as from within herself.

Cracks in the Wall: *Desengaño 6, Amar sólo por vencer*

So let us turn back to externals, to the question of how clothes make the woman in the following story, *Desengaño 6,* as Esteban becomes the talented

servant girl Estefanía in order to court beautiful young Laurela from
within her household. To what extent does "he" become a "she"? Is this a
simple case of disguise that has no effect on some deeper nature of the
subject, or does it either reflect or effect a gender transformation, or at
least a blurring of gender categories? Amy Kaminsky (1988) points out that
clothing is not empty decoration in Zayas's novellas, but a carefully coded
and symbolic text-within-the-text that itself advances the narrative, and
would have been as clearly comprehensible to readers of Zayas's day as it
was to the characters of her frame narrative. But once again, Zayas's text
seems to work at "cross purposes." The letter that Laurela leaves for her father when she runs off with Esteban telling why he had been "transfor-
mado de caballero en dama" (transformed from a gentleman into a lady)
(*Desengaños,* 327) virtually demands an ironic reading, since the reader
knows by this point that Esteban was never a true lady nor a true gentleman; yet in her concluding commentary, the frame-heroine Lisis condemns Esteban's "engaño de transformarse en Estefanía" (deception of
transforming himself into Estefanía) (*Desengaños,* 331), juxtaposing the deceit with the view that it was, in some sense, a transformation. The verb
"transformarse" (to transform oneself), not used in other Zayas cross-
dressing episodes, appears repeatedly in this story, and, in contrast to the
case of Estela in *El juez de su causa,* the narrator does include details to
make the physical change plausible.[17] She describes Esteban as good-
looking and young enough (nineteen or twenty) not yet to have grown a
beard, and describes the process of transformation in some detail:

> Compró todo lo necesario para transformarse en doncella, y no te-
> niendo necesidad de buscar cabelleras postizas, porque en todos
> tiempos han sido los hombres aficionados a melenas, aunque no
> tanto como ahora, apercibiéndose de una navaja, para cuando el
> tierno vello del rostro le desmintiese su traje, dejando sus galillas a
> guardar a un amigo . . . se vistió y aderezó de modo que nadie juz-
> gara sino que era mujer, ayudando más al engaño tener muy buena
> cara, que con el traje que digo, daba mucho que desear a cuantos le
> veían. (*Desengaños,* 298)

> (He bought everything needed to transform himself into a lady's
> maid, not having any need to search for false tresses, because men
> have always been fond of long hair, although not so much as now,
> supplying himself with a razor for the time when the soft fuzz on his

face should belie his dress, leaving his few trappings in the care of a friend . . . he dressed and adorned himself in such a way that no one would guess but that he was a woman, helped along in the deception by the fact that he had a good face that, with the dress I mentioned, provoked desire in all those who saw him/her.)[18]

If we take pronouns as a measure of gender change, Zayas's pronouns transform Esteban into Estefanía more thoroughly than they turn Aminta into Jacinto in the second novella. The narrator consistently uses feminine adjectives and pronouns for Estefanía. In the scene in which Estefanía reveals to Laurela that she is a he, then retracts that assertion at Laurela's anger (319–21), narrative pronouns too switch back and forth. As Laurela tosses and turns the night after the revelation, decides that she prefers the reality of Esteban over that of Estefanía, and determines that she loves him, the narrator says that Estefanía came to see Laurela, "quien ya no *la* miraba como Estefanía sino como a *don* Esteban" (who no longer looked at *her* as Estefanía but as *don* Esteban) (322). Like Dustin Hoffman's character in the film *Tootsie,* s/he is quite a success as a woman, for both male and female servants flirt with "her," as does Laurela's father, don Bernardo. When Esteban/Estefanía first applies for the job, saying that her parents have died leaving her poor and untrained except in music and she prefers to serve rather than "hacer otra flaqueza" (to do some other weakness), a male servant comments, "En verdad que tenéis cara más para eso que para lo que pretendéis, y que gastara yo de mejor gana con vos mi jornalejo que con el guardián de San Francisco" (In truth you have the face more for that than for what you seek, and I would more happily spend my wages with you than with the guardian of Saint Francis) (*Desengaños,* 298). And after s/he has sung a lengthy song about mythological transformations and the conversation has turned to the possibility of true love between women, a maidservant says that "yo quisiera saber . . . qué piensa sacar Estefanía de amar a mi señora Laurela, que muchas veces, a no ver su hermosura, y haberla visto algunas veces desnuda, me da una vuelta el corazón pensando que es hombre" (I would like to know . . . what Estefanía thinks to gain from loving my lady Laurela, because many times, if I hadn't seen how lovely she is, and seen her sometimes undressed, my heart gives me a turn thinking s/he is a man) (*Desengaños,* 318).

It is Laurela's father, don Bernardo, who most persistently pursues Estefanía, and through his pursuit of "her," Zayas turns against men the same-sex infatuation that Lope joked about in *Las fortunas de Diana.* As if to underline this, she has the narrator remind the reader of Esteban/Estefanía's dual nature when the enamored don Bernardo asks Estefanía to sing. The narrator, having just used a feminine pronoun twice to refer to Esteban/Estefanía, comments that "no lo rehusó; que como no era mujer más que en el hábito, no la ocupó la vergüenza" (s/he didn't turn it down, for since she wasn't a woman except in dress, she wasn't bothered by shyness) (*Desengaños*, 307). Another instance in which the narrator reminds the reader of that double nature works more to turn the joke on the readers: she describes Estefanía's suffering, tears and fainting caused by jealousy at hearing of marriage offers for Laurela, saying that "la terneza de su amor vencía la fiereza de hombre, y se tenía entendido que Estefanía se había de morir el día que se casase Laurela" (the tenderness of his/her love won out over manly fierceness, and it was understood that Estefanía would die the day that Laurela should marry) (*Desengaños*, 309). The narrative, I suggest, effectively plays with the reader, making the enamored and jealous Estefanía an increasingly sympathetic figure until, as s/he faints when Laurela's engagement to the neighbor Enrique is announced, and they unlace "her" dress, the reader almost dreads, or at least wishes to postpone, the unmasking of "her" disguise. The sympathy is quickly reversed as Esteban abandons the seduced Laurela to her fate, but for the moment the reader, like Laurela's household, has been drawn into a tangled web of ambiguous erotic attachment posed by the lure of the cross-dressed Esteban/Estefanía.

But that is only the beginning of the complexity of Zayas's allusive-elusive treatment of gender positioning. The symbolic structure of *Amar sólo por vencer*, like that of the preceding story, adds an architectural construction to the sartorial one, as the story focuses on walls that contain and divide sexes and classes. Esteban is the son of a carpenter and has violated class division as well as gender separation in his campaign to seduce Laurela. After the fact, he confesses that, "Soy hijo de un pobre oficial de carpintería, que por no inclinarme al trabajo, me vine a este lugar, donde sirviendo he pasado fingiendo nobleza y caballería" (I am the son of a poor artisan in carpentry, and because I wasn't inclined toward work, I came to this place, where in serving I have gotten by through feigning nobility and chivalry) (*Desengaños*, 325). Laurela has been promised to a family friend, Enrique, and they, rather like Pyramus and Thisbe, live *de pared en media* (separated by only a wall) within the same house. After Esteban and Laurela flee that house and he dishonors and abandons her, her father, uncle, and aunt kill her by arranging a telling accident—they weaken a wall so that it collapses on her and kills "la traidora" (the traitor) and her servant, on their return from hearing mass at Atocha on the occasion of Nuestra Señora de Agosto (Our Lady of the Harvest) (*Desengaños,* 330).[19]

Garber points out that cross-dressing generally serves as an index of "category crisis." By this she means

> a failure of definitional distinction, a borderline that becomes permeable, that permits of border crossings from one (apparently distinct) category to another; black/white, Jew/Christian, noble/bourgeois, master/servant, master/slave. The binarism male/female, one apparent ground of distinction . . . between "this" and "that," "him" and "me," is itself put in question or under erasure in transvestism and a transvestite figure, or a transvestite code, will always function as a sign of overdetermination—a mechanism of displacement from one blurred boundary to another. (1992, 16)

The cross-dressed Estefanía is repeatedly linked to just such a generalized category crisis. For example, at the crucial point at which the narrator switches from calling him don Esteban to Estefanía, we find the following paragraph, which, like our opening joke, extends the category crisis to the animal kingdom:

> Preguntáronla el nombre, y dijo que se llamaba Estefania, sin don; que entonces no debía de ser la vanidad de las señoras tanta como la de ahora, que si tiene picaza, la llaman «doña Urraca», y si papagayo, «don Loro»; hasta a una perrita llamó una dama «doña Marquesa», y a una gata «doña Miza». (*Desengaños,* 299)

> (They asked her her name, and s/he said she was called Estefanía, without "don"; for ladies' vanity must not have been then what it is now, for if she has a magpie, they call her "Lady Chatterer," and a parrot, "Sir Parrot"; and one lady even called her little dog "Lady Marquise" and her cat "Lady Pussy Cat.")

In early modern Europe, the role of clothing in marking class and gender distinction was often given legal status in the form of sumptuary laws, as Garber points out (25–36). In Zayas's Spain, sumptuary laws were repeatedly proposed or imposed in general reforms of morals and national

224 Maria de Zayas Tells Baroque Tales of Love and the Cruelty of Men

finance, and they constituted an important part of the Olivares program of reform published in the Articles of Reformation of 1623 (Elliott 1986, 100, 105, 111, 116, 147). Zayas makes effective use of dramatic irony in Estefanía's first song in Laurela's household, a satirical description of decline from Golden Age abundance into a degeneracy of elaborate dress. In the Golden Age, not only did the oaks pour out honey, and the fields fine emeralds, but people lived "sin malicia" (without guile), "cuando no traían / fregonas ni damas / guardainfantes, moños, guardapiés y enaguas; / Cuando los galanes calzaban abarcas, / no medias de pelo, / que estén abrasadas" (when neither kitchen maids nor ladies wore hoop skirts, top-knots, petticoats, and underskirts; when young gallants wore sandals, not cross-gartered silk stockings) (*Desengaños*, 300–301). In the present Age of Iron, Father Time has gone to the court of Jupiter to complain that only flatterers now wear gold and silk, and to condemn "los diversos trajes/con que [la mentira] se disfraza" (the diverse habits with which [lying] disguises itself) (*Desengaños*, 302). He pleads that old women be required to display their gray heads, women their hair and men their baldness, and that everyone return to wearing the simple old-fashioned garments of their ancestors' era, sending French finery back to France. Father Time accompanies his proposals for sartorial reform with other social measures: (1) that beggar women be gathered together in houses and put to work for their food; (2) that procuresses be exiled to the hills; (3) that complaisant husbands pay attention to the "magic wands" with which their wives find the means to eat and dress well and wear gold and rich fabrics; (4) that slanderers who speak ill of women be sent to war; and (5) that the use of the title *don* (sir) be taxed and the proceeds distributed to the poor. Although Jupiter does nothing but table Time's complaints for further study, it is significant that the satire's climax is the proposal to tax the use of "don," a regular ingredient of conservative complaints against social climbers.

In virtually every story Zayas's narrators voice scorn for members of the lower classes and for those who attempt to ascend beyond their "proper" station. In the following story, which, as we will see, also involves an offense against gender categories, she elaborates the satire against this practice yet more harshly; saying that some houses in Madrid are as overrun with "dones" as tombs are with worms, clearly marking it as indicative of a decay of the social order akin to the decay of death.[20] Therefore, if Garber is correct in reading cross-dressing as an anxiety-displacement mechanism, then presumably anxiety in the case of the Estefanía story is being displaced from the recognizable crises of sexual license and class category to the field of gender division.

In the frame section concluding this story, Lisis organizes her harangue against male deceit and men's responsibility for the downfall of women around the themes of transformation and construction. First, again criticizing Esteban's transformation into Estefanía and his lengthy pursuit of Laurela that never produced true love, she says that he appeared to make himself into a Petrarch for Laurela.[21] But in order to deceive women, men will transform themselves as many times as "Prometheus," she says, clearly confusing that fire-stealing god with Proteus, the divine symbol of original matter. Then she cites several women legendary for their construction or defense of city walls and their gender-crossing activity. Men also cause married women to fall, says Lisis, since few women are capable of the penitence of a Saint Theodora of Alexandria. According to legend, that penitent was the wife of Gregory, prefect of Egypt, and having committed a grave sin, she fled her home to a male monastery some eighteen miles from Alexandria. Dressed as a man, she lived a life of extreme austerity there for many years without being recognized as a woman until after her death. She was even accused by a young woman of being the father of the woman's child and, accepting the slander, took the baby into her care.[22]

Next, Lisis names Artemis, as a model of the ever mourning widow who no longer exists. She is praised in Alvaro de Luna's volume (1466) of illustrious women, perhaps combining two figures: Artemisia I of the first half of the fifth century B.C., blended with the Greek queen of Caria, sister and wife of King Mausolus, who ruled alone for about three years after his death in the fourth century B.C. Although Zayas paints her as a widow eternally crying on her husband's tomb, she was most famous for the great monument—known as the Mausoleum and considered one of the Seven Wonders of the World—she had built for her husband on his death and for which she summoned the most famous carpenters of her day, and for her astute defense of her city against an army invading from Rhodes. She lured the troops off their ships and within the city walls, then occupied their ships and defeated the trapped army; taking the ships bedecked for victory back to Rhodes, she tricked the inhabitants into thinking that this fleet was their own men returning victorious, and conquered their city. She later defeated the fleet of Xerxes as well (Luna 1891, 236–40).

Finally, Lisis contrasts the vulnerability of a young woman such as Laurela, conquered by a campaign such as Esteban's, to the fabled strength of the walls of Babylon. Before a seductive transformation such as that of Esteban young women will fall, "que no son las murallas de Babilonia, que tan a costa labró Semíramis" (for they are not the walls of Babylon that Semíramis built at such cost) (*Desengaños*, 333). Zayas says no more about Semíramis here, but surely her readers would have associated this character with the transgression of protective borders as well as with their construction. The beautiful Semíramis, a blend of fertility goddess and the historical queen Sammuramat, who ruled in Mesopotamia from 811–808, was well known in Zayas's time as an erotic symbol for uncontained, gender-crossing feminine ambition. Lope de Vega's play about her from 1603 is lost, but *La Gran Semíramis* of Cristóbal de Virués, written between 1579 and 1590, was published in 1609, and Zayas and her public may have known one or both parts of Calderón's *La hija de aire*.[23] Surely they were familiar with the concepts that she had arranged her husband's death to secure power for herself, and that she later imprisoned her look-alike son and ruled disguised as him. Putting together these gender and species-crossing transformations and the architectonic element in both Esteban's past and that of Artemis and Semíramis, I suggest that if we apply to this tale a metonymic reading such as that proposed in Chapter 6, we can see the fate of Laurela as indicative of an implicit if unspeakable understanding that boundaries of gender and class may be social constructions, more sartorial and conventional than natural, but that for women any complicity in the transgression of those barriers can be fatal.

But if the constructed nature of gender division is one of the logical limits of this transvestism that can only be inferred metonymically, what of its other suggestion, that of lesbian love? The narrator distances it in two ways: (1) by advancing the possibility of love between women in the suspect voice of Esteban/Estefanía, who refutes it on resuming male dress; and (2) by ridiculing it through the laughter of all "sensible" listeners. For example, when Laurela tells Estefanía that s/he will be for her not a servant, but a sister and friend, Estefanía answers that she is "tan enamorada (poco digo: tan perdida), que maldigo mi mala suerte en no haberme hecho hombre" (so in love—that's an understatement: so head over heels—that I curse my bad luck in not having been made a man.) She responds to Laurela's question of what s/he would do if s/he were a man: "Amarte y servirte hasta merecerte, como lo haré mientras viviere; que el poder de amor también se extiende de mujer a mujer, como de galán a dama." (Love you and serve you to earn your love, as I will do as long as I live; for the power of love also extends between women, as between a lover and his lady) (*Desengaños*, 306). This conversation produces great laughter from all hearers.[24] The suggestion of sexually ambiguous love is also voiced by Estefanía in a song of jealousy organized around multiple mythological lovers, including Narciso and Hermafrodito. Admiring the skill with which Estefanía plays both the male and female roles as she sings, Laurela says:

> —Cierto, Estefanía, que si fueras, como eres mujer, hombre, que dichosa se pudiera llamar la que tú amaras.
> —Y aun así como así —dijo Estefanía— pues para amar, supuesto que el alma es toda una en varón y en la hembra, no se me da más ser hombre que mujer; que las almas no son hombres ni mujeres, y el verdadero amor en el alma está, que no en el cuerpo; y el que ·amare el cuerpo con el cuerpo, no puede decir que es amor, sino apetito, y de esto nace arrepentirse en poseyendo; porque como no estaba el amor en el alma, el cuerpo, como mortal, se cansa siempre de un manjar, y·el alma, como espíritu, no se puede enfastiar de nada. (*Desengaños*, 317)

> ("Certainly, Estefanía, if you were such a man as you are a woman, any woman you loved could call herself blessed."
> "And even as things are," said Estefanía, "because in order to love, understanding that the soul is the same in the male as in the female, it's all the same to me being a man as a woman; for souls are neither men nor women, and true love is in the soul, and not in the body; and he who loves the body with the body, cannot say that it is love, but appetite, and from that, repentance is born in possession; because love was not in the soul, and the body, being mortal, always tires of one plate, and the soul, as spirit, cannot be surfeited with anything.")

The discussion continues, with Estefanía arguing for the superiority of spiritual, incorporeal love between souls, which never dies, over corporeal love, which is quickly satiated and fickle (*Desengaños*, 317). On revealing his true gender to Laurela, however, Esteban contradicts this argument directly, saying she should have known he was a man from his sighs, his tears, and the sentiments in his verses, because "¿quién ha visto que una dama se enamore de otra?" (who has ever seen one lady fall in love with another?) (320). Thus, in one breath, the story explicitly disavows the possibility of lesbian love—albeit in the suspect voice of Esteban—and suggests at the same time that the discourse of platonic love is itself a kind of philosophical cross-dressing, a strategic veiling of physical desire that men use to seduce the women they pursue.

Bearded Love: *Desengaño 7, Mal presagio casar lejos*

If we read intertextually between this story and the next, however, the implication of lesbian attraction cannot be laughed away. In the frame commentary that bridges the two, Lisis talks about the color of true love, which she says should be only white, in its purity and chastity, and golden, for its firmness in conserving that purity. She continues:

> El amor de ahora que usáis, señores caballeros, tiene muchas colores: ya es rubio, ya pelinegro, ya moreno, ya blanco, ya viudo, ya soltero, ya civil y mecánico, ya ilustre y alto. *Y Dios os tenga de su mano, no le busquéis barbado, que andáis tan de mezcla, que ya no sabéis de que color vestirle.* Para conseguir esto, es fuerza que hagáis muchas mujeres malas." (*Desengaños*, 334; emphasis added)

> (The love that you now employ, gentle sirs, has many colors: sometimes it's blond, sometimes black haired, sometimes dark, sometimes white, sometimes a widower, sometimes single, sometimes ordinary and mean, sometimes illustrious and lofty. *And may God grant that you don't seek for it bearded, for you are now going around so mixed up that you don't know with what color to dress it.* In order to accomplish this, it's necessary for you to make many women bad.)

The primary meaning of "barbado" is of course "bearded," and hence "masculine," "substantial," and so on. The *Diccionario de autoridades,* however, also includes an interesting proverb that associates falsity with mixed beard and hair colors: "Falso por natura, cabello negro, y la barba rubia," (False by nature, black hair and a blond beard) which is said to mean that "los que tienen la disformidad de tener el pelo de la cabeza negro, y la barba rubia, ordinariamente son falsos, infieles y peligrosos" (those who have the deformity of having black hair and a blond beard are ordinarily false, faithless, and dangerous). I read this association of a prohibited "bearded love," "mixture," and changeable color as a suggestion of homosexual love, quickly countered by redirecting the reader's focus toward illicit heterosexuality. Similarly, I believe, Zayas, having raised the suggestion of lesbian attraction, reshapes and redirects that possibility of deviance from the accepted heterosexual norm in her next story, *Desengaño 7, Mal presagio casar lejos* (Marry Afar: Portent of Doom).

This tale takes the level of violence against women up yet another peg, as all four daughters in one family marry foreigners, and all are killed by them.[25] Doña Blanca, the heroine, whose parents have died, has been promised by her brother to a prince of Flanders whose father is a great power in that country. The marriage has been made to suit the political interests of the Crown,[26] and doña Blanca accepts it reluctantly, but imposes a condition that the prince come to Spain to court her for a year, which he is happy to do in order to visit Spain, although his father is displeased at the idea. When others laugh at her demand for this unnecessary, artificial courtship before an agreed-upon marriage, doña Blanca defends it with a lengthy argument for the concept of a loving marriage built on a knowledge of the partner one takes. Saying that no one buys a dress or a jewel sight unseen, she insists that he should win her will and demonstrate through the gallantries of courtship that he will be an affectionate husband. Furthermore, she maintains the hope that should the prince prove to be other than the handsome, intelligent, and agreeable man that the marriage contract promised, she would not be obliged to accept him, but could go to a convent instead. Although she does find the prince handsome and well spoken, doña Blanca is overcome with melancholy as the courtship begins. Trying to explain, she can only say that

> en cuanto haberme parecido bien, te puedo jurar que yo soy la apasionada. Y en cuanto a desear que el año del concierto estuviese cumplido, te doy mi palabra que quisiera que durara una eternidad. Y asimismo te prometo que no sé de qué me procede este disgusto, si ya no es de pensar que tengo de ausentarme de mi natural y de mi hermano, y irme a tierras tan remotas como son adonde he de ir; mas tampoco me parece es la causa ésta, ni la puedo dar alcance, aunque más lo procuro. (*Desengaños*, 342–43)

> (as for having appealed to me, I can swear to you than I am passionately fond of him. And as for wanting the agreed-upon year to be completed, I give you my word that I would prefer that it lasted an eternity. And by the same token I assure you that I do not know from what my displeasure stems, if it isn't from thinking that I have to leave my native [land] and my brother and depart for such re-

mote lands as those to which I have to go; but that doesn't seem to
me the cause either, nor can I grasp it, however much I try.)

The paradox that the skilled, apparently sincere, courtship of a handsome young prince—a courtship that delights all of Blanca's ladies-in-
waiting—causes her such sadness can be explained as Blanca's—and
Zayas's—intuition of the (f)utility of the discourse of courtly love with
which he addresses her. Lacan linked that discourse to the inevitable impasse in the relation between the sexes, to the fact that, as he reiterated "Il
n'y a pas de rapport sexuel" (There is no such thing as a sexual relationship) (1975, 355). The demands for proof of love and commitment that
the two sexes address to each other are asymmetrical and can never fit together like the two halves of the mythical locket that (mis)identifies every
sexed baby cast off from the (m)Other and ever searching for its missing
half. The arrows on the sexuation graph (see diagram, Chapter 4, page 132
above) indicating object choice may point across the sexual divide, but
their aim is not reciprocal; hence, although the two sexes unite physically,
the emotional demands that they make of a partner are not complementary. The discourse of courtly love serves to mask this impasse, "an altogether refined way of making up for the absence of sexual relation by pretending that it is we who put an obstacle to it" (Lacan 1982, 141). As Zizek
puts it, courtly love is "a strict fictional formula, . . . a social game of 'as if,'
where a man pretends that his sweetheart is the inaccessible Lady" (1994,
91), at once the object of his desire and the force that prevents the attain-
ment of that desire (96). It heightens the value of the object of desire by
placing an external hindrance that appears to thwart desire, hence maintaining the fantasy that the object would be attainable if that hindrance
were removed (94). Georges Duby (1992), from a literary and historical
perspective, describes the phenomenon of courtly love in terms consonant
with Lacan's evaluation of its function. Recognizing this "courtly neurosis"
(255) as in origin a literary creation and a literature of escape, Duby
stresses its fantasy value and its organization around the pleasure in desire
itself, in anticipation of an infinitely postponed satisfaction. He underlines
the fact that despite the power it apparently gave to women, it was a man's
game. Duby also links it to something closer to a "real" obstacle or wall between the sexes in the aristocratic practice of early separation of the sexes,
a separation that fostered male homosexuality and a male fascination with
and fear of feminine mystery and power. Courtly love was, says Duby, a useful instrument of social discipline for both sexes—in the case of women, to
discourage frivolity, duplicity, and unbridled lust—"for restraining those

traits that provoked anxiety in men, for confining the female sex within a web of carefully orchestrated rituals, for drawing woman's sting by diverting her combativeness to the harmless realm of sport" (262).

The prince skillfully articulates this discourse of suffering service to a distant lady, as in the following sonnet he sings to doña Blanca:[27]

> No quiere, dueño amado, el dolor mío
>   tan áspero remedio como ausencia,
>   que si hay valor, cordura, ni paciencia
>   para sufrir, aunque sufrir porfío.
> Tratadme con desdenes, con desvío,
>   con celos; aunque es tanta su violencia,
>   haréis de un firme amor clara experiencia,
>   aunque me vuelva con mi llanto un río.
> Que como yo me vea en vuestros ojos,
>   dulces nortes de amor, estrellas mías
>   en quien las dichas de mi suerte espero,
> alegres, tristes, con cien mil enojos
>   darán aliento a mis cansados bríos;
>   pero cuando no os veo, desespero.
> Si más que a mí no os quiero,
>   si veros me da vida,
>   tenelda, si no os veo, por perdida.
>   (*Desengaños*, 344)

(My suffering, beloved lady, does not want such a harsh remedy as absence, if there is courage, prudence, and patience to suffer, although I persist in suffering.

Treat me with disdain, with avoidance, with jealousy; be they ever so violent, you will perform a certain trial of a firm love, 'tho' you turn me into a river of tears.

For as long as I see myself in your eyes, polestar of my love, my stars, in which I hope for the blessing of my fortune,

be they happy, sad, or show a thousand angers, they will give life to my exhausted spirit, but when I do not see you, I despair.

If I do not love you more than myself, if seeing you gives me life, consider my life lost if I do not see you.)

Protestations of suffering enslavement to the distant Lady notwithstanding, this courtly love rhetoric masks the fact that the apparently servile mas-

culine lover enjoys the dominant position, a fact violently and melodramat-
ically unmasked in the remainder of this story.[28] Zizek recognizes the realities of the underlying power relationship:

> The courtly image of man serving his Lady is a semblance that con-
> ceals the actuality of male domination; . . . the masochist's theatre is
> a private *mise en scène* designed to recompense the guilt contracted
> by man's social domination; true, the elevation of woman to the sub-
> lime object of love equals her debasement into the passive stuff or
> screen for the narcissistic projection of the male ego-ideal (1994,
> 108). Lacan himself points out how, in the very epoch of courtly
> love, the actual social standing of women as objects of exchange in
> male power-plays was probably at its lowest.

Zizek concedes this and goes on to suggest that courtly love discourse also
serves the feminine position: "This very semblance of man serving his Lady
provides women with the fantasy-substance of their identity whose effects
are real: it provides them with all the features that constitute so-called 'femininity' and define woman not as she is in her *jouissance féminine,* but as she
refers to herself with regard to her (potential) relationship to man, as an
object of his desire" (1994, 108).[29]

While Zayas displays women's pleasure in the discourse of courtly love in
other stories, in this tale she underlines its contrary effect. Although it was
doña Blanca who instituted this yearlong "entretenimiento de amor y
prueba de entendimiento" (entertainment of love and proof of understanding) (*Desengaños,* 347), she finds no pleasure in it except as a means
of delaying her departure from her home. Zayas depicts her as mixing tender love for the prince with rivers of tears even before the reports of her
sisters' martyrdom at the hands of foreign husbands dresses their wedding
celebrations in mourning. In the political "convenience" of the marriage
and the economic terms that Blanca employs in justifying the courtship,[30]
we can read an understanding that in a patriarchal culture organized
through the interchange of women, courtship constitutes the one brief period prior to their contractual transfer out of the paternal household in
which women are granted at least the enjoyment of the fiction of a certain
freedom of choice. But Blanca's enjoyment in this fiction is submerged in a
melancholic foreboding whose cause she cannot name, except in a lament
that she will have to "ausentarse de su natural" (absent herself from her na-
ture/native land.)[31]

"Natural" is, I suggest, a highly ambiguous term that allows Zayas to elide "nature" and "native land" in a story that, on a first level, projects the impasse between the sexes on political divisions—on difference of nationality. The prince's disaffection for Blanca begins as soon as she is in his possession and becomes visible as soon as they leave Madrid and she is out of her brother's power. María, the much loved lady-in-waiting who accompanies her, tries to lift Blanca's sadness "de haber dejado su paternal albergue, y irse a vivir desterrada para siempre de él" (at having left her paternal shelter, and going to live exiled forever from it) (*Desengaños*, 349). But as soon as they board ship for Flanders and he has "la inocente palomilla fuera de todo punto de su nido" (the innocent little dove completely out of her nest) (*Desengaños*, 349), his clear distaste for her brings them to discord, to quarrels that he frames in terms of nationality, as will her cruel father-in-law when they reach Flanders (see Chapter 9 below).

Projection of the sexual impasse on political divisions is only partial, however. Zayas shows women as the victims of male political rivalries, but she also paints an empathy and community among women that is only interrupted by their subordination to the dictates of men. In the very next sentence after Blanca's harsh reception by her father-in-law, the narrator focuses the enmity on Flemish *men,* not women, as she says that doña Blanca's one respite from suffering was provided by the prince's sister, doña Marieta, with whom she forms an immediate and intimate friendship:

> Con esta señora trabó doña Blanca grande amistad, cobrándose las dos tanto amor, que si no era para dormir, no se dividía la una de la otra, comunicando entre ellas sus penas que gustos tenían tan pocos, que no las cansaba mucho el contarlos, porque tan poco estimaba su esposo a la señora Marieta, como el príncipe a doña Blanca. (*Desengaños*, 350)

> (With this lady doña Blanca struck up a great friendship, the two women gaining so much love for each other that except to sleep, the one didn't separate from the other, sharing between them their sorrows, for they had so few pleasures that recounting them did not tire them much, because lady Marieta's husband valued her as little as the prince did doña Blanca.)

Furthermore, after doña Blanca is bled to death at her father-in-law's command, she is lamented equally by Spanish and Flemish women, as "llo-

rando se cercaron todas de ella, españolas y flamencas, que en el sentimiento tanto lo mostraban las unas como las otras" (crying, they all drew
around her, Spanish and Flemish women, for in their grief, one group
showed it as much as the other) (*Desengaños*, 364). The fate of Marieta also
locates hostilities between the sexes rather than between nations, since her
husband is a cousin and therefore presumably Flemish. One day a manservant of Marieta's is found stabbed to death. Her father orders his death silenced rather than investigated, and two days later Marieta is garroted by
her father and husband, for equally mysterious causes, since Marieta is too
honest to be suspected of any wrongdoing except perhaps the error of her
friendship with doña Blanca.

The greater reason for the prince's disaffection for doña Blanca resides
closer to the *other* meaning of her "natural" (nature)—at least inasmuch as
we (mis)use "nature" to indicate gender identity and object choice. On ar-
riving in Flanders, doña Blanca finds that her husband has a much favored
page boy, Arnesto:

> Tenía el príncipe un paje, mozo, galán, y que los años no pasaban
> de diez y seis, tan querido suyo, que trocara su esposa el agasajo
> suyo por el del paje, y él tan soberbio con la privanza, que más
> parecía señor que criado. El tenía cuanto el príncipe estimaba, con
> él comunicaba sus más íntimos secretos, por él se gobernaba todo, y
> él tan desabrido con todos, que más trataban de agradarle que al
> príncipe. (*Disengaños*, 350–51)

> (The prince had a page, a handsome young man, whose age was not
> more than sixteen, so much loved by him that his wife would have
> exchanged her reception for that of the page, and he [was] so arro-
> gant with his favored status that he seemed more like a lord than a
> servant. He possessed everything the prince valued, with him he
> shared his most intimate secrets, he was ruled in everything by him,
> and he was so disagreeable with all that they tried harder to please
> him than the prince.)

Suspecting that her husband's indifference to her is due to an affair with
some other woman arranged by the page, she follows her husband to his
room one day,

> sospechando que tenía en él la dama causa de sus celos, . . . en-
> trando con mucho sosiego, por no ser sentida, llegó hasta la cama

del príncipe, en que dormía ordinariamente, que con ella era por gran milagro, y halló . . . [*sic*] ¿Qué hallaría?

Quisiera, hermosas damas y discretos caballeros, ser tan entendida que, sin darme a entender, me entendiérades, por ser cosa tan enorme y fea lo que halló. Vio acostados en la cama a su esposo y a Arnesto, en deleites tan torpes y abominables, que es bajeza, no sólo decirlo, mas pensarlo. Que doña Blanca, a la vista de tan horrendo y sucio espectáculo más difunta que cuando vio el cadáver de la señora Marieta, mas con más valor, pues apenas lo vio, cuando más apriesa que había ido, se volvió a salir, quedando ellos, no vergonzosos ni pesarosos de que los hubiese visto, sino más descompuestos de alegría, pues con gran risa dijeron:

—Mosca lleva la española. (*Desengaños*, 360)

(suspecting that he had in it the lady who was the cause of her jealousy . . . entering very quietly so as not to be heard, she came to the prince's bed, in which he normally slept, for it was a great miracle when he slept with her, and found . . . [*sic*] What would she have found?

I wish, lovely ladies and prudent gentlemen, that I were so expert that you might understand me without my making myself understood, because what she found was such a monstrous and ugly thing. She saw her husband and Arnesto lying in the bed, in such obscene and abominable delights that it is vile not only to say it but even to think it. And doña Blanca, at the sight of such a horrendous and dirty spectacle, more dead than when she saw the lady Marieta's cadaver, but more courageous, since she had scarcely seen it when, more quickly than she had come in, she turned to go, leaving them, not ashamed or sorry that she had seen them, but breaking up with joy, since roaring with laughter, they said: "That bugged the Spanish woman.)

Telling her faithful servant that what she has seen will cause her death, she nevertheless takes the bed out into the patio and burns it, saying that she will "morir vengada . . . a lo menos en el teatro donde se comete su ofensa y la mía, con tan torpes y abominables pecados, que aun el demonio se avergüenza de verlos" (die avenged . . . at least in the theater where his offense and mine is committed with such obscene and abominable sins that even the devil is ashamed to see them) (*Desengaños*, 361). Her act of bedburning is a symbolic execution of Spanish justice, since men convicted of sodomy in Spain were burned alive, in Castille by the civil courts, in Aragon by the Inquisition (Kamen, 1985, 271–72). Blanca presents herself as the victim convicted in this foreign land of perversion and injustice in which "los reos . . . quedan reservados para ser mis verdugos" (the criminals . . . are themselves my executioners). Until divine justice punishes them, she can only burn the theater of the crime and threaten to one day extend the act to Arnesto himself.[32] In retaliation for her daring and for her verbal threat against Arnesto, her father-in-law and the page boy bleed her to death, over the objections of the prince. Admiring her beauty as she faints from loss of blood, the prince is moved to compassion for this "deshojada azucena" (leafless lily) and begs that she be spared. His father rejects that plea, accusing him of being "half woman" in terms that blend gender hostility with xenophobia:

> Calla, cobarde, traidor, medio mujer, que te vences de la hermosura y tiene más poder en ti que los agravios. Calla otra vez, te digo, muera; que de tus enemigos, los menos. Y si no tienes valor, repara tu flaqueza con quitarte de delante. Salte fuera y no lo veas, que mal se defenderá ni ofenderá a los hombres quien desmaya de ver morir una mujer. Así tuviera a todas las de su nación como tengo a ésta. (*Desengaños*, 363)

> (Shut up, coward, traitor, half woman yourself if beauty conquers you and has more power over you than affronts. Shut up I say again, let her die; the fewer your enemies are, the better. And if you don't have the courage, make up for your weakness by getting out of the way. Go outside and don't watch it, because he who faints at seeing a woman die will ill defend himself or offend other men. Would that I had all women of her nation the way I have this one.)

In her sequencing of *Desengaño 6* and *Desengaño 7,* and in the frame commentary on the colors of love that connects them, I suggest, Zayas has in effect cross-dressed the issue of homosexual desire. She raises the idea of love between women in *Desengaño 6,* but both advances and rejects it in the unbelievable voice of Esteban. That refusal is seconded by the laughter of all "sensible" observers within the story. But Zayas never has a purportedly neutral or moralizing narrative voice discount the idea of love between women, Platonic or sexual. She follows that story with *Mal presagio casar lejos,* safely distancing that possibility of homosexuality by displacing it onto the opposite sex and another land where it becomes—almost—mentionable.

But this does not yet exhaust the displacements that Zayas effects in dealing with illicit desire and the situation of women. At the same time that she partially displaces the problem of the sexual impasse toward that of national difference, she shifts blame for the mistreatment of women in patriarchal society toward a political "other," onto Blanca's father-in-law as Flemish patriarch, a man belonging to a nation resting on the borderline between ally and enemy. We will return to the subject of her interweaving of the personal and the political in this and other stories, in Chapter 9.

Those displacements along with others reveal the ideological conflict between gender and class identity that both animates and restricts Zayas's ability to challenge patriarchal gender definitions. Because definitions of "nature," "sex," gender roles, and sexual object choices are deeply implicated in a given sociopolitical order, a writer of Zayas's conservative position could not launch a frontal attack on them, however unjust she might declare the restrictions that that order places on women. She shows cross-dressed women possessing "masculine" courage and discretion (*La burlada Aminta* and *El juez de su causa*), but only when they have been ripped out of social order by male abuse, and in the latter case, she distances the "sadistic" prolongation of feminine power by discussing it through a male narrator. She does narrate through a woman's voice two episodes of male-to-female cross-dressing, rare in her day when such a cross was dressing "down" in the gender hierarchy. But like the few male authors who penned such scenes, she made Esteban/Estefanía a lower-class male who ascends by presenting himself as a poor noblewoman. Technically speaking, Octavia's brother don Juan in *Desengaño 2* is noble, but Zayas underlines the moral baseness that allowed him to adopt the traitorous medium of feminine attire to avenge his sister's seduction by don Carlos: "pensó una traición que sólo se pudiera hallar en un bajo y común hombre, y no de la calidad que don Juan era" (he thought of a betrayal that could only be found in a base and common man, not of the quality of don Juan) (*Desengaños,* 190). Rather than directly confronting the question of what is "natural" and what "cultural" in gender definition, she raises the questions implicitly in her uses of cross-dressing, but displaces any explicit answer toward definitions by ethical qualities, class, and nationality. Good women such as Estela are not just women, but noblewomen, angels of devotion and loyalty; the sexually aggressive woman (Claudia) who cross-dresses to pursue a man and renounces her Christian fate to boot dies impaled by royal edict in an alien land; and men who do not desire women are either subhuman (as is don Marco, an "asparagus" as well as a social climber), or nameless foreign princes.

8

The Undead and the Supernatural

The Supernatural, Now and Then

While Zayas's challenges to gender definition were restricted by her loyalty to an aristocratic sociopolitical order, that conservatism facilitated rather than restricted her freedom in crossing other barriers—in violating the frontiers between life and death and between natural and supernatural causality. Comparable plot elements were familiar to readers of other popular genres in her era, in hagiographic stories and *comedias,* particularly saints' plays, and they were employed by other contributors to the novella vogue as well, if less insistently or strikingly than by Zayas. Fully half her stories in each volume include the use of magic or some form of "undeath"— an interpenetration or communication between the living and the dead. In this chapter, I will explore the orthodoxy and unorthodoxy of her usage: its grounding in beliefs that enjoyed both psychic utility and theological and popular support in Counter-Reformation Spain, and her subtle reworking of the figuration of magic and death in women's defense.

In the Introduction, I suggested that Zayas's tales find a newly sympathetic audience among postmodern readers with a taste for cinematic and novelistic explorations of occult powers, vampire stories, and the combinations of eroticism and deadly violence that fill theaters and book stands.[1] Our fascination with such irrational visions of human experience derives, however, from a cosmology significantly different from that of Zayas, separated from it by the triumph of rationalism and a faith in the scientific method that largely replaced the "magic mentality" (Caro Baroja 1966, 8) of the premodern and early modern periods. Lost faith in the ability of reason and scientific progress to solve the ills of humankind may have encouraged a renewed credence in the existence of supernatural and infrarational forces that prevail over the efforts of human consciousness. Yet in a late twentieth-century context, these admissions play against a continuing scientific-rationalist discourse and hence often take on an "as if" quality or suggest a symbolic or allegorical relationship to other threats in the "real" world.[2] Zayas, in contrast, presents magic and the living dead with a straightforward seriousness, as unquestioned elements of a cosmology in which divine power effaces the life-death frontier and desperate men and women yield to the demonic lure of magic.

The world of Zayas's stories involves a magical view of permeable borders between the individual and the natural world.[3] Such a permeability was characteristic of all the major cosmologies prevailing in the Renaissance, according to Ioan Couliani (1987); none of them excluded the possibility of magic, since they were all "based on the idea of *continuity* between man and the world"—a continuity between the individual *pneuma*, or spirit, and the cosmic one. As an attempt to dominate the forces of nature, magic was the forerunner of modern science, as Susan Paun de Garcia (1992) points out.[4] Magicians were not persecuted by the church before the thirteenth-century ascendance of Aristotelian philosophy, which placed the earth in a position of ontological inferiority in the cosmos as a site of flux, generation, and corruption and denied the existence of natural magic, thereafter considering magic either divine or demonic. Says Paun de García,

> En los siglos XVI y XVII no se dudaba de la existencia de poderes sobrenaturales. Más bien, había un concepto dualístico de orden y poder que dividía el universo entre la luz y la oscuridad, el bien y el

mal, Dios y el Demonio. Por lo tanto, como observa Oswald Spengler, "Los mitos de María y los mitos del Demonio se formaron juntos, el uno era imposible sin el otro. El no creer en cualquiera de los dos era pecado mortal. Se rendía culto a María por medio de la oración, y al Demonio por medio de encantos y exorcismos." (43, citing Spengler, *The Decline of the West*)

(In the sixteenth and seventeenth centuries, the existence of supernatural powers was not doubted. Rather, there was a dualistic concept of order and power that divided the universe between light and darkness, good and evil, God and the devil. Therefore, as Oswald Spengler, observed, "The myths of Mary and the myths of the Devil formed together, the one was impossible without the other. Not believing in either of the two was a mortal sin. One paid homage to Mary through prayer, and to the Devil through spells and exorcisms.")

Zayas puts the supernatural to work considerably more than does Cervantes in his novellas. He maintained a skeptical attitude toward magic and the operation of demonic power, as Forcione points out in his analysis of *El coloquio de los perros* (The Dialogue of the Dogs). In his grotesque portrayal of Cañizares as "the monster at the center of the labyrinth" of moral evil (1984, 59), Cervantes reveals the psychology of the sinner while casting doubts on the truth of witches' reports of congress with the devil and the existence of magic power to work metamorphoses. At the same time, however, says Forcione, Cervantes "was well aware of the imaginative power of the myth of witchcraft . . . and exploited its theological implications to pursue to its most profound depths his major theme of the nature of evil" (1984, 71). In the *Persiles,* as Diana de Armas Wilson demonstrates, Cervantes repeatedly juxtaposes apparently supernatural events with overtly rational explanations of their natural explanation by one or another skeptic. "Moving toward a rationalism that admits and even admires the supernormal, Cervantes' vision in this text is future-related, anticipating both the Enlightenment and the reaction it would generate in the Romantic period, with the naturalizing of the supernatural" (Wilson 1991, 32). Discussing the move away from the magical view, Charles Taylor ascribes it to the development of a new "inwardness" in the wake of the Protestant Reformation which brought with it a sense of self-possession rendering the earlier view a kind of outmoded, primitive thralldom to external forces (Roper 1994, 5).

Significantly, Zayas's first use of magic in her first collection and her first deployment of the "undead" in the second occur in the third tale in each, both of which also happen to be rewrites of a Cervantes story (see Chapter 3 above), as if she were deliberately reinscribing his tales in the older, magical order. Amezúa attributes Zayas's use of the supernatural and marvelous to the combination of her feminine character and a superstitious age, calling it "cosa lógica, porque a la común credulidad de entonces en las artes supersticiosas juntaba ella su condición femenina. La mujer fué siempre mucho más crédula que el hombre" (logical, because to the then common credulity in the superstitious arts, she joined her feminine condition. Woman was always much more credulous than man) (1948, xxviii). Melloni (1976, 86–87) considers Zayas's serious treatment of magic and the supernatural a faithful reflection of the orthodox position of the Catholic church and a mark of her conservative ideology. At a first level of analysis, this is at least partly true, inasmuch as Counter-Reformation imposition of orthodoxy foreclosed the pre-Enlightenment movement described by Taylor and clearly visible in Cervantes.

Adorno, analyzing what he called "authoritarian irrationalism" as a predictable accompaniment of modernity, argued that certain historical situations bring out ever-present possibilities in human beings, and that the anxiety and insecurity that accompanies the decline of social systems can be channeled by individuals or institutions away from objective reasons, focusing paranoid tendencies through supernatural and irrational "causes" such as astrology and the occult. He sees this process behind Counter-Reformation witch-hunting, "when an attempt was being made to artificially reconstruct a social order that by that time had become obsolete" (Adorno 1994, 122).[5] The role of magic in Zayas in general accords with Adorno's hypothesis, for it is concentrated in her first collection rather than the second, in which, as we will see in the following chapter, she comes much closer to confronting the role of historical events and of the patriarchal family and political structures in determining the unhappy fate of women.

Rather than simply labeling her first-volume reliance on magic a reflection of Counter-Reformation orthodoxy or feminine susceptibility to superstition, therefore, we should analyze just how she uses it. Montesa, in his extensive and perceptive analysis of Zayas's use of magic and the supernatural, has set a good example in this regard. While he too sees it as a reflection of the debate over sorcery and witchcraft in her day, he goes much deeper, viewing it as an adjunct of her treatment of the erotic and as a method for exploring the deeper realities of a logically irrational world (1981, 236–51).

Sham Magic, Demonic Trickery, and Suicide

Zayas's first presentation of magic in *El castigo de la miseria* offers a more cynical than skeptical vision of its operation, and significantly alters its gendered trajectory. Rather than displaying the physical and spiritual sickness of a woman convinced she is a witch, Zayas gives us a sham male "enchanter" who preys on the pathetic gullibility and despairing greed of don Marcos. After his wife, Isidora, has departed with his fortune, her "nephew" Agustín and the servant Inés, don Marcos encounters Isidora's other servant, Marcela, in the street, seizes her, and tries to shake out of her a confession of the location of the clothing and jewels she had stolen when she left the house on the night of the marriage. She convinces him that doña Isidora had made her steal and hide the clothes and jewels and tells him that her future husband knows how to conjure devils and will be able to make them reveal the destination of Isidora and his fortune. The enchantment is a sham, performed with a mumbo-jumbo conjuration over an ancient-looking copy of *Amadís de Gaula* and a tortured, burned cat. The turning point of the episode is not the conversion experience of a "heroic dog" confronting a "malevolent female" (Forcione 1984, 156) as Berganza drags the transported Cañizares out to public view, nor does it produce the possibility of a cure, physical or spiritual. Rather, its most spectacular moment is the explosively flaming death of a cat tortured by a false magician in order to extort more money from don Marcos, and it foreshadows not a potential cure but his proximate death in despair for the loss of his fortune. In this male-narrated story, Zayas first presents "magic" as a hoax nourished by human greed and gullibility.

Nevertheless, Zayas's first version of *El castigo de la miseria* then reaffirms the existence of demonic forces as she brings on the devil himself to facilitate the miser's death by suicide. She eliminated this episode in the 1638 version, in which don Marcos dies of a fatal fever brought on by the shock of losing his fortune and compounded by his encounter with the "demonic" cat. With one exception, all subsequent editions of the story, including that of Amezúa and its modern descendants, derive from this version. Although Sandra Foa drew attention to the different ending in the 1637 edition some years ago, it is not yet readily available and I therefore include it as Appendix 2. In this ending, don Marcos recovers from his fever and, despairing, goes out to hang himself by the light of the moon. Zayas describes his route with unaccustomed precision, telling her readers that he goes in the direction of the "nombrado Colegio de Doña Maria de Aragón" (renowned School of Doña María de Aragón) and is heading downhill near "aquella puente que han hecho nueua en aquel camino" (that new bridge that they built on that route) (Zayas y Sotomayor, 1637b, 126) when he encounters a man he takes to be the marriage broker, Gamarra. This precision will be repeated in her other stories involving the supernatural, as she sets the locus of uncanny events with abundant concrete detail that anchors them in a mundane or specific reality unusual in her idealistic style.[6]

In the original ending of *El castigo de la miseria,* Don Marcos and Gamarra trade stories of misfortune and plans to hang themselves from the nearby trees. The marriage broker relates a convoluted story of gambling debts and his stealing from the house of his employer, the duke of Osuna, that would take him to the gallows if discovered. Since he prefers to die by his own hand, he has brought a rope, which is long enough for both of them. He prepares two nooses and attaches them to two trees. A young man who has been resting under a tree and has seen don Marcos talking to someone the man cannot see, on seeing don Marcos hang himself from a branch, runs off to tell the corregidor what is happening. When officials return to the scene, they find don Marcos hanging from the tree but only an empty noose in the other, and no one in the duke's household who has ever heard of Gamarra. From this evidence and the invisibility of don Marcos's interlocutor, they conclude that "el tal era el demonio, que por desesperar a don Marcos, auia venido con aquel engaño, y que le auia sucedido a su gusto, como parecia" (he was the devil, who had appeared with that trick to make don Marcos despair, and it had gone according to his wish, it seemed) (Zayas y Sotomayor 1637b, 126–27).

The demonic suicide ending confronts us with four questions: (1) why did Zayas end her rewriting of the Cervantine tale with such an episode? (2) what psychic truth did it have for her? (3) how does it relate to the view of suicide in her day? and (4) why, in view of the inclusion of other suicides in her stories, did she eliminate it in the second version? Foa, who thinks that Zayas has reduced Cervantes' protagonists to one-dimensional caricatures, seconds Segundo Serrano Poncela's opinion that her intent in this tale is to "censurar la avaricia y valorizar la astucia feminina" (censure avarice and exalt feminine astuteness) (Foa 1977, 75). In light of the metonymic punishment of "pussy" and the final reduction of doña Isidora to begging (see Chapter 3 above), it is hard to see this story as an exaltation of feminine astuteness, but Zayas certainly does censure avarice, and intended, in both versions, "to punish fully and relentlessly Don Marcos for his sin, rather than to allow him to repent and redeem himself" (Foa 1977, 78). In the first version Zayas emphasizes the gravity of his sin by adding: "conforme merecía su miseria; porque un miserable no es bueno sino para el infierno, adonde todos quantos allá están, lo son" (as his miserliness deserved, because a skinflint is no good for anything but hell, where all the residents are wretches) (Zayas y Sotomayor 1637b, 127). The second registers the reaction of the inscribed audience with the words: "Con grandísimo gusto oyeron todos la maravilla que don Alvaro dixo, viendo castigado a don Marcos" (They heard the marvel that don Alvaro told with the greatest of pleasure, seeing don Marcos punished), The only unpardonable masculine sin in Zayas's amorous "theology" is not a sin of the flesh but material greed. She may allow faithless lovers or even brutal torturers of women to repent, but a man whose *objet a* of desire is not woman but wealth and wealth alone worships a false god; he has sold his soul to the devil and cannot be redeemed. Don Marcos freely admitted that "su honra era su dinero" (his honor was his money) (*Novelas,* 154) and that his heart was with the six thousand ducats that Isidora and Agustín had carted off (*Novelas,* 156). In providing don Marcos the rope with which to hang himself, the devil is not driving him to despair. That has already been accomplished by the loss of his treasure and compounded by the false spell and the mocking letter from doña Isidora, in which she offers to cohabit with him again if he can get together another six thousand ducats. "El desesperado don Marcos" (The despairing don Marcos) was already heading downhill in search of a tree from which to hang himself when he met the devil in the shape of the marriage broker. The devil only facilitates or accelerates the collection of an overdue loan.

Although we speak of don Marcos's death as suicide, Zayas uses the theologically weighted term *desesperarse* (to despair) that indicted the ultimate sin—despairing of God's infinite capacity for forgiveness of sin.[7] To die by one's own hand in such a condition of despair meant that one's soul was condemned to hell, and suicides could not be buried on holy ground, although exceptions could be made for those whose despair was attributed to insanity (Martínez Gil 1993, 150–52).

Within Zayas's fictional world, in the first version of *El castigo,* don Marcos's master does secure holy burial for him using the excuse of insanity: "Dieron de todo quenta a su amo de don Marcos, el cual mandó, que le

enterrasse, sacando licencia, para que fuesse en sagrado, dando por disculpa de su desesperacion, que estaua loco" (They gave an account of
everything to don Marcos's master, who ordered that he be buried, securing permission for it to be in holy ground, giving as an excuse for his despair that he was crazy); but to this her narrator adds a moralizing commentary that, like the frame-section reactions, definitively condemns don
Marcos to hell: "que esta es la vanidad del mundo, honrar el cuerpo,
aunque el alma esté donde la deste miserable" (and this is the world's vanity, to honor the body although the soul may be where that of this miser is)
(Zayas y Sotomayor 1637b, 127).

The extensive research of Martínez Gil on the treatment of death in
Hapsburg Spain demonstrates that the demonically directed end of don
Marcos is perfectly consonant with received ideas—both theological and
popular—concerning the end of life. The devil was an undisputed reality
for the church, and many of the writers of the "Artes de bien morir" (or
manuals for dying) that proliferated in the first half of the seventeenth
century maintained that he appeared in various guises to many, if not all,
human beings in the hour of their death, in the final battle for eternal control of their souls (cited in Martínez Gil, 359, 369–70). According to
Nicolás Díaz, the devil appeared at "la muerte de aquellos que él conforme
a la vida que viuieron, y al descuydo que en él la tuuieron, tiene por cierto
que se han de condenar" (the death of those whom he shapes to the life
they lived, and by their lack of attention to him in life, he is sure that they
must be condemned). The debate was not *whether* the devil appeared, but
the frequency with which he did, and how to separate true demonic ap-
paritions from the natural torments of the final illness and the mental de-
rangement they might cause. Many *Arte* authors maintained that the devil
did not have to show himself openly but could take form in the imagination of the moribund person, where he would shape "formas feísimas, som-
bras pavorosas, imágenes diabólicas, y extravagantes, con que lo amenazan,
lo horrorizan, hasta conducirlo si pueden a la desesperación" (very ugly
forms, terrifying ghosts, diabolical and extravagant images, with which they
menace him and horrify him, until they lead him if they can to desperation) (cited in Martínez Gil 1993, 370–71). Such visions, obviously, would
not be discernable to others, but only to those whom God had chosen to
favor or punish.[8]

As Zayas first penned the melodramatic finale of *El castigo de la miseria*,
don Marcos succumbs to a fever that observers believe will be fatal to him,
but no priest is summoned to assist him to a good death. He recovers suffi-

ciently to dress and go out to end his life by his own hand, and there encounters the devil in the guise of the marriage broker. That the devil should appear to claim a man whose single-minded devotion to material gain had already placed him in league with the devil is perfectly consistent with the picture of the death struggle in many *Artes de bien morir.* That he should appear in the form of the marriage-broker offering him a rope to hang himself is psychologically consistent with the structure of his desire and with the common-sense proverb of "giving someone enough rope to hang themselves." The marriage broker dangled before don Marcos his *objet a* of desire—substantial wealth in the form of binding himself in marriage to a wealthy woman. When that *objet a* vanished into thin air along with the lady who presumably possessed it, all he has left is the bond proffered by the marriage broker, transformed into the rope with which to hang himself. That the devil was invisible to an observer is also consistent with the belief that the devil could really be present in visions limited to the agonist whose soul was in dispute. There is, therefore, no theological reason why Zayas should have eliminated the episode, for it only underlines the central point of the story, the idea that a miser who loves gold more than women or his very soul is a damnable member of the human race.

Nor is there evidence of Inquisitorial intervention or of any difficulty with securing the approval of censors.[9] She does not eliminate the deaths by suicide in two other stories in the *Novelas amorosas,* that of the feminine antagonists Adriana of the first story, *Aventurarse perdiendo* (Venturing and Losing), and Lucrecia in the sixth, *El desengaño amando y premio de la virtud* (The Road to Disillusionment and the Prize for Virtue).[10] Nor does she shy away from including violently self-inflicted death in the *Desengaños,* in which the endings of both the first and last tales include suicides.[11] Therefore we can presume that neither Zayas nor the censors objected to including suicide per se. Foa suggests that given the inquisitorial climate of the day, Zayas may have been persuaded to eliminate the episode because it made the climax of the tale "an impressive triumph by the Devil" (1977, 79). This is a plausible hypothesis given the overall effect of the episode, albeit in artistic more than in theological terms. Although Zayas restricts the role of the devil to that of an accomplice to an already despairing don Marcos, the ambiguous fascination of his appearance projects backwards in one's retrospective experience of the tale. By externalizing and concretizing the demonic, life-killing nature of an all-consuming desire for cold metal, it overshadows and colors the reader's view of preceding events in such a way as to detract from the personal responsibility of this miser for his own sad end.

In her narratives, Zayas employs the terms *devil, demonic,* or *diabolic* with a considerable range of representative values, from metaphorical to literal.[12] At the most figurative end of her signifying scale, she applies it to paint characters as hyperbolically ugly—the "endemoniado negro" (devilishly black) stable boy who is the object of Beatriz's lust in *El prevenido engañado* (*Novelas,* 183) or the "negra y endemoniada dama" (the black and devilish woman) who took Elena's place in *Desengaño 4* (*Desengaños,* 237). At a midpoint between figurative and literal, she employs it to qualify seductive or destructive stratagems as monstruously evil. For example, she calls don Juan's disguise as a woman to rape Camila an "invención diabólica" (*Desengaños,* 197) and speaks of the "espíritu diabólico" (diabolic spirit) that sent Inés in "endemoniado encanto" (a devilish spell) to don Diego's bed (*Desengaños,* 277, 289). She describes as a "prevención diabólica" (diabolic plan) the letters planted to accuse Beatriz of conspiring against her host the duke in *Desengaño 9* (*Desengaños,* 441), and labels the ruse used to make don Dionís kill the innocent Magdalena an "endemoniado enredo" (devilish plot) (*Desengaños,* 495). In her Manichaean world, however, even when Zayas's use of these terms is most figurative, we can still trace their connection to a literal belief in the existence of the devil as origin or inspiration of evil. She marks out the path frequently, pointing to the devil as motivator of villainous or desperate acts. When don Juan decided to dress as a woman to rape Camila, he was "vencido del demonio" (conquered by the devil), and "reinó en Carlos el demonio" (the devil ruled in Carlos) to make him poison her (*Desengaños,* 193, 195). She underscores most insistently the operation of the devil in the last *desengaño,* as Florentina says that "hablaba y obraba el demonio" (the devil spoke and worked) to inspire her maid to suggest that they trick don Dionís into killing Magdalena. "Seguíamos todas lo que el demonio nos inspiraba" (We all followed what the devil inspired us to do) says Florentina, and later, when don Dionís unleashes his fury, the devil makes her unable to confront him and curtail it: "el demonio, que ya estaba señoreado de aquella casa, me ató de suerte que no pude" (the devil, who was now lord of that house, tied me so that I couldn't) (*Desengaños,* 494, 496).

Finally, and most relevant to the ending of *El castigo de la miseria,* Zayas's narrator credits don Dionís's suicide to the devil, saying that

> insistido del demonio, puso el pomo de la espada en el suelo y la punta en su cruel corazón diciendo:

—No he de aguarder a que la justicia humana castigue mis delitos,
que más acertado es que sea yo el verdugo de la justicia divina.

Se dejó caer sobre la espada, pasando la punta a las espaldas, llamando al demonio que le recibiese el alma. (*Desengaños*, 499)

(set on by the devil, he put the pommel of his sword on the floor
and its point to his cruel heart saying: "I will not wait for human justice to punish my crimes, for it is more fitting that I should be the
executor of divine justice."

He let himself fall on the sword, its point sticking out through his
back, calling on the devil to receive his soul.)

Don Dionís is, of course wrong in theological terms in committing the ultimate sin of succumbing to the devil's call to despair. Inés, walled in to
starve and rot in *Desengaño 5,* also feels tempted to kill herself, but prays for
divine assistance to resist the devil's lure. Through the wall, she tells her
rescuer that "muchas veces me da imaginación de con mis propias manos
hacer cuerda a mi garganta para acabarme; más luego considero que es el
demonio, y pido ayuda a Dios para librarme de él" (many times I imagine
making a noose around my throat with my own hands to finish myself off;
but then I reflect that it is the devil [that gives me that image] and I ask
God's help to free myself from him) (*Desengaños*, 286).

However close and powerful or remote and figurative the connection to
the devil we see in Zayas's use of "demonic" and "diabolic," it never cancels
the operation of free will in the characters' choice to accept demonic direction, as do don Dionís and the black maid of *Desengaño 4;* or to resist it
as do the black stable boy and doña Inés. In only two tales other than the
first version of *El castigo* does Zayas bring on the devil in person, these
being *El jardín engañoso* and *Desengaño 9.* In both, his intervention serves to
dramatize or sensationalize the formidable opposition confronting guiltless or virtually guiltless women. Hence, I suggest that Zayas's decision to
excise the original ending of *El castigo* should not be attributed to institutional, religious censorship, but to her own authorial recognition that removing the literal intervention of the devil better centered don Marcos's
guilt where she wishes to situate it—in the personal, freely assumed sin of
overweening lust not for women but for wealth.

Masculinized Magic

With or without the devil, however, the world of magic to which Zayas introduces us in this story is unusually masculine. Rather than offering a

quintessentially female witch like Cervantes' Cañizares, she shows us a false male "sorcerer" extorting money from a gullible male, who is in turn driven to despair by the devil himself. As multiple studies of the history of magic and witchcraft in early modern Europe have demonstrated, those accused of involvement in such crimes were, by an overwhelming proportion, women (Sánchez Ortega 1992; Sallman 1993). Both the classical and Judeo-Christian traditions depicted women as a source of evil and capable of irrational connection with supernatural powers. The association of women with matter, the flesh, and sexuality made them the predictable sources of love magic in particular, and the social marginalization of women encouraged their cultivation of sorcery as a source of support in fact as well as in the popular and institutional fancy. Yet without departing from a grounding in the real and imagined practice of witchcraft in her day, Zayas cross-dresses it or otherwise projects its negative power onto a demonized "other" safely distanced from her personal definition of the true woman, who is Spanish and noble.

The practice of magic in the Renaissance was divided into two classes, one the domain of men, the other primarily of women. Zayas's first "sorcerer" is engaged in the masculine world of magic, the learned use of occult arts in the pursuit of wealth. This brand of necromancy, nourished by Neoplatonic magic, by scholarly forms of divination from the Jewish and Arab tradition, and by astrology and alchemy, was mainly the preserve of learned, elite males. Such workers of magic dedicated their efforts to fashioning talismans that could make a man powerful and invulnerable and to "conjuring up spirits that could foretell the future and reveal the location of hidden treasures" (Sallman 1993, 455)—exactly the goal for which don Marcos employs his sorcerer. That Marcela's boyfriend should name the demon he calls up "Calquimorro, demonio de los caminos" (Anymoor, devil of the highways) (*Novelas*, 161) is predictable as well. Apart from Arab input to the art of necromancy, Moriscos were popularly believed to have left large caches of treasure buried in secret locations after their forced dispersal in the 1570's and expulsion in 1609. And behind all types of magic lurks the devil, repeatedly invoked by all tormented and tormenting characters in Zayas, and brought visibly on the scene in at least three of her stories: *El castigo de la miseria* (A Miser's Reward), *El jardín engañoso* (The Deceitful Garden) and *Desengaño 9, La perseguida triunfante* (Triumph over Persecution). But even leaving the devil himself out of the count, Zayas shows more males than females practicing magic.

She also entrusts to men as much as to women the practice of the second class of magic, that devoted to Eros. Of the four practitioners of love magic whom she creates, one is a Moor (*Desengaño 5*),[13] one is a student from Alcalá (*Desengaño andando y premio de la virtud*, and two are Italian women (*La fuerza del amor* and *Desengaño amando*), one of whom uses witchcraft on her own behalf, the other for hire. Feminine use of magic is thus distanced by making it a practice of foreign women.

The first episode of recourse to love magic also demonstrates Zayas's awareness of the relationship between recourse to magic and the powerlessness of women in a patriarchal society. Laura in *La fuerza de amor* (The Power of Love) has been brought up in a completely masculine family following her mother's death in giving birth to her. Although her father and two older brothers love Laura, they leave her alone to deal with her philandering, abusive husband don Diego, moving away from their home in Naples so as not to witness his physical abuse of her and her emotional suffering. They depart after a scene in which Laura's screams draw them to her room, where don Diego's blows have left her bathed in blood, and Carlos pulls out a dagger to stab him. But don Diego, seeing the danger, *embraces* Carlos to stop the blow, and Laura further paralyzes him with her plea, "¡Ay hermano mío, mira que en esa vida está la de tu triste hermana!" (Ay, look, my brother; in that life lies that of your sad sister!) Zayas thus literalizes the power of the homosocial bonds that stay his hand from intervening to protect his abused sister, and verbalizes the internalized as well as real feminine dependency that contributes to their power.

In despair after their departure, Laura enlists the aid of the *hechicera* (sorceress). She turns to magic only when she finds herself totally isolated, with no other power or court to which she can appeal; her decision thus accords with Adorno's observation of the relative rationality of recourse to magic in certain times and circumstances: "In former periods, superstition was an attempt, however awkward, to cope with problems for which no better or more rational means were available" (1994, 37).[14] The sorceress charges her to bring the hair and teeth of a hanged man to work a spell to bring her errant husband home, and as Laura gathers courage to go to the dread site, she laments the complete absence of anyone to whom she can turn:

¿A quién contaré mis penas que me las remedie? ¿Quién oirá mis quexas que se enternezca? ¿Quién verá mis lágrimas que me las enxugue? Nadie por cierto, pues mi padre y hermanos, por no oírlas me han desamparado, y hasta el cielo, consuelo de los afligidos, se hace sordo por no dármele. (*Novelas,* 241)

(To whom will I relate my sufferings so that s/he will relieve them? Who will hear my complaints and be moved? Who will see my tears and dry them for me? No one, certainly, since my father and brothers have abandoned me so as not to hear them, and even heaven, consolation of the afflicted, deafens itself in order not to give it to me.)

Not only do men turn a deaf ear and a blind eye to cruelty to women, but as "legislators of the world," they keep women ignorant and defenseless, actively conditioning them in such a way that they are incapable of seeking their own remedies. Laura protests:

¿Por qué, vanos legisladores del mundo, atáis nuestras manos para las venganzas, imposibilitando nuestras fuerzas con vuestras falsas opiniones, pues nos negáis letras y armas? ¿El alma no es la misma que la de los hombres? Pues si ella es la que da valor al cuerpo, ¿quién obliga a los nuestros a tanta cobardía? Yo aseguro que si entendierais que también había en nosotras valor y fortaleza, no os burlarais como os burláis; y así, por tenernos sujetas desde que nacemos vais enflaqueciendo nuestras fuerzas con los temores de la honra, y el entendimiento con el recato de la vergüenza, dándonos por espadas ruecas, y por libros almohadillas. (*Novelas,* 241–42)

(Why, vain legislators of the world, do you tie our hands against revenge, rendering our forces unfit for service with your false opinions, since you deny us arms and education? Isn't our soul the same as that of men? Well, if the soul is what gives the body courage, what forces ours to so much cowardice? I assure you that if you understood that there was also courage and strength in us, you would not deceive us as you do; and therefore, in order to keep us in subjection from our birth you proceed to weaken our forces with fear for our honor, and [you weaken] our understanding with concern for shame, giving us in place of swords, spindles, and in place of books, embroidery frames.)

Yet while Zayas has Laura level this charge against masculine designs, she also reveals the pressure of her conservative ideology at work as she separates the major religious and political institutions (in the form of the Inquisition and the viceregal system of governance) from her critique of patriarchal practices. As Laura turns to the sorceress, the narrator, Nise, attributes the proliferation of *hechiceras* in Italy to the absence of the Inquisition:

> Hay en Nápoles en estos enredos y supersticiones tanta libertad, que públicamente usan sus invenciones, haciendo tantas y con tales apariencias de verdades, que casi obligan a ser creídas; y aunque los confesores y el Virrey andan en esto solícitos, como no hay el freno de la Inquisición, y los demás castigos no les amedrentan, porque en Italia lo más ordinario es castigar la bolsa. (*Novelas*, 238–39)

> (There is so much liberty in Naples in these mischiefs and superstitions, that they practice their inventions publicly, performing so many and with such appearance of truth that they almost oblige one to believe them; and although the confessors and the viceroy are heedful of this, since there is not the restraint of the Inquisition and no other punishments frighten them, because in Italy it is most common to punish their pocketbooks.)

Nise inserts skeptical terms intended to cast a prudent doubt on the truth of their power—superstition, *enredo* (mischief), *embuste* (trick)—or calls their witchcraft a money-extorting occupation.[15] The efficacy of erotic magic is never put to the test in this story, however, because Laura's mere presence in the gruesome chapel is enough to waken her brother from a deep sleep with the extrasensory perception that his sister is in danger. Thus she sustains the feminine fantasy of the "man-who-would-understand" in the form of a loving brother's telepathic response.[16] As he comes galloping toward Naples, his horse stops dead still before the chapel and he rescues Laura, taking her home to tell her story, first to her family and then to the ruling viceroy. Not just any viceroy, but one with whom Zayas very possibly had a personal connection (see Chapter 1 above), don Pedro Fernández de Castro, count of Lemos, on whom she bestows lavish praise: "nobilísimo, sabio y piadoso príncipe, cuyas raras virtudes y excelencias no son para [ser] escritas en papeles, sino en láminas de bronce y en las lenguas de la fama" (most noble, wise, and pious prince, whose rare virtues and excellence deserve to be written not on paper, but on bronze plaques and on the tongues of fame) (*Novelas*, 245). The viceroy calls don

Diego to account and he repents and promises to mend his ways, but Laura elects to enter the convent rather than return to her repentant husband. Again, not just any convent, but a Concepción convent, an order to which Zayas has also been linked, and which she calls a "convento noble, rico y santo" (a noble, rich and saintly convent) (*Novelas*, 247).

In this first engagement with erotic magic, Zayas thus shows why women turn to sorcery, yet she preserves powerful institutions from her general-ized critique of masculine practices.[17] (We will examine further her divided or self-limiting challenge in Chapter 9.)

In the story that follows, Zayas most exploits the theme of magic, credit-ing it with real effects while spelling out the orthodox Christian explana-tion of the (limited) source of demonic power. She also uses it to both comic and spectacular effect in this tale. Competing for the attentions of her lover, don Fernando, with an older Italian woman, Lucrecia, who is "grandísima hechicera" (a great sorceress), doña Juana seeks the assistance of a student at Alcalá. Between them, they use magic for the same three primary purposes for which women employed it historically, according to Sánchez Ortega's study of Inquisition records: (1) to determine a man's amorous intentions; (2) to obtain a man's love; and (3) to recover the af-fection or ardor of a cold or straying lover (1992, 61). The student gives Juana magic rings, inset with green stones, that she is to wear while quizzing don Fernando about his intentions. After doing so, however, Juana entrusts the rings to a servant girl who wears them while drawing water, washing clothes, and performing other tasks. And when the student recovers the rings, the two demons who inhabit them jump out and pum-mel him to a pulp for allowing them to be thus abused. Nevertheless, they reveal that Fernando has no intention of marrying Juana. Juana then de-cides to attempt to transport a former lover back from Naples to marry her, and the student teaches her spells and incantations to that end. The spells have a dramatic effect—by the third day, Octavio appears to tell Juana that he has died and to complain that she continues to torment him in death as she did in life. This emissary from the underworld explains to her the di-vine source of apparently demonic arts:

> Advierte que aunque el demonio es padre de mentiras y engaños, tal vez permite Dios que diga alguna verdad en provecho y utilidad de los hombres, para que le avisen de su perdición, como ha hecho contigo, pues por la boca del estudiante tiene avisado tu peligro. Teme, que te dixo que estás en los infiernos. . . . Y no pienses que

he venido a decirte esto por la fuerza de tus conjuros, sino por particular providencia y voluntad de Dios, que me mandó que viniese a avisarte desto y decirte que si no miras por ti, ¡ay de tu alma! (*Novelas*, 267)

(Take note that although the devil is the father of lies and deceits, God may permit him to tell some truth for the benefit and utility of men, to warn them of their perdition, as he has done with you, for you were notified of your danger through the student's mouth. Be fearful, for he told you that you are in hell. . . . And don't think I have come to tell you this through the power of your spells, but through the special providence and will of God, who ordered me to come to warn you of this and to tell you that if you don't look out for yourself, woe be unto your soul!)

This messenger gets Juana's full attention and the next day she too enters the Concepción convent, with a dowry partly supplied by Fernando.

This is not the end of the novella's magic effects, however. Lucrecia continues to exercise her craft as don Fernando marries another women, Clara. She takes her revenge using a method that, according to Inquisition records, both men and women attributed to *hechiceras*—she casts a spell on him that saps his strength for six months, then others that cause him to dislike his wife, whom he abandons to follow Lucrecia to another city. When his wife follows him there and takes a job as a servant in the house, he does not even recognize her until one day when Lucrecia is ill and gives Clara the task of feeding a very special rooster she keeps in a chest in the attic. Clara finds the fowl and takes off the glasses Lucrecia has put on the rooster, whereupon her husband immediately recognizes her. Lucrecia also has a wax statue of a man with powers like the effigy that don Alonso employed in *Desengaño 5;* she sinks a pin into it and throws it into the fire, before committing suicide when her spell over Fernando is broken. The hen, the wax figures, and the pins were all elements in the repertoire of tools of "sympathetic magic" described in Inquisition trials of women accused of witchcraft.[18] Zayas is thus fictionalizing elements that would also have been taken seriously by most of her readers. She creates a symbolic fictional auto-da-fé as the authorities burn Lucrecia's body and all the instruments of her witchcraft. This allows Zayas to dramatize the real effects of her magic, yet provide the reassurance that a combination of human watchfulness and diligence, the care of the Divine overseer, and the might of terrestrial political/religious institutions can bring such malign manipulators to their deserved end.

In Lacanian terms, we might say that this presentation of magic and its power over human subjects is a formalization of the anxiety caused by the formulation of the subject in alienation, in which our sense of "self" is dependent on the message received from the Other. The lack of autonomy, the vulnerability to external forces and institutions, is attributed to magical objects and to malign spirits who manipulate them to control our actions. Thus the compulsions experienced as alien that dominate conscious life can be demonized. Elaine Pagels demonstrates the long history of the demonizing of variously defined enemies of the faith in Judeo-Christian tradition. Even theologians such as Saint Augustine, who denied ontological existence to evil, still evoked Satan in sermons and prayers when communicating with a community of believers who experienced their own struggle against evil as a combat with unremitting demons, internal or external (Pagels 1995, 179–82). Classically, the demonic label is directed toward religious dissenters; Zayas follows this pattern in having her false first sorcerer invoke a demon named Calquimorro, and in investing in a Moorish *hechicero* the power to control doña Inés's body, if not her spirit. The duel of magic is capped by the gendered cosmic test of supernatural power in *Desengaño 9,* in which the devil lends his magic support to Federico's pursuit and persecution of Beatriz while the Virgin defends her. Inasmuch as the Other is in part the other sex, it is understandable that the principal locus for demonic power figured by a woman writer such as Zayas would be masculine and behind it all, the devil himself.

The Living and the Undead

If the boundary between natural and supernatural causality is porous in Zayas's fictional world, that between life and death is equally permeable. Visions and voices of the dead regularly intervene in the world of the living, and bodies or parts of bodies linger on the threshold between death and life to transmit both terrifying and salvific messages from the other side. As the ultimate unknowable experience in human existence, death has always possessed a fascination, but attitudes toward it have varied considerably over the centuries, as Ariès in particular has shown us (1974; 1981). He traces the slow evolution from a medieval "tamed death" to a more personalized confrontation with the end of life in early modern Europe that he called "one's own death," and thence to a death projected on others ("thy death") in Romanticism, followed by "forbidden death" in the modern era. Openly expressed fascination with death and violent dismemberment in the late twentieth century seems particularly striking, perhaps, because it follows a century or more during which society handled death by silencing, hiding and denying it. Quite the opposite was the case in Counter-Reformation Spain, however. Martínez Gil points out that the early seventeenth century saw a resurgent fixation on death, including an emphasis on its macabre aspects even greater than that of the fifteenth century with its *danzas de la muerte* (1993, 316–21, 348). Remembrance and representations of death took center stage in religious discourse and in literary and artistic formulations of Baroque *desengaño*. In the era of Gracián's *Criticon*, Quevedo's *El sueño de la muerte*, and the memento mori paintings of Valdés Leal, what is unique in Zayas's stories is not the interpenetration of life and death, but the mode and ends toward which she mobilizes the dead in her stories of love.

Making the (Un)dead Speak

Counter-Reformation insistence that the faithful should conduct their lives with a continuous focus on the inevitable end of death is in a sense a Symbolic-order endeavor directed at overcoming the impasse in human experience that is posed by the silence of death. Freud observed: "My death is unimaginable. Even the unconscious is convinced of its immortality."[19] Dreamers never dream their own deaths, however vividly they may perceive in sleep the fear of that event, or the death of others. At the same time, the fear of death and dissolution inhabits conscious life, however variously human beings may attempt to defend themselves against the threat of this inevitable enigma. Christian doctrine, of course, upholds the foreclosure of death through belief in the immortality of the soul and the eventual resurrection of the body. Yet following the positive estimation of human potential and the valuing of terrestrial life that arose in the Renaissance, Counter-Reformation law imposed the belief that enjoyment of eternal life in bliss rather than in perpetual torment could only be secured by the sacrifice of earthly pleasures, by the *mortification* of the flesh. Freud posited that the result of a thorough imposition of superego control could be a "pure culture of the death drive" ("The Ego and the Id," 1974, 19:53). The resurgent fixation on death that Martínez Gil documents in seventeenth-

Juan Valdés Leal, *In Ictu Oculi.* Oil on canvas. Iglesia del Hospital de la Santa
Caridad, Sevilla (photo: Art Resource, New York)

century Spain and the sensual presentation of its macabre horror may find
an immediate material cause in visitations of plague, economic crisis, and
political decline, as he suggests, but it is also a psychic response to Reformation demands for the mortification of the flesh as the paradoxical route
to immortality.

Given the association of woman with matter, woman qua flesh, images of
the death that at once lures and threatens were often figured as women.[20]
While the skull or a fleshless and vaguely masculine skeleton served in
most memento mori as the reminder of death, death personified often
took on feminine form, in literary and in plastic representations. In the *Ro-*

mance del enamorado y la muerte, for example, death is "una señora tan blanca, / muy más que la nieve fría" (a woman so white, much more that the cold snow), who lures a lover to a fatal attempt at union with his beloved. In *La carta del cartujo,* death appears as a beautiful woman from the torso up, a skeleton below, while another painting represents death/woman with a vertical division (Martínez Gil 1993, 341). Quevedo paints a similarly fused death/woman in *Sueño de la muerte,*[21] as does Gracián in *El Criticón:*

> Entró finalmente la tan temida reina [la muerte], ostentando aquel su tan extraño aspecto a media cara; de tal suerte, que era de flores la una mitad y la otra de espinas; la una de carne blanda y la otra de huessos; muy colorada aquélla y fresca, que parecía de rosas entreveradas de jazmines, muy seca y muy marchita ésta. (1980, part 3, *crisi* 11, p. 773)

> (Finally the most feared queen [death] came in, displaying her strange appearance in half-face; in such a way that one half was of flowers and the other thorns, the one of soft flesh and the other bones; that one very rosy and fresh, that looked like roses intermixed with jasmine, this one very dry and withered.)

Zayas too deploys images of deathly horror in female flesh, albeit to a different end, as we shall see. But when she animates the voice of death from beyond the tomb to warn her protagonists against their impending fate, death comes clothed in masculine flesh. Her first protagonist, the visionary dreamer Jacinta of *Adventurarse perdiendo,* dreams the death of her fantasy-come-to-life love in the form of a masculine death's-head. Jacinta "sees" don Félix's death in advance, dreaming that she receives his head in a box. This sort of violation of time, space, and the frontier of death is a regular unconscious occurrence in the forum of dreams and is easily accommodated both in ancient and modern understandings of the nature of dreams. In Artemidorus's category of day-residue dreams (Artemidorus Daldianus 1975, 14, 20), as in modern schemes of dream interpretation, a dream such as Jacinta's is understood as a natural expression of anxiety. Inasmuch as Zayas's contemporaries ascribed to the ancient view that some dreams were divinely inspired messages, however, they could also read Jacinta's dream as a supernatural communication. And we can characterize it as a strategically ambiguous introduction to the waking visions or appearances of the dead in her other stories. Don Felix's head "speaks" to Jacinta from beyond the tomb inasmuch as she interprets it as emblematic of his death and the death of her dream of requited love.

Zayas's next emissary from the other side of the death frontier does come in fully supernatural form, however, and speaks his warning with the power of a divine dispenation, as Octavio answers doña Juana's summons in *El desengaño andando y premio de la virtud*. Abandoned by don Fernando, Juana uses the student magician's powers to summon this former suitor back from Naples to Spain to marry her. Following the magician's instructions, she conjures up Octavio's presence within three sessions. She hears a noise at the closed door and feels a cold wind on her face, and then Octavio enters the room, laden with chains, surrounded by flames, and giving fearful sighs. His first words are a challenge: "¿Qué me quieres, doña Juana, qué me quieres? No bastaba haber sido mi tormento en vida, sino que en muerte y todo te precias de dármele" (What do you want of me, doña Juana, what do you want of me? Wasn't it enough to have been my torment in life, without you boasting of giving me torment in death too?) (*Novelas*, 267). He tells her that he was killed leaving a gambling house, and although he is suffering terrible torments, his death will not be eternal. In other words, he is in purgatory rather than hell.[22]

Over the centuries, purgatory came to be conceived as an intermediate space and time of waiting, in which the soul, or *anima*, separated from the body at death would be purged while waiting for the second coming and final judgment, or the cancellation of personal debt for sin. It was according to Ariès a space related also to old pagan beliefs, a limbo in which unsatisfied shades wandered, to linger at the scene of their sins or deaths and to appear to the living, at least in visions and dreams (Ariès 1981, 66–68, 153). Martínez Gill comments:

> Durante siglos, los muertos habían impuesto a los vivos su presencia cotidiana; el triunfo del purgatorio había supuesto su apartamiento y reclusión. Andando el tiempo, esa lejanía abocaría al olvido, olvido de la muerte, olvido de los muertos, nuevo sistema de manifestar el rechazo que hace el ser humano de un fenómeno irracional que, después de padecerlo tantos siglos, aún no comprende. (509–10)

> (For centuries, the dead had imposed on the living their daily presence; the triumph of purgatory had entailed their withdrawal and

seclusion. With the passage of time, that distance would pass into forgetting, forgetting death, forgetting the dead, a new system of demonstrating the rejection by human beings of an irrational phenomenon which, after suffering it for so many centuries, they still do not understand.)

But in Zayas's day, as her stories demonstrate vividly, this repression of death was still far away. Although purgatory was in a sense created to confine waiting souls to a space separated from the living, whether spirits wandered beyond it or not, communication between the living and the dead was not broken, however much the church attempted to limit it to the channels of prayer and *sufragios* (good works to benefit souls in purgatory) (Martínez Gil 1993, 508).

The supernatural emissaries that Zayas animates in this story also contravene the limits of terrestrial chronology with views into the future akin to those that now draw people to such films as *Back to the Future* or *Terminator 2*. The devils contained in the rings provided by the magician deliver—along with a beating—a dire report on the present and future of don Fernando and doña Juana: "¿Piensas que se ha de casar con ella? No por cierto, porque juntos como están acá, están ardiendo en los infiernos, y de esa suerte acabarán, sin que ni tú ni ella cumpláis vuestro deseo" (Do you think he'll marry her? Surely not, because together as they are here, they are burning in hell, and they will end in that way, without either you or she fulfilling your desire) (*Novelas,* 263). Octavio reiterates that time-effacing vision of eternal torment: "Teme, que te dixo [el estudiante] que estás en los infiernos" (Be fearful, for [the student] told you you are in hell) (*Novelas,* 267). Like the Polaroid snapshot of the future love and destruction left to the heroine of *Terminator 2,* Zayas gives Juana a vision of an eternal future already operant. But like the young hero of *Back to the Future,* she is also afforded the opportunity to affect that future-past-present. Octavio adds to his warning the possibility of a soul-saving reprieve conceded her by a benevolent God if she mends her ways:

> Dale gracias [a Cristo] porque te avisa enternecido de tu perdición, porque le costaste su sangre y morir en una Cruz. . . . Y no pienses que he venido a decirte esto por la fuerza de tus conjuros, sino por particular providencia y voluntad de Dios, que me mandó que viniese a avisarte desto y decirte que si no miras por ti, ¡ay de tu alma! (*Novelas,* 267)

(Thank [Christ] because, moved by your perdition, he warns you, because you cost his blood and death on a Cross. . . . And don't think I have come to tell you this through the power of your spells, but through the special providence and will of God, who ordered me to come to warn you of this and to tell you that if you don't look out for yourself, woe be unto your soul!)

After this brief sermon, Octavio leaves as he came, moaning and dragging his chains behind him. Juana, terrified by this heavenly warning, feels that an accumulation of divine warnings capped by the appearance of Octavio means that her death is near and resolves the next day to enter a convent.

Zayas thus introduces her readers to the presence of the "living dead" with a dramatic vision of a masculine *alma en pena* who is careful to justify the possibility of his appearance in theologically acceptable terms. Juana's method in conjuring him up is a damnable act of black science, *nigroman-cia*.[23] Nevertheless, belief in appearances of such *animas* continued, much fed by stories told by nuns and priests. The official position of the church was cautious, but did include the possibility of appearance of souls from heaven, purgatory, or even, very occasionally, from hell, as a divinely con-ceded miracle sent for the good of the living, to console, advise or protect them (Martínez Gil 1993, 505–6). The possibility that such visions might be a demonic temptation, however, wrapped them in a terrifying atmosphere, even for a strong spirit such as that of Saint Teresa. And the terror was aug-mented by the belief that anyone who saw such an *alma en pena* was des-tined to die within the year (507–8). Hence Juana's determination to end her sinful life and her dabbling in magic arts and to enter a convent as quickly as possible.

Two more male bodies speak their warnings from the other side of death in Zayas's *Desengaños amorosos*. In a preliminary episode in *Desengaño 10*, Don Gaspar, pursuing the source of painful moans in the cellar of the home of women of easy virtue he frequents, digs up the body of a young gentleman, dead but still emitting soulful groans. This curious, brief episode will be analyzed at length in Chapter 9; here we need only note that don Gaspar reads the moaning corpse as a divine warning that deters him at least temporarily from the pursuit of illicit amorous pleasures.

Zayas makes a much more eloquent male corpse central to *Desengaño 3, El verdugo de su esposa*, her version of the widely circulated story "Los dos amigos" (The Two Friends). That story is also the base of the Cervantine tale inserted in the first part of *Don Quixote*, "El curioso impertinente," which was in its turn the touchstone for Zayas's narrative.²⁴ "Los dos ami-gos" in Zayas are don Pedro and don Juan, inseparable friends in Palermo since childhood. When Don Pedro marries the beautiful Roseleta, don Juan at first keeps a prudent distance from the newlyweds' home, but re-turns on don Pedro's insistence, falls passionately in love with Roseleta—without the perverse wife-testing intervention of Cervantes' Anselmo—and begins to court her assiduously. After the failure of her angry and eloquent efforts to dissuade don Juan, Roseleta tells her unsuspecting husband of don Juan's courtship and shows him love notes he has sent her. Feigning an obligatory business trip, don Pedro has Roseleta arrange a love tryst with don Juan at their country home and organizes an ambush for his treacherous friend. But don Juan is saved by his devotion to the Virgin Mary, who makes a hanged man the vocal instrument of her intervention. On the road out of town, don Juan hears the bells sound the Ave Maria and stops to pray to the Virgin, begging her forgiveness for the sin he was about to commit and for her protection and intercession to secure her di-vine Son's pardon as well. As he then passes the spot where three men had been hanged that day for robbery, one of them calls his name. Amazed, don Juan stops and the man explains that God has worked the apparently impossible, saving his life because he was innocent. Don Juan cuts him down and the hanged man then insists on entering the villa in his stead; don Juan watches in hiding and sees don Pedro and his servants attack the man, throw his now twice-dead body in a well, and weight it down with stones. As the thoroughly shaken don Juan returns to the city, he sees the three robbers hanging from the trees as he first found them. The next day, after begging don Pedro's forgiveness and recounting the miracle that saved him, don Juan enters a Carmelite monastery.

But not even this miraculous intervention can save Roseleta in Zayas's version. Don Pedro's love for his wife does not withstand public gossip about the case, the stings of being labeled the man who killed a hanged man, and the lures of a former lover of don Juan, Angeliana, angelic only in name. When Roseleta sends a threatening note to her rival, Angeliana convinces don Pedro that Roseleta was in fact guilty of adultery and they carefully plan her murder, effected by don Pedro's surreptitious removal of a bandage while she is being bled to cure a throat ailment. She bleeds to death and don Pedro marries Angeliana. He also again attempts to kill don Juan, but fails. In the listeners' discussion after the story, the men exoner-ate don Pedro on the grounds that a husband has the right to defend his honor against the slurs of the public, whether well or ill founded. The women judge him guilty, and then wonder why God saved don Juan and allowed Roseleta to suffer. Both sexes concur in Lisis's concluding summation that God's designs are incomprehensible, to which she adds her judgment that "a Roseleta le había dado Dios el cielo padeciendo aquel martirio, porque la debió de hallar en tiempo de merecerle, y que a don Juan le guardó hasta que le mereciese con la penitencia" (God had given Roseleta heaven, suffering that martyrdom, because he must have found her at the right time to deserve it, and he spared don Juan until he should merit it with his penitence) (*Desengaños,* 223).

Zayas thus reverses virtually all the cause-and-effect relationships of the tale as Cervantes told it, beyond the basic situation of a male friendship destroyed by rivalry over a beautiful woman. Where Cervantes makes the tragic tale a study of homosocial bonding and mimetic desire played out in the testing of Camila (Wilson 1987), Zayas centers it on a much simpler, direct rivalry for possession of the beautiful Roseleta, compounded by the inconstancy of men, the inevitable mobility of masculine desire, and the existence of a female rival. For the complex psychological interplay that eventually proves Cervantes' Camila to be indeed an "imperfect animal," Zayas substitutes a melodramatic intervention by a dead man animated by the Virgin Mary that is nevertheless insufficient to save a "perfect" wife.[25] Cervantes, as Wilson says, makes the story a "test of wife-testing," as shared cultural fictions drive Anselmo to self-destruct in midsentence while the once-passive Camila becomes mistress of her own fate by staging a consummate representation of another cultural myth, a Lucrece-style suicide attempt. In contrast, Zayas's narrator repeatedly links this story to the preceding one about the rape and poisoning of her innocent Camila to preach that a wife accused of adultery cannot save herself either by silence and seclusion, nor by speaking out, as had Roseleta—only to invite her own murder while being treated for a *throat ailment.* Even the miraculous resurrection of a dead man serves only to save a guilty man, not an innocent woman.[26] In the patriarchal order of her stories, men may even overcome the silence of death, but Symbolic Order language affords virtuous women no medium for survival. Women, her tales of disillusionment imply, can only speak their innocence through their bodies, in death.

Love Over Death

In one work from the *Novela amorosas,* however, Zayas tells through a male narrator a miracle tale of love that triumphs over death. In the two-part story *El imposible vencido,* the "undead" take the form of a false ghost and a true resurrection by love.[27] Friends and neighbors in Salamanca since childhood, don Rodrigo and Leonor were born under the star of the fatally separated lovers Pyramus and Thisbe, says the narrator. Their desire to marry is rejected by Leonor's parents on economic grounds, since Rodrigo as a second son does not dispose of a fortune equal to that of Leonor, an only daughter of wealthy parents. They promise her to don Alonso instead, and don Rodrigo departs to serve as a soldier in Flanders. Leonor promises to wait for three years for him, then falls in what appears to be a dead faint on seeing him dressed for departure in deathlike colors, straw and black, "colores de su fortuna" (the colors of his fortune) (*Novelas,* 333) as the coach arrives at the place of death: "[el] lugar de la muerte . . . en el que se habían de apartar las almas de los cuerpos" (the place of death . . . where souls had to separate from bodies) (*Novelas,* 333). Although the tale thus opens with a generous dose of tragic notes centered on love, separation, and death, its overall tone is quite the opposite, as the miraculous finale is preceded by a scene of the "walking dead" that is a hoax, more comic than terrifying. Zayas repeats the sequence she employed in the first version of *El castigo de la miseria,* proceeding from hoax to "real" supernatural events.

In the first part of the story, don Rodrigo will put a false ghost to death and in the second he brings a true corpse to life with the strength of his love and Christ's intervention. Serving the duke of Alba, he enters combat with a chain-rattling "ghost" in pursuit of love. The duke of Alba dispatches him to the house of doña Blanca, a beautiful widow whose home is "haunted" by what proves to be an enamored married neighbor on stilts, decked out with chains that he rattles trying to frighten off servants and gain access to the lady.[28] When don Rodrigo knocks him to the ground and reveals the hoax, the false ghost becomes a true *alma en pena* as he is condemned to death by beheading.[29] Doña Blanca then joins the numerous Flemish beauties seeking don Rodrigo's attentions, but the narrator assures us that although he is courteous to them, his constant love for doña Leonor is such that it could resurrect the Golden Age. Through a bedswitch ruse, he negotiates doña Blanca's marriage to his friend, don Beltrán, long her suitor, by agreeing to a love tryst with her one night, at which don Beltrán takes his place. Meanwhile, Leonor's mother has overheard her lamenting don Rodrigo's prolonged absence, her parents have a false letter sent saying he has married a Flemish woman, and she is thereupon married to don Alonso. Rodrigo duly returns to Salamanca,[30] now a captain rewarded for his military service with membership in the Order of Santiago and four thousand ducats of income. The newlywed and miserable Leonor, seeing him from her balcony, falls dead from the shock. After her burial the distraught don Rodrigo bribes a sacristan to let him into her tomb, and as he prays to Christ before a crucifix in front of her coffin, she lifts her hand to her head, beginning to return to life. This sort of resurrection-by-love occurs in a number of versions by other authors, but Zayas is unusual in her insistence that Leonor was really, truly dead, not just drugged or in a coma.

As she does other supernatural occurrences, Zayas grounds the miracle in a plethora of detail about the rituals of burial and marriage, as don Rodrigo and Leonor defend the legality of their union. We are told that her marriage to don Alonso was invalid because she had given her word and a *cédula* to don Rodrigo, that she had been deceived and forced to marry by her parents, and that even if that marriage had been legal, it had been dissolved by her death. We follow their process through the full marriage rites prescribed by the Council of Trent—the publication of the banns three times in the cathedral in Salamanca in the hearing of her parents and don Alonso, their wedding and the consummation of the marriage, and how they come to "velar" or to publicly consecrate their union one month later in the Salamanca cathedral, where after the ceremony her mother finally recognizes that this beautiful bride is indeed her dead daughter.[31] Don Alonso, interested principally in recovering the dowry he lost at Leonor's death, brings suit and attempts to disrupt the postwedding festivities. At his insistence, the corregidor has the disputed bride sequestered under neutral custody, a fairly common practice instituted to insure that the sacrament of marriage was freely undertaken by the parties involved, not forced on them by their families (Casey 1989, 95–101). The case is then passed from civil to ecclesiastical authorities, and the reader learns that Leonor had never permitted the consummation of her marriage to don Alonso, that she was watched for thirty-six hours rather than the requisite twenty-four, and that her death was certified by three doctors before burial.[32] The narrator tells us twice that Leonor never regained her color, her pallor constituting for the rest of her life the proof of passage through the valley of death.

Contrasting elements of the first and second episodes of this tale illuminate the underlying fantasy of the power of true love as Zayas tells it through a male narrator. In the first, a false ghost pursues illicit desire (the "ghost" being alive and married) and the bed-switch substitution by which doña Blanca is married to the "wrong man" is legitimized as a consequence

of her independent pursuit of satisfaction of desire and subsequent acceptance of the consummated union. Leonor, on the other hand, proves her
constant love by refusing satisfaction to the husband forced on her by
parental deceit. The final key to that fantasy, however, occurs in the ultimate resolution of the case by students at the University of Salamanca.
After the bishop has heard the evidence, he consults with a famous professor at the university,[33] and the latter, because the case is so serious and he
does not want to decide it alone, tells it to students in his class, explaining
to them the rights of each party. The students decide the case, shouting in
unison: " '¡Désenla a don Rodrigo; désenla a don Rodrigo, que suya es!' "
(Give her to Rodrigo, give her to Rodrigo, for she is his!) This judgment is
reminiscent of the biblical story of Pontius Pilate passing to an assembled
crowd the responsibility for the fate of Christ (Mark 15:1–15; Matthew
27:11–26; Luke 23:1–25; John 18:28–19:16)—the Christ who had inter-
ceded for the grieving don Rodrigo, and Christ through God's love for humanity was also resurrected from the dead for their salvation. The underlying fantasy of the story is thus that of a perfect satisfaction of desire in an
ideal love that overcomes the triple opposition of the law: as it is exercised
in parental authority, in civil and ecclesiastical institutions, and in the final
law of nature, that of death. It thus becomes a rewriting of the story of salvation through resurrection of the flesh, akin to the maternal rewriting of
the fall of humankind that Zayas constructs in *El jardin engañoso* (see Chapter 2 above). The narrator, don Lope, concludes the story with the happily-
ever-after ending of enduring love and survival through a son, as

> don Rodrigo gozó de la hermosa doña Leonor muchos años,
> aunque pocos según su amor. . . .
>
> Murió doña Leonor primero que su marido, si bien se llevaron el
> uno al otro pocos meses, dejándole un hijo que hoy vive casado,
> siendo en su tierra muy querido. (*Novelas,* 367)

> (don Rodrigo enjoyed the lovely doña Leonor for many years, al-
> though they seemed few according to his love. . . .
>
> Doña Leonor died before her husband, although the one pre-
> ceded the other by only a few months, leaving him a son who today
> is living, married, and much loved in his land.)

Telling Bodies

In the violent world of the *Desengaños amorosos,* however, what Zayas shows
her readers is not a love that triumphs over death, but love that brings

death in its wake to virtually all the heroines of these stories, except for a lucky five who find timely refuge in a convent. The death she displays is different from the literary representation of the philosophy of *desengaño* in a writer such as Gracián, or the memento mori iconography of the plastic arts. They figure the death that inhabits all earthly existence in vaguely masculine skeletons or in alluring female flesh. She exhibits not the death present in life but the death threat—physical as well as emotional—within amorous relationships.[34] Whereas Zayas's masculine undead return to tell their stories in words, the eloquence women display in death is corporeal, not verbal.

Her presentation of death as a spectacle in which ultimate truth is written in the body is grounded in the concern for a "good death" that Martínez Gil links with the emergence of the preaching orders and the printing press, and that was reinvigorated by the influence of Jesuit pedagogy (1993, 50–62). *Artes del bien morir* appeared and proliferated in the early modern period at a time when the manner in which the individual faced the moment of death and of individual judgment came to be seen as the dramatic turning-point that would guarantee eternal life or condemnation (32–33). Death was a spectacle in which a tranquil expiration and a beautiful corpse were testimony of salvation, even of sainthood if the corpse displayed particular beauty, whiteness, fragrance, light, and most particularly, incorruptibility. Saint Theresa of Avila's death was a paradigmatic example, as P. de Ribadeneira's describes it in *Flos Sanctorum:*

> Acabando de expirar quedó su rostro hermoso en gran manera, blanco como el alabastro sin arruga ninguna, aunque solía tener hartas por ser vieja, las manos, y los pies con la misma blancura, todos hermoseados con manifiestas señales de la inocencia y santidad que en ellos avía conservado. Fue tan grande la fragancia del olor que salía de su santo cuerpo al tiempo que la vestían, y adereçauan para enterrarla, que trascendía por toda la casa. (Cited in Martínez Gil 1993, 167)

> (Her death completed, her face stayed most beautiful, white as alabaster without a single wrinkle, although she had had abundant ones because she was old, her hands and feet of the same whiteness, all transparent, . . . and as soft to the touch as if she were alive. All her members became beautified with clear signs of the innocence and sanctity that she had conserved in them. The fragrance that

emerged from her saintly body when they dressed her and prepared her for burial was so great that it spread throughout the whole house.)

The triumphal death of saints was often depicted with signs of heaven opening to receive their souls, as in the death of the Franciscan friar Fator, described by M. Escudero de Cobeña:

> Antes que el ánima le saliese del cuerpo, vieron todas las gentes una claridad tan grande desde su cuerpo, que llegaba al cielo y oían las gentes muchas músicas, unas abajaban por la claridad y otras subían. Al parecer de los oyentes eran ángeles y decían. "Ven amigo del Señor." Quedó su cuerpo tan odorífero y con tanta fragrancia de olor después de muerto, que a todos admiraba, y dan gracias a el Señor por ello. Turó [sic] este olor tres o cuatro días. (Cited in Martínez Gil 1993, 170)

> (Before his soul left his body, everyone saw a great light from his body that reached heaven, and they heard much music, some descending on the light and others ascending. It seemed to the hearers that they were angels and said, "Come, friend of the Lord." His body became so odiferous and with such sweet fragrance after death that it astounded everyone, and they gave thanks to the Lord for it. This fragrance lasted three or four days.)

As she depicts good and bad deaths inscribed in the flesh, then, Zayas is employing a code well known to her readers. What is notable in her stories, however, is their almost exclusive focus on the female body. Males deaths, whether violent or tranquil, are mentioned in passing but virtually never described;[35] female deaths, as in contemporary horror films, are lingeringly depicted. In horror films, Clover suggests, this phenomenon distances castration anxiety for the primary audience of such films, adolescent males (1992, 35, 51–53). Bronfen (1992) posits that in paintings and literary works of the eighteenth and nineteenth centuries, death itself is kept at bay for the masculine artists and their audience through the aestheticized death of a beautiful woman, a privileged site of alterity. A different psychic mechanism seems to underlie this practice in Zayas's novellas, however, as the following sequence of examples will demonstrate.

In her first volume of stories, feminine death is restricted to the heroines' actively desiring antagonists, beginning with doña Adriana in the first novella, *Aventurarse perdiendo.*[36] Her suicide by poison when rejected by don Félix inscribes in her swollen, blackened body the ugly death of those condemned to hell for despair. We see this cadaver through the eyes of her suffering mother:

> Quien a este punto viera a la triste de su madre, de creer es que se le partiera el corazón por medio de dolor, porque ya de traspasada no podía llorar, y más cuando vieron que después de frió el cuerpo, se puso muy hinchada, y negra, porque no sólo consideraba el ver muerta a su hija, sino haber sido desesperadamente. (*Novelas,* 55)

> (Whoever should see her poor mother at this moment could believe that the pain would break her heart, already so pierced that she could not cry, and even more so when they saw that after the body was cold, it turned very swollen and black, because she was not only pondering seeing her daughter dead, but also having died in despair.)

In the *Desengaños amorosos,* feminine martyrs to love abound, and the innocence of the majority is written in the beauty of their corpses, like that of Roseleta of *Desengaño 3:* "hallaron la hermosa dama muerta, que como se había desangrado, estaba la más bella cosa que los ojos humanos habían visto" (they found the lovely lady dead, and since she had bled to death, she was the most beautiful thing that human eyes had seen) (*Desengaños,* 221). In *Desengaño 4,* don Martín recounts scenes of good and bad death in a melodramatic and literal black-and-white contrast, which he prefaces with the declaration that God not only rewards innocent sufferers (with a good death) but arranges it so that the body (as well as the soul) will be honored: "Cuando Dios, que no se olvida de sus criaturas y quería que ya que había dado (como luego se verá) el premio a Elena de tanto padecer, no quedase el cuerpo sin honor, ordenó lo que ahora oiréis" (When God, who does not forget his creatures and now that he had given Elena the reward for so much suffering—as will be seen later—desired that her body should not remain without honor, ordered what you will now hear) (*Desengaños,* 250). The black maid who had falsely accused Elena of adultery confronts the death most feared—a sudden death that finds her in a state of sin, without time for confession and absolution:

La negra, que acostada estaba, empezó a dar grandes gritos, diciendo: —¡Jesús, que me muero, confesión!—, . . . y entrando adonde la negra estaba, la hallaron batallando con la cercana muerte. Tenía el rostro y cuerpo cubierto de un mortal sudor, tras esto, con un temblor que la cama estremecía, y de rato en rato se quedaba amortecida, que parecía que ya había dado el alma, y luego volvía con los mismos dolores y congojas a temblar y sudar a un tiempo. (*Desengaños*, 250–51)

(The black woman, who was in bed, began to shout loudly, saying: "Jesus, I am dying, confession!" . . . and going in where the black woman was, they found her battling with her approaching death. Her face and body were covered with a fatal sweat, and after this, with a trembling that shook the bed, and from time to time she fainted and it seemed that she had already given up her soul, and then she would return with the same pains and anguish to trembling and sweating at the same time.)

She insists that they call don Jaime to confess her guilt to him:

—Señor mío: en este paso en que estoy no han de valer mentiras ni engaños. Yo me muero, porque a mucha priesa siento que se me acaba la vida. Yo cené y me acosté buena y sana, y ya estoy acabando. Soy cristiana, aunque mala, y conozco, aunque negra, con el discurso que tengo, que ya estoy en tiempo de decir verdades, porque siento que me está amenazando el juicio de Dios. Y ya que en la vida no le he temido, en la muerte no ha de ser de ese modo. Y así, te juro, por el paso riguroso en que estoy, que mi señora está inocente, y no debe la culpa por donde la tienes condenada a tan rigurosa pena. (*Desengaños*, 251)

(My lord: in the straits I am in, neither lies nor deceits have any use. I am dying, because I feel that my life is finishing very quickly. I dined and went to bed happy and healthy and now I am expiring. I am a Christian, although bad, and I know, although I am black, with the reason I possess, that I have come to the time to tell truths, because I feel that God's judgment is threatening me. And although I haven't feared it in life, in death it will not be that way. And thus, I swear to you, by the desperate pass in which I am, that my lady is in-

nocent, and does not deserve the guilt for which you have her condemned to such a severe punishment.)

Rather than giving her the pardon and priestly absolution for which she
begs, don Jaime deals her immediate death with a dagger. He rushes to
free doña Elena from her cell only to find her the very portrait of a saintly
death:

> Entrando dentro, vio a la desgraciada dama muerta estar echada
> sobre unas pobres pajas, los brazos en cruz sobre el pecho, la una
> mano tendida, que era la izquierda, y con la derecha hecha con sus
> hermosos dedos una bien formada cruz. El rostro, aunque flaco y
> macilento, tan hermoso, que parecía un ángel, y la calavera del
> desdichado y inocente primo junto a la cabecera, a un lado.
> (*Desengaños*, 252)

> (Going within, he saw the unfortunate lady dead, lying on some mis-
> erable straw, her arms making a cross on her breast, one hand—the
> left one—stretched out, and with the right hand, forming with her
> lovely fingers a well-shaped cross. Her face, although thin and ema-
> ciated, so lovely that she looked like an angel, and the skull of her
> ill-starred and innocent cousin next to the head of her bed, at one
> side.)

The narrator reiterates the contrast as the two women's burials are prepared, saying that "la negra . . . parecía un retrato de Lucifer" (the black
woman . . . looked like a portrait of Lucifer) while Elena "cada hora
parecía estar más hermosa" (seemed to be more beautiful every hour)
(*Desengaños*, 254).

Zayas's repeated portrayal of divine honor paid to the female body
counters the traditional characterization of woman as an imperfect animal.
Women were considered so inferior to men that some questioned whether
they could be resurrected as women in heaven. Nicolás Díaz, for example,
said, "En principio parece que todos debieran resucitar hombres, pues 'las
mugeres nacen fuera de la intención de la naturaleza' " (In principle, it
seems that all should be resurrected as men, since "women are born outside the design of nature"). Yet continuing with the Aristotelian distinction
of the female as an imperfect being who nevertheless serves perfectly the
needs of the species, he concludes that they will in fact be resurrected as
women because sexual difference " 'conviene a la perfección de la especie

humana' " (suits the perfection of the human species). Furthermore, he concluded, "En el cielo la mujer ya no estará sujeta al hombre, como sucede en esta vida a causa de su flaqueza e imperfecto entendimiento, 'porque en la bienaventurança no ha de aver estas faltas' " (In heaven the woman will no longer be subject to the man, as occurs in this life because of her weakness and imperfect understanding, "because in heavenly bliss there will be no faults") (cited in Martínez Gil 1993, 487).

The corollary to Zayas's insistence on the worthiness of the female body is the imprint of materiality on a woman's being.[37] This is not to say that she defines a woman's identity or "essence" as coterminous with her body. Speaking in her own authorial voice in the "Al que leyere" preface, she alternated between essentialist and constructionist views of women, and in *Desengaño 5,* don Diego and the corregidor both insist that doña Inés was innocent of adultery with don Diego, since his use of her body took place when she was dispossessed of her senses, judgment, understanding, and will. Yet in this tale, as in *Desengaño 2,* in which Camila was raped by don Juan despite her best efforts to keep herself out of the reach of his attentions, the violation of their bodies leaves a lingering mark. Camila immediately hid her shame in a convent for a year, and her inconsolable husband Carlos hid in his home while the public debated her culpability: "Divulgóse el caso por la ciudad, andando en opiniones la opinión de Camila. Unos decían que no quedaba Carlos con honor si no la mataba; otros, que sería mal hecho, supuesto que la dama no tenía culpa, y cada uno apoyaba su parecer" (The case became known throughout the city, Camila's reputation being put in question. Some said that Carlos would not have honor if he did not kill her; others, that that would be a bad deed, since the lady was not guilty, and everyone supported his own opinion) (*Desengaños,* 194). She only returned home on the insistence of her father-in-law, who was convinced of her innocence—and concerned with the continuation of his line. When she does emerge from the convent, she refuses all adornments, keeping her body wrapped in a rough monastic habit.[38] But Carlos refuses to eat or sleep with her, and she lives the life of a martyr, her eyes never dry of tears, confessing frequently and without seeing or being seen by anyone. Carlos eventually gives her a poison that fails to kill her, but rather swells every part of her body but her head to monstrous size, in which penance she lives for six months before being summoned to heaven:

> Reinó en Carlos el demonio, y la dio un veneno para matarla; mas no le sucedió así, porque debía de querer Dios que esta desdichada y santa señora padeciese más martirios para darle en el cielo el pre-

mio de ellos. Y fue el caso que no la quitó el veneno luego la vida, mas hinchóse toda con tanta monstruosidad, que sus brazos y piernas parecían unas gordísimas columnas, y el vientre se apartaba una gran vara de la cintura; sólo el rostro no tenía hinchado. Nunca se levantaba de la cama, y en ella estaba como un apóstol, diciendo mil ejemplos y dando buenos consejos a sus criadas. De esta suerte vivió seis meses, al cabo de los cuales, estando sola en su cama, oyó una voz que decía: «Camila, ya es llegada tu hora.» Dio gracias a Dios porque la quería sacar de tan penosa vida; recibió sus sacramentos, y otro día en la noche murió, para vivir eternamente. (*Desengaños*, 195)

(The devil reigned within Carlos, and he gave her poison to kill her; but it didn't turn out that way, because God must have wished that this ill-starred and saintly lady should suffer more martyrdom in order to reward her for it in heaven. And it happened that the poison did not kill her right away, but swelled her up to such a monstrous size that her arms and legs looked like very fat columns and her stomach stuck out a yard from her waist; only her face did not swell up. She never got up from bed and in it she was like an apostle, recounting a thousand exemplary cases and giving good advice to her maids. She lived this way for six months, at the end of which, alone in her bed, she heard a voice that said, "Camila, your hour has come." She gave thanks to God for wanting to take her out of this painful life, received his sacraments, and the next night she died, to live eternally.)

In the case of doña Inés in *Desengaño 5, La inocencia castigada* (Innocence Punished), her husband, brother, and sister-in-law wall in the flesh that has offended them, turning it into a macabre spectacle of death-in-life that the narrator describes in painful detail, from her blindness to her worm-eaten flesh, as we have seen in the previous chapter. She concludes by describing its effect on viewers: "No hay más que decir, sino que causó a todos tanta lástima, que lloraban como si fuera hija de cada uno" (There is nothing more to say except that it caused everyone so much sorrow that they cried as if she were the daughter of each one of them) (*Desengaños*, 287). After her rescue, her beauty is restored, but not her sight, and twenty years later she is still living a saintly life in a convent, the narrator tells us, reiterating several times her continued blindness.

Given the narrator's insistence on doña Inés's innocence, readers often question the poetic justice and narrative logic of this blindness. The most obvious interpretation might be the virtue of blindness to the temptations of the world, or blindness as a path to insight into transcendent truth and spiritual values. However, the only possible link to such themes in Zayas's narrative is the commentary of the nun, doña Estefanía, on the preferability of her divine Husband, who forgives all offenses, to earthly men, who blame women not only for their actions but also for their very thoughts, and are invariably cruel in punishment. While Zayas emphasizes beginning in her first story the importance of the eyes in awakening desire, her narrator tells us that doña Inés married in obedience to her brother and to escape the cruel tutelage of her sister-in-law rather than in response to her own desire for her husband.

I suggest, rather, that the blindness is a misplaced, synecdochic punishment. It is inflicted on the eyes of the woman whose beauty arouses desire in the eyes of others, envy in those who do not possess her, and a thirst to punish her in the flesh on the part of her cruel sister-in-law. The narrator tells us that it was her beauty that brought her misfortune—"Por ésta le vino la desgracia, porque siempre la belleza anda en pasos de ella" (Her misfortune came became of this, because beauty is always on the path of it) (*Desengaños,* 266)—when as a married woman she first came before the public eye:

> Siendo doncella, jamás fue vista, por la terrible condición de su hermano y cuñada; más ya casada, o ya acompañada de su esposo, o ya con las parientas y amigas, salía a las holguras, visitas y fiestas de la ciudad. Fue vista de todos, unos alabando su hermosura y la dicha de su marido en merecerla, y otros envidiándola y sintiendo no haberla escogido para sí, y otros amándola ilícita y deshonestamente, pareciéndoles que con sus dineros y galanterías la granjearían para gozarla. (*Desengaños,* 266)

> (As a maiden, she was never seen, on account of the terrible character of her brother and sister-in-law; but once married, either accompanied by her husband or with women relatives and friends, she went out to the town merriments, visits, and parties. She was seen by all, some praising her loveliness and the good fortune of her husband in meriting her, and others envying her and lamenting not having chosen her for themselves, and others loving her illicitly and

dishonestly, considering that with money and gallantries they would win her favor to enjoy her.)

Over and over, the narrator shows us the figure of doña Inés in the eyes of others. Innocent and in love with her husband, she paid no attention to men's attention, "por parecerle que con su honestidad podía vencer cualesquiera deseos lascivos de cuantos la veían" (because it seemed to her that with her honesty she could conquer any lascivious desires of those who saw her) (*Desengaños*, 267). Nor did she hide from don Diego's nightly courtship below her balcony, thinking it directed at other women in her street. If she had realized their object, the narrator says, "de creer es que pusiera estorbo al dejarse ver" (one can believe that she would have put hindrances in the way of her being seen) (*Desengaños*, 267). We see her in the eyes of the corregidor, his ministers of justice, and her brother, walking the streets of her city in a hypnotic trance, clad only in her slip. After the investigation, the reason her husband gives for the move to Seville is "por quitarse de los ojos de los que habían sabido aquella desdicha, que los señalaban con el dedo" (to remove themselves from the eyes of those who had known that disgrace, [and] who pointed the finger at them) (*Desengaños*, 283).

There is no rational, logical, *conscious* justice that can explain why doña Inés should be punished with permanent blindness for the desire she aroused in others. Yet the implicit message of this story and that of Camila and Carlo is that the being of a woman whose body has been illicitly enjoyed, even against her will, bears a material stain for which she must do penance in the material world, a penance always cruelly and unjustly imposed by her husband and others linked to her by flesh and blood. Zayas's narrator closes the story proper with the observation: "Quiso Dios darla sufrimiento y guardarle la vida, porque no muriese allí desesperada, y para que tan rabioso lobo como su hermano, y tan cruel basilisco como su marido, y tan rigurosa leona como su cuñada, ocasionasen ellos mismos *su* castigo" (God wished to give her suffering and conserve her life, so that she might not die there in desperation, and so that such a ravenous wolf as her brother, and such a cruel basilisk as her husband, and such a rigorous lioness as her sister-in-law might themselves cause *their/(her)* punishment) (*Desengaños*, 288; emphasis added). The ambiguous reference of the concluding adjective, is on the one hand, characteristic of Zayas's loose sentence structure,[39] and on the other, inherent in the Spanish language, in which *su* can mean either his, hers, theirs, or yours. The most obvious reading is that (God willed that) in punishing doña Inés, her husband, brother, and sister-in-law might punish themselves, but it could also be read as (divinely ordained that) they be the instruments of her punishment. With a discrete grammatical distancing of divine will from the cruel punishment, both readings are true to the sequence of her fiction.

The overlapping reference of the possessive adjective is also true to the gender structure of the honor code, to its overlapping of possession of the flesh and responsibility for its defense and punishment. Marriage vows made of the married couple "one flesh," and every reader of Golden Age drama remembers multiple plaints in which fathers and brothers as well as husbands lament that their honor is centered in that fragile vessel, the weak and tempting flesh of woman. If we relate those laments to the structure of the ego, the construction of the superego, and the deadlier side of *jouissance,* we can gain insight into the unconscious truth of the honor code whose operation Zayas conceals/reveals in this tale. Because the human subject can only know itself in alienation, by reflection or analogy with another human being, the ego is not "being itself" but a mask over anxiety caused by the original split in knowledge—the need to seek ourselves outside ourselves, in the form of imaginary identifications, projections, and transferences (Ragland 1995, 39). Desire is therefore dialectical, it "always rephrases the implicit questions: What am I [to you]? What am I worth in the lane of the social gaze? That is, what do I lack? How can I reify myself as ideal?"[40] "A child learns its position in society by submitting to the myths, roles, and rules of its social order, and internalizing them, thereby acquiring the superego" (Ragland 1995, 60–61). The founding structure of the superego is the principle of prohibition, the law of the *Nom/Non du père;* expressed in terms of the honor code, it stipulates that one may not legitimately enjoy any partner other than that permitted by patrilinear marriage rules. The gendered corollary rule within the honor code was that in order to protect his honor—say, his ego, or his sense of individual worth as he knows himself in the eyes of others—a man must enforce at all costs his right to control the enjoyment of any woman linked to him by blood or marriage, a right that will inevitably be challenged by other men seeking to destroy his sense of worth by enjoying her. The feminine version of that injunction was the obligation to defend honor not only through the woman's own chastity but also through identification with a man who was able to defend it or to cast out the flesh that offended his/their honor or to do both. Hereby enters into operation the deadly side of *jouissance* as the drive to maintain consistency, the illusion of the ego as an integrated "self," even at the cost of (self)-destructive actions. This "deadlier side of *jouissance* appears in haunting gazes and voices" (Ragland 1995, 91)—recognized by doña Inés's husband as "the eyes of those who had learned of that disgrace [and] were pointing the finger at them" (*Desengaños*, 283). Borrowing Ragland's words,

> Insofar as the first form of the superego is created by the primordial castrating power of the gaze that judges, thereby promoting ideals, superego injunctions will forever after intersect in the projective optics of imaginary relations. . . . That is, since *jouissance* is tethered to the Other—not the other, as we think—individuals find themselves inexplicably burdened by death weights or inertias that do not really correspond to realities 'outside.' Although people project guilt and blame onto others, such projections are actually narcissistic identifications with unconscious ideals of "self." (1995, 90–91)

The "death weight" that drives the (self)-destructive actions of Inés's relatives is the narcissistic identification with her flesh, which, although it does not in physical fact correspond to outside reality, is consciously expressed as well as unconsciously suffered under the honor code. With that identification comes obedience to the injunction that their/her illicitly enjoyed flesh must be punished, walled away from judging eyes of the Other to destroy itself in darkness. The same identification with the offending feminine flesh motivates Carlos's "demonic" poisoning of the innocent Camila in *Desengaño 2*.

By seeing Zayas as a deeply divided writer who subscribes to the fundamental ideology of patriarchal Spain yet seeks to defend women's autonomous value, we can understand the logic of her qualified defense of feminine flesh that, however unwillingly, offends the honor code. Beatriz, the martyr-queen of *Desengaño 9*, wiser to the ways of the world than doña Inés, was able to foresee the danger of her brother-in-law's desire and, with a combination of her own intelligence and the protection of the Mother of God, was able to defend herself against his attempts to seduce, rape, and kill her. Hence the eyes her husband ordered gouged out could be miraculously restored and all other attempted violations of her person miraculously reversed. Nevertheless, she chooses to follow the only truly safe path for women in such a society, espoused in a lengthy concluding commentary on the tale of Inés by the nun, Estefanía, who later narrates Beatriz's story—that of electing an all-forgiving divine Husband and removing themselves from the sight of the world.

Love and Death—Bis

Paralleling the position as eighth novella in the *Novelas amorosas* of the male-narrated fantasy of love's triumph over death in *El imposible vencido,* we find a very different vision of love and death in *Desengaño 8,* one that might be described as a feminine love *of* death.[41] For Pedro, a wealthy nobleman from Jaén, transmission from father to son of family wealth and unsullied blood are more important than life itself. Like Jacinta's father in the first *novela,* he wants his entire patrimony to go to his son Alonso, and is therefore determined that his daughter Mencía enter a convent so that he will not be obliged to provide her a dowry. To keep her from marrying the wealthy and generous don Enrique, who wants to marry her with or without a dowry, he and his son kill Mencía on the pretext that she would thus have sullied their blood by mixing it with that of a commoner, since don Enrique's grandparents were *labradores* (farmers). While don Pedro preserves himself from implication by a trip to Seville, don Alonso traps Mencía while she is writing a letter to don Enrique, summons a priest to help her confess, and stabs her to death before dispatching his page with Mencía's note to lure Enrique to his death.[42] Answering her summons, don Enrique is greeted with a miraculous warning: at a touch of his hand, the window of her room opens with a bang and in it, he sees her cadaver, bathed in a marvelous luminosity, her wounds bleeding as if freshly made.[43] A weak, delicate voice coming from the direction of her cadaver tells him that she has been killed for his sake and warns him to save himself:

> —Ya, esposo, no tienes que buscarme en este mundo, porque ha más de nueve horas que estoy fuera de él, porque aquí no está más de este triste cuerpo, sin alma, de la suerte que le miras. Por tu causa me han muerto, mas no quiero que tú mueras por la mía, que quiero me debas esta fineza. Y así, te aviso que te pongas en salvo y mires por tu vida, que estás en muy grande peligro, y quédate a Dios para siempre. (*Desengaños,* 382–83)

> (Now, husband, do not look for me in this world, because I left it more than nine hours ago, for here there is nothing more than this body, without a soul, as you see it. Because of you they have killed

me, but I don't want you to die because of me and I want you to owe
me this favor. And thus, I warn you to get to a safe place and look
out for your life, for you are in great danger, and God keep you
forever.)

Enrique is so mortally paralyzed by the vision of her, however, that he remains transfixed. Alonso and a friend, in the street at the same time, do
not see this vision, and Alonso stabs him twenty-two times and leaves him
for dead. Thanks to the intervention of "su Madre Santísima," (his Most
Holy Mother), Enrique survives, joins the Franciscan order, and dedicates
his fortune to building a humble convent and in it, a chapel with a vault to
which he brings Mencía's body, miraculously still bleeding and beautiful a
year after death:

> habiendo muchos testigos que se hallaron a verle pasar que, con
> haber pasado un año que duró la obra, estaban las heridas cor-
> riendo sangre como el mismo día que la mataron, y ella tan her-
> mosa, que parecía no haber tenido jurisdicción la muerte en su her-
> mosura. (*Desengaños*, 385)

> (having many witnesses who found on seeing her pass by that, al-
> though the work had lasted a year, her wounds were bleeding as on
> the very day that they killed her, and she was so lovely that it seemed
> that death had no jurisdiction over her beauty.)

Zayas gives us in Mencía one instance of a woman who breaks the silence of death with speech, but her otherworldly words of warning have no
effect. Only the spectacle of her bleeding corpse registers on Enrique. His
survival instead is attributed to the intervention—presumably silent—of
the Most Holy Mother. She who is (not) Queen of Heaven, to whom, of
whom, and for whom men speak, and whose efficacy (for men) is spoken
by male cadavers.[44]

Alonso becomes a soldier in Naples, lavishly supported by his father
until the latter learns that his son has married a beautiful, virtuous, and
noble but poor young woman, Ana. Furious that his son had thus blocked
his plans to marry him to a rich noblewoman, he disinherits Alonso, his
wife, and his infant son. Hoping to regain his father's favor, with the en-
couragement and assistance of a friend, Marco Antonio, Alonso kills his
wife. Zayas describes the killing with an abundance of macabre detail and

pathetic effects:[45] convinced one evening to leave the son she is nursing to
see the viceroy's departure, the young "lamb" is beheaded while eating an
empanada in a garden, with one blow of a knife Alonso had sharpened for
the occasion. They throw her headless body in a well in the garden, but it
sticks halfway down, where Marco Antonio's elderly woman servant finds it
while trying to draw water to clean the house next morning, a cleaning that
presumably would have started in the garden with the table and chair that
she found drenched in blood. The clothing on Ana's cadaver is described
in minute detail, as is the scene of her grandfather's recognition of it when
it is put on display in the public plaza. But the narrator begs her listeners
to imagine for themselves the reaction of Ana's mother when he has the
body taken home: "Hízolo llevar a su casa, donde no hay que decir cómo le
recibiría su madre. Los oyentes lo juzguen que yo no me atrevo a contarlo"
(They had her carried home, where I don't have to say how her mother received her. Let my hearers judge, for I don't dare relate it) (*Desengaños*,
396). Alonso and Marco Antonio bury her head in a cave by the marina
just before boarding a galley to follow the viceroy's convoy. On the return
to Spain, however, they are caught stealing silk stockings in Genoa and are
returned to Naples. Alonso readily confesses guilt for Ana's murder as well
as for that of his sister, Mencía, for he says he has been unable to sleep for
two months because of recurrent dreams in which he sees his sister threatening him with a knife. In one last macabre scene on the scaffold, Alonso
asks his executioners to stay their hands long enough to bring him his
wife's head, whose burial spot he describes. It was miraculously preserved,
as they found, "sacándola tan fresca y hermosa como si no hubiera seis
meses que estaba debajo de tierra" (taking it out as fresh and lovely as if it
hadn't spent six months underground) (*Desengaños*, 398). He takes it in his
hands, addressing it tearfully: "—Ya, doña Ana, pago con una vida culpada
la que te quité sin culpa. No te puedo dar más satisfacción de la que te doy"
(Now, doña Ana, I pay with a guilty life for taking your guiltless life away. I
cannot make greater amends than that which I give you) (*Desengaños*, 398).

The avaricious don Pedro's reaction to the news of his son's death is anything but tearful, however. Barely pausing during a game of cards, he
reshuffles the deck and, pronouncing that "más quiero tener un hijo de-
gollado que mal casado" (I would rather have a son beheaded than badly
wed) (*Desengaños*, 398), he continues his game.

There seems no way to avoid describing this macabre surfeit of blood,
pathos and beautifully incorruptible feminine cadavers as a fundamentally
masochistic fantasy. The narrator, in her prefatory diatribe, attacks the in-

constancy of masculine desire, the blindness of feminine credulity in men's deceitful words, and the injustice of men's denigration of all women, on whom they indiscriminately project their own sins and those of the bad, free, man-chasing women whose only real affront to them is to their pockets. She concludes by announcing that the objective of her tale, as of all their *desengaños,* is to demonstrate the existence of good, innocent women who suffer without guilt the cruelty of men. And indeed, Zayas displays Mencía and Ana as martyrs to the cruelty of the quintessential patriarchal father, obsessed with preserving intact and unsullied his wealth and noble blood. To do so requires denying any responsibility toward or dependence on the feminine (or plebeian) Other. In contrast to other stories, in which the initial genealogies are given, here the narrator never mentions a wife, a mother for Mencía and Alonso, as if don Pedro were the solitary, self-sufficient generator of his line. To preserve his solipsistic domain, he employs his son as the instrument to kill the sister who would mix his blood with the (wealthy) bloodline of *labradores,* and to regain his favor and wealth, the same son beheads the (noble) poor wife who gives him his only surviving male heir. Both women die in streams of blood, leaving bodies whose miraculously incorruptible beauty testify to their innocence and sanctified status as martyrs to masculine cruelty.

Observations offered by Kristeva and Cixous help illuminate Zayas's understanding of women's position in paternal society and the unconscious truth of this melodramatic tale. Cixous suggests that in a parallel to masculine castration into the Symbolic order, decapitation serves as a literal or symbolic operation to subject the disorderly feminine chatter and laughter that disrupts the order of the masculine economy. "If masculinity is culturally ordered by the castration complex, it might be said that the backlash, the return, on women of this castration anxiety is its displacement as decapitation, execution, of woman, as loss of her head" (Cixous 1981, 43). That masculine economy, she posits, is based on debt, on a price for everything, on returns, knowledge and power. The feminine text that opposes it has tactility, touch, says Cixous, a touch that passes through the ear. Or we might say in Zayas, the ear and the eye: the ear in the semi-oral diction of her text (see Chapter 10 below) and the eye, in the vividly melodramatic images of bleeding women that she crafts in *Desengaño 8.* "Writing in the feminine is passing on what is cut out by the Symbolic, the voice of the mother, passing on what is most archaic . . . the movement of the text, doesn't trace a straight line. I see it as an outpouring . . . which can appear in primitive or elementary texts as a fantasy of blood, of menstrual flow,

etc." (Cixous 1981, 54). Discussing the efficacy of monotheism as fundamental to social organization in the Judeo-Christian tradition, Kristeva
states: "As the principle of a symbolic, paternal community in the grip of
the superego . . . monotheism represses, along with paganism, the greater
part of agrarian civilizations and their ideologies, women and mothers"
(1986a, 141). While Zayas carefully isolates her saving God from the operation of terrestrial patriarchy, she shows this principle in operation in don
Pedro's family in the elimination of the mother, the sister, and the daughter-in-law, as well as the wealthy prospective son-in-law of *labrador* origins
who might sully don Pedro's bloodline—or more truthfully, contest his exclusive control of patrimony. Although the monotheistic God generally
speaks only to men, Kristeva says, woman in fact knows "more about Him;
indeed, she is the one who knows the material conditions, as it were, of the
body, sex and procreation, which permit the existence of the community,
its permanence and thus man's very dialogue with his God" (1986a, 140).[46]
Zayas reveals this knowledge implicitly, by making the sacrificial female
body the instrument that facilitates men's rapprochement with God—the
good Enrique as a monk in the Franciscan order, and the bad Alonso in a
penitent confession before his death. Yet in an economy in which woman's
desire is Saint Augustine's "body sense," a private and personal good set
against the public, common, "unchangeable" good of the paternal community, to consent to that good is to eat of the forbidden fruit proffered by the
serpent in the garden to Eden, to risk expulsion from paradise by opposing
"the sublimating Word and paternal legislation" (Kristeva 1986a, 144).
Within the confines of that order, all that remains for woman, suggests
Kristeva, is "to pit herself constantly against that opposite in the very movement by which she desires it, to kill it repeatedly and then suffer endlessly:
a radiant perspective on masochism, a masochism that is the price she
must pay in order to be Queen" (1986a, 144).

The three ballads contained in *Desengaño 8* underline the organizing
structure of this masochistic fantasy. The feminine narrator sets before us
two males whose poems of desire anticipate the site/sight of the death that
their love will bring to the desired woman. While courting Mencía, Enrique sang outside her window a ballad that paints the eyes in competition
with the memory for possession of the image of his beloved, who is, he concludes, "Deidad . . . en quien mis ojos/ adoran de Dios el ser" (Goddess
. . . in whom my eyes adore God's being), at whose feet he kneels as an
adoring slave, continually renewing the surrender of his soul to her. He
sings this at the window that one day would open miraculously to set be-

fore his eyes the spectacle of her martyred body. Alonso, lamenting an evening when rain kept doña Ana from going with her mother and sisters to the garden where he courted her, composed a ballad in which he paints himself burning in the purgatory of her absence, his soul drowning in pain:

> Muerto de mis propias penas,
>   y en ellas penando estoy;
>   que es purgatorio tu ausencia;
>   tu vista, gloria mayor
>   (*Desengaños*, 389)

(Dead from my own sufferings, I am still suffering in them, for your absence is purgatory; seeing you, the greatest glory.)

He will later put her to death in another garden and will end his life confessing tearfully to her beautiful severed head before the executioner dispatches him to pay for his crimes in purgatory or in hell. In these two ballads, Zayas reveals her recognition that the adored woman is ultimately a dead woman and, conversely, that her death secures that adoration.

Lisis ends the evening with a curious song on the pain of subjection to an imagined love. Its first stanzas are laments of a suffering lover familiar in courtly and Petrarchan lyrics, but the poetic voice then reveals that her pain is an elected torment, at once self-punishing and self-preserving:

> No quise ver lo que adoro,
>   y adoro lo que no he visto;
>   porque amar lo que se goza
>   comodidad la imagino.
>   Yo me quité la ventura,
>   y lloro haberla perdido;
>   mi voluntad es enigma,
>   mi deseo, un laberinto.
>   El cautiverio apetezco,
>   de la libertad me privo,
>   y negándome a las dichas,
>   ya por las dichas suspiro.

(I did not want to see what I adore, and I adore what I have not seen, because I imagine that loving what one enjoys is comfort.

I took away my happiness, and I cry over having lost it; my will is an
enigma, my desire a labyrinth.
I hunger for captivity, I deprive myself of freedom, and denying myself bliss yet for bliss I sigh.)

She concludes her song with an invocation of a desired death as the only
resolution to the enigma: "Mas ¡ay de mí! que de una y otra suerte, / el
remedio que espero es en la muerte! (But woe is me! for either one way or
the other, the remedy that I await is death!) (*Desengaños*, 401).

Desengaño 8 thus closes with a lyrical feminine invocation to a desired
death, a death that we can see not as a dissolution into nothingness, but an
elevation to the fantasy position of honored queen as the story's heroines
leave behind two men to keep them alive in memory, one paying in purgatory or hell for his cruelty to his beloved, the other praying beside her sanctified body.

From her orthodox position, then, Zayas freely crosses the frontiers between natural and supernatural spheres. She partially shifts away from
(noble, Spanish) women and toward men, foreigners, or infidels the association with magic, and clothes warning specters of death in masculine
flesh. Taking up a masculine narrator's voice, she depicts a fantasy of the
triumph of love over death in this life, but in her pessimistic second volume, the only refuge for women is a masochistic fantasy of love and honor
for their beautiful, martyred flesh after death.

9

Familiar Enemies

The Enemy Without

Where does the misery come from? Or, as Jacqueline Rose refocuses that question posed to Freudian theory by Wilhelm Reich—where does sexual violence against women come from? (Rose 1989, 25–29). Is its origin public or private, social or psychic?[1] The level of violence in Zayas's *Desengaños amorosos* provokes the same question, but an overview of the collection as a whole allows no single, unqualified answer.

The narrator of *Desengaño 7, Mal presagio casar lejos* (Marry Afar: Portent of Doom), points explicitly toward a source "outside," attributing the malevolence toward women to political "others"—Italian and Portuguese husbands, and in particular a Flemish father-in-law, more enemies than allies of Spain and Spanish women. As "la inocente corderilla" (the innocent

little lamb) Blanca bleeds to death over her husband's protests and the
Flemish patriarch says he would like to be able to dispose of all Spanish
women as he does her, the narrator blames the prince's coldness toward
Blanca on his father and his page boy lover, Arnesto. She calls both of
them "tyrants," and compares Blanca's death to that of Seneca, saying that
"como Séneca, [Blanca] rindió la vida a la crueldad de los tiranos y el alma
al cielo" (like Seneca, Blanca surrendered her life to the tyrants' cruelty
and her soul to heaven) (*Desengaños,* 364).[2]

Zayas's association of the deceptive rhetoric of courtly love and of homosexuality with exaggerated patriarchal authority demonstrates a fascinating insight into the implication of the political order in the "private"
dilemmas of women. We have already considered in Chapter 7 how courtly
love discourse masks the sexual impasse, the fundamental noncomplemen-
tarity of masculine and feminine aims in a heterosexual relationship. At
the same time, it served reigning political interests from the late medieval
period through Zayas's century. Georges Duby (1992), describing the nature and function of the model of courtly love in medieval courts, points
out that despite the power it apparently attributed to the lady served, it was
really "a man's game." It was "first and foremost a criterion of distinction
within masculine society" (256), says Duby, a discourse and ritual that
marked aristocratic separation from the animality of the lower classes.
Duby also links the fantasy value of courtly love literature to the practice of
the early separation of the sexes in court society, a separation that fostered
male homosexuality and male fascination with and fear of feminine mystery and power. Although this discourse was clearly literary rather than social in origin, Duby attributes the widespread and relatively rapid adoption
of this "courtly neurosis" (255) to its political as well as psychic utility. Em-
phasizing self-restraint, friendship, and loyalty, the courtship ritual
schooled young men in the same virtues demanded of them by their lord
and "reinforced the ethics of vassalage on which the whole political structure of the time rested" (261). It also served to discipline women, controlling presumed feminine traits of frivolity, duplicity, and unbridled lust that
provoked masculine anxiety. It was a device, says Duby, "for confining the
female sex within a web of carefully orchestrated rituals, for drawing
woman's sting by diverting her combativeness to the harmless realm of
sport. The game of love did not disturb and in fact strengthened the social
hierarchy in which women were subordinate to men. Once the game was
over and everyone returned to serious business, the *amie* returned to the
place God intended for her kind, her 'gender,' under the strict authority of
the man on whom she depended as wife, daughter, or sister" (262–63).

As Joan Kelly (1984) argues in her classic essay, "Did Women Have a Renaissance?" the infusion of Neoplatonic spirituality into the discourse of love from the Renaissance onward did nothing to improve women's relative status within that hierarchy. Kelly's evaluation of the novelty and extent of the reduction of women's power by a Renaissance separation of public and private spheres and the restriction of women to a devalued private zone has been contested (Brown 1986). Still valid, however, is her demonstration of the relationship between the Neoplatonic love discourse—spiritual refinement through willing submission to the service of an unreachable, chaste ideal woman—and the reduction of courtiers to impotence and dependence on powerful princes and a centralized monarchy. In Kelly's words:

> The likeness of the lady to the prince . . . both masks and expresses the new dependency of the Renaissance noblewoman. In a structured hierarchy of superior and inferior, she seems to be served by the courtier. But this love theory really made her serve—and stand as a symbol of how the relation of domination may be reversed, so that the prince could be made to serve the interests of the courtier. The Renaissance lady is not desired, not loved for herself. Rendered passive and chaste, she merely mediates the courtier's safe transcendence of an otherwise demeaning necessity. (Kelly 1984)

The reversal of the relation of domination and the service is psychic, not political. That is, the lover acquires the desired spiritual refinement by voluntarily serving the unreachable lady, who stands as a symbol of the powerful prince whom the lover must serve. The discourse of love thus functions to veil inescapable political dependency behind a fiction of elective and elevating masculine subordination to the ideal woman in the sexual relation.

The second and third elements of our triad of courtly love discourse, homosexuality and patriarchal authority in *Desengaño 7,* have been lucidly analyzed by Paul Julian Smith. Likening the understanding of Zayas to that of Irigaray, he delineates the relationship between homosexuality and patriarchy in this story: " 'Hom(m)osexualité' (sexual commerce between men) is the logical result of a system which persists in excluding women. In this 'circulation of the same' women can figure only as objects of exchange and can never transcend a state of permanent exile. The dominant male culture thus promotes an overt exogamy (marriage across the national boundaries requiring the exchange of women) and a covert endogamy

(exclusive relations between men which ensure the oppression of women)"
(Smith 1989, 36).

In *Desengaño 7,* Zayas devotes the first third of the tale to an exaggerated
account of the courtship rituals that apparently empower the idealized
lady, then reveals its falsity as the fate of Blanca and her sisters dramatizes
the true defenselessness of women in a hierarchical and "hom(m)osexual"
commerce between men. Although her brother loves her, to further the
political interests of the crown he serves, he marries her to the son of "[un]
gran potentado [de Flandes]" (a great Flemish potentate) (*Desengaños,*
339). Zayas portrays that potentate as the epitome of arbitrary patriarchal
authority, a man who possesses the power of life or death over all those be-
neath him and who operates according to his own will alone, restrained by
neither fear of God nor the social order.[3] He dispenses death to under-
lings, be they servants or his very daughter, with swift and summary injustice and perverse cruelty. His authority is not supreme, however, but is limited by the subjection of Flanders to the Spanish monarchy, as Zayas's
readers knew and as she underlines by saying that the severe punishment
of Flanders by the duke of Alba was punishment for the murder or Blanca.
She could therefore expect her readers to understand the Fleming's enmity toward Spanish women, the lineage and the nation they represent, as
a hatred for a power that limited his authority. A similar enmity toward
Spanish women on the part of Portuguese and Italians is named as the
cause of the death of Blanca's sisters, whose marriages the readers presumes also to have been made for reasons of political (mis)alliance. The
Flemish prince's very definition of masculine subjectivity consists of an aggressively competitive power to eliminate all opposition, as he rejects his
own son's "feminine" plea to spare Blanca's beauty:

> Calle, cobarde, traidor, medio mujer, que te vences de la hermosura
> y tiene más poder en ti que los agravios. Calla otra vez, te digo,
> muera; que de tus enemigos, los menos. Y si no tienes valor repara
> tu flaqueza con quitarte de delante. Salte fuera y no lo veas, que mal
> se defenderá ni ofenderá a los hombres quien desmaya de ver morir
> una mujer. Así tubiera a todas las de su nación como tengo a ésta.
> (*Desengaños,* 363)
>
> (Shut up, coward, traitor, half woman yourself if beauty conquers
> you and has more power over you than affronts. Shut up, I say
> again, let her die, the fewer your enemies are, the better. And if you

don't have the courage, make up for your weakness by getting out of the way. Go outside and don't watch, because he who faints at seeing a woman die will ill defend himself or offend other men. Would that I had all the women of her nation where I have this one.)

For such an exaggeratedly masculine subject, women are the enemy in that they constitute the excluded sexual other of the unconscious,[4] here literalized in *Desengaño 7* as both sexual and political opposition to the masculine subject's quest for unchallenged preeminence.[5] The old prince dislikes being obliged to permit his son's departure for Spain to court Blanca and attacks her for this lengthy, foreign "madness" on their arrival in Flanders, thus putting her on notice that she is in the court of her enemies. But the young prince was happy to leave his father's domain briefly and go to Spain to play out the courting ritual Blanca demanded. And he played well the role of the suffering, faithful gallant pleading for the favors of a sovereign "dueño" (owner/lord/lady), the significantly ambiguous title given the love object in courtship. As Duby and Kelly point out, courtiers whose sociopolitical existence depended on pleasing an all-powerful prince were cast in an analogous subordinate role and were schooled for it by the rituals of courtship. Zayas dedicates a lengthy harangue in the concluding frame of the *Desengaños* to the "feminizing" effect of service at court and to a degeneration of military-chivalric ethics, both of which she relates to male verbal abuse of women. Men today, she says, are reluctant to serve as soldiers and to defend women against foreign invaders. They only sport the insignia of a gentleman on their chests as an adornment, akin to their use of luxurious stockings and long curly locks. Rather than fighting alongside their king in the field, they spend their time in the gardens of the Prado and by the river, "llenos de galas y trajes femeniles, y los pocos que le acompañan [al rey], suspirando por las ollas de Egipto" (decked out with adornments and effeminate garb, and the few who do accompany him [the king], sighing for the fleshpots of Egypt) (*Desengaños,* 505).[6] All of this degenerate, ignoble behavior, she says, stems from their low regard for women.

Naming practices in *Desengaño 7* afford another window on the operation of the sexual-political hierarchy. Neither the prince, nor his father, nor any of the foreign husbands of Blanca's sisters, nor her brother, carry proper names in the narrative; they are positions in the field of power relationships that need be designated only by title and nationality. The women, in contrast, are referred to by their given names. Their claim to social being is not positional and institutional, but derivative and relational. Their value is constituted only in relation to males, as media of exchange between empowered male subjects or instruments and objects of revenge in the competition for power between rival males.[7] Only three males are individually named, for very different reasons. In a telling narrative lapse, Zayas gives not one but two different names to the one male who has neither institutional power nor exchange value, but only instrumental worth—Blanca's brother's chamberlain, who is sent to Flanders with Blanca and who is to marry her lady-in-waiting, María. Zayas first calls him Jorge, then switches to Gabriel several pages later.[8]

Arnesto, like the women, is designated by a given name; lover of the young prince and collaborator with his father, he draws his value not from institutional position but by constituting himself as an object of desire.

> El tenía cuanto el príncipe estimaba, con él comunicaba sus más íntimos secretos, por él se gobernaba todo, y él tan desabrido con todos, que más trataban de agradarle que al príncipe. . . . algunas . . . o por burlas o veras, le decía [a Blanca] que más quería a su paje que no a ella. (*Desengaños*, 351)

> (He had everything the prince valued, he shared his most intimate secrets with him, he was ruled by him in everything, and he was so disagreeable with everyone that they tried harder to please him than the prince. . . . some people . . . whether as a joke or in truth, said to her [Blanca] that he loved his page more than he did her.)

In the figure of Arnesto, Zayas literalizes the perception that in a culture that so forecloses feminine subjectivity, the circuit of desire operates only between males.[9] Given her institutional and ideological allegiance, however, Zayas dramatizes this relationship between patriarchal structures and homosexuality at a saving distance from the heartland of Hapsburg Spain.

The third male specifically named, the duke of Alba, functions as the instrument of just revenge and as the psychic *cordon sanitaire* between the barbaric cruelty of foreign patriarchs, which can be fictionally imagined, and their Spanish counterparts, whose fundamental legitimacy she never directly challenges. In a phrase curiously appended to the report of Blanca's death as a martyrdom that outstrips that of her sisters, Zayas reworks historical causality to make her death rather than religious dissent and separatist rebellion the cause of the duke's punishingly repressive government in Flanders.[10]

Muerta la hermosa doña Blanca tan desgraciadamente, porque no envidiase la desdicha de sus hermanas, si es don para ser envidiado, dejando bien qué llorar en aquellos Estados, pues los estragos, que tocaron en crueldades, que el duque de Alba hizo en ellos, fue en venganza de esta muerte. (*Desengaños*, 364)

(The lovely doña Blanca so haplessly dead, so that she shouldn't envy the misfortunes of her sisters, if that is a gift to be envied, leaving so much to cry over in those States, since the damages, that bordered on cruelties, that the Duke of Alba inflicted on them was in revenge for this death.)

From a Lacanian perspective, the duke of Alba serves Zayas as a partial embodiment of the fantasy of the existence of an Other of the Other that would guarantee the consistency of the Symbolic order (Zizek 1994). With his intervention, that of the king, and signs or assurances of celestial favor for martyred women, Zayas provides her readers with a reassuring fiction that the suffering of such women has transcendent meaning. For example, she says that the innocence of doña Mayor, Blanca's older sister, was proved "y el rey había severamente castigado a su marido, con lo cual se moderó en parte el color de su muerte, juzgándola gozaba en el cielo la corona de mártir" (and the king had punished her husband severely, with which the coloring of her death was partially moderated, judging that she was enjoying the crown of a martyr in heaven) (*Desengaños*, 349). That Blanca received such a heavenly crown is made materially visible in her incorrupt body, the beautiful cadaver brought home to Spain: "También sacaron el cuerpo de doña Blanca para traerle a España, que estaba tan lindo como si entonces acabara de morir (señal de la gloria que goza el alma)" (They also removed the body of doña Blanca to bring her to Spain, and she was as lovely then as if she had just died—a sign of the glory her soul was enjoying) (*Desengaños*, 365).

The following tale, *Desengaño 8, El traidor contra su sangre* (Traitor to His Blood), brings the misery and sexual violence against women "back home" to Spain. But in doing this, Zayas hedges around this particular case with multiple guarantees of the existence of an "Other of the Other," both terrestrial and celestial, as a kind of palisade to curtail the potential extension of this case to an implicit criticism of the paternal order fundamental to the sociopolitical structure of Hapsburg Spain.[11] As in the third novella, the explicitly labeled root of masculine antisocial behavior in this disenchantment is greed, linked to a secondary but hyperbolic concern for preservation of the purity of blood. The narrator underlines the fact that don Pedro is in fact more interested in money than noble blood by making doña Ana the daughter of a member of the Order of Santiago, and describing don Pedro's reaction to the news of their marriage:

> Loco de enojo, le escribió una carta muy pesada, diciéndole en ella que ni se nombrase su hijo, ni le tuviese por padre, pues cuando entendió que le diera por nuera una gran señora de aquel reino, que engrandeciera su casa de calidad y riqueza, añadiendo renta a su renta, se había casado con una pobre mujer, que antes servía de afrenta a su linaje que de honor. (*Desengaños*, 391)

> (Out of his mind with anger, he wrote him a very harsh letter, telling him in it that he should not call himself his son, nor hold him as his father, for when he had believed that he would give him as daughter-in-law a great lady of that realm who would augment their house both in quality and wealth, adding income to their income, he had married a poor woman, who served more as an affront to their line than as an honor to it.)

Don Pedro says that if doña Ana were at hand, he would dispose of her as he had doña Mencía. Failing that, he passes a sentence of economic strangulation on the newlyweds that will lead in rather short order to their physical deaths. He announces that he will not send one cent more to his son; he will consume all the patrimony himself playing cards rather than allowing doña Ana to enjoy it: "Pensaba dar tan buen cabo de su hacienda, que cuando él muriese no hallase ni aun sombra de ella; que más quería jugarla a las pintas, que no que la gozase la señora doña Ana de Añasco" (He planned to finish off his estate so thoroughly that when he died, not a shadow of it would be left; for he preferred to gamble it playing faro[12] rather than having lady doña Ana de Añasco enjoy it) (*Desengaños*, 391). The news of his son's execution reaches him while he is playing cards, and his reaction is similarly callous (see below).

Don Pedro's dedication to card-playing has a greater significance than just that of marking his hard-heartedness. Numerous Christian moralists condemned this diversion as an invention of the devil, a nefarious pastime associated with disorder, blasphemy, greed, squandering of wealth, and a host of other social and moral ills.[13] Luque Faxardo, for example, in a substantial treatise titled *Fiel desengaño contra la ociosidad y los juegos* (1603) says that

el naipe es un instrumento de juego con que se desperdicia y mal
logra el tiempo, el edificio de las virtudes se pone por tierra, la hacienda se consume y en mil ocasiones se acaba el [*sic*] sufrimiento,
los hombres se muelen, desbarátanse los patrimonios, aunque sean
muy gruesos. (Luque Faxardo 1955, 1:104–5)

(playing cards are an instrument with which time is wasted and ill-
spent, the structure of virtues is brought to earth, wealth is consumed and in a thousand occasions ends in suffering, men are
ground up, patrimonies squandered, although they may be very
large.)

Luque Faxardo cites Plato, Saint Gregory, Saint John Chrysostom, and numerous other authorities in attributing a demonic origin to card-playing,
and he points out the infernal end to which it leads:

El modo es diabólico, sus invenciones de Lucifer, que yo no hallo en
ellas huellas de cristiandad. El Padre eterno, como plantas no suyas,
mandará arrancarlas de raíz y, echándolas al fuego eterno, que también estos fulleros son Sinagoga de Satanás, que hacen cabildo para
destruir hombres, allá arderán como gavilla de estopa; que así lo
dice el Espíritu Santo: "Las juntas de pecadores son estopa dis-
puesta para el infierno"; ejerciten sus crueldades impías, que todo
es secarse más para disponer la materia al fuego. (1955, 2:44–45)

(The fashion is diabolic, its inventions those of Lucifer, for I do not
find in them the marks of Christianity. The eternal Father will order
them pulled out as alien plants and, throwing them on the eternal
fire—for these card sharps are a Synagogue of Satan, who conspire
to destroy men—there they will burn like bundles of sackcloth; for
thus says the Holy Spirit: "Assemblies of sinners are sackcloth ready
for hell"; let them exercise their ungodly cruelties, for all of it is just
to dry up more to prepare material for the fire.)

Don Pedro's card-playing thus classes him with the forces of evil and foreshadows the divine justice that will punish his self-centered cruelty.

We might, furthermore, read a more subtle critique of masculine self-
absorption in the card game Zayas has don Pedro play. Writers in Renaissance and Baroque Spain frequently used the terminology of card games
symbolically or allegorically (Etienvre 1982). Some authors built double
meanings on the name of the game alone, as does Zayas in *El castigo de la*

miseria, when don Marcos refuses to "jugar al hombre" (to play the man), the game much loved by Marcela, doña Isadora and her "nephew" Agustín (see Chapter 6 above). Others combined the symbolism of the name of the game with symbolic readings of the values of the four suits or individual cards, or with allegorical applications of the rules of the game. This was the technique employed by Luis Mejía de la Cerda in his 1625 *auto sacramental, El juego del hombre* (Mejía de la Cerda 1915). The basic concept of the *auto* relies on the title of the game, as Christ "plays man" in a match against the devil for human souls. The allegory also evokes in some scenes the rules of the game, and the secular and Catholic values of the suits, "oros" (gold), "copas" (chalices), "espadas" (swords) and "bastos" (clubs), as well as the symbolism of the face cards "rey" (king), "caballo" (horse) and "sota" (knave). Zayas does not give us such a full-fledged allegory, but rather a suggestive allusion that rests, I suggest, on wordplay with the name of the game and the nature of the cards in the deck. Don Pedro is "jugando a las pintas," playing a game that depends on finding two matching cards in a series. According to the definition in the *Diccionario de autoridades* (1737), it consisted of turning cards face up, first for the opponent, then for the dealer, and continuing to turn cards up alternately until one or the other found a card like the player's initial card, thereby gaining points.

We should note that the face cards in the deck don Pedro would have used included no worthy female figure; the original series of four, king, queen, knight, and jack, was reduced to three in Italy and Spain through eliminating the queen, whereas the knight was dropped in England and France (Etienvre 1982, 424). The feminine was reintroduced into the card system inasmuch as the jack or knave, called the "sota" in Spanish, was represented with a certain femininity, but in a vulgarized if not scabrous form, as we can see in modern definitions of *sota:* (1) literally, that which is underneath; (2) jack or knave in cards, and (3) hussy or brazen woman. In Etienvre's words, "Encore faut-il ne pas se méprendre sur cette féminité, car elle est toujours ridicule et vulgaire, parfois même scabreuse, ce qui est en quelque sorte une façon d'évincer la dame une seconde fois" (One should still not misunderstand that femininity, because it is always ridiculous and vulgar, sometimes even scabrous, which is in some sense a means of evicting the lady a second time) (1982, 424).

Pinta (stripe) also means the identifying external mark by which the good or bad quality of a thing is known, akin to the proverbial meaning in English of knowing a person by their stripes. *No quitar pinta* is defined in the *Autoridades* as "frase que significa parecerse con grandísima semejanza a otro; no sólo en la apariencia exterior, sino también en el genio y operaciones" (a phrase that means to resemble another very closely, not only in external appearance, but also in character and actions). Again, English employs similar phrases with *stripe*, as in "two men of the same stripe." Don Pedro, both at the card table and in life, plays a game that excludes women as legitimate participants and in which the objective is to produce a matching card, a son of the same "pinta," or stripe, as the greedy old man.

The cruel patriarch don Pedro presides over a hom(m)osocial economy that tolerates women only as long as they add wealth to the family patrimony rather than siphoning it off in the form of dowries or even maintenance of future heirs. In the end, the son Alonso, plagued by guilty dreams of his sister's death, and cognizant of the justice of his death as payment for the murder of his innocent wife, is partially exonerated. The narrator lays guilt instead at the feet of the father and Alonso's friend Marco Antonio, a curious character, whom Zayas describes as a peculiar Italian phenomenon known as a "clérigo salvaje," or "wild priest," one who wears clerical robes and lives on an income from the church without having studied for the priesthood or being ordained. As an accomplice to the designs of a cruel patriarch, he takes the place occupied by Arnesto in the previous story. Why Zayas would include such a character is something of a puzzle. One might see him as a distant echo of the role of corrupt priests and monks in the novels of Boccaccio, Bandello, and Marguerite de Navarre. On the other hand, combining the role of Marco Antonio with that of the priest whom Alonso calls to confess Mencía—who tries to dissuade him but is ultimately most interested in saving his own life—one might see it as a subtle and cautious insinuation of clerical impotence to prevent the victimization of women, or even their implication in its barbarity.[14]

Any such suggestion, like the potentially contagious critique of the patriarchal order, is quarantined by the intervention of terrestrial and divine justice. Over and over, Zayas's narrator speaks of the hand of God behind the events of the story. To give just one example, she explains the robbery in Genoa by saying that "ya Dios, ofendido y cansado de aguardar tan enormes delitos, como don Alonso cometía, para que pagase con su sangre culpada la inocente que había derramado en las muertes de su hermana y esposa" (now God, offended and tired of waiting, for such enormous crimes as don Alonso was committing, for him to pay with his guilty blood the innocent blood he had shed in the deaths of his sister and wife) (*Desengaños*, 396). Ultimate divine reward for the martyred women is signaled in the miraculous body of doña Mencía and the head of doña Ana, perfectly preserved after six months' burial in a cave. Reference to divine direction of events, either visible or beyond human comprehension, occurs in all her stories, of course, but not always with the frequency and insistence of this tale. More significant, I suggest, is the multiple invocation of well-known figures of the Spanish nobility, at least four of whom are named in this story. The second episode of the story is very specifically anchored in time and place—in Naples—at the time of a change of viceroys, which gives the opportunity for naming three nobles who served in that office between 1610 and 1620: Pedro Fernández de Castro Andrade y Portugal, seventh count of Lemos; his brother, Francisco Ruiz de Castro y Portugal, and Pedro Téllez de Girón, third duke of Osuna. Two more officials are named in connection with the pursuit of don Alonso and Marco Antonio, one don Antonio de Lerma, a sergeant put in charge of a squadron of soldiers sent after them, and Alvaro de Bazán, marquis of Santa Cruz, general of the galleys in which they were fleeing. It is of course possible that the events of the story, if not "un verdadero caso" (a true case) as the narrator proclaims,[15] did have a basis in fact, or that Zayas had some personal or familial connection with the officials named (see Chapter 1 above). Zayas's invocation of the wife of the ninth count of Lemos as "mi señora" (my lady) does suggest some personal relationship. Whatever the connection, the effect within the fiction is that of setting off the injustice of the "fictional" don Pedro of Jaén against the system of justice administered by a series of commendable Spanish authority figures.[16]

In the end, God himself serves as the final guarantor that the designs of such a cruel patriarch will not prevail, as the narrator ends the story with an ironic divine punishment. When don Pedro says of his executed son, "Better dead than badly wed" and goes back to his card game, God intervenes:

> Mas Dios, que no se sirve de soberbios, le envió el castigo de su crueldad pues antes de un mes, una mañana, entrando los criados a darle de vestir, le hallaron en la cama muerto, dejando una muy gruesa hacienda, ¿a quién sino al nieto cuya madre tanto aborreció? Que, como los criados le vieron muerto, dando cuenta a la justicia, . . . sabiendo cómo tenía aquel nieto, se avisó la muerte de don Pedro a don Fernando, y, sabida, él, su nuera con el niño dejando a Italia, se vinieron a Sevilla, donde hoy, a lo que entiendo vive, y será don Pedro Portocarrero y Añasco, de algunos veinte y ocho años. (*Desengaños*, 399)

(But God, who is not pleased by arrogant people, sent him the punishment for his cruelty, for before the month was out, one morning,
when his servants came into his room to help him dress, they found
him dead in bed, leaving a great fortune, to whom but the grandson
whose mother he so abhorred? For, when the servants saw that he
was dead, notifying the authorities, . . . knowing how he had that
nephew, don Fernando was advised of the death of don Pedro, and
thus informed, he, [and] his daughter-in-law leaving Italy with the
child, they came to Seville, where he lives today I understand, and
he would be don Pedro Portocarrero y Añasco, now some twenty-
eight years old.)

In the end, then, Zayas contains the critique of patriarchy at home as a fundamentally flawed structure by having God cast out the bad apples and by
showing us an earthly system of justice that rewards the deserving heir. But
for his daughter and daughter-in-law, on this earth, the misery spread by
don Pedro was irreversible.

History as Context and Symbol in Zayas

Where, then, does Zayas situate the source of women's misery? Does it
come from a familiar enemy, with an *r*—or a familial one? What is the relationship between Zayas's use of political history and her presentation of
the situation of women in the patriarchal family? In addressing that issue, I
would like to detach the *r* and the *l* and make them stand for the problem
of the relationship between history and narrative fiction, between the *r* and
the *l* as "reality" and as "literature" inasmuch as they are roughly dichoto-
mous in our perception. I am not particularly concerned with the attempt
to somehow look "through," behind, or around literary structures at the
problematics of recovering a prethematized "historical reality."[17] My concern is not with narrative in history but rather with history in narrative fiction. More specifically, I would like to examine the presentation of historical event, of historical time, and of *a*-historical time in Zayas's novellas.

Time is inseparable, apparently, from our perception of both poles of
the rough dichotomy I have posed between "reality" and "literature." It is
inextricably intertwined with how we comprehend our existence and how
we tell the stories of our lives, "real" or fictional. According to the

Thomistic psychology that prevailed in Golden Age Spain, perceptions were attributed to the *sensus communis,* a psychophysical cerebral power that gathered together the impressions emanating from the diverse external senses—vision, hearing, tactile sense, and so on, and blended them into a coherent image, or phantasm.[18] According to the theory of perception put forward by Dr. Rodolfo Llinas, however, the process of perception may work quite differently (Blakeslee 1995). Our perception of objects may not occur in space, on a sort of "Cinemascope screen in the brain where all the pieces come together" (p. C10) as in Saint Thomas's *sensus communis.* Rather, Dr. Llinas suggests that highly fragmented sensory perceptions are stored in separate areas of the cerebral cortex. The messages from the activated cells in the cerebral cortex are then bound together not in space but in *time,* through the rhythmic scanning system of the central brain structure called the thalamus. "The sensory messages of sight, sound, smell and touch, are . . . bound together not in a single place but in a single instant of time" (p. C10). During sleep, too, even when the senses are relatively inactive, the images we see in dreams occur in similar rhythmic coordination of cellular activity. In cognition, in our perception of reality, both physical and psychic, timing is everything.

If we broaden our vision from the single instant and object, to complex objects of knowledge, time is equally important. David Carr, in his study *Time, Narrative, and History,* draws on the phenomenology of Husserl and Heidegger to argue that our experience of existence is temporal, that even such limited perceptions or actions as hearing a melody or serving a tennis ball depend on relating past and future segments of the perception or action. Says Carr: "The bedrock of human events, then, is not just sequence but configured sequence"; human time is not just the tick-tock of the clock, the formless flow of time, but configured time (1986, 44). For Paul Ricoeur, that configuration is accomplished through narrative, which synthesizes the heterogeneous into beginnings, middles, and ends. According to Ricoeur, narrative is less a description of reality than its redescription in the mode of "as if," a poetic ordering of our experience of time (Carr 1986, 14–15). From the perspective of developmental psychology, however, Jerome Bruner argues that we learn this "as if" mode at an early age. Bruner notes that "there is compelling evidence to indicate that narrative comprehension is among the earliest powers of mind to appear in the young child and among the most widely used forms of organizing human experience" (1991, 9). Narrative is a fundamental tool in what Bruner calls the "cultural tool kit" with which we achieve a knowledge of social reality.

We organize our lives by telling them as stories, to ourselves and to others[19] (Carr 1986, 61).

Nor are the stories in which and through which we live told in a vacuum. They are learned, repeated, and modified in an inherited cultural tradition and a given social context, these together supplying the language in which stories are told, the norms for their content, and the canonical shapes on which they are modeled. The norms can be breached, of course, and the canons altered, but if the stories are to be believable, they must maintain some degree of referentiality to their cultural context.[20] It is this referential grounding in a given social context that makes fiction of an earlier age both a lure and a trap for readers who look to those stories for evidence of the lived experience of centuries past. Which brings us to the question of history as context in the novellas of María de Zayas.

In considering history as context in her stories, then, we can look first at the historical context of their composition. Most of the first ten were written in the early 1620s, the beginning of the reign of Philip IV. Within the overall sense of decline in seventeenth-century Spain, this was a relatively optimistic era. The second volume was written in the dark decade of the 1640s and repeatedly recalls the traumatic events of those years. Readers tempted to invent a biography for Zayas (by identifying her with the fate of her heroines) often speculate about some personal disappointment with the male sex as a cause of the strident denunciation of men and the violence pervading her second volume; however, barring a major archival discovery of documentation of her life, we can never know this.[21] What we do know, through the satirical portrait of Zayas in the *Vejamen* (see Chapter 1 above), is that she experienced the Catalonian rebellion at close range, but from the divided position of a Castilian witness of the event. It is not surprising, therefore, that the crisis years of their creation should be, if not the proximate cause of the violence of the *Desengaños,* the medium through which she expressed her rancor over the situation of women.

Amezúa, as we have seen (Chapter 2), took at face value the declarations of Zayas's narrators that their stories are true histories, and praised "doña María" as a supremely realistic writer, faithfully portraying the texture of life in court society under the Hapsburg monarchy. Goytisolo mocked Amezúa's naive reading, arguing that her "crossword puzzle plots" are more nourished by literary traditions than by any simple reflection of "reality." His evaluation of the stories' realism is surely more accurate than Amezúa's. Nevertheless, the judicious reader can garner some sense of the social structures and social preoccupations of Zayas's day from her texts.

For example, despite her ardent defense of women's intellectual and moral equality with men, her description of family genealogies invariably concentrates on the paternal line, evidence of the pervasive weight of the patriarchal order. Aristocratic class prejudice is painfully obvious in her texts, in diatribes against servants and social climbers. We can even see something about living quarters; for example, that even members of the upper class lived in multiple-family dwellings.[22] The extent to which her fictional renditions of the language and rituals of courtship reflect social practice is harder to evaluate, since they were so thoroughly entwined with literary traditions. But one novella, *El imposible vencido* (Triumph over the Impossible), gives us a detailed picture of post-Tridentine marriage rites (see Chapter 8 above); other stories corroborate the relationship traced by James Casey (1989, 75–85) between the nature of the dowry system and inheritance laws—particularly female inheritance—and an aristocratic preference for endogamy, to hold family property together. And the collection as a whole dramatically demonstrates the limited options open to "decent" women in Golden Age Spain. Zayas argues vehemently for women's equality, in theory, in the frame portions of the collection; but in the enclosed stories, more thoroughly dominated by the circular relationship between social customs and narrative models, she presents no viable alternatives for aristocratic women other than marriage within their social class, withdrawal to a convent either as a secular resident or a nun, or death. Nevertheless, as we have seen in previous chapters, Zayas does subtly shift the narrative paradigms that she inherited.

We can appreciate one way in which she shifts the paradigm by noticing the differences in her configurations of time and historical event in her two volumes. To begin, I will look at the first phrases of several stories—just the beginnings, because as all good writers and readers know, first sentences set the tenor and direction of the tale.

Let us begin to sing of the Muses of Helikon, / who hold the great and holy mount of Helikon, / and dance on tender feet round the violet spring / and the altar of Kronos' mighty son. (Hesiod 1987, 29)

Before there was any earth or sea, before the canopy of heaven stretched overhead, Nature presented the same aspect the world over. (Ovid 1955)

Once upon a time there lived a king and queen who were grieved, more grieved than words can tell, because they had no children. (Perrault 1961)

Por entre las ásperas peñas de Montserrat, suma y grandeza del poder de Dios y milagrosa admiración de las excelencias de su divina Madre . . . subía Fabio, ilustre hijo de la noble villa de Madrid. (*Novelas*, 37)

(Among the rough crags of Montserrat, sum and grandeur of the power of God and miraculous admiration of the excellence of his divine Mother . . . climbed Fabio, illustrious son of the noble city of Madrid.)

No ha muchos años que en la hermosísima y noble ciudad de Zaragoza, divino milagro de la Naturaleza y glorioso trofeo del Reino de Aragón, vivía un caballero noble y rico, y él por sus partes merecedor de tener por mujer una gallarda dama. (*Novelas*, 401)

(Not many years ago in the most beautiful and noble city of Zaragoza, a divine marvel of Nature and glorious trophy of the Kingdom of Aragón, lived a noble and rich gentleman, and he for his part worthy of having as his wife an elegant lady.)

The five stories that begin with those sentences are Hesiod's *Theogony,* Ovid's *Metamorphoses,* Perrault's "The Sleeping Beauty," and the first and last stories in María de Zayas's first volume, the *Novelas amorosas.* The first sentence of her last *desengaño*, in contrast, differs significantly from those openings:

Estando la católica y real majestad de Felipe III, el año de mil seiscientos diez y nueve, en la ciudad de Lisboa, en el reino de Portugal, sucedió que un caballero, gentilhombre de su real cámara, a quien llamaremos don Gaspar . . . (*Desengaños,* 471)

(While his Catholic and Royal Majesty Philip III, in the year sixteen hundred nineteen, was in the city of Lisbon, in the Portuguese realm, it happened that a gentleman, a gentleman-in-waiting in his royal chamber, whom we will call don Gaspar . . .)

The striking difference in this opening is the very specific anchoring of this story in historical time and place—Philip III's 1619 journey to Lisbon for the swearing-in of the future Philip IV before the Portuguese *cortes.*

References to well-known points in time and space are standard features of the idealistic and conventional world of the *novela cortesana.* In both volumes, Zayas situates virtually all her stories in cities within the Hapsburg realm, generally described in minimal and formulaic terms as very noble, rich, famous, or a combination of these.[23] As Montesa Peydro (1981) points out, although the geographic settings are perfunctory and conventional, they all sound familiar to Zayas's readers and help to bring this idealistic system in direct contact with her readers' experience. He believes that her evocation of what he calls a "macrorrealidad" (macroreality) through references to historical events and famous personages serves the same purpose, that of creating a system of referentiality that lends verisimilitude to her tales.

Without questioning the truth of Montesa's assertion, I would argue that Zayas's use of space and time has more complex expressive purposes or effects. When she does pay attention to the particular physical characteristics of a location, she does so for symbolic or atmospheric purposes related to the central action and theme of the particular tale, as we have seen in considering *Aventurarse perdiendo* and *Desengaño 4* (Chapters 4 and 6, respectively). And the configurations of time in the two volumes differ significantly.

In the prevailing time paradigm of the first volume, *specific* historical time and events are not given particular importance. Although the social structures, like the city names, situate the stories in the world of Hapsburg Spain as Zayas and her readers knew it, the "macroreality" of famous names and events, when adduced, serves as background or as a functional element of the plot. Within that overall context, the time that matters to her heroes and heroines is cyclical—their position within the family in the natural cycle of birth, marriage, and death. The opening sentences of nine of the ten stories in this first volume contain no specific time referent; the mode of human experience they establish is closer to the time paradigms of myth and folklore than to the linear historical time with which Zayas opens her last *desengaño.*[24] The conditions set out for the beginning of the first heroine's entry into a tumultuous history of desire are the death of her mother and the emotional absence of her father, who only cares about her brother. Historical events are mentioned in this story—the war in Flanders and the siege of Mamora[25]—but in that first volume they figure only as the far-off wars that take noble young gallants away from the women who love them. They supply one of the obstacles to achievement of true love that are necessary to a good story.[26]

The closing story of this volume, *El jardín engañoso,* is a qualified miracle tale that hinges on a magical erasure or reversal of time. As we have seen in Chapter 5, it is the only Zayas story told by a female narrator that ends in successful, enduring, socially approved marriage for two sisters, with the classic happy ending "vivieron muchos años con hermosos hijos" (they lived many years with lovely children). Zayas inherited from Boccaccio and Timoneda the basic elements of that plot—the suitor, the generous husband, and the May-in-January garden created by a magician. But by making the magician the devil himself, having the miraculous garden be a product of a Faustian pact, and adding a Cain-and-Abel rivalry, Zayas makes that story an implicit reversal of the biblical story of the fall of humanity into original sin and death. The garden thus becomes a false earthly paradise created by carnal desire, one made by the devil rather than God, and its disappearance is not a punishment for sin but redemption from committing it. And in Zayas, it is a mother who tells the story and another mother who weds her daughter to the man whose generosity defeats the devil of illicit desire. In this magical/miraculous reversal of time, Zayas closes her first volume with a tale whose timelessness is akin to that of folklore, legend, and myth.

What is the importance of this configuration of time? David Carr, as we observed earlier, argues that there is no unbridgeable gap between historical narrative and life in history, at least in Western culture, since our lived experience, for us both as individuals and as social groups, is configured narratively, with an understanding of the present that is both retrospective and projective. Carr adds a coda, however, in which he admits that universalizing his argument, or carrying that of Ricoeur to its logical conclusions, implies relegating cultures that experience time as nonlinear to the category of subhuman or infantile (1986, 179–83). Carr suggests that "perhaps the great literary works of our culture, no doubt starting with the Bible, have inculcated in us a tendency to live our lives as stories" (184). And the organizing perspective of those "stories we live" has been overwhelmingly masculine.[27]

Julia Kristeva, however, argues that such a linear experience of time is not universal even within Western culture. Citing Nietzsche's contrast between cursive and monumental time, Joyce's reference to "father's time" versus "mother's species," and the association of woman with space rather

than time in numerous matriarchal religions and in Plato, Kristeva says
that women's involvement with reproduction and its biological rhythms
links female subjectivity to a cyclical and monumental temporality that,
like numerous non-Western civilizations and mystical experiences, has little to do with linear time (1986b). Kristeva's explanation of the phenomenon of "Women's Time," as she calls it, is not quite as essentialist as such
an abbreviated summary makes it sound. She is not a full-fledged biological determinist. Rather, she argues that sexual difference translates into
difference in relationships "toward the symbolic contract which *is* the social contract: a difference then, in the relationship to power, language and
meaning" (196). The challenge for succeeding generations of women
since the emergence of a feminist consciousness, says Kristeva, has been to
find a satisfactory balance between that feminine space of *jouissance* and incorporation in the Symbolic order, the social contract of historical time
(199–208). Women can elect incorporation in the Symbolic order and its
linear time, and men can reject it. But the prevailing time paradigm in
Zayas's first volume, I would argue, has much in common with this nonlinear "Women's Time," and appropriately concludes with a story told by a
mother that implicitly reverses the biblical creation story of humanity's fall
in and into time.

In the second volume of 1647, in contrast, historical events move to the
foreground or assume an important symbolic relationship to the course of
personal histories in a number of stories. The first *desengaño* is set in Catalonia and the last in Portugal, and in both, the chain of violence and
death is literally and symbolically linked to a rebellious enemy within the
house. The narrator of the first tale, *La esclava de su amante* (Slave to Her
Own Lover), states that "dentro en mi casa estaba el incendio" (the confla-
gration was within my house) (*Desengaños*, 130). The father of Isabel Fajardo, the first-person narrator of the first *desengaño*, goes to Catalonia to
fight the rebels, and the heroine and her mother follow him as far as
Zaragoza. There they are lodged in the house of a noble widow, whose son
don Manuel, frustrated by Isabel's resistance to his amorous demands,
rapes her. In her attempts to convince him to "make an honest woman of
her" by marrying her, she literally sells herself into slavery,[28] and follows
him to Sicily, Algiers, and back to Spain, where, like many of Zayas's heroines, she eventually enters a convent.[29] Both volumes of Zayas's stories thus
open with first-person retrospective accounts of amorous misfortune, since
the heart of the first novella is Jacinta's account to Fabio. Whereas the precondition for Jacinta's vulnerability to desire was a natural event—the
death of her mother—it is political rebellion and personal violence that

initiate the *desengaño*. Here, in full immersion in "men's time," the time of linear history, a daughter is separated from her father and mother by the violence of war and rape.[30]

Zayas, I suggest, anticipated the twentieth-century feminist slogan "The personal is political"—but did so in reverse. In the opening and closing stories of her second volume, the political is made personal. The heroine of the first *desengaño* spells this out:

> Sucedió en este tiempo el levantamiento de Cataluña, para castigo de nuestros pecados, o sólo de los míos, que aunque han sido las pérdidas grandes, la mía es la mayor: que los muertos en esta ocasión ganaron eterna fama, y yo, que quedé viva, ignominiosa infamia. (*Desengaños*, 129)

> (The uprising of Catalonia took place at this time, as a punishment of our sins, or of mine alone, for although the losses have been great, mine is the greatest: for those who died on that occasion gained eternal fame, and I, who remained alive, ignominious infamy.)

In this story, *Desengaño 7*, and *Desengaño 10*, Zayas symbolically links the political crisis within the Hapsburg monarchy to the vulnerability of women within patriarchal family structures. As Lévi-Strauss (1969, 65, 478–93) demonstrates, the exogamous exchange of women has been fundamental to the structure of society, preventing dangerous fission of the social group. Fray Martín de Córdoba recognized the sociopolitical value of such exchange in *El jardín de las nobles doncellas,* a fifteenth-century treatise written to support Isabella of Castille's candidacy to the throne. He attributes three functions to women, the first being that of continuing the species and the second, of preventing fornication; regarding the third, Fray Martín says:

> La otra utilidad—de la creación de la fembra—es reconciliación de paz; e ésto es especial entre los reyes. Acaece que han contienda los grandes señores sobre partimiento de tierras e de lugares, e con una hija hacen paz, traban parentesco. Donde, no solamente los grandes señores, mas todo el humanal linaje, se puede ligar por matrimonio. (Cited in Vigil 1994, 12–13)

> (The other utility—of the creation of the female—is the reconciliation of peace; and this is especially so between kings. It happens that great lords have disagreements about the division of lands and set-

tlements, and with a daughter they make peace, forge kinship.
Whereby, not only great lords, but all the human lineage can be
bound through matrimony.)

Unfortunately, "el humanal lineaje" (the human lineage) is not so securely
bound by the exchange of women. Social and political rebellions regularly
outstrip the capacity of peacekeeping bonds, and women are often innocent victims of warfare, as we all know. Sometimes this is simply because of
their proximity to the zone of conflict, as in the case of Isabel, whom Zayas
makes the symbol of women's fate when there is a fire "within the house,"
here a rebellion within the political family of the Spanish Hapsburg
monarchy. In other cases, the victimization of women is more deliberate
and pointed. The converse of the peacemaking value of female exchange
is the utility of women as pawns through whom rivals can wage "war"
against powerful males or against a political order whose dominance the
rival can perhaps not openly attack.[31] As we have seen in Chapter 8, the
honor system and the implication of noble male identity in the "flesh" of
related females increases these women's vulnerability to reprisals. Zayas
shows us this victimization on an individual level in *Desengaño 2,* as don
Juan rapes Camila and her offended husband then poisons her. She also
gives us a hyperbolic demonstration of its operation on a larger and more
political scale in *Desengaño 7,* as the political marriages of doña Blanca and
her sisters fail to assuage resentment against Spanish dominance in subject
territories, and they pay for that failure in the flesh.[32]

That such a link between political conflict and the victimization of
women exists in fact as well as in Zayas's literary fancy has been sadly
demonstrated recently by the systematic use of rape in Bosnia. The warring
factions in that conflict tell their stories differently, of course. Which
demonstrates again that the stories we tell, like the stories we live, depend
on our relationship to the Symbolic order of language, money and power.
And the way we organize those stories, like the way our brain orders sensory perceptions, depends on timing, on the way we live in time.

The Enemy Within

The misery that women suffer in Zayas's stories does not all originate "outside," in the social order, however. Nor does it all stem from men's cruelty,

duplicity, or inconstancy. Many of her tales include at some point a sexually aggressive female antagonist. The general pattern in such tales is that of supportive female relatives versus the "bad woman" who is unrelated—the stranger. The pattern, however, is broken in three very significant places. In the frame narrative, the heroine Lisis's antagonist is a cousin, and in the last story in each collection, the competition is between two sisters. Significantly, these two concluding stories are told by Lisis's mother and Lisis herself. *Desengaño 10, Estragos que causa el vicio* (The Ravages of Vice), has troubled or at least puzzled many readers on several counts, most particularly because the violence in this story is unleashed by the female protagonist. Why, they ask, would Zayas conclude her championship of women with a story about such a "bad" one?

Structurally, the story is puzzling as well. Loose, episodic construction is a characteristic of all Zayas tales, but in the last novella, the logic of the narrative articulation is particularly problematic. Lisis opens this last *desengaño* with a declaration that she is shunning all rhetorical decoration and obscurity, speaking only the direct language given her by her nature and her parents. Then she relates two adventures of don Gaspar, a young Spanish nobleman temporarily in Portugal. One night when he is entering a large house to visit a lady friend who lives on the third floor, he is frightened by moans coming from a ground-floor storage room. Finding a recently disturbed section in its dirt floor, he digs with a hook and to his horror, brings up with it the face of a man recently buried. When he and helpers disinter "aquel cuerpo, que se lamentaba como si tuviera alma" (that body, which moaned as if it had a soul) (*Desengaños*, 473), they find in one pocket of the richly attired young man love notes from a woman and "la bula," the papal bull that granted special privileges such as exemption from fasting and abstinence to those who participated in the Reconquest, or Crusades, or otherwise supported the Catholic faith.[33] Neither the bull nor the love notes give the man's name, so don Gaspar arranges his burial and taking it as an "aviso de Dios para que se apartase de casa donde tales riesgos había" (warning from God that he should stay away from a house in which there were such risks) (*Desengaños*, 474), stops visiting the lady. Shortly thereafter, however, he sees two beautiful sisters at mass and falls in love with one, doña Florentina, who lives with the other, doña Magdalena, and Magdalena's husband, don Dionís. Florentina lives closely guarded with her sister in don Dionís's house, and don Gaspar is not even able to bribe a servant to help him present his case. The narrator inserts the interesting comment that don Gaspar had no luck with the servants because the Spanish are little liked by the Portuguese "que, con vivir entre nosotros, son nuestros enemigos" (who, although they live among us, are our enemies) (*Desengaños*, 476). This story was written and published in the decade of the 1640 Portuguese rebellion against Spanish rule, which the Spanish were never able to crush.

After two months of fruitless efforts, one night as he passes by the house, don Gaspar finds Florentina nearly dead on the ground, takes her to his residence, and sends for both a doctor and a priest, as she wants to confess before dying. She survives, and tells a horror story of desire, betrayal, and violence. Having fallen madly in love with her sister's husband, she refused all offers of marriage, eventually confessed her love to don Dionís and carried on a passionate affair with him for four years until a loyal maidservant of Florentina offered to betray Magdalena so that don Dionis would kill her and marry Florentina. She made it look as if Magdalena were having an affair with a handsome young page, and don Dionís killed them and then continued to slaughter everyone else in the house, including the maidservant, who confessed to the betrayal. Leaving Florentina for dead, he killed himself by falling on his sword. Florentina was saved by a black slave, who put herself in the path of his fury, allowing Florentina to escape to the street, where don Gaspar found her. This story cures don Gaspar of his infatuation, and he returns to Castilla, while Florentina, with the dowry inherited from Magdalena and don Dionís, enters a convent and becomes a nun.

The last bizarre element in this violent tale is Lisis's evaluative commentary blaming the death of the "honest and virtuous" Magdalena not on her "sister" but on "an infamous servant."[34] She launches into a violent diatribe against servants, calling them "domesticated animals" and "unpardoning enemies" whom one pampers only to have them turn on their masters like lions on their keeper:

> [A] Doña Magdalena no le sirvió el ser honesta y virtuosa para librarse de la traición de una infame sierva, de que ninguna en el mundo se puede librar; porque si somos buenas, nos levantan un testimonio, y si ruines, descubren nuestros delitos. Porque los criados y criadas son animales caseros y enemigos no excusados, que los estamos regalando y gastando con ellos nuestra paciencia y hacienda, y al cabo, como el león, que harto el leonero de criarle y sustentarle, se vuelve contra él y le mata, así ellos, al cabo al cabo, matan a sus amos, diciendo lo que saben de ellos y diciendo lo que no saben, sin cansarse de murmurar de su vida y costumbres. Y es lo

peor que no podemos pasar sin ellos, por la vanidad, o por la hon-
rilla. (*Desengaños*, 508)

(Being honest and virtuous didn't help doña Magdalena free herself from the betrayal of an infamous servant, from whom no
woman in the world can free herself; because if we are good, they
bear false witness against us, and if [we are] wicked, they reveal our
crimes. Because serving men and maidservants are domesticated animals and unforgiving enemies, whom we pamper, spending on
them our patience and fortune, and in the end, like a lion who
turns on the keeper who has raised and maintained him and kills
him, so they, in the end, kill their masters, telling what they know
about them and saying what they don't know, never tiring of gossip-
ing about their lives and habits. And the worst of it is that we can't
get along without them, either for vanity, or for poor honor.)

Vitriol against servants is a repeated motif in Zayas's stories, but the disso-
nance between the merits of their actions and the self-serving treachery
the narrators charge against them is particularly revealing in this instance.
In launching this charge, Lisis has switched to the perspective of Magdalena rather than that of Florentina, who had been the center of the story
itself both as subject and object of desire. She effaces Florentina's viewpoint, crucial role, and very existence as she concentrates her venom on
the nameless maidservant. As she narrated the story, Lisis had described
the maid's actions as demonically inspired, but not as self-serving; rather, it
was an attempt to save the soul and the honor of her mistress, Florentina,
with whom she had been raised since childhood, an effort that cost the
maid her own life and soul. All the other servants of the house showed only
loyalty and honesty, including a black slave girl who died saving Florentina's life by shielding her from don Dionís's avenging sword.

How can the reader meaningfully articulate these seemingly disparate
elements: the promise of speaking natural language, the diatribe against
servants, the location in Portugal, the enemy within, and particularly the
revelation of a not-quite-dead speaking body, with its love notes and papal
bull and the violent slaughter survived only by the desiring sister who
caused it? If we read for a linear, logical progression, we will not find it. I
suggest however, that if we read this story metonymically, looking for the
relation of contiguity between the discontinuous elements, we will find a
meaning that is as much repressed as revealed by their articulation.

My own reading finds their conjunction in the idea of "the enemy within." Like the name of Yahweh, it can only be evoked indirectly, in the laterally connected elements—the threat posed by servants, or the relationship between the Portuguese and Spain. We can also read the anonymous dead body as the threat of death within the house of Eros. His pockets contain authorized access to forbidden pleasures in the papal bull and love notes and we, like don Gaspar, attribute his death to the pursuit of those pleasures. Yet his is a desiring body that will not quite die, that continues to speak despite hasty burial in the cellar of the house. Zayas draws no overt logical parallels between this bizarre episode and the central story of Florentina and Magdalena, and the dead body episode seems buried and forgotten as the story proceeds. Significantly, however, Lisis alludes to it precisely at the moment don Gaspar finds the moribund Florentina in the street, moaning in tones that "frightened don Gaspar more than those he heard in the cellar [cueva]" (477). She too can be read, I suggest, as the desiring body, or desire itself as the resilient enemy within the body of woman. Since Zayas, like Freud, considers active libido appropriate only to the male, the buried but unsilenced voice of desire with whom she is implicitly linked is masculine.

Obviously, Florentina is the *enemy within* Magdalena's house. Her name is significant, because "Florentina" is a diminutive of "Flora," the name of the Roman goddess of flowers and by extension of all vegetation, of the cycles of nature, and thence of sex.[35] In Spain, the order of her representation came to be reversed, and her name became synonymous with illicit female sexuality. Pérez de Moya's mythological dictionary describes her as a famous Roman whore who left her earnings to the Roman people. They built a temple to her, later cleaning up her reputation by calling her goddess of the flowers.[36] Zayas does not make her "little whore" Florentina a true sister, however. She and Magdalena were brought up as loved and loving sisters and only learned after their parents' death that they were both born of earlier marriages of their parents, and were thus not related by blood. On her marriage, Magdalena took Florentina to her new home, "pensando," said Florentina, "que traía una hermana y verdadera amiga, y trujo la destrucción de ella" (thinking—said Florentina—that she was bringing a sister and a true friend, and she brought the destruction of the house) (*Desengaños*, 490).

Since the female antagonist in previous stories had been unrelated, it seems significant that in the frame and in the last story in each collection, the threat is brought within the house, so to speak. In the story immediately preceding this, the antagonist is a true brother, the prince Federico who falls passionately in love with the queen Beatriz, his brother's wife (see Chapter 5 above). The novella *Al fin se paga todo* also includes a treacherous, desiring brother, and a Cain-Abel rivalry between blood brothers is a significant factor in *El jardín engañoso*. That Zayas makes Magdalena and Florentina only sisters by marriage has no effect on the plot as such, and I therefore attribute it to the author's resistance to bringing "the enemy within" as close as a blood sister, daughter of the same mother and father, and hence a kind of double of one's "self." In the evaluative commentary immediately following the tale, Lisis excludes actively desiring woman from their own sex and class, asserting that "las malas no son mujeres" (the bad ones are not women) and if one finds "en las de alta jerarquía . . . travesuras y embustes . . . ésas son más bestias fieras que las comunes" (in those of high rank . . . pranks and fibs . . . those women are wilder beasts than common women) (*Desengaños*, 503–4). Florentina alone survives the holocaust she provokes and becomes a nun, and several other actively desiring Zayas protagonists also become nuns, while passive, virtuously innocent heroines tend to be killed or live out their lives as secular residents of convents. The unspoken message thus written into Zayas's plots is that desire is like the servant within the house: indispensable, semiautonomous, and ultimately uncontrollable, a kind of domesticated lion. It cannot be, will not be, exterminated, but can only be contained by its sublimation as religious passion and by a return to an imaginary or real bonding with the mother in the female society of a convent.

But if we can find a coherence of disparate elements in Zayas's last tale only by means of a metonymic contiguity in terms of "the enemy within," how do we reconcile that form of reading with the Lisis/Zayas proclamation of her natural, unadorned style? Certainly it is clear that she shuns the intricate verbal wit of a Quevedo, for example. But to uphold her claim that she speaks/writes in a language learned from her nature and her parents requires a very different understanding of the acquisition and function of language from that which Zayas probably intended to convey, a concept we have learned from the language-centered psychoanalytic theories of Lacan and Lacanian disciples—and their feminist critics, such as Kristeva and Irigaray. While Lisis/Zayas may claim to speak directly, in a simple style accessible to all, in my own experience of teaching Zayas, I find that students who have had no particular difficulty reading Luis de León or Cervantes, for example, protest that Zayas is impenetrable until they learn to deal with her disjunctive, looping syntax. Furthermore, as I have argued earlier (see Chapter 6), I believe that disjunctive signifying process extends beyond the level of the sentence to the articulation of the narrative as a whole, and it is that which requires a metonymic reading, a reading that looks for the central object not in direct naming but in laterally related allusion.[37]

Jane Gallop (1985), in her playful reading of Lacan on metaphor and metonymy, first links metaphor with a patent, vertical, male, phallic construction of meaning, and metonymy with the feminine, with linear oppression or repression of meaning, with the invisible female genitalia. But she goes on to point out that the phallus in Lacanian terms only operates when it is veiled, and that the vertical bar of the plus sign in Lacan's equation for metaphor crosses a horizontal bar; that metonymy can function phallically if the feminine is seen as dominant, as the phallic mother, and that metaphor cannot exist without the linearity of metonymy, which was always already there, and is what makes metaphor possible. Ragland-Sullivan concurs with Gallop's association of metonymy with the feminine, but adds the important caution that the link is not biological but cultural, in the cultural traditions associated with the feminine on which women generally model their identity.[38]

We might think of the reading/writing process in Zayas not only in terms of a metonymy linked to the feminine, but also in light of the interaction that Kristeva describes between the symbolic and semiotic orders. For Kristeva, as for Lacan, entry into the Symbolic order, the domain of paternal law and of language, is an essential step in the construction of subjectivity, in the achievement of a socially functional sense of bounded, if permeable, identity. Kristeva, however, posits the existence of a preverbal semiotic modality that precedes the symbolic and coexists with it, disrupting its rational, univocal order.[39] The semiotic is a modality of drives, of instinctual energy charges organized by the primary processes of condensation and displacement into what Kristeva calls a *chora*, a kind of nonspatial receptacle of drive energy and ephemeral stases ordered in relation to the maternal body. It finds its expression not in the rationally communicative function of language, but in rhythm, color, tone, and intensity, and in the way they distort or disrupt the linear order of philosophical discourse. Although the semiotic is essential to the aesthetic signifying process, it cannot find expression without entry into the symbolic order that permits representation.

The articulation of Zayas's tales seems to me illustrative of the creative interaction of the symbolic and semiotic that Kristeva describes. Without separation from the maternal and submission to the Name-of-the-Father there would be no tale, for there would be no language. Furthermore, narrativity is embedded in social practice in a mutually reinforcing relationship that would have made the construction and reception of a direct challenge to the master plot (active male subject/passive female object) virtually impossible in a literary and cultural tradition as strongly patriarchal as that of seventeenth-century Spain. Feminine resistance to that narrative—and social—order surfaces, then, not within the discrete episodes of Zayas's plots as such, but in the gaps and ruptures that disrupt their logical, linear progress, and in the ellipses separating apparently unrelated details. In a sense, this signifying process is another kind of enemy within, the disruptive force associated with the feminine and with the maternal that will not be contained in the rational paternal narrative order.

To articulate meaning through the sort of metonymic reading that I suggest requires that the reader acknowledge that s/he, in positing the points of contiguity supposedly hidden in the ellipses of narrative, is as much writing as reading meaning. To read thus becomes a dialectic between what Kristeva calls two *sujets en procès,* subjects in process or on trial, author and reader, in which meaning is never fully and finally inscribed, but always emerging in the intersections of their dialogue. It was Zayas's stories that first led me to psychoanalytic theory, and to the pleasures of this sort of dialogic encounter with her texts. In suggesting the readings I have posited in the foregoing chapters, my hope is therefore to broaden and enrich the engagement that other readers may establish with the product of Zayas's imaginative art.

PART IV

En-closure

10

Framing the Tale

Most viable works of literature tell us something about how they are to be read,
guide us toward the conditions of their interpretation
—Peter Brooks, *Reading for the Plot: Design and Intention in Narrative*

I opened Part II with the suggestion that Zayas asks her readers to read her
novellas with their mothers in mind. But is it fair to say that her *Sarao*
(soiree) also guides us toward conditions of interpretation in any way akin
to the collaborative articulation of meaning that I have suggested in concluding the preceding chapter? On the surface, we can say yes, inasmuch
as a collaborative articulation mimics the fictional device of her frame narrative, in which a variety of narrators speak to entertain the ailing Lisis and
debate the meaning of their narratives. She, fictionally instructed by their
tales, performs the final telling act, followed by a didactic commentary in
which her authorial "I" blends with that of Zayas herself, as we shall see.
However, inasmuch as the process of articulating meaning advanced by
Kristeva is open-ended and multiple, always somewhat differently wrought
by each unique writer-reader dialectic, we must say no. Zayas states clearly

in the voice of her first narrator, and those of the fictional speakers who follow her, that she has one message—to warn women against yielding to desire. Or perhaps she has two, if we add the injunction to men to respect women in word as well as deed. But I would argue that this two-level, yes and no answer proves the point—that the driving energy of Zayas's fictional world is located both in what she says and in the unconscious truth she seeks to suppress. The frame tale itself becomes in Zayas's hands a kind of narrative containing act, a fictional device designed to focus the exemplary power of her twenty tales toward the delivery of her primary explicit message. To understand Zayas's particular use of the frame tale, I would like to approach it through a brief consideration of the function of artistic frames, in a larger sense, and of the nature and function of the frame tale in Zayas's predecessors in the novella tradition.

First let us imagine a fond father or mother who in a burst of parental enthusiasm puts a child's first tempera painting in a real frame and hangs it on the wall. What is the significance of that frame? In the mind of parent and child, at least, it says, this is not just a five-year-old's play with color, this is important; this is ART. Now, working in reverse, if we call to mind a favorite painting, whether it be a Velázquez, Monet or Picasso and, in our mind's eye remove its frame, does it diminish it in some way? Does it make more tenuous the stature of that image as a work of art? I would be tempted to say that it does, until I think of a small print I have of one of my favorite paintings, La Tour's *Education of the Virgin*.[1] It has no frame, just a tack holding it to the wall above the desk in my office, yet looking at it transports me to another realm of aesthetic as well as educational purity. I would deduce from this mental exercise that the declaration of aesthetic value can be either internally or externally coded.

If we turn to theater, we find the same to be the case. Theaters with a proscenium arch and a stage curtain need no mediating *dramatic* frame or prologue to define the dramatic world. But dramatic prologues are an important constituent of Spanish Renaissance drama from Juan del Encina forward, when plays were performed in improvised theaters and playwrights were defining the conventions of drama for their audiences. Although prologues gradually disappeared in the public theaters, they continued as a vital part of the street performances of the *autos sacramentales* (allegorical religious drama) for the annual Corpus Christi celebration. Informal street theater today, too, requires some kind of frame definition. This may be effected by a barker, or a lone performer who attracts a group of spectators. On the other hand, the separate, aesthetic realm may in this case too be worked internally, by opening the dramatic action with a heightened theatrical rhetoric—"overacting"—which marks this interaction as distinct from the everyday world of the street itself. Once a semicircle of spectators forms, they themselves mark out the limits of the aesthetic "object," within which space, time, and being have the peculiar doubleness of drama. While most mature human beings respect the integrity of the object thus demarcated, the frame is not impermeable. Naive spectators do sometimes behave like don Quixote before Maese Pedro's puppet show; Henry Sullivan (1983, 386) cites two cases of twentieth-century spectators of a German version of Calderón's *La dama duende* (The Phantom Lady) who got carried away and intervened across the frame at least verbally. And the Argentine dramatist Osvaldo Dragún told me that when in the last days of the military regime, his troop, using theater as a political weapon, performed his works wherever they could gather a crowd in the streets of Buenos Aires, one play in particular caused "framing" problems. In his brief play, *Historia de un hombre que se convertió en perro* (Story of a Man Who Turned into a Dog), as the title indicates, the main character is transformed from a speaking human being into a barking dog. As he was reduced to barking, the spectators might have understood the political point being made, but all the neighborhood dogs saw was a new interloper in their territory, and the only way the troop could keep them from attacking was by, shall we say, turning up the theatrical rhetoric, and, in solidarity with the "caninized" actor, all barking ferociously until the "real" dogs retreated.

Presumably, most of us are not mongrel readers. While we acknowledge the thorny problem of the ontology of fictional discourse, in practice we are generally able to recognize the presence of a fictional text by its own combination of external and internal markers: externally the book as a physical object in itself, and the liminary elements that Genette (1987, 7–8) calls the "paratexte" of the work—title, preface, epigraph, and so on, and internally by stylistic clues. The latter may be as close to the time-honored "Erase una vez" (Once upon a time) as is the opening sentence of Cervantes' novella, *La ilustre fregona* (The Illustrious Kitchen Maid): "En Burgos, ciudad ilustre y famosa, no ha muchos años que en ella vivían dos caballeros principales y ricos" (In the illustrious and famous city of Burgos, not many years ago there lived two high-born and rich gentlemen) (1990, 297). Or the clues may appear more subtly and slowly, as in *La fuerza de la sangre* (The Power of Blood): "Una noche de las calurosas del verano volvían de recrearse del río, en Toledo, un anciano hidalgo, con su mujer, un niño pequeño, una hija de diez y seis años y una criada. La noche era clara; la hora, las once; el camino, solo, y el paso, tardo" (One of those hot summer nights, in Toledo, an elderly gentleman was returning from an outing to the river with his wife, a small boy, a sixteen-year-old daughter, and a serving girl. The night was clear, the hour, eleven o'clock, the road, deserted, and their pace, slow) (1990, 239). Even in this second case, the special rhythm of the second sentence would alert most readers that they are not perusing a seventeenth-century equivalent of a police report.

If these subtle forms of framing are, in practice, generally sufficient to delimit a fictional text, what, then, are the purpose and function of the much more assertive framing devices used by Boccaccio in the *Decameron* (c. 1350), Chaucer in the *Canterbury Tales* (1386–1400) (and their Eastern predecessors), and the many novella writers who followed in that tradition? Why did Cervantes in his *Novelas ejemplares* (Exemplary Novels) (1613) dispense with the frame and why did Lope personalize it in the *Novelas a Marcia Leonarda* (Stories for Marcia Leonarda) (1621–24)?[2] Why did the majority of Spanish novella writers of the 1620s and 1630s follow the example of Cervantes rather than Lope? Finally, the question of most interest to me, why did Zayas, who wrote her first stories in that same era, opt to build a frame tale around her two-volume collection of novellas?[3]

In tackling these questions, I would like to make one more preliminary detour through a fairly recent use of the frame tale, the Rob Reiner film *The Princess Bride,* which I would describe as a romance packaged for postmodern cynics. And very effectively packaged indeed. Anyone who has a teenage child has probably seen at least bits of this film more times than they can count, and my daughter reports that at the mere mention of it, her college friends launch into gleeful recitals of their favorite lines. The film opens with the sound of a child's cough, followed by strains of "Take Me Out to the Ball Game" and a view of a Nintendo-style baseball game on a television screen. The young boy playing it is ill and confined to his room, but is less than delighted when his grandfather arrives to visit bearing a present—"a *book*??"—and proposing to read to him the story that his father read to him when he was sick, that he read to the boy's father, and will now read to him. The boy is unenthusiastic but when his grandfather assures him that it has lots of sports in it, he says he'll try to stay awake. What the grandfather reads is a classic tale of a poor, gallant hero named Wesley who defeats an evil prince, Humperdink, and wins his beautiful ladylove, Buttercup, all seasoned generously with humor, magic, and valor. At key points in the narrative, the camera cuts back to the boy, now fully engrossed in the tale, but interrupting the reading when the story seems to depart from his ideal paradigm, or when Wesley and Buttercup spend too much time kissing.

This cinematographic frame tale contains most of the major elements of classic literary frames. The first is the motif of illness. In Boccaccio's frame, this illness is without—the plague raging through Florence, from which the seven ladies and three gentlemen retreat both physically and psychologically, recounting stories in the safe haven of beautiful gardens in country estates. More often, the sickness is within. In the twelfth-century *Disciplina clericalis* of Petrus Alfonsi, a dying Arab transmits his wisdom to his son by telling him a series of stories and proverbs containing moral lessons (Gittes 1991, 59).[4] The pretext for storytelling in María de Zayas's novellas is the illness of the heroine of the frame tale, Lisis, whose friends gather to entertain her and speed her convalescence by telling stories. In Zayas's tale, as in numerous stories in novella collections, the true illness is *doubly* within, for the physical symptoms are the result of *mal de amor*—in the case of Zayas's Lisis, suffering caused by jealousy and disappointment in love, as her beloved don Juan neglects her for her cousin Lisarda. Boccaccio too, in his "Proemio," cites his former suffering of frustrated passion and offers his stories as pleasure, counsel, and cure for the "charming ladies" who suffer love's melancholy (1982, 2–3). Zayas's frame narrative seems, until the very end, to posit two possible remedies for the suffering of unrequited love: on the one hand, Lisis is promising to marry another man, the adoring don Diego;[5] on the other, the enclosed narrators hammer home the point that their tales are to warn women against the pitfalls of desire and male treachery, and in the opening frame section of the second volume, the reader is given a hint that in the throes of a renewed, life-threatening episode of *mal de amor*, Lisis has reconsidered that promise: "tuvo lugar su divino entendimiento de obrar en su alma nuevos propósitos si bien a nadie lo daba a entender, guardando para su tiempo la disposición de su deseo, mostrando a don Diego y a la demás familia . . . un honesto agrado" (her divine understanding had time to work within her soul new intentions, although she didn't suggest them to anyone, saving the resolution of her desire for its proper time and displaying to don Diego and the rest of the family a modest charm) (*Desengaños*, 116). This hint is reinforced visually at the opening of the third night of the *sarao*. Lisis appears without the dress and jewels sent her by don Diego for their betrothal; she and doña Isabel are attired in white, thus matching the white Concepcionista habit of the nun, doña Estefanía. With their dazzling, diamond-studded white garb, they are "like Venus in beauty and Diana in chastity." Only after Lisis narrates Florentina's tale and moralizes on it does Zayas exclude a possible worldly remedy for *mal de amor.* Taking the hands of doña Isabel and doña Estefanía, Lisis announces her retirement to the closed, feminine world of the convent, where she will observe the fate of "los demás" (the others)—which in context seems to mean that this inner narrator plans to observe the future of protagonists of the tales that she and her friends have told.

Another element that Reiner's cinematic frame shares with literary frame tales is that of a physical separation from the everyday world, a separation that permits storytelling. Often the frame underlines the horror and threat of the outside world. Boccaccio describes the physical and social ravages of the plague in gruesome detail, and Marguerite de Navarre's narrators in the *Heptameron* narrowly escape war, violent bandits, and a roaring flood.[6] Zayas, and later Mariana de Carvajal, mark the separation in terms of temperature, contrasting the inner warmth of the Madrid residence where the storytellers gather with the icy December temperatures without.[7] They meet, Zayas says,

> una tarde de las cortas de Diciembre, cuando los hielos y terribles nieves dan causa a guardar las casas y gozar de los prevenidos braseros, que en competencia del mes de Julio, quieren hacer tiro a las cantimploras y lisonjear las damas, para que no echen menos el Prado, el río y las demás holguras que en Madrid se usan. (*Novelas,* 29)

> (one of the short December afternoons, when the ice and terrible snow give cause for staying home and enjoying the readied braziers that, in competition with the month of July, want to rival the water-cooling jugs and please the ladies so that they will not miss the Prado, the river, and the other enjoyments customary in Madrid.)

In painting such a scene, Zayas and Carvajal link their settings with the folklore tradition of storytelling "alrededor de la lumbre" (around the fire), a tradition also evoked by the very titles of two earlier Spanish novella collections, Timoneda's *El Patrañuelo* (Tall Tales) (1567) and Eslava's *Noches de invierno* (Winter Nights) (1609).[8] I would hardly be original in suggesting that the comfort of companionship and a crackling fire that is proffered in the frame settings is a physical translation of the psychic or metaphysical "warmth," comfort, or "cure" provided by narrative itself, as it models a meaningful design for human life, for a cold, chaotic existence in which order and purpose are rarely self-evident.

For the contained narratives to offer that comfort, however, the frame space of storytelling must draw its intended audience into the order of make-believe through an attractive and credibly familiar portal. Reiner shows the grandfather entering a comfortable middle-class home, probably in a suburb of Chicago, since the boy wears a Bears T-shirt and the grandfather's dress and accent suggest the European immigrant communities that decades ago marked the speech of Boston, New York, and Chicago. Given the customary restriction of women to private, domestic spaces, it should not surprise us that most early modern women writers also chose a domestic setting for their narratives. This is as true of Zayas and Carvajal as it is of Christine de Pizan in her *Cité des dames*.[9] We should put "domestic" in quotes, however. The frame space constructed by Carvajal really does transmit a flavor of an idealized domesticity for the lesser nobility inhabiting a multifamily residence in Madrid.[10] While Zayas also sets her frame in a multifamily residence, the atmosphere she seeks to create is rather one of aristocratic luxury, courtly elegance, and formality. Her storytellers gather in a room hung with panels of green velvet and tapestries that, rather like perspective scenery in court theaters, invite participants to transport themselves imaginatively into the Arcadian woods and the exotic gardens of Babylon. *Crowning* the room, in Zayas's description, is a dais supplied with silver-trimmed, green velvet cushions and a chaise lounge serving as the *throne* for Lisis, yet more richly adorned in gold-trimmed green brocade.[11] "Desiring readers," Zayas paints a narrative portal designed to lure them with the attractive luxury and atmosphere of nobility to which they aspired in an era in which the imitation of aristocratic values and styles permeated all levels of society.[12]

Reiner's grandfather, like the narrators of many frame tales, represents the wise man (or woman) who instructs an inexperienced listener through an entertaining tale. In the eighth-century frame narrative *Panchatantra*, the three doltish young sons of a mighty king learn worldly and political wisdom from the tales of a wise man (Gittes 1991, 9–10). In don Juan Manuel's *El conde Lucanor*, the wise old servant Petronio provides the guidance requested by the count in the form of exemplary tales. Whereas the American grandfather reads to a boy, Boccaccio, Lope de Vega, and many other writers of novella collections posit a primarily female readership. Zayas's narrators, however, address a mixed audience, both within the frame and as presumed readers of the collection, exhorting women to attend the warnings in the tales, and entreating men to hear or read them with a chivalrous spirit and an open mind.

This dialogue with a fictive audience is, of course, one of the primary functions of the frame tale, as Amy Williamsen (1991) demonstrates in the case of Zayas. Anne Cayuela, in her study of the liminary apparatus of seventeenth-century Spanish fiction, points out that reading is a communicative act in which one of the parties is absent, and that publication in print made works available to a large and heterogeneous audience. One result is an emphasis, in the liminary apparatus, on the nature of the destinatee and on the concrete aspects of the communicative act (1994, 81, 123–24). The prologue, in a kind of act of seduction, creates an image both of the author and of the implied or ideal reader in order to obtain not only a reading, but a particular kind of reading.[13] Two of our novella authors perform this image-creating function quite literally: Cervantes, in the self-portrait he paints in the prologue to his *Novelas ejemplares;* and Lope de Vega, who depicts his fictive destinatee Marcia Leonarda in glowing color. The fully personified communicative act in frame narratives make this image-operated seduction of the reader yet more dramatic, particularly in frames such as those of Marguerite de Navarre and María de Zayas, which involve extensive exchange between fictional narrators and their listeners. This function of the frame is of the utmost importance in Zayas's collection, as we will see.

First, however, I would like to consider two other perspectives on the nature and function of frames, theories that focus more on the other end of the author to "real" world relation, that of the sociohistorical and ideological context and the author's use or omission of a frame tale. Katharine Gittes provides a fascinating perspective on the relation between cultural structures and frame narratives in her study of an early time period, tracing the development of the tradition from early Eastern tales to Chaucer and Christine de Pizan. With reiterated apologies for the imprecision of the terms "Eastern" and "Western,"[14] Gittes draws a fundamental contrast between East and West in the metaphysical conception of the world. The East, rooted in nomadic tribal life, saw the world as open and appreciated the infinite variety and limitless renewability of life. Early Arabic literary forms, such as the pre-Islamic ode, or *qasida,* and the tenth- and eleventh-century Arabic picaresque, or *maqamah,* have a loose, open-ended, linear structure, organized not by a unifying theme or idea but by the perspective of the speaker or central character (Gittes 1991, 34–45). Hence, a collection such as the *The Thousand and One Nights,* the product of a culture that avoids rounding off numbers, preferring 1001 as the expression of a large, indefinite number (Gittes 1991, 33, 46).

Gittes traces the Western view of a more closed universe back to Greek mathematical principles, to the preference of Pythagoras for geometry over algebra, and for what Gittes describes as "[a] concept of organization, a notion of unity, in which the whole has greater importance than the parts. . . . Pythagoras, voicing what had been implied in Greek thought before his time, stated that the universe is harmonious because all its parts are related to one another mathematically. He thought that mathematical order lay behind the apparently mysterious, arbitrary, and chaotic workings of nature" (1991, 24). This insistence on harmony, unity, and the orderly subordination of the part to the whole underlies the literature, art and architecture, and worldview passed on from Greece and Rome to medieval European philosophers (29).

Medieval Spain served as the bridge over which the frame-tale collection, along with so many other elements of Eastern culture, reached the West. The collection of tales known as the *Panchatantra,* much of which seems to have originated in India and the Near East, acquired in its eighth-century Arabic translation an open-ended frame in which a wise man tells stories to educate a king's sons who had previously refused instruction (Gittes, 1991, 8–20). Augmented and renamed, with an Arabic touch, *Kalilah and Dimnah,* the collection came to Europe through the Arab conquest. When Alfonso X had it translated in the thirteenth century, it became, according to a recent editor, Thomas Irving, "the first extensive piece of prose literature in the popular language of Spain" and "a point of confluence in the streams of Arabic and Spanish civilization" (*Kalilah and Dimnah* 1980, xi). It also furnished the model for the widely read *Disciplina clericalis* that the converted Spanish Jew Petrus Alfonsi wrote first in Arabic, then translated into Latin. That work, according to Gittes, "ranks above all other works in bridging "Eastern" and "Western" narrative traditions and in funneling Arabic content and structure to European medieval vernacular writers (1991, 57).[15] The frame narrative tradition that developed thereafter, according to Gittes, bore the continuing tension between open and closed structures, between the attraction of symmetry and the suspense of the indefinite (113). Further, she says,

> the earliest Arabic frame narratives suggest that medieval Arabs perceived the natural world as a world where boundaries and structure, if they exist, are not especially desirable. The later European frame

narratives, notably the *Decameron,* the *Confessio* and the *Canterbury Tales* suggest the reverse; that even though the natural world appears disorderly, the medieval Christian longed to see a spark ... which would give the sensation that underneath the disorder lies a comforting divine harmony, perhaps ordered along Pythagorean lines. The harmony hinted at in these fourteenth-century frame narratives is a harmony which the reader will see and fully comprehend in the afterlife. What looks like disorder on earth is God's order misperceived. (148)

H. H. Wetzel, beginning in time approximately where Gittes leaves off, traces the development of the novella from the late Middle Ages to Cervantes, in a more closely deterministic fashion. He relates the presence or absence of a developed narrative frame—as well as the predominance of different types of novellas—to the relative stability or flux in the political and ideological structures of the age. Within the stable order of feudalism and medieval Christianity, collections of *exempla* did not require an elaborated narrative frame, for order was perceived to be supplied by Divine Providence, whose operation the *exempla* helped to explain allegorically. Says Wetzel, "It was not by chance that the first European collections of *novelas* appeared at the end of the thirteenth century in southern and central Italy; in that "anarchic" land, the autonomy of the towns and of their citizens was most advanced, the social order profoundly overturned by the nascent preponderance of the merchant bourgeoisie and orthodox faith heavily buffeted by the revaluation of man, a new consciousness of his own value and the effect of major heretical movements" (1981, 46). Within this turbulent world, Boccaccio supplied a harmonious fictional order to contain the chaos of reality, the social breakdown brought on by the plague, "a symbolic index of the danger which threatened to dissolve the civic, religious and moral norms of the society" (47). That Boccaccio felt empowered to supply such an order and felt the need to do so, Wetzel relates to the sociopolitical order of Florence in his day, where a commoner such as Boccaccio could participate actively in both the financial and political life of the city, and where social norms were in flux and civic equilibrium precarious, as the bourgeois "virtues" of a modern economy intermingled with traditional aristocratic codes of conduct. With the refeudalization of the fifteenth and sixteenth centuries, frame narratives were either weakened or omitted by authors who enjoyed no true political power, being limited to a subordinate role in princely courts (50). For his mid-sixteenth-century-collection, Bandello constructed no organizing frame but dedicated each of his 214 stories to one of a variety of notable figures in the courtly society he knew. Wetzel relates this practice to his dependent position within an Italy whose cities no longer enjoyed the relative autonomy of Boccaccio's Florence, but were buffeted by European power contests on Italian soil, and in which the discovery of the New World and the Reformation were transforming the mental as well as the physical world (53). That Marguerite de Navarre, on the other hand, constructed a highly elaborated narrative frame within a rigidly hierarchical political structure, Wetzel attributes to her privileged position, one of true authority as queen of France, albeit a France torn by religious dissension. Hence the importance of the lengthy discussions by her quite fully developed frame personalities, who express profound differences of viewpoint (50–51).[16] And finally, in the declining empire of seventeenth-century Spain, Cervantes, says Wetzel, "made a virtue of the necessity of renouncing the frame" (54). He exchanged the powerlessness of a *hidalgo* without even the comfort of a subordinate position at court "for the empowerment of a gifted artist who constructed fictive reality to his own image and dissolved the contradictions of reality through well-known literary devices such as recognitions, found children, etc." (54–55). One might contest his evaluation of Cervantes renunciation of the frame in the light of that author's announcement of a future work that has the sound of a framed novella collection, *Semanas del jardín*. On the other hand, Wetzel might claim vindication in the fact that such a collection never saw the light of day.

If we bring the theories of Gittes and Wetzel to bear on Zayas's choice of a fully developed frame narrative, the results are contradictory. From the scarce documentation of her life, we can say that she probably enjoyed a somewhat more secure socioeconomic position than did Cervantes, as the daughter of Fernando de Zayas, who was at one time the majordomo of the count of Lemos and who was named corregidor of an estate of the Order of Santiago in 1638 (Barbeito Carneiro 1986, 165–72). In no way could we argue that she enjoyed true political authority, as did Marguerite de Navarre. At best we could claim for her, as she does for herself, a position of moral authority as self-appointed spokeswoman for women within an absolutist, resolutely patriarchal Counter-Reformation society that denied them any legitimate independent agency.[17] By Gittes's categories, this was an ideologically closed society, one that would foster the containment of difference, of the chaotic multiplicity of reality, within a strictly controlling frame, but by those of Wetzel, it would make the erection of such a frame impossible for a powerless female.

Zayas does not use the frame as a format for true discussion of philosophical difference, as does Marguerite de Navarre, but rather as an arm of philosophical combat in the defense of women. She makes of it, we might say, a "thesis" frame narrative.[18] And it is the effective propagation of her thesis, I believe, that motivates her use of such a frame.

To demonstrate the rhetorical strategy operative in Zayas's use of the frame, however, we will first have to move inside it, to examine her tactics from the perspective of two elements of internal narrative design: (1) the relationship of the enclosed tales to the tradition of exemplary narrative; and (2) the import of such "superficial" aspects of style as her descriptive technique and use of titles, titles of individual tales and of the volumes that contain them.

The title *Novelas amorosas y exemplares* that heralded her first volume of stories adhered tenaciously to her collection in subsequent editions. Faced with the 1625–34 ban on the publication of novels and volumes of plays, Zayas apparently altered the original title of her manuscript from "Novelas amorosas y exemplares" to "Honesto y entretenido Sarao" (Decorous and Entertaining Soiree) when submitting it for censorial approval,[19] and her second volume was published with the title *Parte segunda del Sarao y entretenimiento honesto.* She substitutes for the maligned generic title "novela" the term "maravilla" (marvel) in her first volume and "desengaño" in the second. Nevertheless, the approval and license given her first volume in 1635 by the *vicario general* in Zaragoza, Juan Domingo Briz, refers to her "novelas," and all editions of her first volume carry the title *Novelas amorosas y exemplares* on the title page. Furthermore, despite Zayas's efforts to overturn that title, all editions of the two parts together from 1659 forward reverted to the earlier form, being called *Primera y segunda parte de las novelas amorosas y exemplares de Doña María de Zayas y Sotomayor.* My concern here, however, is less with her avoidance of the morally and aesthetically suspect generic title "novela" than with the term "ejemplar."[20]

Zayas was writing toward the end of the two-century period, from the fifteenth to the seventeenth centuries that Leonardo Olschski has labeled the "age of exemplarity" (cited in Lyons 1989, 12, 247), in which reliance on the use of the example to support the general statement was fed by a variety of factors, including humanism, religious crisis, a rapidly expanding body of knowledge, and a turn toward proof through experimentation and observation. But the expanding and diversifying world of experience made this age at the same time a period of crisis for the *exemplum* and related rhetorical figures, as John Lyons (1989), Karlheinz Stierle (1998), and Timothy Hampton (1998) demonstrate. Lyons presents example as a basic rhetorical figure that can be traced back as far as Aristotle's *Rhetoric* and *Topics,* wherein it constitutes one of the two means of producing belief, the first being example, or *paradeigma,* the second enthymeme or syllogism (1989, 4, 6).[21] Arguing that the lack of critical attention to example as a rhetorical figure may derive from its capacity to appear as a direct representation of reality, Lyons posits it as always engaged in supporting or restructuring systems of belief. It might qualify, he believes, as "the most ideological of figures, in the sense of being the figure that is most intimately bound to a representation of the world and that most serves as a veil for the mechanics of that representation" (ix). In the early modern period, examples were viewed as possessing both cognitive and ethical value; they were mostly chosen to arrive at "a common ground of belief" that writers and readers could recognize as reality, on the one hand. On the other, in accord with repeated justifications of literature for its ability to provide examples of conduct to imitate or shun, examples were "aimed at direct behavioral modification" (x, 12–13).

More immediately, Zayas writes in the shadow of Cervantes' regeneration of the novella form with his collection of *Novelas ejemplares.*[22] In his preface—that important "paratextual" threshold in which an author seeks to set the terms that guide the reading of his text (Genette 1987, 7–8)— Cervantes vigorously defends the exemplarity of his stories. In consonance with the humanist predilection for example that rested on its capacity to serve *both* as model of conduct for imitation and as model for writing (Lyons 1989, 13), Cervantes characterizes his tales as exemplary first in terms of content, second in terms of their form.[23] Over the centuries, some readers—from Lope de Vega to Américo Castro—have disputed the legitimacy of Cervantes claim for exemplarity. As Forcione points out, Lope was judging Cervantes' narratives in terms of a narrow concept of exemplarity, one that can be contained in a title and summed up in moralizing sentences and aphorisms. On the other hand, Castro in his later years condemned many of the novellas as hypocritical accommodations to received ideas and values by a Cervantes whom Castro judged to have sacrificed his critical authenticity and innovative independence of thought on the altar of literary success and social acceptance.[24] But Forcione persuasively argues that Cervantes, having absorbed and made his own the Christian humanism that flourished in Spain in his youth, and possessing a thorough familiarity with a wide variety of literary genres and modes, did indeed craft stories that were exemplary both in content and form. Combining and reshaping traditional genres and bringing into dialogue a diversity of subjective perspectives, he challenges his readers to free themselves from stock responses and comfortably familiar beliefs (Forcione 1982, 19–30). Forcione also suggests that Cervantes rejected the use of a courtly narrative frame because it traditionally enclosed *exempla* within a "dogmatic monologism" contrary to the Baktinian dialogism and thoughtful freedom with which he sought to empower his tales (6, 87–88, n. 78). Subsequent Spanish novella writers shunned his dialogic model, says Forcione; rather, "as the frame in María de Zayas's novella collection indicates, [they] returned to the pre-Boccaccian dogmatic monologism characteristic of medieval *exempla*, an idiom which they found well suited to the proclamation of the life-denying philosophy of *desengaño*" (1982, 88 n. 78).[25]

Although "dogmatic monologism" is a reductive description of Zayas's narrative discourse as a totality, it is a fair characterization of the surface of her texts and the external structure of the collection. From the first paragraph of the first tale, her narrators present their stories as a warning to women not to yield to unrestrained desire, as true and living examples of unfortunate women from whose fate they should learn to mistrust masculine desire in its multiple, deceptive disguises. While about half of the protagonists of the "marvels" of love in Zayas's first volume achieve wedded bliss, in the second, not a single protagonist enjoys such an end and only an occasional narrator or secondary character does so, schooled by the violence he or she has witnessed. But to classify her discourse as "dogmatic monologism" is to overlook the tension between the overt—even strident—didacticism of her sermonizing narrators and the unconscious knowledge of the nature of desire that generates, organizes, and energizes the stories they tell, from the dreams of Jacinta in *Aventurarse perdiendo* to the enemy within of *Desengaño 10.*

Zayas acknowledges the separation between ideal surfaces and murky depths as she describes Lisis's appearance and the setting in which she presents herself at the beginning of the *sarao.*

> Coronaba la sala un rico estrado, con almohadas de terciopelo verde, a quien las borlas y guarniciones de plata hermoseaban sobre manera, haciendo competencia a una vistosa camilla, que al lado del vario estrado había de ser trono, asiento y resguardo de la bella Lisis, que como enferma pudo gozar desta preeminencia, era asimismo de brocado verde, con fluecos y alamares de oro, *que como tan ajena de esperanzas en lo interior, quiso en lo exterior mostrar tenerlas.* (*Novelas,* 31–32; emphasis added)

(Crowning the room was a rich dais, with pillows of green velvet made exceedingly handsome with tassels and silver trim, competing with a splendid chaise lounge at the side of the unusual dais that was to be the throne, seat, and shelter of the beautiful Lisis, who because of her illness[26] could enjoy this preeminence, that was also of green brocade, with gold fringes and tassels, *who since she was so devoid of hope inside, wanted on the outside to demonstrate having it.*)

Pfandl (1933, 369), by whose Victorian standards Zayas's fiction was not in the least exemplary, called her *Sarao* "un edificio gótico estropeado por arquitectos renacentistas y barrocos" (a Gothic edifice spoiled by Renaissance and Baroque architects). Pfandl was morally offended by the darkly perverse human conduct he saw within those Gothic/Baroque structures, particularly that "obscene *novella*" *El prevenido, engañado* and the "sadistic" tale *El juez de su causa*.[27] Américo Castro also employed an architectural image in expressing his disdain for exemplarity in general, comparing its objective to that of monumental Baroque structures, built by makers conscious of existing in a time of crisis and designed to overwhelm observers' senses, with the following consequence: "En las artes figurativas . . . lo proyectado hacia el exterior predominaba sobre el sentimiento de intimidad" (In the figurative arts . . . that which was projected toward the exterior predominates over the sense of intimacy) (1967, 453). What is, then, the relation between exteriority and interiority, between surface and depth, in her fictions?

Lyons asserts that exteriority is in fact one of the basic characteristics of example,[28] a procedure for argumentation through evidence that can be *seen*. It gestures outside the writer's own discourse toward some commonly-accepted textual referent or referential world, diverting attention from the authoritarian nature of the discursive general statement by in effect saying " 'see for yourself' " (1989, 28). Such exteriority carried to an extreme may operate as spectacle, a spectacle intentionally created for its effect on an audience. That is precisely the stated goal of Zayas's "exemplary love stories." But spectacular exemplarity can be directed toward very different ends. Lyons cites in particular the use of example as spectacle in Machiavelli and Marguerite de Navarre. The latter makes use of "a kind of disjointed imaging" in what Lyons calls her "fictions of self-discovery," her discovery not of a universal ideal but of the irreconcilability of diverse human perspectives and of the distance between the real and the true, between the external world and spiritual meaning (29, 72–117). Machiavelli, on the

other hand, recommends to princes the strategic use of example to control
and dissimulate. He advocates the use of carefully selected historical examples to conceal undesirable truths as much as to reveal exemplary behavior,
and to reshape communal memory of the past, thereby guiding the expectations for the future that memory generates. Further, recognizing the irrational nature of human behavior, he favors the use of spectacular exemplary punishment as a rational strategy designed to turn that irrationality
in the direction desired by the ruler (Lyons 1989, 29, 35–71). In both authors, however, we see a divergence between spectacular surfaces of the example and the deeper knowledge of human nature that lies behind or
emerges from its use.

As the description of Lisis in her salon demonstrates, there is at first
reading an almost hyperbolic exteriority in Zayas's fictions. She presents
the great majority of her characters as one-dimensional ideal types of
virtue, beauty, and gallantry, or their polar opposites. Significantly, her descriptive technique relies heavily on prepositioned adjectives, for both the
characters and their settings: "un rico estrado," (a rich dais) "una vistosa
camilla" (a luxurious/showy chaise lounge) or "la bella Lisis" (the beautiful Lisis). (English translation cannot render the full effect of this abundance of prepositioned adjectives, since pre-positioning is the norm in
English, not the exception.) The opening description of *Aventurarse perdiendo* is characteristic:

> Por entre las *ásperas peñas* de Monserrat, suma y grandeza del poder
> de Dios y *milagrosa admiración* de las excelencias de su *divina Madre,*
> donde se ven en *divinos misterios,* efectos de sus misericordias, pues
> sustenta en el aire la punta de un *empinado monte,* . . . el *milagroso y
> sagrado templo,* tan adornado de riquezas como de maravillas . . . y el
> mayor de todos aquel *verdadero retrato* de la *Serenísima Reina* de los
> Angeles y Señora nuestra . . . subía Fabio, *ilustre hijo* de la *noble villa*
> de Madrid, lustre y adorno de su grandeza; pues con su *excelente en-
> tendimiento* y *conocida nobleza, amable condición* y *gallarda presencia* la
> adorna y enriquece tanto como cualquiera de sus *valerosos fun-
> dadores* y de quien ella, como madre, se precia mucho. (*Novelas,*
> 37–38; emphasis added)

> (Among the *rugged peaks* of Monserrat, summit and greatness of the
> power of God and *miraculous admiration* of the excellencies of his *di-
> vine Mother,* where so many *divine mysteries* are seen, effects of her

compassion, since the point of a very steep mountain sustains in the air . . . the *miraculous and sacred temple*, as adorned by riches as by marvels . . . and the greatest of all is that *true portrait* of the *Most Serene Queen* of the Angels and Our Lady . . . climbed Fabio, *illustrious son* of the *noble city* of Madrid, luster and adornment of her greatness; for with his *excellent understanding* and *acknowledged nobility, kind nature* and *gallant bearing* adorns and enriches her as much as any of the *valiant founders* whom she, as mother, so prizes.)

Zayas uses adjectives not to particularize but to underline inherent characteristics of a salon, a mountain, a temple, or a man or woman, and to load each object with a value judgment as she moves it into the reader's line of vision. Furthermore, her descriptions of clothing, with their minute and loving attention to detail, far exceed the physical descriptions of her characters. For example, when Zayas introduces doña Ana in *Desengaño 8*, she tells us only that she is barely fifteen and more beautiful than any other woman in the city, despite her poverty. We are not told even whether she is fair or dark, only that this "tierna y descuidada corderilla" (tender and unprepared little lamb) (*Desengaños*, 389) whom don Alonso will sacrifice to paternal greed is noble, honest, and beautiful and lives modestly within her home (*Desengaños*, 387). When her headless body is retrieved from the well, however, we see her attire in glowing color:

> Tenía vestido un faldellín francés con su justillo de damasco verde, con pasamanos de plata, que como era verano, no había salido con otro arreo, y un rebociño negro que llevaba cubierto, unas medias de seda nacarada, con el zapatillo negro que apenas era de seis puntos. (*Desengaños*, 395)

> (She was wearing a French underskirt with its bodice of green damask, with silver braid, for since it was summer, she had not worn any other ornament when she went out, and a little black shawl that she took to cover up, flesh-colored silk stockings, and a black slipper that was barely a size 6.)

Clothing and furnishings socially constitute and situate Zayas's characters far more vividly than do her generic moral and physical descriptions. In describing Lisis in her salon, Zayas zigzags between the heroine and her surroundings so that the two almost blend as one dazzling entity, with no

336 María de Zayas Tells Baroque Tales of Love and the Cruelty of Men

clear point of reference to differentiate the character and her setting. She configures her characters in the romance tradition of a close correspondence between ideal beauty, moral purity, and aristocratic elegance and an equivalent correlation between base origins, ugliness, and sin. Her stories are written to appeal to a society permeated by the values of a resurgent aristocratism, in which all classes mimicked aristocratic demeanor to the best of their economic possibilities and escaped the realities of their existence in avid consumption of stories controlled by courtly codes.

Nevertheless, as Zayas reveals to the reader in her opening description of Lisis, all this dazzling exterior display may be a lie, a strategic concealment of a very different intimate prospect, in which the display of external brilliance is in inverse proportion to the bleak internal reality. Or perhaps one should say, to the unremitting ferment of life bubbling behind or below formal and conscious external structures. Our linguistic resources and the thought processes they facilitate make it difficult to consider the surface-depth question other than in spatial terms. Yet the dichotomies we set up may themselves be a false separation, a focus on surfaces that ignores the invisible life-giving activity that inhabits, shapes, and sustains those surfaces. Scientists have recently been paying increasing attention to the importance of bacterial activity within the human body taking place from the moment of birth, and to the operation of microbes in shaping the planetary skin, its rocks, seas, gases, metals, and minerals, as seen, for example, in the recently discovered Serra Pelada goldfields in Amazonian Brazil.[29] The difficulty is that we seem to be unable to see both "levels," as it were, at the same time, to contemplate simultaneously the surface and depth, the gleam of a nugget of gold and the microbes that concentrated it, the desirable skin of the beloved and the organs that sustain his or her life,[30] the formal, conventional and didactic discourse of Zayas's stories with the mechanisms of desire they invoke.[31]

Nor is this energizing tension (between hidden desire and ideal surface) the only strain that disrupts the exemplary "monologue." Lisis gives voice to another yawning fault line in the preface to her narration of *Desengaño 10:* "¡Oh, quién tuviera el entendimiento como el deseo, para saber defender a las hembras y agradar a los varones!" (Oh, that I had understanding equal to my desire, to know how to defend females and please males!) (*Desengaños,* 470).[32] As Lisis/Zayas articulates this wish in concluding the narrative preface, the frame heroine's narrative voice blends with that of Zayas herself, confronting male objections to the *Sarao,* its publication, and the possibility that men will buy the book only to condemn it.

She/they conclude with a flourish of bravado, saying that nevertheless she *writes* without fear. How to defend women within a patriarchal order that discounts women intellectually, metaphysically, and morally and abuses them physically, without risking rejection by the masculine subjects she desires, the masculine readers she courts, and the hierarchical sociopolitical order she upholds? Only in the subjunctive mode of wish fulfillment can Lisis/Zayas imagine an understanding capable of reconciling these mutually exclusive goals:

> Veis aquí, hermosas damas, cómo quedando yo con la victoria de este desafío, le habéis de gozar todas, pues por todas peleo. ¡Oh, quién tuviera el entendimiento como el deseo, para saber defender a las hembras y agradar a los varones! Y que ya que os diera el pesar de venceros, fuera con tanta erudición y gala, que le tuviérades por placer, y que, obligados de la cortesía, vosotros mismos os rindiérades más. Si es cierto que todos los poetas tienen parte de divinidad, quisiera que la mía fuera tan del empíreo, que os obligara sin enojaros, porque hay pesares tan bien dichos, que ellos mismos se diligencian el perdón. (*Desengaños*, 470–71)

> (Here you see, lovely ladies, how as I achieve victory in this challenge, you all enjoy it, since I fight for all of you. Oh, if I only had understanding equal to my desire, to know how to defend females and please males! And since I would give you pain in defeating you, would that I could do so with so much erudition and elegance that you [yourselves] would surrender yourselves yet further. If it is true that all poets have a touch of divinity, would that mine were of such empirical heights that it might obligate you without angering you, for there are injuries so well phrased that they procure their own pardon.)

> De todas estas damas habéis llevado la represión temiendo . . . (*Desengaños*, 471)

> (You have borne the rule of all these ladies in fear because . . .)

The passage as a whole is a classic example of the rhetorical strategy Zayas adopts, from the "Al que leyere" preface of the *Novelas* to the concluding paragraph of the *Desengaños,* an alternation between aggression and seduction as she addresses her desired and desiring readers. It is another "trick of the weak" akin to those that Josefina Ludmer (1991) identifies in Sor Juana's *Carta Atenagórica*, the alternation between conflicting terms adopted by a woman writer confronting a powerful masculine addressee from the socially and intellectually restricted position afforded women. Unlike Sor Juana, however, Zayas is openly confrontational, and she whirls from stance to stance, addressing now men, now women, attacking and curtseying, flattering and reviling, nagging and commanding, with a rhetoric that works its effect not with cool reason and linear logic but with the piling-on of passion. From a brief opening invocation addressed to a female public, in which she adopts an aggressive stance, depicting herself as sword-wielding defender of all women in the duel between the sexes, she retreats to the modest decorum of authorial humility, of not knowing how to please men as she defends women. And for the remainder of the passage, her implied addressee is male, as in "Al que leyere." She reiterates her desire to please those masculine addressees, to find the learning, "gala," the divine gift of poetic creativity needed to bring them pleasure in their defeat.

As Lisis/Zayas continues, she—again like Sor Juana—negotiates a feminine discursive entry into the public order of letters by blurring the distinction between public and private spheres, extending the private world of the courtly *sarao* and oral storytelling in which women were readily admitted into the public sphere of literary publication:

De todas estas damas habéis llevado la represión temiendo porque aún no pienso que están bien desengañadas de vuestros engaños, y de mí la llevaréis triunfando, porque pienso que no os habré menester sino para decir bien o mal de este sarao, y en eso hay poco perdido, si no le vale, como he dicho, vuestra cortesía; que si fuera malo, no ha de perder el que le sacare a luz, pues le comprarán siquiera para decir mal de él, y si bueno, él mismo se hará lugar y se dará el valor. Si se tuvieren por bachillerías, no me negaréis que no van bien trabajadas y más, no habiéndome ayudado del arte, que es más de estimar, sino de este natural que me dio el Cielo. Y os advierto que escribo sin temor, porque como jamás me han parecido mal las obras ajenas, de cortesía se me debe que parezcan bien las mías, y no sólo de cortesía, mas de obligación. Doblemos aquí la hoja, y vaya de desengaño, que al fin se canta la gloria, y voy segura de que me habéis de cantar la gala. (*Desengaños,* 471)

(You have borne the rule of all these ladies in fear because I still do not believe that they are thoroughly disenthralled of your deceits, and you will bear mine in triumph because I do not believe that I will need you except to speak good or evil of this *sarao,* and in that there is little lost, if as I have said, your courtesy does not defend it; for if it should be bad, the publisher will lose nothing, for they will buy it if only to speak ill of it, and if it is good, it will make its own place and its own worth. If they [the stories] should be considered prattle [nonsense], you will not deny that they are well wrought and more, not having relied on art, which is more to be respected, but on this nature [natural talent] that Heaven gave me. And I warn you that I write without fear, because the works of others have never seemed bad to me, and hence I deserve the courtesy that mine should appear good, not only out of courtesy but obligation. Let us mark the page here, and may it go as a disenthrallment, since in the end, victory is sung and I go assured that you will sing my praise.)[33]

In a complex sentence whose referential poles are not clearly fixed, she suggests that in the private space of the courtly sarao, men tolerate feminine "represión" (dominance, control, or curbs) fearing, or rather hoping, that the women they desire are not disillusioned about the deceitful nature of their desire, and they will bear her dominance "triunfando" (in triumph). Her syntactical shifts leave grammatically unclear just whose triumph this will be. She appeals to (masculine) courtesy at the same time that she vaunts her authorial independence, in a swirl of clauses saying that (1) her own desire for them (men) is only for their approval of her work; (2) people will buy her *soirée* if only to speak ill of it; (3) she deserves the courtesy she affords other authors; (4) she deserves respect for her natural, heaven-sent talent and for the merits of her work.

But in negotiating this entry into the public sphere by linking sexual and narrative desire, by linking masculine (sexual) desire for acceptance by the women they court with her desire for acceptance in the masculine world of letters, Zayas skims over the surface of the other fundamental tension that permeates her work. Her tactics for containing this tension emerge clearly when we compare the function of the frame narrative of *The Princess Bride* with the polemically exemplary end Zayas gives her frame narrative and the authorial postscript with which she seals it.

The frame narrative of Reiner's film shows "postmodern" viewers how a boy moves from playing electronic games to giving avid attention to a traditional romance. At first, he objects at the "kissing parts" and tells his grandfather to skip them, although his grandpa assures him, "Someday you may not mind so much." That "someday" arrives by the end of the story, when he tells his grandfather *not* to skip the description of the sublime final kiss of Wesley and Buttercup.

What has changed his mind? The story, of course. Peter Brooks suggests that narrative accomplishes what is logically unthinkable. "It is the ordering of the inexplicable and impossible situation as narrative that somehow mediates and forcefully connects its discrete elements, so that we accept the necessity of what cannot logically be discoursed of" (1985, 10). For example, in the Grimm brothers tale "All Kinds of Fur" described by Brooks, a folktale recounts a series of trials undergone by a king who would marry his own daughter, showing us narrative as a way of thinking, a way of accepting the prohibited or impossible, in this case incest. Jerome Bruner seconds Brooks's concept of the function of narrative and adds several important observations: (1) that human beings, from their earliest years, perceive and organize existence through narrative; (2) that narrative *constitutes* reality as much as it reflects it; and (3) that changes in narrative paradigms may reshape not just plots, but also modes of thought.

The Reiner frame shows narrative moving an Oedipal boy to acceptance of the—for him—previously unthinkable: that the objective of a hero is not just excelling at sports or defeating the evil antagonist, but should include blissful, lasting union with an ideal member of the opposite sex—the traditional plot that, however unrealistic, aligns sexual and narrative desire as well as assuring the continuation of the species.

Zayas, however, confronted a much more formidable logical obstacle. Within the genre of the "novela amorosa," she sought to implant the conviction that heterosexual union is *not* the desired goal but a fatal trap for most women, and that true happy endings can only be found by sublimating desire for any corporeal male and rejoining the mother in the feminine world of the convent. In her concluding authorial postscript directed to "Fabio" and signed in her own name, Zayas directly confronts the contradiction between the reader/hearer expectations aroused by her chosen literary form and the conclusion to which she drives her tales:

> Ya, ilustrísimo Fabio, por cumplir lo que pedistes de que *no diese trágico fin a esta historia,* la hermosa Lisis queda en clausura, temerosa de que algún engaño la desengañe, no escarmentada de desdichas propias. *No es trágico fin, sino el más felice que se pudo dar,*

pues codiciosa y deseada de muchos, no se sujetó a ninguno. Si os duran
los deseos de verla, buscadla con intento casto, que con ello la hal-
laréis tan vuestra y con la voluntad tan firme y honesta, como tiene
prometido, y tan servidora vuestra como siempre, y como vos
merecéis; que hasta en conocerlo ninguna le hace ventaja.

Doña María de Zayas Sotomayor
(*Desengaños,* 510–11; emphasis added)

(Now, most illustrious Fabio, to comply with what you asked, *that
I not give this story a tragic end,* the lovely Lisis remains cloistered,
fearful that some deceit might disenthrall her, not chastised by her
own misfortunes. *It is not a tragic ending, but rather the happiest that
could be given her, for desiring and desired by many men, she made herself
subject to none.* If your desire to see her continues, search her out
with a chaste intention, for with that you will find her as much yours
and with her affection as steady and honest as she has promised,
and as much your servant as ever, and as you deserve; for even in
recognizing that, no woman exceeds her.

Doña María de Zayas Sotomayor)

To surmount the contradiction between her chosen narrative form and
the use to which she puts it, Zayas not only tells story after story of the fatal
effects of desire, but also *models* in her frame narrative the reeducative effect of those stories. As she concludes the narration of Florentina's history,
Lisis announces that she has been "desengañada" (disenthralled) not by
personal experience, but by "ciencia" (knowledge), by the lesson she has
learned from the fate of other women, both within the *desengaños* that her
friends have told and in the "real time" that has transpired "outside" the
fiction in Madrid during the fictional time span of the *sarao,* since "martes
de carnestolendas de este presente año de mil seiscientos cuarenta y seis"

The signature of María de Zayas y Sotomayor, from the autographed manuscript
of her play, *La traición en la amistad,* MS Res. 173. Biblioteca Nacional de Madrid

(Shrove Tuesday of the present year one thousand six hundred forty-six) (*Desengaños*, 509). Thus schooled "en cabeza ajena," (by others' mistakes) she breaks her engagement to don Diego and retreats with her mother to the safety of convent walls: "me acojo a sagrado y tomo por amparo el retiro de un convento, desde donde pienso (como en talanquera), ver lo que sucede a los demás" (I take sacred refuge and take as my shelter the withdrawal to a convent, from where I plan—as if behind a barricade—to see what happens to the rest) (*Desengaños*, 509). Who are "los demás" (the rest) whose fate Lisis will observe, her fellow characters in the frame narrative? The characters in the stories they have narrated? Figures in the fictionalized "outside" of 1646 Madrid? Or the readers whose attention she claims?

Zayas repeatedly blurs narrative levels, particularly in the second volume, and most insistently in its concluding tale and frame. Melloni, Welles, and other critics have called attention to this aspect of her work. Montesa, in particular, provides an excellent analysis of Zayas's frame and of the four layers of narrators and narratees she creates: (1) Zayas-Fabio; (2) narrator-reader; (3) narrators (frame characters)-hearers (frame characters); and (4) narrators (characters within the stories)-hearers (characters within the stories). He shows how she creates distance-effacing confusion by crisscrossing those levels at strategic moments, through a variety of techniques: (1) strategically placed autobiographical narration;[34] (2) narrators who speak of *writing* the tale for inclusion in this *book,* and (3) the addition of the final paragraph in Zayas's own voice, directed to Fabio. While some readers may regard these confusions errors, Montesa is certainly right to assert that they are a deliberately chosen technique, one that works to reduce the distance between fiction and experience to bring the message of her thesis novel to her public, and to immerse her public in the world of her *sarao.* He links it with parallel techniques in other Baroque art, most notably painting and the theater. In painting, it compares to the figures that look out at the spectator, the *mise-en-abîme* of scenes within scenes, and the confusion of planes effected by the play of mirrors of Velázquez's masterpiece *Las meninas.* Like Lope's drama of the conversion of the actor Ginés, *Lo fingido verdadero,* it aims at erasing the border between fictive and objective reality, between performance and lived experience. This, Montesa believes, is Zayas's response to Baroque anxieties concerning the nature of being (1981, 351–76).[35]

One further narrative detail, which Montesa overlooks, proves yet more conclusively that Zayas's confusion of narrative planes is deliberate. Both he and Melloni discuss at some length the last paragraph, in which Zayas speaks to a certain "Fabio" in her authorial voice. Melloni (1976, 16) calls this "mysterious addressee of the collection" a rabbit pulled out of a magic hat, a rhetorical trick like the Marcia Leonarda to whom Lope dedicated his efforts and his metanarrative commentaries. Montesa calls him "este desconocido personaje, Fabio, que no había aparecido anteriormente" (this unknown character, Fabio, who had not previously appeared) and gives him a concrete existence outside the novelistic work: "Es un amigo personal de la autora a quien, indirectamente, dedica su obra y con el que, al parecer, había mantenido algunas conversaciones sobre ella." (He is a personal friend of the author, to whom, indirectly, she dedicates her work and with whom she apparently had several conversations about it) (1981, 373). Without disallowing the possibility of such a personal addressee, I would point out that in fact, a Fabio *has* appeared before within her fictional world, in the opening story of the collection, as the pilgrim climbing Montserrat who discovered Jacinta, listened to her story, and brought her back to society, where she chose exactly the same secular life in the convent that Lisis has just elected, consoled by visits from Celio. Hence, Zayas's address to Fabio and her invitation to satisfy his desire to see Lisis with chaste visits to her convent binds together the ending of this last tale, the frame plot, and that of the first narrative. We might even say that it makes the entire collection one long multiepisodic exemplary story of the education of Jacinta/Lisis told to Fabio from beginning to end.

Zayas's collection thus demonstrates an exaggeration of the iterativity and multiplicity that Lyons names as the first characteristic of example. According to Lyons, "Multiplicity . . . stresses the redundancy of example within a single moment (that is, the way speakers or writers give several at once as if to support a point), while iterativity stresses the way an example that explicitly points to an event that happened once actually stands for many similar events occurring through time" (1989, 27).

I would point out, along with the reappearance of Fabio, two other significant clues to Zayas's fusion of stories and of the lives of characters within or between them. The first is an "error" in Lisis's farewell address to the *sarao* participants, "corrected" and annotated in Yllera's edition. Lisis addresses her disappointed suitor not as don Diego but as don Dionís as she justifies to him her retirement on the basis of the ten preceding *desengaños*. In all editions up through 1734, this speech began, "Y así, vos, señor don Dionís . . . advertid que no será razón que, deseando yo desengañar, me engañe; no porque en ser vuestra esposa pueda haber engaño, sino porque no es justo que yo me fíe de mi dicha, porque no me siento más firme que la hermosa doña Isabel" (And thus, you, don Dionís . . . note that it would not be reasonable, if I want to disillusion [others], that I should deceive myself; not because there can be deception in being your wife, but because it is not just that I should trust in my good fortune, for I do not feel stronger than the lovely doña Isabel), whose story awoke her fear. Continuing, Lisis names in turn the tragic fate of each heroine of the *Desengaños:* Camila, Roseleta, Elena, doña Inés, Laurela, doña Blanca, doña Mencía, doña Ana, and doña Beatriz—whose life could be saved only by the intervention of the Mother of God—and doña Magdalena. Lisis tops off her tragic roll call with the tirade against servants as the "enemy within" discussed in Chapter 9. This confusion of don Diego and don Dionís points toward the unconscious logic of the volume, in which each tale is in a sense a variant replaying of the preceding story or stories, with Lisis bringing it to a conclusion by conflating her suitor with the husband/lover of Magdalena and Florentina as she chooses not to risk their fate.

The second clue is that Zayas gave a title only to the first *desengaño, La esclava de su amante* (The Slave of Her Lover). The story that constitutes *Desengaño segundo* was fused in the early editions with the first *desengaño,* and succeeding tales were headed only "Second night," "Third night," and so forth. The moralizing or descriptive titles of the other tales were added by the publisher of the 1734 edition. Rather than viewing this editorial state only as an indication of hasty and careless publication, we can see in it evidence that Zayas presents the succeeding tales as modulations of the first, an iterative example of the fate of women who enslave themselves to love. In her closing paragraph, Zayas contrasts their subjection to the freedom Lisis achieves, as she tells Fabio that it is the happiest ending possible, since Lisis, "desiring and desired by many, subjected herself to no one" (*Desengaños,* 510–11).

The name Zayas suggests for the enveloping addressee is significant, for it evokes the fictional addressee of the "Epístola moral a Fabio" attributed to Andrés Fernández de Andrada.[36] This well-known poem was the culmination of the Horatian epistle cultivated by Boscán, Garcilaso, and all the major Spanish Golden Age poets (Rivers 1988). Fernández de Andrada's poetic epistle begins by warning "Fabio" against imprisoning himself in courtly ambitions and ends as the poet announces his retirement from the world and invites his friend to join him:

> Fabio, las esperanzas cortesanas
> prisiones son do el ambicioso muere

y donde al más activo nacen canas.
El que no las limare o las rompiere,
ni el nombre de varón ha merecido,
ni subir al honor que pretendiere.

. . . .

Ya, dulce amigo, huyo y me retiro
de cuanto simple amé: rompí los lazos.
Ven y sabrás al grande fin que aspiro,
antes que el tiempo muera en nuestros brazos.

(Alonso 1978, 22)

(Fabio, the hopes of courtiers are shackles in which the ambitious man dies and even the most active candidate grows gray.
He who doesn't use a file on them or break them does not deserve to be called a man or to rise to the position he seeks. . . .
At last, sweet friend, I flee and withdraw from everything that in my simplicity I love; I have broken the bonds: come and you will see the great purpose to which I aspire, before time dies away in our arms.)

(Trans. Rivers 1988, 251–58)

Fabio is also the addressee of Rodrigo Caro's single notable work, "Canción a las ruinas de Itálica." And Quevedo, in two versions of his sonnet "Llama a la Muerte" (Call to Death) and "Salmo 16" (Psalm 16), whose opening line is "Ven ya, miedo de fuertes y de sabios" (Come now, fear of the strong and the wise), laments the disappearance of "Fabios," "Curios," and "Decios."[37] As James Crosby's note to these lines points out, Quevedo alludes to Roman heroes and consuls. In the case of Fabio, the model would have been the Roman general and statesman Fabius Maximus Cunctator, Quintus (d. 203 B.C.), whose cautious delaying tactics and strategy of attrition against Hannibal's invading Carthaginian army allowed Rome to recover and take the offensive in the Second Punic War. He took over after conventional Roman generals had been repeatedly beaten by Hannibal during the long campaign in the Italian peninsula. Fabius would seem to be ready for battle, drawing Hannibal to mobilize his army, but then would withdraw out of distance. The Fabian Society, founded in London in 1883–84 with the objective of establishing socialism through evolutionary rather than revolutionary means took its name from that Fabius, for his strategy of avoiding pitched battles, achieving victory over stronger forces through patience and elusive tactics of attrition. His namesake, Fabio, could therefore well serve as addressee for a literary-philosophical consideration of the best strategy for dealing with a powerful antagonist, whether that be the lure of advancement at court, for Fernández de Andrada, or that of amorous engagement with the opposite sex, in Zayas's novellas.

The name Fabio was also associated with contenders under the sign of Venus. Many Fabios appeared on the stage of Golden Age theater, engaged either directly or in a supporting role in its love plots. "Fabio" was the third most frequent first name in Lope's character lists, figuring in more than eighty of his plays, as well as in thirty by Calderón and twenty-two by Tirso de Molina (Morley and Bruerton 1968; Tyler and Elizondo 1981). Sometimes Fabio would be secondary gallant, but more often he played a supporting role, as a servant to one of the leading characters, as he does in Zayas's own play, *La traición en la amistad*. He could also be a participant— or a pawn—in love intrigues at that less elevated level, as is the Fabio of Lope's *El perro del hortelano*. Quevedo cast himself as an enamored and disdained Fabio in a comic "autobiographical" ballad, "Parióme adrede mi Madre, / !Ojalá no me pariera!" (My mother gave birth to me on purpose / Would that she hadn't!). His litany of all the ways nature and fortune have mistreated him concludes with the stanza "Aquesto Fabio cantaba / A los balcones y rejas / De Aminta, que aun de olvidarle / Le han dicho que no se acuerda" (Fabio sang this at the balcony and grill of Aminta, whom they tell him doesn't even remember him enough to forget him) (Quevedo Villegas 1981, 401–8).[38]

Blending the amorous Fabio with the supportive, philosophical friend in her opening and closing figures, Zayas leaves her desired male readers with an ideal masculine model in her Fabio, parallel to the feminine model posed in Lisis. Fabio, as the understanding listener, chastely desiring admirer, and supportive helper, has multiple counterparts in her narrative world—don Martín in *La burlada Aminta;* Carlos, Laura's brother in *La fuerza del amor;* the marquis don Sancho in *Desengaño amando, y premio de la virtud;* Carlos in *El jardín engañoso;* and don Felipe, alias Luis, in *Desengaño 1, La esclava de su amante,* They anticipate a frequent figure in nineteenth-century novels by women, the "man who understands" (Hirsch, citing A. Rich; see Chapter 4 above).[39]

In her elaborated and plotted frame and the iterativity of her exemplary tale, Zayas moves in the opposite direction from Madame de La Fayette. As Lyons points out, in *La Princesse de Clèves* the French writer undercuts the ability of example to support a general statement (1989, 217) and demonstrates in her plot that examples are not applicable to or predictive of future events and courses of action. "As *La Princesse de Clèves* and *Zayde* demonstrate repeatedly, passage from a partial, concrete representation to a general rule or from a general rule to a partial, concrete representation is an act of fiction" (233). The example can no longer serve as a reliable link between the individual and authoritative sources of knowledge. Mme. de La Fayette also effectively internalizes the frame and paves the path for the transition from novella to novel, says Lyons (217–40). Zayas, in contrast, resurrects and elaborates the frame, giving it a plot that makes it in effect the twenty-first tale, the concluding model that demonstrates not only the best course to adopt in the game/war of love, but also the power of fiction to set its public on that course. Zayas's decision to employ such a frame tale, I propose, is not aesthetically motivated by a need to delimit and organize fictional worlds, but polemically designed to enhance the power of the narrative to transcend the limits of fiction and to reorganize her readers' modes of thought. At the same time, she uses it as a spectacular containing act for the tensions and conflictive desires that energize her narratives.

Nevertheless, I would suggest that it is the perception of those irresolvable tensions that provides the continuing fascination of her novels for readers through the centuries. We are drawn far less by the surface exemplarity of her work than by its narrative energy, its discursive contradictions, and the ellipses that beg the reader to fill them, to complete the text in an imaginative interactive reading process beyond the limits of the page. This too I believe Zayas intuited, and she inscribes it in her paragraph-long epilogue to Fabio, inviting a continued discussion of how best to find a happy ending, in narrative and in the flesh, for the dance of desire.

Conclusion

"You're *finishing* a book on María de Zayas? Amazing!" That is only a fantasy question, but in fact it is a more valid query than those I quoted in my introduction. Despite the burgeoning interest in Zayas and the multiplying numbers of articles, editions, and lectures on her work, book-length studies are slow in appearing. Surely others who have embarked on them find, as I have, that it is easier to start a study of her twenty stories than to decide that it is finished. Whatever approach we choose, her fictions lead us down too many paths. The task of drawing together into a coherent and meaningful synthesis the multiple threads of my own study is a daunting endeavor.

Zayas, as we have seen, faced a formidable challenge herself in attempting to contain the tensions that pervade her narratives securely within the framework of the didactic lesson she sought to teach. She posed for herself a next-to-impossible task in narratological terms within her chosen genre, that of turning storytelling against its own motive energy, desire. Inasmuch as the genre of the *novela amorosa* is fueled, within the story, by the desire for a sexual object or the social objective of marriage, using it to warn men and women away from the dangerous waters of desire is antithetical to its inherent structure. We can presume that Zayas was aware of that contradiction because she concluded her first volume with three success stories, "marvels" of love triumphant that could exist in the realm of fantasy where narrative can accomplish feats not objectively possible in the everyday world. The aptly titled eighth novella, *El imposible vencido* (Triumph over the Impossible) is a male-narrated fantasy of love that conquers the ultimate enemy, death. Such a miracle tale, in Zayas's cosmology of permeable frontiers between life and death, the natural and supernatural, could conceivably be accomplished with a love so strong that it calls forth divine intervention in the natural order. The fantasy nature of the last novella, *El jardín engañoso* (The Deceitful Garden), however, is acknowledged even by the mother who narrates this mythical reversal of the fall into sin and the expulsion from paradise, a fantasy of marriage negotiated outside the paternal economy of socially instrumental exchange of women, in an order of gifts and generosity capable of overcoming fratricidal jealousy, lust, and the devil himself. Success stories well situated to lure readers on to a second volume, with the promise of ten more stories beginning with a frame-narrative betrothal and ending with a wedding.

The unreality of the intervening success story, *El juez de su causa* (The Judge of Her Own Case)—in which the cross-dressed heroine rises to the post of viceroy on the strength of her valor and intelligence—is not metaphysical but social. The uniqueness of this fantasy in her collection confronts us with the other impasse in Zayas's narrative world—that of defending the moral and intellectual equality and capacity of women while maintaining a conservative aristocratic ideology and upholding the very concepts of social propriety and obligation, class distinction, institutional rectitude, and the patriarchal honor code that held women in a subordinate position. That was for her the more insurmountable antithesis. Although through feminine narrators and in her own authorial voice she vigorously asserts women's capacities and attacks the educational disadvantages and social practices that restrict their development, she devises no new plots that demonstrate those assertions. Rather, she navigates around that impasse diegetically in the penultimate novella of this first volume by having a male narrator tell a familiar story inherited from a line of male authors that included Boccaccio, Timoneda, and Lope de Vega. Even in this story, however, the heroine does not initiate such a bold departure from social norms voluntarily, but only after she has been ripped out of the social order by kidnapping, and at the end she transfers the honors she has earned to the lover whose life she has saved. In the darker second volume, the two women who put on male dress and the freedom of movement it brings and who invade masculine terrain are the treacherous antagonist Claudia of the first story, who dies impaled on a stake, and the saintly queen Beatriz in the next to last, who is given her masculine garb and miraculous curative medicine by the Mother of God.

This socio-ideological impasse did not, however, prevent Zayas from subtly recasting masculine literary models from a feminine perspective. In *El juez de su causa*, for example, simply by extending Estella's term of office and her trial of Carlos, she makes this familiar tale uncomfortable for many readers, even "sadistic" in the view of some male critics. In virtually all her stories, she shows that falling in love and marrying is not the end of the story for women but only one episode, and that what really proves a woman's character is what she does later, when love dies or marriage sours.

Her deployment of the gender-destabilizing motif of cross-dressing is rather different from the prevalent modes in male-authored novellas and *comedias*. Her heroines do not dress "up" in men's clothes to pursue errant lovers or to wreck bloody vengeance on the whole male sex, but don masculine garb protectively, when male abuse has cast them out of their place in the social order. Rather, it is males who cross-dress as women aggressively, to secure sexual satisfaction or revenge by a deceitful invasion of women's domain. The use of magic, so generally attributed to women both in fact and fiction, she reassigns to men, Moors, or foreigners. The dreadful specter of death arrives dressed in masculine guise rather than in alluring feminine flesh—not only in the scores of violent attacks visited on women, but also in the cautionary visions of speaking dead men. Women, on the other hand, speak the truth of their life and death not in words but in their bodies, displaying their guilt or innocence after death in swollen, blackened flesh or in sweet beauty miraculously preserved. Furthermore, when we examine closely the tone and content of the tales she tells through masculine narrators, either explicitly (i.e., as participants in the frame gathering), or as internal tale-tellers, we can see that she reveals in them masculine fears and fantasies about women. She is imaginarily capable, as it were, of changing seats on the train and occupying a masculine angle on the sexual divide, but with a provisional and ironic pose, for she turns those tales back on their tellers with humor.

Inasmuch as the desire that drives narrative is also desire for meaning, Zayas could, at least for censors and other appropriately disposed readers, overcome the narratological antithesis and accomplish her didactic objective by countering the energetic lure of the love story with a steady stream of sermonizing and, particularly in the second volume, with melodramatic examples of the lethal consequences of desire, multiplied to monstrous dimensions and related with stomach-turning graphic detail. Furthermore, by intertwining her heroine's stories and crisscrossing levels of discourse so that they merge at the end into one iterative example of disillusionment with heterosexual love, she leaves far behind the few miracle tales of love in the first volume, all but forgotten in the fatal tallies of the second volume, in which the only success story is that of surviving the voyage through the sea of desire, of navigating one's way back to the safe feminine haven of the convent walls.

Yet even as she steers her last protagonists, Florentina and Lisis, behind those walls, Zayas still keeps the motor energy of the drive of desire engaged. She paints the resplendent beauty of Lisis, Estefanía, and Isabel, and has Estefanía acknowledge mockingly how convent residents entertain the fruitless suits of the men who continue to court them. Zayas personalizes this continuing heterosexual contact, telling us that Florentina is happy to exchange letters with don Gaspar, as Jacinta enjoyed visits from Celio, and in her own authorial voice, she invites her "friend" Fabio to visit Lisis in her convent to discuss the felicity of her chosen life. In that authorial epigraph, Zayas characterizes Lisis's life as ideal because it confers autonomy while sustaining her desirability: "No es trágico fin, sino el más felice que se pudo dar, pues *codiciosa y deseada de muchos,* no se sujetó a ninguno" (It is not a tragic ending, but rather the happiest that could be given her, for *desiring and desired by many men,* she made herself subject to none) (*Desengaños,* 510–11; emphasis added). In the last story, *Estragos que causa el vicio* (The Ravages of Vice), telling us that both don Gaspar and the friend who helps him rescue Florentina are in love with her, Zayas keeps alive in the reader's mind the possibility that this lusty antiheroine will repeat the marital success of Hipólita of *Al fin se paga todo* (Just Desserts), who survived the death of the three men who desired her to marry her rescuer, bringing along an inherited fortune. Since feminine desire for the phallus is in part desire for the status and security it offers in the social order, and status within the more worldly convents of Baroque Spain relied not only on saintliness but also on economic power, Zayas leaves Florentina enjoying the convent equivalent of a successful marriage, having inherited the fortunes of Magdalena and don Dionís that will enable her to live a life of luxury within the convent akin to that of Serafina and Gracia in *El prevenido engañado* (Forewarned but Not Forearmed).

Thus, Zayas's second volume may seem to contain the drive of desire within the limits of her didactic objective as Florentina, Lisis, Isabel, and Estefanía depart for their convents, but it does so by repressing rather than erasing the basic narratological antithesis of her collection. The last *desengaño, Estragos que causa el vicio,* lays the ground for the "return of the repressed from the future" (Zizek 1991, 188) in terms of the history of her reception. Seventeenth-century censors such as Pio Vives might approve her fictions as "un asilo donde puede acogerse la femenil flaqueza más acosada de importunidades lisonjeras, y un espejo de lo que más necesita el hombre para la buena dirección de sus acciones" (a sanctuary in which the womanish weakness most besieged by flattering importunities can find refuge, and a mirror of that which man most needs for the right ordering of his actions) (Zayas 1649, fol. A2r). But when her fictions began to draw critical attention again from the late nineteenth century forward, generations of critics would link *Estragos* with *El prevenido engañado* and *Al fin se paga todo* to challenge her credentials as a feminist on the grounds that she wrote about "bad women."

Can we classify her as a genuine "feminist"? Was her declared advocacy of women's moral and intellectual equality with men sincere, and was improving women's condition one of the primary objectives of her fictions? To apply the term "feminist" to a seventeenth-century writer is anachronistic, yet the question has been much debated by her twentieth-century readers, and the answer continues to concern us, whatever terminology we employ. The answer is unquestionably yes, in my opinion. She was not a philosophically consistent feminist, it is true. She presented her case for women not with rigorous, linear logic, but with passionate argumentation, with shifting, sometimes contradictory tactics and rhetoric, and she hammers it in through the cumulative effect of her harangues against the abuse of women and the pathos of her fictional examples. The opposing view of feminine weakness, moral and intellectual, might be more coolly argued and certainly held the advantage of general and long-standing acceptance. But Laquer and other modern students of the history of sexual categorization have demonstrated that the assignation of women to an inferior position in the gender hierarchy did not originate in scientifically rigorous observation either, nor was it philosophically consistent. And more philosophically trained twentieth-century critics of masculine hegemony such as Fuss and Gayatri Spivak have found that philosophical consistency is not necessarily the most effective strategy for advancing the interests of disadvantaged groups.

Why, then, did she include in both collections not only multiple feminine antagonists but also stories centered on morally dubious feminine protagonists? Amezúa considered her presentation of "bad women" evidence of her "realism," and in this case the term is not badly chosen, although his concept of a transparent realism is superficial. Zayas understood the nature of sexual desires and fears, those of men as well as those of women. The stories centered on "bad women" are mostly narrated by men and reflect masculine fears of women who might deceive, control, or, worst of all, laugh at them. In the tales narrated by women, "bad women" generally operate as feminine antagonists, competing for the heroine's lovers. They, too, represent common feminine fears of the "Other Woman," who occupies what might be called a "holding place" in the feminine psyche, ready to be filled by the appearance, real or imagined, of a competitor for the attention of the desired man. Florentina of *Estragos* could be viewed as an embodiment of the fearsome "Other Woman" from the position of Magdalena, which is the perspective Lisis takes in compiling her final list of feminine martyrs. But I believe she also represents Zayas's recognition of the multiple sources of violence against women. It may come from without, from "foreigners"— from political structures, inasmuch as women serve as pawns and sometimes scapegoats in a masculine competition for power, as in *Desengaño 7, Mal presagio casar lejos* (Marry Afar: Portent of Doom). Or it can originate within the family, as in *Desengaño 8, Traidor de su sangre* (Traitor to His Own Blood)— in the greed and cruelty of patriarchs who consider women useful only as a means of increasing the family fortune through marriage, or for propagating sons of their own stripe. Or the violence can arise in fraternal jealousy, as in so many Zayas tales, including the last in the first volume and the penultimate *desengaño,* in which she links it with the devil himself and his competition with God and the Mother of God for the souls of men and women. But Zayas's first and last *desengaños* demonstrate that violence can also be nourished by the "enemy within"—the persistently treacherous and rebellious desire within the house in *Desengaño 1, La esclava de su amante* (Slave of Her Lover). Or, finally, in *Estragos,* within the body of woman herself, in the indomitable force of desire, the essential servant that is the domestic enemy in Zayas's narrative world. Hence, Zayas in the sequence of her last four tales, brings the source of violence ever closer in to its original and intimate origin within every human being, within the divided subject herself. She made her stories a working-through of desire, in two senses: as a good storyteller, she used it as an essential servant to narrative; and as a perceptive observer of human nature, she crafted stories that she hoped might enable women to manage, or at least to survive, that indispensable domestic enemy.

Survival, for her typical heroine, consists of a working-through of desire that leads from the house of the father to that of the husband and from there to the feminine world of the convent, back to the "house of the mother." Does this pattern constitute in Zayas a (m)Other plot, a narrative alternative to the Oedipal "masterplot"? Yes and no. No, in that she was not able to break out of the loop between narrative possibility and lived experience to envision any viable alternative for women beyond those sanctioned in the paternal order, marriage or life in a convent. Yes, in that the choice of convent life is in Zayas primarily a choice of the safe haven of feminine society, a circling back to psychic attachment to the mother, rather than a religious calling, as espoused by spiritual leaders, to marry the perfect Divine husband. Yes, if one sees the episodic structure of her stories as reflecting a feminine kind of sexual pleasure, more diffuse, cyclical, and prospective than the linear, retrospective trajectory of masculine sexual pleasure that animates the Oedipal plot, according to Winnett. Yes, in that Zayas's interwoven tales anticipate the preference for stories with multiple protagonists that Biruté Ciplijauskaité (1988, 208) observes in many late twentieth-century women writers, stories that are decentralized and present the tale through a polyphony of voices in dialogue. No, in that she gives us no more than hints of a story behind the convent walls, of a *jouissance* on the feminine side of the sexual divide. Like other truths of feminine experience, perhaps, Zayas does not find such a story tellable in the mold of masculine language and literary models except by suggestion, by her swirling, convoluted style and by the metonymic structure of her stories. That paratactic construction too allows her to circumnavigate her ideological impasse, by repressing the key terms that she cannot or does not openly name.

Like those unspoken terms, the knowledge of unconscious structures that Zayas displays in her stories is implicit rather than explicit. She recounts the story of desire like a native speaker, one who possesses an implicit knowledge of a language system, its lexicon and grammatical structures. We can best approach them, I suggest, like second-language learners, who have to acquire an explicit knowledge of the rules of that language and of the nuances and the limitations of its vocabulary in order to hear and understand what she has to say. The vigorous energy of her narratives combined with the puzzling gaps in their structure invites readers to question the unspoken depths of human motivation and interaction partly hidden under their melodramatic exteriority. Intriguing sign-posts in her fictions—from Jacinta's dream in the first story to the moaning dead body that prefaces the last—launched me on a drive to acquire the knowledge to explain them, sending me to study theories of the psyche from Aristotle to Kristeva as well as the novella tradition and the cultural context in which she wrote. As I seek to draw together the threads of this study, however, I acknowledge that I cannot—and would not—attempt to tie them into some Gordian knot that would secure *the* meaning of her fictions and the truth of her intentions for all time and for all other readers. Zayas's fictions, for the reasons I have underlined, require an interactive reading process. Readers will bring to the filling-in of her gaps their own questions and understandings, conscious and unconscious, entering the narrative world of her *Sarao* from their own perspectives, and thereby renewing the dialogue of desire that Zayas animated nearly four centuries ago.

Appendix I:
The First Ending of *El castigo de la miseria*

Fué tanta la pasion que don Marcos recibio con esta carta, que le dio una calentura accidental, de tal suerte que bien pensaron los que le vian, que era llegado su fin. Estuuo assi hasta las ocho de la noche, y a essa hora tomó su capa, y se salio de casa de aquel su amigo, y guió ázia el nombrado Colegio de Doña Maria de Aragon, que, como era Verano, aunque el Sol yua siguiendo su viage a las playas Indias, la Luna, por estar en su principio, como el Sol dexaua desierta de su luz la tierra, yua ella ocupando, con sus plateados rayos, los lugares que quedauan vazios de luz. Y baxando la cuesta abaxo, el desesperado don Marcos, guió ázia aquella puente que han hecho nueua en aquel camino, donde encontró con vn hombre, que tuuo por cierto ser Gamarra, el que hizo el contrato de sus negras bodas, el qual le dixo: Donde bueno, señor don Marcos, por esta parte, y a esta hora. Donde puede ir vn hombre tan desuenturado como yo (respondio el) sino a colgarme de vno destos arboles, para que se acaben mis desuenturas. O señor Gamarra, y que casamiento el mio, si a V.m. le sucede todo como yo le desseo, tan mal le irá como a mi, yo le prometo que le he hallado en parte, que a traer espada, yo tomára vengança de sus engaños, que V.m. ha sido el faraute de todos los que me ha hecho aquella traydora que me dio por muger. Ya he sabido (replicó Gamarra) lo que passa, y le juro que me ha llegado al alma su desdicha, a no estar a tiempo de vengarle yo mismo por mis manos, le diera disculpa, mas yo vengo con la mayor pesadumbre que ninguno en el mundo puede tener, tal que he salido de mi casa con proposito de ahorcarme, porque mas quiero morir a mis manos, que no en vna horca. Essa honrada determinacion me trae a mi, amigo Gamarra (dixo don Marcos) porque despues [*sic*] que me veo corrido de quantos me miran, no quiero alma, ni vida; mas para que vea si ay otro mas desdichado que yo, me aueys de contar que os ha sucedido, y luego, como buenos amigos, dispondremos nuestra vida, y nuestra muerte. Que quereys saber mas, de que si aqui no me quito la vida (dixo Gamarra) mañana me han de ahorcar en la plaça de Madrid, y es el caso, que yo seruía aqui a vn

señor, ques el Duque de Osuna, y de quien soy muy priuado, con gran es-
tremo, diome a guardar vnas joyas que tenia que dar a vna dama, llegue
con ellas a vna casa de juego, puseme a jugar, y de lance, en lance, parando
mas a menudo que deuia, quien juega lo ageno, enfin lo perdi todo: vien-
dome tan desesperado, y que la perdida monta mas de mil ducados, estaua
que perdia mi juycio. Preguntome vn guarda ropa del Duque, que que
tenia, es mi amigo, contele mi desdicha, y el conmouido della, me dio las
llaues de su guarda ropa, y me dixo, que entrasse, y sacasse lo que
quisiesse, que el me guardaria las espaldas: hizelo assi, agradeciendole el
bien que me hazia, é yo tome vnas colgaduras de seda, y oro, y otras cosas,
que bien valian el precio de mi perdida; y yendo a salir, dio conmigo el
mayordomo, como me vio sobarcado, [sic] asio de mi, yo que vi lo que me
importaua el huirle, dexé, no solo el hurto, mas la vida en las manos, junto
con las llaues, y me escape, dexando quando sali de casa preso al guarda
ropa, que si le aprietan, há de dezir la verdad, y yo he de padecer como
reo. Temiendo esto, tomé este cordel, y me vine aqui donde vn arbol
destos, y vos, seran testigos de mi desuentura, y no todos los ojos de la
Corte, y si vos venis con esse mismo intento, aqui ay arboles, y cordel para
los dos; y diziendo esto, sacó de la faltriquera el cordel. Agradeciole don
Marcos el socorro, y pidiole hiziesse los laços para entrambos, lo qual hizo
con mucho desenfado, y priessa, poniendolos en dos arboles, que estauan
juntos. Todas estas platicas estaua oyendo vn hombre que estaua recostado
debaxo de vn arbol, descansando de que auia llegado al rio, y buelto, y
aunque via a don Marcos hablar, y que le respondian, como no via con
quien, estaua tan turbado, que aun el resuello no ossaua que saliesse de su
boca, y mas quando vio que el pobre desesperado, se echó el laço al cuello,
y se arroxó de vna rama en que se auia subido. Y como a este punto se
oyessen vnos grandes ahullidos, disparó a correr la cuesta arriba, mas
ligero que vna aguila, y no paró hasta la casa del Corregidor, donde, entrando en su presencia, contó lo que auia sucedido, y como aquel hombre
quedaua ahorcado, y que a la cuenta otro se auia ahorcado con el, segun lo
que hablaua, y el otro respondia, aunque el no auia visto mas de vno. Y tras
esto contó todo lo que les auia oydo, diziendo que el otro se llamaua
Gamarra, y que dixo ser criado del Duque de Osuna, y como el
Guardaropa estaua preso. El Corregidor, y la mas gente que pudo, con el
hombre, fueron al lugar dicho, donde, con luzes que lleuaron, porque ya
la Luna yua escondiendose, hallaron al miserable don Marcos colgado del
arbol, y en el otro junto a el, vn laço, mas no auia nada en el. Quitaronle de
alli, con harta lastima de su alma, y traxeronle a la carcel, donde a el, y al

que dio la noticia, pusieron en ella, hasta la mañana, que hizieron pesquisa, de quien fuesse el muerto, y esto fue facil de saber, por algunos papeles que le hallaron en las faltriqueras, y assi mismo la carta de doña Isidora, y no faltó quien le conociesse por criado de aquel señor, a quien seruia. Fueron a informarse en casa del Duque de Osuna, de aquel Gamarra que dezian, del qual no hallaron nueua, ni señas de tal hombre; porque ni era verdad el ser criado del Duque, ni la perdida de las joyas, ni prisión del Guardaropa, por donde coligieron, junto con lo que el hombre dezia que oia hablar, y no via quien, que el tal era el demonio, que por desesperar a don Marcos, auia venido con aquel engaño, y que le auia sucedido a su gusto, como parecia. Dieron de todo quenta a su amo de don Marcos, el qual mandó, que le enterrassen, sacando licencia, para que fuesse en sagrado, dando por disculpa de su desesperacion, que estaua loco, que esta es la vanidad del mundo, honrar el cuerpo, aunque el alma esté donde la deste miserable; mandó assi mismo escriuir este sucesso, el qual ha venido a mi poder, junto con lo que le sucedio a doña Isadora, que fue, que estando en Barcelona aguardando las galeras para embarcarse para Napoles, vna noche, don Agustín, y su Inés, la dexaron durmiendo, y con los seys mil ducados de don Marcos, y todo lo demas que tenian, se embarcaron. Y llegados a Napoles, el asentó plaça de soldado, y la hermosa Ines, puesta en paños mayores, se hizo Dama Cortesana, sustentando con este oficio, en galas, y regalos a su don Agustin. Doña Isidora se boluio a Madrid, donde, renunciando el moño, y las galas, anda pidiendo limosna de puerta en puerta. La qual me contó mas por entero esta marauilla, y yo me determiné a escriuirla, para que vean los miserables, el fin que tuuo este, y no hagan lo mismo, escarmentando en cabeça agena.

Con grandisimo gusto oyeron todos la marauilla que don Aluaro dixo, viendo castigado a don Marcos, conforme merecia su miseria; porque vn miserable no es bueno sino para el infierno, adonde todos quantos allá estan, lo son. Y viendo que don Alonso se preuenía para la suya, trocando su asiento con Alvaro, hizo don Juan señas a los músicos, los cuales cantaron así (Zayas 1637b, 124–27).

Appendix II: Plots Summaries

Novelas amorosas y ejemplares

I. *Aventurarse perdiendo*

Told by Lisarda, Lisis's rival for don Juan's affections.

Fabio, a young gentleman from Madrid, climbing Montserrat to visit the monastery there, finds Jacinta disguised as a boy, lamenting her misfortunes. He realizes she is a woman and entreats her to tell him her story.

As a girl of sixteen growing up in Baeza (Andalusia), Jacinta's mother has died and her father pays attention only to his son. Jacinta dreams one night of a handsome lover with a cape over his face. When in her dream she pulls back the cape, he stabs her to the heart with a dagger. She wakes up in love with this phantom, who later materializes as Félix, a neighbor long off at war. He courts her secretly at night.

Félix's cousin Adriana is also in love with him. He first humors her mother's request to court her, then obeys Jacinta's demand that he tell Adriana he is already engaged to another woman. Adriana warns Jacinta's father that his daughter is offending the family honor and then commits suicide. Jacinta and Félix flee from her father, taking refuge in a convent. Félix goes out one night, is attacked by Jacinta's father and brother, kills the brother, and has to leave the country. He goes to serve in Flanders.

Jacinta's father intercepts all letters from Félix and sends a false letter announcing his death. Jacinta takes a religious habit. Six years later he reappears, she breaks her religious vows, and they get a papal dispensation to allow their marriage after a year in which they are not to cohabit.

During the waiting period, Félix goes off to war again in Mamora while Jacinta stays with his aunt and her daughter, Guiomar, in Madrid. Jacinta dreams of receiving a letter from Félix with a box that she thinks will contain jewels, but on opening it, she finds it contains his head. She later learns that he has drowned at sea. Rather than returning to the convent, she stays with Guiomar and her mother.

Some time later, she falls in love with Celio, a friend of Guiomar, when he is boasting of his coldness to another woman's love. At first flattered and attentive, he loses interest quickly and leaves for Salamanca. She follows him but is misled and robbed by her escort and takes refuge in the mountain of Monserrat, disguised as a boy shepherd.

Fabio tells her that Celio treats all women this way and that he has already taken orders in the priesthood. At Fabio's urging, Jacinta leaves Monserrat and returns with him to Madrid to enter a convent, in which she will live as a secular resident, continuing in her love for Celio and content with seeing him. Félix's sister Guiomar, whose mother has died, joins Jacinta in the convent.

II. *La burlada Aminta y venganza del honor*

Told by Matilde.

Aminta's father and mother die when she is twelve or fourteen, entrusting her to the care of her father's brother, the captain don Pedro, in Segovia. Don Pedro has one son, Luis, who is a soldier in Italy, and it is agreed that Aminta will marry him on his return. Meanwhile, she has many suitors in Segovia, including one "don Jacinto," a young man who comes there on business with his "sister" Flora. With Flora's help and the mediation of Elena, a merchant's widow and neighbor of Aminta, he seduces her, she leaves home and goes with him to the vicar, who performs the betrothal ceremony, and then spends the night with him in the inn where he and Flora are staying. As the news of Aminta's disappearance spreads, Jacinto kills Elena to prevent being identified, takes Aminta (now calling herself doña Vitoria) to the house of doña Luisa, a widowed relative of his who lives on the outskirts of town, and leaves for Valladolid with Flora. Don Martín, doña Luisa's son, returns home and they tell Aminta that "Jacinto" is really Francisco, that he is already married to a woman in Madrid who has returned to her parents because of his escapades, and that Flora is his longtime lover. Don Martín, smitten by Aminta, overhears her laments in her room and, unlocking her door, keeps her from opening her veins and offers to avenge her honor and marry her. She declares that she will avenge herself and they follow Jacinto to Valladolid, with Aminta dressed as a page and don Martin as a muleteer. Aminta serves Jacinta and Flora for a month, then, hearing that don Pedro has died and her cousin has returned and seeks revenge, stabs Jacinto to death in the heart and Flora in the throat and chest and departs, locking the door behind her. She and don Martín leave in a carriage for Madrid, changing clothes on the way so that when the corregidor encounters them they go unrecognized. They marry and live in Madrid under feigned names and doña Luisa comes to live with them.

III. *El castigo de la miseria*

Told by don Alvaro.

Don Marcos comes to Madrid at twelve with his father, a poor, very old gentleman from Navarre, and secures the position of page in the house of a prince. Thanks to a supremely miserly form of life, he accumulates six thousand ducats by the age of thirty. With the appearance of wealth and the services of a marriage broker, doña Isidora, a woman who presents herself as the thirty-six-year-old widow living with her handsome young "nephew" Agustín, lures don Marcos into marrying her. On their first wedded morning they are awakened early by a servant, Inés, and don Marcos finds doña Isidora's teeth in his whiskers, her hair on the pillow, and her fifty-five-year-old wrinkles plainly visible; what has disappeared are jewels and wedding finery, stolen by the maid Marcela who has unlocked a door and disappeared during the night. In short order other creditors come for the silver and clothing he thought were Isidora's, the owner returns to reclaim the house, and doña Isidora flees with Agustín and Inés, don Marcos's money and everything else they could carry. He can find no trace of them, but does encounter Marcela, who convinces him of her innocence and has him hire a magician (her boyfriend), to conjure up demons to reveal the whereabouts of his wealth. The "demon" is a tortured cat, who leaves don Marcos in a faint. He then receives a letter from doña Isidora berating him for his miserliness and saying that she will happily live as his wife again if he gathers another six thousand ducats. Doña Isidora is reduced to begging in Madrid after Agustín and Inés embark one night with all the stolen goods for Naples, where he becomes a soldier and she a courtesan.

In the revised version of the story, don Marcos falls so gravely ill from the passionate shock of doña Isidora's letter that he dies. In the ending of the first version, he recovers and, going out to hang himself, encounters the marriage broker, Gamarra, who says that he plans to do the same rather than be executed in the plaza the next day for gambling away jewels entrusted to him by his employer. He carries enough rope for both and don Marcos does hang himself, but the other noose is later found empty

and no trace of Gamarra remains, whereupon it is decided that it was the
devil who had driven don Marcos to despair.

IV. *El prevenido, engañado*

Told by don Alonso.

Don Fadrique, a rich young gentleman in Granada, falls in love with
Serafina, although she favors don Vicente. She agrees to marry him but de-
lays, alleging illness, and one night he sees her come out of the house and
give birth in an outbuilding. He saves the baby, Gracia, and has her
brought up strictly enclosed in a convent, sends Serafina a message of rejection, and leaves town. Serafina becomes a nun.

Fadrique then goes to Sevilla and falls in love with a widow, Beatriz, who
says that in honor of her dead husband, she won't marry for three years.
After courting her for some time, he gets inside the house one night and
sees her going to the stables to care for a dying black man, Antonio, whose
lover she has been. Antonio dies and she then sends Fadrique a note saying
she will marry him immediately. He sends her a note suggesting she mourn
her black lover another year, leaves for Madrid, and Beatriz marries another suitor.

With his cousin don Juan, he courts the married Ana and her cousin Violante. Ana tells Juan to bring Fadrique to take her place in bed with her
husband so that she can enjoy a night with don Juan, and after a long night
of fear, he discovers that the "husband" was Violante. He carries on an affair with her for several months but she rejects marriage, and then he finds
her in bed with a brother of Ana's husband, who "shoots" at him with a
shoe. When Ana laughs at him, he beats her and leaves.

Going to Naples and Rome he has several other affairs with clever and
deceitful women. On his return to Granada, a duchess in Catalonia invites
him to enjoy the afternoon with her while her husband is away hunting.
Caught by the unexpected arrival of the husband, she locks him in a closet
and makes a game of telling her husband she has a lover shut up there,
then laughing at her "joke."

Fadrique, now resolved to marry a simple woman, marries the convent-
raised Gracia, and has her put on a suit of armor every night to guard his
bed and his honor. When he returns from a trip, she tells him innocently
how a young man from Córdova showed her another, pleasanter way for
married people to spend the night. Resigned, he lives with her for a num-

ber of years and leaves his fortune to her on the condition that she become
a nun in the convent where Serafina is. He writes Serafina a letter telling
her that Gracia is her daughter, and mother and daughter end their years
happily, spending her inheritance in building a large convent.

V. *La fuerza del amor*

Told by Nise.

Laura, whose mother died giving birth to her, is the third child of don
Antonio de Garrafa, lord of Piedrablanca, four miles from Naples. She
grows up in Naples with her two older brothers, who love her dearly, particularly the younger, don Carlos. Don Diego courts Laura and they marry,
but in time he loses interest in his wife and spends increasing amounts of
time at the table and in the bed of Nise, a former lover. When Laura complains, he abuses her verbally and then physically. Her brother Carlos intervenes once when he is beating her and would have killed Diego had she
not stopped him. Her father and brothers, finding it painful to see her so
abused, move to their home in Piedrablanca.

Laura turns to a sorceress in hopes of regaining her husband's affections. The sorceress tells her to bring her the beard, hair, and teeth of a
hanged man. To get them, she goes alone at night to a chapel by the side
of the road that leads to Piedrablanca, in which executed criminals are
hung to decompose. While she is in this fearful place, her brother Carlos
awakens from sleep shouting, with the conviction that his sister is in danger. Saddling a horse, he gallops toward Naples and the horse stops and refuses to budge when they reach the chapel. He finds Laura there and takes
her back to Piedrablanca. Don Antonio returns to Naples and complains to
the Viceroy. Laura tells her story and chooses to retire to a convent, although the repentant don Diego begs her not to and says he will have the
viceroy put Nise in a convent instead, but Laura insists. Don Diego is killed
in battle and Laura becomes a nun.

VI. *El desengaño andando, y premio de la virtud*

Told by Filis.

Fernando, the only son of a moderately wealthy widow in Toledo, courts
and wins doña Juana with the promise of marriage, but puts off marrying
her on the pretext of his mother's opposition. Doña Juana's parents have

died and she has no other relatives in Toledo. Lucrecia, an older woman from Rome who is a friend of doña Juana and who has become wealthy practicing sorcery, uses her art to enchant Fernando and to take him away from Juana. Juana appeals to a student from Alcalá, who gives her two magic rings to find out the truth. A servant borrows them and washes clothes with them on and the demons in them beat the student but reveal the truth, that don Fernando will not marry her. She then uses a spell and summons a former lover, who appears from purgatory to tell her she will burn eternally in hell if she doesn't reform. She asks Fernando for a dowry to enter a convent and he gives it to her.

Fernando, who has accumulated large gambling debts, then marries Clara, a merchant's daughter, thinking she is rich, but her father leaves for the Indies with what money there is. Don Fernando mistreats Clara, particularly after his mother dies, and goes to Seville with Lucrecia. The marquis don Sancho is in love with Clara but she accepts neither his attention nor his help in her financial straits. Leaving their two daughters with doña Juana in the convent, she goes to Seville and serves as a maid to Fernando and Lucrecia for a year. She eventually discovers the secret of Lucrecia's hold over Fernando—a chained and blinded rooster. Removing the blinders, she frees her husband from the spell. Lucrecia commits suicide and Clara takes the ill Fernando back to Toledo and nurses him until he dies from the effects of Lucrecia's sorcery. She then marries the marquis and they live happily and have many children. Her daughters by don Fernando, with a dowry provided by don Sancho, become nuns in doña Juana's convent.

VII. *Al fin se paga todo*

Told by don Miguel.

Don García, a young noble from Madrid now in Valladolid with the court of Philip III, sees doña Hipólita thrown out of a house one freezing night and takes her to his inn. She is married to don Pedro, the elder of two brothers. The younger, don Luis, who lives next door, also loves and continues to court her, but she rejects his attentions. After eight years of marriage, she becomes enamoured of don Gaspar, a Portuguese soldier. She tells a string of sensual and comic mishaps in their attempts to meet. One night she takes her bed out into the garden to meet don Gaspar when her husband has gone hunting, but he returns and joins her in the garden bed, so that when don Gaspar arrives, his only satisfaction is a kiss while her

husband sleeps. Then she smuggles her would-be lover into the house, but
it catches on fire; another time, he gets stuck trying to climb into the window and has to flee, frame and all. In their final misadventure, her husband returns home quickly to "do his necessities" and she hides don Gaspar in a trunk. Thinking he has died of suffocation, she has to enlist the
help of don Luis to remove him and the trunk. He revives, but threats from
don Luis cure him of further interest in Hipólita. Don Luis, however, becomes insistent. One night he lets out the horses so that don Pedro has to
get up to retrieve them. Then he sneaks through the attic into Hipólita's
house and bed. She thinks he is her husband and they make love, then her
husband return with the same in mind and the next day at mass don Luis
lets her know he has enjoyed her. Finding the passageway between the
houses he has used, she sneaks over the next night and kills Luis and, leaving the bloody knife in her house, she flees to the inn of don Gaspar. He
beats her, throws her out, and leaves for Lisbon, but is killed on the road by
a robber. While don García is hiding Hipólita in his inn, Don Pedro is
charged with his brother's murder. Don García takes her to a convent and
she writes to the authorities to tell them what has happened. Don Pedro is
pardoned and wants her back but she refuses and he dies within the year,
leaving his fortune to Hipólita. She marries don García, who had continued to court her in the convent, giving him both wealth and children.

VIII. *El imposible vencido*

Told by don Lope.
Don Leonor and don Rodrigo grow up as neighbors in Salamanca and
love each other from childhood Since Rodrigo is a younger son, however,
her parents promise her to another man, and his parents send him to Flanders. She promises him in secret not to wed another man for three years.
In Flanders, don Rodrigo solves the mystery of the phantasm that seems
to haunt the house of a lovely Flemish widow, doña Blanca, revealing that
the chain-rattling nightly visits are really those of don Arnesto, a married
neighbor enamored of her who hopes thus to gain access to her bedroom.
He and the servant who helped him are executed. Blanca falls in love with
don Rodrigo and although he humors her, he cooperates in a bed-switch
trick to marry her to a Spaniard, don Beltrán, who has long loved her.
Leonor's parents, hearing her lament don Rodrigo's four-year absence,
send a false letter to Rodrigo's parents saying he has married a rich Flemish woman, and Leonor submits to marriage to don Alonso (although

never to its consummation). Rodrigo is given a habit of the Order of Santiago and a four-thousand-ducat income for his service in Flanders and goes back to Salamanca to marry Leonor, only to find her already married. She, seeing him pass in the street, falls in a dead faint, is declared dead, and is buried. Rodrigo bribes the sacristan to open the tomb to embrace her. In the tomb, he prays to Christ and she comes back to life. He smuggles her out, takes her to Ciudad Rodrigo, and summons his parents there. On the advice of a theologian they publish the banns and are married in the church in Salamanca in the presence of her parents and don Alonso, who do not react to the names since they are sure she is dead. Only at the end of the wedding ceremony does her mother recognize her. Her first husband calls the corregidor to intervene and he passes the case to ecclesiastical authorities. The bishop consults a famous professor, who in turn presents the case to his students. They declare in favor of Rodrigo, and he is finally named her true husband, since she had been forced to break her first promise to him and had really died, dissolving that forced marriage. She never regains her color but lives many years happily with her husband. They have one son.

IX. *El juez de su causa*

Told by don Juan, Lisis's first love.

Carlos, a gentleman of Valencia, loves Estela, but her parents promise her in marriage to an Italian count. Claudia, in love with Carlos, dresses as a man and serves as his page. Amete, son of a rich man in Fez, has been a slave of Carlos's father, but his rescue has now been arranged. He is also in love with Estela and, with Claudia's help, kidnaps her and takes her to Fez, where Claudia renounces her faith and marries Amete's brother.

Estela resists the pretensions of Amete, who then mistreats her. She is tricked a second time by Claudia, this time with the promise of escape; when they leave the house, they are found by Amete, who tries to rape her, but Xacimín, a Moorish prince, hears her cries and rescues her. He condemns Amete and Claudia to death, and gives Estela money, jewels, freedom, and help to go where she chooses.

Estela chooses to go to Tuniz dressed as a man and using the name Fernando to serve the emperor Charles V in his war against Barbarroja. The emperor gives her a habit of Santiago for saving him in battle. She encounters Carlos, who has been jailed on suspicion of having kidnapped and killed her but has escaped and is serving as a soldier. She makes him her secretary but continually questions him about his love for Estela. The emperor names her viceroy of Valencia and Carlos's case is brought before her. She prolongs his anguish and lets it appear that he will be condemned again, but finally reveals her identity. The emperor makes her princess of Buñol and the habit of Santiago, Estela's income, and the post of viceroy are awarded to Carlos. They marry and have beautiful heirs.

X. *El jardín engañoso*

Told by Laura, Lisis's mother.

Two brothers in Zaragoza, Jorge, the elder and sole heir and his younger brother, Federico, court two sisters, Constanza and Teodosia. Constanza accepts don Jorge's courtship with restraint, but Teodosia despises Federico and secretly loves don Jorge. She tells him that Constanza really loves Federico, and Jorge kills his brother and flees. The girls' father dies, leaving the care of the substantial estate and the daughters in the hands of their mother.

Two years later the noble but poor Carlos arrives in Zaragoza and, taking up residence in front of Constanza's house, falls in love with her. He makes himself a friend of the family, cultivating in particular the mother's affection. Pretending he is mortally ill, he leaves his "fortune" to Constanza, and on his recovery, he marries her. She does not resent the trick, but appreciates him as a considerate husband.

Don Jorge returns to Zaragoza and again pursues Constanza, who rejects his attentions. After a year, Teodosia falls ill and Constanza, recognizing that her love for don Jorge is the cause, asks him to marry her sister, but he says he only wants her. Exasperated, Constanza tells him she will only respond if he can create a beautiful garden in front of her window by the next morning. Don Jorge makes a pact with the devil to give his soul in exchange for the miraculous garden. Seeing it the next morning, Constanza asks her husband to kill her to prevent dishonor, but he says he will kill himself instead. Don Jorge, amazed, grabs his sword and absolves Constanza of her promise. The devil, not to be outdone, gives up his claim on don Jorge's soul. Don Jorge marries Teodosia and all live happily and have many children. No one ever knows that don Jorge killed Federico until after his death, when Teodosia pens a manuscript recounting the story that is discovered after she dies.

Desengaños amorosos

Desengaño 1 (La esclava de su amante)

Told by "Zelima," a supposedly Moorish slave whose friendship is crucial in helping Lisis recover her health. As she begins narrating her own story, she reveals that she is really doña Isabel Faxardo, who went as a young woman from Murcia to Zaragoza when her father served there during the Catalonian uprising. They lodge in the house of a widow, whose daughter Eufrasia becomes close friends with Isabel, and whose son don Manuel courts her, rapes her, and promises marriage but postpones it.

Don Manuel renews an old relationship with doña Alejandra, a married woman with a complicitous husband. To escape from the competition between Alejandra and Isabel, don Manuel sails with the admiral of Castille, who is going as viceroy to Sicily. Don Felipe, a suitor from Isabel's youth in Murcia who followed her to Zaragoza and serves in her houshold under the name don Luis, warns her of Manuel's plans and she leaves home, taking jewels and money. Her father dies from the shock of her disappearance. In order to follow Manuel, she dresses as a Moorish slave and has Octavio, a former servant, sell her to the admiral's majordomo. Luis in turn follows her. On an outing to an island off Sicily, don Manuel, Isabel, and Luis are kidnapped and taken to Algeria, where their captor gives them to his daughter, Zaida. Zaida loves Isabel tenderly, falls passionately in love with don Manuel, and arranges to take all of them back to Spain. They arrive at Zaragoza six years after Isabel left. Zaida plans to be baptized and don Manuel tells Isabel that he will marry Zaida rather than her. Don Luis stabs him to death and flees, Zaida commits suicide with his dagger, and Isabel seeks out Octavio and has him sell her again, to Lisis's uncle. When "Zelima" tells his wife Leonor that he is pursuing her, Leonor sends her to Lisis. Finishing her story, she announces her wish to become a nun.

Desengaño 2 (La más infame venganza)

Told by Lisarda, Lisis's rival.

Octavia and Juan are the two children of a Spaniard who went to Milan as a soldier, gambled away the larger part of his fortune, and married there. Don Carlos, son a rich senator, courts Octavia and seduces her on a false promise of marriage, saying that it will have to be postponed because his father is determined to marry him to a rich woman. Her brother Juan is

away from Milan, studying, until their father is killed in battle and don
Juan can come to Milan to enjoy gambling and women without his father's
restraint. He keeps Octavia shut up at home and in need of everything.
Don Juan kills a man and has to flee to Naples, and Carlos thus has free access to Octavia again; within two years, he has tired of her. A friend of the
senator dies, leaving his daughter Camila extremely rich. She is not as
beautiful as Octavia but very virtuous. At his father's urging, Carlos agrees
to put Octavia in a convent and marry Camila. He convinces Octavia that it
is only a temporary recourse because his father knows of their relation and
threatens them. He marries Camila and then writes to Octavia suggesting
that she become a nun. Her brother Juan returns to Milan, surprised to
find her in a convent, and she tells him her story and asks him to avenge
her dishonor. He threatens and cajols her into becoming a nun, and then
begins to court Camila as his means of revenge. She pays him no attention
and says nothing to her husband, believing that her own virtue and reclu-
sion will protect her. But don Juan dresses in one of his sister's best dresses,
secures entry into Camila's bedroom, tells her of Carlos's relation with Octavia, and rapes her at knifepoint, then departs announcing his identity
and threatening to kill Carlos too. He and his two companions hide in a
convent and nothing more is heard of him. Camila also goes to a convent,
where she stays for a year, until the senator, convinced of her innocence,
persuades her to come home. Carlos will neither sleep nor eat with her
and, after a year, poisons her. Her body, but not her head, swells to enormous proportions and she lives thus for six months before hearing a voice
announcing her death. Carlos disappears and the senator remarries to sire
more children.

Desengaño 3 (*El verdugo de su esposa*)

Told by Nise.

Both sons of Spaniards resident in Palermo, don Juan and don Pedro
grow up as inseparable friends. Don Pedro marries Roseleta and don Juan
stops going to his house, but Pedro insists that he return. He does, and seeing her, envies his friend's luck, falls in love with her, tries to resist temptation, falls ill, and explains his suffering as passion for Angeliana, whom in
fact he has already enjoyed under promise of marriage. But after some two
months, don Juan declares his love to Roseleta and begins to court her.
She tells him to stop or she will tell her husband, and when he persists, she
shows don Pedro the notes his friend is sending her. Furious, he has her

send a note inviting don Juan to meet her at their country estate. Don Pedro leaves town, then doubles back to the estate and hides there. Roseleta also lets don Juan see her leave town for the estate, but she then returns to Palermo by another route.

Leaving Palermo for the estate, don Juan hears the bells ring the Ave Maria and stops to pray to the Virgin, asking her forgiveness for what he is about to do, and her intercession with her Son to protect him. Continuing on his way, he passes three robbers who had been hanged by the side of the road and one of them calls him by name, says that God has miraculously saved his life because he was innocent, and has don Juan cut him down. When they arrive together at the estate, the robber insists that don Juan hide while he goes to the garden door. Don Pedro and servants burst forth firing pistols, shoot the robber, and throw him in a well while don Juan watches from in hiding. He comes out and starts toward the estate, but the robber, dripping blood, stops him, telling him that he was and is dead, but that the Virgin Mary allowed him to appear as don Juan to save him. Returning home, he sees the robber still hanging from his noose. In the morning, he astounds don Pedro and Roseleta by appearing alive, begs their forgiveness, and enters a monastery.

As people gossip about the event, don Pedro's love for Roseleta turns to hate; Angeliana, angry at losing don Juan because of Roseleta, seeks out don Pedro and becomes his lover, not hiding the relationship at all. Roseleta sends her a threatening note, whereupon Angeliana retaliates by telling don Pedro that Roseleta had really been don Juan's lover and they plan how to kill her. He stays away from Angeliana for two months, then while she is being bled for a throat ailment, he removes the bandage while she sleeps and she bleeds to death. He feigns grief, but marries Angeliana within three months. He also tries to kill don Juan, but the Mother of God continues to protect him.

Desengaño 4 (*Tarde llega el desengaño*)

Told by Filis. Internal first-person narrator, don Jaime de Aragón.

Don Martín is returning to Toledo from Flanders when his ship sinks in a storm. He and a companion are washed ashore on Gran Canaria Island and are taken in by don Jaime de Aragón, owner of a large and lovely castle. At dinner, don Jaime has a small door off the dining hall opened and a beautiful but very thin and roughly dressed blond woman emerges and crawls under the table, where she eats scraps and bones and is served water in a skull she carries. A very ugly black woman, richly dressed and bejeweled, is ushered in ceremoniously at the same time and don Jaime seats her at the table. After the meal, don Jaime tells his visitors his story.

While he was a young soldier in Flanders, he received a mysterious invitation and, led blindfolded at night by an old servant, was taken to a luxurious residence where he was entertained lavishly by a woman whose beauty he could only feel, not see, in the darkness. Afterward, she gave him money and jewels and invited him to return for the same favors every night but pledged him not to try to see her or learn her identity. After a month, a friend told him that his absence each night and his new wealth were making people say he was a thief. The next night, he marked the door of his lover's house with a blood-soaked sponge and talked her into letting him see her beauty. She was Madame Lucrecia, the widowed only daughter of a rich and powerful old prince. But the next day when he demonstrated by courting her openly in the street that he had broken the pledge of secrecy, rather than dispatching the old nighttime guide, she sent six armed men to kill him. He survived and returned to Gran Canaria, where the death of his parents had left him a rich man. But he could not forget Madame Lucrecia.

At mass one Holy Week he saw Elena, who was a portrait of Lucrecia, but as poor as she was noble, virtuous, and beautiful. He married her and lived happily with her for eight years, until a maid—the black woman now presiding in his house—told him Elena was having an affair with a handsome young cousin who lived with them while studying for the priesthood. He took the whole household from the city to the castle in the country and burned the cousin alive, saving his skull to serve as a drinking vessel for Elena, who now eats under his table while the black maid enjoys the position of lady of the house. They have lived thus for two years.

That night after all have retired, the black woman cries out that she is dying and calls for don Jaime to confess that her accusation of Elena was false, a self-protective and vengeful lie. She had fallen in love with the cousin, who rejected her advances and joined Elena in chastizing her. Don Jaime stabs her to death instantly and runs to release Elena only to find her dead in a saintly pose. He tries to kill himself and when don Martín stops him, he goes mad. Don Martín goes back to Toledo and marries his cousin.

Desengaño 5 (*La inocencia castigada*)

Told by doña Laura, Lisis's mother.

Doña Inés, whose parents have died, is happy to marry at eighteen to escape the rigorously guarded life imposed on her by her brother and his cruel wife. She is living happily with her husband, seeing the society of her city (near Seville) for the first time. Don Diego falls in love with her but she is not even aware that his courtship is directed at her. A neighbor offers to help him, borrows the dress doña Inés ordinarily wears on the pretext of loaning it to a niece for her wedding, puts it on a prostitute who looks like Inés and has don Diego meet her alone, in an almost dark room. He believes that he is possessing doña Inés. After the dress is returned, he speaks to her one day at mass and when she denies any contact with him, he mentions the dress and the neighbor. She tells him to come to her house the next day when her husband is leaving for Seville. She has called the corregidor and has him hide while don Diego tells his story; the neighbor woman is given two hundred lashes and exiled from the city for six years.

Don Diego then turns to a Moorish sorcerer. He makes a figure of doña Inés, nude, with a pin through the heart and a candle on her head. When he lights the candle, the sleeping doña Inés arouses and, in a trance, comes to don Diego's bed, staying there until he sends her away. The spell works and he enjoys nightly visits from doña Inés for more than a month, although she never speaks and thinks each morning that she has been having wicked dreams. One night as she walks through the streets clad only in her shift, she is seen by the corregidor making nightly rounds with officers and Inés's brother Francisco, and the effect of don Diego's candle-figure is demonstrated.

The corregidor refuses doña Inés's request to kill her and declares her innocent, but her husband, brother, and sister-in-law move to a house on the outskirts of Seville and wall her into a tiny space, feeding her only bread and water for six years while her flesh is consumed by vermin and she goes blind in the darkness. A neighbor finally hears her lament through the wall and she is rescued. Her family jailors are executed and she enters a convent, regaining her beauty but not her sight.

Desengaño 6 (*Amar sólo por vencer*)

Told by Matilde.

Don Esteban falls in love with Laurela, the third daughter of noble and wealthy parents in Madrid, dresses as a woman and, calling himself Estefanía, secures a position as maid in her house to be near her. He earns her affection with his musical talent and tells everyone he loves her and that love is a question of souls, not gender. Servants of both sexes and Laurela's father are interested in "Estefanía." He is sick with jealousy when Laurela visits a neighbor to whom her parents have promised her in marriage. Esteban then reveals that he is a man and convinces Laurela to run away with him, but after one night with her becomes fearful of the consequences and admits that he is the son of a carpenter and is already married. She stays with an aunt and uncle for a year until one day while she is at mass her father and uncle weaken a wall so that it falls on her and a maid, killing them both. Her sisters both enter a convent and her mother joins them after the father's death.

Desengaño 7 (*Mal presagio casar lejos*)

Told by doña Luisa, a widow.

Four sisters and a brother of royal blood are left orphans by the death of their father and mother. The oldest sister marries in Portugal and takes the youngest with her. Her husband sends a page with a letter implicating her falsely in infidelity and kills her; the youngest escapes by jumping out a window, breaking both legs, and spends the rest of her life in bed. The second sister marries in Italy. For praising the looks of a Spanish captain, her husband strangles her with her own hair while she is washing it and then poisons their four-year-old son.

Before her sisters are killed, Blanca, the third and most beautiful, is promised by her brother to a Flemish prince. She would have preferred to enter a convent but consents reluctantly, on the condition that the prince come to Spain to court her for a year. The prince courts her assiduously and she finds him pleasing yet grows more melancholy as the year passes. Between the celebration of her betrothal and the wedding, the news of her sisters' deaths arrives. After the wedding they depart for Flanders, and the prince turns lukewarm and quarrelsome. In Flanders, her father-in-law greets her by demonstrating his hatred of her and all Spanish women. She is also mistreated by the prince and his much favored young page, Arnesto.

She finds a fast friend, however, in her sister-in-law Marieta, married to a cousin who is as cold to her as the prince is to Blanca.

Within several months, for mysterious reasons, a manservant of Marieta is killed, and rather than investigating the case, her husband ties her to a chair in the dining hall and garrots her in front of her father, who had sentenced her to death. When the doors are opened, Blanca faints at the sight and the prince protests as well. Blanca, knowing her turn will be next, distributes her jewels to her Spanish ladies-in-waiting, writes her brother a letter, and dispatches it to Spain.

Four months later, she goes into the prince's bedroom one afternoon, suspecting she will find him with another woman but finds him instead in bed with Arnesto, who laughs at her horror at the sight. Announcing that what she has seen will be her death, she has the bed taken out to the patio and burned. That night, she calls her Spanish confessor, takes communion, gives him a chain and rings, and asks him to leave this place of danger and to tell her brother she was dying. The next day, Arnesto and her father-in-law bleed her to death over the protests of the prince. Her brother arrives and, gathering troops, attacks the princes, father and son, and they and many others are killed. The duke of Alba's punishment of the Flemish is said to be in revenge for Blanca's death.

Desengaño 8 (*El traidor contra su sangre*)

Told by doña Francisca.

Don Pedro, a proud, cruel, and greedy man in Jaén, has a son, don Alonso, and a daughter, Mencía. He wants to keep all their wealth for the son and tries to make Mencía become a nun, refusing to give her a dowry to marry and turning down all suitors. Don Enrique, a wealthy man from Granada, wants to marry her without a dowry but don Pedro refuses his request because his grandparents were commoners. He continues to court her and they exchange marriage vows. Enrique had previously been involved with a married woman, Clavela, who frequents the house of a mother and daughter also visited by don Alonso and tells don Alonso of Enrique's courtship of Mencía. Alonso and his father plan to kill them, but wait to do so until don Pedro goes to Seville on business. Alonso then catches her writing Enrique a note, locks her in her room, summons a priest to confess her, then stabs his sister over and over, sends Mencía's note to Enrique, and waits in the street to kill him. When don Enrique arrives that night, Mencía's window opens by itself and he sees her still-bleeding body bathed in a mysterious light, and her voice warns him that she is dead and pleads that he save himself. He is frozen by the sight and don Alonso and a friend stab him and flee. Enrique survives, becomes a Franciscan monk, builds a chapel, and has Mencía's still-bleeding body interred there.

Don Alonso goes to Naples, where he enjoys generous financial support from his father. He makes friends with an "unlicensed priest," Marco Antonio, and falls in love with doña Ana de Añasco, grandaughter of a Spanish nobleman, don Fernando. He marries her and they have a son but when don Alonso tells his father, he disinherits him for marrying a poor woman. In hopes of regaining his father's favor, Marco Antonio and don Alonso behead doña Ana at supper in Marco Antonio's garden, throw her body in the well, bury her head in a cave in the marina and embark for Spain. The baby's hungry cries waken the grandmother, and the next day doña Ana's grandfather identifies by its clothes the body put in the plaza after a serving woman found it in the well.

Don Alonso and Marco Antonio are arrested in Genoa, where they have stolen some silk stockings. They are brought back to Naples and sentenced to be executed. Don Alonso, repentant, asks that they bring doña Ana's head to him so he may beg forgiveness before his death. Although six months have passed, it is still fresh and lovely. When the news of don Alonso's death is brought to his father, he says he would rather have his son dead than badly wed and continues playing cards, but dies shortly thereafter and doña Ana's son inherits his fortune.

Desengaño 9 (*La perseguida triunfante*)

Told by doña Estefanía, a nun and cousin of Lisis.

King Ladislao of Hungary marries princess Beatriz of England, sending his younger brother Federico to arrange the betrothal and bring her to Hungary. Federico falls madly in love with her but restrains his passion at first. Ladislao and Beatriz live happily together for a year until Ladislao departs to defend his realm against attack. He leaves governing power jointly in the hands of Beatriz and Federico. The latter takes advantage of this to declare his passion and pursue her. After trying in vain to dissuade him, she has a golden cell built and imprisons him in it. The queen rules so well for a year that her vassals do not miss either Federico or the king. When the returning king nears the city, she frees Federico, who has refused to bathe, shave, or change his clothes. He goes in this state to meet the king and tells him she imprisoned him because he refused *her* sexual advances.

The king believes Federico and orders that the queen be taken to the wildest forest, where her eyes are put out and she is left as food for beasts.

Beatriz is praying to God and His Mother when she hears steps and a woman's consoling voice. The visitor restores Beatriz's eyes, gives her bread, fruit, and water, leads her to a lovely meadow, and departs, encouraging her to persist in her virtuous ways, pleasing to God. Here she is found by a German, Duke Octavio, who has been hunting. He takes her back to his palace and his wife, where she lives under the name Rosismunda.

Ladislao has meanwhile begun to doubt the truth of Federico's accusation and to lament his harshness. Federico goes to look for Beatriz, intending to rape and kill her, but he finds no trace of her until an ugly man dressed as a scholastic appears. He says he is a learned magician and will help Federico achieve his desires if he will promise never to confess it, even in the face of death, to which the prince agrees. The doctor tells him that Beatriz is in Germany with her sight restored and that by raping and killing her, he can become king of Hungary. Federico convinces the king that he has found the remains of Beatriz's clothes and that heaven, seeing her guilty, has consented in her death. The king nevertheless refuses to remarry and names Federico his heir. After a year, Federico and the doctor travel to Germany and, with Federico's appearance transformed by a magic ring, they enter the palace. The doctor, who can make himself invisible, plants treasonous letters in Rosismunda's sleeve and then announces to the duke that he has learned of a plot to kill him. The houshold is searched and the letters found in her sleeve. She is taken back to the spot where they found her. Her queenly dress magically reappears, but so does Federico, intent on rape and killing. Beatriz's marvelous visitor arrives and removes her from his arms, replacing her with a raging lion who leaves him badly wounded before the doctor saves him.

Her savior takes her this time to a shepherd's hut. The emperor and empress pass by, see and summon Beatriz, and their six-year-old son loves her on sight. He insists that she return to the palace and care for him, even sleeping in the same bed. The doctor again reveals her whereabouts to Federico, takes him to the palace, and instructs him to enter the prince's chamber, put a sleeping herb under Beatriz's pillow, and stab the prince to death, leaving the bloody dagger in her hand. When they are thus discovered the next morning, the emperor orders her taken and beheaded. Beatriz's protectress appears again to rescue her from her executioners' hands and take her to faraway peaks to live as a hermit in a cave. The prince revives as he is about to be buried and demands Florinda, as he called her.

Beatriz lives happily in her cave for eight years and the doctor cannot discover her whereabouts. Then one morning, her protectress appears with all the attributes of the Virgin Mary and reveals that she is the Mother of God. She gives Beatriz a man's clothes and herbs and tells her to go with them to Hungary, where many are dying from a plague. She tells Beatriz that her herbs will cure anyone who confesses all their sins before her; but will be fatal if any sin is not confessed. Her fame quickly spreads as she cures all sufferers, and the king sends for her to cure Federico, who is gravely ill. With the king's promise to forgive him for what he is about to say and over the protests of the doctor, Federico confesses all. Ladislao is despairing but Beatriz reveals her identity and is instantly transformed to all her queenly glory and the Virgin appears beside her while the doctor disappears in an explosion of demonic sulphurous smoke.

Although Ladislao wants Beatriz to live again as his queen, she goes to a convent, taking all her ladies-in-waiting with her. Ladislao has her sister Isabel brought from England to marry Federico and then becomes a monk as well.

Desengaño 10 (*Estragos que causa el vicio*)

Told by Lisis.

During the reign of Philip III, a gentleman of the royal chambers named don Gaspar accompanied the king on a trip to Lisbon. There, he began visiting the youngest of four sisters, who lived in part of a distinguished residence. Entering one night by a back door to which they have given him a key, he hears moaning coming from a cellar and finds a freshly buried body of a young man, dead but still moaning. He has the unidentified man buried and takes it as a divine warning to stay away from such a house.

Then he sees two beautiful sisters at mass, Magdalena and Florentina. Magdalena is married to don Dionís, and Florentina lives with them, in such close seclusion that don Gaspar has no luck approaching her. But one night he finds Florentina in the street, nearly dead from sword wounds, takes her to his inn, and has her cared for. When she regains consciousness, she tells him to take ministers of justice to don Dionís's house, where they find a massacre. She tells him that although she and Magdalena were raised as sisters, they were born of previous marriages of their father and

mother, Florentina's mother having died in giving birth to her. When don
Dionís courts and marries doña Magdalena, Florentina also falls in love
with him, eventually tells him so and they are lovers for some four years
and vow to marry after doña Magdalena dies. She confesses the truth to a
priest one Holy Week, he puts the fear of hell in her, and she tells a maid
who has been with her from childhood. The maid tells her it is just as likely
she will die first and will go to hell in guilt; she suggests that they arrange
for doña Magdalena to die, since she in her innocence will earn a martyr's
crown in heaven, and once married, Florentina will be able to make sacrifices and penitence like David and secure forgiveness. The maid tells don
Dionis that Magdalena is betraying him with a handsome young servant
and arranges a nighttime scene that supports her false testimony. Don
Dionís kills him and doña Magdalena, two of her maids, two pages, and
three kitchen slaves. Florentina's maid, repentant and horrified, tells him
her testimony was false, that she arranged it so he would marry Florentina,
and he kills her. Florentina appears and he tries to kill her, but a black
kitchen slave puts herself between them, giving her time to escape. He
then falls on his sword and she stumbles to the street.

Hearing this story kills don Gaspar's love for Florentina as well, and he
counsels her to become a nun. She does so, maintaining a friendly correspondence with don Gaspar, who returns to Toledo and marries. Although
Florentina eventually confesses her own role in the massacre, the king pardons her and she inherits don Dionís's fortune.

Appendix III: Charts of Stories

Story	Narrator(s)	Protagonist(s)	Father	Mother	P's Fate Children Convent	Setting, Historical Context	Facilitators
Frame Tale		Females:	(Dead)	(Present)		Madrid	
		Lisis	Dead	Laura[1]			
		Lisarda	Dead	Present			
		Matilde	Dead	Present			
		Nise	Dead	Present			
		Filis	Dead	Present			
		dª Isabel Faxardo[2]	Dead	Living			
		dª Luisa[3]	–	–			
		dª Francisca	–	–			
		dª Estefanía[4]	–	–			
		Males:	(Present)	(Dead)			
		don Juan	don Francisco	Dead			
		don Alvaro	Present	Dead			
		don Miguel	Present	Dead			
		don Alonso	Present	Dead			

Story	Narrator(s)	Protagonist(s)	Father	Mother	P's Fate Children Convent	Setting, Historical Context	Facilitators
Aventurarse perdiendo	Lisarda	Jacinta	Living, uncaring	Dead	Married, Nun, Widowed, Scorned, Convent[7]	Baeza[6]	Sarabia
						Mamora Montserrat	Fabio
		-d Felix	Living	Living	Dies	Valencia	
		-dª Adriana	Dead	Present[8]	Suicide		
		-Celio	–	–	Holy Orders	Madrid	
La burlada Aminta	Matilde	Aminta	Dead[9] Uncle Pedro (dies)	Dead & aunt living	Seduced, Abandoned, Kills Jacinto Marries d. Martín[12] No Children	Segovia War w/Duke of Savoy[11] Unnamed City Madrid	d Elena[10]
		-d Jacinto[13]	–	–	Killed		
		-wife dª María[14]	Living	Living	–	–	d Luisa[15]
		-"sister" Flora[16]	–	–			
		-d Martín[17]	Dead	doña Luisa	Marries Aminta		

Castigo de la miseria	dAlvaro						
		don Marcos	Dead	Dead[18]	Marries, duped, Dies[19]	Madrid	Marriage-broker Gamarra
		-dª Isidora	—	—	Begger		
		-Agustínico[20]	—	—	Soldier		
		—Inés, criada	—	—	Cortesan		Marcela
Prevenido, engañado	dAlonso						
		don Fadrique	Dead	Dead	Marries Gracia	Granada	
		-Serafina	Living	Living	Nun[21] Daughter, Gracia[22]		
		-dª Beatriz[23]			Marries[24]	Seville[25]	
		-dª Violante	Dead?[26]	Dead?	New lover[27]	Madrid[28] Marries	
		-Anonymous	—	—	Married	Naples	
		- "	—	—	Kills husband	Rome	
		- Duquesa	—	—	Married	Catalonia	
		- dª Gracia	Dead[29]	Absent (Nun)	Marries, Lover, Neighbor Nun[30]	Granada	

Story	Narrator(s)	Protagonist(s)	Father	Mother	P's Fate Children Convent	Setting, Historical Context	Facilitators
La fuerza del amor	Nise	Laura	d Antonio	Dead[31]	Married Forgotten Convent Nun	Naples	Sorceress ESP, brother Carlos, horse
		-d Diego Pinatelo	Living	Living	Killed, war	War of Phil. III w/Duke of Savoy	
		-Nise	–	–	Lover of d Diego		
Desengaño amando, y premio de la virtud	Filis	d Fernando	Dead	Living[32]	Dies, Witchcraft, Dies Repentant	Toledo	
		-dª Juana	Dead	Dead	Nun		Student/ magician Octavio
		-Lucrecia	–	–	Lover Suicide	to Sevilla	Spells Rooster/Specs Wax figure, pin
		-dª Clara	Merchant, leaves	Dead?	Married, 2 daughters Working Servant Remarries, Children		

Play	Head	Member			Fate	Location	
Al fin se paga todo	don Miguel	-Marqués don Sancho	Dies[33]	—	Buries Fernando / Marries Clara		Juana[34]
		dª Hipólita	Living[35]	Living	Convent / Remarries (d García) / Children[36]	Valladolid, Court, Phil III	Maid
		-d Pedro	—	—	Dies		
		-d Luis	—	—	Killed by Hipólita		
		-d Gaspar	—	—	"Dies," Chest Killed		
		-d García	—	—	Marries Hipólita		don García
El imposible vencido	don Lope	dª Leonor	d Francisco	dª María	Married, Dies, Married, Has son	Salamanca[37]	
		d Rodrigo	Living	Living	Married	Flanders, Duque de Alba governor sack, Amsterdam[38] Ciudad Rodrigo	Prayer
		dª Blanca[39]	widow	—	Married by bed-switch		
		-d Arnesto	—	—	"Ghost" Executed		Servant

Story	Narrator(s)	Protagonist(s)	Father	Mother	P's Fate Children Convent	Setting, Historical Context	Facilitators
		–d Beltran	–	–	Married		d Rodrigo
		d Alonso	–	–	Loses		
El juez de su causa	don Juan	Estela	Living	Living	Kidnapped Viceroy Married Princess Children	Valencia Fez Tuniz, Carlos V vs Barbarroxa Italy France	Xacimín
		–d Carlos	Living	Living Viceroy	Married		
		–Claudia	–	–	Page Marrd, Zayde Executed		servant[40] Amete
		–Zayde	Living, Bajá	–			
		–Conde it.			Rejected		
		–Amete	Living, Bajá		Executed		
El jardín engañoso	dª Laura	Constanza	Dies (before main plot)	Fabia	Married 2 sons	Zaragoza	Trick of Carlos
		–don Jorge	Living	Living	Marries Teodora		Trick of Devil

Desengaño 1
(La esclava
de su amante) — "Zelima"

Character					
-Carlos	–	–	Marries Children		Fabia Old nurse
-Teodosia	Dies	Fabia	Marries Jorge Children		
-Federico	Living	Living	Killed by Jorge		
dª Isabel Faxardo	Dies (flight of Isabel)	Living[41]	Raped "Slave"[43] Kidnapped Nun	Murcia Rebelión, Cataluña Zaragoza Carnival[46]	Claudia[42] Octavio[44] Leonisa[45]
-d Felipe (Luis)	–	–	Servant, Kills d Manuel Disappears Killed, war[48]	Admiral/ Viceroy[47] Alicante	
-d Manuel	Dead	Living	Killed	Algeria Zaragoza Valencia Madrid	
-Alejandra	–	–	–		
-Zaida	Living	–	Suicide		

Story	Narrator(s)	Protagonist(s)	Father	Mother	P's Fate Children Convent	Setting, Historical Context	Facilitators
Desengaño 2 (La más infame venganza)	Lisarda	Octavia	Dies (battle)	Dies after husband	Lover of Carlos Convent[49] Nun	Milan War 1614?[50]	
		-d Carlos	Living	Dead[51]	Disappears		
		-Camila	Dead[52]	-	Married to Carlos Raped by Juan Poisoned, Carlos		
Desengaño 3 (El verdugo de su esposa)	Nise	d Pedro	Dead?[53]	-	Kills Roseleta Marries Ang.	Palermo[54]	Virgin Mary Hanged Man
		-Roseleta	-	-	Bled to death		
		-d Juan	Dead?	Dead?	Convent		
		-Angeliana	Dead	Dead	Marries Pedro		
Desengaño 4 (Tarde llega el desengaño)	Filis (d Martín) (d Jaime)	d Jaime de Aragón	Dead[55]	Dead	Lover, Lucrecia Nearly killed Marries Elena Insane	(Toledo)[56] Flanders Gran Canaria	
		-Lucrecia (widow)	Príncipe	-	Orders Jaime's assassination		

Desengaño (narrator)	Character			Fate	Location	Role
Desengaño 5 (*La inocencia castigada*) dª Laura (widow)	-Elena	Dead	Dies[57]	Married / Starved	City near Seville; Seville	Neighbor
	-cousin	-	-	Burned		Prostitute (Dress)
	-black maid	-	-	Dying, Stabbed		Corregidor
	dª Inés	Dead	Dead	Married / Bewitched / Walled up / Blind / Convent[58]		Neighbors
	-d. Alonso	-	-	Executed[59]		Archbishop
	-d Diego	-	-	Jailed;[60] Executed?		Sorcerer (statue)
Desengaño 6 (*Amar sólo por vencer*) Matilde	Laurela	Living (d Bernardo)	Living	Seduced / Abandoned / Killed[62]	Madrid	Aunt, uncle[61]
	-d Esteban (Estefanía)	Living	Living	Disappears		
	-wife	-	-			
	-d Enrique	-	Living	With parents		

Story	Narrator(s)	Protagonist(s)	Father	Mother	P's Fate Children Convent	Setting, Historical Context	Facilitators
Desengaño 7 (*Mal presagio casar lejos*)	dª Luisa (viuda)	dª Blanca	Dead	Dead	Married / Killed by father-in-law	Spain[63] Flanders	dª María[64] d Jorge[65]
		-Flemish prince	Living	–	Killed / Punished by Duke de Alba		Arnesto[66]
		dª Mayor	Dead	Dead	Married / Killed by husband[68]	Portugal[67]	
		dª María	Dead	Dead	Legs broken		
		dª Leonor	Dead	Dead	Married,[69] strangled, son poisoned	Italy	
		srª Marieta	Living	–	Married[70] Killed[71]		
Desengaño 8 (*El traidor contra su sangre*)	dº Francisca	dª Mencia	d Pedro	–	Secretly married; Killed,[73] Bleeding	Jaen	Gonzalo[72]
		-d Enrique	Living	Living	Secretly married; Monk		

Desengaño	Narrator	Character			Fate	Setting	Characters
		-Clavela[74]	—	—	Married Disinherited Naples Jailed[77]	Seville	Mother & daughter[75]
		d Alonso	d Pedro	—	Garrotted	VII Count of Lemos viceroy, Duke of Osuna; Others named; Genoa	Friend[76] Marco Antonio[78]
		-dª Ana de Añasco	Dead; grand- father living	Living	Married child[79] Beheaded[80]		
Desengaño 9 (La perse- guida triunfante)	Estefanía (monja)	Beatríz (Queen)	Living	Living	Married Blinded Exiled Serial per- secutions Hermit Physician Nun	England Hungary Germany	Virgin Mary Duke Octavio Devil Magic ring Peasants Emperor Prince
		Ladislao (King)	Dead	Dead	Married Abdicates Monk		
		-Federico	Dead	Dead	Allied to devil Cured King Marries Isabela[81]		

Story	Narrator(s)	Protagonist(s)	Father	Mother	P's Fate Children Convent	Setting, Historical Context	Facilitators
Desengaño 10 (Estragos que causa el vicio)	Lisis	don Gaspar	–	–	Marries[82]	Lisbon Felipe III 1619 trip to Portugal	Moaning body d Miguel[83]
		-Florentina[84]	Dead[85]	Dead[86]	Lover of d.Dionís Nun		
		–don Dionís	–	–	Married Suicide		Confessor Maid
		–Magdalena	Dead	Dead	Married Killed		

1. Also a narrator in both volumes.

2. Added as "Zelima" at beginning of *Desengaños,* along with three other new narrators; "Moorish slave" given to Lisis by her mother's sister; pleasure in her friendship helps cure Lisis. They are like "two loving sisters."

3. A widow. She and her sister, doña Francisca, who is single, have recently come to live in the same house in which Lisis lives. Both are said to be lovely young women and "bien entendidas" (of clear understanding).

4. A nun and Lisis's cousin. She has left the convent temporarily to recover from a fever.

5. Added in frame section following first novella; receives Lisis's favors after second, making don Juan jealous.

6. Don Felix returns from Flandes accompanying doña Leonor de Portugal, countess of Gelves, to Zaragoza when her husband don Diego Pimental is viceroy. Jacinta and Félix go to Rome, then back to Madrid.

7. Guiomar joins Jacinta in convent after her mother's death.

8. Sister of don Félix's father; another sister lives with her. Two other sisters in a convent, to which Félix takes Jacinta when they are caught courting by her father and brother. Don Félix has another widowed "relative" (later called his aunt) in Madrid, with a daughter, doña Guiomar, with whom Jacinta goes to live.

9. Father dies when she is twelve or fourteen, puts her in care of his younger brother Pedro and his wife.

10. Lives in lower floor of don Pedro and Aminta's house. "A woman in between a lady and a servant. She had been the wife of a merchant"; helps don Jacinto.

11. Pedro's only son, to whom he wants to marry Aminta, is serving in Italy in this campaign. Earlier mention of Philip II giving Pedro habit of Santiago.

12. Under assumed name; doesn't claim inheritance from father, because of cousin don Luis to whom she had been betrothed.

13. True name, don Francisco, as doña Luisa reveals.

14. Separated from Jacinto and living in her parents' house in Madrid.

15. Relative of don Jacinto, newly arrived and not well known in Segovia, lives on outskirts of town. Mother of don Martín, she joins them in Madrid after their marriage and expresses delight with her daughter-in-law.

16. Well connected through powerful relatives in court, according to doña Luisa; otherwise would have been executed for "her well-known appetites."

17. Only son of doña Luisa.

18. Before he came to court with elderly father, she died when he was twelve, "of a sudden pain in the side."

19. In first version, committing suicide with rope provided by the devil in the guise of marriage-broker Gamarra.

20. Also called Agustín, and don Agustín, "nephew"/lover of doña Isidora. .

21. After don Fadrique breaks engagement with accusing note; possible death of baby she abandoned weighs on her conscience, "the motive for her endeavoring with her life and penitence not only to achieve forgiveness of her sin, but the name of saint, and she was held as such in Granada" (*Novelas,* 141).

22. Apparent father don Vicente, who was courting Serafina; don Fadrique leaves baby in charge of his aunt.

23. Widow and relative of don Fadrique's friend don Mateo.

24. After her black lover dies and don Fadrique rejects her, suggesting she mourn the death of her black lover at least a year, she marries another suitor.

25. Staying several months in house of rich relative.

26. Resides with her cousin, doña Ana—in a "separate room" after her marriage (163) but with a connecting door.

27. Younger brother of her brother-in-law, doña Ana's husband.

28. Fadrique stays in one of several houses of an uncle in the "barrio del Carmen"; the uncle is rich, has only one son and heir, don Juan, whom he has betrothed to a rich cousin; the marriage is delayed because she is only ten years old.

29. Don Vicente, repenting his ill treatment of Serafina, tries to get her to leave the convent and marry him, but when she refuses, he falls ill and dies.

30. Stipulated in will by don Fadrique that she should become a nun with her mother.

31. Died at Laura's birth, but says "her father's discretion filled this lack reasonably well" (178).

32. Can't or won't control wild only son, who is wasting inheritance. Fernando's excuse for not marrying Juana; when she goes into convent, wants to marry Fernando, thinking that will settle him down. She "puts her eyes" on Clara, arranges marriage; defends Clara when son mistreats her; her death removes last shield for Clara, last restraint on Fernando

33. Death of father makes it possible for don Sancho to marry Clara (at first only wanted to be her lover).

34. Offers to take Clara's four- and five-year-old girls while Clara goes to Sevilla; also to "treat them as her own" and provide dowry for them to be nuns with her if Clara doesn't return; gives Clara money; very happy with "her new daughters."

35. Her parents do not figure in the story after her first marriage.

36. With don García, not in eight-plus years of marriage with don Pedro.

37. Two references to descendents either of son or of student judges having relatives on royal council. Interesting reference to famous professor.

38. Dates mistaken. Duke of Alba not in command when the sack took place.

39. Daughter of Flemish woman and Spaniard.

40. Old man, helps her get post as page to don Carlos.

41. Becomes a nun with her daughter (see closing paragraphs of *Desengaños*).

42. "Doncella" (lady's maid) who served as Isabel's personal maid; much loved "por habernos criado [juntas] desde niñas" (because we were brought up [together] since we were girls.)

43. Following don Manuel to Sicily, she disguises herself as slave and arranges to be sold to his majordomo; after the kidnapping and return to Zaragoza, don Manuel's rejection of her for Zaida and his killing by don Felipe, she has Octavio sell her again in Valencia; she is bought by an uncle of Lisis, whose wife, Leonor, gives her to Lisis because her husband is pursuing "Zelima."

44. An old servant living nearby, whose dismissal had made the place which don Felipe/Luis occupied.

45. Maid of wife of majordomo, with whom "Zelima" became very friendly.

46. Carnival (Carnestolendas) is the time setting in the frame narrative as well.

47. When the admiral of Castille is named viceroy of Sicily. Ylleras note identifies him as probably Juan Alfonso Enríquz de Cabrera (d.1647), ninth admiral of Castille and fifth duke of Medina de Rioseco, gentleman in Philip IV's household, his major, on the Councils of State and War, and viceroy of Naples (*Desengaños* 149 n. 14).

48. See "epilogue" section of final frame.

49. At urging of Carlos, supposedly only until father's wrath calms.

50. "Ocasionáronse en este tiempo las largas y peligrosas guerras de aquellos reinos, que no solas lloran ellos, sino nosotros, pues de esto se originó entrársenos en España y costarnos a todos tanto como cuesta" (At that time, there occured the long and dangerous wars in those realm, that we lamented as well as they, because the entry into Spain stemmed from that, and its costing everyone all that it costs." Yllera (*Desengaños*, 179 n. 2) notes this as "An allusion to the hostilities begun in 1614 when Carlos Manuel I, Duke of Savoy, fought against Spain, reclaiming Monferrato in his grandaughter's name, at the death of his son-in-law, the duke

Francisco IV (1612). But it seems that this event makes the author think of the uprising in Catalonia."

51. Never mentioned; but father remarries and has children after Carlos disappears.

52. In his will, Camila's father names father of Carlos her tutor.

53. Friendship of don Pedro and don Juan attributed to friendship of their fathers, and the hanged man says the Virgin saved him because of a mass he has said every Saturday in the chapel where his parents are buried.

54. Protagonists don Pedro and don Juan are sons of Spaniards who have gone to serve in Sicily, married, and remained there.

55. Both parents die between the Lucrecia and Elena episodes, the mother first, followed within a year by the father.

56. City of origin and ultimate destination of enclosed observer/narrator, don Martín.

57. Dies six years after daughter's marriage.

58. "Living the life of a saint" but the narrator doesn't say she became a nun.

59. Along with her brother don Francisco and sister-in-law.

60. The sorcerer disappeared; don Diego is jailed, tried by the Inquisitor General and "does not reappear."

61. Sister of don Bernardo and her husband.

62. Killed by father, aunt, and uncle, who bring a wall down on her. Two sisters became nuns, and her mother with them when she is widowed.

63. No city given.

64. Much loved servant and confidant of doña Blanca, goes to Flanders with her.

65. Manservant of Blanca's brother; also accompanies her to Flanders; later called don Gabriel. He and doña María marry; their daughter, also called María, marries a close relative of doña Blanca—parents of narrator.

66. Sixteen-year-old page with whom the prince has a homosexual relationship.

67. Vague mention of Spanish king punishing "el reo."

68. Along with various Spanish maids. Sister, doña María, who had accompanied her to Portugal and heard a page's denunciation of the trap set by husband, broke her legs jumping from a window to save herself.

69. For her praising a Spanish captain as handsome, husband killed both wife and 4-year-old son.

70. To a cousin; still very young and living with her father. But later said to be twenty-four years old.

71. Garrotted by father and husband two days after a manservant of hers had been stabbed to death, apparently at the order of father and husband as well.

72. Servant in house of doña Mencía who served as go-between.

73. Stabbed to death by brother; her dead but still-bleeding corpse warns don Enrique to save himself.

74. Married but living freely. Rejected by don Enrique after he falls in love with doña Mencía, she accepts don Alonso, to work her revenge.

75. Socially acceptable if too free in receiving visits, friends of both Clavela and don Alonso. Taken prisoner for their complicity in death of Mencía, but saved by money.

76. Assisted with attack on don Enrique.

77. In Genova for robbing colored stockings.

78. "Prevete salvaje"—a priest in dress only, who receives income from the church.

79. Inherits cruel grandfather's fortune. Living in Sevilla, 28-year-old don Pedro Portocarrero y Añasco.

80. Execution of don Alonso delayed so he can reveal whereabouts of the head; dug up fresh as when it was buried six months earlier.

81. Beatríz's younger sister.

82. After rescuing and nursing Florentina back to health, her horror story cures him of love for her; he returns to Toledo and marries.

83. Relative of don Gaspar, also in king's service; also enamored of Florentina.

84. She and Magdalena were raised as sisters through parents' remarriages, but are not blood relations.

85. On the death of both parents, both "sisters" were left in the care of Magdalena's maternal uncle, who hoped they would become nuns so he could continue to benefit from their estate.

86. Her true mother died giving birth to her; her father married Magdalena's mother when Magdalena was four years old.

Notes

Introduction

1. The epigraph is quoted from *Novelas amorosas y ejemplares,* ed. Agustín C. de Amezúa (Zayas y Sotomayor 1948). Subsequent quotations from this first volume will be drawn from this 1948 edition by Amezúa, identified as *Novelas* followed by the page number; or from the 1637 princeps, indicated as (Zayas y Sotomayor 1637b).

2. The same situation prevailed in Spain, as Montesa points out: "María de Zayas es hoy día, literariamente hablando, una gran olvidada. Una perfecta desconocida no sólo para el público lector, sino incluso para muchos universitarios que apenas si llegan a conocer su nombre" (María de Zayas is today, speaking in terms of literature, completely forgotten. Totally unknown, not only to the reading public, but even for many university students, who scarcely know her name) (Montesa Peydro 1981, 33).

3. See, for example, Mariscal, 1991, Kurtz 1994, and Greer 1991b and 1990.

4. Henry Sullivan (1990) makes this point with regard to Golden Age drama.

5. See Spitzer 1947.

6. According to statistics offered by Sarah Nalle (1989), approximately 10 or 11 percent of the female population of Cuenca, Madrid, and Toledo could read, as opposed to perhaps 60 percent of the male population. Significantly, the title of this prefatory section is expressed in the subjunctive mood; "To him who may read" would be the literal translation.

7. As an example of the latter, I would cite the opening paragraph of the first story told by Lisarda, which contrasts "las flacas fuerzas de las mujeres" (women's slender forces) with the "claros y heroicos entendimientos de los hombres" (men's clear and heroic understanding) (*Novelas,* 37). For further consideration of her address to male readers, see Chapters 3 and 10.

8. Furthermore, the bulk of the following "Prólogo de un desapasionado" (Prologue by a Dispassionate Reader) consists of an appeal to the reader to buy her book, whatever it costs, rather than seek a "free read" in a bookstore, or borrow the book from someone else. This prologue is sometimes attributed to Castillo Solórzano; Cayuela lists a number of other prologues that makes similar critiques of freeloading readers, including that to Tirso's *Cigarrales de Toledo* and Quevedo's *Buscón* (Cayuela 1994).

9. See Clayton 1989 for an analysis of the approaches of Brooks, Leo Bersani, and Teresa de Lauretis.

10. Elizabeth Grosz points out that "fascination" means both "to entice *and* trap, seduce *and* contain. Mutual fascination [of psychoanalysis with women and vice versa] is always a risky business. Lacan suggests that it is the consequence of an imaginary identification in which the self strives to incorporate the other in an act as aggressive as it is loving. It is never clear who, snake or snake-charmer, is mesmerized by whom" (Grosz 1990, 6–7).

11. Object choice as well as gender play a role also. Kristeva's mother-centered revision of Freud and Lacan has a powerful allure in reading a woman writer such as Zayas; yet a number of feminist critics and theorists reject her equation of the feminine with the maternal and her normative assumption of heterosexuality. See, for example, Butler 1990, 79–93.

12. The first problem with Lacanian theory for many women readers is his privileging of the phallus as the primary signifier, the marker of sexual difference and of the separation from the nurturing (m)Other that initiates one's assumption of a necessarily gendered subjectivity within language. It has not been easy for women to read what Ragland-Sullivan calls the "other Lacan," the Lacan who underlines that the phallus does not equal the penis, that there is no more independence, security, or completion of being in assuming the masculine position of "having" the phallus than there is adopting the feminine position of being the "not-all" who knows herself to be not all, and in relation to whom man sustains his fantasy of being all (Ragland-Sullivan 1991). Zizek makes the point that there is no link between the biological opposition of male and female and the "two asymmetrical antinomies of symbolization (the 'masculine' side that involves the universality of the phallic function grounded in an exception; the 'feminine' side that involves a 'non-all' field which, for that very reason, contains no exception to the phallic function)"; they represent two heteronomous systems grafted together, so that our sexuality is a *bricolage* (Zizek 1994, 155). Explanations of sexual division are related to various philosophical attempts to move from the Particular to the Universal. They are often based on an exclusion which is necessary to guarantee the consistency of the posited Universal. Male and female are not two parts of a Whole, but "two (failed) attempts to symbolize this Whole" (Zizek, 1994, 160).

13. Credit—or blame—for this joke goes to a friendly psychiatrist I met several years ago on a flight to an MLA convention, but whose name I never learned. If not rent, at least apologies for liberties taken with the "property" are due to Freud, who pointed out in "Creative Writers and Day-Dreaming" (1974, 9:141–53) that building the castles in the air we call daydreams is a normal human activity, and that only when such fantasies become "over-luxuriant and over-powerful" should they be associated with neurosis or psychosis.

14. The path between psychoanalysis and literature carries two-way traffic, however. Two of Freud's central concepts, the Oedipus complex and narcissism, were modeled on literary/mythic figures (see "Totem and Taboo," [1974, 13:1–161] and "Leonardo da Vinci and a Memory of His Childhood" [1974, 11: 59–137]; Freud believed that poetic insight often perceived the same structures that he found in clinical observation, and that ideal psychoanalytic training should include "the history of civilization, mythology, the psychology of religions, literary history, and literary criticism" (quoted in Lacan, "Discours de Rome," Wilden 51). Lacan, with his focus on the role of language in structuring the unconscious and the constitution of subjectivity in the Symbolic and Imaginary orders, supports Freud's list and would add to it rhetoric, dialectic, grammar and poetics. See "Discours de Rome," in Wilden 1981, 51, 59; see also Lacan 1977, 144–45, 147.

15. For succinct explanations of the Imaginary order, see Grosz 1990, 31–48 and Wright 1992, 173–76.

16. Contemporary film criticism perhaps makes more evident than does literary criticism the interrelationship between the Symbolic and Imaginary orders and the role of suture in hiding the lack in and of the Real. See, for example, Silverman, 1988.

17. Ruth Anthony El Saffar and Diana de Armas Wilson make a similar point in *Quixotic Desire,* justifying the utility of psychoanalytic criticism, which takes place on the border between two disciplines, as psychoanalysis rediscovers its literary origins, and literary critics avail themselves of a psychoanalysis that at its best demonstrates how, "in both literary and interpretive texts, . . . the psyche functions as an organizing principle, constantly creating itself through the images and lexicons out of which it gains material expression" (1993, 3).

18. "In the transference, desire passes through what Lacan calls the 'defile of the signifier': it enters the Symbolic order, where it can be reordered, reread, rewritten. While other

'transactional' models of reading could be proposed, the model of the psychoanalytic transference has the advantage of imaging the productive encounter of teller and listener, text and
reader, and of suggesting how their interaction takes place in a special 'artificial' medium,
obeying its own rules—those of the symbolic order—yet vitally engaged with the histories and
intentions of desire" (Brooks 1985, 234–35). Flieger (1989, 197) summarizes Freud's last description of transference, from *An Outline of Psychoanalysis,* as follows: "The transference is a
replay of the original oedipal drama, in which the patient sees in the analyst 'the return, the
reincarnations of some important figure out of his childhood or past,' who is generally 'one
or the other of the patient's parents, his father or his mother,' onto whom he 'transfers' the
earlier affect and with whom he may replay the earlier drama in an act of 'aftereducation'
which resolves earlier conflicts." For Lacan's (1981) rereading of Freud on transference, and
for a gentle critique—and partial acceptance—of the application of the transference model
to literary criticism, see Jacques-Alain Miller 1991.

19. *Text* for Kristeva is not a neutral descriptive term, it should be noted, but designates a
particular kind of avant-garde writing permeated with what she calls the semiotic disposition,
which invites, if not requires, the active participation of the reader in the signifying process.

20. While the episodic structure of her narrative can be attributed to the influence of
other narrative paradigms such as the romance or the picaresque novel, the primary models
of the novella furnished Zayas by Boccaccio and Cervantes were more tightly constructed and
her departure from the brevity and linear logic of those models is significant, as I hope to
demonstrate.

21. Admittedly, such selectivity involves a certain amount of distortion, particularly in the
case of Lacan. The difficulty of Lacan's texts, in style as in content, constitutes a deliberate
challenge to the humanist concept of man as a rational, unified subject at the center of history and in control of his own thought and action. Any attempt to simplify that discourse
therefore misrepresents its spirit, and the commentaries of faithful disciples of Lacan often
become nearly as dense as his own.

Chapter 1

1. Serrano y Sanz published the certificate of her baptism, which took place on 12 September 1590 in the Madrid parish of San Sebastián, but gave the mother's name as Catalina,
rather than María, as the certificate shows. Boyer (xi) gives the mother's name as Ana, but
does not specify her source. Godparents at the baptism were Diego de Santoyo and Juana de
Cardona, and Bernabé Gonzálex and Alonso García were witnesses. Her father, baptized in
the same parish, was the son of Luisa de Zayas and Francisco de Zayas; her maternal grandparents were Antonio de Sotomayor and Catalina de Zayas (Barbeito Carneiro 1992, 165–66);
(Yllera 1983, 15–16).

2. Fernández de Navarrete may have been the initiator of the speculative biographies of
Zayas in his 1854 essay on the history of the Spanish novel. He suggested in the form of a
rhetorical question that residence in Zaragoza because of the "dulces lazos que fijan la suerte
de las criaturas" (sweet ties that fix the fate of lasses) might explain her publication there.

3. The fifth novella, *La fuerza del amor,* and part of the eighth *desengaño* take place in
Naples when he was viceroy, and don Félix departs for Naples on the ships waiting to transport the count of Lemos in the first novella, *Aventurarse perdiendo.* References to the count are
laudatory; the narrator of the *La fuerza del amor* describes him as "nobilísimo, sabio y piadoso
príncipe, cuyas raras virtudes y excelencias no son para escritas en papeles, sino en láminas de
bronce y en las lenguas de la fama" (most noble, wise, and pious prince, whose rare virtues
and excellence deserve to be written not on paper, but on bronze plaques and on the tongues
of fame) (*Novelas,* 245). Filis, the narrator of the fourth *desengaño,* includes among her list of
learned women Catalina de Zúñiga y Sandoval, wife of the sixth count of Lemos, and Isabel,
narrator of the first *desengaño,* calls the wife of the ninth count, Ana Girón, "mi señora la con-

desa" (my lady the countess) and attributes to her the ballad she sings in the introduction to the second night of the *Desengaños.*

4. Her poems figured in the preliminaries of *La fábula de Píramo y Tisbe* (1621) and *Prosas y versos del pastor de Clenarda* (1622) by Miguel Botello, *Orfeo en lengua castellana* (1624) by Juan Pérez de Montalban, *Experiencias de amor y fortuna* (1626) by Francisco de las Cuevas, and *El Adonis* (1632) by Antonio del Castillo de Larzával.

5. According to King 1963, 81–82; and Sánchez, 1961, 215–17.

6. I am grateful to Willard King for bringing this play to my attention.

7. I find no documentation for a "Targelia" of Thebes. No such personage is listed in Smith's (1849) three-volume compendium of Greek and Roman biographies, nor in the catalogs of the heroic women of Boccaccio or Alvaro de Luna. Lope has perhaps confused the name of some Greek equivalent of Claudia and Cornelia with "Thargelia," one of the major festivals of Apollo at Athens. See the entries in the *Enciclopedia universal ilustrada . . . Espasa-Calpe* and the *Encyclopedia Britannica,* 15th ed., s.v. "Thargelia."

8. For the publication history, see Yllera 1983. A second, corrected edition of the first volume was printed in Zaragoza in 1637, and included small but significant changes to her preface and the third novella, *El castigo de la miseria.* See below and Chapters 6 and 8. Yllera (1983, 69) observes that the Madrid licenses for the *Novelas* give its title as *Honesto y entretenido sarao,* perhaps indicating a title change made to placate the moralist opposition to literature of entertainment in that decade. This title was dropped on publication in Zaragoza, but reappeared in the title of the second volume. See Chapter 10.

9. In *Fama posthuma a la vida y muerte del Doctor Frey Lope Félix de Vega Carpio. Y elogios panejíricos a la inmortalidad de su nombre . . . Solicitados por el Doctor Juan Pérez de Montalvan* (Madrid, 1636) and *Lágrimas panegíricas a la temprana muerte del gran poeta, y teólogo ensigne Juan Pérez de Montalban . . . Recogidas i publicadas por Don Pedro Grande de Tena* (Madrid, 1639) (Serrano y Sanz 1975, 589).

10. For a description of similar *vejámenes,* see Carrasco Urgoiti 1965.

11. I am much indebted to Belén Atienza for this summary and analysis of the *Vejamen.*

12. Atienza, who is now studying the figure of the madman in Lope's *comedias* in relation to medical as well as literary traditions, suggests that this burlesque introduction served to caricature the women as "mujeres de vida alegre," since hospitals were associated with the treatment of venereal diseases even more than with madness.

13. They were *Certamen poetico de Nuestra Señora de Cogullada . . .* published in 1644, in the Hospital Real y General, like Zayas's *Novelas;* and the *Contienda poética, que la Imperial Ciudad de Zaragoza Propuso a los Ingenios Españoles en el fallecimiento del Serenissimo Señor, Con Balthasar Carlos de Austria . . . ,* published in 1646 (Jiménez Catalán 1925).

14. Cf. Sancho's comment to doña Rodríguez in *Don Quixote* part II: "hay tanto que trasquilar en las dueñas, según mi barbero, cuanto será mejor no menear el arroz, aunque se pegue" (Cervantes Saavedra 1971, 810–11) (there's so much to shear in those duennas, according to my barber, that it would be better not to stir the rice, even though it sticks) (1957, 797) and the following episode of the "bearded" *dueñas.* Rodríguez Marín provides a collection of literary examples of the reputation of duennas as go-betweens (Cervantes Saavedra 1928, 7:340–45).

15. See Trope 1994, 355–56.

16. The *Vejamen* apparently circulated quite widely, according to Brown, who lists nine surviving manuscripts of it.

Chapter 2

1. That the term "maravilla" is preferred to the designation "novela," disdained as too vulgar, Foa (1979, 104) attributes to the association of the latter term with the licentiousness

of the form as developed by Boccaccio, and the growth in seventeenth-century Italy and Spain of the poetics of *meraviglia,* which, as James V. Mirollo describes it, sought to provoke *admiratio* in the reader through the combination of the supernatural, surprise achieved through plot, and stylistic *agudeza,* or wit. Cayuela (1994) relates it more immediately to the ban on publication of works of fiction and *comedias* between 1625 and 1634. Juan de Piña, in the prologue to his *Varias fortunas* (Diverse fortunes) (1627) reveals the strategy of avoiding censure by rebaptizing his fictions: "Que bien sabía eran fábulas, y las auía mudado el nombre, y auía entendido la fullería a escusar nuevos memoriales, y persocuciones [*sic*]" (That he well knew that they were fables [i.e., fictional tales] and had understood the trick to avoid new memorandums and persecutions) (cited in Cayuela 1994, 50). See also Chapter 10.

2. As Bourland (1973), Place (1923, 7–8), and Amezúa (1948, xvii) point out, other Spanish authors of novellas had earlier adopted the model of a social gathering as a frame for storytelling. Eslava's 1609 *Noches de inverno* (Winter Nights) also employs a social gathering format, one that is more significant and interesting than the anecdotes related in it. None, however, tailors it to the same didactic or polemical shape that Zayas makes of the frame. See Chapter 10 below.

3. See Nancy D'Antuono (1983). A volume containing Spanish versions of 14 (of 214) Bandello stories was published in 1589. The translator, Millis y Godínez, acknowledges that he has based his translations on the much lengthened French adaptations of Bouisteau and Belleforest, "añadiendo o quitando cosas superfluas, y que en el español no son tan honestas como debieran, atento que la francesa tiene algunas solturas que acá no suenan bien" (adding or removing superfluous things that in Spanish are not as decent as they should be, mindful that the French language possesses some laxities that do not sound good here) (Bandello 1943, 7).

4. Place compiled a fairly comprehensive survey of possible Zayas sources in his 1923 study of Zayas, and subsequent critics have identified others as well. These will be indicated in discussions of the individual Zayas tales.

5. The play (Vega Carpio 1928) is a different but thematically related story in which a cross-dressed queen becomes the judge of her husband who had ordered her killed to marry another woman. My thanks to José Antonio Rodríguez Garrido for locating this play and securing a copy for me.

6. Montesa Peydro (1981) describes all editions known to him, and Yllera (1983, 82–99) gives details of editions, translations, and adaptations and indicates common errors of attribution.

7. Guiomar Hautcoeur (1998?) includes Zayas as a significant contributor to the popularity of the Spanish novella in France. She attributes to the novella, identified with the *comedia* in the mind of its public, a significant role in the evolution of the novel in France.

8. In at least one English edition, Cervantes gets credit for three Zayas stories. A volume titled *A Week's Entertainment at a Wedding. Containing six surprising and diverting Adventures . . . Written in Spanish by the Author of Don Quixot, and now first translated into English* published in London in 1710, contained six novels, none of them by Cervantes. Three were Zayas stories, *Desengaño 8* and *10,* and the seventh *novela, Al fin se paga todo* (Williams 1950, 77).

9. Our current practice of individual exegesis and critical commentary on literary readings may have had its origins in the Protestant Reformation and the tradition of individual interpretation of the Bible that then extended to other texts. See Lionel Gossman 1994, 27.

10. Cited as it appears in the 1705 Barcelona and the 1712 Valencia edition.

11. Few copies of this edition appear to have survived. Yllera, having located no other copy, followed Montesa's description of a personal copy. I have consulted the only copy I found in the United States, in the Ellis Rare Book Room of the Library of the University of Missouri, Columbia: PRIMERA / Y / SEGVNDA / PARTE DE LAS / NOVELAS AMOROSAS, Y EXEMPLARES / de Doña Maria de Zayas, y Sotomayor, / natural de Madrid. / CORREGIDAS, Y EN-

MENDADS EN ESTA / *vltima impression.* / [woodcut: thistle] / Impresso en Valencia, por Antonio Bordazar, / año 1712. / *A costa de Joseph Cardona, Mercader de Libros* [title page framed by woodcut border].

12. "Argumentoso" is defined in the *Diccionario de autoridades* as "ingenioso, laborioso y solícito" "ingenious, hardworking, and diligent" and "picante" also implies "spicy" or "racy."

13. Lola Luna (who omits Zayas's name from her list of the literary women he includes) finds in this appendix evidence that thanks to the diffusion of Erasmian ideas regarding the education of women and Castiglione's model of the courtly woman, by the seventeenth century the qualities that could earn women inclusion in the (limited) ranks of exemplary women had been expanded to include intellectual virtues, along with nobility, chastity, modesty, and saintly virtue (Luna 1996, 32–36).

14. "Complete" in that they contain all ten novellas from the two parts; her confrontational "Al que leyere" prologue was omitted from the 1638 octavo edition of the *Novelas* and from all subsequent editions prior to that of Amezúa. See Julian Olivares's forthcoming edition of the *Novelas* in Cátedra. My thanks to him for supplying this information.

15. I am grateful to Laura Bass for locating for me the information on Fiel de Aguilar and Lampillas.

16. See Susan Kirkpatrick 1989.

17. See Jagoe 1993 and Blanco 1989.

18. The "entertaining" literature for those of undiscriminating taste was often described in terms of literal consumption, and both the categories and terminology have persisted through the twentieth century. For example, Montesinos (1955), discussing confusion in reading tastes in the early part of the nineteenth century, refers ironically to an anonymous critic of *Los vicios de Madrid* (The Vices of Madrid) as "un lector de novelas [que] se engulle las de doña María de Zayas—de las que luego se afirma que «no valen nada»" (a novella reader who gobbles up those of María de Zayas—and then affirms that they "aren't worth a thing") (44).

19. She publishes four *novelas: Aventurarse perdiendo, El castigo de la miseria, La fuerza del amor;* and *El desengañado amado y premio de la virtud* [*sic*], and four *desengaños:* numbers 3, 5, 8, and 10 in Yllera's (1983) edition, *El verdugo de su esposa, La inocencia castigada, El traidor contra su sangre,* and *Estragos que causa el vicio.*

20. Pardo Bazán's apologia reflects a selective and personal reading of Zayas's use of magic (see Chapter 5), as well as an implicit defense and explanation of her own introduction of the supernatural in a number of stories. She reads *La inocencia castigada* as "[un] curioso relato donde, más bien que patrañas mágicas, veo un caso de *sonambulismo y sugestión hipnótica a distancia,* —interpretado como entonces se podía interpretar" ([a] curious tale where, rather than magic hoaxes, I see a case of *sonambulism and hypnotic suggestion at a distance* —interpreted as they could be interpreted then) (15). On other counts too, her appreciation of Zayas reflects her own position and practices as an aristocratic, outspoken writer who wrote about all classes of society, tried to harmonize Naturalism with Catholicism, and ardently defended women's rights and education for women. She applauds Zayas for her vigorous advocacy of women's rights and clear condemnation of the injustice of their legal and societal subjection, seeing in her a continuation of the vigor of Queen Isabelle, opposed to the degradation of women that accompanied a general decline in Spain, visible under the later Hapsburgs and fully developed, in Pardo Bazán's view, under the Bourbon regime that had been restored to power in her day after the failure of the First Republic.

21. Not all critics of those decades were as consistent and thoroughgoing in their dislike of Zayas's work. Writing in 1901, James Fitzmaurice-Kelly showed a penchant for her novelas, which he described as "spicy." Citing Ticknor, he defended her by saying: "Sobre los grados de indecencia no hay nada escrito. Doña María no tiene la pretensión de considerarse como un moralista didáctico; brilla por otras cualidades más literarias, por su golpe de vista real, por su cínico humorismo, por sus dotes narrativas, por sus admirables retratos de personajes y

cuadros de costumbres, y por su malicia picaña de excepcional sabor" (There is nothing written about levels of indecency. Doña María doesn't have the pretension of considering herself a moralist didact; she shines for more literary qualities, for her admirable portraits of characters and national customs, and for the exceptional flavor of her shameless maliciousness) (Fitzmaurice-Kelly c. 1901, 457). Later, however, in the midst of the Roaring Twenties, his enthusiasm has waned; he substitutes for praise of Zayas's literary gifts a recitation of the use of her fiction by Scarron, Molière and Beaumarchais. Again citing Ticknor, he lays the blame for the "indecency" of her stories on the tenor of the times: "No reinando ninguna casta austeridad entre las damas de honor de la corte de Felipe IV, no la exijamos tampoco a las que escribían" (With no austere chastity reigning among the ladies-in-waiting of the court of Philip IV, let us not demand it either of women who wrote.) (Fitzmaurice-Kelly 1926, 297).

22. "These stories have unquestionable value in that they reflect, as in a mirror, the tendencies of the age. In the elaborate and detailed descriptions of social entertainments, artistic decorations and dress, we are better able to penetrate into the customs, the tastes and the foibles of a period which has ever been replete with interest, and, as we read, we are gradually aware that unconsciously the author wove into her narrative the spirit and atmosphere of the society in which she moved" (13:212–13).

M. V. de Lara, in surveying Spanish women writers in 1932, also considered Zayas the first "theorizing feminist" to consciously comment on the conditions of the female sex in Spain, and a possible influence on Sor Juana. Lara says that the objective of defending women justifies her didactic use of "crude realism," and considers her reputation for immorality unjust, at once a product of the situation of Spain in her day and of foreign imitations of her work (Lara 1932, 31–35).

23. Just what developments in the cultural history of mid-twentieth century Spain led him to undertake this edition is a question I have posed but for which I do not as yet have a satisfactory answer. I suspect that it is related to the effects of uneven modernity in Franco's Spain combined with a backward-looking, authoritarian regime, which Stephanie Sieburth describes in *Inventing High and Low* (1994). To republish her works would fit with the reverence for the literary traditions of Golden Age Spain and the nostalgia for the aura of past imperial glory and Catholic orthodoxy that that regime attached to them. It would be an implicit recognition of the importance of women writers and readers and a selection likely to appeal to a wider popular audience, while containing that opening by dubbing the form, as did Amezúa, a *novela cortesana,* a "court novella," and critiquing her works in accord with the terms of nineteenth-century literary criticism in Spain, as Goytisolo would point out.

24. She draws her stories, he says, not from earlier storytellers but from "la vida, que le brinda generosamente casos y sucesos a porfía, muchos y más extraordinarios e inauditos que su propia fantasía hubiera podido imaginar" (life, which generously and insistently offers her events and cases more abundant, extraordinary and unheard of than her own fantasy could have imagined) (1948, xvii); "la vida de entonces era tan varia y rica, las pasiones y afectos tan dinámicos y desapoderados, los caracteres tan indómitos y recios, tan inquieta y prodigiosa la existencia de las gentes, que bien pudieron ocurrir y tomarlos ella del medio circundante" (life was then so varied and rich, passions and emotions so dynamic and disavowed, personalities so indomitable and rough, people's lives so restless and wondrous, that they could easily happen and she could take them from the society around her) (xxvii).

25. "Si las criaturas humanas que en toda obra de ficción crea o traslada cualquier escritor de una realidad vista por él son como un reflejo mimético de su alma, un trasunto más o menos fiel de su temperamento, el de doña María hubo de ser a la cuenta vehemente y ardoroso por demás" (If the human creatures that any writer in every work of fiction creates or copies from the reality he sees are a mimetic reflection of his soul, a more or less faithful copy of his temperament, doña María's had to have been on balance impassioned and excessively ardent) (1948, xvii).

26. "Hay en ella como una intuición latente de la psicología femenina, del corazón de la

mujer, que la hace escribir, con un precioso rasgo de su pluma, que 'una cosa es mirar, y otra ver', rasgo revelador de su don innato de observación consciente de cuanto la rodea, cualidad esencial en todo buen novelista" (There is in her something like a latent intuition of feminine psychology, of a woman's heart, that makes her write, with a precious stroke of the pen, that 'looking is one thing and seeing another', a revealing characteristic of her innate gift of observation, aware of everything that surrounds her, an essential quality in any good novelist) (xix); Her use of the supernatural and marvelous is, according to Amezúa, "cosa lógica, porque a la común credulidad de entonces en las artes supersticiosas juntaba ella su condición femenina. La mujer fué siempre mucho más crédula que el hombre" (logical, because to the credulity then common in the superstitious arts she added her feminine condition. Women were always more credulous that men) (xxviii).

27. Walter Kendrick, in *The Secret Museum: Pornography in Modern Culture,* decided that it was impossible to define pornography, whether ancient or modern, elite or popular. Says Williams, "Kendrick decides that the only workable definition of pornography . . . is simply whatever representations a particular dominant class or group does not want in the hands of another, less dominant class or group. Those in power construct the definition of pornography through their power to censor it" (Williams 1989, 11–12).

28. María del Pilar Palomo (1976) also dedicates several pages to Zayas in her interesting analysis of the structure of the "novela cortesana" (courtly short stories, the term Amezúa applied to the genre of the novella in seventeenth-century Spain). Following the development of the genre from its roots in *Calila e Dimna* through don Juan Manuel and Boccaccio, she divides them into two basic forms: (1) a structure of "juxtaposed" tales, each independent of the others, such as that of Cervantes *Novelas ejemplares.* This group includes many collections told within a unifying social frame as in the case of Boccaccio and Zayas; and (2) "coordinated" stories that are constructed within the universe of an overall narrative, as in Tirso's *Deleitar enseñando.* Her study of Zayas concerns primarily the relationship between the stories and frame narrative. See Chapter 10.

29. Spaniards and many foreign Hispanists as well, says Goytisolo, continue to demonstrate a willed blindness to anything but canonical views of the Spanish Golden Age as an era of honor and faith. One of the most interesting elements of this rich and insightful article is his thesis that the repression of eroticism in Spanish letters was a product not only of the Counter-Reformation or a bourgeois rejection of animality for rationality, but also of a particular Castilian response to the caste conflict in early modern Spain, in which sensuality was associated with a repudiated Islamic heritage.

30. The Williamsen-Whitenack (1995) collection of essays contains a useful bibliography of Zayas studies up to 1975 as well as a number of important articles. Particularly useful for my own focus are those of Dorfkle, El Saffar, and Stroud and that of Williamsen, who adds to her earlier insights on the importance of the ironic mode and gendered discourse in Zayas.

31. See Jameson's discussion of the role of envy and loathing in animating the dialectic of group and class identity. "Whatever group or identity investment may be at work in envy, its libidinal opposite always tends to transcend the dynamics of the group relationship in the direction of that of class proper," says Jameson (1993, 36). He proposes as one of the objectives of cultural studies the analysis of the interplay of these overlapping, sometimes conflicting, subject positions. Such an analysis, however difficult, "restores to culture its hidden inner meaning as the space of the symbolic moves of groups in agonistic relation to each other" (38–39).

Chapter 3

1. Pfandl calls this an "obscene novel" and says that "casi no es más que una libertina enumeración de diversas aventuras de amor, porque su pretendido profundo sentido (la

cuestión de si verdaderamente la mujer ha de ser tonta para ser fiel) no aparece hasta muy tarde y con poca claridad" (it is little more than a libertine enumeration of various amorous adventures, because its supposed profound meaning—the question of whether a woman really has to be foolish to be faithful—only appears belatedly and with little clarity) (1933, 369). See also Felten, 1978, 96–99.

2. María del Pilar Oñate did not include Zayas in her survey of the history of feminism in Spanish literature.

3. Even the voice of the preface is, in Zayas as in all other authors, that of a fictionalized authorial persona, as is evident in Genette's survey of the many poses common in prefaces (1987, 150ff.).

4. See also Teresa de Lauretis's revisitation of this debate and the reductive dichotomy set up in the U.S. between the explanations of sexuality of Freud and Foucault (de Lauretis 1998).

5. We see such an essentialist concept of feminine writing employed in regard to Zayas both negatively and positively, explicitly and implicitly, in critics as diverse as Pfandl and Sylvania, Amezúa and Paul Julian Smith. Alison Weber (1990), however, presents a persuasive case for Saint Theresa's use of an *écriture féminine* as a strategy, a discourse of subordination.

6. In Laqueur's words, "Almost everything one wants to *say* about sex—however sex is understood—already has in it a claim about gender. Sex, in both the one-sex and the two-sex worlds, is situational; it is explicable only within the context of battles over gender and power" (1990, 11). The relationship between the definition of the human physiology and the interests of the state is foregrounded by Huarte de San Juan as the fundamental justification for his treatise *El examen de ingenios para las ciencias*. Huarte offers his study to the king as the best grounds for efficient utilization of the capacities of his subjects, based on a comprehension of the physiological basis of differing human capacities. See his two "Proemios," to the king and to the reader (149–65), and the introduction by Guillermo Serés, 26–30. As we will see below, Zayas reacted to Huarte's definition of the humoral inferiority of women, overturning its terms.

7. Some degree of essentialism is perhaps inevitable in positing a specifically feminine experience.

8. This translation is at best an approximation of this tricky and important passage. Boyer translates "engaños de pensado" as "clever thinking," but admits that a more literal translation is "intentional deceptions." *De pensado* is defined in *Autoridades* as "intentional" or "with forethought"; *agudo* can mean "sharp," keen-edged," "witty," or "clever," and is thus close to the colloquial use of "sharp"; "ingenio" or "wit," a vital concept in Baroque literary esthetics, meriting a book-length exposition by Gracián (1998). *Engaño* is an equally central term in the philosophy of the Baroque. Covarrubias defines it as a trick or deception performed with wit and astuteness and connects its derivation with the French term *enginnier* because "el que engaña es ingenioso y astuto" (he who deceives is witty and astute); ([1611] 1979, 519). *De pensado* according to the *Diccionario de autoridades* ([1732] 1979) means "de intento, u con consideración antecedente" (intentionally, or considered in advance).

9. Huarte's book was put on the Inquisition's list of forbidden books in Portugal in 1581 and in Spain in 1583. The principal objections of the theologians were that his insistence on the organic foundation of intelligence conflicted with the fundamental doctrines of free will and the immortality of the soul. Huarte's revised version was published posthumously in 1594. See Serés's introduction (Huarte de San Juan 1989, 110–13).

10. The first story of creation in Genesis that recounted God's simultaneous creation of man and woman in his image might be recovered, or the creation story otherwise rewritten to dignify women. See Surtz 1990 for an account of the creation story as told by Sor Juana de la Cruz. The prevailing version, of woman's secondary creation from Adam's rib, with the assignation of guilt to Eve for trespassing God's commandment, generally served to justify the sub-

ordination of women to men and the Pauline injunction of feminine silence. But resolute defenders of women reinterpreted this story as well, assigning first guilt to Adam and saying that while he was made of the dust of the earth, Eve was wrought from a more worthy matter, the flesh of man. See Espinosa 1990, 149–54 and Rodríguez del Padrón 1884, 88–89. For an account of fifteenth-century defenses of women, see Matulka 1931, 3–37. In the second half of the fifteenth century, Teresa de Cartagena, a nun and daughter of the *converso* rabbi Pablo de Santa María, argued that men were superior to women only in physical strength, a balance necessary for human survival, that God had made women as well as men and could endow any woman with the capacity to write, as he had given her the capacity to write two religious treatises, the *Arboleda de los enfermos* (Grove for the Ill) and the *Admiraçion operum dey* (Admiration of the Works of God). She, like Zayas, argues that custom alone keeps women from writing (Vicente García 1989).

11. Laquer posits that from the Greeks through the seventeenth century the predominate model of sex was a one-sex model, not the two-sex model of radical dimorphism, of anatomical and physiological incommensurability between males and females that has prevailed since the eighteenth century (Laqueur 1990, 1–6, 79–88). In her thorough study of medieval accounts of sexual difference, however, Cadden (1993) demonstrates that his description is overly simplistic, and Laquer (1990, 30–35 and 254 n. 25) admits the existence of a kind of two-sex model at least as early as Aristotle's definition of the female as material, male as form.

12. Covarrubias's *Tesoro de la Lengua* of 1611 has no entry for *ovaries*, only for *testicles*, but the *Diccionario de autorides* of 1737 does include not one but two, the first of which is architectural—they are described as "cierta especie de moldura tallada en forma de huevos, con una listilla que los guarnece" (a certain kind of molding cut in the form of eggs, with a little ribbon decorating them)—and the second anatomical: "Se llaman en la Anatomía los testículos de la hembra. . . . Tienen también las mugeres dos testículos, que los modernos Anatómicos llaman *ovarios*, porque demuestran que están llenos de huevos" (They are called in Anatomy the female testicles. . . . Women also have two testicles, which modern Anatomists call *ovaries*, because they show that they are full of eggs).

13. Huarte describes at length the different balances of heat with dryness or wetness that he judges optimal for development of the three mental faculties of understanding, imagination, and memory (321–46).

14. For example: "Los niños que se engendran de simiente fría y seca, como son los hijos habidos en la vejez, a muy pocos días y meses después de nacidos comienzan a discurrir y filosofar; porque el temperamento frío y seco . . . es muy apropriado para las obras del ánima racional" (Children who are engendered from cold and dry seed, as are sons had in old age, within a few days and months of being born begin to reason and philosophize; because the cold and dry temperament . . . is very apt for works of the rational spirit) (316). Teresa Soufas shows that other women writers also took advantage of the ambiguities and contradictions of humoral theories of gender differences to claim for themselves the creative intellectual powers associated with the coldness of the melancholic temper so widely associated with women only in terms of negative irrationality and emotional instability (Soufas 1996a).

15. In contrast, women of "good condition," possessing a full measure of cold, damp feminine humors, are not upset by anything, laugh at every occasion and sleep well, according to Huarte (616).

16. For examples of this practice by other women writers, see Scott (1994) and Sabat-Rivers 1987. I am happy to acknowledge my debt to two "foremothers" who helped me in the work of identifying Zayas's learned women: Nina Scott for her article on Sor Juana's list of exemplary women, which gave me invaluable information and important source indications, and Rolena Adorno, who provided me with copies of Scott's article in its preliminary and final forms.

17. See Yllera's notes in her edition of the *Desengaños* (Zayas y Sotomayor 1983, 230–32) for an identification of these women.

18. According to a modern editor of Lucan, his wife did play a role in the transmission of his poems: "Presumably, Lucan's papers, including the ms of the *Pharsalia*, came into the hands of Polla Argentaria after the deaths of her husband, his uncles and his father in 65 C.E" (Joyce introduction to Lucan, xiv).

19. See the forthcoming work of Shifra Armon on these ties.

20. See Irigarary 1994, Nye 1994, and Halperin 1990.

21. I render "lecciones de opinión" as "influential lessons" on the authority of the definition given in the *Diccionario de Autoridades* for "hacer opinión": "Vale ser hombre cuyo dictamen sirve por autoridad en qualquier materia" (indicates being a man whose opinion [or judgment] serves as an authority on any matter.) Zayas uses the verb "hacer" and Aspasia clearly was an influential figure in Athenian political and intellectual life. Boyer translates the phrase as "theoretical lessons," but neither the *Diccionario de Autoridades* nor Covarrubias's *Tesoro* lends support to that rendering.

22. He describes a literary/philosophical tradition in Socratic literature of Plato's day in which courtesans—Theodote or Aspasia—figured as teachers of men, primarily on erotic topics, which is the role apparently given Aspasia in two lost Socratic dialogues bearing her name, by Antisthenes and Aeschines. Halperin suggests that Plato followed the tradition of attributing a discourse on love to a woman, but in separating his erotic theory from that of Aeschines, he chose to make Diotima not a courtesan but a priestess, since prophetesses were also considered to have privileged access to religious wisdom (122–24).

23. Calderón, however, includes it in his dramatic reworking of the story of her life in *La gran Cenobia* (1959b), an early play about the mutability of fortune and the nature of legitimate rule. See de Armas (1986, 68–86).

24. Luna states that "é fállase que sopo las letras de Egipto, é que aprendió las Griegas por enseñanza de Longino, varón filósofo; por ayuda de lo qual facen memoria, que sopo todas las historias" (it happened that she knew the letters of Egypt and learned those of Greece from the teaching of Longinus, a philosophical man; on account of which they record that she knew all the histories) (Luna 1891, 278).

25. Zayas's source for this detail may well have been Calderón's dramatic reworking of Zenobia's life story in *La gran Cenobia*, performed in 1625 (Shergold and Varey 1961, 278), when Zayas was writing her *Novelas*, and included in the *Primera parte* of his *comedias* published in 1636. In that play, a treacherous court lady describes Zenobia with grudging admiration: "Su industria y valor es tal / que los triunfos que recibe / de día, de noche escribe; / libro que *Historia oriental* / llama" (Her industry and courage is such that the triumphs she achieves by day, she writes by night, in a book she calls the *Eastern History*) (Calderón de la Barca 1959b, 496).

26. The text is in this case that of the first edition of Zaragoza (1637b, fol. q7r). Between this princeps and the later version used by Amezúa, certain corrections were made in the text. One minor change was made in this sentence, a displacement of a connecting *y*. The later version reads: "que paso en silencio y por no alargarme, porque . . ." This weakens the causal explanation of her omission of more famous foremothers. In the first version she stops in order to avoid prolixity *and* because she presumes everyone knows all this. In the second, she passes over them in silence *and* in order to avoid prolixity, because they already know all this.

27. Upper-class women were tutored at home, to a greater or lesser degree. Beginning in the sixteenth century, schools for girls were established in convents, but these seemed to have been primarily for middle-class girls. Lower-class women were generally illiterate. Formal higher education was closed to women. The question of women's education is well treated by Vigil (1994, 39–60).

28. Cervantes' "friend" says that his difficulty in finding the learned authors and quotations to write a respectable preface can be easily solved by using a book that lists them all, from A to Z. As Martín de Riqueur's note to the relevant passage points out, this is a jibe at Lope's provision of an alphabetized list of authorities cited in his works *El peregrino en su patria*

and *Isidro* (Cervantes Saavedra 1971, 1:20, 24, and n. 20). My thanks to Elisa Rhodes for making this connection.

29. Zayas does not overtly define women as the weaker sex in her preface, but her narrators do explicitly place them in that position at strategic points in her stories, beginning with the opening paragraph of her first *novela,* which contrasts the "flacas fuerzas de las mujeres" (weak wills of women) with the "claros y heroicos entendimientos de los hombres" (clear and heroic understanding of men) (*Novelas,* 37).

Chapter 4

1. This reminder of men's debt to women is not Zayas's invention or innovation, of course. It was a standard feature in debates about the nature of women. See, for example, Castiglione (1967, 243). In Calderón's *El alcalde de Zalamea,* Pedro Crespo includes it in his advice to his son Juan as he leaves to become a soldier: "No hables mal de las mujeres; / la más humilde, te digo / que es digna de estimación, / porque, al fin, dellas nacimos" (Don't speak ill of women; the humblest one, I tell you, is worthy of respect, for, in the end, we are born of them) (Calderón de la Barca 1981, 245). Lope, in *El premio del bien hablar,* extends it past the nine-month debt. The hero, don Juan, who twice duels with men who verbally abuse women, says "Que es honrar a las mujeres / deuda a que obligados nacen / todos los hombres de bien / por el hospedaje / que de nueve meses, deben y es razón que se pague; / que, puesto que son las lenguas / espadas, para templarse / quiso Dios que las pusiesen / en los pechos de sus madres" (that to honor women is an obligation of all men of goodwill from birth, for the debt of nine months' lodging, and it is right that they should pay it; for, since tongues are swords, God wanted them to be put to their mothers' breasts to be tempered) (Vega Carpio 1859, 375). Rather, it is Zayas's use of it as the concluding and presumably climactic argument of her preface that is significant.

2. As Giorgio Barberi Squarotti (1983) points out, the ingenious construction of this confession lies partly in the fact that he saves for the end and prefaces with long lament the only true sin, which at the same time is the most remote in his personal history as well as insignificant. The power of this confession is derived from Ciappalletto's appropriation of religious rhetoric—the rhetoric of confession—so thoroughly that he cannot be discovered, and the rhetoric itself gives it the power to make falsehood true, as true miracles are performed on his grave.

3. Guido Almansi, after reviewing the multiple interpretations of the story and quoting the weeping Ciappelletto, summarizes: "The critic Muscetta has argued in a revealing passage that the grief of the hardened old paederast over the way he offended his mother shows great psychological finesse. But what does this last formula really mean? In whose particular brain is this finesse supposed to be located? In Cepperello's? In Boccaccio's? Or in that of Muscetta and myself and thousands of other readers ogling and salivating at the outrageous spectacle of a nasty old queer weeping made-up tears over his poor dead mother who bore him inside her for nine long months? This is the critical point: if this one story sanctions literature as falsehood, then this particular scene sanctions the act of reading as a descent into transgression and indecency" (1975, 49).

4. There is a psychic logic to this infantile "first word" that we can comprehend through Lacanian explanations of the entry of the subject into the Symbolic order. It is the intervention of the third term, the phallic signifier, that breaks up the mythic mother-infant symbiosis. The infant learns by experience that s/he is not the "phallus," the desire of the (m)Other, that she comes and goes, that she desires elsewhere as well. She is, therefore, a "puta" (whore). At the same time, it is the rupture of that mythic symbiosis by the third term or phallic signifier that makes possible and necessary the child's acquisition of language. (One does

not need to name what is always present, or felt to be present.) The child takes up language him/herself to survive, to negotiate that loss. For a related analysis of the role of the maternal in the *Coloquio* from the perspective of Kristeva's theory of abjection, see Garces 1993.

5. See Bourland 1973, 10, and her bibliography. Anne Cayuela's dissertation provides a valuable update and extension of Bourland's data.

6. "He pensado que tienen las novelas los mismos preceptos que las comedias, cuyo fin es haber dado su autor contento y gusto al pueblo, aunque se ahorque el arte, y esto, aunque va dicho al descuido, fue opinión de Aristóteles" (I have thought that the same precepts apply to novellas as to *comedias*, whose objective is for the author to please the people, although art be hanged, and this was Aristotle's opinion, even if it is carelessly stated) (Vega Carpio 1988, 103). Given Lope's ironic play with conventions in the metanarrative "intercolunios" (interstices) in *Marcia Leonarda* (e.g., the reference to Aristotle precisely in the moment of proclaiming freedom from classical precepts), this cannot be taken as a straightforward theoretical statement. However, the interpenetration of themes, imagery, styles of characterization and plotting strategies between the novella and the *comedia* are clear in Lope's four novellas, as they are in Tirso's *Cigarrales de Toledo*. See Brownlee 1981 for a discussion of the Lope's debate with Cervantes on the novella form.

7. Cervantes' complex development of character and open-ended dramatic works also set him apart—in fact made his *comedias* and *entremeses* (interludes) unsaleable to Golden Age theater companies. Yet Francisco Sánchez (1993) argues that his works are organized around theatrically designed scenes. Plots migrate freely from *comedias* and *entremeses* to novellas and back again; e.g., in Cervantes' *El celoso extremeño* and *El viejo celoso* .

8. Lugo y Dávila's full title is *Teatro popular: Novelas morales para mostrar los géneros de vidas del pueblo y afectos, costumbres, y pasiones del ánimo con aprovechamiento parar todas personas*. In his "Introducción a las novelas," Lugo y Dávila is one of the first to attempt a theoretical definition of prose fiction as a genre. He grounds it on the same Aristotelian concept of imitation regularly cited for drama, as the following passages demonstrate: "Esta fábula [la novela] es imitación de la acción, y no dijo de las acciones, porque no le es permitido a la novela abrazar más que una acción, así como la tragedia" (This tale [the novella] is an imitation of the action, and I do not say 'actions' because it is not permissible for the novella to include more than one action, as in tragedy) (1906, 22); "Digo que la novela es un poema regular, fundado en la imitación; porque toda la poética, según la definió Aristóteles, es imitación de la naturaleza" (I say that the novella is a regular poem, based on imitation; because all poetry, as Aristotle defined it, is an imitation of nature) (24); and he uses the same metaphor applied to the theatre from Cicero to Shakespeare and Lope, calling it a mirror in which human events are reflected and men find examples of the conduct they should follow or avoid (26).

9. Mothers were similarly scarce in drama elsewhere in early modern Europe; Eric Nicolson says that women were catalogued in relationship to men, in "normative roles—the virginal maid, chaste wife, and celibate widow—and transgressive ones—adulteress, prostitute, courtesan, and procuress" (Nicholson 1993, 296). The omission of the mother from such a list is linked by Coppélia Kahn to "a patriarchal conception of the family in which children owe their existence to their fathers alone; the mother's role in procreation is eclipsed by the father's, which is used to affirm male prerogative and male power" (Kahn 1986, 35–36). Shakespeare did, however, create noteworthy mothers in *Hamlet* and *Coriolanus* and in his late romances, and Amy Williamsen-Cerón (1984) has pointed out the danger of imprecise generalizations in her analysis of two significant exceptions to the rule of maternal absence, the mother-daughter pairs in Lope's *La discreta enamorada* and in Mira de Amescua's *La casa del tahur*. Faliu-Lacourt (1979) also suggests that critics have overlooked the significance of mothers who are present in the *comedia*, particularly in the works of Guillén de Castro.

10. Taking into account unpublished convent drama written by women such as Lope's daughter might well alter and enrich the overall picture. But female-authored dramas re-

cently published by Soufas (1996b) follow the masculine paradigm in omitting representation of mothers.

11. In their introduction to *Quixotic Desire*, El Saffar and Wilson (1993, 13) posit a parallel between an increasing focus in post-Freudian psychoanalysis on the mother-child relationship neglected by Freud in his focus on the father figure, and a "fascination with and focus on the mother . . . in the later works of Cervantes."

12. See Sánchez 1993, 46–56 and Forcione 1982, 375–76, 386–87.

13. The mothers of both Ricaredo and Arnesto also attempt to further the love interests of their sons in *La española inglesa*. Ricaredo's mother convinces his father to allow him to marry Isabela, and Arnesto's mother, the *camarera mayor* to the queen, pleads his case with the queen, who has promised Isabela to Ricaredo. The mother of the duke in *La señora Cornelia* is a shadowy blocking figure to her son's open marriage to Cornelia, much less threatening than corresponding paternal figures in Zayas.

14. Preciosa (*La fuerza de la sangre*), Leonisa (*El amante liberal*), Isabela (*La española inglesa*), Leocadia (*La fuerza de la sangre*).

15. Cornelia (*La señora Cornelia*) and Leocadia (*Las dos doncellas*); Teodosia, in *Las dos doncellas*, does refer to her parents as living. Costanza, the product of don Diego's rape of her noble mother, has been raised without knowing her mother, who died when she was young. Mother-daughter separation is not the rule in all novella collections, however. In the stories of Céspedes y Meneses, mothers play an extremely important role, as both helpers and obstacles in the path of true love for their daughters. Lope includes mothers, but not as significant actants.

16. Kristeva describes the abject as a pre-object, or pseudo-object, that only surfaces in breaches in secondary repression; it is the "object" of primary repression, the first insecure division of the "je" from the preceding and enveloping (m)Other. "L'abject nous confronte . . . à nos tentatives les plus anciennes de nous démarquer de l'entité *maternelle* avant même que d'ex-ister en dehors d'elle grâce à l'autonomie du langage. Démarquage violent et maladroit, toujours guetté par la rechute dans la dépendance d'un pouvoir aussi sécurisant qu'étouffant" (Kristeva 1980). "The abject confronts us . . . with our earliest attempts to release the hold of the *maternal* entity even before ex-isting outside of her, thanks to the autonomy of language. It is a violent, clumsy breaking away, with the constant risk of falling back under the sway of a power as securing as it is stifling" (1982, 13).

17. Melloni (1976, 91) finds mothers nearly nonexistent in Zayas, and Montesa says that the few mothers who are included are hazily drawn and powerless:

> No es un factor *útil* a la hora de complicar el desarrollo de los hechos y, por tanto, queda marginado. Se le cita en ocasiones, pero es un personaje desdibujado, sin características propias. De ello podemos deducir el papel secundario que en la realidad desempeñaba. La única faceta destacable es el amor a los hijos. A veces sufre, impotente y distante, la agresividad que el padre desarrolla contra la hija (II, 6), pero carece de autoridad o persuasión para evitarla . . . su carácter es más bien blando y consentidor, especialmente para los hijos varones que, en cuanto alcanzan cierta edad, escapan a su autoridad. (Montesa Peydro 1981, 276–77)

> (She is not a *useful* factor at the time of complicating the development of events and therefore remains marginal. She is mentioned occasionally but is a sketchy character, without her own characteristics. From that we can deduce the secondary role that she played in reality. Her only noteworthy facet is love for her children. Sometimes she suffers, powerless and distant, the aggressiveness that the father develops against their daughter (II, 6), but she lacks authority or persuasive power to avoid it . . . rather, her character is bland and permissive, especially for her sons who, as soon as they reach a certain age, escape her authority.)

18. In the *Desengaños*, Zayas gives explicit narrative voice exclusively to women, and therefore adds female narrators to replace the silenced males, but does not mention the presence or absence of their mothers.

19. In the *Heptameron* of Marguerite de Navarre, in contrast, the five male and five female storytellers narrate and debate from more individualized and explicitly divergent perspectives, but never draw into two such rigidly separated camps.

20. Zizek makes the point that there is no link between the biological opposition of male and female and the "two asymmetrical antinomies of symbolization (the 'masculine' side that involves the universality of the phallic function grounded in an exception; the 'feminine' side that involves a 'non-all' field which, for that very reason, contains no exception to the phallic function); they represent two heteronomous systems grafted together, so that our sexuality is a *bricolage*" (1994, 155). Explanations of sexual division are related to various philosophical attempts to move from the Particular to the Universal, moves often based on an exclusion which is necessary to guarantee the consistency of the posited Universal. Male and female are not two parts of a Whole, but "two (failed) attempts to symbolize this Whole" (160).

21. This includes *Desengaño 4,* whose explicit narrator is female, but within which the internal narrating voice is masculine.

22. For a related reading of the importance of maternal absence in Zayas focused on her *Desengaño 5,* see Cruz 1996.

23. Jacinta's first-person narrative within this narrative also begins with a statement of the exemplary value of her tale of passion and the suffering it has caused. For an analysis of Zayas's work in the tradition of the *exemplum,* as well as of the rhetorical strategy of her contradictory invocation of women's frailty and men's clear and heroic understanding, see Chapter 10 below.

24. Of the many occurrences of this motif in narrative fiction as well as in the crossdressed abandoned heroines of the *comedia,* the most famous today is Cervantes' Dorotea, in part 1, chap. 28 of *Don Quixote.*

25. See Feal 1993 for a related reading of the Sierra Morena as don Quixote and Cardenio's retreat from the law of the "Terrible Father" to the Imaginary and the pure yet threatening maternal womb of nature.

26. Surviving a perilous storm at sea, a group of lovers in Castillo Solórzano's *Lisardo enamorado* (1613) find themselves near "aquella áspera montaña de Monserrat, sitio venerado de tantas naciones por ser erario santo de la más preciosa joya de los cielos, en quien puso tantos primores su divino artífice" (that rugged mountain, Montserrat, a site venerated by so many nations for being the holy treasury of the heavens' most precious jewel, so exquisitely worked by the divine artisan). They all decide to express their gratitude by visiting "el divino santuario de la Madre del Verbo divino" (the divine sanctuary of the Mother of the divine Word) (Castillo Solorzano 1947, 255). The reunited and reconciled lovers in Cervantes' story *Las dos doncellas* also make a pilgrimage, first to Montserrat and then to Santiago, but Cervantes does not mention that it is a shrine to Mary, saying only that "en tres días llegaron a Monserrate, y estando allí otros tantos, haciendo lo que a buenos católicos cristianos debían, con el mismo espacio volvieron a su camino, y sin sucederles revés ni desmán alguno llegaron a Santiago" (Cervantes Saavedra 1990, 386).

27. In her introduction to *El Monserrate Segundo* (1602) by Cristobal de Virués (1984, 24–25), Hicks lists among the distinguished sixteenth-century pilgrims Carlos V, Maximilian of Austria, don Juan de Austria, the duke of Alba, the duke of Saboya, and Philip II, who made several visits.

28. In Zayas's first story, after visiting the monastery, Fabio climbs to the remote "Cave of Saint Anthony, "la más áspera como prodigiosa, respecto de las cosas que allí se ven; tanto de las penitencias de los que las habitan, como de los asombros que les hacen los demonios" (the most rugged as well as the most marvelous, with respect to the things that are seen there, both the penitence of those that inhabit them and the amazing things the demons do to them)

(*Novelas*, 38). The reunited lovers in Castillo Solórzano's *Lizardo enamorado* (1629) ascend the mountain "a ver las devotas hermitas de ella donde les edificaron grandamente las estrañas penitencias de aquellos santos hermitaños que habitaban aquellos devotos oratorios" (to see the devout hermitages on it where they were greatly edified by the strange penitence of those saintly hermits who inhabit those devout oratories) (Castillo Solorzano 1947, 261). Engravings of Montserrat also show the mountain dotted with hermitages, and some are surrounded by vignettes of the life of Darin.

29. The last two lovers, don Jaime and Dorothea, do not appear physically in Montserrat but their story is related there by don Jaime's page (Castillo Solórzano 1947, 281–92). One lover, don Lope, driven mad by (well-deserved) frustration in love, is cured during the pilgrimage; don Gutierre, whose beloved was killed by a rival, remains as a hermit.

30. The Cervantine criticism of Diana de Armas Wilson provides several superb examples of such a fruitful critical dialogue. See Wilson 1993.

31. At least in his early formulation of the theory of dream interpretation, Freud indicated that the meaning of dream symbols was individual and contextual, and emerged through the dreamer's own interpretation of their latent and displaced significance. He did add material to later editions of *The Interpretation of Dreams* that encouraged the idea of the existence of a fixed code, a sort of universal dictionary of symbolism in dreams that has been further reified by certain of his psychoanalytic followers and by trivializing "Freudian" readings of literary works. Lacan has rejected this later Freudian approach (Wilden 1981, 232; Ragland-Sullivan 1986, 166–75).

32. See *The Interpretation of Dreams*, 9, 145 and "Creative Writers and Day-Dreaming." Diana de Armas Wilson quotes Freud's conclusion to a 1932 lecture on the "dark continent" of femininity: " 'Turn to the poets, if you want to know more about femininity.' " Wilson continues: "As psychoanalysis, . . . turns the question of femininity back to literature, at last heeding Freud's own advice, literature will be held to a fuller accounting of earlier representations of love and sexuality" (1991, xiv–xv). Freud's sentence in full: "If you want to know more about femininity, enquire from your own experiences of life, or turn to the poets, or wait until science can give you deeper and more coherent information." (1974, 22:135).

33. See Greer 1991b, 62–72 and Stein 1993, 144–74. Mercury says: "Yo le he de representar / en las fantasmas de un sueño / toda su historia, con que / alentado a un mismo tiempo / y desconfiado viva; pues ignorando y creyendo, / ni aquello le tendrá soberbio" (I will present his history to him in the phantasms of a dream so that he might live encouraged and doubting at the same time, for not knowing and believe, neither the one will make him arrogant) (Calderón de la Barca 1959a, 1827).

34. See, for example, Calderón's *auto sacramental El verdadero Dios Pan*, or Sor Juana's *El cetro de José*. Heffernan (1988, 202–10) reports in detail the dreams of Saint Perpetua, an "allegorized foretelling" of her impending martyrdom, dreams she considered sent by God.

35. Fray Luis de León, after an interview with Lucrecia, concluded that her interesting dreams showed no "sure sign of God," but rather were the product of a "vertiginous spirit," and suggested exorcism rather than punishment (Kagan 1990, 121).

36. Saint Teresa describes the wounding dart of love in *Las moradas* (1588). See the Sixth *morada*, chap. 2 (Teresa de Jesús 1972, 57).

37. Bernini's rendition of Saint Teresa in ecstasy is key to Lacan's explanation of a feminine *jouissance* beyond the phallus. See Lacan (1982, 137–61), and Jacqueline Rose's observations in the introduction to that volume, p. 52.

38. Dorothy J. Thompson (1994), lecturing on records of dreams by Greek and Egyptian dreamers in Ptolemaic Saqqara in the second century BC, observed that dreams were given great importance for their predictive value; that they owed their content to hopes and fears, to everyday concerns, both sexual and economic, of the dreamers; that they drew much of their imagery from the visual content—geographic, architectural, and religious, of their cultural context; and that literary echoes frequently appear in their recording.

39. For a reading of Fabio as ideal analyst, see my earlier version of part of this chapter in Greer 1995, 96–98.

40. Lucrecia de León too dreamed of a mysterious "Miguel" who first appeared masked and imprisoned, then in many other guises: prophet, shepherd, a monarch who is a "New David," and finally as her husband. Kagan comments: "Miguel's varied personae are difficult to interpret, but it seems likely that Miguel-Piedrola represents Lucrecia's conception of the good governor, compared to Philip [II], the bad governor. If one chooses a Freudian interpretation, Lucrecia's marriage to Miguel and her elevation to queen reads as an Oedipal fantasy in which Lucrecia rejects her evil dream father, the king, and displaces him by marrying Miguel, the ideal governor-father" (Kagan 1990, 73).

41. This is a polysemous phrase, since *sueño* means both "sleep" and "dream" in Spanish, and *pesado* has multiple meanings: deep or heavy, bothersome or impertinent, offensive, hard, strong, or violent, and laden with humors or vapors.

42. Bergmann 1990, 168. She coins this phrase in analyzing the poetic portraits of women written by Sor Juana Inés de la Cruz, and Octavio Paz's puzzled vacillation in reading them. Bergmann terms the portraits "a direct confrontation with the cultural constitution of the female as the passive object of contemplation. . . . The female object of desire, treated as a passive statue in male poetic discourse, is revealed in Sor Juana's poetry to have been listening all along, and to be capable of mimicking the same discourse in a disconcerting way" (168). According to Clover, active female gaze in modern horror movies is a characteristic of the sexually repressed "Final Girl," whose partial appropriation of phallic characteristics is important in her capacity to survive and to "castrate" her assailants in the climactic scenes (1992, 48–49).

43. Matthew Stroud has studied the importance of this phenomenon in Zayas's *comedia*, *La traición en la amistad*, in relation to Lacan's theory of the gaze (Stroud 1995, 156–58). It is, he says, the look of the other or the gaze "that opens up for the subject the realization that one is not complete" (156–57). In a brief summary of Lacan's complex theory, Stroud comments, "Of great importance is the fact that it is not merely a matter of the subject's seeing the other, or the subject's being seen by the other, but rather that one sees oneself being seen by the other. In a real sense, one is defined by the gaze of others, of the Other" (156–57 n. 73). See also "Voyeurism/Exhibitionism/The Gaze" in Wright (1992, 447–50). In this entry, Elizabeth Grosz criticizes the use of a Sartrean concept of the look by certain feminist film critics, who characterized it as objectifying, subjugating, and masculine. As Grosz says, while certain "uses" of vision can objectify and reinforce patriarchal power relations, vision itself cannot be conceived as masculine.

44. The economic subtext of Zayas's stories merits an extended exploration. Attention should be paid not only to overtly discussed issues such a dowries, mayorazgos, venality in official circles and servants' quarters, etc., but also in its figuration through dress. For example, even in the perilous moment when Jacinta leaves her house at night, she remarks that she is in the street barefoot and wearing nothing but a "faldellín de damasco verde, con pasamanos de plata" (a petticoat of green damask, with silver braid) (*Novelas,* 57). The articles of Charnon-Deutsch and Kaminsky offer intelligent insights on these topics.

45. Eyes and scopic effects are important throughout her novels. One of her more interesting poems is the décima in *Desengaño 8:* "De la memoria, los ojos / se quejan" (My eyes complain of memory).

46. Quevedo employs similar imagery in a sonnet about a wound of love, but from a masculine perspective it figures not the onset of desire but the pain of rejection and the inability to see the beloved's face:

> Soñé que el brazo de rigor armado,
> Filis, alzabas contra el alma mía,
> diciendo: "Éste será el postrero día
> que ponga fin a tu vivir cansado."

Y que luego, con golpe acelerado
me dabas muerte en sombra de alegría,
y yo, triste, al infierno me partía,
viéndome ya del cielo desterrado.
    Partí sin ver el rostro amado y bello;
mas despertóme deeste sueño un llanto,
ronca la voz, y crespo mi cabello.
    Y lo que más en esto me dio espanto
es ver que fuese un sueño algo de aquello
que me pudiera dar tormento tanto.

(I dreamed. Filis, that you raised your arm in rigor against my soul, saying 'This will be the final day that will put an end to your weary life'; and then, with a swift blow you gave me death in the shadow of (your) joy and I, forlorn, left for hell, seeing myself already exiled from heaven. I left without seeing your beautiful, beloved face; but a cry woke me from this dream, my voice hoarse, my hair curled. And what most terrified me was seeing that the dream was but a part of that which gives me such torment.) (1969, 529).

47. Freud explained heterosexual male development as proceeding through an Oedipus complex of love for the mother and rivalry with the father, which is resolved by the operation of castration anxiety when the boy recognizes the absence of a penis in the female genitals, gives up incestuous desire for the mother and identifies with the father. After relinquishing the idea of the father as the girl's first love, Freud eventually came to posit penis envy (the castration complex) as the pivotal factor that initiates rather than resolves the female Oedipus complex, engineering a double turn: of erotogenic zone (clitoral to vaginal) and of object choice, from the mother, now resented for bringing the girl into the world so "ill equipped," to the father and thence to other possessors of the penis capable of providing the ultimate penis-substitute, a baby. Freud's largely discredited explanation of female sexuality has raised controversy, from the statements of Ernest Jones, Karen Horney and Melanie Klein in the 1920s, to the sarcasm of Irigaray.

48. Freud does not see the adoption of these positions as bound by anatomy, however. For him, all human beings are initially bisexual and take on psychic gender by suppressing primarily either the active, masculine element or the passive, female side of their nature. The suppression is never total, nevertheless. In Freud's essay "A Child is Being Beaten" (1974, 17:177–204), we can see the close relationship between the constructions of fiction and the complex fantasies of masochism.

49. Foa (1979, 78–100) comments on the pervasiveness of images of war in Zayas's description of the relation between the sexes, and relates it to the philosophy of the epoch. By the second volume, "husband" has become a synonym for "enemy": "un marido, que con este nombre se califica de enemigo" (a husband, for with this name he is classed as an enemy) (Desengaños, 428).

50. See "Guiding Remarks for a Congress on Feminine Sexuality" in Lacan 1982, 92–93.

51. See, in particular, Silverman 1988, and Clover.

52. Flaubert addressed this flexibility from the author's standpoint in his classic declaration, "Madame Bovary, c'est moi." For an analysis of cross-gender audience identification, see Clover 1992, 234–35, 237.

53. E.g., Tirso in the comedia En Madrid y en una casa: "Pintan al competidor como a un Narciso los celos" (act 3, line 1262); and in Doña Beatriz de Silva, in which the emperor is called "un Narciso" (893); or Ruíz de Alarcón, in La verdad sospechosa, act 2, lines 1341–43, describing don García's pretense of being an indiano rico: "que debió de imaginar / que aquí le ha de aprovechar / más ser Midas que Narciso" (Ruiz de Alarcón 1982, 391).

54. See, for example, 95–96, 102, 112. Parker (1968) rejects Pfandl's psychological reading as irrelevant, blind to the "logic of literary influences" (272); the significant sources for her *auto* were for Parker not psychic division but literary traditions—use of the language of human love to represent the relationship between the human soul and God learned from the Song of Songs and mystic writings as well as the Calderonian model for the allegorical use of classical mythology in constructing the *auto sacramental*.

55. Freud postulated a primary narcissism tied to ego-libido, or the self-preservation instinct, followed by a secondary narcissism that he saw as a way station between infantile auto-eroticism and object love. In Freud's theory, complete achievement of the transition to object love marks the masculine position, while for the female, puberty "seems to bring about an intensification of the original narcissism, and this is unfavorable to the development of a true object-choice with its accompanying sexual overvaluation" (1974, 14:88). A person who loves by the narcissistic type may choose as object, said Freud "(a) what he himself is (i.e. himself), (b) what he himself was, (c) what he himself would like to be, [or] (d) someone who was once part of himself" ("On Narcissism" 1974, 14:90). Freud also says: "The determinants of women's choice of an object are often made unrecognizable by social conditions. Where the choice is able to show itself freely, it is often made in accordance with the narcissistic ideal of the man whom the girl had wished to become" (1974, 22:132–33).

56. Recognition of the relevance of the Eco and Narcissus myth to mystical love is not unique to Sor Juana. Parker describes two other autos that utilize it—with less "poetic imagination" than Sor Juana (Parker 1968, 263), and Paz recognizes as a possible source the Epistola VI of Francisco de Aldana to Arias Montano, in which the contemplative soul is depicted as Eco before the divine Narcissus: "y ¿qué debiera ser, bien contemplando, / el alma sino un eco resonante / a la eterna Beldad que está llamando / y, desde el cavernoso y vacilante / cuerpo, volver mis réplicas de amores / al sobrecelestial Narciso amante" (and what, considering well, could the soul be but an echo resonating to the eternal Beauty that calls it, and from a cavernous and hesitant body, returns my loving replies to the loving Narcissus of the highest heaven?) (Aldana 1957, 59).

57. The suggestion of an androgynous appeal in Narcissus is not unique to Zayas. Guillén de Castro evokes the association comically in the opening scene of *El Narciso en su opinión* when his lackey Tadeo calls himself "entre lacayo y paje, / un criado hermofradita" (between lackey and page, a hermaphrodite servant) (1968, 27). His vowel confusion of *o* and *a* suggests a related gender confusion in his master's pride in his "hermosura."   '

58. This is not unique to Zayas, of course. A cautionary attitude toward any purely human, terrestial satisfaction is a part of the philosophy of *desengaño*. She is unique, however, in her depiction of the violence done to women.

59. In doña Alda's dream in the lovely ballad "En Paris está doña Alda," the death of love is prefigured as an inescapable bird of prey, and the truth of Roldán's death in Roncesvalles arrives in a bloodstained letter.

60. See the excellent exposition "death drive (Freud)" by Elisabeth Bronfen in Wright 1992.

61. See below on desire as lack.

62. Given the frequency with which Zayas and countless other Golden Age writers refer to virginity as a jewel, an obvious implication is that the jewel that is not there, when Jacinta opens the box, is her own virginity.

63. The Other is not necessarily the biological mother, but any first nurturer who is the locus of the infant's primary, undifferentiated identifications. "By separation, the subject finds, one might say, the weak point of the primal dyad of the signifying articulation, in so far as it is alienating in essence. It is in the interval between these two signifiers that resides the desire offered to the mapping of the subject in the experience of the discourse of the Other, of the first Other he has to deal with, let us say, by way of illustration, the mother. It is in so far

as his desire is beyond or falls short of what she says, of what she hints at, of what she brings out as meaning, it is in so far as his desire is unknown, it is in this point of lack, that the desire of the subject is constituted" (Lacan 1981, 218–19)

64. "Demand in itself bears on something other than the satisfactions it calls for. It is demand of a presence or of an absence—which is what is manifested in the primordial relation to the mother, pregnant with that Other to be situated *within* the needs that it can satisfy. . . . Thus desire is neither the appetite for satisfaction, nor the demand for love, but the difference that results from the subtraction of the first from the second. . . . For both partners in the relation, both the subject and the Other, it is not enough to be subjects of need, or objects of love, but they must stand for the cause of desire" (Lacan 1977).

65. See pages 127–28.

66. Describing his optical model of this metaphor, Lacan says:

> You will then see that it is in the Other that the subject is constituted as ideal, that he has to regulate the completion of what comes as ego, or ideal ego—which is not the ego ideal—that is to say, to constitute himself in his imaginary reality.
>
> But, certainly, it is in the space of the Other that he sees himself and the point from which he looks at himself is also in that space. Now, this is also the point from which he speaks, since in so far as he speaks, it is in the locus of the Other that he begins to constitute that truthful lie by which is initiated that which participates in desire at the level of the unconscious. (1981, 144)

67. In fact, it is a sonnet plus *estrambote,* an added concluding triplet. Poetic form thus seems to mimic psychic structure—recapitulation of a triangulated desire by a triplet appended to the sonnet form.

68. In the long, lyrical passage that evokes this relationship in the left column, she says: "Women doubtless reproduce among themselves the strange gamut of forgotten body relationships with their mothers." In the right-hand column that records the history of that relationship in religious discourse, she says, "The Virgin especially agrees with the repudiation of the other woman (which doubtless amounts basically to a repudiation of the woman's mother) by suggesting the image of A woman as Unique" (Kristeva 1987, 257–58). Michie (1989) discusses the continuing problem that recognition of the "other woman" has presented for feminist criticism.

69. Another mother-daughter pair represent in literal terms, the "place" of the threat of feminine rivalry in *Desengaño 8.* It is in the house of these noble but too free women and with their assistance that the "other woman" Clavela denounces the love between Mencía and Enrique that leads directly to the death of Mencía, and indirectly to that of doña Ana.

70. Fabio's function is akin to that which Hirsch (crediting Adrienne Rich) calls the "man-who-would-understand," a common device among nineteenth-century women writers. Such men help women negotiate sexual difference and accomplish the transition from mother to father; they help the heroine negotiate a socially and fictionally acceptable situation both within and without conventional marriage and avoid a full repetition of her mother's story (Hirsch 1989, 57–63): "Women writers do not simply hand their heroine from mother to father; they attempt to compensate for the loss of mothers by replacing authoritative fathers with other men who, endowed with nurturing qualities, might offer an alternative to patriarchal power and dominance. The female fantasy which emerges from this will to difference can be understood in Adrienne Rich's terms as the fantasy of 'the-man-who-would-understand,' the man who, unlike the father, would combine maternal nurturance with paternal power" (57–58).

71. Women not as sexual objects but as an ideal community. See Chapter 7 for discussion of the suggestion of homosexual and lesbian relationships in *Desengaños 6* and *7*.

72. In an earlier explanation (Greer 1995), I employed Nancy Chodorow's description of the cultural effects of how male-female definitions are effected and affected by the fact that women do virtually all the fundamental nurturing of infants. As Mitchell points out (Lacan 1982, 37 n. 4), her work might be classed as a sociologically oriented study of the process of gender *imprinting* and the reproduction of gender roles based on an assumed sexual identity. It is useful as a first approach to describing the interaction between social practice and culturally embedded narrative paradigms, and is more immediately accessible and acceptable for many women readers, but does not offer the profound engagement with the problem of the definition of sexual identity of Freudian and Lacanian theory.

73. Translation of the symbols representing the two genders on the upper half begins with the upper line on the masculine side: "There exists a subject who is not subject to castration," the "Ur-father" who can have access to all the women, and whose phallic *Nom/Non* "castrates" his sons and daughters, effecting their separation (partial for feminine subjects) from the mother and their concurrent induction into the Symbolic order. The lower line on the masculine side represents the necessary identification with and subjection to the paternal law for masculine subjects: "All subjects are subject to castration." On the feminine side of the graph, the top line is translated as "There does not exist a subject who is not subject to castration." There is no "Ur-mother" within the Symbolic order; hence the barred *La* below the line as well. Entry into subjectivity depends on separation from the mother by the intervention of the Third Term, the phallic signifier. Separation for feminine subjects is never complete, and the lower line therefore translates as "No subject is fully castrated," fully identified with and subordinated to the paternal signifier. See Fink 1991, from which this diagram is drawn. Or, in other words, female infants are taught to build their gender identity on similarity with the mother, whereas male infants are enjoined to build theirs on difference from her (Ragland-Sullivan 1991, 50–51).

74. See, for example, the importance for don Martín of Elena's mother's presence in *Desengaño 4*, discussed in Chapter 6.

75. Among protagonists who enter convents, women who have actively desired and pursued their lovers are more likely to become nuns, while those who have been more passive victims of male desire more often choose secular convent life. The difference will be explored in Chapter 5. In the case of the more passionate women, such as Serafina in *El prevenido engañado* (Forewarned but Not Forearmed), Zayas does emphasize their penitence.

76. Laura, of *La fuerza de amor* (The power of love), says that "ella estaba desengañada de lo que era el mundo y los hombres, y que así no quería más batallar con ellos, . . . Y que supuesto esto, ella se quería entrar en un monasterio, sagrado poderoso para valerse de las miserias a que las mujeres están sujetas" (she was disillusioned with the world and with men and didn't want to have to struggle with them any longer. . . . And in view of this, she wanted to enter a convent, a sturdy sanctuary that defends women against the miseries to which they are subjected) (*Novelas*, 246). In *El prevenido engañado* (see preceding note), at the death of don Fadrique, who had raised and married Gracia, Serafina's abandoned baby, "entró doña Gracia monja con su madre, contenta de haberse conocido las dos, porque como era boba, fácil halló el consuelo, gastando la gruesa hacienda que le quedó en labrar un grandioso convento, donde vivió con mucho gusto" (doña Gracia became a nun in the same convent with her mother, happy that the two knew each other, because since she was foolish, she easily found consolation, spending the large fortune left her in building a grand convent where she lived pleasantly) (*Novelas,* 21).

Chapter 5

1. The second novella, *La burlada Aminta* (Aminta Deceived), also ends in marriage, but only after Aminta has, as Paul Julian Smith puts it, assumed the "law of the dagger and the phal-

lus" by cross-dressing as a man and killing her seducer and the older woman who is his lover.
She then marries another man, but they move to Madrid and live under an assumed name.

2. The *Decameron*, day 10, story 5, a condensation of the version of the story in his earlier
work, *Filócolo* (1338), itself a lengthy telling of an episode in the famous French romance,
Floire et Blanchefleur.

3. According to Madelon Sprengnether (1989), contemporary women writers also frequently rewrite the fall, and often using garden imagery. Such rewritings, she finds, recount
the fall as the loss of the mother, and differ from traditional accounts in that they do not
scapegoat the woman.

4. Don Jorge, however, appears in various ways to resist "castration," subjection to the
Nom/Non du père; or paternal law; he has not followed Constanza's insistence that he ask her
father for her hand in marriage, and both the killing of his brother and his pact with the devil
take place outside the city walls; Gartner, in his perceptive reading of this story, says that both
actions occur in the same place. This is true only inasmuch as both are in the unlocalized
space outside the walls that symbolically mark the bounds of civilization and of law.

5. The 1637 princeps has "las damas" (the ladies) instead of "ellas" ([feminine] they).

6. Carlos does "pay" an old woman servant who assists him in this deceit. Zayas regularly
describes relationships between masters and servants in venal terms.

7. This emphasis on "regalos" could be *read* negatively, of course, in terms of the reiterated misogynist theme in Golden Age literature of the cost of courting women, their demand
for gifts, jewels, coaches, and other luxuries. But the shift begins with the mother's attentions
to her daughters and the only subsequent negative connotation linked to these "regalos" is
that of male self-interest in adopting this mode.

8. *The Franklin's Tale* in Chaucer is a thematically similar story, and it includes the issue of
class.

9. She reiterates this idea near the end of the story, describing don Jorge's grateful
prayer to God (*Novelas*, 421).

10. Brownlee (1995), who makes this story her test case for considering Zayas's novels
"both paradigmatically baroque and strikingly post-modern," suggests that rather than cele-
brating the referentiality of language and the importance of "keeping one's word" in earlier
versions of the tale, Zayas uses it to explore the dark and intricate labyrinths of post-lapsarian
language, revealing its power to deceive.

11. She closes her *Sarao*, "prometiendo si es admitido con el favor y gusto que espero, segunda parte, y en ésta el castigo de la ingratitud de don Juan, mudanza de Lisarda y boda de
Lisis, si como espero, es estimado mi trabajo y agradecido mi deseo, y alabado, no mi tosco estilo, sino el deseo con que va escrito" (promising if it is received with the favor and pleasure
that I hope, a second part, and therein the punishment of don Juan's ingratitude, Lisarda's
change of heart, and Lisis's wedding if as I wish, my work is esteemed and my desire gratefully
received and praised, not my unpolished style, but the desire with which it is written) (*Novelas*, 423).

12. Charnon-Deutsch observes: "A reading of Zayas' stories supports Irigaray's contention
that a female 'subject' cannot be imagined in masculinist discourse because the object of her
stories is not only to complain that women are objects but to support the systems which objectify women" (26).

13. For a "body count," see Vollendorf 1995.

14. Roper points out in regard to Protestant marriage in the era of the Reformation that
"production was organized in household-based units," of an urban household with married
master of one of the guild-organized crafts in charge of unmarried apprentices and journey-
men as well as his children and his wife, who held the position of mistress of a small household. Adulterous couples thus upset the economic as well as the social system and often
ended up in exile (Roper 55–56). Zayas's love stories are based on and written for a society

whose economic and political organization was very different, and in fact did often accommodate integrating into the socioeconomic order illegitimate children at least of royalty and the high nobility, but the practical difficulty of doing so for a land-based aristocracy operating under a system of *mayorazgo* probably is a factor in this attenuated "happy ending" for Aminta.

15. When doña Clara's merchant father leaves for the Indies without paying his daughter's dowry, "la madre de don Fernando, viendo su inocencia y virtud, volvía por ella y le servía de escudo" (don Fernando's mother, seeing her innocence and virtue, stood up for her and served as her shield). She dies within a few years, however, "perdiendo en ella doña Clara su escudo y defensa, y don Fernando el freno que tenía para tratarla tan ásperamente como de allí adelante hizo" (doña Clara losing with her a shield and defense, and don Fernando the restraint that he had against treating her as roughly as he did from then on) (*Novelas,* 272).

16. The narrator depicts doña Ana's maternal concern briefly but effectively: "muy madre, quiso criar a sus pechos" (very much a mother, she wanted to nurse him herself) (*Desengaños,* 391). She also describes her anxiety to return to care for her baby just before she is beheaded.

17. In *El jardín engañoso* (The Garden of Deceit), the narrator refers to "Constanza y Teodosia, con su madre *y las demás criadas*" (Constanza y Teodosia, with their mother *and the other maids*) (*Novelas,* 421). Zayas's adjectivization is sometimes careless, but as it fits the pattern of plotting, I think we can take it as further indication of a subtle association of active mothering with social degradation.

18. When after don Fernando's death she marries a Marquise, they have sons rather than daughters.

19. Foa (1979, 168–80), following the suggestion of Place (1923, 48–52) that the source of the tale is the "Patraña 21" of Juan de Timoneda, analyzes the differences in the treatment of the theme by Timoneda and Zayas as well as the influence of Cervantes on the narrative technique in this story. Grieve links it with the Crescentia-saga and the Florence of Rome stories (1991, 88 n. 6, 101). My thanks to José Antonio Rodríguez-Garrido for calling my attention to the medieval romance (see below) and for his clear and cogent study of the history of this story.

20. Cf. the importance of eyes from the outset of first story. As Grieve (1991, 99) points out, the blinding and the restoration of her sight by her mysterious protectress represents the suffering of a feminine martyr, the power of the "Mother of God," and also serve to contrast physical with moral blindness.

21. Rodríguez-Garrido notes that the number eight derives from the Marian tradition; the Immaculate Conception of the Virgin is celebrated on December 8, and her birth on September 8.

22. "Beatriz . . . antes de su muerte, escribió ella misma su vida, como aquí se ha dicho con nombre de desengaño; pues en él ven las damas lo que deben temer, pues por la crueldad y porfia de un hombre padeció tantos trabajos la reina Beatriz, que en toda Italia es tenida por santa, donde vi su vida manuscrita, estando allá con mis padres" (Beatriz . . . before her death, herself wrote her life, told here under the name of a disenchantment; since in it ladies see what they should fear, since because of the cruelty and persistence of a man, queen Beatriz suffered so many trials that she is held as a saint in all of Italy, where I saw the manuscript of her life, when I was there with my parents) (*Desengaños,* 467). One can read this statement as evidence of Zayas herself having been in Italy with her parents and having read the tale in a manuscript. Whether this is true or not, the statement also serves to set her account apart from widely-known versions such as that of Timoneda to preserve the fiction that all *desengaños* are true-life accounts.

23. The romance, preserved in manuscript in the Escorial and published by Benaim de Lasry, is an indirect Spanish prose translation (through a lost Galician translation) of a thirteenth-century French version in verse by Gautier de Coincy. The "Crescentia legend" seems

to have originated in India, traveling to Europe before the end of the eleventh century, and is closely related to another group of tales known as those of "Florence of Rome" (Benaim de Lasry 1982, 18–23).

24. Heffernan (1988, 149–50) remarks on the episodic construction of many saints' lives, which he relates to that of the late classical writer Suetonius's biographies *Lives of the Twelve Caesars* in obliging the reader to provide intellectual order. *La perseguida triunfante* is the most episodic of Zayas's stories, but the logical coherence or progression of the episodes is not problematic for the reader, since the hagiographic model of a series of trials is clear and is in fact announced by the divine Mother in her first appearance to Beatriz: "aunque Dios ha permitido darte este martirio, aún no es llegado tu fin, y te faltan otros que padecer; que a los que Su Divina Majestad ama, regala así" (although God has allowed you to be given this martyrdom, your end is not yet come and there will be others to suffer, for His Divine Majesty gives these gifts to those whom he loves) (*Desengaños,* 431). The next most episodic story is *El prevenido engañado* (see Chapter 6).

25. Zayas implicitly acknowledges her Alfonsine source, attributing to him the characterization of men's hearts as dense forests populated with wild beasts that she employs in the sermon against men she adds at this point in the narrative.

26. The narrator describes how the devil works on the Emperor's brother:

> donzel de tan grant beldat que en ninguna tierra non podería fallar más fermoso nin de mejor donaire si el diablo non lo engañara. Mas el diablo, que es sotil & apercebido de mal & fazedor de todas maldades lo fizo ser necio & triste & desmayado, ca bien cuydara engañar más ayna por él la santa emperatrís ca por otro omne, ca él bien sabe quál sabor ha el omne mançebo de la mugier, & cómmo la plaz con ella. . . . Por aquel donzel, que tanto era fermoso, venía el diablo con sus tentaçiones & con sus antojamientos tentar la buena dueña.

> (a youth of such great beauty that one could not find in any land one more handsome nor charming if the devil had not deceived him. But the devil, who is clever and prepared with evil and worker of all wrongs made him foolish and sad and weak, for he could more easily deceive the saintly empress through him than through another man, because he knew well what a taste for a woman the young man has, and the pleasure he takes with her. . . . Through that youth, who was so handsome, the devil came with his temptations and his fancies to tempt the good lady.) (Benaim de Lasry 1982, 179)

27. In the "Santa enperatrís" romance, the heroine chooses to become a nun married to Christ rather than resume married life as the empress of Rome, but neither the Emperor nor her ladies follow her model in rejecting earthly ties. The empress further chooses to mortify her flesh by living as an "emparedada," walled in a tiny space and directing her (spiritual) gaze only toward heaven; the romance may well have served as inspiration for parts of Zayas's *Desengaño 5* (see below).

28. Residence of laywomen in convents and of mothers and daughters and other close female relatives in the same religious community was also a historical reality in Zayas's day. For example, Catalina Arana, the mother of María de Jesús Agreda, convinced her husband to become a lay Franciscan and to convert their home into a Concepcionista convent, where she remained with her two daughters (Artola 1992, 218). Angela de Azevedo, who served as lady-in-waiting to Philip IV's first wife, Queen Isabel, and wrote at least three plays, entered a Benedictine convent with her only daughter after her husband's death (Soufas 1997, 1). See also Echániz on mothers and daughters as *freilas,* or lay sisters, of the Order of Santiago (1996, 14, 21–22 n. 57) and Vigil on convent life (1994, 208–15).

29. "The war is with men, not with mankind—with pungent realities, not abstract forms. The struggle is often depicted in a crudely misanthropic manner" (Heffernan 1988, 189).

30. The Immaculate Conception was widely and vigorously defended in Spain in the sixteenth and seventeenth centuries, but it only earned the status of official Church dogma in 1854, the year Fernández de Navarrete included Zayas in his survey of the history of the Spanish novel. The Assumption of the Virgin was not accepted by the Vatican as dogma until 1950, the year of the publication of Amezúa's edition of the *Desengaños* (Kristeva, 1987, 244; Sullivan 1989, 249–50).

31. Timoneda's Geroncia also changes names, becoming Clariquea—like the wandering heroine of the Greek romance *Teagenes y Clariquea*— and then Pelegrina, when she discovers the miraculous herb cure.

32. The "inda" ending makes this association positive, in contrast to the negative link associated with other sexually active namesakes of Flora (see Chapter 6 below).

33. According to the research of Sarah Nalle, the Virgin often occupied this position in the popular mind (lecture at Princeton University, Fall 1996).

34. Several Zayas critics have noted this. Gartner, for example, suggests that in Zayas's universe of false texts of seduction and silenced true narratives, women can only escape the inscription on their bodies of the consequences of economies of male desire by retreat to the convent. Yet that space is outside the limits of narrative, a possible alternative suggested but not explored.

35. Whether the metaphorical relationship of language to experience, the bar between the signifier and the signified is in this case different in kind or only in degree from that which operates in other areas of human existence is a question outside the parameters of this study.

36. This poem in the voice of a feminine divine power appears in *Thunder: Perfect Mind,* one of the Gnostic Gospels discovered in 1945 that represent early Christian teachings—perhaps as early or earlier than the canonical gospels. In contrast to the masculine gods of Judaism, Christianity, and Islam, the divinity reflected in many of these texts is conceived of as a dyad, containing both masculine and feminine elements (Pagels 1989, xiii-xxiii, 48–49).

Chapter 6

1. See Lacan's train station image of gender placement in the Introduction, pages 9–10.

2. While the five male and five female narrators of the *Heptameron* narrate and debate from clearly individualized and explicitly divergent perspectives, they never draw into two formally, even rigidly separated camps such as those marked out by the mother/daughter, father/son alignment in Zayas's opening frame.

3. Williamsen, however, points out the irony embedded in Zayas's text through the incorporation of implied readers whose reactions are differentiated by gender; her own experiment with modern-day readers confirmed a more literal reading by masculine readers and a more ironic reading by feminine readers. She argues that Zayas's stories, rather than rigidly supporting the honor code, use irony to challenge "the very 'foundations' of the patriarchal order" (Williamsen 1991, 647).

4. Foa (1977) analyzes the connection between this story and Cervantes and some of the ways in which Zayas's literary technique and personal vision differ from that of Cervantes in the *Casamiento engañoso*. She makes only a brief reference to the transformation of the *Coloquio* dogs into a cat and does not develop its significance.

5. Goytisolo considered these humorous scenes, along with certain episodes of magic, Zayas's best writing: "En ellas . . . el estilo se aligera y desembaraza de los clisés que lastran y dificultan la lectura de sus obras, consiguiendo a momentos una eficacia dramática (o cómica) digna de los mejores escritores de aquel tiempo" (In them . . . her style lightens and frees itself of the clichés that weigh down and render reading her works difficult, achieving at times a dramatic (or comic) effectiveness worthy of the best writers of that era) (1977, 106).

Melloni, on the other hand, eliminates *El castigo* from her study because it doesn't fit in her scheme of Zayas's narrative technique: "perché obbediente a diversi criteri letterari, e pertanto a diverse regole compositive" (because it obeys other literary criteria, and therefore other rules of composition) (6 n. 11).

6. Luce Irigaray and Jane Gallop also appropriate Freudian and Lacanian concepts, at once using them at an ironic distance and parodying their phallocentrism, or phallogocentrism.

7. See "Leonardo da Vinci and a Memory of His Childhood," in Freud 1974, 11:94–95.

8. Kaplan, in her examination of the relationship between "perversions" and social pressure to conform to gender stereotypes, finds the same complexity in male fetishist's attraction to the "phallic woman":

> Traditionally in most cultures, the female genitals are thought of and represented as damaged organs. In the mind of the fetishist the damaged female genitals must undergo interminable imaginary reparations to be eternally revived as a phallus. The woman whom the fetishist endows with this fictitious genital is transformed into the proverbial "phallic woman." Now that the term "phallic woman" has come into common usage, it is popularly used to refer to any powerful, authoritative, "masculine" woman. However . . . the fundamental phallic woman is a woman who embodies a stereotype of denigrated femininity: a Playboy bunny, a centerfold, a call girl, a whore, a go-go dancer, a wife who submits to her husband's demands that she dominate him or urinate on him, the slave who has the power to generate erections in her master because she is imagined as having a phallus hiding under her silky veils. The phallic woman, even when she plays the role of a dominating sadist with pointy breasts and spike heels, is a demeaned and 'castrated' woman, a woman who has been temporarily repaired for the purpose of creating erections in the man who is paying the bill (1992, 35).

9. Cf. also the work of Jessica Benjamin (1988), who from an object-relations approach, discusses the fantasy of the omnipotent mother, a defense against the perception of lack of infantile omnipotence. She posits the possibility of space within the mother-child dyad for recognition of the other's subjectivity without the intervention of the third term.

10. Hearing this "maravilla" (marvel) is meant to serve women as an "[un] aviso para que no se arrojen al mar de sus desenfrenados deseos" (a warning not to throw themselves into the sea of their unrestrained desires) (*Novelas*, 37).

11. See, for example "Anal Eroticism and the Castration Complex" in *Three Case Histories* (261–79) or "Character and Anal Erotism" (1974, 9:168–75).

12. Perhaps because his single-minded desire is for money, Zayas does not leave him with the added punishment of venereal disease, as Cervantes does his Alférez.

13. The "magician" here is a false *mago,* but that he is masculine is significant. See Chapter 8.

14. At the same time, the name stands in ironical relationship to the "marco" as a half-pound measure of gold or silver coins, to signify himself through money. Isi*dora* is a similarly ironic name, for this woman is far from the gift don Marcos takes her to be, despite the rooting of her name in the Greek word for gift.

15. This is Foa's interpretation of the difference in the tales. She sees the general seventeenth-century climate of political and social "desengaño" (disillusionment) in Spain reflected in the war between the sexes in Zayas's novels, and more particularly in the dominance of this tale by "la astucia, primera ley de la vida. . . . Zayas presenta aquí un cuadro bastante sombrío de la humanidad. En su novela no hay ni una nota de esperanza: todo es engaño, crueldad, falta de piedad y de compasión. La visión del mundo que expone María de

Zayas es mucho menos optimista que la de Cervantes—en su novela no hay absolutamente ninguna esperanza de redención. Esto explica gran parte de los cambios que ella ha introducido en su obra" (shrewdness, the first law of life. . . . Zayas presents here a fairly somber view of humanity. In her novella there is not a note of hope: everything is deceit, cruelty, lack of pity, and compassion. The vision of the world that María de Zayas sets out is much less optimistic than that of Cervantes—in her novela there is absolutely no hope of redemption. This explains in large part the changes that she has introduced in her work) (1979, 144–45).

16. Sor Juana made an intriguingly parallel substitution of a cat for another Cervantine animal, parodying literary portraiture of women in the *ovillejo* (rondel) "El pintar de Lisarda la belleza" (On Painting the Beauty of Lisarda). She plays on (1) the anecdote twice cited in *Don Quixote,* part II, about the bad painter Orbaneja who painted "Lo que saliere" (Whatever comes out) and then to prevent confusion, labeled his ill-formed creation *Este es gallo* (This Is a Cock); (2) Don Quixote's extension of the example to the bad poet Mauleón who translated *Deum de Deo* as "Dé donde diere" (Let him give where he will) (Cervantes Saavedra 1971, part II, 562, 1051; 1957, 549, 1033); and probably (3) Calderón's alteration of the rooster to a cat in Gil's version of the anecdote in *La devoción de la cruz*. Sor Juana says of her commission to paint Lisarda: "Yo tengo de pintar, dé donde diere, / salga como saliere, / aunque saque un retrato / tal que, después, le ponga: *Aquéste es gato*" (haphazardly; let the picture come out as it will, even if it produces a portrait on which afterwards a label will have to be attached: *This is a cat*) (Juana Inés de la Cruz 1987, 71). The paraphrase is that of Bergmann (1990).

17. The gendered pronoun is deliberate here, since the masculine perspective predominates in Darnton's history of the treatment of cats.

18. As Menton points out, this is a positive rather than menacing association between cats and the lover who figures as an alternative to the rational, capitalistic, and bureaucratic world. The protagonist says of la Maga " 'Preferíamos encontrarnos en el puente, en la terraza de un café, en un cine-club o agachados junto a un gato en cualquier patio del Barrio Latino' " (We preferred to meet on the bridge, on a café terrace, in a cine club or squatting next to a cat in some patio in the Latin Quarter); or in another instance: " '[. . .] un viejito tomando sombra en un rincón, y los gatos, siempre inevitablemente los minouche morrongos miau-miau kitten kat chat cat gatto grises y blancos y negros y de albañil, dueños del tiempo y de las baldosas tibias, invariables amigos de la Maga que sabía hacerles cosquillas en la barriga y les hablaba un lenguaje entre tonto y misterioso, con citas a plazo fijo, consejos y advertencias.' " (an old man taking the shade in a corner and cats, always inevitably the *minouche morrongos miau-miau,* kitten *kat chat* cat *gatto* grey and white and black and dawn-colored, owners of time and the warm paving stones, invariable friends of Maga who knew how to tickle them on the stomach and talk to them in a language half foolish, half mysterious, with dates to meet, advice and warnings) (Menton 1998, 38).

19. See "The Metaphoric and Metonymic Poles," in Jakobson 1975, 90–96.

20. She cites Philip's reliance on the counsel of his daughter, Isabel Clara Eugenia of Austria, and Isabel's wisdom and courage in governing Flanders. She also refers without specific names to "the sisters of the emperor Charles V" of whom the most notable in this regard were Catalina, the wife of John III of Portugal, who assumed the regency on his death in the minority of her grandson Sebastian, and María (1505–58), who married Louis II, king of Hungary and Bohemia; widowed in 1526, she governed in the Low Countries for twenty-five years. In Yllera's words, "She was a woman of great intelligence, protectress of artists and poets, and collected an excellent library" (Zayas y Sotomayor 1983, 229 n. 6).

21. In this field she names two women: (1) the countess of Lemos, Catalina de Zúñiga y Sandoval, sister of Philip III's favorite, Lerma, who was chief lady-in-waiting to Philip's wife, Queen Margarita of Austria, and governess of Margarita María, wife of Emperor Leopold I of Austria, whom she praises for her "excellent understanding" and a knowledge of Latin unequaled by any learned male; and (2) a Franciscan nun, Eugenia de Contreras of the convent

of Santa Juana de la Cruz, also distinguished for her command of Latin and of theology according to Zayas, and for the lively wit of her poetry and prose, by Montalbán's testimony (*Desenganos* 229–30 and n. 9).

22. Zayas cites three women in this category: (1) María Barahona, a nun in the Convent of the Concepción Jerónima, known for her musical ability as well as her poetry; (2) the dramatist Ana Caro Mallén de Soto (see Chapter 1); and (3) Isabel de Ribadeneira—whom she calls a lady-in-waiting of the countess of Gálvez but who Serrano y Sanz says was a Franciscan nun—whose poetry she praises highly, as did Lope de Vega in his *Laurel de Apolo* (*Desengaños*, 230 and nn. 10–12).

23. As Apuleius tells the story, Psyche, the youngest of three daughters of a king, was so beautiful that people left off worshipping the divine Venus to celebrate this new, human Venus. Enraged, the goddess sent her son Cupid to punish Psyche, marrying her with the least of men, the most abject and disgraced in the world. But Cupid fell in love with Psyche when he saw her. He therefore arranged that an oracle tell the king that to save his kingdom he must abandon Psyche on a mountain, leaving her dressed for a "funereal wedding" with the cruel monster destined to be her husband, A gentle breeze takes her to a beautiful field, in front of a handsome palace. Entering it, she is entertained as a queen. At night, in darkness, Cupid comes to her bed, tells her he is her husband and that she can enjoy a life of perfect happiness as long as she does not try to learn his identity. But under the influence of her jealous sisters she becomes fearful and curious and one night takes a lantern to see him and a knife to kill the "monster" she has never seen. On seeing his beauty, she is so enchanted that she accidently lets a drop of burning oil fall on him. He awakens and disappears, furious. She searches for him desperately throughout the world and submits to impossible trials imposed by her divine mother-in-law, who hopes they will kill her. In the last of these, she must descend to the underworld and bring back to Venus a box of beauty cream from Proserpina. Curiosity overtakes her again and she opens the box and falls into an apparently fatal sleep, but Cupid intervenes and convinces Jupiter to pardon her and give her divine immortality as his wife. In the traditional allegorical interpretation of the tale, Psyche figured the human soul in search of divine love.

24. De Armas follows the story from the twelfth-century French romance *Partonopeus de Blois* through various prose versions: Masuccio's *Novelle* (1476); Bandello's *Novella* 25 of his *Quarta parte* (1573); Céspedes y Meneses's *El soldado Píndaro; Los efectos que hace amor,* from Castillo Solórzano's collection *Los alivios de Casandra* (1640), and the Zayas version. He also summarizes its appearance in various *comedias:* Lope de Vega's *La viuda valenciana;* Tirso's *Amar por señas, Quien calla, otorga,* and *La celosa de sí misma;* Calderón's *La dama duende;* and Ana Caro's *El conde Partinuplés.* The forty-third story in the *Heptameron* of Marguerite de Navarre also tells a version of this story in which a chalk mark reveals the invisible mistress to be a hypocritical woman who wants to enjoy a sensual affair while maintaining an unblemished reputation of virtuous severity. Calderón also uses the Pysche-Cupid myth without gender reversal in the court play *Ni Amor se libra de amor* and two *autos sacramentales.*

25. The ages that don Jaime assigns to himself do not tally chronologically; they function as indicators of stage of life, of relative youth and maturity, rather than of actual years.

26. De Armas also considers Zayas's version of the "Invisible Mistress" story in connection with the second episode. He speculates that "it may have been included to balance the shock of the brutal husband's behavior with the cruelty of a woman" (45), but notes that it is an unequal balance, since don Jaime escaped cruelty, whereas Elena "emerges as a creature imprisoned by her society, a society ruled by men" (46). In a recent article, he suggests that Zayas's version of the first episode is a response to the misogynist version of the story in *El soldado Píndaro* by Céspedes y Meneses, and that Maino's painting of Mary Magdalene next to a cross as well as a skull may have suggested Zayas's addition of Elena dying with her arms in a cross. De Armas concludes that "unlike her saintly prototype she does not have to repent, since she did

not sin against her husband. The cross she has to bear is that of male sinfulness. . . . Zayas . . . points to the wisdom of women, their saintliness and godliness. In striving for angelic goodness, they are often crossed by men and must bear the cross of living in patriarchal society" (1998, 15).

27. "Così adunque alla stolta giovane adivenne delle sue beffe, non altramenti con uno scolare credendosi frascheggiare che con un altro avrebbe fatto, non sapiendo bene che essi, non dico tutti ma la maggior parte, sanno *dove il diavolo tien la coda*. E per ciò guardatevi, donne, dal beffare, e gli scolari spezialmente" (Boccaccio 1985, 699).

28. See Zizek 1991, chaps. 5 and 6; and Lacan 1981, where he depicts the antinomy between the eye viewing an object and the gaze, on the side of the object rather than the "seeing" eye: "In the scopic field, everything is articulated between two terms that act in an antinomic way—on the side of things, there is the gaze, that is to say, things look at me, and yet I see them. This is how one should understand those words, so strongly stressed in the Gospel, *They have eyes that they might not see.* That they might not see what? Precisely, that things are looking at them" (109). See also his chap. 2, n. 47, on the nature of (dis)possession by the gaze.

29. The referent of "a vista de ojos" is ambiguous; it could refer to his not having patience to try to witness the offending relationship between Elena and her cousin, or could not tolerate that others should know or see it.

30. See Lacan's (1981) discussion of this painting; and Zizek 1991, 90–91.

31. The candlelit procession of the black maidservant is ironically reminiscent of that deployed by doña Estefanía in Cervantes' *La fuerza de la sangre.*

32. "The Hebrew and Latin words for skull, (*Golgotha, calvarium*) served as powerful reminders of the place where Christ had been crucified. At the foot of the Cross, which was also thought to mark the place of Adam's burial, the first sinner's skull had become the holy cup meant to gather the New Adam's precious blood. The striking image of the penitent woman drinking out of her lover's skull may have been suggested to Marguerite by the dramatic representation of Adam's skull turned into chalice on the Golgotha" (Rigolot 1994, 60).

33. In *Al fin se paga todo,* don García mentions being tempted to play Tarquin to the "Lucrecia" whom he has discovered, but overcomes his desire to rape the woman he has found unconscious in the street. He has, perhaps, the wrong Lucrecia in mind when he exercises this restraint, as she proves to have been less than pure. Rather than kill herself, she has killed the brother-in-law who pursued and possessed her, taking advantage of his knowledge that she was attempting to pursue a love affair with another man.

34. Cesar had been a cardinal but renounced his ecclesiastical career when Louis XII of France made him duke of Valentinois in 1499 and led French and mercenary troops to undertake the conquest of the region of Romagna, of which he became duke in 1501.

35. In Calderón's *La dama duende,* his version of the "Invisible Mistress," Honig (1972) read a shadow of incest in don Luis's dark frustration and doña Angela's remark that she is denied the sun and married to two brothers.

36. The Zayas stories involving competition between brothers or sisters are *Al fin se paga todo, El jardín engañoso, Desengaño 9,* and *Desengaño 10.* In the *El patrañuelo* of Timoneda, in contrast, the first, fifth, and thirteenth stories revolve around incest or the threat thereof.

37. From a Jungian perspective, Erich Neumann has made the Psyche-Eros myth a tale of prototypical female development, but another Jungian, María von Franz, suggests that it is rather the development of man's projection of the feminine, of what men fear in the feminine, split off and disowned (Labouvie-Vief 1994, 15). In Zayas's version, the latter is unquestionably the case.

38. The "residue of the castration threat lies behind the paranoid fantasy of the *vagina dentata,* the sexually insatiable woman who exhausts men and depletes them of their sexual 'resources' " (Grosz 1990, 135).

39. See Kristeva 1980; and Dianne Chisholm's "Uncanny," in Wright 1992, 436–40.

40. In Kristeva's theory of abjection, the installation of the "father of individual prehistory" in the pre-mirror stage provides a pole of identification that permits an incipient separation from the immediate presence of the enveloping maternal, abjected as the infant turns toward the magnet of primary love and primary identification, a pattern or model as yet sexually undifferentiated, but "always already within the symbolic orbit, under the sway of language" (1987, 27). For Kristeva, thus "the whole symbolic matrix sheltering emptiness is thus set in place in an elaboration that precedes the Oedipus complex" (27). This object of love is a metaphor for Kristeva, the constitutive metaphor or "unary feature" that locates it within the symbolic code. She draws the idea of the unary feature from Lacan, quoting from his *Ecrits*, "The Subversion of the subject and dialectic of desire" (Lacan 1977, 306): " 'Take just one signifier as an emblem of this omnipotence [of the other's authority], that is to say of this wholly potential power (*ce pouvoir tout en puissance*), this birth of possibility, and you have the unary feature (*traite unaire*), which, by filling in the invisible mark that the subject derives from the signifier, alienates this subject in the primary identification that forms the ego ideal' " (Kristeva 1987, 387 n. 18).

41. Lucrecia is not sexually innocent, of course, but her "cruelty" toward don Jaime is reactive, a response to his violation of their secret, signifying a move away from unquestioning attachment to her and toward loyalty to the paternal order.

42. See the discussion of the value of women in Greek tragedy in Zeitlin 1990.

43. Pardo Bazán left these two stories out of her collection for their "mucha crudeza" (great crudeness) while at the same time recognizing their merit (see Chapter 2). This charge of "crudeza" and Victorian prudery is understandable from readers such as Ticknor and Pfandl, but less so from the pen of the author who wrote the opening scenes of Perucho scrambling for food among the dogs in *Los pazos de Ulloa* and who depicted the sensuality of the developing incestuous desire in the cave scene in *La madre naturaleza*.

44. His own servant later kills him and steals the jewels, but is caught and before being hanged, confesses to having killed don Gaspar, who had stolen the jewels from doña Hipólita.

45. Freud suggests that that fantasy arises from the male subject's "infantile narcissistic relations with the mother, where he is affirmed as the object of her desire, the phallus for her. He is positioned here, and in adult relations, as the subject who has what the (m)other lacks. His position as phallic is conditioned on women's valorized, 'superior' position coupled with their real social powerlessness (this repeats the characteristics of the phallic mother). In short, he displaces his infantile narcissism onto the extraneous love object, and by projecting her as an extension of himself, is able to receive his narcissistic investment back" (Grosz 1990, 127, citing Freud, "Five Lectures on Psychoanalysis," in Freud 1974, 11:168ff.).

46. The consequences for the embodied "ghost" are tragic, however, as he is executed. The metonymic relationship between this episode and the final "resurrection" of doña Leonor merits further study. See Chapter 5.

Chapter 7

1. Judith Butler, for example, resisting the solution of sex as given by nature, and gender by cultural constructions, says that sex may also be a politically motivated construct in that "gender must also designate the very apparatus of production whereby the sexes themselves are established. As a result, gender is not to culture as sex is to nature; gender is also the discursive/cultural means by which 'sexed nature' or 'a natural sex' is produced and established as 'prediscursive,' prior to culture, a politically neutral surface *on which* culture acts" (1990, 7).

2. Lope mocks the conventionality of that device in his novella version of the *Juez de su causa* story, *Las fortunas de Diana* (The Fortunes of Diana) in one of the metafictional "intercolunios" addressed to his inscribed reader, Marcia Leonarda. When Diana/Celio enters the service of the *mayoral* of the duque de Behar, relates Lope:

Silveria, hija suya, . . . desde que entró en su casa no . . . había quitado [los ojos] de su rostro.

Paréceme que dice vuestra merced que claro estaba eso, y que si había hija en esa casa se había de enamorar del disfrazado mozo. Yo no sé que ello haya sido verdad; pero, por cumplir con la obligación del cuento, vuestra merced tenga paciencia. (1988, 77)

(Silveria, his daughter, . . . since he entered the house . . . hadn't taken her eyes off his face.

It seems to me your grace is saying that of course, if there was a daughter in the house, she had to fall in love with the disguised youth. I don't know that that would have been true; but to meet the requirements of the story [I ask] your grace to have patience.)

3. Lope's Diana in *Las fortunas de Diana* also uses the name of her lover (and of the son she has borne him). This is an intuition into a subject's identification with her symptom/cause of desire; see Zizek 1991, 130–40.

4. The story does not originate with Lope of course. Significant elements of the plot appear in Boccaccio, Lope de Vega, Timoneda and elsewhere. See Chevalier 1982.

5. Parker renders the Latin *dilatio* as "dilation," which does not conform strictly with its contemporary use in English, in which its principal meaning is "expansion." English does retain that sense in the adjective "dilatory," however, and the *Random House Unabridged Dictionary* includes under *dilate* the meaning "to speak at length; expatiate" and also "to describe or develop at length," although the later sense is listed as archaic.

6. *Dilatio* as a fundamental characteristic of romance narrative was connected in the Renaissance, says Parker, with the wiles of enchantresses who lure the unwary into corruption (1987, 10–11).

7. The possessive adjective in Spanish does not mark the gender of the possessor, but rather agrees with the object in gender and number. To render this gender neutrality, in such translations I write *his/her*, and also *s/he* where English requires a gendered pronoun not needed in Spanish, in which verb forms do not require use of a subject pronoun.

8. In *Opuscules et lettres,* ed. Louis Lafuma (Paris: Aubier-Montaigne, 1955), 166–66. Recounted by Louis Marin in the finale, "The Legitimate Usurper, or The Shipwrecked Man as King," of the *Portrait of the King* (1988, 215–38).

9. There is one case of female-to-male cross-dressing, in *Desengaño 9.* Queen Beatriz dresses as a male on instructions from "La Madre de Dios," as we have seen in Chapter 5.

10. There are certain exceptions involving male to female transvestism, notably Guillén de Castro's *La fuerza de la costumbre* (The Power of Habit) and a few other plays in which the *gracioso* cross-dresses as a female to further his master's pursuit of a (female) love object. Interesting exceptions also exist in court dramas such as Tirso's *Aquiles* and Hercules in Calderón's *Fieras afemina Amor* (Love Tames the Savage Beast).

11. For example, describing Octavia's initial resistance to Carlos's courtship, she says, "Así lo hiciera siempre, que así no fuera causa de las desdichas que después sucedieron" (Would that she had always done the same, for then she wouldn't have been the cause of all the misfortunes that later took place) (*Desengaños,* 172); when Octavia listens to his serenade, Lisarda comments that "en esto se ve cuán flacas son las mujeres, que no saben perseverar en el buen intento. Y aun por esta parte disculpo a los hombres en la poca estimación que hacen de ellas" (in this we see how weak are women, who don't know how to persevere in their good intentions. And even on this count I exonerate men in the low estimation they have of them) (*Desengaños,* 177). Expressing ambivalence about Octavia's request that don Juan seek revenge against Carlos for her, she adds a diatribe against women who do *not* seek revenge with

their own hands or those of another, nor leave it to heaven to settle the balance, but rather continue the chain of vice by allowing themselves to be deceived by another man as well.

12. Although Zayas never explicitly connects this story with Saint Oria, or Aurea, this picture of the mortification of the flesh between narrow walls is probably inspired at least in part by that most famous of the "emparedadas"—devout women who in the medieval era chose to live in very small cells under the rule of a monastery. In Berceo's *Poema de Santa Oria,* both Oria and her teacher Urraca choose to live as *emparedadas* (1981, 97, 99). She was rewarded for her devotion with several heavenly visions, in which one of the three virgin martyrs who are her guides shows her the glorious seat being prepared for her in heaven. To earn it, says her guide, she must remain *emparedada* all her life (115). In another, the Virgin Mary reaffirms her glorious future and tells her the sign will be suffering a painful mortal illness (123–24). After her death, her saintly mother Amuña—later buried close to her daughter in a cave hear the church San Millán de Suso—has a vision in which Oria tells her that she was accompanied in her passage into heaven by the Virgin Mary and her earlier saintly virgin guides, and that she resides with the innocents put to the sword by Herod for Christ (134, 138). For more information on the *emparedadas,* see the forthcoming study of women's spirituality in Spain by Elisa Rhodes, to whom I am indebted for drawing my attention to Santa Oria.

13. In *Encore,* Lacan writes:

> L'amour lui-même . . . s'adresse au semblant. Et, s'il est vrai que l'Autre ne s'atteint qu'à s'accoler . . . au *a,* cause du désir, c'est aussi bien au semblant d'être qu'il s'adresse. Cet être-là n'est pas rien. Il est supposé à cet objet qu'est le *a* .
>
> Ne devons-nous pas retrouver ici cette trace qu'en tant que tel il répond à quelque imaginaire? Cet imaginaire, je l'ai désigné expressément de l'*I,* ici isolé du terme *imaginaire.* Ce n'est que de l'habillement de l'image de soi qui vient envelopper l'objet cause du désir, que se soutient le plus souvent . . . le rapport objectal. (Lacan 1975, 85)
>
> (Love itself . . . addresses a semblance. And, if it is true that the Other cannot be reached except by clinging to it . . . or to [object] *a,* the cause of desire, it is also a semblance of being that it addresses. That being is not nothing. It is attributed to that object that is the *a.*
>
> Shouldn't we rediscover here that trace that as such, corresponds to some imaginary register? I have expressly designated that imaginary register by the capital letter I, separate in this case from the [general] term "imaginary." It is only through the costuming of the image of the self that the object as cause of desire comes to be contained, and which, in most cases, is sustained by the object relation.)

14. (Zizec 1991, 136–37). My rendering of Lacan's diagram, from chap. 8, "Le savoir et la vérité" (Knowledge and truth) of Seminar 10, *Encore,* is inspired by Zizek's use of this diagram to illustrate the ambiguous and disturbing ontology of certain aspects of the Real in the short stories of Patricia Highsmith (Zizek 1991, 133–37), and in particular, Highsmith's story "The Black House," of which he says:

> The example of the "black house" demonstrates clearly the purely *formal* nature of the "object small *a* ": it is an empty form filled out by everyone's fantasy. In contrast, the protuberances at the Austrian cemetery are almost too present, they are in a way a formless content forcing upon us the massive, inert presence, their nauseous, glutinous bulk. It is not difficult to recognize, in this opposition, the opposition between *desire* and *drive:* the object small *a* names the void of that unattainable surplus that sets our desire in motion, while the pond exemplifies the inert object, the embodiment of the enjoyment around which the drive circulates. The opposition between desire and

drive consists precisely in the fact that desire is by definition caught in a certain dialectic, it can always turn into its opposite or slide from one object to another, it never aims
at what appears to be its object, but always "wants something else." The drive, on the
other hand, is inert, it resists being enmeshed in a dialectical movement; it circulates
around its object, fixed upon the point around which it pulsates. (133–34)

15. See the interpretation of this story by Anne Cruz, who finds in it an expression of
Zayas's increasing skepticism regarding female friendships as well as family ties, and of the impossible desire to return to female origins, "to the 'no man's land' that is the un(dia)critical
and undifferentiated maternal" (Cruz 1996, 48). She observes that Inés's innocence is prefigured in her name, a Spanish version of "Agnes," associated with the Latin *agnus*, or lamb, and
reads her final blindness as the confinement of the luring and threatening feminine: "She becomes an unseeing sign to be gazed on, Medusa-like, by others" (47).
    16. I thank Kristina Ríos for this observation, made in a seminar presentation and paper
at New York University in the fall of 1994.
    17. Zayas uses some form of "transformarse" six times in this story, but not in any other
cross-dressing episode. Her only use of it in the first volume refers to don Marcos, who "con la
sutileza de la comida, se vino a transformar de hombre en espárrago" (with the sparcity of his
food, came to transform himself from a man into an asparagus) (*Novelas*, 126); in the *Desengaños*, she uses it once in reference to the poor noble Felipe who out of love for doña Isabel,
took a job serving in her house under the name Luis, once in relation to the transformation
of the slave Zelima into the lady doña Isabel (*Desengaños*, 258) and once in the hagiographic
tale of doña Beatríz.
    18. See note 7, this chapter.
    19. Presumably Zayas was deliberately ironic in locating Laurela's death on the day of the
celebration of the Assumption of the Virgin, 15 August, *agosto* in Spanish meaning both August and harvest. It is said that the festival may be a Christianization of a pagan harvest celebration dedicated to Artemis (Thompson and Carlson 1994, 17).
    20. The passage reads as follows:

> Nadie hace ostentación de los «dones» como en España, y más el día de hoy, que han
> dado en una vanidad tan grande, que hasta los cocheros, lacayos y mozas de cocina le
> tienen; estando ya los negros «dones» tan abatidos, que las taberneras y fruteras son
> «doña Serpiente» y «doña Tigre». Que, de mi voto, aunque no el de más acierto,
> ninguna persona principal se le había de poner. Que no ha muchos días que oí llamar
> a una perrilla de falda «doña Jarifa», y a un gato «don Morro». Que si Su Majestad
> (Dios le guarde) echara alcabala sobre los «dones», le había de aprovechar más que el
> uno por ciento, porque casas hay en Madrid, y las conozco yo, que hierven de «dones»,
> como los sepulcros de gusanos. Que me contaron por muy cierto que una labradora
> socarrona de Vallecas, vendiendo pan, el otro día, en la plaza, a cualquiera vaivén que
> daba el burro, decía: «Está quedo, don Rucio.» Y queriendo partirse, empezó a decir:
> «don Arre», y queriendo pararse «don Jo». (*Desengaños*, 350)

(No one brandishes [the titles of] "sir and lady" as in Spain, and more than ever nowa-
days, when they have grown to such vanity that even coachmen, lackeys, and kitchen
maids use them; those black titles having sunk so low that tavern and fruit-selling
women are "Lady Serpent" and "Lady Tiger." And, in my opinion, although it may not
be the most successful plan, no principal person ought to use it. Because not many
days ago, I heard a lapdog called "Lady Elegance" and a tomcat "Sir Miaow." And if His
Majesty (God save him) should impose a sales tax on "sir" and "lady," it would yield
him more than one percent, because there are houses in Madrid, and I know them,

that are teeming with "sirs" and "ladies" like tombs with worms. And they told me as truth that a sly peasant girl from Vallecas, selling bread the other day in the plaza, whenever her donkey swayed would say, "Hold still, Sir Donkey." And wanting him to leave, she began to say: "Sir Giddap" and wanting him to stop, "Sir Whoa."

21. "¿Quién le vio tan enamorado, tan fino, tan celoso, tan firme, tan hecho Petrarca de Laurela, como el mismo Petrarca de Laura . . . ?" (Who saw him so enamored, so refined, so jealous, so firm, made such a Petrarch to Laurela as Petrarch himself to Laura . . . ?) (*Desengaños*, 330) only to see his devotion evaporate as soon as she succumbed. This anticipates the critique of the fictionality of courtly-love discourse implicit in the plot of the following *desengaño*, discussed below.

22. Butler 1934; Zayas y Sotomayor 1983, 332 n. 24; and *Bibliotheca Sanctorum*.

23. For the controversy over the date—and the authorship—of this two-part play, see Cruickshank 1984 and Rose 1976. For details on the Semíramis myth/legend, see Gwynne Edwards's introduction to Calderón de la Barca 1970.

24. The dismissal through ridicule is repeated in other shorter scenes, and one extended one, following another declaration by Estefanía of her love for Laurela:

> Empezaron todas a reírse, y don Bernardo preguntó qué enigmas eran aquéllas.
>
> —¿Qué enigmas han de ser —dijo doña Leonor—, sino que Estefanía está enamorada de Laurela desde el punto que la vio, y lamenta su ausencia celebrando su amor, como habéis visto?
>
> —Bien me parece —respondió don Bernardo—, pues de tan castos amores bien podemos esperar hermosos nietos.
>
> —No quiso mi dicha, señor mío —dijo Estefanía—, que yo fuera hombre; que, a serlo, sirviera como Jacob por tan linda Raquel.
>
> —Mas te quiero yo mujer que no hombre —dijo don Bernardo.
>
> —Cada uno busca y desea lo que ha menester —respondió Estefanía.
>
> Con esto y otras burlas, que pararon en amargas veras, se llegó la hora de acostarse, diciendo Laurela a Estefanía la viniese a desnudar, porque desde luego la hacía favor del oficio de camarera. (*Desengaños*, 308–9)

(They all began to laugh, and don Bernardo asked what those enigmas were.
> "What enigmas can they be," said doña Leonor, "other than that Estefanía has been in love with Laurela since s/he saw her, and laments her absence celebrating her/his love, as you have seen?"
> "That seems fine to me," answered don Bernardo, "because from such chaste loves we can well expect lovely grandchildren."
> "My fortune did not grant, my lord," said Estefanía, "that I might be a man; for if I were one, I would serve her as Jacob served the pretty Rachel."
> "I like you better as a woman than as a man," said don Bernardo.
> "Everyone searches for and desires what he needs," responded Estefanía.
> With this and other jokes, that ended in bitter truths, the bedtime hour arrived, with Laurela telling Estefanía to come and help her undress, since of course s/he also did her the favor of serving as her lady-in-waiting.)

25. The fate of the first three is disposed of quickly in the opening paragraphs. The oldest was married to a Portuguese man, who stabbed his wife to death on finding her reading a letter that he himself had sent to her as if from a Castilian gentleman. The youngest sister, who had accompanied her to Portugal, broke her legs jumping from a window to escape being stabbed as well. The next daughter was married to an Italian who strangled her to death with

her own hair and then poisoned their four-year-old son after she made an innocent comment that a certain Spanish captain was handsome.

26. "Por conveniencias a la real corona y gusto de su hermano" (for the convenience of the Crown and the wishes of my brother) (*Desengaños*, 339).

27. It is a sonnet with an added *estrambote* of two heptasyllables and one hendecasyllable. Zayas's reworking of traditional literary forms includes a number of variants on classic verse patterns.

28. The song Blanca sings lamenting the prince's disdain after their arrival in Flanders reflects the reversal of their position, repeating much of the same imagery. E.g., "¿Qué gusto tiene tus ojos / de ver los ojos, que un tiempo / dueños llamaron los tuyos, / dos copiosas fuentes hechos? / . . . Muy a mi costa les quitas / el imperio que tuvieron: / mas tú te llevas la gloria / y ellos pasan los tormentos. / . . . ¿Quién me dijera algún día / esta ingratitud que veo? / ¡Ah, finezas de hombre ingrato, / y cómo en humo se fueron!" (What pleasure do your eyes take in seeing turned into two copious fountains the eyes you once called beloved? . . . At great cost to me you take from them the rule they had, but you take away their glory and they suffer torments. . . . Who might have told me some day of the ingratitude I see? Oh, courtesies of an ungrateful man, how much smoke they became!) (*Desengaños*, 352–54).

29. In subsequent sections, Zizek suggests that one reading of the sadistic torture of the woman in the film *Blue Velvet* would be a drastic attempt to jolt a woman out of her passivity and depression, but finally acknowledges that the fundamental motive is that of masking masculine impotence. When we set Zayas's story in its full political context, a similar implication of masculine impotence hidden behind a mask becomes visible. See Chapter 9.

30. She asks, Why would one question the wisdom of the woman who would "avisarse del caudal que lleva en su esposo? Todas cuantas cosas se compran se procuran ver, y que, vistas, agraden al gusto, como es un vestido, una joya. ¿Y un marido, que no se puede deshacer de él, como de la joya y del vestido, ha de ser por el gusto ajeno?" (inform herself about the wealth she gets in her husband? Everything people buy they try to see, and be sure that, seen, they please one's taste, such as a dress or a jewel. And a husband, whom one cannot get rid of like a jewel or a dress, has to be [acquired] according to another's taste?) (*Desengaños*, 340)

31. There are two definitions for "natural" as a noun given in the *Diccionario de autoridades:* (1) "El genio, índole, o inclinación propia de cada uno. Dícese también del instinto e inclinación de los animales irracionales" (The temperament, character, or inclination belonging to each person. It is used also for the instinct or inclination of irrational animals); and (2) "el que ha nacido en algún Pueblo o Reino" (he who was born in some town or kingdom).

32. "Preguntóle el atrevido paje que por qué causa se hacía aquel exceso. A quien respondió doña Blanca que la causa era su gusto, y que agradeciese no hacía en él otro tanto; mas que algún día lo haría, o no sería doña Blanca" (The bold page asked her on what cause she committed that excess. To which doña Blanca answered that the cause was her will, and that he should be thankful that she didn't carry out another one against him; but that some day she would do it, or she would not be doña Blanca) (*Desengaños*, 361).

Chapter 8

1. One student in this category remarked after reading Zayas, "She's a trip!" Rather than being repelled by the levels of irrational violence in her tales, she found reading her fiction a voyage through altered states of consciousness accessible without the need for a mind-altering drug.

2. An obvious example is the popularity of vampire movies in the era of AIDS; an erotic bite that confers a wearying and painful immortality functions as a "virtual reality" scenario that reverses the threat of a virus spread by sexual activity.

3. See Lyndal Roper's study of witchcraft trials in early modern Germany (1994).

4. As have Ioan Couliano (1987), Bertrand Russell in the *History of Western Philosophy*, and various historians of religion and science.

5. We should note, however, that in Spain witch-hunting was in general circumscribed rather than exacerbated by the intervention of the Inquisition, in comparison with the fever that swept Germany, for example.

6. See, for example, her description of the *humilladero* (roadside chapel) near Naples in *La fuerza del amor* (The Power of Love), worthy of inclusion among Ariès's catalog of charnel houses and ossuaries.

7. Martínez Gil (1993, 149) says that the term *suicide* became current with the increased valoration of the individual around the beginning of the industrial revolution, and although it appeared in the seventeenth century, used by English philosophers and by casuists, it was not used in France until the mid-eighteenth century.

8. Martínez Gil is citing Nicolas Díaz, *Tratado del juyzio final en el qual se hallarán muchas cosas muy provechosas, y curiosas* (Valladolid 1588, fol. 115v), and Francisco Arana, *Muerte prevenida o christiana preparación para una buena muerte* (Seville, 1736?, 278).

9. The Inquisition did order the suppression of the ending of one story by Zayas's friend Pérez de Montalban beginning with the 1632 Index of Prohibited Books. The story "La mayor confusión" (The Greatest Confusion) from the collection *Sucesos y prodigios de amor* (1626) is a tale of incest in which a widowed mother, enamored of her own son, one night takes the place of a servant he has courted and becomes pregnant by him. Years later the brother falls in love with his own sister/daughter and marries her despite all the obstacles that the mother imposes, short of revealing her sin, which she only communicates to him in a letter to be read posthumously. Reading it after her death causes him such anguish that he dies in a few weeks. The Inquisition's censors seem to have been operating in that case more from prudishness than a concern for didactic value or religious dogma, for they ordered the erasure only of the last two paragraphs in which the son anguishes over what course to take and dies, and the young woman retires to a convent. The censor was probably offended by the fairly open discussion in the first excised paragraph of his impossibility of either occupying the marriage bed knowing that his wife is his sister/daughter, or avoiding it without revealing to her the reason. As excised, the story ends with the mother's confessional letter (Pérez de Montalbán 1949, 129–66). For the list of works on this list, see Márquez 1980, 263–67.

10. Adriana poisons herself after don Félix rejects her in the first story, leaving a note on her body explaining the reason and cause of her death. She is nevertheless given a Christian burial, "facilitando su riqueza y calidad los imposibles que pudiera haber, habiéndose ella muerto por sus manos" (her wealth and quality overcoming the opposition there could have been, having died by her own hand) (*Novelas*, 56), as the narrator comments ironically. Lucrecia enjoys no such preferential treatment after she stabs herself to death when Clara reveals her use of black magic (*Novelas*, 287).

11. In the first *desengaño*, after don Felipe kills don Manuel, the Moorish woman Zaida whom don Manuel has promised to marry pulls a dagger from his belt and stabs herself to death. Don Manuel is buried "como a cristiano" (as a Christian) and Zaida "como a mora desesperada" (as a despairing Moor) (*Desengaños*, 165). In the last tale, don Dionís falls on his own sword after slaughtering the rest of the household. The narrator simply observes that the authorities bury all the dead, without further comment.

12. With the exception of *El castigo de la miseria*, references to the devil and the demonic are much more frequent in the *Desengaños* .

13. Explaining the Moor's magic powers, the narrator says that "como ajenos de nuestra católica fe, no les es dificultoso, con apremios que hacen al demonio, aun en cosas de más calidad" (since they are aliens to our Catholic faith, it is not difficult for them, with pressures that they apply to the devil, even in things of greater quality) (*Desengaños*, 276).

14. Malinowski reached similar conclusions in his study of the recourse to magic in what

he calls "primitive" societies, and Gmelch extends it to contemporary society in his report of the practices of professional baseball players, who develop superstitious rituals in proportion to the factor of chance in their performance (Gmelch 1985; Malinowski 1985).

15. Paun de García posits for Zayas a fundamentally skeptical attitude toward sorcery, offering as evidence the phony conjuring act in *El castigo de la miseria* and the narrator's use of the term "embustera hechicera" (lying sorceress) in *La fuerza de amor,* and contrasts this with other stories in which magic spells are presented as efficacious. I suggest, however, that Zayas uses *embustes* and derivative terms more in the sense of "trick" than "fraud" and that their use does not therefore necessarily imply skepticism. She calls Marcela's boyfriend an "embustero" (trickster, liar): "llevaron a la carcel al embustero y su criado" (they took the trickster and his servant to jail) (*Novelas,* 162), and implies a similar economically motivated exploitation on the part of the sorceress who sends Laura to the chapel, citing her interest in bleeding the lady's pocketbook. In the next novella, however she uses the term *embustes* to describe effective spells. For example, she says that Lucrecia, like the Moorish magician in *Desengaño 5,* could draw her lover to her from his house: "Lucrecia se valía de más eficaces remedios, porque acontecía estar el pobre caballero en casa de doña Juana, y sacarle della, ya vestido, ya desnudo, como le hallaba el engaño de sus hechizos y embustes" (Lucrecia made use of more effective remedies, for it would happen that while the poor gentleman was at doña Juana's house, she would take him out of it, whether dressed or undressed, however the deception of her spells and tricks found him) (*Novelas,* 260). She also speaks of the "embustes" with which Lucrecia blinded don Fernando (*Novelas,* 282).

16. See Chapter 4, note 70, and Chapter 10.

17. In so doing, she displays an attitude toward authority that Adorno describes as characteristic an "authoritarian personality," one evincing a biphasic attitude common in totalitarian regimes. The person exhibits obedience, even a masochistic submissiveness, toward higher-ups and a disdain for inferiors that can extend to sadistic treatment of them (Adorno 1994, 6–7, 20–27). Zayas in this story as elsewhere regularly displays her disdain for servants, believing that "a los criados no es menester darles tormento para que digan las faltas de sus amos, y no sólo verdades, pues saben también componer mentiras; y así los llama un curioso poeta en prosa, común desdicha de los que no se pueden servir a sí mismos" (it is not necesary to torment servants to make them tell their masters' failings, and not only the true ones, for they also know how to make up lies; and therefore a curious prose-poet calls them the ordinary misfortune of those who can't wait on themselves) (*Novelas,* 231–32). For a related Lacanian analysis of obscene enjoyment by the postmodern subject that extends to contemporary events in Bosnia, see Zizek 1991, 141–69; 1994, 203–17.

18. Sánchez Ortega cites the case of an Isabel Maesso, tried in 1670 when a neighbor accused her of possessing a box with suspicious contents. It was found to contain "two pieces of heart-shaped wax, one pierced from top to bottom with three pins, and the other pierced through the thickest part with a needle; and another piece of wax in the shape of a stomach, with a hole" (198). She also tells us that María Estevan included a black hen in the ingredients of a potion designed to cure a man's impotence (203).

19. "Thoughts for the Times on War and Death," cited in Ragland 1995, 102.

20. This is understandable either in Aristotelian language, of woman as matter and man as form; or in Lacanian terms, of woman as the lost original promise of a mythical primary *jouissance* beyond the phallus that marks sexual difference, separation, and the possibility of identity. Describing the Freudian concept of the death drive Elisabeth Bronfen observes that "both 'death' and 'woman' function as Western culture's privileged tropes for the enigmatic and for alterity. . . . like the death drive, which articulates that death is not outside but rather inextricably inhabiting life, femininity also is not a reassuringly canny opposite to masculinity, but rather is inside the masculine, inhabiting it as 'otherness, as its own disruption' [citing Shoshana Felman, "Rereading Femininity," *Yale French Studies* 62 (1981): 41]. As manifesta-

tions of such a force of oscillation, both death and femininity not only call into question rigid categories, but also mark the absence of a fixed place within culture. They function as the foundation and condition of culture's representational systems, as *telos* and origin, yet themselves exist nowhere as reference for this representation [citing Teresa de Lauretis 1984, *Alice Doesn't: Feminism, Semiotics, Cinema,* 13]" (Bronfen, in Wright 1992, 53).

21. Quevedo's description is as follows:

> Entró una que parecía mujer muy galana y llena de corona, cetros, hoces, abarcas, chapines, tiaras, caperuzas, mitras, monteras, brocados, pellejos, seda, oros, garrotes, diamantes, serones, perlas y guijarros. Un ojo abierto y otro cerrado, vestida y desnuda de todas colores. Por el un lado era moza y por el otro era vieja. Unas veces venía despacio y otras aprisa. Parecía que estaba lejos y estaba cerca. Y cuando pensé que empezaba a entrar, estaba ya a mi cabecera.

> (There entered what seemed to be a very elegant woman, decked out with crowns, scepters, sickles, sandals, clogs, tiaras, cowls, miters, capes, brocades, furs, silk, gold, garrotes, diamonds, panniers, pearls and pebbles. One eye open and the other closed, partly dressed in all colors and partly naked. On one side she was young and on the other old. Sometimes she came slowly and other times rapidly. She seemed to be far away and she was close. And when I thought she was just beginning to come in, she was already at the head of my bed.) (1989, 238–39; translation modified).

22. Although Octavio clearly indicates that he is suffering in purgatory, in the chains, flames, and sighs with which he arrives, and in his own words: "estoy en las mayores penas que puede pensar una miserable alma, que aguarda en tan grandes dolores la misericordia de Dios" (I am in the greatest suffering imaginable for a wretched soul that waits for God's compassion in great pain) (*Novelas,* 267), Zayas does not use the term *purgatory.* It was in general circulation in her day, as evidenced by the definition in Covarrubias's 1611 dictionary: "Lugar en las partes infernas, donde están las almas de los fieles que murieron en gracia purgando lo penal de sus pecados, los quales son ayudadas con los sacrificios y sufragios de los vivos, y con el tesoro de la Yglesia e indulgencias" (A place in the infernal regions where the souls of the faithful who died in grace are purging their sins with penalties, who are assisted with the sacrifices and good works of the living, and with the treasury of the Church and indulgences) (889). In fact, as Henry Sullivan demonstrates, the existence of purgatory, rejected by Protestant Reformers, was warmly defended by Catholic polemicists, particularly the Jesuits, during the Counter-Reformation (1996, 67). Nevertheless, Zayas only employs the word *purgatorio* metaphorically, in the context of the suffering caused by unrequited love: in a ballad that don Diego has his servant-musician sing while courting Laura in *La fuerza del amor* (228); in another sung by don Alonso courting doña Ana in *Desengaño 8* (389); and in Federico's self-justification before he writes a declaration of love to include among official papers he and Beatriz read during king Ladislao's absence (*Desengaños,* 416).

23. The Council of Trent had condemned such practices: "hazer oraciones, y conjuros, para que se aparezcan las Almas, y declaren cosas que dessean saber, que se haze por vn arte llamada vulgarmente Nicromancia, la qual está proyuida, y es grauísimo pecado vsar della, con la qual el demonio, se aparece, y dize ser Alma, y da a entender lo que quiere" (praying and making spells to make Souls appear and state things they want to know, which is done with an art popularly called Necromancy, which is prohibited and it is a very grave sin to make use of it, with which the devil appears and says he is the Soul, and states what he wants believed) M. Carrillo, *Explicación de la bula de los difuntos en la qual se trata de las penas y lugares del Purgatorio; y como pueden ser ayudadas las Animas de los difuntos, con las oraciones y sugragios de los*

vivos (*Explanation of the [Papal] bull of the dead in which the places and penalties of Purgatory are considered; and how the Souls of the dead can be helped with prayer and suffering of the living*) (in Alcalá de Henares 1615, fol. 22, cited in Martínez Gil, 504.

24. Diana de Armas Wilson (1987) has given us a superb example of how meaning can be located between texts in her study of the intertextuality of this Cervantine tale. A similar analysis of Zayas's tale would have to focus as much on what she subtracts from Cervantes' version as what she adds—in particular, her erasure of the intriguing study of homosocial bonding and sexual desire as the desire of the Other that Cervantes traces between Anselmo and Lotario. Her response to a number of the motifs in Cervantes appears in the discussions between the frame-tale characters that precede and follow the story. Like Cervantes, Zayas makes questions of narrative veracity and verisimiltude, originality, and poetic justice the topics of discussion between characters in the larger fiction. Her narrator Nise also reacts at some length to a topic posed by Cervantes through Lotario, the level of responsibility properly assigned to woman, an "imperfect animal" in the Aristotelian classification.

25. Place (1923), tracing Zayas's sources, found no clear antecedent for the Virgin's intervention through a hanged man. He does cite as a possibility a tale of a poor gentleman who comes back to life to help his friend win a tournament and the hand of the king's daughter. Her inspiration for that motif seems more likely to have derived at least in part from the folkloric antecedents to Tirso's *El burlador de Sevilla* that circulated throughout Europe, of an exchange of invitations between a live man and a dead man, in which he is saved from being carried to hell because he has prepared for his visit with holy water, a cross, or some other holy relic. In the frame introduction to the story, Nise compares the fate of Camila, raped by don Juan after hiding his pursuit of her from her husband, in the previous tale, with that of Roseleta, whose report to her husband of "the pretensions of another don Juan" did not save her, despite divine intervention (*Desengaños,* 201). Zayas's repeated use of a woman deliberately bled to death in this and other stories also points toward a theatrical source, Calderón's *El médico de su honra*.

26. Centuries before, Apuleius included the resurrection of the dead as witnesses on charges of adultery in *The Golden Ass,* but his speaking dead men come back to accuse, not defend, their wives (Apuleius 1995, bk. 2, para. 27–29 and bk. 9, para. 31).

27. For this story, as Place (1923) points out, Zayas could draw inspiration from a wide variety of novelistic and folkloric sources, from Boccaccio and Bandello to the legend of the lovers of Teruel.

28. A curious note is that Zayas gives the name Arnesto to the man masquerading as a ghost, as she does the homosexual page boy lover in *Desengaño 7*. Both stories are set in Flanders under the governorship of the Duke of Alba as well.

29. This episode is clearly inspired by a story of Castillo Solorzano, "La fantasma de Valencia" (The Ghost of Valencia), from *Tardes entretenidas* (1992, 85–125), in which a don Rodrigo returns from serving the Duke of Alba in Flanders to find his dead brother's house "haunted" by a lover pretending to be a ghost in order to be with the woman he loves. This ghost has better luck; his act is approved by the lady as well, and gains him the opportunity to consummate their secret marriage and thus establish his claim to her over the man chosen by her family.

30. Zayas reorders history by saying that the Duke sends him with the news of the sack of Antwerp, which did not occur until several years after the Duke was replaced as governor. See chapter 9 below.

31. The paternal social structure grounds identity in a name that may not be unique. On hearing her named in the banns, they think that in a city like Salamanca, there would be others by the same name and surname. But the recognition scene suggests that the mother-daughter connection is not fully contained under paternal law, but partly inscribed in the flesh, in a "language of the heart."

Su madre de doña Leonor, con menos sufrimiento que los demás se levantó, y llegán-
dose cerca della la estuvo mirando atentamente, y como de todo punto la conociese,
con pasos desatentados se fué a abrazar con ella, diciendo:

—¡Ay, querido Leonor, hija mía! ¿y cómo es posible que tu corazón puede sufrir el
no hablarme? (*Novelas*, 363)

(Doña Leonor's mother, with less difficulty than the others got up and coming close to
where she was, looking at her attentively, and as soon as she had fully recognized her,
went bewildered to embrace her, saying: "Ay, beloved Leonor, my daughter, how is it
possible that your heart can suffer not speaking to me?")

32. This story perhaps exploits to dramatic effect a fear of being buried alive that we tend
to associate with such stories as that of Poe, but Martínez Gil depicts this fear as surfacing in
the seventeenth century, when certain reports or wills speak of waiting inordinate amounts of
time—from thirty-six hours to three days—before burying someone who dies a sudden death
(1993, 356–59).

33. I would suggest that this might be in part a tongue-in-cheek allusion to Fray Luis de
León, indeed a famous professor at Salamanca, and certainly well known to feminine readers
also for his treatise on the proper conduct of a Christian wife, *La perfecta casada* (The Perfect
Wife) (1583).

34. In this her *desengaños* are akin to the blend of desire and death in some Quevedo poetry.

35. The only exceptions to this are the lingering death from the effects of Lucrecia's witchcraft of the repentant don Fernando in *Desengaño amando y premio de la virtud;* and to a lesser
extent, that of don Marcos in *El castigo de la miseria*, particularly in the first version that concluded with his suicide. At the risk of falling into a circular argument, one might suggest that
both these males have been feminized by their subjection to the powerful, desiring woman;
that as Paul Julian Smith says, the law of the phallus has been inverted, not overturned.

36. Lucrecia also commits suicide in *Desengaño amando,* and Claudia, who had cross-
dressed to serve as don Carlos's page and later married a Moor, is executed in *El juez de su
causa.* There is an interesting symmetry in the fact that in the first story of the *Novelas,* it is the
desiring female antagonist, the "bad" rival, who dies by suicide when her desire in thwarted,
whereas in the last novel of the second volume, only the desiring "bad" woman Florentina survives the generalized massacre she unleashed.

37. I am indebted to Laura Bass for this insight with regard to *Desengaño 5,* which she is
exploring in a forthcoming article on this story.

38. "Se vino a su casa tan honestamente vestida, que en lo que vivió no se puso más galas
que las que sacó del convento, que era un hábito de picote" (She came home so honestly attired that as long as she lived she put on no more finery than that which she wore out of the
convent, which was a habit made of goat hair) (*Desengaños*, 194)

39. Sonia Piloto di Castri, in the preface to her translation to Italian of the *Novelas
amorosas,* to Italian, observes of Zayas's style:

In genere tende a dilungarsi in periodi formati da un accumulo di proposizioni sobur-
dinate, spesso complicate da tortuose perifrasi: un esuberante suseguirsi e alternarsi di
relative, causali, finali, avversative, ecc., fra le quali è difficile districarsi e dove i
soggetti, spesso non esplicitati, si confondono in una ridda di imprevedibili alternanze.
Spezzare questi periodi significava per il traduttore non solo fare di un lunghissimo
enunciato una serie di frasi brevi, ma anche decifrare le frasi ellittiche, identificando e
portando in luce i soggetti sottintesi, separare ed evidenziare le proposizioni reggenti

dalle secondarie, speso non immediatamente individuabili. Un'operazione non semplice. (Zayas y Sotomayor 1995, xix)

(In general she tends to meander in long sentences formed of an accumulation of subordinate propositions, often complicated by tortuous periphrases: an exuberant succession and alternation of relative, causal, final and adversatives clauses, etc., which it is difficult to unravel and where the subjects, often not explicit, merge in a whirl of unpredictable alternation. Breaking up these sentences means for the translator not only making a series of short sentences from a very long enunciation, but also deciphering the elliptical phrases, identifying and bringing to light implied subjects, separating and making evident principal propositions from the secondary ones, often not easily individualized. Not a simple operation.)

40. (Ragland 1995, 90). I have added the parenthetical "to you" in the first question to clarify the nature of desire as the difference between the satisfaction of a (physical) need and the demand for love or recognition by the Other.

41. The only other element that the novella and the *desengaño* have in common is that the declared obstacle to lovers' union is economic. Don Rodrigo overcomes this by earning a knighthood in the Order of Santiago for his military service as a preliminary accomplishment before his greater feat of bringing Leonor back to life through prayer and establishing the validity of their marriage. But no human effort can overcome the greed, pride, and cruelty of the misogynist patriarch in *Desengaño 8*.

42. This story and the previous one abound with reminiscences of Calderón's wife-murder play *El médico de su honra*. While the death by bleeding occurs in *Desengaño 7*, the names in this tale are multiply reminiscent of Calderón's characters. Instead of the just or cruel king, Pedro is here a cruel noble father. The lovers too bear the same names, Mencía and Enrique, and a page functions rather like Clarín in revealing the murder after the fact.

43. The episode is described thus:

En el pequeño retrete había gran claridad, no de hachas ni bujías, sino una luz que sólo alumbraba en la parte de adentro, sin que tocase a la de afuera. Y más admirado que antes, miró a ver de qué salía la luz, y vio al resplandor de ella a la hermosa dama tendida en el estrado, mal compuesta, bañada en sangre, que con estar muerta desde mediodía, corría entonces de las heridas, como si se las acabaran de dar, y junto a ella un lago del sangriento humor. (*Desengaños*, 382)

(There was a great brightness in the little dressing room, not from torches or candles, but a light that only illuminated the inside, without touching the part outside. And more amazed than before, he looked to see where the light came from and saw in its splendor the lovely lady stretched out on the dais, disordered, bathed in blood that, even with her having been dead since midday, still flowed from her wounds as if they had just been given to her, and next to her a lake of the sanguinary humor.)

44. The Mother of God does speak to Beatriz in *Desengaño 9* as she rescues her time and again, but she addresses her when they are alone, or her voice is not heard by others present at the scene. Even in the climactic confrontation with the demonic doctor at the end of that tale, when the assembled crowd does see the "Mother of God, Queen of the Angels and our Lady" with her hand on Beatriz's right shoulder, she remains silent and it is the devil who speaks, saying, "¡Venciste, María, venciste! ¡Ya conozco la sombra que amparaba a Beatriz, que hasta ahora estuve ciego!" (You won, Mary, you won! Now I recognize the shadow that protected Beatriz, 'tho' until now I was blind!) (*Desengaños*, 465).

45. Perhaps most pathetic are the hungry cries of the son who wakes in her absence; see Chapter 5.

46. I find a delightful corroboration of Kristeva's insight in the commentary of a woman who is expert in a very different discourse, that of biological science. The Science section of the 15 October 1996 *New York Times* featured several articles on the vital role microbes play at the lowest, oldest, and most fundamental frontiers of life, between the living and the nonliving. They shape the earth's surface and sustain the vital processes of the human body. Dr. Abigail Salyers, a microbiologist at the University of Illinois, concluded, "We should love them. They're like our mother. They clean up our messes."

Chapter 9

1. Against Freud's theory of the death drive, Reich argued for a social origin of misery, in an oppression by the external world, thus creating a rigidly artificial dichotomy that has negative consequences both for psychoanalysis and for feminist concerns, says Rose. Her answer is that "violence is not something that can be located on the inside or outside, in the psychic or the social . . . but rather something that appears as the effect of the dichotomy itself. I want to suggest that feminism, precisely through its vexed and complex relationship with psychoanalysis, may be in a privileged position to recast this problem, refusing the rigid polarity of inside and outside together with the absolute and fixed image of sexual difference which comes with it and on which it so often seems to rely" (Rose 1989, 28).

2. In Zayas's day, Seneca was popularly considered Spanish because of his birth in Córdoba. Connecting the invocation of the "Spanish" Seneca as model for Blanca's martyrdom with the condemnation of "tyrants" and the fate of Blanca and her sisters in the hands of foreign husbands, we can see in this story Zayas's consideration of the question of empire and the price women pay for men's political ambitions. Earlier in the story, when doña Blanca was lamenting the prince's coldness toward her since their arrival in Flanders, she had painted her husband as Nero in his cruel tyranny: "Préciate de tu crueldad; / cantarás como otro Nero, / viendo que se abrasa el alma / adonde tienes tu imperio" (Boast about your cruelty; you will sing like another Nero, seeing that the soul is consumed where you have your empire) (*Desengaños*, 354). In her image, he reigns in her soul as Nero did in Rome, and takes cruel delight in seeing it consumed in flames.

3. Blanca's maidservant María begs her to dissemble to protect herself from "esa cruel gente, tan poderosos, con ser tan grandes señores, que ni temen a Dios ni al mundo" (those cruel people, who being such great lords, fear neither God nor the world) (*Desengaños*, 361).

4. See Chapter 6 and Zizek's (1994) discussion of Otto Weiniger's antifeminism.

5. For example, when Blanca complains of the young prince's neglect, he responds that Spanish women are tiresome and that any foreigner who mixes his blood with theirs deserves punishment. Blanca retorts that her deception was greater than his and her blood as noble as his: "Mayor le merece la española que entendiendo viene a ser señora, deja su patria donde lo es, por hacerse esclava de quien no la merece" (A greater one awaits the Spanish woman who, understanding that she is coming to be lady of the house, leaves her country where she is one in order to become the slave of one who does not deserve her) Her father-in-law snaps: "No seáis tan atrevida, doña Blanca . . . que os cortaré yo las alas. Con qué soberbia os remontáis, que no sé yo cuándo pensasteis vos, ni vuestro linaje, llegar a merecer ser esposa de mi hijo" (Don't be so bold, lady Blanca, for I will clip your wings. How arrogantly you soar high, for I don't know when you or your line thought you would succeed in deserving to be my son's wife) (*Desengaños*, 355).

6. Her harangue had a *very* contemporary pertinence in 1646, when Zayas says she was writing this second volume. Olivares's policies, particularly his attempts to impose taxes and obligatory military service on the nobility, had in recent years provoked what Marañon called "the strike of the great nobles," and few answered the call to arms in 1640, many nobles argu-

ing that they were only obliged to serve when accompanying the king. Overcoming Olivares's opposition, the king did travel to Aragón to take command close to the front in 1642, and each subsequent year through 1646. See Domínguez Ortíz 1955; Elliott 1986, 610; Stradling 1988, 120.

7. The eldest sister is called "doña Mayor" (literally, lady Elder), perhaps in recognition of the limited advantage of being the oldest sister, in order of preference for marriage and size of dowry.

8. The latter name is more appropriate, as marking an ironic reversal of the role of the archangel Gabriel. Rather than carrying to Mary the news of the miraculous conception of the savior, this Gabriel is entrusted with carrying to Blanca's brother the news of her imminent martyrdom at the hands of her Flemish enemies. Later married to Blanca's serving lady María, he fathers another María, who passes the story along to her descendants, including doña Luisa, the narrator of the story. That Zayas consciously made this connection with the archangel is highly unlikely, however. A more practical suggestive source for the name Gabriel, given the patronymic link if not one of kinship, might have been Gabriel de Zayas (d. 1595), secretary of state under Philip II and responsible for northern affairs and, as the "eyes and ears" of the duke of Alba at court, much involved with policy toward the Netherlands (Maltby 1983).

9. Once the homosexual relationship between the prince and Arnesto is revealed, the reader is led to interpret preceding mysterious violence as related intrigue.

10. Alba became governor of the Netherlands in 1567, in the wake of the April 1566 "Request of the Nobles" in which they asked for suspension of the Inquisition and of executions in the Netherlands and for consideration of their grievances in Madrid; and after the August 1566 iconoclastic sack of church property that followed Philip's rejection of the suggested policy of tolerance. He established a Council of Trouble that became known as the "Council of Blood" for executing over one thousand and condemning another seven thousand to death, from humble citizens to high nobles (Maltby 1983). Alba loomed large in Zayas's imagination, it appears, but her placement of him in history was more imaginative than precise. In the novella *El imposible vencido* (Triumph over the Impossible) she has him dispatch Rodrigo to carry back to Spain the news of the sack of Antwerp. In fact, Alba had been replaced as viceroy in Flanders by Luis de Requesens in 1573 and don Juan de Austria had recently been given command when the Antwerp sack occurred in 1576 (Kamen 1983). Whereas Lope de Vega plays ironically with altering history in *Las fortunas de Diana* to call attention to the role of the narrator, Zayas's rewriting of the deeds of the duke of Alba involves no irony, but rather a mental rearrangement of history to suit her version of poetic truth or poetic justice.

11. Vollendorf (1995) accurately links *Desengaño 7* and *Desengaño 8* as explorations of the misogynist violence in paternal cultures, and characterizes the *Desengaños* in general as tales in which Zayas reorders from a feminist perspective the focus on the body as a spectacular site for the production of truth that Foucault found characteristic of the criminal justice systems of western Europe up until Zayas's era. Vollendorf mislabels *Desengaño 8* as *El verdugo de su esposa*, the title applied to *Desengaño 3* (or *4*). More significant than this understandable error, I believe, she ignores the sociopolitically conservative self-limitation of Zayas's critique of the fundamental structures of Hapsburg Spain. For example, she disregards the complicating factor of the last *desengaño*, in which a woman ignites and survives the generalized violence provoked by her desire.

12. "Jugar a las pintas" and faro, the old game favored by highborn gamblers in Europe, are similar but not identical, at least as the first is described in the *Diccionario de Autoridades* (see below).

13. For an excellent study of the symbolism of cards in early modern Spain, including references to a variety of criticisms of them, see Etienvre 1982. I thank Belén Atienza for calling my attention to the association of cards with disorder and evil, and to Etienvre's study.

14. The narrator reports that don Alonso responds to his dissuasion by telling him that if

he says a word to anyone within a week, he will cut him in little pieces. "Temió tanto el clérigo que, no dudando estaba tan en peligro como la dama, habiéndoselo prometido, no vio la hora de verse fuera de aquella casa y aun después no acababa de asegurarse estaba en salvo, por lo cual no se atrevió a dar cuento del caso, hasta que estuvo público" (The priest was so afraid that, not doubting that he was as much in danger as the lady, having promised him [don Alonso], he couldn't wait for the minute he found himself outside that house and even afterwards he couldn't convince himself that he was safe, for which he didn't dare to reveal the case until it was public) (*Desengaños*, 381).

15. The multiple reminiscences of *El médico de su honra* demonstrate that even if the story does indeed have a factual base, it is also indebted to a powerful literary model.

16. Another possible reading might be one akin to political readings of *El burlador de Sevilla*, that see the powerlessness of the assemblage of kings and nobles to stop the abuses of don Juan as a critique of corrupt earthly regimes that requires divine intervention. However, Zayas does not foreground the corruption as does Tirso. Cf. Márquez Villanueva 1996, especially section 3.

17. The impossibility of such an enterprise has been well demonstrated by Hayden White, Paul Ricoeur, and David Carr (1986), among others.

18. This phantasm, once immediately present to the mind, could then be engraved in the memory, from which it could be voluntarily recalled as a presence from the past, and could be reshaped in the imagination (Brennan 1937).

19. As Carr puts it: "Louis Mink was thus operating with a totally false distinction when he said that stories are not lived but told. They are told in being lived and lived in being told. . . . And here I am thinking only of living one's own life, quite apart from the social dimension, both cooperative and antagonistic, of our action, which is even more obviously intertwined with narration" (61).

20. For much of this description, I am indebted to Bruner's 1991 article. As he puts it, "Culture always reconstitutes itself by swallowing its own narrative tail—Dutch boys with fingers in the dike" (19).

21. William Clamurro (1988) suggests that the relationship between politics and passion is the reverse: that the violent clash between erotic passion and the social demands of the honor code that destroy the agonists of these *desengaños* serves to symbolize a sense of social disintegration and ideological conflict within an aristocratic class committed to anachronistic codes of behavior.

22. For such details of the texture of everyday life, however, the *Navidades de Madrid* (1663) by her feminine literary successor, Mariana de Carvajal, is a richer source, albeit penned by a much less accomplished and interesting storyteller.

23. The third story in each volume departs from this formulaic setting and description. Both are versions of Cervantine tales. For the relationship between *El castigo de la miseria* and Cervantes' *El casamiento engañoso* and *El coloquio de los perros*, see Chapter 6. For Zayas's reworking of "El curioso impertinente" in *Desengaño 3* (*El verdugo de su esposa*), see Chapter 8.

24. The story that is a partial exception to this paradigm is *Al fin se paga todo*. Its opening sentence sets it in Valladolid, while the court of Philip III was resident there. However, that specific time period and location are of no particular importance to the tale itself, which is closer to the model of Boccaccio's *beffas* (practical jokes) than most of her stories.

25. From the standpoint of a twentieth-century reader, one could argue that both the war in Flanders and the seige of Mamora *do* have symbolic importance; they were both components of costly campaigns whose eventual loss was as certain as the ultimate frustration of the dream of a fully satisfying and enduring sexual relationship. However, it would be hazardous to speculate that Zayas intuited this when she wrote this story, at least a decade if not two before the 1648 Treaty of Münster recognized the independence of the United Provinces.

26. For example, in *La burlada Aminta*, Aminta is promised to her cousin, who is away fight-

ing in the war with the duke of Savoy when don "Jacinto" lays seige to her, and in *El imposible vencido,* doña Leonor's parents send a false letter saying that Rodrigo has married a Flemish woman while he serves under the duke of Alba in Flanders. (See note 10, this chapter).

27. As Elaine Pagels's work on early Christianity has demonstrated, the story that the canonical Bible itself tells exemplifies the deliberate exclusion of the feminine voice. The Judeo-Christian concept of God, like that of Islam, but unlike those of all the other major religions, excludes any feminine principle from the divinity. Early Christianity was open to women, even as preachers and teachers, however, and one tradition included Mary Magdalene as a most favored disciple of Christ. Most of the Gnostic Gospels followed the first creation story in Genesis—in which men and women were created equally and simultaneously in God's image—describe God in equally masculine and feminine terms, and allow an equal participation in social, political, and religious structures of their communities. But such feminine participation in the principle of divinity and the priesthood was excluded as Christianity established itself as an orthodox, institutional religion (Pagels 1988, 1989).

28. She imprints the marks of her enslavement to passion in the S-clavo, "esclavo" (S + nail = slave) marks on her cheeks, as Chanon-Deutsch points out. Interestingly, that device is virtually the same as the Lacanian sign for the subject, divided by desire.

29. In the course of these events, Isabel's father dies of a heart attack from the shock; a faithful but poor rival for her affections, don Felipe, kills don Manuel when he declares that he intends to marry a beautiful Moorish woman instead of doña Isabel; the Moorish woman commits suicide; don Felipe disappears and is eventually killed in an unspecified war; and Isabel enters a convent.

30. Yllera suggests that in the second *desengaño* Zayas also has in mind the Catalonian rebellion rather than the hostilities begun in 1614 by Carlos Manuel I, duke of Savoy, to reclaim Monferrato. The narrator, Lisarda, comments: "Ocasionáronse en este tiempo las largas y peligrosas guerras de aquellos reinos, que no solas lloran ellos, sino nosotros, pues de esto se originó entrársenos en España y costarnos a todos tanto como cuesta" (The long and dangerous wars of those realms were stirred up at that time, which not only they lament but we do as well, since from this grew the entry into our Spain and costing all of us as much as it costs) (*Desengaños,* 179 and n. 2).

31. For an excellent consideration of the manner in which in Lope's *comedias* male homosocial desire and struggle for dominance is carried out through rivalry over women, see Yarbro-Bejarano 1994, particularly chaps. 5, 7, and 8.

32. In her stories Zayas also shows us—willingly or perhaps inadvertently, given her conservative social ideology—an awareness of how women suffer the consequences of class tensions. Esteban/Estefanía's attempt to climb out of his social class causes Laurela's death in *Desengaño 6;* and the unwillingness of the cruel and greedy father of *Desengaño 8* to allow his daughter to marry the son of wealthy *labradores* (farmers) leads to her death as well as that of the poor but noble doña Ana.

33. See Baldwin 1967 and the *Diccionario de autoridades.* The latter says of the Bula de la Santa Cruzada, "Es la que se publica y se concede a los Reinos de España, y contiene muchas gracias, indultos y privilegios, siendo entre ellos muy conocido el de poder los que la toman comer huevos y lacticinios en los días de ayuno de la Quaresma: y ésta suele llamarse por antonomasia la bula" (It is that which is published and granted to the Kingdoms of Spain, and it contains many favors, exoneration and privileges, the best known among them being that those who take it can eat eggs and dairy products during fast days of Lent, and this is usually called the bull by antonomasia).

34. Since Lisis is both narrator of the tale and commentator on it, the break between the plotted story and the framing commentator is less pronounced in this case. The commentary also includes the harangue against feminized, cowardly men who abuse women verbally and are unwilling to defend them militarily against enemies "outside," as discussed above.

35. Flora is the name Zayas gives to the aggressively desiring female antagonist in the sec-

ond story of her first collection, and she is explicity linked to the Roman model as the heroine laments, "¡Ay Flora cruel, más traidora y engañosa que la pasada, por quien en Roma
tienen en tan poco las de tu nombre!" (Ay, cruel Flora, more treacherous and deceitful that
the previous one, for whom those of your name are held in such low regard) (*Novelas*, 105)
     36. The passage proceeds:

> San Agustín hace mención de una famosa ramera, que los romanos canonizaron por
> deesa, llamada Flora. Esta, siendo en gran manera hermosa, vendía su cuerpo a cuan-
> tos querían, mas si no la daban gran suma de dinero, no admitía a nadie; y como con
> este torpe oficio hubiese allegado mucho, cuando murió, dejando gran cantidad de
> dinero, dejó al pueblo romano por su heredero, mandando comprar rentas para que
> cada año le hiciesen solemnes fiestas en memoria suya. El pueblo romano aceptó la
> herencia con cargo y obligación de solemnizar la fiesta de una tal mujer, y no con-
> tentándose con esto, pasaron más adelante de lo que había pedido, que fué hacerla
> templo y señalarla sacrificios y dedicarla por deesa. Y como después de mejor mirado,
> considerasen ser afrenta tener por deesa una mujer pública, por quitar el mal sonido,
> mandaron que la llamasen la deesa de las flores, y que presidiese a ellas, y que tuviese
> cargo de que los árboles floreciesen bien, para que dello procediesen frutos en abun-
> dancia, y que dedicada por deesa destas cosas, podía muy bien ser adorada por tal, y así
> quedó canonizada por deesa; y porque el pueblo recibiese bien esto, constituyeron fi-
> estas bien regocijadas y deshonestas, conforme a la torpedad de la deesa cuyas eran.
> (Pérez de Moya 1595, 82–83)

> (Saint Augustine mentions a famous whore, whom the Romans canonized as a god-
> dess, named Flora. She, being extremely beautiful, sold her body to all who desired it,
> but if they did not give her a great sum of money, she did not admit anyone; and as she
> gathered a great deal from this indecent occupation, when she died, leaving a great
> quantity of money, she left the Roman people as her inheritor, ordering the purchase
> of annuities so that every year they would make solemn celebrations in her memory.
> The Roman people accepted the inheritance with the charge and obligation of solem-
> nizing the celebration of such a woman, and not content with that, they went beyond
> what she had asked and made her a temple and designated sacrifices and dedicated
> them to her as a goddess. And looking at it better afterwards, they considered it to be
> an affront to have a prostitute as a goddess, and in order to remove the bad tone, they
> ordered that they call her the goddess of flowers, and that she preside over them, and
> that she should be credited with the ample flowering of the trees so that they might
> produce fruit in abundance, and that dedicated as goddess of these things, she could
> well be adored as such, and thus she became canonized as a goddess; and in order that
> the people might receive this well, they established very delightful and lewd festivals, in
> conformity with the indecency of the goddess whose festival they were.)

     In Calderón's *El mágico prodigioso*, lines 2220–21, Justina complains that she is being
treated worse than a prostitute when Lelio and Floro accuse her of having a lover hidden in
her house: "¿Viéronse Laia ni Flora / en afrentas semejantes?" (Did either Laia or Flora find
themselves in similar affronts?) As noted in the McKendrick/Parker edition, Cervantes also
names this Flora in the prologue to *Don Quixote:* " 'Si tratárades de . . . mujeres rameras, ahí
está el obispo de Mondoñedo, que os prestará a Lamia, Laida y Flora' " ("If you should deal
with . . . women prostitutes, you have there the bishop of Mondoñedo, who will lend you
Lamia, Laida and Flora"). Cervantes refers to a letter in the *Epístolas familiares* of Antonio de
Guevara in which Guevara recounts the lives of the three courtesans (Calderón de la Barca
1992).

37. I do not mean to suggest that nonlinear narrative creation of meaning is unique to women's writing. Kristeva's theory of the poetic text concentrates on male writers. And as Forcione (1984), has demonstrated, Cervantes' most powerful linked stories, *El casamiento engañoso* and *El coloquio de los perros,* generate meaning through what he terms a "fugal" organization (126), or the "dialectic and dialogic movement" (179) of apparent narrative disorder.

38. "Insofar as the feminine has been mythologized on the side of shadows, desire, and dreams, if not as the very source of the enigmata of aesthetics, the masculine clings instead to *logos* and identifies knowledge with the visible, with method, the provable. Jane Gallop is on the right track in *Reading Lacan* when she links metonymy to the feminine and meaphor to the masculine, but not because of the biological literalism she implies [Gallop 1985, 126]. Metaphor and metonymy are not gender specific. Woman may *seem* universalizeable because culture identifies her with the silence of the drives that Lacan called the real, even if she does not recognize this as a knowledge about *jouissance.* Neither sex is assured of a universal function in terms of knowledge, then" (Ragland-Sullivan 1991, 73).

39. "This modality is the one Freudian psychoanalysis points to in postulating not only the *facilitation* and the structuring *disposition* of drives, but also the so-called *primary processes* which displace and condense both energies and their inscription. Discrete quantities of energy move through the body of the subject who is not yet constituted as such and, in the course of his development, they are arranged according to the various constraints imposed on this body—always already involved in a semiotic process—by family and social structures. In this way the drives, which are 'energy' charges as well as 'psychical' marks, articulate what we call a *chora:* a nonexpressive totality formed by the drives and their stases in a motility that is as full of movement as it is regulated" (Kristeva 1984).

Chapter 10

1. My print carries the attribution of Georges de La Tour, but according to the catalog of the exhibit of La Tour's work in the National Gallery of Art in 1996–97, some art historians believe that, while the original conception was Georges's, the execution of the work may be in large part that of his son Etienne (Conisbee 1996, 124).

2. Juan de Piña goes Cervantes one further, in a witty near-abolition of the prologue as well as the frame narrative in his collection of novellas published in 1624. He reduces it to two sentences: "El *Prólogo* se introduze a suma de lo impresso: dilatado, nunca visto de la ociosidad. Las *Novelas exemplares y prodigiosas historias* deste libro dizen la brevedad que afectan, como el *Prólogo* " (The Prologue presents itself as a summation of what is printed, postponed, never seen by idle readers. The *Exemplary novels and prodigious stories* of this book, like its Prologue, bespeak the brevity to which they aspire) (1987, 33). Piña transfers the explanatory and apologetic function of the standard prologue to a complex epilogue.

3. She appears to have written at least eight of the stories and to have been preparing them for publication about 1625, when the preferred style was Cervantes' frame-less model (see Chapter 1). As noted in earlier chapters, the third novella in each volume is a rewriting of a Cervantes story.

4. Illness is also a motif in numerous French collections: Philippe de Vigneulles, *Les Cent Nouvelles Nouvelles* (The Hundred New Novels), Le Seigneur de Cholières, *Les Après-disnees du Seigneur de Cholières* (The After-Dinner Stories of the Lord of Cholieres), and others (Losse 1994, 63). In Mariana de Carvajal's *Navidades de Madrid* (Christmas in Madrid) (1993), the lady of the house has been confined to the house caring for her ailing, elderly husband and, curiously, it is his death near the Christmas season that makes the storytelling possible.

5. At the end of the first volume, their betrothal is promised for the first day of the new year, and along with it, a second part of the *sarao* (soiree), in which don Juan's ingratitude will be punished, Lisarda's affections will change and Lisis will wed. In the opening frame of the

second volume, however, the reader is informed that Lisis's affliction with *mal de amor* grew so grave that it became life threatening, until the companionship of the "Moorish slave" Zelima/Isabel started her on the road to recover. The promised betrothal/narrative celebration was therefore postponed for more than a year, until the recovered Lisis accedes to the wishes of don Diego and her mother and sets the celebration for the last three nights of the coming carnival season, in which the entertainment is to culminate on the last night in her betrothal.

6. As Lyons (1989, 76–78) points out, however, the refuge they take, in a Franciscan monastery, is in a moral sense at least, the heart of the danger, as Franciscan monks, both in the frame and enclosed tales, represent the threat of religious hypocrisy. The same could be said of Zayas's frame "refuge," for the courtly gathering of men and women revolves around the same lure and threat of amorous desire central to her stories.

7. Reiner also suggests a winter cold—there is a heavy blanket on the boy's bed and a shot of the mother opening the drapes over his window shows a wintry-looking glimpse of other suburban rooftops. Carvajal describes the arrival of "el riguroso invierno armado de sus espesas nieves y empedernidos yelos" (the severe winter armed with thick snows and rock-hard ice) and the organizer of the social gathering in which stories are told again names the cold: "Ocho días nos quedan para llegar a la Pascua, y siendo domingo la Nochebuena, pues los fríos son tan grandes y tenemos tribuna dentro de casa, paréceme que estos cinco días de Pascua y lo restante de las vacaciones no dejemos a nuestra viuda" (We still have eight days before Christmas, and since Christmas Eve is on Sunday, since the cold is so great and we have a tribune within the house, it seems to me that for these five days of Christmas and the rest of the vacation we should not leave our widow) (1993, 16, 17).

8. Eslava's first tale depicts the possible economic effect of *mal de amor*, with a story that tells how one of the frame participants lost a ship due to the immoderate passion of its young captain.

9. Marguerite de Navarre is an exception to this rule, and understandably so, given her position in the French court. See the discussion of her frame according to Wetzel's theory below.

10. Doña Lucrecia, the hostess of the storytelling gathering, is said to live in a house "labrada a la malicia" (literally, built with guile or cunning), the sort of one-story residence favored by the lesser nobility in Madrid because it exempted them from the obligation of housing royal servants and other courtesans who flooded the capital when Philip II transferred it to Madrid, as Catherine Soriano's note to Carvajal's text informs us. Carvajal adds a number of realistic touches, such as telling us that doña Lucrecia lives in the center of the house so that she can rent out the better exterior rooms. But she also describes it as having a beautiful garden that with its fruit trees, flowers, fountains, and statuary might be a miniature copy of the nearby gardens of El Prado.

11. The drawing room (*sala*) is, we are told, "cercada de muchas filas de terciopelo verde" (surrounded with many panels of green velvet) and "aderezada de unos costosos paños flamencos, cuyos boscajes, flores y arboledas parecían las selvas de Arcadia o los pensiles huertos de Babilonia. Coronaba la sala un rico estrado, con almohadas de terciopelo verde, a quien las borlas y guarniciones de plata hermoseaban sobre manera, haciendo competencia a una vistosa camilla, que al lado del vario estrado había de ser trono, asiento y resguardo de la bella Lisis" (adorned with expensive Flemish tapestries, whose woodland scenes, flowers, and groves looked like the forests of Arcadia or the hanging gardens of Babylon. Crowning the room was a luxurious dais, with cushions of green velvet, made exceedingly handsome by gold tassels and trim, in competition with a striking chaise lounge at the side of the unusual dais that was to be the throne, seat, and shelter of the lovely Lisis) (*Novelas*, 31–32).

12. See Melloni 1976, 89–100, for a discussion of the relation of Zayas's technique to the escapist aspirations of her readers.

13. Cayuela, who attributes this comparison to Virginie Rejaud, says:

Séduire, en effet, suppose de se représenter l'autre, de construire l'image à laquelle on désir que l'autre s'identifie. Et qu'est-ce que le lecteur fictif sinon l'image de l'Autre? Ne peut-on se représenter la construction de ce lecteur comme un mouvement analogue à celui de la séduction? Car, comme dans la séduction, l'enjeu est bien d'amener l'autre à participer à la création de l'illusion qui sans lui resterait "lettre morte." Séduire suppose aussi de donner une image de soi, de se représenter aux yeux de l'autre, en fonction de l'image qu'on a de lui et de la relation qu'on veut établir avec lui. (1994, 321–22, citing Virginie Rajaud, "La séduction, clé pour une analyse de la réception littéraire," *CREER*, Paris III, Séance du 8 Juin 1990)

(Seduction, in effect, involves representing the other to oneself, constructing the image with which one wishes the other to identify. And what else is the fictive reader if not the image of the Other? Cannot one represent the construction of this reader as a move analogous to that of the seduction? Because, as in seduction, the object is to induce the other to partake in the creation of the illusion which without him would remain a "dead letter." Seduction presupposes also giving an image of oneself, of representing oneself in the eyes of the other in accord with the image that one has of him and of the relation that one wishes to establish with him.)

14. Gittes cites María Rosa Menocal's study of the insistent repression of the substantial impact in medieval Europe exercised by Arabic culture, both as the source of learning, of literary traditions, and of material well-being, and as a negative pole against which theologians and writers such as Dante reacted.

15. Menocal (1987, 139–42) argues that Boccaccio scholars have paid too little attention to the importance of the Arabic and Hebrew inspiration and Arabic or Andalusian sources in the *Decameron,* as, for example, the model of scatological tales within a didactic frame provided him by Petrus Alfonsi's *Disciplina clericalis.*

16. Wetzel is thus closer to Marcel Tetel's reading of a fundamental ambiguity, indeed a Manichaean duality, in the *Heptameron* (1981) than to Paula Sommer's assertion of an ascendance of Protestant faith (1984).

17. In his insightful book *Contradictory Subjects,* George Mariscal says that in this Spanish society, "[the] aristocratic subject . . . is undeniably a masculinist construct; virtually all forms of subjectivity in this period depended on different degrees and kinds of 'maleness,' rather than on the historically more recent male/female binomial" (1991, 27). Since Mariscal rightly argues that subjectivity (roughly equivalent to agency) is based on exclusions, what one is *not* as much as what one is—for example, not *converso* nor lower class, this argument displays a curious blindness, because the *first* exclusionary ground for subjectivity in Golden Age Spain is "not female" and subjectivity therefore is grounded in the male-female polarity.

18. Montesa, in his excellent discussion of her use of the frame, also describes her collection as a whole as an "obra *de tesis* " (Montesa Peydro 1981, 351; emphasis in the original).

19. See Cayuela 1994, 58 and Moll 1982. The approval by Ioseph de Valdiuielso dated 2 June 1636 (actually 1626) refers to it thus: "Este honesto, y entretenido Sarao, que me mandó ver el señor don Iuan de Mendieta" (This decorous and entertaining Soiree, that don Juan de Mendieta ordered me to examine) and the license conceded by Mendieta, *vicario general* for Madrid, states that "damos licencia para que se pueda imprimir, e imprima este libro; Tratado honesto, y entretenido Sarao" (we give a license to allow printing, and let this book be printed; Seemly treatise and entertaining Soirée).

20. Various critics consider the reasons why Zayas and other Spanish novella writers avoided the term *novela.* For a very substantial discussion of the history of the use and avoidance of that designation, see Cayuela, 47–79 and 361–70.

21. Lyons, noting the general occlusion from critical view of example as a basic rhetorical

figure, traces the development of the term and its bifurcation into *example* and the Latin word *exemplum* on the one hand, and on the other its vernacular forms (including the Spanish form *ejemplo*), the latter coming to mean in common critical usage either a particular genre or literary device, " 'a short narrative used to illustrate a moral point' " as Robert P. apRoberts defines it in the *Princeton Encyclopedia of Poetry and Poetics* (Lyons 1989, 9–10).

22. Cervantes' composition of that apparently contradictory title, combining the morally and aesthetically suspect genre label "novela" with the concept of exemplary content, set the pattern for many of the novella writers who followed him. "C'est avec Cervantes que la *novela* s'affiche comme telle pour la première fois sur un frontispice, dans un titre qui renseigne le lecteur à la fois sur la forme et le contenu: *Novelas ejemplares*. Ce titre crée ailleurs un courant titulaire que sera emprunté par quelques auteurs tout au long du XVIIème siècle" (It is with Cervantes that the novella advertises itself as such for the first time on a frontispiece, in a title that informs the reader at the same time about the form and the content: *Exemplary novels*. This title also creates an entitling practice that will be borrowed by various writers throughout the seventeenth century) (Cayuela 1994, 365–66).

23. Regarding their exemplary content, Cervantes says, "Heles dado nombre de *ejemplares*, y si bien lo miras, no hay ninguna de quien no se pueda sacar algún ejemplo provechoso; . . . Una cosa me atreveré a decirte: que si por algún modo alcanzara que la lección de estas *Novelas* pudiera inducir a quien las leyera a algún mal deseo o pensamiento, antes me cortara la mano con que las escribí que sacarlas en público" (I have named them "exemplary," and if you look at it well, there is not one from which some beneficial example cannot be drawn; . . . I will be so bold as to say one thing to you: that if in some way it should come about that reading these *Novellas* could induce the reader to some evil desire or thought, I would rather cut off the hand with which I wrote them than publish them) (1990, 8–9). In terms of form, he declare that "yo soy el primero que he novelado en lengua castellana; que las muchas novelas que en ella andan impresas, todas son traducidas de lenguas extranjeras, y éstas son mías propias, no imitadas ni hurtadas. Mi ingenio las engendró y las parió mi pluma, y van creciendo en los brazos de la estampa" (I am the first person who has "novelized" in the Castilian language; for the many novellas that circulate in publication in that tongue are all translated from foreign languages, and these are mine alone, neither imitated nor stolen. My wit engendered them and my pen gave birth to them, and they are growing up in the arms of the press) (9).

24. See Vega Carpio 1988, 48; Castro 1972; and Forcione's discussion of their critiques (1982, 1–18). See also Forcione 1989.

25. While this argument seems a fair characterization of the unique qualities of Cervantes' novelistic art, its accuracy is questionable as a sweeping generalization of the discourse, framed or unframed, of all his followers in that genre. Juan de Piña in particular cannot be so simply dismissed.

26. Boyer's readable translation of this passage underlines the symbolic importance of the insistence on the color green as symbol of hope. She has also disentangled its syntax in ways I avoid, for reasons explored below. Her translation reads: "The room was crowned by a rich dais piled high with mountains of green velvet cushions ornamented with splendid silver embroidery and tassels. To one side of the dais was a luxurious couch that was to serve as seat, sanctuary, and throne for the lovely Lysis who, because of her illness, could enjoy this distinction. It was green brocade with gold trimming and fringe, the green symbolizing a hope she did not really feel" (Zayas y Sotomayor 1990, 9).

27. He also criticized the episodic nature of her stories, calling *El prevenido* nothing more than a libertine enumeration of adventures in love, and seeing no relation whatsoever between the two adventures of don Jaime in *Desengaño 4*. Given his distaste for the diverse manifestations of sexual desire that Zayas makes visible, it is not surprising that he was unwilling and unable to perceive the unconscious logic that binds these episodes together. Particular stories that he rejects leads us to the other tension operative in that Baroque structure.

28. The other characteristics he lists are iterativity or multiplicity (see below), discontinuity, rarity, artificiality, undecidability, and excess (Lyons 1989, 27–34).

29. See the articles by William J. Broad, "Bugs Shape Landscape, Make Gold," and Sandra Blakeslee, "From Birth, Body Houses Microbe Zoo," and "Microbial Life's Steadfast Champion," in the "Science Times" section of *The New York Times*, 15 October 1996, C1, C3, C7–8. Scientists found that the goldfield, for example, may have been formed by the work of swarms of microbes who concentrate the gold by assembling it in a pure state on their cell surfaces.

30. See, in this regard, Zizek's discussion of "feminine" or "bodily" depth and the "pure-skin" surface of the Symbolic order, in conjunction with the David Lynch film *Blue Velvet* and Deleuze's conception of the Sense-Event in *The Logic of Sense* (Zizek 1994, 122–33).

31. Cervantes' stories give us a sense that he is attempting to bridge this gulf, to explore the intermediate regions between surface and depth, often through the use of a double who serves as a living alter-ego of the hero or heroine. Yet in a sense he admits the impossibility of such an exploration, in that he "kills" Anselmo in *El curioso impertiente* when he is in the very act of self-exploration, self-revelation or confession, with his body half in bed, half over his desk, dying with pen in hand.

32. Zayas employs the word *hembra* (female) only four other times in her entire collection: (1) in *Aventurarse perdiendo*, saying that Félix's father had three children, the oldest and youngest "hembras" and a middle male child, Félix; (2) in *Desengaño 4*, as don Jaime stabs the black slave to death calling her a deceiving, evil female; (3) in *Desengaño 6*, as Esteban/Estefanía argues for the possibility of true love between two women, arguing that the soul is the same in the male and the female; and (4) within *Desengaño 10*, as Florentina's servant calls herself the world's most evil female and the only one who deserves to die for causing Magdalena's death with her plot to save Florentina.

33. Zayas here plays on the expression "cantar la gala, o la gloria" (to sing the praise, or the glory) defined in the *Diccionario de Autoridades* as "celebrar la acción heróica, e insigne de algun sugeto, que aventajó a los demás, y sobresalió en ella" (to celebrate the heroic and illustrious action of some subject who excelled in it and surpassed others).

34. Jacinta's account at the level of inner narrator in the first novella, *Aventurarse perdiendo*, and that of Florentina in *Desengaño 10* and the autobiographical first *desengaño* told by the frame character Isabel/Zelima.

35. Montesa postulates that in Zayas, this technique derives from "vivencia" (lived experience).

> La intercambiabilidad de autor-ente de ficción en la literatura es reflejo de una concepción de la existencia en la que nada es fijo ni estable. . . . El continuo cambio de perspectivas a que se nos somete en las novelas de Zayas es una manera de *relativizar* el cosmos, ofreciéndonos el espectáculo de una experiencia total, sin divisiones, en la que con tanto derecho entre nuestra ficción como nosotros. . . . La interpenetración ilógica de planos narrativos es un modo de a-racionalidad, como lo era la brujería, la superstición, el subconsciente o lo sobrenatural . . . lejos de desarrollar una función *desintegradora* del mundo, tienen como fin *integrar* en una unidad más amplia todas las *formas de ser* que somos capaces de experimentar. . . . Es buscar una lógica nueva, superior, desestructurar un mundo en el que el pensamiento tiene la primacía, y ordenarlo de nuevo de un modo en el que el sistema de subordinación no es fijo. (Montesa 1981, 375–76)
>
> (The interchangeability between author and fictional being in literature is a reflection of a concept of existence in which nothing is fixed or stable. . . . The continual change of perspective to which the novellas of Zayas submit us is a means of *relativizing* the cosmos, offering us the spectacle of a total experience, undivided, in which our fictions, like us, enter very rightly. . . . The illogical interpenetration of narrative planes is an a-

rational method, as was witchcraft, superstition, the subconscious, or the supernatural
. . . far from developing a disintegrative function toward the world, they have as their
end *integrating* in a larger unity all the *forms of being* that we are capable of experienc-
ing. . . . It is to look for a new, superior logic, to deconstruct a world in which thought
holds primacy, and order it again according to a method in which the system of subordination is not fixed.)

36. I thank Belén Atienza for bringing this work to my attention.

37. The relevant lines are, in "Llama a la Muerte": "Fallecieron los Curios y los Fabios"
([All] the Curios and Fabios have died); and in Salmo 16, "Por tal manera Curios, Decios,
Fabios / fueron" (In that way Curios, Decios, and Fabios have gone).

38. The poem was written before 1627 and published in the first edition of his *Sueños y dis-
cursos* in that year, and Zayas could thus have read it when she was writing her novellas. James
O. Crosby adds notes questioning whether this poem is really autobiographical, because of
the comic tone and because he uses "el nombre ficticio de Fabio . . . para amantes ridículos
y desdichados" (the fictitious name Fabio . . . for ridiculous and ill-fated lovers) more than
once. In fact, however, Crosby only cites one other poem, another ballad, that "en la simulada
figura de unas prendas ridículas, burla de la vana estimación que hacen los amantes de semejantes favores" (in the simulated figure of some ridiculous garments, mocks the vain regard
lovers hold for such favors). In the ballad "aquel sacristán famoso / aquel desdichado Fabio"
(that famous sacristan, that unfortunate Fabio) has been collecting tokens of his love for
"Benita": "cubriendo con cuatro cuernos / de su bonete de paño / más de mil que tú, Benita,
/ le has puesto con otros tantos" (covering with the four horns of his wool biretta more than a
thousand that you, Benita, have put on him with as many men). Quevedo describes in his
characteristically grotesque, satirical style the tokens—a shoe, a garter, a ribbon, a portrait—
as Fabio debates how best to dispose of them, and thinks perhaps burning might be best since
they came from devil (Quevedo Villegas 1981, 439–44).

39. Zayas also gives us a phantasmatic diabolic version of such a supportive, understanding friend in *Desengaño 9,* in the Count Fabio who is the supposed correspondent for the sedi-
tious letters planted in the sleeve of Rosismunda/Beatriz in the palace of Duke Octavio.

Works Cited

Adorno, T. W. (1994). *Adorno: The Stars Down to Earth and Other Essays on the Irrational in Culture.* New York: Routledge.

Aldana, F. de. (1957). *Poesías.* Madrid: Espasa-Calpe.

Almansi, G. (1975). *The Writer as Liar: Narrative Technique in the "Decameron."* London: Routledge & Kegan Paul.

Alonso, D. (1976). "La correlación en la estructura del teatro calderoniano." In *Calderón y la crítica: Historia y antología,* edited by M. Durán and R. González Echevarría, 2:388–454. Madrid: Editorial Gredos.

———., ed. (1978). *La "Epístola moral a Fabio," de Andrés Fernández de Andrada.* Madrid: Editorial Gredos.

Amezúa y Mayo, A. de. (1950). Prologue to *Desengaños amorosos: Parte segunda del Sarao y entretenimiento honesto de Doña Mariá de Zayas y Sotomayor,* by M. de Zayas y Sotomayor, vii-xxiv. Madrid: Aldus, S. A. de Artes Gráficas.

Amezúa y Mayo, A. G. de. (1948). "Prólogo del colector." In *Novelas amorosas y ejemplares,* by María de Zayas y Sotomayor, vii-l. Madrid: Aldus, S. A. de Artes Gráficas.

Anthony [El Saffar], R. (1993). "Violante: The Place of Rejection." In *The Prince in the Tower: Perceptions of "La vida s sueño,"* edited by F. A. de Armas, 165–82. Lewisburg: Bucknell University Press.

Anthony El Saffar, R., and D. de Armas Wilson, eds. (1993). *Quixotic Desire: Psychoanalytic Perspectives on Cervantes.* Ithaca: Cornell University Press.

Antonio, N. (1783–88). *Bibliotheca hispana nova; sive, Hispanorum scriptorum qui ab anno MD ad MDCLXXXIV.* Matriti, J. de Ibarra.

Apuleius. (1995). *The Golden Ass.* Oxford: Oxford University Press.

Ariès, P. (1974). *Western Attitudes Toward Death: From the Middle Ages to the Present.* Baltimore: Johns Hopkins University Press.

———. (1981). *The Hour of Our Death.* Oxford: Oxford University Press.

Arquiola, E. (1988). "Bases biológicas de la feminidad en la España moderna (siglos XVI y XVII)." *Asclepio: Revista de historia de la medicina y de la ciencia* 40 (1): 297–315.

Artemidorus Daldianus. (1975). *The Interpretation of Dreams: "Oneirocritica."* Park Ridge, N.J.: Noyes Classical Studies.

Artola, A. M. (1992). "Sor María de Jesús Agreda y la clausura concepcionista." In *1 Congreso Internacional del Monacato Femenino en España, Portugal y América, 1492–1992,* 2:213–220. León: Universidad de León.

Baker, E. (1990). "La problemática de la historia literaria." In *Texto y sociedad: Problemas de historia literaria,* edited by B. Aldaraca, E. Baker, and J. Beverley, 12–18. Atlanta, Ga.: Rodopi.

Baldwin, M. W. (1967). "Bulla Cruciata." In *New Catholic Encyclopedia,* 2: 881–82. New York: McGraw Hill.

Bandello, M. (1943). *Historias trágicas.* Madrid: Ediciones Atlas.

Barbeito Carneiro, I. (1986). "Escritoras madrileñas del siglo XVII (Estudio bibliográfico-crítico)." Ph.D. diss., Universidad Complutense.

———. (1992). *Mujeres del Madrid barroco: Voces testimoniales.* Madrid: Dirección General de la Mujer de la Comunidad de Madrid.

———. (1990). *Novelle.* Edited by E. Mazzali. Milan: Rizzoli.

Barberi Squarotti, G. (1983). "Quattro confessioni." In *Il potere della parola,* 97–127. Naples: Federico Ardia.

Benaim de Lasry, A. (1982). *Two Romances: A Study of Medieval Spanish Romances and an Edition of Two Representative Works.* Newark, Del.: Juan de la Cuesta.

Benjamin, J. (1988). *The Bonds of Love: Psychoanalysis, Feminism, and the Problem of Domination.* New York: Pantheon Books.

Berceo, G. de. (1981). *Poema de Santa Oria.* Madrid: Clásicos Castalia.

Bergmann, E. (1991). "The Exclusion of the Feminine in the Cultural Discourse of the Golden Age: Juan Luis Vives and Fray Luis de León." In *Permanence and Evolution of Behavior in Golden-Age Spain: Essays in Gender, Body, and Religion,* edited by A. Saint-Saëns, 123–36. Lewiston: Edwin Mellon Press.

———. (1990). "Sor Juana Inés de la Cruz: Dreaming in a Double Voice." In *Women, Culture, and Politics in Latin America,* 151–72. Berkeley and Los Angeles: University of California Press

Bersani, L. (1969). *A Future for Astyanax: Character and Desire in Literature.* Boston: Little, Brown.

Bibliotheca Sanctorum. (1961?-1970).12 vols. Rome: Instituto Giovanni XXIII nella Pontificia Università Lateranense.

Blakeslee, S. (1995). "How the Brain Might Work: A New Theory of Consciousness." *New York Times,* March 21, 1995, C1, C10.

Blanco, A. (1989). "Domesticity, Education, and the Woman Writer: Spain 1850–1880." In *Cultural and Historical Grounding for Hispanic and Luso-Brazilian Feminist Literary Criticism,* edited by H. Vidal, 371–94. Minneapolis: Institute for the Study of Ideologies and Literature.

Boccaccio, G. (1881). *Delle donne famose.* Bologna: Presso Gaetano Romagnoli.

———. (1982). *The Decameron.* New York: New American Library.

———. (1985). *Decameron.* Milan: Arnoldo Mondadori.

Borges, J. L. (1956). *Ficciones.* Buenos Aires: Emecé.

Bourland, C. (1973). *The Short Story in Spain in the Seventeenth Century.* New York: Burt Franklin.

Bouza Alvarez, F. J. (1991). *Locos, enanos y hombres de placer en la corte de los Austrias.* Madrid: Temas de Hoy.

Boyer, H. P. (1990). Introduction to *The Enchantments of Love,* by María de Zazas y Sotomayor. Berkeley and Los Angeles: University of California Press.

Brennan, R. E. (1937). *General Psychology: An Interpretation of the Science of the Mind Based on Thomas Aquinas.* New York: Macmillan.

Bronfen, E. (1992). *Over Her Dead Body: Death, Femininity, and the Aesthetic.* New York: Routledge.

Brooks, P. (1985). *Reading for the Plot: Design and Intention in Narrative.* New York: Vintage Books.

———. (1987). "The Idea of a Psychoanalytic Literary Criticism." *Critical Inquiry* 18:334–48.

Brown, J. C. (1986). "A Woman's Place Was in the Home: Women's Work in Renaissance Tuscany." In *Rewriting the Renaissance: The Discourses of Sexual Difference in Early Modern Europe,* edited by M. W. Ferguson, M. Quilligan, and N. J. Vickers, 206–26. Chicago: University of Chicago Press.

Brown, K. (1987). "Context i text del *Vexamen* d'Academia de Francesc Fontanella." *Llengua i Literatura Catalanes* 2:172–252.

Brownlee, M. S. (1981). *The Poetics of Literary Theory: Lope's "Novelas a Marcia Leonarda" and Their Cervantine Context.* Madrid: José Porrúa Turanzas.

———. (1995). "Postmodernism and the Baroque in María de Zayas." In *Cultural Authority in Golden Age Spain,* edited by M. S. Brownlee and H. U. Gumbrecht, 107–27. Baltimore: Johns Hopkins University Press.

Bruner, J. (1991). "The Narrative Construction of Reality." *Critical Inquiry* 18:1–21.

Bush, A. (1993). "The Phantom of Montilla." *Quixotic Desire: Psychoanalytic Perspectives on Cervantes,* edited by R. Anthony El Saffar and D. de Armas Wilson, 264–91. Ithaca: Cornell University Press.

Butler, J. (1990). *Gender Trouble: Feminism and the Subversion of Identity.* New York: Routledge.

Butler, R. A. (1934). *The Lives of the Saints.* London: Burns Oates & Washbourne.

Cadden, J. (1993). *Meanings of Sex Difference in the Middle Ages: Medicine, Science, and Culture.* Cambridge: Cambridge University Press.

Calderón de la Barca, P. (1959a). *Las fortunas de Andrómeda y Perseo.* In *Obras completas.* Vol. 1 (*comedias*). Edited by A. Valbuena Briones, 1:1817–60. Madrid: Aguilar.

———. (1959b). *La gran Cenobia.* In *Obras completas.* Vol 1 (*comedias*). Edited by A. A. Valbuena Briones, 1:481–515. Madrid: Aguilar.

———. (1970). *La hija del aire.* Edited by G. Edwards. London: Tamesis.

———. (1981). *El Alcalde de Zalamea.* Madrid: Clásicos Castellanos.

———. (1992). *El mágico prodigioso: A Composite Edition and Study of the Manuscript and Printed Versions.* Edited by M. McKendrick. Oxford: Clarendon Press.

Caro, A. (1993). *Valor, agravio y mujer.* Edited by L. Luna. Madrid: Castalia.

Caro Baroja, J. (1966). *Las brujas y su mundo.* Madrid: Alianza Editorial.

Carr, D. (1986). *Time, Narrative, and History.* Bloomington: Indiana University Press.

Carrasco Urgoiti, M. S. (1965). "Notas sobre el vejamen de academia en la segunda mitad del siglo XVII." *Revista Hispánica Moderna* 31:97–111.

Carvajal, M. de. (1993). *Navidades de Madrid y noches entretenidas en ocho novelas.* Madrid: Comunidad de Madrid.

Casey, J. (1989). *The History of the Family.* Oxford, Basil Blackwell.

Castiglione, B. (1967). *The Book of the Courtier.* New York: Penguin Books.

Castillo Solórzano, A. de. (1854). *La Garduña de Sevilla y anzuelo de las bolsas. Novelistas posteriores a Cervantes.* Edited by C. Rosell y López, 2 (BAE, vol. 33): 169–234. Madrid: M. Rivadeneyra.

———. (1947). *Lisardo enamorado.* Madrid: Gráficas Ultra.

———. (1992). *Tardes entretenidas.* Barcelona: Montesinos.

Castro, A. (1967). *Hacia Cervantes.* Madrid: Taurus.

———. (1972). *El pensamiento de Cervantes.* Barcelona: Noguer.

Castro y Belvis, G. de. (1968). *El Narciso en su opinión.* Madrid: Taurus.

Cayuela, A. (1994). "L'appareil liminaire des libres de fiction en prose, contribution à l'histoire de la lecture en Espagne au XVIIème siècle," Ph.D. diss., Université Stendhal Grenoble III.

Cervantes Saavedra, M. de. (1928). *El ingenioso hidalgo Don Quijote de la Mancha.* Edited by F. Rodríguez Marín. Madrid: Tipografía de la Revista de Archivos, Bibliotecas y Museos.

———. (1957). *Don Quixote of La Mancha.* Translated by W. Starkie. New York: New American Library.

———. (1971). *Don Quijote de la Mancha.* Edited by M. de Riquer. Barcelona: Editorial Juventud.

———. (1990). *Novelas ejemplares.* Edited by F. Gutiérrez. Barcelona: Editorial Juventud.

———. (1992). *Exemplary Novels.* Edited by B. W. Ife. Warminister, Aries & Phillips.

Charnon-Deutsch, L. (1991). "The Sexual Economy in the Narrative of María de Zayas." *Letras Femeninas* 17:15–28.

Chase, Cynthia. (1989). "Desire and Identification in Lacan and Kristeva." In R. Feldman and J. Roof, eds., *Feminism and Psychoanalysis,* 65–73. Ithaca: Cornell University Press.

Chevalier, M. (1982). "Un cuento, una comedia, cuatro novelas. (Lope de Rueda, Juan Timoneda, Cristóbal de Tamariz, Lope de Vega, María de Zayas)." In *Essays on Narrative Fiction in the Iberian Peninsula in Honour of Frank Pierce,* edited by R. B. Tate, 27–39. Oxford: Dolphin.

Ciplijauskaité, B. (1988). *La novela femenina contemporanea (1970–1985): hacia una tipología de la narración en primera persona.* Barcelona: Antropos.

Cixous, H. (1980). "The Laugh of the Medusa." In *New French Feminisms: An Anthology,* edited by E. Marks and I. de Courtivron, 245–64. Amherst: University of Massachusetts Press.

———. (1981). "Castration or Decapitation?" *Signs* 7:41–55.

Cixous, H., and C. Clément. (1988). *The Newly Born Woman.* Minneapolis: University of Minnesota Press.

Clamurro, W. H. (1988). "Ideological Contradiction and Imperial Decline: Toward a Reading of Zayas's *Desengaños amorosos.*" *South Central Review* 5:43–50.

Clayton, J. (1989). "Narrative and Theories of Desire." *Critical Inquiry* 16:33–53.

Clover, C. J. (1992). *Men, Woman, and Chain Saws: Gender in the Modern Horror Film.* Princeton: Princeton University Press.

Conisbee, P. (1996). *Georges de La Tour and His World: Catalogue of the Exhibition at the National Gallery of Art and the Kimbell Art Museum, Fort Worth, 1996–1997.* New Haven: Yale University Press.

Couliano, I. P. (1987). *Eros and Magic in the Renaissance.* Chicago: University of Chicago Press.

Covarrubias Orozco, S. de. ([1611] 1979). *Tesoro de la lengua castellana o española.* Madrid: Ediciones Turner.

Cruickshank, D. (1984). "The Second Part of *La hija del aire.*" *Bulletin of Hispanic Studies* 61:286–94.

Cruz, A. J. (1996). "Feminism, Psychoanalysis, and the Search for the M/Other in Early Modern Spain." *Indiana Journal of Hispanic Literature,* no. 8: 31–54.

D'Antuono, N. L. (1983). *Boccaccio's "Novelle" in the Theater of Lope de Vega.* Madrid: Jose Porrúa Turanzas.

Darnton, Robert. (1984). *The Great Cat Massacre and Other Episodes in French Cultural History.* New York: Basic Books.

de Armas, F. A. (1998). "Psyche's Fall and Magdalene's Cross: Myth and Hagiography in María de Zayas's *Tarde llega el desengaño.*" In *Estudios en honor de Janet Pérez: El sujeto femenino en escritoras hispánicas,* edited by S. Cavallo et al., 3–15. Potomac, Md.: Scripta Humanistica.

———. (1986). *The Return of Astraea: An Astral-Imperial Myth in Calderón.* Lexington: University of Kentucky Press.

de Lauretis, T. (1984). "Desire in Narrative." In *Alice Doesn't: Feminism, Semiotics, Cinema.* Bloomington: University of Indiana Press.

———. (1998). "The Stubborn Drive." *Critical Inquiry* 24:851–77.

Diccionario de Autoridades. (1979). Edited by Real Academia Española. Madrid: Editorial Gredos.

Diogenes Laertius. (1931). *Lives of Eminent Philosophers.* Harvard University Press.

Domenéch, F. (1994). *La traición en la amistad de María de Zayas. Entreactos de la tragicomedia de los jardines y campos sabeos de Feliciana Enríquez de Guzmán. La firmeza en la ausencia de Leonor de la Cueva y Silva.* Madrid: Asociación de Directores de Escena de España.

Domínguez Ortíz, A. (1955). "La movilización de la nobleza castellana en 1640." *Anuario de Historia del Derecho Español* 25:799–822.

Duby, G. (1992). "The Courtly Model." In *Silences of the Middle Ages,* edited by C. Klapisch-Zuber, 2:250–66. Cambridge: Harvard University Press, Belknap Press.

Echaníz, M. (1996). "Spaces of Women's Religiosity in the Military Order of Santiago in Late Medieval Castile (Twelfth to Sixteenth Centuries)." In *Spanish Women in the Golden Age: Image and Realities,* edited by M. S. Sánchez and A. Saint-Saëns, 3–22. Westport, Conn: Greenwood Press.

Elliott, J. H. (1986). *The Count-Duke of Olivares: The Statesman in an Age of Decline.* New Haven: Yale University Press.

———. (1990). *Imperial Spain, 1469–1716.* London: Penguin Books.

Enciclopedia universal ilustrada europeo-americana: etimologías sánscrito, hebreo, griego, latín, árabe, lenguas indígenas americanas, etc.: versiones de la mayoría de las voces en francés italiano, inglés, alemán, portugués, catalán, esperanto. Edited by Espasa-Calpe. ([1907] c. 1930). Madrid: Espasa-Calpe.

Espinosa, J. de. (1990). *Diálogo en laude de las mugeres.* Albolote (Granada), Ediciones A. Ubago.

Etienvre, J.-P. (1982). "Le symbolisme de la carte à jouer dans l'Espagne des XVIe et XVIIe siècles." In *Les Jeux à la Renaissance: Actes du XXIIIe Colloque International d'Études Humanistes, Tours, Juillet 1980,* edited by P. Ariès and J.-C. Margolin, 421–44. Paris: Librarie Philosophique J. Vrin.

Faliu-Lacort, C. (1979). "La madre en la comedia." In *La mujer en el teatro y la novela del siglo XVII: Actas del IIᵉ Coloquio del Grupo de Estudios sobre Teatro Español (G.E.S.T.E.),* 39–59. Toulouse: Institut d'Études Hispaniques et Hispano-Américaines, Université de Toulouse-Le Mirail.

Feal, C. (1993). "Against the Law: Mad Lovers in *Don Quixote.*" In *Quixotic Desire: Psychoanalytic Perspectives on Cervantes,* edited by R. Anthony El Saffar and D. de Armas Wilson, 179–99. Ithaca: Cornell University Press.

Felten, H. (1978). *María de Zayas y Sotomayor: Zum Zusammenhang zwischen moralistischen Texten und Novellenliteratur.* Frankfurt am Main: Klostermann.

Fernández de Navarrete, E. (1854). *Bosquejo histórico sobre la novela española: Novelistas posteriores a Cervantes,* Edited by C. Rosell y López, 2:v-c. Madrid: M. Rivadeneyra.

Fiel de Aguilar, M. B. (1787). *La literatura española demostrada por el erudito don Nicolas Antonio.* Madrid: Imprenta Real.

Fink, B. (1991). " 'There Is No Such Thing as a Sexual Relationship.' " *Newsletter of the Freudian Field* 5:59–85.

———. (1995). *The Lacanian Subject.* Princeton: Princeton University Press.

Fitzmaurice-Kelly, J. (1926). *Historia de la literatura española.* Madrid: Ruiz Hermanos.

———. (c. 1901). *Historia de la literatura española desde los orígenes hasta el año 1900.* Madrid: La España Moderna.

Flieger, J. A. (1989). "Entertaining the Ménage à Trois: Psychoanalysis, Feminism, and Literature." In *Feminism and Psychoanalysis,* edited by R. Feldstein and J. Roof, 185–208. Ithaca: Cornell University Press.

Foa, S. M. (1977). "Humor and Suicide in Zayas and Cervantes." *Anales Cervantinos* 16:71–83.

———. (1979). *Feminismo y forma narrativa: Estudio del tema y las técnicas de María de Zayas y Sotomayor.* Valencia: Albatros Hispanófila Ediciones.

Forcione, A. K. (1982). *Cervantes and the Humanist Vision: A Study of Four "Exemplary Novels."* Princeton: Princeton University Press.

———. (1984). *Cervantes and the Mystery of Lawlessness: A Study of "El Casamiento Engañoso* and *El Coloquio de los Perros."* Princeton: Princeton University Press.

———. (1989). "Afterword: Exemplarity, Modernity, and the Discriminating Games of Reading." In *Cervantes's "Exemplary Novels" and the Adventure of Writing,* edited by M. Nerlich and N. Spadaccini, 331–52. Minneapolis: Prisma Institute.

Foucault, M. (1982). "Afterword: The Subject and Power." In *Michel Foucault: Beyond Structuralism and Hermeneutics.* Edited by H. L. Dreyfus and P. Rabinow, 208–26. Chicago: University of Chicago Press.

———. (1984). "What Is an Author." In *The Foucault Reader.* Edited by P. Rabinow, 101–20. New York: Pantheon Books.

Freud, S. (1974). *The Standard Edition of the Complete Psychological Works.* Edited by J. Strachey. London: Hogarth Press and the Institute of Psycho-Analysis.

———. (1989). *The Freud Reader.* Edited by P. Gay. New York: W. W. Norton.

Fuss, D. (1989). *Essentially Speaking: Feminism, Nature, and Difference.* New York: Routledge.

Gallop, J. (1985). *Reading Lacan.* Ithaca: Cornell University Press.

Garber, M. (1992). *Vested Interests: Cross-Dressing and Cultural Anxiety.* New York: Routledge.

Garces, M. A. (1993). "Berganza and the Abject: The Desecration of the Mother." In *Quixotic Desire: Psychoanalytic Perspectives on Cervantes.* Edited by R. Anthony El Saffar and D. de Armas Wilson, 292–314. Ithaca: Cornell University Press.

Gartner, B. S. (1989). "María de Zayas y Sotomayor: The Poetics of Subversion." Ph.D diss., Emory University.

Genette, G. (1987). *Seuils.* Paris: Éditions du Seuil.

Gil y Zárate, A. (1844). *Manual de literatura, segunda parte: Resumen histórico de la literatura española.* Madrid: Boix.

Gittes, K. S. (1991). *Framing the "Canterbury Tales": Chaucer and the Medieval Frame Narrative Tradition.* New York: Greenwood Press.

Gmelch, G. "Baseball Magic." (1985). In *Magic, Witchcraft, and Religion: An Anthropological Study of the Supernatural,* edited by A. C. Lehman and J. E. Myers, 295–301. Palo Alto: Mayfield.

Gossman, L. (1994). "History and the Study of Literature." *Profession* (26–33).

Goytisolo, J. (1977). "El mundo erótico de María de Zayas." In *Disidencias.* Barcelona: Seix Barral: 63–115.

Gracián, B. (1980). *El Criticón.* Edited by S. Alonso. Madrid: Cátedra.

———. (1998). *Arte de ingenio, Tratado de la Aguneza.* Edited by E. Blanco. Madrid: Catedra.

Greer, M. R. (1990). "Bodies of Power in Calderón: *El nuevo palacio del Retiro* and *El mayor encanto, amor.*" In *Conflicts of Discourse: Spanish Literature of the Golden Age,* edited by P. Evans, 145–65. Manchester, Manchester University Press.

———. (1991a). " 'Authority' in *Comedia* Editions: Tirso de Molina's *Santa Juana.*" In *Editing the "Comedia" II,* edited by M. McGaha and F. P. Casa, 67–95. Anne Arbor, Mich.: Michigan Romance Studies.

———. (1991b). *The Play of Power: Mythological Court Dramas of Pedro Calderón de la Barca.* Princeton: Princeton University Press.

———. (1995). "The M(Other) Plot: Psychoanalytic Theory and Narrative Structure in María de Zayas." In *María de Zayas: The Dynamics of Discourse,* edited by A. Williamsen and J. Whitenack, 93–114. London: University Presses of America.

Grieve, P. E. (1991). "Embroidering with Saintly Threads: María de Zayas Challenges Cervantes and the Church." *Renaissance Quarterly* 44: 86–106.

Griswold, S. C. (1980). "Topoi and Rhetorical Distance: The 'Feminism' of María de Zayas." *Revista de Estudios Hispánicos* 15:97–116.

Grosz, E. (1990). *Jacques Lacan: A Feminist Introduction.* New York: Routledge.

Halperin, D. M. (1990). "Why Is Diotima a Woman?" *One Hundred Years of Homosexuality, and Other Essays on Greek Love,* 113–51. New York: Routledge.

Hampton, T. (1998). "Examples, Stories, and Subjects in *Don Quixote* and the *Heptameron.*" *Journal of the History of Ideas* 59 (4): 597–611.

Hautcoeur. (c. 1998). "La *novela* espagnole du Siècle d'Or en France de 1615 à 1715: Contribution à une poétique du genre romanesque au XVIIe siècle." Ph.D. diss., University of Paris III.

Heffernan, T. J. (1988). *Sacred Biography: Saints and Their Biographers in the Middle Ages.* Oxford: Oxford University Press.

Heiple, D. (1991). "Profeminist Reactions to Huarte's Misogyny in Lope de Vega's *La prueba de los ingenios* and María de Zayas's *Novelas amorosas y ejemplares.*" In *The Perception of Women in Spanish Theater of the Golden Age,* edited by A. K. Stoll and D. L. Smith, 121–34. Lewisburg: Bucknell University Press.

Hesiod. (1987). *Hesiod's Theogony.* Cambridge, Mass.: Focus Information Group.

Hirsch, M. (1989). *The Mother/Daughter Plot: Narrative, Psychoanalysis, Feminism.* Bloomington: Indiana University Press.

Honig, E. (1972). *Calderón and the Seizures of Honor.* Cambridge: Harvard University Press.

Huarte de San Juan, J. (1989). *Examen de ingenios para las ciencias.* Madrid: Cátedra.

Irigarary, L. (1994). "Sorcerer Love: A Reading of Plato's *Symposium,* Diotima's Speech." In *Feminist Interpretations of Plato,* edited by N. Tuana, 181–95. University Park: Pennsylvania State University Press.

Jagoe, C. (1993). "Disinheriting the Feminine: Galdós and the Rise of the Realist Novel in Spain." *Revista de Estudios Hispánicos* 27:225–48.

Jakobson, R. (1975). *Fundamentals of Language.* The Hague: Mouton.

Jameson, F. (1993). "On 'Cultural Studies.' " *Social Text* 34:17–52.

Jiménez Catalán, M. (1925). *Ensayo de una tipografía zaragozana del siglo XVII.* Zaragoza: Tipografía "La Académica."

Juana Inés de la Cruz, S. (1987). *Obra selecta.* Barcelona: Planeta.

Kagan, R. L. (1990). *Lucrecia's Dreams: Politics and Prophecy in Sixteenth-Century Spain.* Berkeley and Los Angeles: University of California Press.

Kahn, Coppélia. "The Absent Mother in King Lear." In *Rewriting the Renaissance: Discourse of Sexual Difference in Early Modern Europe,* edited by M. W. Ferguson, M. Quilligan, and N. J. Vickers. Chicago: University of Chicago Press.

Kalilah and Dimnah. Edited by T. Irving. (1980). Newark, Del.: Juan de la Cuesta.

Kamen, H. (1983). *Una sociedad conflictiva: España, 1469–1714.* Madrid: Alianza Editorial.

———. (1985). *La Inquisición española.* Barcelona: Editorial Crítica.

Kaminsky, A. K. (1988). "Dress and Redress: Clothing in the *Desengaños amorosos* of María de Zayas y Sotomayor." *Romanic Review* 79 (2): 377–91.

Kaplan, E. Ann. (1992). *Motherhood and Representation.* New York: Routledge.

Kelly, J. (1984). *Women, History, and Theory*. Chicago: University of Chicago Press.

King, W. F. (1963). *Prosa novelística y academias literarias en el siglo XVII*. Madrid: Boletín de la Real Academia.

Kirkpatrick, S. (1989). *Las Románticas: Women Writers and Subjectivity in Spain, 1835–1850*. Berkeley and Los Angeles: University of California Press.

Kristeva, J. (1980). *Pouvoirs de l'horreur*. Paris: Editions du Seuil.

———. (1982). *Powers of Horror: An Essay on Abjection*. New York: Columbia University Press.

———. (1984). *Revolution in Poetic Language*. New York: Columbia University Press.

———. (1986a). "About Chinese Women." In *The Kristeva Reader*. Edited by T. Moi, 138–59. New York: Columbia University Press.

———. (1986b). "Women's Time." In *The Kristeva Reader*. Edited by T. Moi, 186–213. New York: Columbia University Press.

———. (1987). *Tales of Love*. New York: Columbia University Press.

Kurtz, B. E. (1994). "Illusions of Power: Calderón de la Barca, the Spanish Inquisition, and the Prohibition of *Las órdenes militares* (1662–1671)." *Revista Canadiense de Estudios Hispánicos* 18 (2): 189–217.

Labouvie-Vief, G. (1994). *Psyche and Eros: Mind and Gender in the Life Course*. Cambridge: Cambridge University Press.

Lacan, J. (1975). *Le Séminaire, XX: Encore*. Paris: Éditions du Seuil.

———. (1977). *Écrits: A Selection*. Translated by A. Sheridan. New York: W. W. Norton.

———. (1981). *The Four Fundamental Concepts of Psycho-Analysis*. Translated by A. Sheridan. New York: W. W. Norton.

———. (1982). *Feminine Sexuality. Jacques Lacan and the "École Freudienne."* Edited by J. Mitchell and J. Rose. New York, W. W. Norton.

Lampillas, X. (1789). *Ensayo histórico-apologético de la literatura española contra las opiniones preocupadas de algunos escritores modernos italianos*. Madrid: Josefa Amar y Borbon.

Laqueur, T. (1990). *Making Sex: Body and Gender from the Greeks to Freud*. Cambridge: Harvard University Press.

Lara, M. V. de. (1932). "De escritoras españolas, II: María de Zayas y Sotomayor." *Bulletin of Spanish Studies* 9:31–37.

Lévi-Strauss, C. (1969). *The Elementary Structures of Kinship*. Boston: Beacon Press.

Lida de Malkiel, M. R. (1975). *La tradición clásica en España*. Barcelona: Editorial Ariel.

Lista y Aragón, A. (1844). *Ensayos literarios y críticos*. Seville: Calvo-Rubio.

Llorente, J. A. (1822). *Observations critiques sur le roman de Gil Blas de Santillane*. Paris: Moreau.

Losse, D. N. (1994). *Sampling the Book: Renaissance Prologues and the French "Conteurs."* Lewisburg: Bucknell University Press.

Lucan. (1993). *Pharsalia*. Ithaca: Cornell University Press.

Ludmer, J. (1991). "Tricks of the Weak." In *Feminist Perspectives on Sor Juana Inés de la Cruz*, edited by S. Merrim, 86–93. Detroit: Wayne State University Press.

Lugo y Dávila, F. de. (1906). *Teatro popular (Novelas)*. Madrid: Librería de la Viuda de Rico.

Luna, A. de. (1891). *Libro de las virtuosas é claras mujeres*. Madrid: Sociedad de Bibliófilos Españoles.

Luna, L. (1996). *Leyendo como una mujer la imagen de la Mujer*. Barcelona: Anthropos.

Luque Faxardo, F. de. (1955). *Fiel desengaño contra la ociosidad y los juegos*. Madrid: Real Academia Española.

Lyons, J. D. (1989). *Exemplum: The Rhetoric of Example in Early Modern France and Italy*. Princeton: Princeton University Press.

Malinowski, B. (1985). "Rational Mastery by Man of His Surroundings." In *Magic, Witchcraft, and Religion: An Anthropological Study of the Supernatural*, edited by A. C. Lehman and J. E. Myers, 289–94. Palo Alto: Mayfield.

Maltby, W. S. (1983). *Alba. A Biography of Fernando Alvarez de Toledo, Third Duke of Alba, 1507–1582*. Berkeley and Los Angeles: University of California Press.

Marin, L. (1988). *The Portrait of the King*. Minneapolis: University of Minnesota Press.

Mariscal, G. (1991). *Contradictory Subjects: Quevedo, Cervantes, and Seventeenth-Century Spanish Culture*. Ithaca: Cornell University Press.

Márquez, A. (1980). *Literatura e Inquisición en España (1478–1834)*. Madrid: Taurus Ediciones.

Márquez Villanueva, F. (1996). *Orígenes y elaboración de "El burlador de Sevilla."* Salamanca: Ediciones Universidad.

Martínez Gil, F. (1993). *Muerte y sociedad en la España de los Austrias*. Madrid: Siglo XXI de España.

Matulka, B. (1931). *The Novels of Juan de Flores and Their European Diffusion: A Study in Comparative Literature*. New York: Institute of French Studies.

McKendrick, M. (1991). *Theatre in Spain, 1490–1700*. Cambridge: Cambridge University Press.

Mejía de la Cerda, L. (1915). "*El juego del hombre*." *The Romanic Review* 6 (3): 239–82.

Melloni, A. (1976). *Il sistema narrativo di María de Zayas*. Torino: Quaderni Iberoamericani.

Meltzer, F. (1987). "Editor's Introduction: Partitive Plays, Pipe Dreams." *Critical Inquiry* 13:215–21.

Menocal, M. R. (1987). *The Arabic Role in Medieval Literary History: A Forgotten Heritage*. Philadelphia: University of Pennsylvania Press.

Menton, S. (1998). "El gato emblemático." *La Goceta del Fondo de Cultura Económica* 232:37–39.

Michie, H. (1989). "Not One of the Family: The Repression of the Other Woman in Feminist Theory." In *Discontented Discourses: Feminism/Textual Intervention/Psychoanalysis*, edited by M. S. Barr and R. Feldstein, 15–28. Urbana: University of Illinois Press.

Miller, J.-A. (1991). "Language: Much Ado About What." In *Lacan and the Subject of Language*, edited by E. Ragland-Sullivan and M. Bracher, 21–35. New York: Routledge.

Miller, P. C. (1994). *Dreams in Late Antiquity: Studies in the Imagination of a Culture*. Princeton: Princeton University Press.

Molho, M. (1993). "Cervantes and the 'Terrible Mothers.'" In *Quixotic Desire: Psychoanalytic Perspectives on Cervantes*, edited by R. Anthony El Saffar and D. de Armas Wilson, 239–63. Ithaca: Cornell University Press.

Moll, J. (1982). "La primera edición de las 'Novelas amorosas y exemplares' de María de Zayas y Sotomayor." *Dicenda: Cuadernos de Filología Hispánica* 1:177–79.

Montesa Peydro, S. (1981). *Texto y contexto en la narrativa de María de Zayas*. Madrid: Dirección General de la Juventud y Promoción Sociocultural.

Montesinos, J. F. (1955). *Introducción a una historia de la novela, en España, en el Siglo XIX*. Madrid: Castalia.

Moore, M. (1982). *The Complete Poems of Marianne Moore*. New York: Penguin Books.

Moreto y Cabaña, A. (1828). *No puede ser.* In *Comedias Escogidas,* 2:3–142. Madrid: Imprenta de Ortega y Compañía.
Morley, S. G., and C. Bruerton (1968). *Cronología de las comedias de Lope de Vega.* Madrid: Editorial Gredos.
Nalle, S. T. (1989). "Literacy and Culture in Early Modern Castile." *Past and Present,* no. 125: 65–96.
Navarre. M. de. (1984). *The Heptameron.* London: Penguin Books.
Nicholson, E. (1993). "The Theater." In *A History of Women: Renaissance and Enlightenment Paradoxes,* edited by N. Z. Davis and A. Farge, 3:295–314. Cambridge: Harvard University Press, Belknap Press.
Nye, A. (1994). "Irigaray and Diotima at Plato's Symposium." In *Feminist Interpretations of Plato,* edited by N. Tuana, 196–216. University Park: Pennsylvania State University Press.
Oñate, M. del Pilar. (1938). *El feminismo en la literatura española.* Madrid: Espasa-Calpe.
Ovid (1955). *The Metamorphoses of Ovid.* Harmondsworth: Penguin Books.
Pagels, E. (1988). *Adam, Eve, and the Serpent.* New York: Random House.
———. (1989). *The Gnostic Gospels.* New York: Vintage Books.
———. (1995). *The Origin of Satan.* New York: Random House.
Palomo, M. del Pilar. (1976). *La novela cortesana (forma y estructura).* Barcelona: Editorial Planeta.
Pardo Bazán, E. (c. 1892). "Breve noticia sobre doña María de Zayas y Sotomayor." In *Novelas de doña María de Zayas,* by María de Zayas y Sotomayor. Edited by E. Pardo Bazán, 3:5–16. Madrid: Agustín Avrial.
Parker, A. A. (1968). "The Calderonian Sources of *El divino Narciso* by Sor Juana Inés de la Cruz." *Romanistisches Jahrbuch* 19:257–74.
Parker, P. (1987). *Literary Fat Ladies: Rhetoric, Gender, Property.* New York: Metheun.
Paterson, A. K. G. (1993). "Tirso de Molina and the Androgyne: *El Aquiles* and *La dama del olivar.*" *Bulletin of Hispanic Studies* 70:105–14.
Paun de Garcia, S. (1992). "Magia y poder en María de Zayas." *Cuadernos de ALDEEU* 8:43–54.
Paz, O. (1988). *Sor Juana, or, The Traps of Faith.* Cambridge: Harvard University Press.
Pérez de Montalban, Juan (1949). *Sucesos y prodigios de amor.* Madrid: Sociedad de Bibliófilos Españoles.
Pérez de Moya, J. (1585). *Philosofía secreta.* Madrid: Francisco Sánchez.
Perrault, C. (1961). *Perrault's Complete Fairy Tales.* New York, Dodd, Mead.
Perry, M. E. (1990). *Gender and Disorder in Early Modern Seville.* Princeton: Princeton University Press.
Pfandl, L. (1933). *Historia de la literatura nacional española en la Edad de Oro.* Barcelona, Sucesores de Juan Gili.
Piña, J. de. (1987). *Novelas exemplares y prodigiosas historias.* Verona: Facoltà di Lingue e Letterature Straniere.
Pizan, C. de. (1982). *The Book of the City of Ladies.* New York, Persea Books.
Place, E. B. (1923). *María de Zayas, An Outstanding Woman Short-Story Writer of Seventeenth Century Spain.* Boulder: University of Colorado Studies.
Plato. (1989). *Symposium.* Indianapolis: Hackett.
Quevedo [Villegas], F. de. (1989). *Dreams and Discourses.* Warminster, Aris & Phillips.
Quevedo Villegas, F. de. (1981). *Poesía varia.* Madrid: Ediciones Cátedra.
———. (1969). *Obra poética.* Madrid: Castalia.

Quint, D. (1993). *Epic and Empire.* Princeton: Princeton University Press.
Ragland, E. (1995). *Essays on the Pleasures of Death.* New York: Routledge.
Ragland-Sullivan, E. (1986). *Jacques Lacan and the Philosophy of Psychoanalysis.* Urbana: University of Illinois Press.
———. (1991). "The Sexual Masquerade: A Lacanian Theory of Sexual Difference." In *Lacan and the Subject of Language,* edited by E. Ragland-Sullivan and M. Bracher. New York: Routledge.
Rigolot, F. (1994). "Magdalen's Skull: Allegory and Icongraphy in *Heptameron* 32." *Renaissance Quarterly* 47 (1): 57–73.
Rivers, E. L., ed. (1988). *Renaissance and Baroque Poetry of Spain.* Prospect Heights, Ill.: Waveland Press.
Rodríguez del Padrón, J. (1884). "Triunfo de las donas." In *Obras de Juan Rodríguez de la Cámara (o del Padrón).* Edited by A. Paz y Meliá, 85–127. Madrid: Sociedad de Bibliófilos Españoles.
Roper, L. (1994). *Oedipus and the Devil: Witchcraft, Sexuality, and Religion in Early Modern Europe.* London: Routledge.
Rose, C. (1976). "Who Wrote the *Segunda parte* of *La hija del aire?*" *Revue Belge de Philologie et d'Histoire* 54:797–822.
Rose, J. (1989). "Where Does the Misery Come From? Psychoanalysis, Feminism, and the Event." In *Feminism and Psychoanalysis,* edited by R. Felstein and J. Roof, 24–39. Ithaca: Cornell University Press.
Ruiz de Alarcón, J. (1982). *Comedias.* Caracas: Biblioteca Ayacucho.
Sabat-Rivers, G. (1987). "Antes de Juana Inés: Clarinda y Amarilis, dos poetas del Perú colonial." *La Torre (Nueva Epoca)* 1 (2): 275–87.
Sallman, J.-M. (1993). "Witches." In *Renaissance and Enlightenment Paradoxes,* edited by N. Z. Davis and A. Farge, 3:295–314. Cambridge: Harvard University Press, Belknap Press.
Sánchez, F. J. (1993). *Lectura y representación: Análisis cultural de las "Novelas ejemplares" de Cervantes.* New York: Peter Lang.
Sánchez, J. (1961). *Academias literarias del Siglo de Oro español.* Madrid: Gredos.
Sánchez Ortega, M. H. (1992). "Woman as Source of 'Evil' in Counter-Reformation Spain." In *Culture and Control in Counter-Reformation Spain,* edited by A. J. Cruz and M. E. Perry, 196–215. Minneapolis: University of Minnesota Press.
Scheman, N. (1988). "Missing Mothers, Desiring Daughters: Framing the Sight of Women." *Critical Inquiry* 15:62–89.
Scott, N. M. (1994). " 'La gran turba de las que merecieron nombres': Sor Juana's Foremothers in "La Respuesta a Sor Filotea." In *Coded Encounters: Writing, Gender, and Ethnicity in Colonial Latin America,* edited by F. J. Cevallos-Candau et al. Amherst: University of Massachusetts Press.
Serrano y Sanz, M. (1975). *Apuntes para una biblioteca de escritoras españolas desde el año 1401 al 1833.* Madrid: Atlas.
Shergold, N. D., and J. E. Varey (1961). "Some Early Calderón Dates." *Bulletin of Hispanic Studies* 38:274–86.
Sieburth, S. (1994). *Inventing High and Low: Literature, Mass Culture, and Uneven Modernity in Spain.* Durham: Duke University Press.
Silverman, K. (1988). *The Acoustic Mirror: The Female Voice in Psychoanalysis and Cinema.* Bloomington: Indiana University Press.
Smith, P. J. (1989). *The Body Hispanic: Gender and Sexuality in Spanish and Spanish American Literature.* Oxford: Clarendon Press.
Smith, W. (1849). *Dictionary of Greek and Roman Biography and Mythology.* Boston, Charles C. Little & James Brown.

Sommers, P. (1984). "Marguerite de Navarre's *Heptaméron:* The Case for the Cornice." *The French Review* 58:786–93.

Soufas, T. S. (1996a). "The Gendered Context of Melancholy for Spanish Golden Age Women Writers." In *Spanish Women in the Golden Age: Images and Realities,* edited by M. S. Sánchez and A. Saint-Saëns, 171–84. Westport, Conn: Greenwood Press.

———., ed. (1996b). *Women's Acts: Plays by Women Dramatists of Spain's Golden Age.* Lexington: University Press of Kentucky.

———. (1997). *Dramas of Distinction: A Study of Plays by Golden Age Women.* Lexington: University Press of Kentucky.

Spitzer, L. (1947). "Soy quien soy." *Nueva Revista de Filología Hispánica* 1 (2): 113–27.

Sprengnether, M. (1989). "(M)other Eve: Some Revisions of the Fall in Fiction by Contemporary Women Writers." In *Feminism and Psychoanalysis,* edited by R. Feldstein and J. Roof, 298–322. Ithaca: Cornell University Press.

Stein, L. K. (1993). *Songs of Mortals, Dialogues of the Gods: Music and Theatre in Seventeenth-Century Spain.* Oxford: Clarendon Press.

Stierle, K. (1998). "Three Moments in the Crisis of Exemplarity: Boccaccio-Petrarch, Montaigne, Cervantes." *Journal of the History of Ideas* 59 (4):581–95.

Stradling, R. A. (1988). *Philip IV and the Government of Spain, 1621–1665.* Cambridge: Cambridge University Press.

Stroud, M. D. (1995). "The Demand for Love and the Mediation of Desire in 'La traición en la amistad.' " In *María de Zayas: The Dynamics of Discourse,* edited by A. R. Williamsen and J. A. Whitenack, 155–69. Madison, N.J.: Associated University Presses.

Sullivan, H. W. (1983). *Calderón in the German lands and the Low Countries: His Reception and Influence, 1654–1980.* Cambridge: Cambridge University Press.

———. (1989). "La misión evangélica de Tirso en el Nuevo Mundo: La Inmaculada Concepción de María y la fundación de los Mercedarios." In *El mundo del teatro español en su Siglo de Oro: Ensayos dedicados a John E. Varey,* edited by J. M. Ruano de La Haza, 248–66. Ottawa: Dovehouse Editions Canada.

———. (1990). "Lacan and Calderón: Spanish Classical Drama in the Light of Psychoanalytic Theory." *Gestos,* año 5, no. 10: 39–55.

———. (1996). *Grotesque Purgatory: A Study of Cervantes's "Don Quixote," Part II.* University Park: Pennsylvania State University Press.

Surtz, R. E. (1990). *The Guitar of God: Gender, Power, and Authority in the Visionary World of Mother Juana de la Cruz (1481–1534).* Philadelphia: University of Pennsylvania Press.

Sylvania, L. E. V. (1922). "Doña María de Zayas y Sotomayor: A Contribution to the Study of Her Works." *Romanic Review* 13:197–213, 14:199–232.

Teresa de Jesús, S. (1972). *Las moradas: Libro de su vida.* México City: Editorial Porrua.

Tetel, M. (1981). "*L'Heptaméron:* Première nouvelle et fonction des devisants." In *La Nouvelle française à la Renaissance,* edited by L. Sozzi and V. L. Saulnier, 449–58. Geneva: Editions Slatkine.

Thompson, D. J. (1994). "Dreams as History? Dreams and Prophecy." Lecture, Princeton University.

Thompson, S. E., and B. W. Carlson, eds. (1994). *Holidays, Festivals, and Celebrations of the World Dictionary.* Detroit, Omnigraphcs.

Ticknor, G. (1866). *History of Spanish Literature.* 3 vols. Boston: Ticknor and Fields.

Timoneda, J. (1986). *El patrañuelo.* Madrid: Cátedra.

Trope, H. (1994). *Locura y sociedad en la Valencia de los siglos XV al XVII.* Valencia: Puvill Libros.

Tyler, R. W., and S. D. Elizondo (1981). *The Characters, Plots, and Settings of Calderón's Comedias*. Lincoln, Nebr.: Society of Spanish and Spanish-American Studies.

Valbuena Prat, A. (1937). *Historia de la literatura española*. Barcelona: Gustavo Gili.

Vega Carpio, L. de. (1776). *El laurel de Apolo*. Madrid: Antonio de Sancha.

———. (1859). *El premio del bien hablar*. In *Obras de Lope de Vega,* 13:372–402. Madrid: Real Academia Española.

———. (1928). *El juez de su causa*. In *Obras de Lope de Vega Carpio*. Edited by E. Cotarelo y Mori, 6:648–93. Madrid: Real Academia Española.

———. (1971). *El peregrino en su patria*. Edited by M. A. Peyton. Chapel Hill: University of North Carolina Studies in the Romance Languages and Literatures.

———. (1980). *La Dorotea*. Edited by E. Morby. Madrid: Clásicos Castalia.

———. (1985). *La Dorotea*. Edited by A. Trueblood and E. Honig. Cambridge: Harvard University Press.

———. (1988). *Novelas a Marcia Leonarda*. Edited by J. Barella. Madrid: Ediciones Jucar.

Vélez de Guevara, L. (1984). *El diablo cojuelo*. Edited by E. Rodríguez Cepeda. Madrid: Cátedra.

Vicente García, L. M. (1989). "La defensa de la mujer como intelectual en Teresa de Cartagena y Sor Juana Inés de la Cruz." *Mester* 18 (2): 95–103.

Vigil, M. (1994). *La vida de las mujeres en los siglos XVI y XVII*. Madrid: Siglo veintiuno de España.

Virués, C. de. (1984). *El Monserrate Segundo*. Edited by M. F. Finch. Valencia: Albatros Hispanófila.

Vocabulario italiano. (1993). Edited by E. de Felice and A. Duro. Torino: Società Editrice Internazionale.

Vollendorf, L. (1995). "Reading the Body Imperiled: Violence Against Women in María de Zayas." *Hispania* 78 (2): 272–82.

Weber, A. (1990). *Teresa of Avila and the Rhetoric of Femininity*. Princeton: Princeton University Press.

Welles, M. L. (1978). "María de Zayas y Sotomayor and Her *Novela cortesana:* A Reevaluation." *Bulletin of Hispanic Studies* 55:301–10.

Wetzel, H. H. (1981). "Eléments socio-historiques d'un genre littéraire: L'histoire de la nouvelle jusqu'à Cervantès." In *La nouvelle française à la Renaissance,* edited by L. Sozzi and V. L. Saulnier, 41–78. Geneva: Editions Slatkine.

Wilden, A. (1981). *Speech and Language in Psychoanalysis: Jacques Lacan*. Baltimore: Johns Hopkins University Press.

Williams, L. (1989). *Hard Core: Power, Pleasure, and the "Frenzy of the Visible."* Berkeley and Los Angeles: University of California Press.

Williams, R. H. (1950). "Review of Amezúa Edition." *Hispanic Review* 18:75–77.

Williamsen, A. (1991). "Engendering Interpretation: Irony as Comic Challenge in María de Zayas." *Romance Languages Annual* 3:642–48.

Williamsen, A. R., and J. A. Whitenack, eds. (1995). *María de Zayas: The Dynamics of Discourse*. Madison, N.J.: Associated University Presses.

Williamsen-Cerón, A. (1984). "The Comic Function of Two Mothers: Belisa and Angela." *Bulletin of the Comediantes* 36:167–74.

Wilson, D. de A. (1987). " 'Passing the Love of Women': The Intertextuality of *El curioso impertinente*." *Cervantes* 7:9–28.

———. (1991). *Allegories of Love: Cervantes's "Persiles and Sigismunda."* Princeton: Princeton University Press.

———. (1993). "Cervantes and the Night Visitors: Dream Work in the Cave of Montesinos." In *Quixotic Desire: Psychoanalytic Perspectives on Cervantes,* edited by

R. Anthony El Saffar and D. de Armas Wilson, 58–80. Ithaca: Cornell University Press.

Winnett, S. (1990). "Coming Unstrung: Women, Men, Narrative, and Principles of Pleasure." *PMLA* 105:505–18.

Wright, E., ed. (1992). *Feminism and Psychoanalysis: A Critical Dictionary.* Oxford: Basil Blackwell.

Yarbro-Bejarano, Y. (1994). *Feminism and the Honor Plays of Lope de Vega.* West Lafayette: Purdue University Press.

Yllera, A. (1983). Introduction to *Parte segunda del Sarao y entretenimiento honesto (Desengaños amorosos),* by María de Zayas y Sotomayor, 11–110. Madrid: Cátedra.

Young-Bruehl, E. (1990). *Freud on Women: A Reader.* New York: W. W. Norton.

Zayas y Sotomayor, María de. (1637a). *Novelas amorosas, y exemplares.* Zaragoza: Pedro Esquer.

———. (1637b). *Novelas amorosas, y exemplares compuestas por . . . , natural de Madrid.* Zaragoza: Hospital Real y General de N. Señora de Gracia, a costa de Pedro Esquer.

———. (1646). *Novelas amorosas y exemplares.* Barcelona: Gabriel Nogues.

———. (1649). *Parte segvnda del sarao, y entretenimiento honesto.* Barcelona: Sebastian de Cormellas.

———. (1948). *Novelas ejemplares y amorosas.* Edited by A. Amezúa y Mayo. Madrid: Aldus, S. A. de Artes Gráficas.

———. (1973). *Novelas completas.* Edited by M. Martínez del Portal. Barcelona: Editorial Bruguera.

———. (1983). *Parte segunda del Sarao y entretenimiento honesto (Desengaños amorosos).* Edited by A. Yllera. Madrid: Cátedra.

———. (1990). *The Enchantments of Love.* Translated by H. P. Boyer. Berkeley and Los Angeles: University of California Press.

———. (1995). *Novelle amorose ed esemplari.* Translated by S. Piloto di Castro. Torino: Giulio Einaudi.

Zeitlin, F. (1990). "Playing the Other: Theater, Theatricality, and the Feminine in Greek Drama." In *Nothing to Do with Dionysius: Athenian Drama in Its Social Context,* edited by J. Winkler and F. Zeitlin, 63–96. Princeton: Princeton University Press.

Zizek, S. (1991). *Looking Awry: An Introduction to Jacques Lacan Through Popular Culture.* Cambridge: MIT Press.

———. (1994). *The Metastases of Enjoyment: Six Essays on Women and Causality.* London: Verso.

Index

Index 465

Fontanella, Francesc
  portrayal of Zayas, 29–34, 74, 301
  Vejamen, 25–33, 35, 301
foremothers, 72–78
frame, 320–21
  in literature, 321–23, 326, 329
  theatrical, 320–21
  in Zayas's works, 321–22, 347
frame narrative
  as communicative act, 95, 326
  in literature, 324–25, 327, 328–29
  Zayas's use of, 14, 319–25, 329–30, 341, 347
Freud, Sigmund
  and castration, 162, 192
  and dreams, 103–5, 107, 412 n. 31
  and feminism, 8, 9
  and libido, 115, 124, 312
  and narcissism, 117, 415 n. 55, 426 n. 45
  and Oedipal model, 191, 414 n. 47
  and the unconscious, 8, 56, 122, 169, 257
La fuerza del amor (*The Power of Love*), 20, 251–53

gaze. *See also* eyes
  of the other, 187–88, 209, 278, 413 n. 43
  power of, 112–13
gender
  identification with, 116, 118, 119–20
  and narrativity, 8, 48, 56, 116
  in Zayas's works, 59–60, 81
gender differentiation, 64, 70–71, 92–93, 199–200, 239, 406 n. 11
gender pronouns, 93, 206–9, 221–22
generosity, 137–40
Gil Blas de Santillane, 46–49
Gil y Zárate, Antonio, 46–47
Golden Age, Spain in
  drama, 90, 209, 210, 277, 346
  life in, 142, 202, 224, 302
  literature, 5, 32, 116–17, 124, 344
greed, 293, 294, 354. *See also* miserliness
guilt, 122–23, 184, 249

hagiography, 144, 148, 155, 196, 239
history
  and narrative fiction, 299, 305
  and women, 307–8
  in Zayas's works, 301, 302, 304–5, 307

homosexuality. *See also* lesbianism
  and courtly love, 230, 288
  and patriarchy, 288–89
  in Spain, 32, 236
  in Zayas's works, 32, 234–36
Huarte de San Juan, Juan, 67–72, 81

imaginary, 11, 167
immortality, 257–58
El imposible vencido (*Triumph over the Impossible*), 198, 265–67, 302, 349
incest, 189–92, 195, 340
La inocencia castigada (*Innocence Punished*)
  and essence of woman, 214–18, 273, 278
  magic in, 52, 213, 216
  sight and perception in, 219, 274–76

El jardín engañoso (*The Garden of Deceit*)
  fratricide in, 136, 350
  generosity in, 137–39
  maternal presence in, 136–37, 140–41, 305
  reversal of Biblical story in, 305, 306, 349
  sexual desire in, 136–37
  supernatural in, 305, 350
  time in, 305–6
Jerome, Saint, 107–8, 150
jouissance
  and essence of woman, 214–16
  feminine, 133, 155, 157, 161, 232, 306, 355
  and male honor, 210, 277–78
  and subjectivity, 124, 133, 193, 210
Juana Inés de la Cruz, Sor, 4, 74, 117–18, 209, 338
El juez de su causa (*The Judge in Her Own Case*)
  cross-dressing in, 198, 201–5, 209
  and gender, 206, 207–9
  sadism in, 198, 205, 350

Kristeva, Julia
  and abjection, 192–93, 410 n. 16, 426 n. 40
  and cult of the Virgin, 99–100, 150
  and language, 12, 313
  and maternal discourse, 157, 167, 192–93, 398 n. 11
  and narcissism, 117
  and psychoanalytic discourse, 9, 313, 355
  and subjectivity, 314
  and time, 305–6